Office for
National Statistics

KV-371-162

United Kingdom
National Accounts

The Blue Book

2017 edition

Editors: Dean Goodway & Sarah Nightingale

Office for National Statistics

ISSN 2040–1612

A National Statistics publication

National Statistics are produced to high professional standards set out in the Code of Practice for Official Statistics. They are produced free from political influence.

About us

The Office for National Statistics

The Office for National Statistics (ONS) is the executive office of the UK Statistics Authority, a non-ministerial department which reports directly to Parliament. ONS is the UK government's single largest statistical producer. It compiles information about the UK's society and economy, and provides the evidence-base for policy and decision-making, the allocation of resources, and public accountability. The Director-General of ONS reports directly to the National Statistician who is the Authority's Chief Executive and the Head of the Government Statistical Service.

The Government Statistical Service

The Government Statistical Service (GSS) is a network of professional statisticians and their staff operating both within the Office for National Statistics and across more than 30 other government departments and agencies.

Copyright and reproduction

Any enquiries regarding this publication should be sent to: info@statistics.gsi.gov.uk

Contents

Contents

All of the tables in this publication can be found on the cd-rom

Acknowledgements and contacts

Acknowledgements

The Blue Book is a collaborative effort. We are grateful for the assistance provided by the various government departments and organisations that have contributed to this book.

Contacts

For information about this publication please contact the editor:

Dean Goodway +44 (0)1633 456869 (blue.book.coordination@ons.gsi.gov.uk)

Specific data enquiries should be directed to the following:

Gross domestic product (GDP):

Rob Kent-Smith +44 (0)1633 651618 (gdp@ons.gsi.gov.uk)

Sector and financial accounts:

Katherine Kent +44 (0)1633 455829 (sector.accounts@ons.gsi.gov.uk)

Household expenditure:

Gareth Powell +44 (0)1633 455969 (consumer.trends@ons.gsi.gov.uk)

Household income:

David Matthewson +44 (0)1633 455612 (saving.ratio@ons.gsi.gov.uk)

General government and public sector:

Jamie Pritchard +44 (0)1633 456722 (jamie.pritchard@ons.gsi.gov.uk)

Central government:

Bob Richards +44 (0)1633 456424 (bob.richards@ons.gsi.gov.uk)

Local government:

Katherine Mills +44 (0)1633 456367 (katherine.mills@ons.gsi.gov.uk)

Public corporations:

Vera Ruddock +44 (0)1633 455864 (vera.ruddock@ons.gsi.gov.uk)

Gross capital formation:

Alison McCrae +44 (0)1633 455250 (gcf@ons.gsi.gov.uk)

UK trade and transfers:

Hannah Finselbach +44 (0)1633 455635 (trade@ons.gsi.gov.uk)

Gross value added by industry:

James Scruton +44 (0)1633 456724 (ios.enquiries@ons.gsi.gov.uk)

Input-output supply and use tables and production accounts:

Robert Doody +44 (0)1633 455803 (robert.doody@ons.gsi.gov.uk)

Non-financial corporations:

Katherine Kent +44 (0)1633 455829 (sector.accounts@ons.gsi.gov.uk)

Financial corporations:

Karen Grovell +44 (0)1633 456103 (karen.l.grovell@ons.gov.uk)

Rest of the world:

Richard McCrae +44 (0)1633 456106 (bop@ons.gsi.gov.uk)

Capital stock:

Kate Davies +44 (0)1633 455617 (gcf@ons.gsi.gov.uk)

National balance sheet:

Dan Groves +44 (0)1633 456341 (capstocks@ons.gsi.gov.uk)

Environmental accounts:

Gemma N Thomas +44 (0)1633 455523 (environment.accounts@ons.gsi.gov.uk)

Flow of funds:

Stuart Deneen +44 (0)1633 456129 (stuart.deneen@ons.gsi.gov.uk)

Other customer enquiries:

ONS Customer Contact Centre +44 (0)845 601 3034 (info@statistics.gsi.gov.uk)

Media enquiries:

+44 (0)845 604 1858 (press.office@ons.gsi.gov.uk)

An introduction to the UK national accounts

What is the Blue Book?

The Blue Book was first published in August 1952 and presents a full set of economic accounts (national accounts) for the UK. These accounts are compiled by Office for National Statistics (ONS). They record and describe economic activity in the UK and, as such, are used to support the formulation and monitoring of economic and social policies.

Chapter 1

Chapter 1 of the Blue Book provides a summary of the UK National Accounts, including explanations and tables covering the main national and domestic aggregates, for example:

- gross domestic product (GDP) at current market prices and chained volume measures

- GDP deflator

- gross value added (GVA) at basic prices

- gross national income (GNI)

- gross national disposable income (GNDI)

- population estimates

- employment estimates

- GDP per head

- the UK summary accounts (the goods and services account, production accounts, distribution and use of income accounts, and accumulation accounts)

Chapter 1 also includes details of revisions to data since the Blue Book 2016.

Chapter 2

Chapter 2 includes:

- input-output supply and use tables

- analyses of GVA at current market prices and chained volume measures

- capital formation

- workforce jobs by industry

Chapters 3 to 7

Chapters 3, 4, 5, 6 and 7 provide:

- a description of the institutional sectors

- the sequence of the accounts and balance sheets

- an explanation of the statistical adjustment items needed to reconcile the accounts

- the fullest available set of accounts providing transactions by sectors and appropriate sub-sectors of the economy (including the rest of the world)

Chapters 8 to 11

Chapters 8, 9, 10 and 11 cover additional analysis and include:

- supplementary tables for gross fixed capital formation (GFCF), national balance sheet and public sector

- statistics for European Union purposes

Chapter 12

Chapter 12 covers:

- UK Environmental Accounts

Chapter 13

Chapter 13 covers:

- flow of funds

Overview of the UK national accounts and sector accounts

In the UK, priority is given to the production of a single gross domestic product (GDP) estimate using income, production and expenditure data. Further analysis is available on the following:

- income analysis at current prices

- expenditure analysis at both current prices and chained volume measures

- value added analysis compiled on a quarterly basis in chained volume measures only

Income, capital and financial accounts are produced for non-financial corporations, financial corporations, general government, households and non-profit institutions serving households.

The accounts are fully integrated, but with a statistical discrepancy (known as the statistical adjustment), shown for each sector account. This reflects the difference between the sector net borrowing or lending from the capital account and the identified borrowing or lending in the financial accounts, which should theoretically be equal.

Financial transactions and balance sheets are produced for the rest of the world sector in respect of its dealings with the UK.

An introduction to sector accounts

The sector accounts summarise the transactions of particular groups of institutions within the economy, showing how the income from production is distributed and redistributed and how savings are used to add wealth through investment in physical or financial assets.

Institutional sectors

The accounting framework identifies two kinds of institutions:

- consuming units (mainly households)

- production units (mainly corporations, non-profit institutions or government)

Units can own goods and assets, incur liabilities and engage in economic activities and transactions with other units. All units are classified into one of five sectors:

- non-financial corporations

- financial corporations

- general government

- households and non-profit institutions serving households (NPISH)

- rest of the world

Types of transactions

There are three main types of transactions.

Transactions in products

Transactions in products are related to goods and services. They include output, intermediate and final consumption, gross capital formation, and exports and imports.

Distributive transactions

Distributive transactions transfer income or wealth between units of the economy. They include property income, taxes and subsidies, social contributions and benefits, and other current or capital transfers.

Financial transactions

Financial transactions differ from distributive transactions in that they relate to transactions in financial claims, whereas distributive transactions are unrequited. The main categories in the classification of financial instruments are:

- monetary gold and special drawing rights

- currency and deposits

- debt securities

- loans

- equity and investment fund shares or units

- insurance, pension and standardised guarantee schemes

- financial derivatives and employee stock options

- other accounts receivable or payable

Summary of changes

The main gross domestic product (GDP) - impacting improvements implemented in the Blue Book 2017 are as follows.

Actual rental and imputed rental

The new approach for private actual rentals brings consistency with the methods for imputed rentals introduced in Blue Book 2016. It also removes the discontinuity in the current price data at 2010, which was due to an interim solution in place since Blue Book 2014. As part of the process of bringing the sources and methods for private actual rentals into line with imputed rentals, we identified and implemented some further improvements to imputed rentals.

Improvements to the recording of GFCF

Following a quality review of software in gross fixed capital formation (GFCF), analysis has shown that elements in the estimates of purchased software – a component of intellectual property products (IPP) – have been double-counted from 2001; this change removes the double-counted element.

The IPP asset will also be impacted as a result of updated data for entertainment, literary or artistic originals.

The recording of transfer costs has also been improved through the use of updated House Price Index (HPI) data and the inclusion of transfer costs (fees and taxes) associated with the buying and selling of players in the sports industries.

Other GDP-impacting improvements include:

- impacts from separating estimates for the households and non-profit institutions serving households sector

- unfunded public sector pensions methodology review

- improvement to illegal activities

- revised estimates of exhaustiveness and concealed income adjustment

- revised estimates of Value Added Tax fraud

- BBC data update

- public sector finances alignment

This Blue Book also includes a range of improvements to the sector and financial accounts. The largest have been separating the households and non-profit institutions serving households (NPISH) accounts; improving the data sources, especially for dividend income of the self-employed; introducing the new securities dealers survey data and methods; and improving the treatment of corporate bonds, shares and dividends methods and data sources.

We have also included the "Revaluation account" and the "Other changes in volume account". This has led to the renumbering of some tables to ensure that the sequence of accounts set out in the European System of Accounts 2010 can be maintained. This has resulted in the financial balance sheets in Chapters 1 and 3 changing their last digit from previously published .9 to .11.

The new table numbering system for Chapters 3, 4, 5, 6 and 7 is as follows.

.9 - Other changes in volume of assets account

.10 - Revaluations account

.11 - Financial balance sheets

All other tables remain unchanged.

For more detailed information surrounding these changes please see Impact of method changes to the national accounts and sector accounts: Quarter 1 1997 to Quarter 2 2017

A series of articles have been published describing the improvements and their impact in detail.

The basic accounting framework

The accounting framework provides a systematic and detailed description of the UK economy, including sector accounts and the input-output framework.

All elements required to compile aggregate measures, such as gross domestic product (GDP), gross national income (GNI), saving and the current external balance (the balance of payments) are included.

The economic accounts provide the framework for a system of volume and price indices, to allow chained volume measures of aggregates such as GDP to be produced. In this system, value added, from the production approach, is measured at basic prices (including other taxes less subsidies on production but not on products) rather than at factor cost (which excludes all taxes less subsidies on production).

The whole economy is subdivided into institutional sectors with current price accounts running in sequence from the production account through to the balance sheet.

The accounts for the whole UK economy and its counterpart, the rest of the world, follow a similar structure to the UK sectors, although several of the rest of the world accounts are collapsed into a single account as they can never be complete when viewed from a UK perspective.

Table numbering system

The table numbering system is designed to show relationships between the UK, its sectors and the rest of the world. For accounts drawn directly from the European System of Accounts 2010: ESA 2010, a three-part numbering system is used; the first two digits denote the sector and the third digit denotes the ESA account. Not all sectors can have all types of account, so the numbering is not necessarily consecutive within each sector's chapter.

The rest of the world's identified components of accounts 2 to 6 are given in a single account numbered 2. UK whole economy accounts consistent with ESA 2010 are given in section 1.6 as a time series and in section 1.7 in a detailed matrix identifying all sectors, the rest of the world and the UK total.

The ESA 2010 code for each series is shown in the left-hand column, using the following prefixes:

- S for the classification of institutional sectors

- P for transactions in products

- D for distributive transactions

- F for transactions in financial assets and liabilities

- K for other changes in assets

- B for balancing items and net worth

Within the financial balance sheets, the following prefixes are used:

- AF for financial assets and liabilities

- AN for non-financial assets and liabilities

What is an account? What is its purpose?

An account records and displays all flows and stocks for a given aspect of economic life. The sum of resources is equal to the sum of uses, with a balancing item to ensure this equality.

The system of economic accounts allows the build-up of accounts for different areas of the economy, highlighting – for example – production, income and financial transactions.

Accounts may be elaborated and set out for different institutional units or sectors (groups of units).

Usually a balancing item has to be introduced between the total resources and total uses of these units or sectors. When summed across the whole economy these balancing items constitute significant aggregates.

Table I.1 provides the structure of the accounts and shows how gross domestic product (GDP) estimates are derived as the balancing items.

The integrated economic accounts

The integrated economic accounts of the UK provide an overall view of the economy. Table I.1 presents a summary view of the accounts, balancing items and main aggregates and shows how they are expressed. The accounts are grouped into four main categories:

- goods and services accounts

- current accounts

- accumulation accounts

- balance sheets

The goods and services account

The goods and services account is a transactions account, balancing total resources, from outputs and imports, against the uses of these resources in consumption, investment, inventories and exports. No balancing item is required as the resources are simply balanced with the uses.

Current accounts: the production and distribution of income accounts

The production account

This account displays transactions involved in the generation of income by the activity of producing goods and services. The balancing item is value added (B.1). For the nation's accounts, the balancing items (the sum of value added for all industries) are, after the addition of taxes less subsidies on products, gross domestic product (GDP) at market prices or net domestic product when measured net of capital consumption. The production accounts are also shown for each industrial sector.

The distribution and use of income accounts

This account shows the distribution of current income (value added) carried forward from the production account and has saving as its balancing item (B.8). Saving is the difference between income (disposable income) and expenditure (or final consumption).

The distribution of income compromises of four sub-accounts:

- primary distribution of income account

- secondary distribution of income

- redistribution of income in kind

- use of income account

The primary distribution of income account

Primary incomes are accrued to institutional units because of their involvement in production or their ownership of productive assets. They include the following:

- property income (from lending or renting assets)

- taxes on production and imports

The following are excluded:

- taxes on income or wealth

- social contributions or benefits

- other current transfers

The primary distribution of income shows the way these are distributed among institutional units and sectors. The primary distribution account is divided into two sub-accounts – the generation and the allocation of primary incomes.

The secondary distribution of income account

This account describes how the balance of primary income for each institutional sector is allocated by redistribution; through transfers such as taxes on income, wealth and so on, social contributions and benefits, and other current transfers. It excludes social transfers in kind.

The balancing item of this account is gross disposable income (B.6g), which reflects current transactions and explicitly excludes capital transfers, real holding gains and losses, and the consequences of events such as natural disasters.

The redistribution of income in kind

This account shows how gross disposable income of households and non-profit institutions serving households, and government are transformed by the receipt and payment of transfers in kind. The balancing item for this account is adjusted gross disposable income (B.7g).

The use of income account shows how disposable income is divided between final consumption expenditure and saving. In addition, the use of income account includes, for households and for pensions, an adjustment item (D.8 – adjustment for the change in pension entitlements), which relates to the way that transactions between households and pension funds are recorded.

The accumulation accounts

These accounts cover all changes in assets, liabilities and net worth. The accounts are structured into two groups.

The first group covers transactions that would correspond to all changes in assets, liabilities and net worth that result from transactions and are known as the capital account and the financial account. They are distinguished to show the balancing item net lending or borrowing.

The second group relates to all changes in assets, liabilities and net worth owing to other factors, for example, the discovery or re-evaluation of mineral reserves, or the reclassification of a body from one sector to another.

The capital account

The capital account is presented in two parts.

The first part shows that saving (B.8g), the balance between national disposable income and final consumption expenditure from the production and distribution and use of income accounts, is reduced or increased by the balance of capital transfers (D.9) to provide an amount available for financing investment (in both non-financial and financial assets).

The second part shows total investment in non-financial assets. This is the sum of gross fixed capital formation (P. 51g), changes in inventories (P.52), acquisitions less disposals of valuables (P.53) and acquisitions less disposals of non-financial non-produced assets (NP). The balance on the capital account is known as net lending or borrowing. Conceptually, net lending or borrowing for all the domestic sectors represents net lending or borrowing to the rest of the world sector.

If actual investment is lower than the amount available for investment, the balance will be positive – representing net lending. Similarly, when the balance is negative, borrowing is represented. Where the capital accounts relate to the individual institutional sectors, the net lending or borrowing of a particular sector represents the amounts available for lending or borrowing to other sectors. The value of net lending or net borrowing is the same irrespective of whether the accounts are shown before or after deducting consumption of fixed capital (P.51c), provided a consistent approach is adopted throughout.

The financial account

This account shows how net lending and borrowing are achieved by transactions in financial instruments. The net acquisitions of financial assets are shown separately from the net incurrence of liabilities. The balancing item is net lending or borrowing.

In principle, net lending or borrowing should be identical for both the capital account and the financial account. In practice, however, because of errors and omissions this identity is very difficult to achieve for the sectors and the economy as a whole. The difference is known as a statistical adjustment.

The other changes in assets account is concerned with the recording of changes in the values of assets and liabilities, and thus of the changes in net worth, between opening and closing balance sheets that result from flows that are not transactions, referred to as "other flows".

This account is further subdivided into:

- other changes in the volume of assets account

- revaluation account

The other changes in the volume of assets account records the changes in assets, liabilities and net worth between opening and closing balance sheets that are due neither to transactions between institutional units, as recorded in the capital and financial accounts, nor to holding gains and losses as recorded in the revaluation account. Examples include reclassifications and write-offs. The balancing item for this account is other changes in volume (B.102).

The revaluation account records holding gains or losses accruing during the accounting period to the owners of financial and non-financial assets and liabilities. The balancing item for this account is nominal holding gains and losses (B.103).

The balance sheet

The second group of accumulation accounts complete the sequence of accounts. These include the balance sheets and a reconciliation of the changes that have brought about the change in net worth between the beginning and end of the accounting period.

The opening and closing balance sheets show how total holdings of assets by the UK or its sectors match total liabilities and net worth (the balancing item). Various types of assets and liabilities can be shown in detailed presentations of the balance sheets. Changes between the opening and closing balance sheets for each group of assets and liabilities result from transactions and other flows recorded in the accumulation accounts, or reclassifications and revaluations.

Net worth
equals
changes in assets
less
changes in liabilities.

The rest of the world account

This account covers the transactions between resident and non-resident institutional units and the related stocks of assets and liabilities. Written from the point of view of the rest of the world, its role is similar to an institutional sector.

Satellite accounts

Satellite accounts cover areas or activities not included in the central framework because they either add additional detail to an already complex system or conflict with the conceptual framework. The UK Environmental Accounts are satellite accounts linking environmental and economic data to show the interactions between the economy and the environment.

See UK Environmental Accounts: 2017 for further information.

The limits of the national economy: economic territory, residence and centre of economic interest

Economic territory and residence of economic interest

The economy of the UK is made up of institutional units that have a centre of economic interest in the UK economic territory. These units are known as resident units and it is their transactions that are recorded in the UK National Accounts.

UK economic territory

The UK economic territory includes:

- Great Britain and Northern Ireland (the geographic territory administered by the UK government within which persons, goods, services and capital move freely)

- any free zones, including bonded warehouses and factories under UK customs control

- the national airspace, UK territorial waters and the UK sector of the continental shelf The UK economic territory excludes Crown dependencies (Channel Islands and the Isle of Man).

ESA 2010 economic territory

Within the European System of Accounts 2010: ESA 2010, the definition of economic territory also includes:

- territorial enclaves in the rest of the world (embassies, military bases, scientific stations, information or immigration offices and aid agencies used by the British government with the formal political agreement of the governments in which these units are located)

But it excludes:

- any extra- territorial enclaves (that is, parts of the UK geographic territory like embassies and US military bases used by general government agencies of other countries, by the institutions of the European Union or by international organisations under treaties or by agreement)

Centre of economic interest

When an institutional unit engages and intends to continue engaging (normally for one year or more) in economic activities on a significant scale from a location (dwelling or place of production) within the UK economic territory, it is defined as having a centre of economic interest and is a resident of the UK.

If a unit conducts transactions on the economic territory of several countries, it has a centre of economic interest in each of them.

Ownership of land and structures in the UK is enough to qualify the owner to have a centre of interest in the UK.

Residency

Resident units are:

- households

- legal and social entities such as corporations and quasi- corporations, for example, branches of foreign investors

- non-profit institutions

- government

- so-called "notional residents"

Travellers, cross-border and seasonal workers, crews of ships and aircraft, and students studying overseas are all residents of their home countries and remain members of their households.

When an individual leaves the UK for one year or more (excluding students and patients receiving medical treatment), they cease being a member of a resident household and become a non-resident, even on home visits.

Economic activity: what production is included?

Gross domestic product (GDP) is defined as the sum of all economic activity taking place in UK territory. In practice a "production boundary" is defined, inside which are all the economic activities taken to contribute to economic performance. To decide whether to include a particular activity within the production boundary, the following factors are considered:

- does the activity produce a useful output?

- is the product or activity marketable and does it have a market value?

- if the product does not have a meaningful market value, can one be assigned (imputed)?

- would exclusion (or inclusion) of the product of the activity make comparisons between countries over time more meaningful?

The following are recorded within the European System of Accounts 2010: ESA 2010 production boundary:

- production of individual and collective services by government

- own-account production of housing services by owner-occupiers

- production of goods for own final consumption, for example, agricultural products own-

- account construction, including that by households

- production of services by paid domestic staff

- breeding of fish in fish farms

- production forbidden by law; as long as all units involved in the transaction enter into it voluntarily

- production from which the revenues are not declared in full to the fiscal authorities, for example, clandestine production of textiles

The following fall outside the production boundary:

- domestic and personal services produced and consumed within the same household, for example, cleaning, the preparation of meals or the care of sick or elderly people

- volunteer services that do not lead to the production of goods, for example, caretaking and cleaning without payment

- natural breeding of fish in open seas

(European System of Accounts ESA 2010 (2013) paragraphs 1.29 and 1.30)

Prices used to value the products of economic activity

In the UK, a number of different prices may be used to value inputs, outputs and purchases. The prices are different depending on the perception of the bodies engaged in the transaction – that is, the producer and user of a product will usually perceive the value of the product differently, with the result that the output prices received by producers can be distinguished from the prices paid by producers.

Basic prices

Basic prices are the preferred method of valuing output in the accounts.

They are the amount received by the producer for a unit of goods or services
minus any taxes payable
plus
any subsidy receivable as a consequence of production or sale.

The only taxes included in the price will be taxes on the output process – for example, business rates and Vehicle Excise Duty, which are not specifically levied on the production of a unit of output. Basic prices exclude any transport charges invoiced separately by the producer. When a valuation at basic prices is not feasible, producers' prices may be used.

Producers' prices

Producers' prices are basic prices
plus
those taxes paid per unit of output (other than taxes deductible by the purchaser such as VAT, invoiced for output sold)
minus
any subsidies received per unit of output.

Purchasers' or market prices

Purchasers' or market prices are the prices paid by the purchaser and include transport costs, trade margins and taxes (unless the taxes are deductible by the purchaser).

Purchasers' or market prices are producers' prices
plus
any non-deductible VAT or similar tax payable by the purchaser
plus
transport costs paid separately by the purchaser (not included in the producers' price).

They are also referred to as "market prices".

The rest of the world: national and domestic

Domestic product (or income) includes production (or primary incomes generated and distributed) resulting from all activities taking place "at home" or in the UK domestic territory.

This will include production by any foreign-owned company in the UK, but exclude any income earned by UK residents from production taking place outside the domestic territory.

GDP
equals
the sum of primary incomes distributed by resident producer prices.

The definition of GNI (gross national income) is gross domestic product (GDP) plus income received from other countries (notably interest and dividends), less similar payments made to other countries.

GDP
plus
net property income
equals
GNI.

This can be introduced by considering the primary incomes distributed by the resident producer units. Primary incomes, generated in the production activity of resident producer units, are distributed mostly to other residents' institutional units.

For example, when a resident producer unit is owned by a foreign company, some of the primary incomes generated by the producer unit are likely to be paid abroad. Similarly, some primary incomes generated in the rest of the world may go to resident units. It is therefore necessary to exclude that part of resident producers' primary income paid abroad, but include the primary incomes generated abroad but paid to resident units.

GDP (or income)
less
primary incomes payable to non-resident units
plus
primary incomes receivable from the rest of the world
equals
GNI.

GNI at market prices
equals
the sum of gross primary incomes receivable by resident institutional units or sectors.

National income includes income earned by residents of the national territory, remitted (or deemed to be remitted in the case of direct investment) to the national territory, no matter where the income is earned.

Real GDP (chained volume measures)
plus
trading gain
equals
real gross domestic income (RGDI).

Real gross domestic income (RGDI)
plus
real primary incomes receivable from abroad
less
real primary incomes payable abroad
equals
real gross national income (real GNI).

Real GNI (chained volume measures)
plus
real current transfers from abroad
less
real current transfers abroad
equals
real gross national disposable income (GNDI).

Receivables and transfers of primary incomes, and transfers to and from abroad, are deflated using the gross domestic final expenditure deflator.

Gross domestic product: the concept of net and gross

The term gross means that, when measuring domestic production, capital consumption or depreciation has not been allowed for.

Capital goods are different from the materials and fuels used up in the production process because they are not used up in the period of account but are instrumental in allowing that process to take place. However, over time, capital goods wear out or become obsolete and in this sense GDP does not give a true picture of value added in the economy. When calculating value added as the difference between output and costs, we should also show that part of the capital goods are used up during the production process (the depreciation of capital assets).

Net concepts are net of this capital depreciation, for example:

GDP
minus
consumption of fixed capital
equals
net domestic product.

Symbols used

In general, the following symbols are used:

.. not available

 nil or less than £500,000

£ billion denotes £1,000 million

United Kingdom National Accounts

The Blue Book
Tables A to C

2017 edition

Editors: Dean Goodway & Sarah Nightingale

Office for National Statistics

Revisions since ONS Blue Book, 2016 edition

	2009	2010	2011	2012	2013	2014	2015
National accounts aggregates at current prices							
Gross domestic product at market prices	10 077	7 438	6 788	10 181	12 991	14 582	19 177
less basic price adjustment	33	45	43	39	114	136	582
Gross value added at basic prices	10 044	7 393	6 745	10 142	12 877	14 446	18 595
Expenditure components at current prices							
National expenditure on goods and services at market prices							
Households	12 373	9 676	9 130	10 749	14 724	17 689	23 879
NPISH[1]	726	788	785	815	−107	−47	−1 510
General government	−736	−950	−1 196	−1 412	−1 539	485	1 234
Gross fixed capital formation	−3 188	−3 501	−3 820	−3 941	−3 015	−1 530	−3 617
Changes in inventories	–	–	–	–	−362	195	2 812
Acquisitions less disposals of valuables	–	–	–	–	−581	−1 602	−6 487
Total exports	1 069	1 431	1 875	1 914	2 271	7 271	6 821
Statistical discrepancy (expenditure)	–	–	–	–	–	–	−3 332
Total imports	167	6	−14	−2 056	−1 600	7 879	623
Income components at current prices							
Compensation of employees	−374	−705	−938	−1 110	4 446	2 952	990
Gross operating surplus							
Public non-financial corporations	3 771	4 370	4 951	5 644	6 121	6 745	7 405
Private non-financial corporations	3 044	3 291	1 102	4 017	−2 471	2 480	8 459
Financial corporations	488	771	1 027	1 017	1 273	1 957	−4 410
General government	–	–	–	–	–	–	−52
Households and NPISH[1]	5 000	4 954	4 537	5 816	6 554	5 558	8 598
Mixed income	−2 603	−6 057	−4 862	−6 308	−4 416	−6 576	−4 602
Taxes on production and imports	751	814	971	1 116	1 311	1 402	2 025
less subsidies	–	–	–	−11	173	64	242
Statistical discrepancy (income)	–	–	–	–	–	–	522

1 Non-profit institutions serving households.

B The sector accounts: Key economic indicators

£ million

			2009	2010	2011	2012	2013	2014	2015	2016
Net lending(+)/borrowing(-) by:										
Non-financial corporations										
Public	CPCM		−906	−3 100	−1 655	−415	925	−1 988	−1 423	−2 512
Private	DTAL		20 136	39 352	39 716	1 299	−26 793	−13 983	−41 126	−19 286
Total	EABO	B.9	19 230	36 252	38 061	884	−25 868	−15 971	−42 549	−21 798
Financial corporations	NHCQ	B.9	−963	−32 110	−14 592	2 819	−20 477	−20 587	−33 263	−43 240
General government										
Central	NMFJ		−151 320	−147 246	−118 941	−129 584	−93 329	−103 294	−77 106	−54 823
Local	NMOE		−8 251	−3 040	−4 614	−8 889	−4 317	−653	−3 853	−9 470
Total	NNBK	B.9	−159 571	−150 286	−123 555	−138 473	−97 646	−103 947	−80 959	−64 293
Households and NPISH[1]										
Households	A99R		73 553	73 533	56 415	58 172	45 472	41 345	55 537	18 229
NPISH	AA7W		8 229	12 198	4 016	4 421	299	−807	1 111	3 014
Total	NSSZ	B.9	81 782	85 731	60 431	62 593	45 771	40 538	56 648	21 243
Rest of the world	NHRB	B.9	59 523	60 415	39 659	72 174	98 219	99 967	100 123	116 799
Private non-financial corporations										
Gross trading profits										
Continental shelf profits	CAGD		21 452	25 379	29 806	25 246	23 470	16 702	10 253	9 575
Others	CAED		221 336	238 724	244 379	248 753	261 837	298 861	312 022	336 456
Rental of buildings	DTWR		15 865	16 526	18 638	18 549	19 354	20 091	18 900	19 763
less holding gains of inventories	DLRA		4 213	8 435	8 798	2 733	3 098	1 465	−3 674	11 295
Gross operating surplus	CAER	B.2g	254 440	272 194	284 025	289 815	301 563	334 189	344 849	354 499
Households sector										
Disposable income, gross	QWND	B.6g	1 079 160	1 092 900	1 111 762	1 166 292	1 208 238	1 243 487	1 317 252	1 339 355
Implied deflator of households and NPISH Individual consumption expenditure Index (2015=100)[2]	CRXA		88.3	89.8	93.3	95.3	97.6	99.4	100.0	101.4
Real households disposable income:										
Chained volume measures (reference year 2015)	DG2V		1 156 187	1 146 658	1 127 087	1 159 707	1 176 905	1 190 413	1 256 881	1 257 784
Index (2015=100)[2]	DG2Z		92.0	91.2	89.7	92.3	93.6	94.7	100.0	100.1
Gross saving	HADA	B.8g	115 084	117 902	104 515	106 016	103 574	106 787	121 559	92 045
Households total resources	HAYW		1 075 938	1 102 516	1 117 921	1 159 679	1 202 309	1 250 706	1 303 427	1 325 372
Saving ratio (per cent)	DG5H		10.7	10.7	9.3	9.1	8.6	8.5	9.3	7.0

1 Non-profit institutions serving households
2 Rounded to one decimal place

C Table C: Sector statistical adjustments

£ million

		2009	2010	2011	2012	2013	2014	2015	2016
Private non-financial corporations	NYPM	14 539	18 885	13 506	−3 486	−2 660	4 367	−22 711	12 269
Financial corporations	NYOX	−14 431	−15 359	963	−2 702	−1 567	−231	13 575	15 359
Public corporations	NYPI	124	640	−415	104	137	786	−315	−310
Central government	NZDW	824	−954	24	556	870	−743	547	247
Local government	NYPC	21	840	399	19	−504	−172	394	−152
Households	NYPA	−7 531	−3 731	−19 229	−15 062	−14 540	−9 161	9 979	−17 889
Non-profit institutions serving households	NYPH	7 907	11 949	−4 884	6 972	4 727	−4 908	−10 701	1 950
Rest of the world	NYPO	−1 451	−12 268	9 640	13 596	13 536	10 062	9 231	−2 763
Total[2]	RVFE	−	−	−	−	−	−	−	−8 711

1 Non-profit institutions serving households.
2 Equals, but opposite in sign to, the residual error observed between GDP measured by the income approach and GDP measured by the expenditure approach.

United Kingdom National Accounts

The Blue Book
Chapter 01: National Accounts at a Glance

2017 edition

Editors: Dean Goodway & Sarah Nightingale

Office for National Statistics

Introduction

This section of the UK National Accounts, The Blue Book: 2017 edition provides an examination of recent trends and important movements for a range of information contained in a number of the subsequent Blue Book chapters. All UK data referred to in this section are consistent with the Blue Book 2017.

GDP and the headline economy

ha ter 1   rovides information on the headline economy, including the latest estimates of UK gross domestic product (GDP), which records how much output was produced in the UK in any given year. In September 2007, Northern Rock became the first UK bank in 150 years to suffer a bank run. To mark the tenth anniversary of the financial crisis, Figure 1 shows how the path of the economy compares with the previous three UK downturns. The financial crisis led to a peak-to-trough fall in output of 6.1%, while it took over five years for the economy to reach its pre-downturn levels. Compared with previous downturns, the effects of the financial crisis were larger in scale.

Figure 1: The last four UK downturns, 1973, 1980, 1990 and 2008

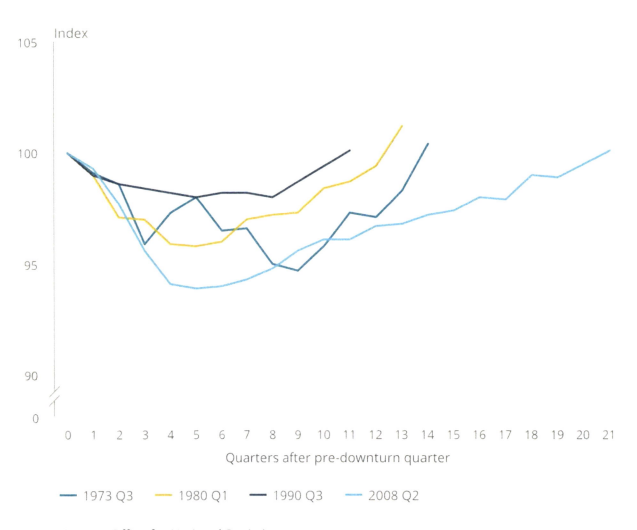

Figure 1: The last four UK downturns, 1973, 1980, 1990 and 2008

Source: Office for National Statistics

Source: Office for National Statistics

Notes:

1. Q1 refers to Quarter 1 (Jan to Mar), Q2 refers to Quarter 2 (Apr to June), Q3 refers to Quarter 3 (July to Sept), and Q4 refers to Quarter 4 (Oct to Dec).

2. Indexed to the pre-downturn peak

Figure 2 shows how UK GDP has evolved over the last 10 years. GDP fell by 0.5% in 2008, then by a further 4.2% in 2009. This was driven by an initial fall in gross capital formation, as gross fixed capital formation fell by 5.1% in 2008 and by 13.8% in 2009[1]. The financial crisis led to a tightening of credit conditions and increased economic uncertainty, which impacted upon the ability and willingness of firms to invest in fixed capital. Household consumption also contracted in this period, falling by 0.6% in 2008 and by 3.3% in 2009. The deterioration in labour market conditions and the outlook for household finances led to a process of household deleveraging, in which households reduced their liabilities relative to income, by paying down debt or cutting down on new borrowing. This led to consumers cutting back on spending.

Figure 2: Contributions to real UK gross domestic product growth by expenditure, 2007 to 2016

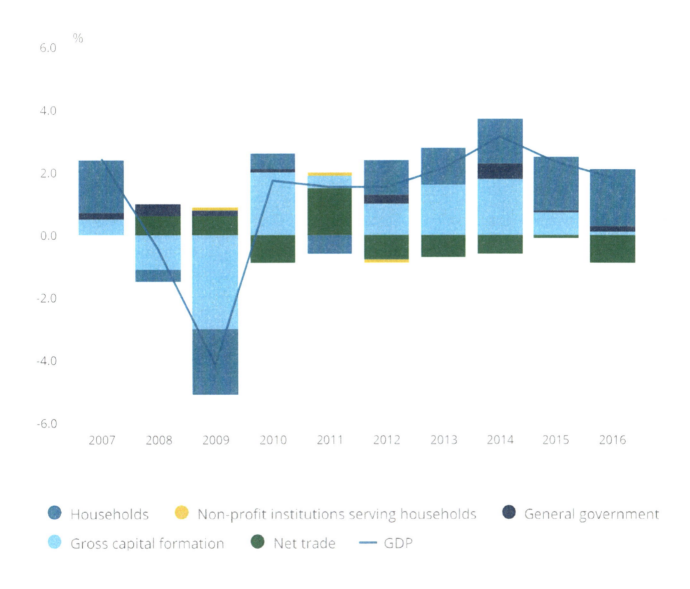

Figure 2: Contributions to real UK gross domestic product growth by expenditure, 2007 to 2016

Source: Office for National Statistics

Notes:

1. Components may not sum to total gross domestic product due to rounding and loss of additivity in data prior to open period. The statistical discrepancy in 2016 is also not displayed.

The economy showed initial signs of a pickup in activity in 2010, when GDP increased by 1.7%. Figure 2 shows that the UK economy has steadily increased in the subsequent years, which in recent years has been driven by growth in consumption and investment, as the factors that weighed on the outlook in the downturn started to unwind. Despite the sterling depreciation associated with the financial crisis, net trade provided little contribution to UK GDP growth in the following years, which to some extent reflects the impact on global demand in this period.

The latest estimates show that GDP grew by 1.8% in 2016, driven primarily by household consumption, which increased by 2.9%. Gross fixed capital formation was more subdued, picking up by 1.3% in 2016. Exports grew by only 1.1%, which was more than offset by the 4.3% increase in imports, as net trade detracted from GDP growth in 2016.

Notes for GDP and the headline economy

1. Gross fixed capital formation (GFCF) is a net investment concept. It refers to the net increase in physical assets in a given period, recording the total value of the acquisitions of fixed assets, less its disposals. It records the net capital expenditure by both the public and private sectors, such as spending on plant and machinery, transport equipment, software, new dwellings and other buildings, and major improvements to existing buildings and structures. GFCF is recorded under gross capital formation, which also records changes in inventories and the acquisitions less disposals of valuables.

Households

The Blue Book allows for an examination of the flow-stock relationship in the national accounts. The non-financial account records the flows in disposable income and how this is allocated by households between consumption and saving. The extent to which savings exceed investment is reflected in the net lending or borrowing position of each domestic sector in the UK and the rest of the world. Changes in the lending or borrowing positions are reflected in the acquisition of financial assets and liabilities by each sector, which is recorded in the financial account.

These financial flows feed into the stock position of financial assets and liabilities that are held by each sector. The change in wealth not only reflects the accumulation of new assets and liabilities, but also the revaluation of existing ones and other changes in volume, as set out in the following equation:

$$\text{Stock}_t - \text{Stock}_{t-1} = \text{Flow}_t + \text{Revaluation Changes}_t + \text{Other Changes in Volume Account}_t$$

For the first time, information on the revaluation changes and other changes in volumes is published in Blue Book 2017, which allows for a full reconciliation of the flow and stock positions of assets and liabilities.

In the national accounts, the economy is grouped into a number of institutional sectors, split by type of activity, ownership and control. This provides us with information on the UK's economic performance and financial position. A comprehensive explanation of the headline sectors, income and capital accounts and the financial balance sheet can be found in the Blue Book. The households account has now been separated from the non-profit institutions serving households (NPISH) account. This section of the Blue Book focuses on recent trends in the household sector.

Households saving ratio

The households saving ratio is the proportion of total household disposable income that is saved [1]. Figure 3 shows how the saving ratio has evolved since 1970 and highlights how this ratio typically increases during an economic downturn. In each of the last four UK downturns, the saving ratio has risen, as households have undergone a process of deleveraging in response to the increased uncertainty around the economic outlook.

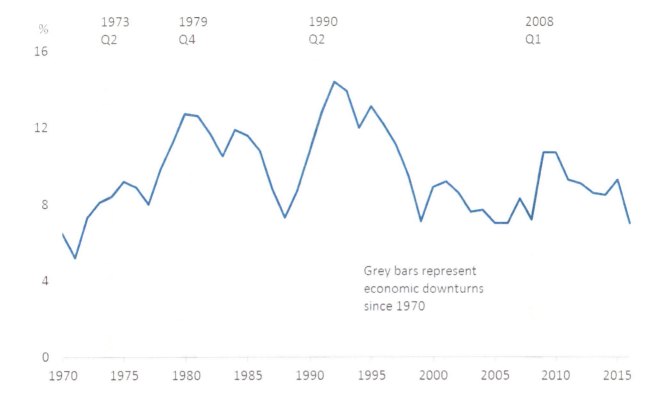

Grey bars represent economic downturns since 1970

In the run-up to the financial crisis, the saving ratio had steadily declined, falling to 7.0%. As economic prospects quickly deteriorated, there was a fall in consumer confidence and households began to save a greater proportion of their income. Credit had been much more readily available to households up until 2007, but households were less able and willing to finance their spending by increasing their financial liabilities as credit conditions tightened during the financial crisis. As such, households became more reliant on saving more of their disposable household resources to finance their expenditure. The saving ratio rose sharply to 10.7% in 2009 and 2010.

In recent years, the households saving ratio has been on a downward trend as consumption growth has outstripped growth in disposable income, which has been relatively subdued. The households saving ratio fell to 7.0% in 2016.

Gross Household Disposable Income

By definition, movements in the saving ratio can be attributed to changes in total available resources and consumption expenditure. Figure 4 shows growth in gross household disposable income (GHDI), decomposed into compensation of employees (CoE) – which includes wages and salaries as well as employers' social contributions – gross mixed income and gross operating surplus (GOS), net property income[2], net social contributions and benefits, net current transfers and taxes on income and wealth.

Figure 4 shows that during the economic downturn there was a slowing in the growth of CoE in 2008 and 2009, which increased by only 1.4% and 0.4% respectively. This was offset by strong growth in households' receipt of social benefits, which helped buffer the fall in GHDI growth. Meanwhile, mixed income and gross operating surplus (GOS) reduced GHDI growth.

As output increased from 2010, GHDI growth has also picked up. That said, it slowed to 1.5% in 2016, which was the weakest annual growth rate since 2010. This slowdown reflected an increase in taxes and falls in net property income, other current transfers, and social contributions and benefits. The largest negative contribution was net property income, driven primarily by a 16.4% fall in dividends from corporations. This is likely to reflect the forestalling of dividends, which were brought forward and paid in 2015, before an increase in taxes on dividends was introduced in April 2016.

Figure 4: Decomposition of gross household disposable income 2007 to 2016

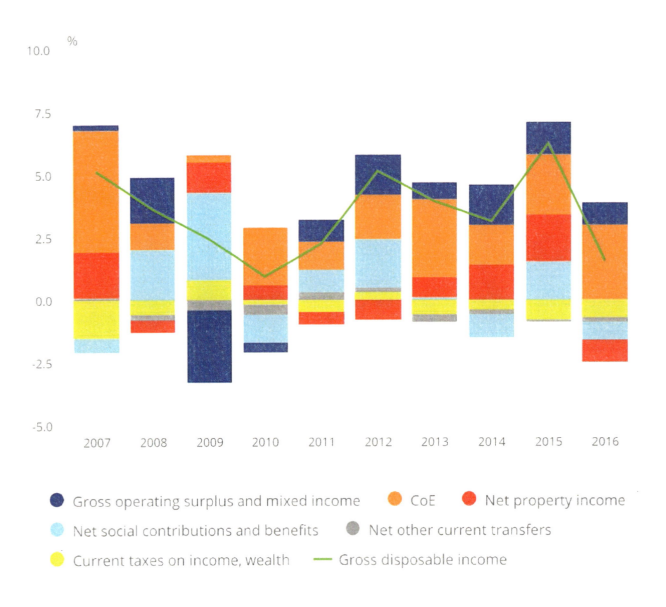

Legend:
- Gross operating surplus and mixed income
- CoE
- Net property income
- Net social contributions and benefits
- Net other current transfers
- Current taxes on income, wealth
- Gross disposable income

Source: Office for National Statistics

Household consumption

As growth in GHDI slowed, nominal household consumption fell and the households saving ratio rose. Figure 5 shows that household consumption fell by 2.6% in 2009. Within household consumption, goods may be classified as durable (such as cars or furniture), semi-durable (such as clothing) or non-durable (such as food). Durable goods are those that can be used repeatedly or continuously over a period of more than a year. These are typically considered to be more discretionary in nature, as consumers can more easily delay their purchase. It is therefore expected that expenditure on these items might slow during periods of lower income growth or heightened uncertainty about the future.

There was a marked slowdown in durable goods consumption during the 2008 to 2009 downturn. In 2007, durable goods consumption increased by 6.9% in volume terms, but this fell by 2.6% in 2009. This slowdown coincided with weaker growth in household incomes, with GHDI falling year-on-year from 5.1% in 2007 to 2.4% in 2009 and an increase in the saving ratio. Meanwhile, annual growth in household consumption of non-durable goods – which comprises just over half of total household goods expenditure – saw a less marked fall during the 2008 -2009 downturn and has been on a steady upward trend since 2009, growing at an average annual rate of 0.3%.

Figure 5: Decomposition of nominal growth in total household final consumption expenditure, UK, 2007 to 2016

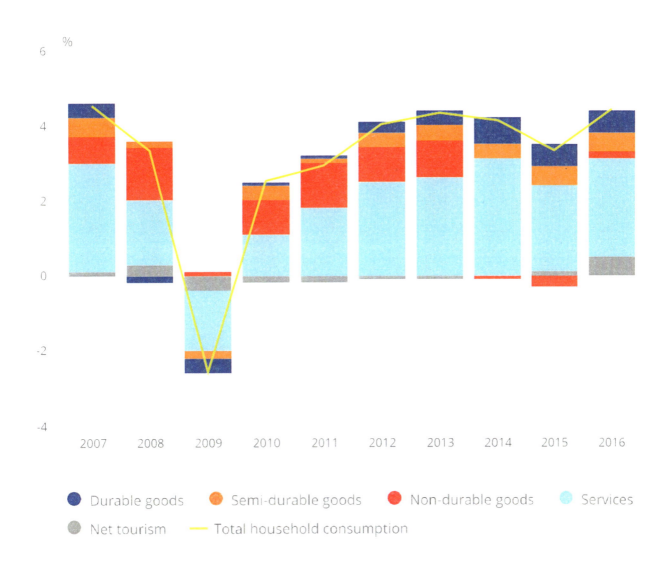

Figure 5: Decomposition of nominal growth in total household final consumption expenditure, UK, 2007 to 2016

Source: Office for National Statistics

The slowdown in GHDI in 2016 coincided with a strong increase in consumption expenditure, with total household consumption growing by 4.4% – its strongest annual growth rate since 2007 (Figure 5) – and was reflected in the fall in the saving ratio.

Net acquisition of financial assets and liabilities by households

If savings exceed investment, that sector is able to finance the borrowing needs of others as there are net resources available. In contrast, if investment exceeds savings, that sector has a borrowing need in order to finance its expenditure. Figure 6 shows the net lending/borrowing position of households from the financial accounts over the period 1997 to 2016 and how this was financed. Positive bars indicate where households have acquired financial assets (for example, deposits and pension assets) while negative bars indicate the acquisition of financial liabilities (for example, loans). If the acquisition of assets exceeds the acquisition of liabilities, this indicates that households are lending to other sectors in the given period.

Figure 6: Net acquisition of households financial assets and liabilities, UK, 1997 to 2016

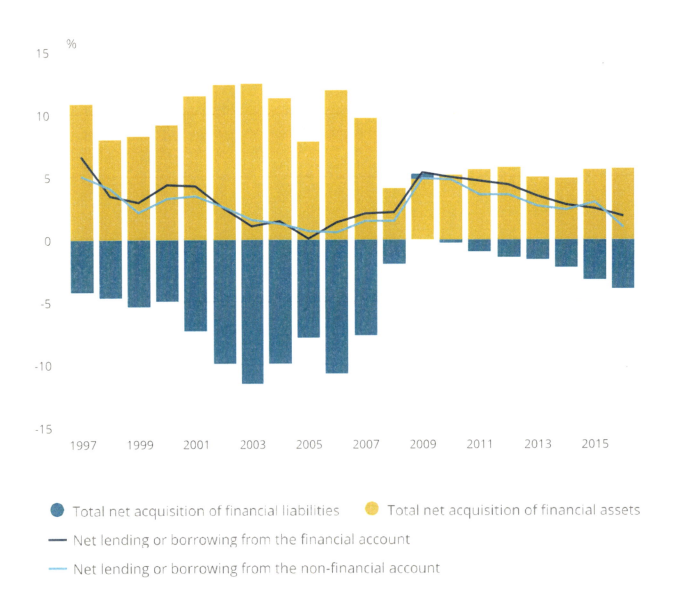

Figure 6: Net acquisition of households financial assets and liabilities, UK, 1997 to 2016

It can be seen that households have been a net lender for this period, reflected in households acquiring more financial assets than liabilities. In the years leading up to the financial crisis, households acquired on average net financial assets equivalent to around 10% of gross domestic product (GDP) per year, while acquiring net financial liabilities of around 8% of GDP. Following the financial crisis, households became more of a net lender, reducing their net acquisition of financial liabilities. This corresponds with the impacts of the downturn on the cost and availability of credit, consistent with the increase in the saving ratio. The acquisitions of long-term loans secured on dwellings, fell from a net increase of £103.9 billion in 2007 to a net increase of £33.9 billion in 2008, as households undertook a process of deleveraging. The net lending position of households increased to 5.3% of GDP in 2009.

Household balance sheet

The saving ratio records how much households save of the flow of total household resources in a given period, but it does not take into consideration the net stock of financial and non-financial wealth of households. The change in wealth in a given period is equal to the accumulation of new assets and the revaluation of existing ones. These revaluation changes can be significant when the gross size of the balance sheet is large, as is the case for households (Figure 7).

Figure 7 shows the net worth (wealth) of households as a share of GDP, decomposed into financial and non-financial assets as well as financial liabilities. It shows that the value of household assets has been relatively evenly split between financial and non-financial assets over the past 10 years, with both types of assets following similar trends over time. While both financial and non-financial assets dipped in 2008 during the crisis, the fall in household net worth was driven largely by a £0.5 trillion fall in non-financial assets – predominantly in the value of land. For the first time, Blue Book 2017 is publishing a dwellings estimate that excludes the value of the land underneath the structure, with a separate estimate for the value of the land. These new estimates show that while the value of dwellings has grown steadily over the past 20 years, it has not kept pace with growth in the value of land. Land value increased from £0.7 trillion to £3.9 trillion between 1996 and 2016 (or by 479%), while the value of dwellings grew by less than half the rate at 203% (increasing from £0.5 to £1.5 trillion over the same period).

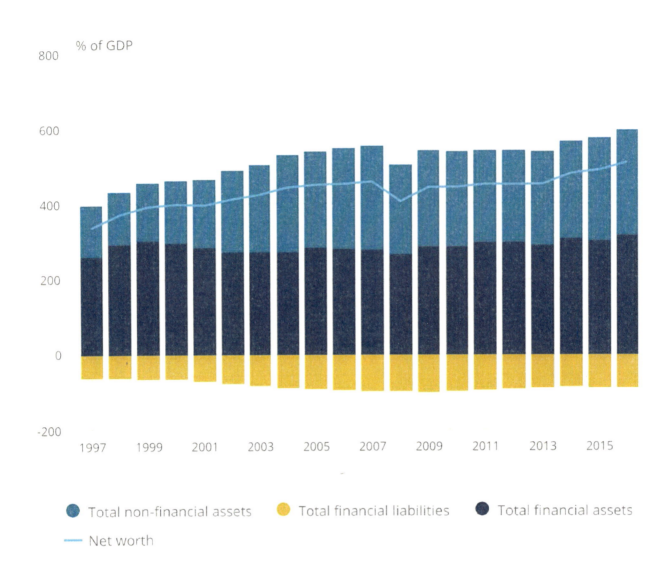

Figure 7: Net worth of households, UK, 1997 to 2016

Source: Office for National Statistics

For the first time, Blue Book 2017 includes information on these revaluations and other changes in volume of assets. These record changes in the value of assets and liabilities, but where there has not been a change in the underlying volume of these stocks. Holding gains and losses are recorded in the former, which may arise because of exchange rate movements or equity price movements.

Figure 8 shows the change in the net stock position of households and non-profit institutions serving households (NPISH), disaggregated into financial flows (net lending/borrowing for the period), other changes to volume of assets and revaluation changes. It shows that while revaluation changes can be particularly large and volatile, much of this volatility can be attributable to revaluations to pensions and insurance, which primarily reflect changes in the discount rate affecting valuations of future flows, rather than equity price or exchange rate movements. In 2016, of the £450 billion increase in the net wealth of households and NPISH 88% was due to revaluation effects.

Figure 8: Change in the net worth of households and non-profit institutions serving households, UK, 1998 to 2016

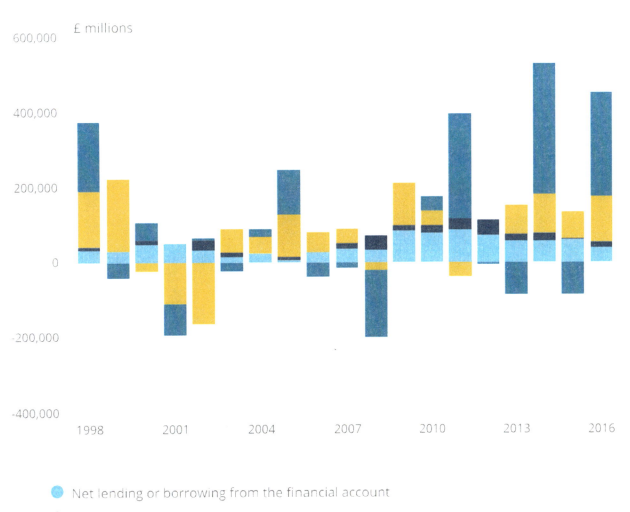

Net lending or borrowing from the financial account

Other changes in volume of assets

Revaluation excluding insurance, pensions and standardised guarantee schemes

Revaluation of insurance, pensions and standardised guarantee schemes

Source: Office for National Statistics

Notes for: Households

3. Total household disposable income is the sum of gross household disposable income and an adjustment for the change in pension entitlements.

4. Income received from financial investments, such as interest on savings or dividends from shares.

Net lending/Borrowing by sector

The income and expenditure of each sector implies a net lending or borrowing position for households, corporations, government and the rest of the world. These flows must sum to zero by definition – for each pound that is borrowed by one sector, there must be a pound that is lent by another.

Figure 9 shows the net lending/borrowing position for each sector in the UK and from the rest of the world. This shows that the net borrowing positions of the corporate and government are offset by net lending from households and the rest of the world. In recent years, the rest of the world has increasingly become a net lender to the UK as the current account deficit has grown to 5.9% of gross domestic product (GDP) in 2016. This has been driven by a fall in net investment income, so the UK has increasingly acquired financial liabilities to finance its borrowing from the rest of the world.

In 2016, households and non-profit institutions serving households (NPISH) were a net lender of 1.1% of GDP. Following the financial crisis, the government budget deficit widened to 10.4% of GDP in 2009. This has narrowed in the intervening period in line with government policy and was 3.3% of GDP in 2016. Following the financial crisis, there was a pickup in capital investment by corporations, which has moved from being a net lender to a net borrower. In 2016, its net borrowing position was 3.3% of GDP.

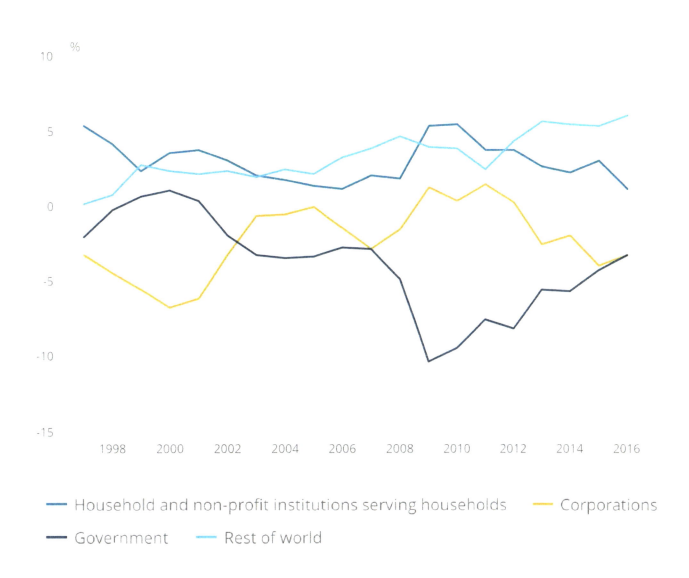

Figure 9: Net Lending/Borrowing

Source: Office for National Statistics

1.1 UK national and domestic product
Main aggregates: Index numbers and values

Current prices and chained volume measures (reference year 2015)

			2009	2010	2011	2012	2013	2014	2015	2016
Indices (2015=100)										
Values at current prices										
Gross domestic product at market prices		B.1*g								
("Money GDP")	YBEU		81.0	83.6	86.6	89.2	92.8	97.3	100.0	103.8
Gross value added at basic prices	YBEX	B.1g	82.6	84.4	86.6	89.4	92.8	97.3	100.0	103.7
Chained volume measures										
Gross domestic product at market prices	YBEZ	B.1*g	88.7	90.2	91.5	92.9	94.8	97.7	100.0	101.8
Gross national disposable income at market prices	YBFP	B.6*g	88.8	91.3	92.6	92.8	94.1	97.6	100.0	102.0
Gross value added at basic prices	CGCE	B.1g	88.9	90.5	91.7	92.9	94.2	97.6	100.0	101.6
Implied deflator										
Implied deflator of GDP at market prices	YBGB		91.3	92.7	94.6	96.0	97.9	99.5	100.0	102.0
Values at current prices (£million)										
Gross measures (before deduction of consumption of fixed capital) at current market prices										
Gross domestic product ("Money GDP")	YBHA	B.1*g	1 529 536	1 579 877	1 635 062	1 685 225	1 752 554	1 837 062	1 888 737	1 961 125
Employment, property and entrepreneurial income from rest of the world (receipts less payments)	YBGG	D.1+D.4	−12 284	960	6 318	−17 499	−35 920	−37 160	−41 811	−49 521
Subsidies (receipts) less taxes (payments) on products from/to rest of the world	QZOZ	-D.21+D.31	2 655	2 945	2 937	2 898	2 926	2 960	3 087	3 327
Other subsidies on production from/ to rest of the world	IBJL	+D.29-D.39	−3 411	−3 059	−3 166	−2 625	−2 455	−2 306	−1 961	−2 431
Gross balance of primary incomes/ gross national income (GNI)	ABMX	B.5*g	1 518 009	1 580 953	1 641 613	1 667 450	1 716 162	1 799 248	1 845 800	1 910 713
Current transfers from rest of the world (receipts less payments)	YBGF	D.5,6,7	14 785	19 596	20 271	20 449	25 280	23 395	22 838	22 025
Gross national disposable income	NQCO	B.6*g	1 503 224	1 561 357	1 621 342	1 647 001	1 690 882	1 775 853	1 822 962	1 888 688
Adjustment to current basic prices										
Gross domestic product (at market prices)	YBHA	B.1*g	1 529 536	1 579 877	1 635 062	1 685 225	1 752 554	1 837 062	1 888 737	1 961 125
Adjustment to current basic prices (less taxes plus subsidies on products)	NQBU	D.21-D.31	137 263	157 849	176 242	179 507	188 124	198 340	203 800	213 478
Gross value added (at basic prices)	ABML	B.1g	1 392 273	1 422 028	1 458 820	1 505 718	1 564 430	1 638 722	1 684 937	1 747 647
Net measures (after deduction of consumption of fixed capital) at current market prices										
Consumption of fixed capital	NQAE	P.51c	190 776	193 371	200 413	207 191	215 935	224 859	231 530	240 255
Net domestic product	NHRK	B.1*n	1 338 760	1 386 506	1 434 649	1 478 034	1 536 619	1 612 203	1 657 207	1 720 875
Net national income	NSRX	B.5*n	1 327 232	1 387 580	1 441 196	1 460 262	1 500 228	1 574 389	1 614 270	1 670 458
Net national disposable income	NQCP	B.6*n	1 312 447	1 367 984	1 420 925	1 439 813	1 474 948	1 550 994	1 591 432	1 648 433
Chained volume measures (reference year 2015, £million)										
Gross measures (before deduction of consumption of fixed capital) at market prices										
Gross domestic product	ABMI	B.1*g	1 675 963	1 704 364	1 729 121	1 754 736	1 790 750	1 845 444	1 888 737	1 922 626
Terms of trade effect ("trading gain or loss")	YBGJ	TGL	−28 229	−21 137	−27 798	−23 261	−12 575	−4 928	−	8 464
Real gross domestic income	YBGL	GDI	1 647 734	1 683 227	1 701 323	1 731 475	1 778 175	1 840 516	1 888 737	1 931 090
Real employment, property and entrepreneurial income from rest of the world (receipts less payments)	YBGI	D.1+D.4	−13 205	1 020	6 554	−17 929	−36 356	−37 197	−41 811	−48 742
Subsidies (receipts) less taxes (payments) on products from/to rest of the world	QZPB	-D.21+D.31	2 855	3 130	3 047	2 969	2 962	2 963	3 087	3 275
Other subsidies on production from/ to rest of the world	IBJN	+D.29-D.39	−3 668	−3 251	−3 284	−2 690	−2 485	−2 308	−1 961	−2 393
Gross balance of primary incomes/ gross national income (GNI)	YBGM	B.5*g	1 635 424	1 684 482	1 708 244	1 713 321	1 741 345	1 802 668	1 845 800	1 881 466
Real current transfers from rest of the world (receipts less payments)	YBGP	D.5,6,7	15 898	20 824	21 028	20 951	25 587	23 418	22 838	21 678
Gross national disposable income	YBGO	B.6*g	1 619 536	1 663 661	1 687 220	1 692 374	1 715 750	1 779 249	1 822 962	1 859 788
Adjustment to basic prices										
Gross domestic product (at market prices)	ABMI	B.1*g	1 675 963	1 704 364	1 729 121	1 754 736	1 790 750	1 845 444	1 888 737	1 922 626
Adjustment to basic prices (less taxes plus subsidies on products)	NTAQ	-D.21+D.31	179 193	179 322	183 640	189 827	203 243	201 472	203 800	211 496
Gross value added (at basic prices)	ABMM	B.1g	1 497 550	1 525 324	1 545 863	1 565 238	1 588 004	1 644 002	1 684 937	1 711 130
Net measures (after deduction of consumption of fixed capital) at market prices										
Consumption of fixed capital	CIHA	P.51c	207 362	211 316	215 079	217 697	221 231	227 491	231 530	236 165
Net national income at market prices	YBET	B.5*n	1 428 862	1 474 078	1 494 100	1 496 720	1 519 691	1 574 713	1 614 270	1 645 285
Net national disposable income at market prices	YBEY	B.6*n	1 412 969	1 453 254	1 473 072	1 475 769	1 494 103	1 551 296	1 591 432	1 623 607

1.2 UK gross domestic product and national income
Current prices

			2009	2010	2011	2012	2013	2014	2015	2016
Gross domestic product										
Gross domestic product: production										
Gross value added, at basic prices		B.1g								
Output of goods and services[1]	KN26	P.1	2 681 932	2 749 082	2 840 463	2 925 877	3 050 105	3 148 781	3 220 900	..
less intermediate consumption[1]	KN25	P.2	1 289 659	1 327 054	1 381 643	1 420 159	1 485 675	1 510 059	1 535 963	..
Total gross value added	ABML	**B.1g**	**1 392 273**	**1 422 028**	**1 458 820**	**1 505 718**	**1 564 430**	**1 638 722**	**1 684 937**	**1 747 647**
Value added taxes (VAT) on products	QYRC	D.211	79 900	95 865	111 437	113 859	118 234	124 211	129 177	133 671
Other taxes on products	NSUI	D.212,4	63 848	68 921	71 100	72 717	76 660	81 425	83 149	89 249
less subsidies on products	NZHC	D.31	6 485	6 937	6 295	7 069	6 770	7 296	8 526	9 442
Gross domestic product at market prices	YBHA	**B.1*g**	**1 529 536**	**1 579 877**	**1 635 062**	**1 685 225**	**1 752 554**	**1 837 062**	**1 888 737**	**1 961 125**
Gross domestic product: expenditure										
Final consumption expenditure		P.31								
Actual individual consumption		P.41								
Household final consumption expenditure	ABPB	P.31	960 854	984 614	1 013 406	1 053 663	1 098 735	1 143 919	1 181 868	1 233 327
Final consumption expenditure of NPISH[2]	ABNV	P.31	50 684	51 276	53 647	53 664	54 428	56 625	56 614	57 005
Individual govt. final consumption expenditure	NNAQ	P.31	205 848	210 597	212 508	217 274	221 294	228 672	233 707	239 469
Total	NQEO	P.41	1 217 386	1 246 487	1 279 561	1 324 601	1 374 457	1 429 216	1 472 189	1 529 801
Collective govt. final consumption expenditure	NQEP	P.32	124 916	126 841	126 270	128 439	126 782	130 342	128 355	130 498
Total final consumption expenditure		P.31								
Households	ABPB	P.31	960 854	984 614	1 013 406	1 053 663	1 098 735	1 143 919	1 181 868	1 233 327
NPISH	ABNV	P.31	50 684	51 276	53 647	53 664	54 428	56 625	56 614	57 005
Total	NSSG	P.31	1 011 538	1 035 890	1 067 053	1 107 327	1 153 163	1 200 544	1 238 482	1 290 332
Central government	NMBJ	P.31	198 936	204 184	209 230	219 559	222 474	233 751	236 928	244 793
Local government	NMMT	P.31	131 828	133 254	129 548	126 154	125 602	125 263	125 134	125 174
Total	ABKW	P.31	1 342 302	1 373 328	1 405 831	1 453 040	1 501 239	1 559 558	1 600 544	1 660 299
Gross capital formation		P.5								
Gross fixed capital formation	NPQX	P.51g	233 395	242 186	251 411	262 820	277 209	300 965	313 189	322 430
Changes in inventories	ABMP	P.52	−14 441	5 458	2 686	1 900	4 712	13 268	7 812	7 937
Acquisitions less disposals of valuables	NPJO	P.53	1 733	73	305	829	4 761	102	−438	2 311
Total gross capital formation	NQFM	P.5	220 687	247 717	254 402	265 549	286 682	314 335	320 563	332 678
External balance of goods and services		B.11								
Exports of goods and services	KTMW	P.6	399 649	445 748	498 862	501 055	519 913	518 925	517 161	547 473
less imports of goods and services	KTMX	P.7	433 102	486 916	524 033	534 419	555 280	555 756	549 531	590 486
Total	KTMY	B.11	−33 453	−41 168	−25 171	−33 364	−35 367	−36 831	−32 370	−43 013
Statistical discrepancy between expenditure components and GDP	RVFD	de	–	–	–	–	–	–	–	11 166
Gross domestic product at market prices	YBHA	**B.1*g**	**1 529 536**	**1 579 877**	**1 635 062**	**1 685 225**	**1 752 554**	**1 837 062**	**1 888 737**	**1 961 125**
Gross domestic product: income										
Operating surplus, gross		B.2g								
Non-financial corporations										
Public non-financial corporations	NRJT		13 093	13 922	14 107	15 023	15 598	15 654	16 198	16 190
Private non-financial corporations	NRJK		254 440	272 194	284 025	289 815	301 563	334 189	344 849	354 499
Financial corporations	NQNV		61 941	46 195	50 507	51 342	52 742	55 628	45 594	46 092
General government	NMXV		22 694	23 892	25 321	26 549	27 441	28 304	29 182	29 763
Households	HABM		126 887	126 512	131 274	141 004	142 603	153 754	163 955	167 434
NPISH	HABV		7 221	7 588	8 186	8 075	9 054	9 398	9 619	9 865
Total	ABNF	B.2g	486 276	490 303	513 420	531 808	549 001	596 927	609 397	623 843
Mixed income	QWLT	B.3g	92 485	89 267	93 393	100 873	106 964	114 160	119 268	127 546
Compensation of employees	HAEA	D.1	795 075	818 959	830 205	849 393	883 501	902 294	930 206	967 754
Taxes on production and imports	NZGX	D.2	168 665	193 572	209 198	214 838	224 453	235 878	243 468	255 140
less subsidies	AAXJ	D.3	12 965	12 224	11 154	11 687	11 365	12 197	13 602	15 608
Statistical discrepancy between income components and GDP	RVFC	di	–	–	–	–	–	–	–	2 455
Gross domestic product at market prices	YBHA	**B.1*g**	**1 529 536**	**1 579 877**	**1 635 062**	**1 685 225**	**1 752 554**	**1 837 062**	**1 888 737**	**1 961 125**
Gross national income at market prices										
Gross domestic product at market prices	YBHA	**B.1*g**	**1 529 536**	**1 579 877**	**1 635 062**	**1 685 225**	**1 752 554**	**1 837 062**	**1 888 737**	**1 961 125**
Compensation of employees		D.1								
Receipts from rest of the world	KTMN		1 176	1 097	1 121	1 124	1 094	1 082	1 295	1 376
less payments to rest of the world	KTMO		1 435	1 486	1 294	1 272	1 420	1 551	1 384	1 735
Total	KTMP	D.1	−259	−389	−173	−148	−326	−469	−89	−359
Subsidies (receipts) less taxes (payments) on products from/to rest of the world	QZOZ	-D.21+D.31	2 655	2 945	2 937	2 898	2 926	2 960	3 087	3 327
Other subsidies on production from/ to rest of the world	IBJL	+D.29-D.39	−3 411	−3 059	−3 166	−2 625	−2 455	−2 306	−1 961	−2 431
Property and entrepreneurial income		D.4								
from rest of the world	HMBN		176 037	174 500	200 529	171 149	157 759	142 463	131 853	132 954
(receipts less payments)	HMBO		188 062	173 151	194 038	188 500	193 353	179 154	173 575	182 116
Total	HMBM	D.4	−12 025	1 349	6 491	−17 351	−35 594	−36 691	−41 722	−49 162
Gross balance of primary incomes/ gross national income (GNI)	ABMX	**B.5*g**	**1 518 009**	**1 580 953**	**1 641 613**	**1 667 450**	**1 716 162**	**1 799 248**	**1 845 800**	**1 910 713**

1 These series are not available for the latest year   2 Non-profit institutions serving households

1.3 UK gross domestic product
Chained volume measures (reference year 2015)

£ million

			2009	2010	2011	2012	2013	2014	2015	2016
Gross domestic product										
Gross domestic product: expenditure approach										
Final consumption expenditure		P.3								
Actual individual consumption		P.41								
Household final consumption expenditure	ABPF	P.3	1 088 615	1 096 462	1 085 891	1 105 308	1 126 255	1 150 513	1 181 868	1 216 008
Final consumption expenditure of NPISH[1]	ABNU	P.3	56 325	55 899	58 155	57 057	56 218	57 081	56 614	56 970
Individual government final consumption expenditure	NSZK	P.31	208 601	211 501	213 967	218 262	222 841	229 143	233 707	237 323
Total	YBIO	P.41	1 352 849	1 363 299	1 357 866	1 380 548	1 405 287	1 436 736	1 472 189	1 510 301
Collective government final consumption expenditure	NSZL	P.32	135 261	133 894	132 026	132 270	128 231	130 744	128 355	128 544
Total	ABKX	P.3	1 488 319	1 497 346	1 490 001	1 512 901	1 533 533	1 567 492	1 600 544	1 638 845
Gross capital formation		P.5								
Gross fixed capital formation	NPQR	P.51g	252 432	263 858	269 573	275 163	284 562	304 735	313 189	317 386
Changes in inventories	ABMQ	P.52	−17 549	5 251	−4 299	−572	2 028	5 548	7 812	3 473
Acquisitions less disposals of valuables	NPJP	P.53	353	−27	−3	142	960	−24	−438	2 195
Total	NPQU	P.5	202 708	231 275	237 014	251 743	277 701	307 997	320 563	323 054
Gross national final expenditure	YBIK		1 681 253	1 723 463	1 722 836	1 761 664	1 810 044	1 875 361	1 921 107	1 961 899
Exports of goods and services	KTMZ	P.6	421 954	446 977	474 841	475 922	479 919	492 660	517 161	522 736
Gross final expenditure	ABME		2 102 718	2 170 151	2 198 708	2 237 968	2 289 798	2 367 507	2 438 268	2 484 635
less imports of goods and services	KTNB	P.7	431 312	468 181	472 265	485 181	500 450	522 796	549 531	572 935
Statistical discrepancy between expenditure components and GDP	GIXS	de	–	–	–	–	–	–	–	10 927
Gross domestic product at market prices	ABMI	B.1*g	**1 675 963**	**1 704 364**	**1 729 121**	**1 754 736**	**1 790 750**	**1 845 444**	**1 888 737**	**1 922 626**
Of which: external balance of goods and services	KTNC	B.11	−9 358	−21 204	2 576	−9 259	−20 531	−30 136	−32 370	−50 199

1 Non-profit institutions serving households

1.3A Composition of UK gross domestic product at market prices by category of expenditure[1]

Current prices

		2009	2010	2011	2012	2013	2014	2015	2016
Gross domestic product: expenditure approach									
Final consumption expenditure	P.3								
Actual individual consumption	P.41								
Household final consumption expenditure	P.3	62.8	62.3	62.0	62.5	62.7	62.3	62.6	62.9
Final consumption expenditure of NPISH[2]	P.3	3.3	3.2	3.3	3.2	3.1	3.1	3.0	2.9
Individual government final consumption expenditure	P.31	13.5	13.3	13.0	12.9	12.6	12.4	12.4	12.2
Total actual individual consumption	P.41	79.6	78.9	78.3	78.6	78.4	77.8	77.9	78.0
Collective government final consumption expenditure	P.32	8.2	8.0	7.7	7.6	7.2	7.1	6.8	6.7
Total final consumption expenditure	P.3	87.8	86.9	86.0	86.2	85.7	84.9	84.7	84.7
Households	P.3	..	..	..	..	..	..	..	..
NPISH	P.3	..	..	..	..	..	..	..	..
Central government	P.3	13.0	12.9	12.8	13.0	12.7	12.7	12.5	12.5
Local government	P.3	8.6	8.4	7.9	7.5	7.2	6.8	6.6	6.4
Gross capital formation	P.5								
Gross fixed capital formation	P.51g	15.3	15.3	15.4	15.6	15.8	16.4	16.6	16.4
Changes in inventories	P.52	−0.9	0.3	0.2	0.1	0.3	0.7	0.4	0.4
Acquisitions less disposals of valuables	P.53	0.1	–	–	–	0.3	–	–	0.1
Total gross capital formation	P.5	14.4	15.7	15.6	15.8	16.4	17.1	17.0	17.0
Exports of goods and services	P.6	26.1	28.2	30.5	29.7	29.7	28.2	27.4	27.9
less imports of goods and services	P.7	28.3	30.8	32.0	31.7	31.7	30.3	29.1	30.1
External balance of goods and services	B.11	−2.2	−2.6	−1.5	−2.0	−2.0	−2.0	−1.7	−2.2
Statistical discrepancy between expenditure components and GDP	de	–	–	–	–	–	–	–	0.6
Gross domestic product at market prices	B.1*g	100.0	100.0	100.0	100.0	100.0	100.0	100.0	100.0

1 Based on table 1.2, components may not sum due to rounding
2 Non-profit institutions serving households

1.3B Composition of UK gross domestic product at market prices by category of income[1]

Percentage

		2009	2010	2011	2012	2013	2014	2015	2016
Operating surplus, gross	B.2g								
Public non-financial corporations		0.9	0.9	0.9	0.9	0.9	0.9	0.9	0.8
Private non-financial corporations		16.6	17.2	17.4	17.2	17.2	18.2	18.3	18.1
Financial corporations		4.0	2.9	3.1	3.0	3.0	3.0	2.4	2.4
Central government		1.0	1.0	1.0	1.0	1.0	1.0	1.0	0.9
Local government		0.5	0.5	0.5	0.6	0.6	0.6	0.6	0.6
Households		8.3	8.0	8.0	8.4	8.1	8.4	8.7	8.5
NPISH[2]		0.5	0.5	0.5	0.5	0.5	0.5	0.5	0.5
Households & NPISH		8.8	8.5	8.5	8.8	8.7	8.9	9.2	9.0
Total	B.2g	31.8	31.0	31.4	31.6	31.3	32.5	32.3	31.8
Mixed income	B.3g	6.0	5.7	5.7	6.0	6.1	6.2	6.3	6.5
Compensation of employees	D.1	52.0	51.8	50.8	50.4	50.4	49.1	49.3	49.3
Taxes on production and imports[3]	D.2	11.0	12.3	12.8	12.7	12.8	12.8	12.9	13.0
less subsidies on products	D.3	0.8	0.8	0.7	0.7	0.6	0.7	0.7	0.8
Statistical discrepancy between income components and GDP	di	–	–	–	–	–	–	–	0.1
Gross domestic product at market prices	B.1*g	100.0	100.0	100.0	100.0	100.0	100.0	100.0	100.0

1 Based on table 1.2, components may not sum due to rounding
2 Non-profit institutions serving households
3 Includes taxes on products

1.4 Indices of value, volume, prices and costs

			2009	2010	2011	2012	2013	2014	2015	2016
Indices of value at current prices										
Gross measures, (before deduction of consumption of fixed capital)										
Gross domestic product at market prices ("Money GDP")	YBEU	B.1*g	81.0	83.6	86.6	89.2	92.8	97.3	100.0	103.8
Gross national income at market prices	YBEV	B.5*g	82.2	85.7	88.9	90.3	93.0	97.5	100.0	103.5
Gross national disposable income at market prices	YBEW	B.6*g	82.5	85.6	88.9	90.3	92.8	97.4	100.0	103.6
Gross value added at basic prices	YBEX	B.1g	82.6	84.4	86.6	89.4	92.8	97.3	100.0	103.7
Chained volume indices ("real terms")										
Gross measures, before deduction of fixed capital consumption at market prices										
Gross domestic product at market prices	YBEZ	B.1*g	88.7	90.2	91.5	92.9	94.8	97.7	100.0	101.8
Categories of GDP expenditure										
Final consumption expenditure	YBFA	P.3	93.0	93.6	93.1	94.5	95.8	97.9	100.0	102.4
Households	CSR9		92.1	92.8	91.9	93.5	95.3	97.3	100.0	102.9
NPISH[1]	CSR8		99.5	98.7	102.7	100.8	99.3	100.8	100.0	100.6
General Government	YBFC		94.9	95.3	95.5	96.8	97.0	99.4	100.0	101.1
Gross fixed capital formation	YBFG	P.51g	80.6	84.2	86.1	87.9	90.9	97.3	100.0	101.3
Gross national final expenditure	YBFH		87.5	89.7	89.7	91.7	94.2	97.6	100.0	102.1
Exports of goods and services	YBFI	P.6	81.6	86.4	91.8	92.0	92.8	95.3	100.0	101.1
Of which: Goods	YBFJ	P.61	79.1	88.1	94.0	92.4	91.5	94.5	100.0	99.1
Of which: Services	YBFK	P.62	85.0	83.8	88.4	91.3	94.7	96.3	100.0	103.6
Gross final expenditure	YBFF		86.2	89.0	90.2	91.8	93.9	97.1	100.0	101.9
Imports of goods and services	YBFL	P.7	78.5	85.2	85.9	88.3	91.1	95.1	100.0	104.3
Of which: Goods	YBFM	P.71	77.1	86.4	87.7	89.7	92.1	96.2	100.0	104.6
Of which: Services	YBFN	P.72	82.1	81.4	80.7	83.9	88.0	91.9	100.0	103.3
Gross national income at market prices	YBFO	B.5*g	88.6	91.3	92.5	92.8	94.3	97.7	100.0	101.9
Gross national disposable income at market prices	YBFP	B.6*g	88.8	91.3	92.6	92.8	94.1	97.6	100.0	102.0
Adjustment to basic prices										
Taxes less subsidies on products	YBFQ	D.21-D.31	87.9	88.0	90.1	93.1	99.7	98.9	100.0	103.8
Gross value added at basic prices	CGCE	B.1g	88.9	90.5	91.7	92.9	94.2	97.6	100.0	101.6
Price indices (implied deflators)[2]										
Categories of GDP expenditure at market prices										
Final consumption expenditure	YBGA	P.3	88.3	89.8	93.3	95.3	97.6	99.4	100.0	101.4
Households	ABJS		88.3	89.8	93.3	95.3	97.6	99.4	100.0	101.4
NPISH	CANI		90.0	91.7	92.2	94.1	96.8	99.2	100.0	100.1
General Government	YBFT		96.3	97.8	98.0	98.7	99.1	99.8	100.0	101.1
Gross fixed capital formation	YBFU	P.51g	92.5	91.8	93.3	95.5	97.4	98.8	100.0	101.6
Total national expenditure	YBFV		93.0	94.1	96.4	97.6	98.8	99.9	100.0	101.6
Exports of goods and services	YBFW	P.6	94.7	99.7	105.1	105.3	108.3	105.3	100.0	104.7
Of which: Goods	BQNK	P.61	100.4	106.3	113.5	113.0	114.4	109.0	100.0	105.5
Of which: Services	FKNW	P.62	87.8	91.7	94.5	95.6	100.7	100.8	100.0	103.8
Total final expenditure	YBFY		93.3	95.2	98.2	99.2	100.8	101.1	100.0	102.2
Imports of goods and services	YBFZ	P.7	100.4	104.0	111.0	110.1	111.0	106.3	100.0	103.1
Of which: Goods	BQNL	P.71	100.4	104.3	112.8	112.2	112.4	107.3	100.0	102.6
Of which: Services	FHMA	P.72	100.7	103.4	105.6	104.0	106.7	103.6	100.0	104.3
Gross domestic product at market prices	YBGB	B.1*g	91.3	92.7	94.6	96.0	97.9	99.5	100.0	102.0
Home costs per unit of output[3]										
Total home costs (based on expenditure components of GDP)	YBGC	B.1*g	93.2	93.4	94.5	96.3	98.5	99.7	100.0	102.2
Compensation of employees	YBGD	D.1	96.3	97.6	97.5	98.3	100.2	99.3	100.0	102.2
Gross operating surplus and mixed income	YBGE	"B.2g,B.3g	89.5	88.1	91.0	93.5	94.9	99.9	100.0	101.3

1 Non-profit institutions serving households
2 Implied deflators are derived by dividing the estimates for each component at current market prices by the corresponding chained volume estimate
3 These index numbers show how employment and operating incomes relate to the implied deflator of GDP at market prices

1.5 Population, employment, income, product and spending per head

			2009	2010	2011	2012	2013	2014	2015	2016
Population and employment (thousands)[1]										
Home population	EBAQ	POP	62 260	62 759	63 285	63 705	64 106	64 597	65 110	65 648
Households population aged 16+										
Self-employed[2]	MGRQ	ESE	3 870	3 990	4 057	4 225	4 262	4 557	4 573	4 766
Employees[2]	MGRN	EEM	25 092	25 017	25 117	25 213	25 515	25 962	26 505	26 760
Total employment[2,3]	MGRZ	ETO	29 156	29 228	29 376	29 697	30 045	30 755	31 284	31 726
Unemployed[2]	MGSC	EUN	2 403	2 497	2 593	2 572	2 474	2 026	1 780	1 633
All economically active[2]	MGSF		31 559	31 726	31 969	32 269	32 518	32 781	33 064	33 360
Economically inactive[2]	MGSI		18 210	18 487	18 678	18 708	18 788	18 908	19 020	19 090
Total[2]	MGSL		49 770	50 212	50 648	50 977	51 306	51 689	52 084	52 450

		2009	2010	2011	2012	2013	2014	2015	2016
Income, product and spending per head £									
at current prices									
Gross national income at market prices	IHXS	24 382	25 191	25 940	26 175	26 771	27 853	28 349	29 105
Gross domestic product at market prices	IHXT	24 567	25 174	25 836	26 454	27 338	28 439	29 008	29 873
Households									
Final consumption expenditure	CRXO	15 433	15 689	16 013	16 540	17 139	17 709	18 152	18 787
Gross disposable income	CRXS	16 391	16 407	16 621	17 354	17 910	18 323	19 304	19 432

		2009	2010	2011	2012	2013	2014	2015	2016
Income, product and spending per head £									
Chained volume measures									
Gross domestic product at market prices	IHXW	26 919	27 157	27 323	27 545	27 934	28 569	29 008	29 287
Gross value added at basic prices	YBGT	24 053	24 304	24 427	24 570	24 772	25 450	25 878	26 065
Households									
Real disposable income	CRXW	18 570	18 271	17 810	18 204	18 359	18 428	19 304	19 160
Adjusted gross disposable income	CRYB	23 239	22 917	22 316	22 666	22 767	22 870	23 763	23 612
Adjusted net disposable income	CRYF	..	..	..	..	..	..	..	..
Final consumption expenditure	CRYJ	17 485	17 471	17 159	17 350	17 569	17 811	18 152	18 523
Actual individual consumption	CRYN	27 247	27 223	26 924	27 174	27 398	27 813	28 172	28 579

1 Components may not sum to totals due to rounding
2 These seasonally adjusted data are 4 quarter annual averages derived from quarterly Labour Force Survey, which does not include those resident in communal establishments except for those in student halls of residence and NHS accommodation
3 Includes people on government-supported training and employment programmes and unpaid family workers

1.6.0 UK summary accounts
Total economy ESA 2010 sector S.1

			2009	2010	2011	2012	2013	2014	2015	2016
Goods and services account		**0**								
Resources										
Output		P.1								
Market output[1]	NQAG	P.11	2 076 126	2 132 346	2 218 597	2 291 276	2 402 285	2 480 212	2 533 954	..
Output for own final use[1]	NQAH	P.12	216 931	221 852	226 648	233 912	242 805	252 428	263 268	..
Non-market output[1]	NQAI	P.13	388 875	394 884	395 218	400 689	405 015	416 141	423 678	..
Total[1]	KN26	P.1	2 681 932	2 749 082	2 840 463	2 925 877	3 050 105	3 148 781	3 220 900	..
Taxes on products	NZGW	D.21	143 748	164 786	182 537	186 576	194 894	205 636	212 326	222 920
less subsidies on products	NZHC	D.31	6 485	6 937	6 295	7 069	6 770	7 296	8 526	9 442
Imports of goods and services	KTMX	P.7	433 102	486 916	524 033	534 419	555 280	555 756	549 531	590 486
Total resources[1]	NQBM	TR	3 252 297	3 393 847	3 540 738	3 639 803	3 793 509	3 902 877	3 974 231	..
Uses										
Intermediate consumption[1]	KN25	P.2	1 289 659	1 327 054	1 381 643	1 420 159	1 485 675	1 510 059	1 535 963	..
Final consumption expenditure		P.3								
By households	ABPB	P.31	960 854	984 614	1 013 406	1 053 663	1 098 735	1 143 919	1 181 868	1 233 327
By NPISH[3]	ABNV	P.31	50 684	51 276	53 647	53 664	54 428	56 625	56 614	57 005
By government		P.3								
For individual consumption	NNAQ	P.31	205 848	210 597	212 508	217 274	221 294	228 672	233 707	239 469
For collective consumption	NQEP	P.32	124 916	126 841	126 270	128 439	126 782	130 342	128 355	130 498
Total by government	NMRK	P.3	330 764	337 438	338 778	345 713	348 076	359 014	362 062	369 967
Total[2]	ABKW	P.3	1 342 302	1 373 328	1 405 831	1 453 040	1 501 239	1 559 558	1 600 544	1 660 299
Gross capital formation		P.5								
Gross fixed capital formation	NPQX	P.51g	233 395	242 186	251 411	262 820	277 209	300 965	313 189	322 430
Changes in inventories	ABMP	P.52	−14 441	5 458	2 686	1 900	4 712	13 268	7 812	7 937
Acquisitions less disposals of valuables[4]	NPJO	P.53	1 733	73	305	829	4 761	102	−438	2 311
Total	NQFM	P.5	220 687	247 717	254 402	265 549	286 682	314 335	320 563	332 678
Exports of goods and services	KTMW	P.6	399 649	445 748	498 862	501 055	519 913	518 925	517 161	547 473
Statistical discrepancy between expenditure components and GDP	RVFD	de	–	–	–	–	–	–	–	11 166
Total uses[1]	NQBM	TU	3 252 297	3 393 847	3 540 738	3 639 803	3 793 509	3 902 877	3 974 231	..

1 These series are not available for the latest year.
2 Non-profit institutions serving households
3 For the total economy, total final consumption expenditure = P.4 actual final
  consumption.
4 Acquisitions less disposals of valuables can be a volatile series but any
  volatility is likely to be GDP neutral as it is offset in UK trade figures

1.6.1 UK summary accounts
Total economy ESA 2010 sector S.1

£ million

			2009	2010	2011	2012	2013	2014	2015
Production account		I							
Resources									
Output		P.1							
Market output	NQAG	P.11	2 076 126	2 132 346	2 218 597	2 291 276	2 402 285	2 480 212	2 533 954
Output for own final use	NQAH	P.12	216 931	221 852	226 648	233 912	242 805	252 428	263 268
Non-market output	NQAI	P.13	388 875	394 884	395 218	400 689	405 015	416 141	423 678
Total	KN26	P.1	2 681 932	2 749 082	2 840 463	2 925 877	3 050 105	3 148 781	3 220 900
Taxes on products	NZGW	D.21	143 748	164 786	182 537	186 576	194 894	205 636	212 326
less subsidies on products	NZHC	D.31	6 485	6 937	6 295	7 069	6 770	7 296	8 526
Total resources	NQBP	TR	2 819 195	2 906 931	3 016 705	3 105 384	3 238 229	3 347 121	3 424 700
Uses									
Intermediate consumption	KN25	P.2	1 289 659	1 327 054	1 381 643	1 420 159	1 485 675	1 510 059	1 535 963
Gross domestic product	YBHA	**B.1*g**	**1 529 536**	**1 579 877**	**1 635 062**	**1 685 225**	**1 752 554**	**1 837 062**	**1 888 737**
Total uses	NQBP	TU	2 819 195	2 906 931	3 016 705	3 105 384	3 238 229	3 347 121	3 424 700
Gross domestic product	YBHA	**B.1*g**	**1 529 536**	**1 579 877**	**1 635 062**	**1 685 225**	**1 752 554**	**1 837 062**	**1 888 737**
less consumption of fixed capital	NQAE	P.51c	190 776	193 371	200 413	207 191	215 935	224 859	231 530
Net domestic product	NHRK	B.1*n	1 338 760	1 386 506	1 434 649	1 478 034	1 536 619	1 612 203	1 657 207

1.6.2 UK summary accounts
Total economy ESA 2010 sector S.1

£ million

			2009	2010	2011	2012	2013	2014	2015
Distribution and use of income accounts		II							
Primary distribution of income account		II.1							
Generation of income account		II.1.1							
Resources									
Total resources (gross domestic product)	YBHA	**B.1*g**	**1 529 536**	**1 579 877**	**1 635 062**	**1 685 225**	**1 752 554**	**1 837 062**	**1 888 737**
Uses									
Compensation of employees		D.1							
Wages and salaries	NQAU	D.11	663 847	672 528	682 715	695 988	723 770	747 138	775 328
Employers' social contributions	NQAV	D.12	131 228	146 431	147 490	153 405	159 731	155 156	154 878
Total	HAEA	D.1	795 075	818 959	830 205	849 393	883 501	902 294	930 206
Taxes on production and imports, paid		D.2							
Taxes on products	QZPQ	D.21	143 748	164 786	182 537	186 576	194 894	205 636	212 326
Other taxes on production	NMYD	D.29	24 917	28 786	26 661	28 262	29 559	30 242	31 142
Total	NZGX	D.2	168 665	193 572	209 198	214 838	224 453	235 878	243 468
less subsidies, received		D.3							
Subsidies on products	NZHC	D.31	6 485	6 937	6 295	7 069	6 770	7 296	8 526
Other subsidies on production	LIUB	D.39	6 480	5 287	4 859	4 618	4 595	4 901	5 076
Total	AAXJ	D.3	12 965	12 224	11 154	11 687	11 365	12 197	13 602
Operating surplus, gross	ABNF	B.2g	486 276	490 303	513 420	531 808	549 001	596 927	609 397
Mixed income, gross	QWLT	B.3g	92 485	89 267	93 393	100 873	106 964	114 160	119 268
Statistical discrepancy between income components and GDP	RVFC	di	–	–	–	–	–	–	–
Total uses (gross domestic product)	YBHA	**B.1*g**	**1 529 536**	**1 579 877**	**1 635 062**	**1 685 225**	**1 752 554**	**1 837 062**	**1 888 737**
less consumption of fixed capital	NQAE	P.51c	190 776	193 371	200 413	207 191	215 935	224 859	231 530
Operating surplus, net	NQAR	B.2n	306 440	308 706	325 072	336 891	346 838	387 888	394 208
Mixed income, net	QWLV	B.3n	81 545	77 493	81 328	88 599	93 192	98 340	102 927

1.6.3 UK summary accounts
Total economy ESA 2010 sector S.1

£ million

			2009	2010	2011	2012	2013	2014	2015	2016
Allocation of primary income account		II.1.2								
Resources										
Operating surplus, gross	ABNF	B.2g	486 276	490 303	513 420	531 808	549 001	596 927	609 397	623 843
Mixed income, gross	QWLT	B.3g	92 485	89 267	93 393	100 873	106 964	114 160	119 268	127 546
Compensation of employees		D.1								
Wages and salaries	NQBI	D.11	663 588	672 139	682 542	695 840	723 444	746 669	775 239	804 241
Employers' social contributions	NQBJ	D.12	131 228	146 431	147 490	153 405	159 731	155 156	154 878	163 154
Total	NVCK	D.1	794 816	818 570	830 032	849 245	883 175	901 825	930 117	967 395
Statistical discrepancy between income components and GDP	RVFC	di	–	–	–	–	–	–	–	2 455
Taxes on production and imports, received		D.2								
Taxes on products		D.21								
Value added tax (VAT)	NZGF	D.211	79 900	95 865	111 437	113 859	118 234	124 211	129 177	133 671
Taxes and duties on imports excluding VAT	NMBU	D.212	–	–	–	–	–	–	–	–
import duties	NMXZ	D.2121	–	–	–	–	–	–	–	–
Taxes on imports excluding VAT and import duties	NMBT	D.2122	–	–	–	–	–	–	–	–
Taxes on products excluding VAT and import duties	NMYB	D.214	61 193	65 976	68 163	69 819	73 734	78 465	80 062	85 922
Total	NVCE	D.21	141 093	161 841	179 600	183 678	191 968	202 676	209 239	219 593
Other taxes on production	NMYD	D.29	24 917	28 786	26 661	28 262	29 559	30 242	31 142	32 220
Total	NMYE	D.2	166 010	190 627	206 261	211 940	221 527	232 918	240 381	251 813
less subsidies, paid		D.3								
Subsidies on products	NMYF	D.31	6 485	6 937	6 295	7 069	6 770	7 296	8 526	9 442
Other subsidies on production	LIUF	D.39	3 069	2 228	1 693	1 993	2 140	2 595	3 115	3 735
Total	NMRL	D.3	9 554	9 165	7 988	9 062	8 910	9 891	11 641	13 177
Property income, received		D.4								
Interest	NHQY	D.41	277 619	226 762	249 097	236 349	208 830	215 247	209 760	210 679
Distributed income of corporations	NHQZ	D.42	216 732	195 681	216 993	220 249	249 354	259 706	276 275	251 488
Reinvested earnings on foreign direct investment	NHSK	D.43	10 986	27 569	29 564	20 517	9 835	–13 463	505	–5 307
Other investment income		D.44								
Attributable to insurance policy holders	L8GN	D.441	42 154	38 448	36 747	35 618	36 529	41 689	28 442	26 770
Payable on pension entitlements	L8GU	D.442	67 817	77 856	74 956	65 918	63 132	77 972	71 412	73 681
Attributable to collective investment fund shareholders		D.443								
Dividends	L8HA	D.4431	3 859	8 090	4 196	4 617	5 216	5 238	5 533	6 167
Retained earnings	L8HH	D.4432	6 037	12 650	6 557	7 222	8 156	8 194	8 652	9 644
Total	L8H3	D.443	9 896	20 740	10 753	11 839	13 372	13 432	14 185	15 811
Total	QYNF	D.44	119 867	137 044	122 456	113 375	113 033	133 093	114 039	116 262
Rent	NHRP	D.45	1 533	1 570	1 571	1 590	1 748	1 762	1 761	1 804
Total	NHRO	D.4	626 737	588 626	619 681	592 080	582 800	596 345	602 340	574 926
Total resources	NQBQ	TR	2 156 770	2 168 228	2 254 799	2 276 884	2 334 557	2 432 284	2 489 862	2 534 801
Uses										
Property income, paid		D.4								
Interest	NHQW	D.41	315 200	272 137	290 933	282 835	255 529	258 855	243 925	245 658
Distributed income of corporations	NHQX	D.42	195 472	174 231	201 461	213 676	234 459	234 898	278 651	251 052
Reinvested earnings on foreign direct investment	NHSJ	D.43	6 878	4 839	–2 368	–885	14 791	4 997	7 354	11 577
Other investment income		D.44								
Attributable to insurance policy holders	L8GP	D.441	43 608	39 480	37 891	36 905	38 158	43 743	29 518	27 714
Payable on pension entitlements	L8GW	D.442	67 817	77 856	74 956	65 918	63 132	77 972	71 412	73 681
Attributable to collective investment fund shareholders		D.443								
Dividends	L8HC	D.4431	3 218	6 694	3 412	3 666	4 127	4 213	4 461	4 916
Retained earnings	L8HJ	D.4432	5 035	10 468	5 330	5 729	6 451	6 596	6 980	7 686
Total	L8H5	D.443	8 253	17 162	8 742	9 395	10 578	10 809	11 441	12 602
Total	NQCG	D.44	119 678	134 498	121 589	112 218	111 868	132 524	112 371	113 997
Rent	NHRN	D.45	1 533	1 570	1 571	1 590	1 748	1 762	1 761	1 804
Total	NHRL	D.4	638 761	587 275	613 186	609 434	618 395	633 036	644 062	624 088
Gross balance of primary incomes / gross national income (GNI)	ABMX	B.5*g	**1 518 009**	**1 580 953**	**1 641 613**	**1 667 450**	**1 716 162**	**1 799 248**	**1 845 800**	**1 910 713**
Total uses	NQBR	T	2 156 770	2 168 228	2 254 799	2 276 884	2 334 557	2 432 284	2 489 862	2 534 801
less consumption of fixed capital	NQAE	P.51c	190 776	193 371	200 413	207 191	215 935	224 859	231 530	240 255
National income, net	NSRX	B.5*n	1 327 232	1 387 580	1 441 196	1 460 262	1 500 228	1 574 389	1 614 270	1 670 458

1.6.4 UK summary accounts
Total economy ESA 2010 sector S.1

£ million

			2009	2010	2011	2012	2013	2014	2015	2016
Secondary distribution of income accounts		II.2								
Resources										
Gross balance of primary incomes/ gross national income(GNI)	ABMX	B.5*g	1 518 009	1 580 953	1 641 613	1 667 450	1 716 162	1 799 248	1 845 800	1 910 713
Current taxes on income, wealth, etc.		D.5								
Taxes on income	NMZJ	D.51	190 532	197 652	204 706	198 737	203 077	206 879	217 794	228 095
Other current taxes	NVCQ	D.59	34 443	35 294	37 436	37 566	39 590	40 958	42 255	42 884
Total	NMZL	D.5	224 975	232 946	242 142	236 303	242 667	247 837	260 049	270 979
Net social contributions		D.61								
Employers' actual social contributions	L8N5	D.611	113 590	128 706	130 153	135 160	140 445	136 010	135 750	143 838
Employers' imputed social contributions	M9WZ	D.612	17 636	17 724	17 337	18 245	19 286	19 146	19 128	19 316
Households' actual social contributions	L8PB	D.613	57 176	58 668	60 401	63 361	64 856	67 209	68 517	73 070
Households' social contribution supplements	L8PX	D.614	67 817	77 856	74 956	65 918	63 132	77 972	71 412	73 681
Social insurance scheme service charge	L8LN	D.61SC	−11 101	−12 568	−14 740	−17 046	−18 324	−18 819	−19 620	−20 318
Total	NQCX	D.61	245 118	270 386	268 107	265 638	269 395	281 518	275 187	289 587
Social benefits other than social transfers in kind		D.62								
Social security benefits in cash	L8QD	D.621	80 825	82 117	83 826	89 187	91 231	93 650	96 461	98 992
Other social insurance benefits	L8QR	D.622	99 996	105 819	108 018	116 908	119 368	117 636	125 769	129 491
Social assistance benefits in cash	MT3C	D.623	105 102	112 257	115 624	118 922	119 646	120 613	121 463	120 963
Total	QZQP	D.62	285 923	300 193	307 468	325 017	330 245	331 899	343 693	349 446
Other current transfers		D.7								
Net non-life insurance premiums	NQBY	D.71	37 750	47 996	45 636	44 589	47 631	41 807	43 129	42 821
Non-life insurance claims	NQDX	D.72	30 364	39 989	38 328	36 218	41 306	36 141	36 177	36 638
Current transfers within general government	NQDY	D.73	124 708	132 310	126 922	128 448	121 658	124 073	121 126	113 778
Current international cooperation	NQEA	D.74	208	223	−87	172	137	150	60	157
Miscellaneous current transfers	QYNA	D.75	59 394	59 184	58 927	66 153	62 383	62 077	61 780	61 833
Total	NQDU	D.7	252 424	279 702	269 726	275 580	273 115	264 248	262 272	255 227
Total resources	NQBT	TR	2 526 449	2 664 180	2 729 056	2 769 988	2 831 584	2 924 750	2 987 001	3 075 952
Uses										
Current taxes on income, wealth etc.		D.5								
Taxes on income	NQCR	D.51	190 475	198 163	204 986	198 942	203 147	206 824	218 041	228 223
Other current taxes	NQCU	D.59	34 443	35 294	37 436	37 566	39 590	40 958	42 255	42 884
Total	NQCQ	D.5	224 918	233 457	242 422	236 508	242 737	247 782	260 296	271 107
Net social contributions		D.61								
Employers' actual social contributions	L8NH	D.611	113 590	128 706	130 153	135 160	140 445	136 010	135 750	143 838
Employers' imputed social contributions	M9X4	D.612	17 636	17 724	17 337	18 245	19 286	19 146	19 128	19 316
Households' actual social contributions	L8PP	D.613	57 115	58 639	60 376	63 338	64 837	67 194	68 506	73 056
Households' social contribution supplements	L8Q5	D.614	67 817	77 856	74 956	65 918	63 132	77 972	71 412	73 681
Social insurance scheme service charges	L8LR	D.61SC	−11 101	−12 568	−14 740	−17 046	−18 324	−18 819	−19 620	−20 318
Total	NQBS	D.61	245 057	270 357	268 082	265 615	269 376	281 503	275 176	289 573
Social benefits other than social transfers in kind		D.62								
Social security benefits in cash	L8QL	D.621	82 873	84 277	86 113	91 472	93 708	96 232	99 140	101 772
Other social insurance benefits	L8QZ	D.622	99 996	105 819	108 018	116 908	119 368	117 636	125 769	129 491
Social assistance benefits in cash	MT3E	D.623	105 153	112 257	115 624	118 922	119 646	120 613	121 463	120 963
Total	NQDN	D.62	288 022	302 353	309 755	327 302	332 722	334 481	346 372	352 226
Other current transfers		D.7								
Net non-life insurance premiums	NQDW	D.71	30 364	39 989	38 328	36 218	41 306	36 143	36 183	36 646
Non-life insurance claims	NQBZ	D.72	37 750	47 996	45 636	44 589	47 631	41 805	43 123	42 813
Current transfers within general government	NNAF	D.73	124 708	132 310	126 922	128 448	121 658	124 073	121 126	113 778
Current international cooperation	NMDZ	D.74	5 021	5 668	6 274	6 122	8 060	7 198	6 823	7 620
Miscellaneous current transfers	NUHK	D.75	60 629	60 667	60 284	67 713	64 421	64 178	63 348	63 062
VAT-based third EU own resource	M9LI	D.761	1 593	2 253	2 197	2 282	2 154	2 388	2 715	2 675
GNI-based fourth EU own resource	M9LJ	D.762	5 163	7 773	7 814	8 190	10 637	9 346	8 877	7 764
VAT and GNI based EU own resources	M9MC	D.76	6 756	10 026	10 011	10 472	12 791	11 734	11 592	10 439
Total	NQDV	D.7	265 228	296 656	287 455	293 562	295 867	285 131	282 195	274 358
Gross disposable income	NQCO	B.6g	1 503 224	1 561 357	1 621 342	1 647 001	1 690 882	1 775 853	1 822 962	1 888 688
Total uses	NQBT	TU	2 526 449	2 664 180	2 729 056	2 769 988	2 831 584	2 924 750	2 987 001	3 075 952
less consumption of fixed capital	NQAE	P.51c	190 776	193 371	200 413	207 191	215 935	224 859	231 530	240 255
Disposable income, net	NQCP	B.6n	1 312 447	1 367 984	1 420 925	1 439 813	1 474 948	1 550 994	1 591 432	1 648 433

1.6.5 UK summary accounts
Total economy ESA 2010 sector S.1

£ million

			2009	2010	2011	2012	2013	2014	2015	2016
Redistribution of income in kind account		II.3								
Resources										
Gross disposable income	NQCO	**B.6g**	**1 503 224**	**1 561 357**	**1 621 342**	**1 647 001**	**1 690 882**	**1 775 853**	**1 822 962**	**1 888 688**
Social transfers in kind		D.63								
Non-market produced	NRNC	D.631	218 394	222 594	225 598	229 597	234 303	240 441	246 362	248 153
Purchased market production	NRNE	D.632	38 138	39 279	40 557	41 341	41 419	44 856	43 959	48 321
Total	NRNF	D.63	256 532	261 873	266 155	270 938	275 722	285 297	290 321	296 474
Total resources	NQCB	TR	1 759 756	1 823 230	1 887 497	1 917 939	1 966 604	2 061 150	2 113 283	2 185 162
Uses										
Social transfers in kind		D.63								
Non-market produced	NRNJ	D.631	218 394	222 594	225 598	229 597	234 303	240 441	246 362	248 153
Purchased market production	NRNK	D.632	38 138	39 279	40 557	41 341	41 419	44 856	43 959	48 321
Total	NRNL	D.63	256 532	261 873	266 155	270 938	275 722	285 297	290 321	296 474
Adjusted disposable income, gross	NRNM	B.7g	1 503 224	1 561 357	1 621 342	1 647 001	1 690 882	1 775 853	1 822 962	1 888 688
Total uses	NQCB	TU	1 759 756	1 823 230	1 887 497	1 917 939	1 966 604	2 061 150	2 113 283	2 185 162

1.6.6 UK summary accounts
Total economy ESA 2010 sector S.1

£ million

			2009	2010	2011	2012	2013	2014	2015	2016
Use of income account		II.4								
Use of disposable income account		II.4.1								
Resources										
Gross disposable income	NQCO	**B.6g**	1 503 224	1 561 357	1 621 342	1 647 001	1 690 882	1 775 853	1 822 962	1 888 688
Adjustment for the change in pension entitlements	NVCI	D.8	55 441	72 826	66 069	54 160	54 162	67 116	46 546	49 674
Total resources	NVCW	TR	1 558 665	1 634 183	1 687 411	1 701 161	1 745 044	1 842 969	1 869 508	1 938 362
Uses										
Final consumption expenditure		P.3								
Individual consumption expenditure	NQEO	P.31	1 217 386	1 246 487	1 279 561	1 324 601	1 374 457	1 429 216	1 472 189	1 529 801
Collective consumption expenditure	NQEP	P.32	124 916	126 841	126 270	128 439	126 782	130 342	128 355	130 498
Total	ABKW	P.3	1 342 302	1 373 328	1 405 831	1 453 040	1 501 239	1 559 558	1 600 544	1 660 299
Adjustment for the change in pension entitlements	NQEL	D.8	55 441	72 826	66 069	54 160	54 162	67 116	46 546	49 674
Gross saving	NQET	**B.8g**	**160 922**	**188 029**	**215 511**	**193 961**	**189 643**	**216 295**	**222 418**	**228 389**
Total uses	NVCW	TU	1 558 665	1 634 183	1 687 411	1 701 161	1 745 044	1 842 969	1 869 508	1 938 362
less consumption of fixed capital	NQAE	P.51c	190 776	193 371	200 413	207 191	215 935	224 859	231 530	240 255
Saving, net	NQEJ	B.8n	−29 854	−5 342	15 098	−13 230	−26 292	−8 564	−9 112	−11 866
Use of adjusted disposable income account		II.4.2								
Resources										
Adjusted disposable income	NRNM	B.7g	1 503 224	1 561 357	1 621 342	1 647 001	1 690 882	1 775 853	1 822 962	1 888 688
Adjustment for the change in pension entitlements	NVCI	D.8	55 441	72 826	66 069	54 160	54 162	67 116	46 546	49 674
Total resources	NVCW	TR	1 558 665	1 634 183	1 687 411	1 701 161	1 745 044	1 842 969	1 869 508	1 938 362
Uses										
Actual final consumption		P.4								
Actual individual consumption	ABRE	P.41	1 217 386	1 246 487	1 279 561	1 324 601	1 374 457	1 429 216	1 472 189	1 529 801
Actual collective consumption	NRMZ	P.42	124 916	126 841	126 270	128 439	126 782	130 342	128 355	130 498
Total	NRMX	P.4	1 342 302	1 373 328	1 405 831	1 453 040	1 501 239	1 559 558	1 600 544	1 660 299
Adjustment for the change in pension entitlements	NQEL	D.8	55 441	72 826	66 069	54 160	54 162	67 116	46 546	49 674
Gross saving	NQCA	**B.8g**	160 922	188 029	215 511	193 961	189 643	216 295	222 418	228 389
Total uses	NVCW	TU	1 558 665	1 634 183	1 687 411	1 701 161	1 745 044	1 842 969	1 869 508	1 938 362

1.6.7 UK summary accounts
Total economy ESA 2010 sector S.1

£ million

			2009	2010	2011	2012	2013	2014	2015	2016
Accumulation accounts		III								
Capital account		III.1								
Change in net worth due to saving and capital transfers account		III.1.1								
Changes in liabilities and net worth										
Gross saving	NQET	B.8g	160 922	188 029	215 511	193 961	189 643	216 295	222 418	228 389
Capital transfers, receivable		D.9r								
Capital taxes	NQEY	D.91r	4 206	2 642	2 936	3 129	4 255	3 886	4 442	4 801
Investment grants	NQFB	D.92r	30 253	29 793	26 455	26 143	23 438	25 100	27 971	25 493
Other capital transfers	NQFD	D.99r	21 102	4 205	4 349	33 356	7 497	7 378	8 742	6 066
Total	NQEW	D.9r	55 561	36 640	33 740	62 628	35 190	36 364	41 155	36 360
less capital transfers, payable		D.9p								
Capital taxes	NQCC	D.91p	4 206	2 642	2 936	3 129	4 255	3 886	4 442	4 801
Investment grants	NVDG	D.92p	29 813	29 596	26 316	26 325	23 754	25 547	28 489	25 983
Other capital transfers	NQCE	D.99p	21 672	5 180	5 448	34 124	8 581	8 558	9 993	7 080
Total	NQCF	D.9p	55 691	37 418	34 700	63 578	36 590	37 991	42 924	37 864
Changes in net worth due to gross saving and capital transfers	NQCT	B.101g	160 792	187 251	214 551	193 011	188 243	214 668	220 649	226 885
Changes in assets										
Changes in net worth due to gross saving and capital transfers	NQCT	B.101g	160 792	187 251	214 551	193 011	188 243	214 668	220 649	226 885
less consumption of fixed capital	NQAE	P.51c	190 776	193 371	200 413	207 191	215 935	224 859	231 530	240 255
Changes in net worth due to net saving and capital transfers	NQER	B.101n	−29 984	−6 120	14 138	−14 180	−27 692	−10 191	−10 881	−13 370
Acquisition of non-financial assets account		III.1.2								
Changes in liabilities and net worth										
Changes in net worth due to net saving and capital transfers	NQER	B.101n	−29 984	−6 120	14 138	−14 180	−27 692	−10 191	−10 881	−13 370
Consumption of fixed capital	NQAE	P.51c	190 776	193 371	200 413	207 191	215 935	224 859	231 530	240 255
Total change in liabilities and net worth	NQCT	B.101g	160 792	187 251	214 551	193 011	188 243	214 668	220 649	226 885
Changes in assets										
Gross capital formation		P.5								
Gross fixed capital formation	NPQX	P.51g	233 395	242 186	251 411	262 820	277 209	300 965	313 189	322 430
Changes in inventories	ABMP	P.52	−14 441	5 458	2 686	1 900	4 712	13 268	7 812	7 937
Acquisitions less disposals of valuables[1]	NPJO	P.53	1 733	73	305	829	4 761	102	−438	2 311
Total	NQFM	P.5	220 687	247 717	254 402	265 549	286 682	314 335	320 563	332 678
Acquisitions less disposals of non-produced non-financial assets	NQFJ	NP	−373	−53	−196	−361	−219	300	209	−160
Statistical discrepancy between expenditure components and GDP	RVFD	de	−	−	−	−	−	−	−	11 166
Net lending(+) / net borrowing(-)	NQFH	B.9n	−59 522	−60 413	−39 655	−72 177	−98 220	−99 967	−100 123	−116 799
Total change in assets	NQCT	B.101g	160 792	187 251	214 551	193 011	188 243	214 668	220 649	226 885

1 Acquisitions less disposals of valuables can be a volatile series but any volatility is likely to be GDP neutral as it is offset in UK trade figures

1.6.8 UK summary accounts
Total economy ESA 2010 sector S.1 Unconsolidated

£ million

			2009	2010	2011	2012
Financial account		III.2				
Net acquisition of financial assets		F.A				
Monetary gold and special drawing rights		F.1				
Monetary gold	NYPU	F.11	–	–	–	–
Special drawing rights	NYPW	F.12	8 522	18	333	111
Total	NQAD	F.1	8 522	18	333	111
Currency and deposits		F.2				
Currency	NYPY	F.21	6 450	1 880	3 149	3 441
Transferable deposits		F.22				
Deposits with UK MFIs[1]	NYQC	F.22N1	577 250	−24 415	65 891	280 257
Of which: foreign currency deposits with UK banks	NYQG	F.22N12	−68 132	−9 673	−74 237	33 889
Deposits with rest of the world MFIs[1]	NYQK	F.22N9	−221 243	195 833	97 393	−190 596
Total	NYQA	F.22	356 007	171 418	163 284	89 661
Other deposits	NYQM	F.29	16 947	−17 556	18 504	−1 901
Total	NQAK	F.2	379 404	155 742	184 937	91 201
Debt securities		F.3				
Short-term		F.31				
Issued by UK central government	NYQQ	F.31N1	25 402	−10 378	10 308	−9 487
Issued by UK local government	NYQY	F.31N2	–	–	–	–
Issued by UK MFIs[1]	NYRA	F.31N5	−63 593	−18 372	−13 132	−3 884
MMIs issued by other UK residents[2]	NYRK	F.31N6	−2 802	769	5 221	−4 122
MMIs issued by rest of the world[2]	NYRM	F.31N9	9 765	−9 467	−2 745	4 781
Long-term		F.32				
Issued by UK central government	NYRQ	F.32N1	171 613	92 881	82 636	100 271
Issued by UK local government	NYRW	F.32N2	−83	−17	595	676
Issued by MFIs and other UK residents[1,6]	KVG9	F.32N5-6	138 434	−250	−38 535	−51 987
Bonds issued by rest of the world	NYSG	F.32N9	31 918	922	−44 862	37 576
Total	NQAL	F.3	310 654	56 088	−514	73 824
Loans		F.4				
Short-term		F.41				
By UK MFIS[1]	NYSS	F.41N1	−208 015	−20 477	−52 628	−27 683
Long-term		F.42				
Direct investment	NYTE	F.421	−46 372	−16 652	−7 372	−11 855
Secured on dwellings	NYTK	F.422	11 076	908	10 691	11 254
Finance leasing	NYTS	F.423	628	−1 053	−392	269
Other long-term loans		F.424				
Other issued by other UK residents	NYTU	F.424N1	32 602	84 809	14 413	−2 685
Total	NQAN	F.4	−210 081	47 535	−35 288	−30 700
Equity and investment fund shares/units		F.5				
Equity		F.51				
Listed UK shares[6]	NYUG	F.511N1	92 180	12 123	4 730	190
Unlisted UK shares[6]	NYUI	F.512N1	64 522	−8 035	−1 084	−47 270
Other equity		F.519				
Other UK equity	NYUK	F.519N6	−4 960	−582	−684	−895
UK shares and bonds issued by other UK residents[6]	NSQJ	F.519N7	–	–	–	–
Shares and other equity issued by rest of the world	NYUQ	F.519N9	22 685	26 353	−1 853	65 314
Investment fund shares/units		F.52				
UK mutual funds' shares	NYUY	F.52N1	26 236	43 191	19 571	18 364
Rest of the world mutual funds' shares	NYVA	F.52N9	9 021	26 256	13 167	18 911
Total[3]	NQAP	F.5	209 684	99 306	33 847	54 614
Insurance, pensions and standardised guarantee schemes		F.6				
Non-life insurance technical reserves	NQBD	F.61	−231	−8 559	−638	1 158
Life insurance and annuity entitlements	M9W7	F.62	4 165	4 917	7 786	430
Pension schemes[4]	MA28	F.6M	65 351	84 471	77 914	66 464
Provisions for calls under standardised guarantees	M9ZJ	F.66	–	–	–	–
Total	NQAW	F.6	69 285	80 829	85 062	68 052
Financial derivatives and employee stock options	MN5F	F.7	−27 634	−43 299	6 124	−39 981
Of which: financial derivatives	NYSI	F.71	−29 194	−44 896	4 491	−41 634
Other accounts receivable	NQBK	F.8	−24 591	−36 948	738	35 940
Total net acquisition of financial assets	NQBL	F.A	715 243	359 271	275 239	253 061

1.6.8 UK summary accounts
Total economy ESA 2010 sector S.1 Unconsolidated

continued

£ million

			2013	2014	2015	2016
Financial account		III.2				
Net acquisition of financial assets		F.A				
Monetary gold and special drawing rights		F.1				
Monetary gold	NYPU	F.11	–	–	–	–
Special drawing rights	NYPW	F.12	43	−14	55	−1 397
Total	NQAD	F.1	43	−14	55	−1 397
Currency and deposits		F.2				
Currency	NYPY	F.21	2 244	3 880	3 766	7 508
Transferable deposits		F.22				
Deposits with UK MFIs[1]	NYQC	F.22N1	40 357	−121 993	10 053	265 463
Deposits with rest of the world MFIs[1]	NYQK	F.22N9	−226 660	52 758	−120 279	111 903
Other deposits	NYQM	F.29	2 527	22 330	5 560	20 320
Total	NQAK	F.2	−181 532	−43 025	−100 900	405 194
Debt securities		F.3				
Short-term		F.31				
Issued by UK central government	NYQQ	F.31N1	−6 487	13 876	6 202	7 554
Issued by UK local government	NYQY	F.31N2	–	–	–	–
Issued by UK MFIs[1]	NYRA	F.31N5	−712	5 095	2 007	13 768
MMIs issued by other UK residents[2]	NYRK	F.31N6	1 563	322	−2 468	430
MMIs issued by rest of the world[2]	NYRM	F.31N9	−22 284	5 688	3 642	−19 494
Long-term		F.32				
Issued by UK central government	NYRQ	F.32N1	63 609	66 740	−3 853	13 235
Issued by UK local government	NYRW	F.32N2	717	496	590	362
Issued by UK MFIs and other UK residents[1,6]	KVG9	F.32N5-6	−4 599	−11 320	−39 749	−6 597
Bonds issued by rest of the world	NYSG	F.32N9	−26 634	54 813	9 640	−92 162
Total	NQAL	F.3	5 173	135 710	−23 989	−82 904
Loans		F.4				
Short-term		F.41				
By UK MFIs[1]	NYSS	F.41N1	−50 656	−103 483	18 474	73 021
Long-term		F.42				
Direct investment	NYTE	F.421	9 581	10 466	−24 328	31 727
Secured on dwellings	NYTK	F.422	12 742	19 473	24 930	38 368
Finance leasing	NYTS	F.423	383	392	386	1 014
Other long-term loans		F.424				
By UK residents	NYTU	F.424N1	43 872	36 054	47 347	37 012
Total	NQAN	F.4	15 922	−37 098	66 809	181 142
Equity and investment fund shares/units		F.5				
Equity		F.51				
Listed UK shares[6]	NYUG	F.511N1	−20 993	−38 587	−26 956	−17 805
Unlisted UK shares[6]	NYUI	F.512N1	−38 877	−3 198	−6 676	−795
Other equity		F.519				
Other UK equity	NYUK	F.519N6	−1 078	−1 400	−1 345	−1 691
UK shares and bonds issued by other UK residents[6]	NSQJ	F.519N7	–	–	–	–
Shares and other equity issued by rest of the world	NYUQ	F.519N9	−8 875	−62 459	−43 059	−60 226
Investment fund shares/units		F.52				
UK mutual funds' shares	NYUY	F.52N1	17 696	25 205	8 391	1 972
Rest of the world mutual funds' shares	NYVA	F.52N9	10 190	7 485	6 164	2 910
Total[3]	NQAP	F.5	−41 937	−72 954	−63 481	−75 635
Insurance, pensions and standardised guarantee schemes		F.6				
Non-life insurance technical reserves	NQBD	F.61	−1 644	5	−2 511	757
Life insurance and annuity entitlements	M9W7	F.62	−8 471	−13 963	56 599	19 617
Pension schemes[4]	MA28	F.6M	67 631	80 161	59 281	63 360
Provisions for calls under standardised guarantees	M9ZJ	F.66	–	27	14	–
Total	NQAW	F.6	57 516	66 230	113 383	83 734
Financial derivatives and employee stock options	MN5F	F.7	42 412	20 854	−82 418	23 495
Of which: financial derivatives	NYSI	F.71	40 710	19 086	−84 240	21 616
Other accounts receivable	NQBK	F.8	−1 611	7 405	686	29 419
Total net acquisition of financial assets	NQBL	F.A	−104 014	77 108	−89 855	563 048

1.6.8 UK summary accounts
Total economy ESA 2010 sector S.1 Unconsolidated

continued

£ million

			2009	2010	2011	2012
Financial account		III.2				
Net acquisition of financial liabilities		F.L				
Special drawing rights	NYPX	F.12	8 654	–	–	–
Currency and deposits		F.2				
Currency	NYPZ	F.21	6 378	2 070	3 250	3 471
Transferable deposits		F.22				
Deposits with UK MFIs[1]	NYQD	F.22N1	203 231	37 738	140 592	161 331
Other deposits	NYQN	F.29	17 148	−17 263	19 070	−2 420
Total	NQCK	F.2	226 757	22 545	162 912	162 382
Debt securities		F.3				
Short-term		F.31				
Issued by UK central government	NYQR	F.31N1	25 975	−2 077	14 454	−18 706
Issued by UK local government	NYQZ	F.31N2	–	–	–	–
Issued by UK MFIs[1]	NYRB	F.31N5	22 398	−85 918	−91 548	4 869
MMIs issued by other UK residents[2]	NYRL	F.31N6	−8 222	4 075	8 865	−5 959
Long-term		F.32				
Issued by UK central government	NYRR	F.32N1	194 266	171 851	124 826	133 873
Issued by UK local government	NYRX	F.32N2	−83	−17	595	676
Issued by UK MFIs and other UK residents[1,6]	KVI5	F.32N5-6	209 304	108 310	40 097	−162 848
Total	NQCM	F.3	443 638	196 224	97 289	−48 095
Loans		F.4				
Short-term		F.41				
By UK MFIs[1]	NYST	F.41N1	−90 615	−37 566	−66 667	6 255
Of which: foreign currency loans by UK banks	NYSX	F.41N12	−39 317	31 047	−28 001	449
By rest of the world MFIs[1]	NYTB	F.41N9	−60 708	98 599	−34 298	20 556
Long-term		F.42				
Direct investment	NYTF	F.421	−34 900	−6 283	−5 088	−251
Secured on dwellings	NYTL	F.422	11 076	908	10 691	11 254
Finance leasing	NYTT	F.423	628	−1 053	−392	269
Other long-term loans		F.424				
Issued by other UK residents	NYTV	F.424N1	−1 285	34 925	19 645	41 801
By rest of the world	NYTX	F.424N9	−17 279	−741	−137	25
Total	NQCN	F.4	−193 083	88 789	−76 246	79 909
Equity and investment fund shares/units		F.5				
Equity		F.51				
Listed UK shares[6]	NYUH	F.511N1	120 036	20 798	5 003	4 979
Unlisted UK shares[6]	NYUJ	F.512N1	104 634	18 467	9 889	−14 619
Other equity		F.519				
Other UK equity	NYUL	F.519N6	−4 908	−528	189	−562
UK shares and bonds issued by other UK residents[6]	NSQK	F.519N7	–	–	–	–
Investment fund shares/units		F.52				
UK mutual funds' shares	NYUZ	F.52N1	26 271	43 235	19 580	18 375
Total[3]	NQCS	F.5	246 033	81 972	34 661	8 173
Insurance, pensions and standardised guarantee schemes		F.6				
Non-life insurance technical reserves	NQDD	F.61	−1 953	−12 463	−945	4 232
Life insurance and annuity entitlements	M9WJ	F.62	4 204	4 950	7 835	436
Pension schemes[4]	MA2L	F.6M	65 351	84 471	77 914	66 464
Provisions for calls under standardised guarantees	M9ZV	F.66	–	–	–	–
Total	NQCV	F.6	67 602	76 958	84 804	71 132
Financial derivatives and employee stock options	MN5Z	F.7	1 561	1 598	1 634	1 654
Of which: financial derivatives	NYSJ	F.71	–	–	–	–
Other accounts payable	NQDG	F.8	−24 945	−36 132	204	36 484
Total net acquisition of financial liabilities	NQDH	F.L	776 217	431 954	305 258	311 639
Net lending(+) / net borrowing(-)		B.9				
Total net acquisition of financial assets	NQBL	F.A	715 243	359 271	275 239	253 061
less total net acquisition of financial liabilities	NQDH	F.L	776 217	431 954	305 258	311 639
Net lending(+) / borrowing(-) from the financial account	NQDL	B.9f	−60 975	−72 683	−30 019	−58 578
Statistical discrepancy between financial and non-financial accounts	NYVK	dB.9	1 453	12 270	−9 636	−13 599
Net lending (+) / borrowing (-) from non-financial accounts	NQFH	B.9n	**−59 522**	**−60 413**	**−39 655**	**−72 177**

UK summary accounts
Total economy ESA 2010 sector S.1 Unconsolidated

£ million

			2013	2014	2015	2016
Financial account		III.2				
Net acquisition of financial liabilities		F.L				
Special drawing rights	NYPX	F.12	–	–	–	–
Currency and deposits		F.2				
Currency	NYPZ	F.21	2 266	3 828	4 017	7 503
Transferable deposits		F.22				
Deposits with UK MFIs[1]	NYQD	F.22N1	–237 016	–130 732	–111 973	285 587
Other deposits	NYQN	F.29	1 692	23 100	5 985	21 044
Total	NQCK	F.2	–233 058	–103 804	–101 971	314 134
Debt securities		F.3				
Short-term		F.31				
Issued by UK central government	NYQR	F.31N1	–14 315	25 809	19 721	12 524
Issued by UK local government	NYQZ	F.31N2	–	–	–	–
Issued by UK MFIs[1]	NYRB	F.31N5	–11 755	22 015	–4 207	20 237
MMIs and other UK residents[2]	NYRL	F.31N6	3 345	332	–2 335	2 942
Long-term		F.32				
Issued by UK central government	NYRR	F.32N1	106 136	64 601	53 250	56 083
Issued by UK local government	NYRX	F.32N2	717	496	590	362
Issued by UK MFIs and other UK residents[1,6]	KVI5	F.32N5-6	46 040	9 955	–47 544	26 704
Total	NQCM	F.3	130 168	123 208	19 475	118 852
Loans		F.4				
Short-term		F.41				
By UK MFIs[1,5]	NYST	F.41N1	–35 696	–145 753	11 862	35 915
By rest of the world MFIs[1]	NYTB	F.41N9	–33 085	106 404	–179 401	–44 463
Long-term		F.42				
Direct investment	NYTF	F.421	–990	18 221	4 813	25 002
Secured on dwellings	NYTL	F.422	12 742	19 473	24 930	38 368
Finance leasing	NYTT	F.423	383	392	386	1 014
Other long-term loans		F.424				
By UK residents	NYTV	F.424N1	50 290	50 332	39 133	30 887
By rest of the world	NYTX	F.429N9	2 173	3 334	5 583	561
Total	NQCN	F.4	–4 183	52 403	–92 694	87 284
Equity and investment fund shares/units		F.5				
Equity		F.51				
Listed UK shares[6]	NYUH	F.511N1	14 122	–25 235	22 674	–94 844
Unlisted UK shares[6]	NYUJ	F.512N1	–1 514	19 066	28 164	139 757
Other equity		F.519				
Other UK equity	NYUL	F.519N6	–740	–1 094	–1 345	–968
UK shares and bonds issued by other UK residents[6]	NSQK	F.519N7	–	–	–	–
Investment fund shares/units		F.52				
UK mutual funds' shares	NYUZ	F.52N1	17 723	25 256	8 482	2 031
Total[3]	NQCS	F.5	29 591	17 993	57 975	45 976
Insurance, pensions and standardised guarantee schemes		F.6				
Non-life insurance technical reserves	NQDD	F.61	–2 033	6	–3 105	936
Life insurance and annuity entitlements	M9WJ	F.62	–8 600	–14 194	57 601	20 437
Pension schemes[4]	MA2L	F.6M	67 631	80 161	59 281	63 360
Provisions for calls under standardised guarantes	M9ZV	F.66	–	27	14	–
Total	NQCV	F.6	56 998	66 000	113 791	84 733
Financial derivatives and employee stock options	MN5Z	F.7	1 703	1 769	1 823	1 880
Of which: financial derivatives	NYSJ	F.71	–	–	–	–
Other accounts payable	NQDG	F.8	–550	9 444	2 638	29 751
Total net acquisition of financial liabilities	NQDH	F.L	–19 331	167 013	1 037	682 610
Net lending(+) / net borrowing(-)		B.9				
Total net acquisition of financial assets	NQBL	F.A	–104 014	77 108	–89 855	563 048
less total net acquisition of financial liabilities	NQDH	F.L	–19 331	167 013	1 037	682 610
Net lending(+) / borrowing(-) from the financial account	NQDL	B.9f	–84 683	–89 905	–90 891	–119 562
Statistical discrepancy between financial and non-financial accounts	NYVK	dB.9	–13 537	–10 062	–9 232	2 763
Net lending (+) / borrowing (-) from non-financial accounts	NQFH	B.9n	**–98 220**	**–99 967**	**–100 123**	**–116 799**

1 Monetary Financial Institutions
2 Money Market Instruments
3 Total F.5 does not always equal the sum of the components listed as some equity components are omitted from this table
4 F.63 Pension entitlements, F.64 Claims of pension funds on pension managers, F.65 Entitlements to non-pension benefits
5 Excluding loans secured on dwellings and finance leasing
6 Prior to 1990, it is not possible to distinguish some elements of F.32N5-6, F.511N1 and F.512N1. These elements are shown combined as F.519N7

1.6.9 UK summary accounts
Total economy ESA 2010 sector S.1

£ million

			2013	2014	2015	2016
Other changes in assets account		III.3				
Other changes in volume of assets account		III.3.1				
Changes in net worth due to other changes in volume of assets		B.102				
Monetary gold and special drawing rights	M9K3	AF.1	–	–	–	–
Currency and deposits	M9LW	AF.2	−3 988	−1 012	26 927	23 101
Debt securities	M9Z9	AF.3	−4 670	−34 871	11 481	−24 198
Loans	N492	AF.4	25 292	−11 016	−42 556	−105 444
Equity and investment fund shares/units	N4B4	AF.5	–	–	–	–
Insurance, pensions and standardised guarantee schemes	N4D6	AF.6	–	–	–	–
Financial derivatives and employee stock options	N4F4	AF.7	–	–	–	–
Other accounts receivable/payable	N4H2	AF.8	−897	−7 225	6 247	3 243
Total	CWTD	**B.102**	15 737	−54 124	2 099	−103 298

1.6.10 UK summary accounts
Total economy ESA 2010 sector S.1

£ million

			2013	2014	2015	2016
Other changes in assets account		III.3				
Revaluation account		III.3.2				
Changes in net worth due to nominal holding gains and losses		B.103				
Monetary gold and special drawing rights	M9K8	AF.1	−2 931	468	−587	1 844
Currency and deposits	M9QZ	AF.2	6 182	−36 333	−25 496	−19 847
Debt securities	N47Z	AF.3	210 976	−22 522	−5 638	147 632
Loans	N4A3	AF.4	−20 481	87 015	11 059	181 289
Equity and investment fund shares/units	N4C5	AF.5	33 375	54 648	173 238	230 681
Insurance, pensions and standardised guarantee schemes	N4E5	AF.6	−816	−1 002	−342	4 433
Financial derivatives and employee stock options	N4G3	AF.7	6 385	−23 000	−1 620	2 177
Other accounts receivable/payable	N4I3	AF.8	2	−101	−107	704
Total	CWU5	**B.103**	232 692	59 173	150 507	548 913

1.6.11 UK summary accounts
Total economy ESA 2010 sector S.1 Unconsolidated

£ billion

			2009	2010	2011	2012
Financial balance sheet at end of period		IV.3				
Non-financial assets	NG2A	**AN**	7 076.1	7 371.6	7 486.7	7 643.9
Total financial assets		**AF.A**				
Monetary gold and special drawing rights		AF.1				
Monetary gold	NYVP	AF.11	6.8	9.1	9.8	10.2
Special drawing rights	NYVR	AF.12	8.9	9.1	9.4	9.1
Total	NYVN	AF.1	15.7	18.2	19.2	19.3
Currency and deposits		AF.2				
Currency	NYVV	AF.21	62.1	64.0	67.2	70.6
Transferable deposits		AF.22				
Deposits with UK MFIs[1]	NYVZ	AF.22N1	3 675.6	3 591.5	3 729.1	4 003.8
Deposits with rest of the world MFIs[1]	NYWH	AF.22N9	2 302.8	2 483.9	2 743.5	2 500.7
Other deposits	NYWJ	AF.29	151.0	133.5	151.6	149.8
Total	NYVT	AF.2	6 191.5	6 272.9	6 691.3	6 724.8
Debt securities		AF.3				
Short-term		AF.31				
Issued by UK central government	NYWP	AF.31N1	38.0	27.5	38.0	28.6
Issued by UK local government	NYWX	AF.31N2	–	–	–	–
Issued by UK MFIs[1]	NYWZ	AF.31N5	92.2	73.4	56.8	56.7
MMIs issued by other UK residents[2]	NYXJ	AF.31N6	12.0	13.5	18.0	14.0
MMIs issued by rest of the world[2]	NYXL	AF.31N9	117.9	113.8	107.0	107.2
Long-term		AF.32				
Issued by UK central government	NYXP	AF.32N1	586.5	698.3	873.2	954.3
Issued by UK local government	NYXV	AF.32N2	1.0	1.0	1.6	2.3
Issued by UK MFIs and other UK residents[1,5]	KVG2	AF.32N5-6	892.7	924.7	912.2	912.7
Bonds issued by rest of the world	NYYF	AF.32N9	886.8	907.8	890.8	931.5
Total	NYWL	AF.3	2 627.1	2 760.0	2 897.5	3 007.4
Loans		AF.4				
Short-term		AF.41				
by UK MFIs[1]	NYYT	AF.41N1	2 503.5	2 468.2	2 372.7	2 285.0
Long-term		AF.42				
Direct investment	NYZF	AF.421	250.1	249.5	226.9	291.9
Secured on dwellings	NYZL	AF.422	1 235.3	1 238.3	1 245.4	1 268.5
Finance leasing	NYZT	AF.423	37.0	36.3	35.9	36.2
Other long-term loans		AF.424				
Issued by other UK residents	NYZV	AF.424N1	750.4	928.7	928.9	943.3
Total	NYYP	AF.4	4 776.2	4 921.0	4 809.7	4 824.9
Equity and investment fund shares/units		AF.5				
Equity		AF.51				
Listed UK shares[5]	NZAJ	AF.511N1	831.4	925.1	723.4	718.3
Unlisted UK shares[5]	NZAL	AF.512N1	651.8	708.2	698.1	670.5
Other equity		AF.519				
Other UK equity	NZAN	AF.519N6	118.9	120.1	121.5	123.6
UK shares and bonds issued by other UK residents[5]	NSRC	AF.519N7	–	–	–	–
Shares and other equity issued by rest of the world	NZAT	AF.519N9	1 730.6	1 878.6	1 817.0	1 922.9
Investment fund shares/units		AF.52				
UK mutual funds' shares	NZBB	AF.52N1	565.1	692.4	677.5	776.5
Rest of the world mutual funds' shares	NZBD	AF.52N9	119.1	156.5	169.4	209.8
Total[3]	NYZZ	AF.5	4 017.0	4 480.9	4 206.8	4 421.6
Insurance, pensions and standardised guarantee schemes		AF.6				
Non-life insurance technical reserves	NZBN	AF.61	62.2	49.4	48.8	49.9
Life insurance and annuity entitlements	M9RO	AF.62	544.8	568.4	543.8	546.4
Pension schemes[4]	M9V4	AF.6M	2 350.8	2 373.6	3 050.7	2 966.2
Provisions for calls under standardised guarantees	M9UI	AF.66	–	–	–	–
Total	NZBF	AF.6	2 957.8	2 991.4	3 643.3	3 562.5
Financial derivatives and employee stock options	MMU5	AF.7	5 279.9	6 421.8	8 165.8	6 958.9
Of which: financial derivatives	NYYH	AF.71	5 275.2	6 417.1	8 161.0	6 954.0
Other accounts receivable	NZBP	AF.8	410.5	386.9	388.8	443.0
Total financial assets	NZBV	**AF.A**	26 275.7	28 253.2	30 822.5	29 962.3

1.6.11 UK summary accounts
Total economy ESA 2010 sector S.1 Unconsolidated

continued

£ billion

			2013	2014	2015	2016
Financial balance sheet at end of period		IV.3				
Non-financial assets	NG2A	AN	8 086.8	8 775.0	9 345.9	9 822.8
Total financial assets		AF.A				
Monetary gold and special drawing rights		AF.1				
Monetary gold	NYVP	AF.11	7.3	7.7	7.1	9.4
Special drawing rights	NYVR	AF.12	9.0	9.0	9.1	8.9
Total	NYVN	AF.1	16.3	16.7	16.2	18.3
Currency and deposits		AF.2				
Currency	NYVV	AF.21	72.8	76.6	80.4	87.8
Transferable deposits		AF.22				
Deposits with UK MFIs[1]	NYVZ	AF.22N1	4 066.0	3 722.0	3 732.9	4 103.7
Deposits with rest of the world MFIs[1]	NYWH	AF.22N9	2 264.7	2 279.1	2 146.4	2 614.3
Other deposits	NYWJ	AF.29	152.2	174.4	180.0	200.4
Total	NYVT	AF.2	6 555.6	6 252.1	6 139.7	7 006.2
Debt securities		AF.3				
Short-term		AF.31				
Issued by UK central government	NYWP	AF.31N1	21.7	35.4	42.4	50.3
Issued by UK local government	NYWX	AF.31N2	–	–	–	–
Issued by UK MFIs[1]	NYWZ	AF.31N5	56.1	65.8	72.4	87.3
MMIs issued by other UK residents[2]	NYXJ	AF.31N6	15.2	16.1	13.5	14.0
MMIs issued by rest of the world[2]	NYXL	AF.31N9	82.2	89.3	96.7	95.2
Long-term		AF.32				
Issued by UK central government	NYXP	AF.32N1	989.8	1 241.4	1 210.6	1 391.8
Issued by UK local government	NYXV	AF.32N2	3.0	3.5	4.1	4.4
Issued by UK MFIs and other UK residents[1,5]	KVG2	AF.32N5-6	896.0	930.1	900.0	981.2
Bonds issued by rest of the world	NYYF	AF.32N9	885.7	939.8	942.0	1 008.4
Total	NYWL	AF.3	2 949.7	3 321.5	3 281.6	3 632.7
Loans		AF.4				
Short-term		AF.41				
By UK MFIs[1]	NYYT	AF.41N1	2 179.0	2 079.1	2 064.6	2 331.8
Long-term		AF.42				
Direct investment	NYZF	AF.421	311.9	300.0	249.6	253.4
Secured on dwellings	NYZL	AF.422	1 280.2	1 301.2	1 327.1	1 366.4
Finance leasing	NYZT	AF.423	36.5	37.3	38.2	39.2
Other-long term loans		AF.424				
issued by otheUK residents	NYZV	AF.424N1	970.4	934.2	967.1	1 090.1
Total	NYYP	AF.4	4 778.1	4 652.0	4 646.7	5 080.9
Equity and investment fund shares/units		AF.5				
Equity		AF.51				
Listed UK shares[5]	NZAJ	AF.511N1	809.3	795.8	767.4	761.7
Unlisted UK shares[5]	NZAL	AF.512N1	674.5	673.9	675.2	695.0
Other equity		AF.519				
Other UK equity	NZAN	AF.519N6	124.5	127.0	128.8	129.9
UK shares and bonds issued by other UK residents[5]	NSRC	AF.519N7	–	–	–	–
Shares and other equity issued by rest of the world	NZAT	AF.519N9	2 033.5	2 112.9	2 138.4	2 444.3
Investment fund shares/units		AF.52				
UK mutual funds' shares	NZBB	AF.52N1	881.8	960.9	1 010.4	1 086.0
Rest of the world mutual funds' share	NZBD	AF.52N9	227.8	224.3	252.2	287.0
Total[3]	NYZZ	AF.5	4 751.4	4 894.8	4 972.5	5 403.9
Insurance, pensions and standardised guarantee schemes		AF.6				
Non-life insurance technical reserves	NZBN	AF.61	48.3	48.3	45.8	46.6
Life insurance and annuity entitlements	M9RO	AF.62	565.6	566.3	605.8	633.9
Pension schemes[4]	M9V4	AF.6M	2 742.9	3 512.1	3 423.2	3 812.8
Provisions for calls under standardised guarantees	M9UI	AF.66	–	–	–	–
Total	NZBF	AF.6	3 356.8	4 126.8	4 074.8	4 493.2
Financial derivatives and employee stock options	MMU5	AF.7	5 600.1	6 251.1	4 577.5	5 404.7
Of which: financial derivatives	NYYH	AF.71	5 595.1	6 246.0	4 572.2	5 399.3
Other accounts receivable	NZBP	AF.8	451.0	459.1	468.4	495.4
Total financial assets	NZBV	**AF.A**	28 458.9	29 974.0	28 177.3	31 535.3

1.6.11 UK summary accounts
Total economy ESA 2010 sector S.1 Unconsolidated

continued

£ billion

			2009	2010	2011	2012
Financial balance sheet at end of period		IV.3				
Total financial liabilities		AF.L				
Special drawing rights	NYVS	AF.12	9.8	10.1	10.1	9.6
Currency and deposits		AF.2				
Currency	NYVW	AF.21	62.7	64.7	68.0	71.5
Transferable deposits		AF.22				
Deposits with UK MFIs[1]	NYWA	AF.22N1	6 601.9	6 610.2	6 953.6	6 980.7
Other deposits	NYWK	AF.29	152.0	134.8	153.5	151.1
Total	NYVU	AF.2	6 816.6	6 809.7	7 175.1	7 203.3
Debt securities		AF.3				
Short-term		AF.31				
Issued by UK central government	NYWQ	AF.31N1	57.5	55.4	69.8	51.1
Issued by UK local government	NYWY	AF.31N2	–	–	–	–
Issued by UK MFIs[1]	NYXA	AF.31N5	360.1	278.3	180.8	185.4
MMIs issued by other UK residents[2]	NYXK	AF.31N6	33.5	38.9	47.5	40.4
Long-term		AF.32				
Issued by UK central government	NYXQ	AF.32N1	822.0	1 021.9	1 280.4	1 392.5
Issued by UK local government	NYXW	AF.32N2	1.0	1.0	1.6	2.3
Issued by UK MFIs and other UK residents[1,5]	KVH7	AF.32N5-6	1 981.5	2 013.1	2 067.9	2 030.5
Total	NYWM	AF.3	3 255.5	3 408.6	3 648.0	3 702.1
Loans		AF.4				
Short-term loans		AF.41				
By UK MFIs[1]	NYYU	AF.41N1	1 599.9	1 497.0	1 371.1	1 362.0
By rest of the world MFIs[1]	NYZC	AF.41N9	733.1	833.1	795.5	829.4
Long-term loans		AF.42				
Direct investment	NYZG	AF.421	337.4	341.5	342.4	469.8
Secured on dwellings	NYZM	AF.422	1 235.3	1 238.3	1 245.4	1 268.5
Finance leasing	NYZU	AF.423	37.0	36.3	35.9	36.2
Other long-term loans		AF.424				
Issued by other UK residents	NYZW	AF.424N1	376.1	489.3	498.3	520.1
Issued by rest of the world	NYZY	AF.424N9	47.5	44.4	42.8	45.2
Total	NYYQ	AF.4	4 366.3	4 479.9	4 331.3	4 531.1
Equity and investment fund shares/units		AF.5				
Equity		AF.51				
Listed UK shares[5]	NZAK	AF.511N1	1 573.6	1 777.2	1 564.8	1 699.9
Unlisted UK shares[5]	NZAM	AF.512N1	1 227.6	1 328.5	1 356.5	1 483.0
Other equity		AF.519				
Other UK equity	NZAO	AF.519N6	127.5	129.7	131.6	134.1
UK shares and bonds issued by other UK residents[5]	NSRD	AF.519N7	–	–	–	–
Investment fund shares/units		AF.52				
UK mutual funds' shares	NZBC	AF.52N1	566.4	694.0	678.8	777.9
Total[3]	NZAA	AF.5	3 495.1	3 929.4	3 731.8	4 094.9
Insurance, pensions and standardised guarantee schemes		AF.6				
Non-life insurance technical reserves	NZBO	AF.61	70.9	58.5	57.5	61.8
Life insurance and annuity entitlements	M9S2	AF.62	549.8	572.3	547.3	554.3
Pension schemes[4]	M9VH	AF.6M	2 350.8	2 373.6	3 050.7	2 966.2
Provisions for calls under standardised guarantees	M9US	AF.66	–	–	–	–
Total	NZBG	AF.6	2 971.5	3 004.4	3 655.5	3 582.2
Financial derivatives and employee stock options	MMW9	AF.7	5 200.3	6 353.9	8 082.5	6 897.5
Of which: financial derivatives	NYYI	AF.71	5 195.6	6 349.1	8 077.7	6 892.6
Other accounts payable	NZBQ	AF.8	403.4	381.6	379.4	429.5
Total financial liabilities	NZBW	**AF.L**	26 518.6	28 377.5	31 013.7	30 450.2
Financial net worth		**BF.90**				
Total financial assets	NZBV	AF.A	26 275.7	28 253.2	30 822.5	29 962.3
less total financial liabilities	NZBW	AF.L	26 518.6	28 377.5	31 013.7	30 450.2
Financial net worth	NQFT	**BF.90**	−243.0	−124.3	−191.1	−487.9
Net worth						
Non-financial assets	NG2A	AN	7 076.1	7 371.6	7 486.7	7 643.9
Financial net worth	NQFT	BF.90	−243.0	−124.3	−191.1	−487.9
Net worth	CGDA	**B.90**	6 833.1	7 247.3	7 295.5	7 155.9

UK summary accounts
Total economy ESA 2010 sector S.1 Unconsolidated

£ billion

			2013	2014	2015	2016
Financial balance sheet at end of period		IV.3				
Total financial liabilities		**AF.L**				
Special drawing rights	NYVS	AF.12	9.4	9.4	9.5	11.1
Currency and deposits		AF.2				
Currency	NYVW	AF.21	73.7	77.6	81.6	89.1
Transferable deposits		AF.22				
Deposits with UK MFIs[1]	NYWA	AF.22N1	6 754.0	6 400.3	6 275.3	7 018.9
Other deposits	NYWK	AF.29	152.7	175.7	181.8	202.8
Total	NYVU	AF.2	6 980.4	6 653.5	6 538.6	7 310.8
Debt securities		AF.3				
Short-term		AF.31				
Issued by UK central government	NYWQ	AF.31N1	36.8	62.6	82.3	94.9
Issued by UK local government	NYWY	AF.31N2	–	–	–	–
Issued by MFIs[1]	NYXA	AF.31N5	173.6	196.4	198.1	236.2
MMIs issued by other UK residents[2]	NYXK	AF.31N6	42.8	45.3	44.3	53.4
Long-term		AF.32				
Issued by UK central government	NYXQ	AF.32N1	1 422.6	1 663.1	1 678.1	1 934.6
Issued by UK local government	NYXW	AF.32N2	3.0	3.5	4.1	4.4
Issued by UK MFIs and other UK residents[1,5]	KVH7	AF.32N5-6	1 884.3	2 008.9	1 970.5	2 083.4
Total	NYWM	AF.3	3 563.1	3 979.7	3 977.4	4 406.9
Loans		AF.4				
Short-term loans		AF.41				
By UK MFIs[1]	NYYU	AF.41N1	1 283.4	1 146.6	1 143.6	1 234.7
By rest of the world MFIs[1]	NYZC	AF.41N9	797.9	857.4	680.9	756.4
Long-term loans		AF.42				
Direct investment	NYZG	AF.421	452.6	431.5	419.4	409.3
Secured on dwellings	NYZM	AF.422	1 280.2	1 301.2	1 327.1	1 366.4
Finance leasing	NYZU	AF.423	36.5	37.3	38.2	39.2
Other long-term loans		AF.424				
Issued by other UK residents	NYZW	AF.424N1	551.5	532.6	567.6	633.1
Issued by rest of the world	NYZY	AF.424N9	57.3	40.2	36.6	38.9
Total	NYYQ	AF.4	4 459.4	4 346.8	4 213.5	4 478.0
Equity and investment fund shares/units		AF.5				
Equity		AF.51				
Listed UK shares[5]	NZAK	AF.511N1	1 931.5	1 933.0	1 938.3	1 960.9
Unlisted UK shares[5]	NZAM	AF.512N1	1 512.2	1 607.2	1 575.6	1 797.2
Other equity		AF.519				
Other UK equity	NZAO	AF.519N6	135.6	139.3	141.9	144.3
UK shares and bonds issued by other UK residents[5]	NSRD	AF.519N7	–	–	–	–
Investment fund shares/units		AF.52				
UK mutual funds' shares	NZBC	AF.52N1	883.7	963.1	1 012.7	1 088.5
Total[3]	NZAA	AF.5	4 462.9	4 642.6	4 668.5	4 990.9
Insurance, pensions and standardised guarantee schemes		AF.6				
Non-life insurance technical reserves	NZBO	AF.61	59.7	59.7	56.6	57.6
Life premiums and annuity entitlements	M9S2	AF.62	574.2	575.7	616.6	641.0
Pension schemes[4]	M9VH	AF.6M	2 742.9	3 512.1	3 423.2	3 812.8
Provisions for calls under standardised guarantees	M9US	AF.66	–	–	–	–
Total	NZBG	AF.6	3 376.8	4 147.6	4 096.4	4 511.4
Financial derivatives and employee stock options	MMW9	AF.7	5 491.5	6 146.5	4 558.7	5 362.2
Of which: financial derivatives	NYYI	AF.71	5 486.5	6 141.3	4 553.4	5 356.7
Other accounts payable	NZBQ	AF.8	439.5	457.0	462.1	485.5
Total financial liabilities	NZBW	**AF.L**	28 783.1	30 383.0	28 524.6	31 556.6
Financial net worth		**BF.90**				
Total financial assets	NZBV	AF.A	28 458.9	29 974.0	28 177.3	31 535.3
less total financial liabilities	NZBW	AF.L	28 783.1	30 383.0	28 524.6	31 556.6
Financial net worth	NQFT	**BF.90**	−324.2	−409.0	−347.3	−21.3
Net worth						
Non-financial assets	NG2A	AN	8 086.8	8 775.0	9 345.9	9 822.8
Financial net worth	NQFT	BF.90	−324.2	−409.0	−347.3	−21.3
Net worth	CGDA	**B.90**	7 762.6	8 365.9	8 998.6	9 801.5

1 Monetary Financial Institutions
2 Money Market Instruments
3 Total AF.5 does not always equal the sum of the components listed as some equity components are omitted from this table
4 F.63 Pension entitlements, F.64 Claims on pension funds on pension managers, F.65 Entitlements to non-pension benefits

5 Prior to 1990 it is not possible to distinguish some elements of AF.32N5-6, AF.511N1 and AF.512N1. These elements are shown combined as AF.519N7

1.7.1

UK summary accounts
2015

Total economy: all sectors and the rest of the world

£ million

		UK total economy	Non-financial corporations	Financial corporations	Monetary financial institutions	Financial corporations except MFI and ICPF[1]	Insurance corporations and pension funds
		S.1	S.11	S.12	S.121+ S.122+S.123	S.124+S.125+ S.126+S.127	S.128+S.129
Production account	I						
Resources							
Output	P.1						
Market output	P.11	2 533 954	2 073 825	246 725			
Output for own final use	P.12	263 268	38 683	4 624			
Non-market output	P.13	423 678		360			
Total	P.1	3 220 900	2 112 508	251 709			
Taxes on products	D.21	212 326					
less subsidies on products	D.31	8 526					
Total resources	TR	3 424 700	2 112 508	251 709			
Uses							
Intermediate consumption	P.2	1 535 963	1 101 827	137 606			
Gross domestic product	**B.1*g**	**1 888 737**	**1 010 681**	**114 103**	**54 724**	**34 409**	**24 970**
Total uses	TU	3 424 700	2 112 508	251 709			
Gross domestic product	**B.1*g**	**1 888 737**	**1 010 681**	**114 103**	**54 724**	**34 409**	**24 970**
less consumption of fixed capital	P.51c	231 530	124 981	8 199			
Net domestic product	B.1*n	1 657 207	885 700	105 904			

		General government	Central government	Local government	Households and NPISH[2]	Households	NPISH	Not sectorised	Taxes less subsidies	Rest of the world
		S.13	S.1311	S.1313	S.14+S.15	S.14	S.15	S.N	D.21-D.31	S.2
Production account	I									
Resources										
Output	P.1									
Market output	P.11	1 038	370	668	212 366	193 604	18 762			
Output for own final use	P.12	3 379	3 006	373	216 582	209 471	7 111			
Non-market output	P.13	360 253	226 034	134 219	63 065	–	63 065			
Total output	P.1	364 670	229 410	135 260	492 013	403 075	88 938			
Taxes on products	D.21							212 326	212 326	
less subsidies on products	D.31							8 526	8 526	
Total resources	TR	364 670	229 410	135 260	492 013	403 075	88 938	203 800	203 800	
Uses										
Intermediate consumption	P.2	162 302	103 083	59 219	134 228	95 097	39 131			
Gross domestic product	**B.1*g**	**202 368**	**126 327**	**76 041**	**357 785**	307 978	49 807	**203 800**	203 800	
Total uses	TU	364 670	229 410	135 260	492 013	403 075	88 938	203 800	203 800	
Gross domestic product	**B.1*g**	**202 368**	**126 327**	**76 041**	**357 785**	307 978	49 807	**203 800**	203 800	
less consumption of fixed capital	P.51c	29 182	18 220	10 962	69 168	59 549	9 619			
Net domestic product	B.1*n	173 186	108 107	65 079	288 617	248 429	40 188	203 800	203 800	

1 Monetary Financial Institutions and insurance corporation and pension funds

2 Non-profit institutions serving households

1.7.2 UK summary accounts
2015
Total economy: all sectors and the rest of the world

£ million

		UK total tconomy	Non-financial corporations	Financial corporations	Monetary financial institutions	Financial corporations except MFI and ICPF[1]	Insurance corporations and pension funds
		S.1	S.11	S.12	S.121+ S.122+S.123	S.124+S.125+ S.126+S.127	S.128+S.129
Distribution and use of income accounts	II						
Primary distribution of income account	II.1						
Generation of income account	II.1.1						
Resources							
Total resources (gross domestic product)	B.1*g	**1 888 737**	**1 010 681**	**114 103**	**54 724**	**34 409**	**24 970**
External balance of goods and services							
Uses							
Compensation of employees	D.1						
Wages and salaries	D.11	775 328	536 290	52 332	26 256	20 077	5 999
Employers' social contributions	D.12	154 878	88 569	13 389	6 717	5 136	1 536
Total	D.1	930 206	624 859	65 721	32 973	25 213	7 535
Taxes on production and imports, paid	D.2						
Taxes on products	D.21	212 326					
Other taxes on production	D.29	31 142	27 890	2 788	1 189	1 069	530
Total	D.2	243 468	27 890	2 788	1 189	1 069	530
less subsidies, received	D.3						
Subsidies on products	D.31	8 526					
Other subsidies on production	D.39	5 076	3 115	–	–	–	–
Total	D.3	13 602	3 115	–	–	–	–
Operating surplus, gross	B.2g	609 397	361 047	45 594	20 562	8 127	16 905
Mixed income, gross	B.3g	119 268					
Statistical discrepancy between income components and GDP	di						
Total uses (gross domestic product)	B.1*g	**1 888 737**	**1 010 681**	**114 103**	**54 724**	**34 409**	**24 970**
less consumption of fixed capital[3]	P.51c	231 530	124 981	8 199			
Operating surplus, net	B.2n	394 208	236 066	37 395			
Mixed income, net	B.3n	102 927					

1.7.2 UK summary accounts 2015

continued

Total economy: all sectors and the rest of the world

£ million

		General government	Central government	Local government	Households and NPISH[2]	Households	NPISH	Not sectorised	Taxes less subsidies	Rest of the world
		S.13	S.1311	S.1313	S.14+S.15	S.14	S.15	S.N		S.2
Distribution and use of income accounts	II									
Primary distribution of income account	II.1									
Generation of income account	II.1.1									
Resources										
Total resources (gross domestic product)	B.1*g	**202 368**	**126 327**	**76 041**	**357 785**	307 978	49 807	**203 800**	**203 800**	
External balance of goods and services										−32 370
Uses										
Compensation of employees	D.1									
Wages and salaries	D.11	132 792	86 599	46 193	53 914	21 033	32 881			1 295
Employers' social contributions	D.12	40 394	21 508	18 886	12 526	5 381	7 145			
Total	D.1	173 186	108 107	65 079	66 440	26 414	40 026			1 295
Taxes on production and imports, paid	D.2									
Taxes on products	D.21							212 326	212 326	−
Other taxes on production	D.29	−	−	−	464	302	162			
Total	D.2	−	−	−	464	302	162	212 326	212 326	−
less subsidies, received	D.3									
Subsidies on products	D.31							8 526	8 526	
Production subsidies other than on products	D.39	−	−	−	1 961	1 961	−			
Total	D.3	−	−	−	1 961	1 961	−	8 526	8 526	
Operating surplus, gross	B.2g	29 182	18 220	10 962	173 574	163 955	9 619			
Mixed income, gross	B.3g				119 268	119 268				
Statistical discrepancy between income components and GDP	di							−		
Total uses (gross domestic product)	B.1*g	**202 368**	**126 327**	**76 041**	**357 785**	307 978	49 807	**203 800**	**203 800**	
less consumption of fixed capital[3]	P.51c	29 182	18 220	10 962	69 168	59 549	9 619			
Operating surplus, net	B.2n	−	−	−	120 747	120 747	−			
Mixed income, net	B.3n				102 927	1 835				

1 Monetary financial institutions and insurance corporation and pension funds
2 Non-profit institutions serving households
3 Consumption of fixed capital for Households and NPISH is made up of
  P.51c1 - Consumption of fixed capital on gross operating surplus plus
  P.51c2 - Consumption of fixed capital on gross mixed income.

1.7.3 UK summary accounts
2015
Total economy: all sectors and the rest of the world

£ million

		UK total economy	Non-financial corporations	Financial corporations	Monetary financial institutions	Financial corporations except MFI and ICPF[1]	Insurance corporations and pension funds
		S.1	S.11	S.12	S.121+ S.122+S.123	S.124+S.125+ S.126+S.127	S.128+S.129
Allocation of primary income account	II.1.2						
Resources							
Operating surplus, gross	B.2g	609 397	361 047	45 594	20 562	8 127	16 905
Mixed income, gross	B.3g	119 268					
Compensation of employees	D.1						
Wages and salaries	D.11	775 239					
Employers' social contributions	D.12	154 878					
Total	D.1	930 117					
Statistical discrepancy between income components and GDP	di	–					
Taxes on production and imports, received	D.2						
Taxes on products	D.21						
Value added tax (VAT)	D.211	129 177					
Taxes and duties on imports excluding VAT	D.212	–					
Import duties	D.2121	–					
Taxes on imports excluding VAT and import duties	D.2122	–					
Taxes on products excluding VAT and import duties	D.214	80 062					
Total	D.21	209 239					
Other taxes on production	D.29	31 142					
Total	D.2	240 381					
less subsidies, paid	D.3						
Subsidies on products	D.31	8 526					
Other subsidies on production	D.39	3 115					
Total	D.3	11 641					
Property income, received	D.4						
Interest	D.41	209 760	15 198	160 246	88 793	38 809	32 644
Distributed income of corporations	D.42	276 275	51 125	100 920	24 753	40 518	35 649
Reinvested earnings on foreign direct investment	D.43	505	−8 190	8 695	91	6 401	2 203
Other investment income	D.44						
Attributable to insurance policy holders	D.441	28 442	153	4 391	5	4	4 382
Payable on pension entitlements	D.442	71 412	–	–			
Attributable to collective investment fund shareholders	D.443						
Dividends	D.4431	5 533	4	4 369	9	559	3 801
Retained earnings	D.4432	8 652	4	6 835	16	872	5 947
Total	D.443	14 185	8	11 204	25	1 431	9 748
Total other investment income	D.44	114 039	161	15 595	30	1 435	14 130
Rent	D.45	1 761	136	36	–	–	36
Total	D.4	602 340	58 430	285 492	113 667	87 163	84 662
Total resources	TR	2 489 862	419 477	331 086	134 229	95 290	101 567
Uses							
Property income, paid	D.4						
Interest	D.41	243 925	30 547	139 601	88 182	49 856	1 563
Distributed income of corporations	D.42	278 651	207 511	71 140	30 217	36 223	4 700
Reinvested earnings on foreign direct investment	D.43	7 354	−2 543	9 897	1 918	6 543	1 436
Other investment income	D.44						
Attributable to insurance policy holders	D.441	29 518		29 518			29 518
Payable on pension entitlements	D.442	71 412		71 412			71 412
Attributable to collective investment fund shareholders	D.443						
Dividends	D.4431	4 461		4 461		4 461	
Retained earnings	D.4432	6 980		6 980		6 980	
Total	D.443	11 441		11 441		11 441	
Total other investment income	D.44	112 371		112 371		11 441	100 930
Rent	D.45	1 761	1 743	–	–	–	–
Total	D.4	644 062	237 258	333 009	120 317	104 063	108 629
Gross balance of primary incomes/ gross national income (GNI)	B.5*g	**1 845 800**	**182 219**	**−1 923**	**13 912**	**−8 773**	**−7 062**
Total uses	TU	**2 489 862**	**419 477**	**331 086**	**134 229**	**95 290**	**101 567**
less consumption of fixed capital	P.51c	**231 530**	**124 981**	**8 199**			
National income, net	B.5*n	**1 614 270**	**57 238**	**−10 122**			

65

1.7.3 UK summary accounts
2015
continued   Total economy: all sectors and the rest of the world

£ million

		General government	Central government	Local government	Households and NPISH[2]	Households	NPISH	Not sectorised	Rest of the world
		S.13	S.1311	S.1313	S.14+S.15	S.14	S.15	S.N	S.2
Allocation of primary income account	II.1.2								
Resources									
Operating surplus, gross	B.2g	29 182	18 220	10 962	173 574	163 955	9 619		
Mixed income, gross	B.3g				119 268	119 268			
Compensation of employees	D.1								
Wages and salaries	D.11				775 239	775 239			1 384
Employers' social contributions	D.12				154 878	154 878			
Total	D.1				930 117	930 117			1 384
Statistical discrepancy between income components and GDP	di							–	
Taxes on production and imports, received	D.2								
Taxes on products	D.21								
Value added tax (VAT)	D.211	129 177	129 177						
Taxes and duties on imports excluding VAT	D.212								
Import duties	D.2121	–	–						3 077
Taxes on imports excluding VAT and import duties	D.2122	–	–						–
Taxes on products excluding VAT and import duties	D.214	80 062	80 062						10
Total	D.21	209 239	209 092						3 087
Other taxes on production	D.29	31 142	30 542	600					
Total	D.2	240 381	239 634	600					3 087
less subsidies, paid	D.3								
Subsidies on products	D.31	8 526	7 358	1 168					–
Other subsidies on production	D.39	3 115	2 497	618					1 961
Total	D.3	11 641	9 855	1 786					1 961
Property income, received	D.4								
Interest	D.41	9 072	8 070	1 002	25 244	24 385	859		83 726
Distributed income of corporations	D.42	10 406	9 428	978	113 824	111 619	2 205		81 394
Reinvested earnings on foreign direct investment	D.43								7 354
Other investment income	D.44								
Attributable to insurance policy holders	D.441	27		27	23 871	23 848	23		1 076
Payable on pension entitlements	D.442	–			71 412	71 412			–
Attributable to collective investment fund shareholders	D.443								
Dividends	D.4431	–		–	1 160	1 078	82		9
Retained earnings	D.4432	–		–	1 813	1 685	128		16
Total	D.443	–		–	2 973	2 763	210		25
Total	D.44	27		27	98 256	98 023	233		1 101
Rent	D.45	1 409	1 409	–	180	25	155		–
Total	D.4	20 914	18 907	2 007	237 504	234 052	3 452		173 575
Total resources	TR	278 836	266 906	11 930	1 460 463	1 447 392	13 071	–	
Uses									
Property income, paid	D.4								
Interest	D.41	46 950	43 214	3 736	26 827	26 193	634		49 561
Distributed income of corporations	D.42								79 018
Reinvested earnings on foreign direct investment	D.43								505
Other investment income	D.44								
Attributable to insurance policy holders	D.441								
Payable on pension entitlements	D.442								
Attributable to collective investment fund shareholders	D.443								
Dividends	D.4431								1 081
Retained earnings	D.4432								1 688
Total	D.443								2 769
Total other investment income	D.44								2 769
Rent	D.45				18	18	–		–
Total	D.4	46 950	43 214	3 736	26 845	26 211	634		131 853
Gross balance of primary incomes/ gross national income (GNI)	B.5*g	**231 886**	**223 692**	**8 194**	**1 433 618**	**1 421 181**	**12 437**	**–**	
Total uses	TU	278 836	266 906	11 930	1 460 463	1 447 392	13 071	–	
less consumption of fixed capital	P.51c	29 182	18 220	10 962	69 168	59 549	9 619		
National income, net	B.5*n	202 704	205 472	-2 768	1 364 450	1 361 632	2 818	–	

1 Monetary financial institutions and insurance corporation and pension funds
2 Non-profit institutions serving households.

1.7.4 UK summary accounts
2015
Total economy: all sectors and the rest of the world

£ million

		UK total economy	Non-financial corporations	Financial corporations	Monetary financial institutions	Financial Corporations except MFI and ICPF[1]	Insurance corporations and pension Funds
					S.121+	S.124+S.125+	
		S.1	S.11	S.12	S.122+S.123	S.126+S.127	S.128+S.129
Secondary distribution of income account	II.2						
Resources							
Gross balance of primary incomes/ Gross national income (GNI)	B.5*g	1 845 800	182 219	–1 923	13 912	–8 773	–7 062
Current taxes on income, wealth etc.	D.5						
Taxes on income	D.51	217 794					
Other current taxes	D.59	42 255					
Total	D.5	260 049					
Net social contributions	D.61						
Employers' actual social contributions	D.611	135 750		51 009			51 009
Employers' imputed social contributions	D.612	19 128	3 568	13 362	315	242	12 805
Households' actual social contributions	D.613	68 517		11 933			11 933
Households' social contribution supplements	D.614	71 412		71 412			71 412
Social insurance scheme service charges	D.61SC	–19 620		–19 620			–19 620
Total	D.61	275 187	3 568	128 096	315	242	127 539
Social benefits other than social transfers in kind	D.62						
Social security benefits in cash	D.621	96 461					
Other social insurance benefits	D.622	125 769					
Social assistance benefits in cash	D.623	121 463					
Total	D.62	343 693					
Other current transfers	D.7						
Net non-life insurance premiums	D.71	43 129		43 123			43 123
Non-life insurance claims	D.72	36 177	4 923	2 181	79	2 035	67
Current transfers within general government	D.73	121 126					
Current international cooperation	D.74	60					
Miscellaneous current transfers	D.75	61 780	–	240	172	68	
VAT and GNI based EU own resources	D.76						
Total	D.7	262 272	4 923	45 544	251	2 103	43 190
Total resources	TR	2 987 001	190 710	171 717	14 478	–6 428	163 667
Uses							
Current taxes on income, wealth etc.	D.5						
Taxes on income	D.51	218 041	32 974	13 674	1 177	10 435	2 062
Other current taxes	D.59	42 255		3 363	3 363		
Total	D.5	260 296	32 974	17 037	4 540	10 435	2 062
Net social contributions	D.61						
Employers' actual social contributions	D.611	135 750					
Employers' imputed social contributions	D.612	19 128					
Households' actual social contributions	D.613	68 506					
Households' social contribution supplements	D.614	71 412					
Social insurance scheme service charge	D.61SC	–19 620					
Total	D.61	275 176					
Social benefits other than social transfers in kind	D.62						
Social security benefits in cash	D.621	99 140					
Other social insurance benefits	D.622	125 769	3 568	81 550	315	242	80 993
Social assistance benefits in cash	D.623	121 463					
Total	D.62	346 372	3 568	81 550	315	242	80 993
Other current transfers	D.7						
Net non-life insurance premiums	D.71	36 183	4 923	2 187	79	2 035	67
Non-life insurance claims	D.72	43 123		43 123			43 123
Current transfers within general government	D.73	121 126					
Current international cooperation	D.74	6 823					
Miscellaneous current transfers	D.75	63 348	4 535	5 697	4 764	933	–
VAT and GNI based EU own resources	D.76	11 592					
Total	D.7	282 195	9 458	51 007	4 849	2 968	43 190
Gross disposable income	B.6g	1 822 962	144 710	22 123	4 774	–20 073	37 422
Total uses	TU	2 987 001	190 710	171 717	14 478	–6 428	163 667
less consumption of fixed capital	P.51c	231 530	124 981	8 199			
Disposable income, net	B.6n	1 591 432	19 729	13 924			

1.7.4
continued

UK summary accounts
2015

Total economy: all sectors and the rest of the world

£ million

		General government	Central government	Local government	Households and NPISH[2]	Households	NPISH	Not sectorised	Rest of the world
		S.13	S.1311	S.1313	S.14+S.15	S.14	S.15	S.N	S.2
Secondary distribution of income account	II.2								
Resources									
Gross balance of primary incomes/ Gross national income (GNI)	B.5*g	231 886	223 692	8 194	1 433 618	1 421 181	12 437	–	
Current taxes on income, wealth etc.	D.5								
Taxes on income	D.51	217 794	217 794						726
Other current taxes	D.59	42 255	13 276	28 979					
Total	D.5	260 049	231 070	28 979					726
Net social contributions	D.61								
Employers' actual social contributions	D.611	84 741	83 240	1 501					
Employers' imputed social contributions	D.612	1 548	834	714	650	313	337		–
Households' actual social contributions	D.613	56 584	55 863	721					–
Households' social contribution supplements	D.614								
Social insurance scheme service charges	D.61SC								
Total	D.61	142 873	139 937	2 936	650	313	337		–
Social benefits other than social transfers in kind	D.62								
Social security benefits in cash	D.621				96 461	96 461			2 679
Other social insurance benefits	D.622				125 769	125 769			–
Social assistance benefits in cash	D.623				121 463	121 463			–
Total	D.62				343 693	343 693			2 679
Other current transfers	D.7								
Net non-life insurance premiums	D.71								2 249
Non-life insurance claims	D.72	447	–	447	28 626	28 234	392		9 195
Current transfers within general government	D.73	121 126	–	121 126					
Current international cooperation	D.74	60	47	13					6 823
Miscellaneous current transfers	D.75	3 479	3 100		58 061	8 465	49 596		6 462
VAT and GNI based EU own resources	D.76								11 592
Total	D.7	125 118	3 153	121 965	86 687	36 699	49 988		36 321
Total resources	TR	759 926	597 852	162 074	1 864 648	1 801 886	62 762	–	248 181
Uses									
Current taxes on income, wealth etc.	D.5								
Taxes on income	D.51				171 393	171 393	–		479
Other current taxes	D.59	1 389		1 389	37 503	37 119	384		
Total	D.5	1 389		1 389	208 896	208 512	384		479
Net social contributions	D.61								
Employers' actual social contributions	D.611				135 750	135 750			
Employers' imputed social contributions	D.612				19 128	19 128			
Households' actual social contributions	D.613				68 506	68 506			11
Households' social contribution supplements	D.614				71 412	71 412			
Social insurance scheme service charge	D.61SC				–19 620	–19 620			
Total	D.61				275 176	275 176			11
Social benefits other than social transfers in kind	D.62								
Social security benefits in cash	D.621	99 140	99 140						
Other social insurance benefits	D.622	40 001	35 323	4 678	650	313	337		
Social assistance benefits in cash	D.623	121 463	94 260	27 203	..				
Total	D.62	260 604	228 723	31 881	650	313	337		
Other current transfers	D.7								
Net non-life insurance premiums	D.71	447	–	447	28 626	28 234	392		9 195
Non-life insurance claims	D.72								2 249
Current transfers within general government	D.73	121 126	121 126	–					
Current international cooperation	D.74	6 823	6 823						60
Miscellaneous current transfers	D.75	19 068	18 966	102	34 048	32 770	1 278		4 894
VAT and GNI based EU own resources	D.76	11 592	11 592						
Total	D.7	159 056	158 507	549	62 674	61 004	1 670		16 398
Gross disposable income	B.6g	338 877	210 622	128 255	1 317 252	1 256 881	60 371	–	
Total uses	TU	759 926	597 852	162 074	1 864 648	1 801 886	62 762	–	248 181
less consumption of fixed capital	P.51c	29 182	18 220	10 962	69 168	59 549	9 619		
Disposable income, net	B.6n	309 695	192 402	117 293	1 248 084			–	

1 Monetary financial institutions and insurance corporation and pension funds
2 Non-profit institutions serving households.

68

1.7.5 UK summary accounts 2015

Total economy: all sectors and the rest of the world

£ million

		UK total economy	Non-financial corporations	Financial corporations	Monetary financial institutions	Financial corporations except MFI and ICPF[1]	Insurance corporations and pension funds
		S.1	S.11	S.12	S.121+ S.122+S.123	S.124+S.125+ S.126+S.127	S.128+S.129
Redistribution of income in kind account	II.3						
Resources							
Gross disposable income	B.6g	**1 822 962**	**144 710**	**22 123**	**4 774**	**−20 073**	**37 422**
Social transfers in kind	D.63	290 321					
Total resources	TR	**2 113 283**	**144 710**	**22 123**	**4 774**	**−20 073**	**37 422**
Uses							
Social transfers in kind	D.63	290 321					
Adjusted disposable income, gross	B.7g	**1 822 962**	**144 710**	**22 123**	**4 774**	**−20 073**	**37 422**
Total uses	TU	**2 113 283**	**144 710**	**22 123**	**4 774**	**−20 073**	**37 422**

1.7.5

UK summary accounts
2015

continued

Total economy: all sectors and the rest of the world

£ million

		General government	Central government	Local government	Households and NPISH[2]	Households	NPISH	Not sectorised	Rest of the world
		S.13	S.1311	S.1313	S.14+S.15	S.14	S.15	S.N	S.2
Redistribution of income in kind account	II.3								
Resources									
Gross disposable income	B.6g	**338 877**	**210 622**	**128 255**	**1 317 252**	1 256 881	60 371	–	
Social transfers in kind	D.63				290 321	290 321	56 614		
Total resources	**TR**	**338 877**	**210 622**	**128 255**	**1 607 573**	1 547 202	60 371	–	
Uses									
Social transfers in kind	D.63	233 707	150 253	83 454	56 614				
Adjusted disposable income, gross	B.7g	105 170	60 369	44 801	1 550 959	1 547 202	3 757	–	
Total uses	**TU**	**338 877**	**210 622**	**128 255**	**1 607 573**	1 547 202	60 371	–	

1 Monetary financial institutions and insurance corporation and pension funds
2 Non-profit institutions serving households

1.7.6 UK summary accounts 2015

Total economy: all sectors and the rest of the world

£ million

		UK total economy	Non-financial corporations	Financial corporations	Monetary financial institutions	Financial corporations except MFI and ICPF[1]	Insurance corporations and pension funds
		S.1	S.11	S.12	S.121+ S.122+S.123	S.124+S.125+ S.126+S.127	S.128+S.129
Use of income account	II.4						
Use of disposable income account	II.4.1						
Resources							
Gross disposable income	B.6g	1 822 962	144 710	22 123	4 774	−20 073	37 422
Adjustment for the change in pension entitlements	D.8	46 546					
Total resources	TR	1 869 508	144 710	22 123	4 774	−20 073	37 422
Uses							
Final consumption expenditure	P.3						
Individual consumption expenditure	P.31	1 472 189					
Collective consumption expenditure	P.32	128 355					
Total	P.3	1 600 544					
Adjustment for the change in pension entitlements	D.8	46 546		46 546			46 546
Gross saving	B.8g	222 418	144 710	−24 423	4 774	−20 073	−9 124
Current external balance	B.12						
Total uses	TU	1 869 508	144 710	22 123	4 774	−20 073	37 422
less consumption of fixed capital	P.51c	231 530	124 981	8 199			
Saving, net	B.8n	−9 112	19 729	−32 622			
Use of adjusted disposable income account	II.4.2						
Resources							
Adjusted disposable income	B.7g	1 822 962	144 710	22 123	4 774	−20 073	37 422
Adjustment for the change in pension entitlements	D.8	46 546					
Total resources	TR	1 869 508	144 710	22 123	4 774	−20 073	37 422
Uses							
Actual final consumption	P.4						
Actual individual consumption	P.41	1 472 189					
Actual collective consumption	P.42	128 355					
Total	P.4	1 600 544					
Adjustment for the change in pension entitlements	D.8	46 546		46 546			46 546
Gross saving	B.8g	222 418	144 710	−24 423	4 774	−20 073	−9 124
Total uses	TU	1 869 508	144 710	22 123	4 774	−20 073	37 422

1.7.6

UK summary accounts
2015

continued **Total economy: all sectors and the rest of the world**   £ million

		General government	Central government	Local government	Households and NPISH[2]	Households	NPISH	Not sectorised	Rest of the world
		S.13	S.1311	S.1313	S.14+S.15	S.14	S.15	S.N	S.2
Use of income account	II.4								
Use of disposable income account	II.4.1								
Resources									
Gross disposable income	B.6g	338 877	210 622	128 255	1 317 252	1 256 881	60 371	–	
Adjustment for the change in pension entitlements	D.8				46 546	46 546			–
Total resources	TR	338 877	210 622	128 255	1 363 798	1 303 427	60 371	–	
Uses									
Final consumption expenditure	P.3								
Individual consumption expenditure	P.31	233 707	150 253	83 454	1 238 482	1 181 868	56 614		
Collective consumption expenditure	P.32	128 355	86 675	41 680					
Total	P.3	362 062	236 928	125 134	1 238 482				
Adjustment for the change in pension entitlements	D.8					46 546			
Gross saving	B.8g	−23 185	−26 306	3 121	125 316	121 559	3 757	–	
Current external balance	B.12								98 145
Total uses	TU	338 877	210 622	128 255	1 363 798	1 303 427	60 371	–	
less consumption of fixed capital	P.51c	29 182	18 220	10 962	69 168	59 549	9 619		
Saving, net	B.8n	−52 367	−44 526	−7 841	56 148	62 010	−5 862	–	
Use of adjusted disposable income account	II.4.2								
Resources									
Adjusted disposable income	B.7g	105 170	60 369	44 801	1 550 959	1 547 202	3 757	–	
Adjustment for the change in pension entitlements	D.8				46 546	46 546			–
Total resources	TR	105 170	60 369	44 801	1 597 505	1 593 748	3 757	–	
Uses									
Actual final consumption	P.4								
Actual individual consumption	P.41				1 472 189	1 472 189			
Actual collective consumption	P.42	128 355	86 675	41 680					
Total	P.4	128 355	86 675	41 680	1 472 189				
Adjustment for the change in pension entitlements	D.8					46 546			
Gross saving	B.8g	−23 185	−26 306	3 121	125 316	121 559	3 757	–	
Total uses	TU	105 170	60 369	44 801	1 597 505	1 593 748	3 757	–	

1 Monetary financial institutions and insurance corporation and pension funds
2 Non-profit institutions serving households.

1.7.7 UK summary accounts
2015
Total economy: all sectors and the rest of the world

£ million

		UK total economy	Non-financial corporations	Financial corporations	Monetary financial institutions	Financial corporations except MFI and ICPF[1]	Insurance corporations and pension funds
		S.1	S.11	S.12	S.121+ S.122+S.123	S.124+S.125+ S.126+S.127	S.128+S.129
Accumulation accounts	III						
Capital account	III.1						
Change in net worth due to saving and capital transfers account	III.1.1						
Changes in liabilities and net worth							
Gross saving	B.8g	222 418	144 710	−24 423	4 774	−20 073	−9 124
Current external balance	B.12						
Capital transfers, receivable	D.9r						
Capital taxes	D.91r	4 442					
Investment grants	D.92r	27 971	4 402				
Other capital transfers	D.99r	8 742	59	1 079	−		1 079
Total	D.9r	41 155	4 461	1 079	−		1 079
less capital transfers, payable	D.9p						
Capital taxes	D.91p	4 442	−	−	−		
Investment grants	D.92p	28 489					
Other capital transfers	D.99p	9 993	1 481	1 079	−		1 079
Total	D.9p	42 924	1 481	1 079	−		1 079
Changes in net worth due to gross saving and capital transfers	B.101g	220 649	147 690	−24 423	4 774	−20 073	−9 124
Changes in assets							
Changes in net worth due to gross saving and capital transfers	B.101g	220 649	147 690	−24 423	4 774	−20 073	−9 124
less consumption of fixed capital	P.51c	231 530	124 981	8 199			
Changes in net worth due to net saving and capital transfers	B.101n	−10 881	22 709	−32 622			
Acquisition of non-financial assets account	III.1.2						
Changes in liabilities and net worth							
Changes in net worth due to net saving and capital transfers	B.101n	−10 881	22 709	−32 622			
Consumption of fixed capital	P.51c	231 530	124 981	8 199			
Changes in net worth due to gross saving and capital transfers	B.101g	220 649	147 690	−24 423	4 774	−20 073	−9 124
Changes in assets							
Gross capital formation	P.5						
Gross fixed capital formation	P.51g	313 189	180 040	9 450	4 916	3 844	690
Changes in inventories	P.52	7 812	7 703	4	−	−	4
Acquisitions less disposals of valuables[2]	P.53	−438	−404	−618	−	−	−618
Total	P.5	320 563	187 339	8 836	4 916	3 844	76
Acquisitions less disposals of non-produced non-financial assets	NP	209	2 900	4	−	16	−12
Statistical discrepancy between expenditure components and GDP	de	−					
Net lending(+) / net borrowing(-)	B.9n	−100 123	−42 549	−33 263	−142	−23 933	−9 188
Total change in assets	B.101g	220 649	147 690	−24 423	4 774	−20 073	−9 124

1.7.7 UK summary accounts
2015
continued

Total economy: all sectors and the rest of the world

£ million

		General government	Central government	Local government	Households and NPISH[3]	Households	NPISH	Not sectorised	Rest of the world
		S.13	S.1311	S.1313	S.14+S.15	S.14	S.15	S.N	S.2
Accumulation accounts	III								
Capital account	III.1								
Change in net worth due to saving and capital transfers account	III.1.1								
Changes in liabilities and net worth									
Gross saving	B.8g	−23 185	−26 306	3 121	125 316	121 559	3 757	−	
Current external balance	B.12								98 145
Capital transfers, receivable	D.9r								
Capital taxes	D.91r	4 442	4 442						
Investment grants	D.92r	13 084	−	13 084	10 485	2 644	7 841		1 433
Other capital transfers	D.99r	3 924	2 806	1 118	3 680	1 076	2 604		1 251
Total	D.9r	21 450	7 248	14 202	14 165	3 720	10 445		2 684
less capital transfers, payable	D.9p								
Capital taxes	D.91p				4 442	4 442	−		
Investment grants	D.92p	28 489	24 937	3 552					915
Other capital transfers	D.99p	3 157	2 012	1 145	4 276	4 254	22		−
Total	D.9p	31 646	26 949	4 697	8 718	8 696	22		915
Changes in net worth due to gross saving and capital transfers	B.101g	−33 381	−46 007	12 626	130 763	116 583	14 180	−	99 914
Changes in assets									
Changes in net worth due to gross saving and capital transfers	B.101g	−33 381	−46 007	12 626	130 763	116 583	14 180	−	99 914
less consumption of fixed capital	P.51c	29 182	18 220	10 962	69 168	59 549	9 619		
Changes in net worth due to net saving and capital transfers	B.101n	−62 563	−64 227	1 664	61 595	57 034	4 561	−	
Acquisition of non-financial assets account	III.1.2								
Changes in liabilities and net worth									
Changes in net worth due to net saving and capital transfers	B.101n	−62 563	−64 227	1 664	61 595			−	
Consumption of fixed capital	P.51c	29 182	18 220	10 962	69 168				
Changes in net worth due to gross saving and capital transfers	B.101g	−33 381	−46 007	12 626	130 763	116 583	14 180	−	99 914
Changes in assets									
Gross capital formation	P.5								
Gross fixed capital formation	P.51g	50 288	31 788	18 500	73 411	60 206	13 205		
Changes in inventories	P.52	−277	−277	−	382	372	10		
Acquisitions less disposals of valuables[2]	P.53	72	72		512	866	−354		
Total	P.5	50 083	31 583	18 500	74 305	61 444	12 861		
Acquisitions less disposals of non-produced non-financial assets	NP		−484	−2 021	−190	−398	208		−209
Statistical discrepancy between expenditure components and GDP	de							−	
Net lending(+) / net borrowing(-)	B.9n	−80 959	−77 106	−3 853	56 648	55 537	1 111	−	100 123
Total change in assets	B.101g	−33 381	−46 007	12 626	130 763	116 583	14 180	−	99 914

1 Monetary financial institutions and insurance corporation and pension funds
2 Acquisitions less disposals of valuables can be a volatile series but any
  volatility is likely to be GDP neutral as it is offset in UK trade figures
3 Non-profit institutions serving households.

1.7.8 UK summary accounts
2015
Total economy: all sectors and the rest of the world. Unconsolidated

£ million

		UK total economy S.1	Non-financial corporations S.11	Financial corporations S.12	Monetary financial institutions (MFI) S.121+ S.122+ S.123	Financial corporations except MFI and ICPF[1] S.124+ S.125+ S.126+S.127	Non-money market funds S.124	Financial corporations except MFI, NMMF and ICPF[2] S.125+S.126+ S.127
Financial account	III.2							
Net acquisition of financial assets	F.A							
Monetary gold and special drawing rights	F.1							
Monetary gold	F.11	–						
Special drawing rights	F.12	55						
Total	F.1	55						
Currency and deposits	F.2							
Currency	F.21	3 766	616	–327	–327	–	–	–
Transferable deposits	F.22							
Deposits with UK MFIs[4]	F.22N1	10 053	37 479	–69 521	–8 638	–56 380	4 637	–61 017
Of which: foreign currency deposits with UK banks	F.22N12	16 186	2 086	14 011	–2 151	14 823	1 008	13 815
Deposits with rest of the world MFIs[4]	F.22N9	–120 279	9 761	–125 569	–61 393	–53 068	–28	–53 040
Other deposits	F.29	5 560	–583	–9 235	–	–9 235	–314	–8 921
Total	F.2	–100 900	47 273	–204 652	–70 358	–118 683	4 295	–122 978
Debt securities	F.3							
Short-term	F.31							
Issued by UK central government	F.31N1	6 202	289	5 592	246	7 158	–528	7 686
Issued by UK local government	F.31N2	–	–	–	–	–	–	–
Issued by UK MFIs[4]	F.31N5	2 007	2 642	356	–342	413	–4 755	5 168
MMIs issued by other UK residents[5]	F.31N6	–2 468	351	–483	39	–580	264	–844
MMIs issued by rest of the world[5]	F.31N9	3 642	4 519	–1 785	5 950	–5 679	8 386	–14 065
Long-term	F.32							
Issued by UK central government	F.32N1	–3 853	–620	–2 325	266	–1 778	–185	–1 593
Issued by UK local government	F.32N2	590	–	185	–	4	1	3
Issued by UK MFIs and other UK residents[4]	F.32N5-6	–39 749	5 684	–45 709	–34 896	–2 943	–1 602	–1 341
Bonds issued by rest of the world	F.32N9	9 640	–369	–6 137	–19 813	5 541	9 808	–4 267
Total	F.3	–23 989	12 496	–50 306	–48 550	2 136	11 389	–9 253
Loans	F.4							
Short-term	F.41							
By UK MFIs[4]	F.41N1	18 474		18 474	18 474			
By rest of the world	F.41N9							
Long-term	F.42							
Direct investment	F.421	–24 328	–25 062	734	–	1 849		1 849
Secured on dwellings	F.422	24 930	–	41 405	32 386	6 757		6 757
Finance leasing	F.423	386	–82	468	–24	492		492
Other long-term loans	F.424							
Issued by other UK residents	F.424N1	47 347	22 497	12 110	–266	4 302		4 302
Issued by rest of the world	F.424N9							
Total	F.4	66 809	–2 647	73 191	50 570	13 400		13 400
Equity and investment fund shares/units	F.5							
Equity	F.51							
Listed UK shares	F.511N1	–26 956	–2	–12 108	503	3 849	6 039	–2 190
Unlisted UK shares	F.512N1	–6 676.0	8 548.0	–1 816	–9 184	6 891	–2	6 893
Other equity	F.519							
Other UK equity	F.519N6	–1 345						
UK shares and bonds issued by other UK residents	F.519N7	–	–	–	–	–	–	–
Shares and other equity issued by rest of the world	F.519N9	–43 059	–11 794	–41 834	–26 212	–12 436	4 870	–17 306
Investment fund shares/units	F.52							
UK mutual funds' shares	F.52N1	8 391	31	35 997	91	248	2 485	–2 237
Rest of the world mutual funds' shares	F.52N9	6 164		6 164		2 877	19 866	–16 989
Total	F.5	–63 481.0	–3 217.0	–13 597	–34 802	1 429	33 258	–31 829
Insurance, pensions and standardised guarantee schemes	F.6							
Non-life insurance technical reserves	F.61	–2 511	–209	–25	–6	–6	–	–6
Life insurance and annuity entitlements	F.62	56 599						
Pension schemes[6]	F.6M	59 281		12 735				
Provisions for calls under standardised guarantees	F.66	14		14	14			
Total	F.6	113 383	–209	12 724	8	–6		–6
Financial derivatives and employee stock options	F.7	–82 418	–3 120	–79 798	10 967	–89 935	–6 775	–83 160
Of which: financial derivatives	F.71	–84 240	–3 120	–79 798	10 967	–89 935	–6 775	–83 160
Other accounts receivable	F.8	686	–1 323	–1 719	18	415	–115	530
Total net acquisition of financial assets	F.A	–89 855.0	49 253.0	–264 157	–92 147	–191 244	42 052	–233 296

1.7.8
continued

UK summary accounts
2015

Total economy: all sectors and the rest of the world. Unconsolidated

£ million

		Insurance corporations and pension funds S.128+S.129	General government S.13	Central government S.1311	Local government S.1313	Households and NPISH[3] S.14+S.15	Households S.14	NPISH S.15	Rest of the world S.2
Financial account	III.2								
Net acquisition of financial assets	F.A								
Monetary gold and special drawing rights	F.1								
Monetary gold	F.11		–	–					–
Special drawing rights	F.12		55	55					
Total	F.1		55	55					–
Currency and deposits	F.2								
Currency	F.21					3 477	2 576	901	228
Transferable deposits	F.22								
Deposits with UK MFIs[4]	F.22N1	–4 503	–969	–2 527	1 558	43 064	42 616	448	–122 026
Of which: foreign currency deposits with UK banks	F.22N12	1 339	–842	–850	8	931	896	35	–145 395
Deposits with rest of the world MFIs[4]	F.22N9	–11 108	3 361	2 997	364	–7 832	–7 832	–	
Other deposits	F.29	–	–6 880	–8 782	1 902	22 258	22 170	88	425
Total	F.2	–15 611	–4 488	–8 312	3 824	60 967	59 530	1 437	–121 373
Debt securities	F.3								
Short-term	F.31								
Issued by UK central government	F.31N1	–1 812	321		321	–	2	–2	13 519
Issued by UK local authorities	F.31N2		–			–	–	–	
Issued by UK MFIs[4]	F.31N5	285	121	–	121	–1 112	–807	–305	–6 214
MMIs issued by other UK residents[5]	F.31N6	58	–2 277	–2 348	71	–59	–28	–31	133
MMIs issued by rest of the world[5]	F.31N9	–2 056	908	908					
Long-term	F.32								
Issued by UK central government	F.32N1	–813	–582		–582	–326	–481	155	57 103
Issued by UK local government	F.32N2	181				405	1 598	–1 193	–
Issued by UK MFIs and other UK residents[4]	F.32N5-6	–7 870	–	–	–	276	874	–598	–7 795
Bonds issued by rest of the world	F.32N9	8 135	17 583	17 583		–1 437	–964	–473	
Total	F.3	–3 892	16 074	16 143	–69	–2 253	194	–2 447	56 746
Loans	F.4								
Short-term	F.41								
By UK MFIs[4]	F.41N1								
By rest of the world	F.41N9								–179 401
Long-term	F.42								
Direct investment	F.421	–1 115							4 813
Secured on dwellings	F.422	2 262	–16 475	–17 678	1 203				
Finance leasing	F.423								
Other long-term loans	F.424								
Issued by other UK residents	F.424N1	8 074	16 180	13 752	2 428	–3 440	–3 440	–	
Issued by rest of the world	F.424N9		–	–					5 583
Total	F.4	9 221	–295	–3 926	3 631	–3 440	–3 440		–169 005
Equity and investment fund shares/units	F.5								
Equity	F.51								
Listed UK shares	F.511N1	–16 460	–12 112	–12 731	619	–2 734	–2 850	116	49 630
Unlisted UK shares	F.512N1	477	–758	–758	–	–12 650	–12 056	–594	34 840
Other equity	F.519								
Other UK equity	F.519N6		–1 345	–1	–1 344	–	–	–	–
UK shares and bonds issued by other UK residents	F.519N7	–	–	–	–	–	–	–	–
Shares and other equity issued by rest of the world	F.519N9	–3 186	93	93		10 476	–8 661	1 342	
Investment fund shares/units	F.52								
UK mutual funds' shares	F.52N1	35 658				–27 637	–29 758	2 121	91
Rest of the world mutual funds' shares	F.52N9	3 287				–	–	–	
Total	F.5	19 776	–14 122	–13 397	–725	–32 545	–45 530	12 985	84 561
Insurance, pensions and standardised guarantee schemes	F.6								
Non-life insurance technical reserves	F.61	–13	–35		–35	–2 242	–2 211	–31	–594
Life insurance and annuity entitlements	F.62					56 599	56 599	–	1 002
Pension schemes[6]	F.6M	12 735				46 546	46 546	–	–
Provisions for calls under standardised guarantees	F.66		–						
Total	F.6	12 722	–35		–35	100 903	100 934	–31	408
Financial derivatives and employee stock options	F.7	–830	–1 219	–1 219		1 719	2 275	–556	3
Of which: financial derivatives	F.71	–830	–1 219	–1 219		–103	453	–556	–
Other accounts receivable	F.8	–2 152	10 064	9 354	710	–6 336	–7 997	1 661	1 085
Total net acquisition of financial assets	F.A	19 234	6 034	–1 302	7 336	119 015	105966	13049	-147575

UK summary accounts
2015
Total economy: all sectors and the rest of the world. Unconsolidated

£ million

		UK total economy S.1	Non-financial corporations S.11	Financial corporations S.12	Monetary financial institutions (MFI) S.121+ S.122+ S.123	Financial corporations except MFI and ICPF[1] S.124+ S.125+ S.126+S.127	Non-money market funds S.124	Financial corporations except MFI, NMMF and ICPF[2] S.125+S.126+ S.127
Financial account	III.2							
Net acquisition of financial liabilities	F.L							
Monetary gold and special drawing rights	F.1							
Special drawing rights	F.12	–						
Total	F.1	–						
Currency and deposits	F.2							
Currency	F.21	4 017		3 849	3 849			
Transferable deposits	F.22							
Deposits with UK MFIs[4]	F.22N1	–111 973		–111 973	–111 973			
Deposits with rest of the world MFIs[4]	F.22N9							
Other deposits	F.29	5 985	–	–4 704		–4 704		–4 704
Total	F.2	–101 971	–	–112 828	–108 124	–4 704		–4 704
Debt securities	F.3							
Short-term	F.31							
Issued by UK central government	F.31N1	19 721						
Issued by UK local government	F.31N2	–						
Issued by UK MFIs[4]	F.31N5	–4 207		–4 207	–4 207			
MMIs issued by other UK residents[5]	F.31N6	–2 335	–2 739	347		347	–56	403
MMIs issued by rest of the world[5]	F.31N9							
Long-term	F.32							
Issued by UK central government	F.32N1	53 250						
Issued by UK local government	F.32N2	590						
Issued by UK MFIs[4]	F.32N5-6							
and other UK residents		–47 544	25 706	–58 846	–10 784	–51 172	261	–51 433
Bonds issued by rest of the world	F.32N9							
Total	F.3	19 475	22 967	–62 706	–14 991	–50 825	205	–51 030
Loans	F.4							
Short-term	F.41							
By UK MFIs[4]	F.41N1	11 862	5 681	–5 653		–8 348	–665	–7 683
Of which: foreign currency loans by UK banks	F.41N12	–7 815	1 824	–14 071		–14 149	–16	–14 133
By rest of the world	F.41N9	–179 401	5 167	–188 786		–193 305	–107	–193 198
Long-term	F.42							
Direct investment	F.421	4 813	638	4 175	–	3 652	–	3 652
Secured on dwellings	F.422	24 930	–1 120					
Finance leasing	F.423	386	267	144	84	60	–	60
Other long-term loans	F.424							
Issued by other UK residents	F.424N1	39 133.00	–8 188.00	26 934		13 921	–75	13 996
Issued by rest of the world	F.424N9	5 583	–	4 754	–	4 754	44	4 710
Total	F.4	–92 694.00	2 445.00	–158 432	84	–179 266	–803	–178 463
Equity and investment fund shares/units	F.5							
Equity	F.51							
Listed UK shares	F.511N1	22 674	11 651	11 023	6 049	4 599		4 599
Unlisted UK shares	F.512N1	28 164	15 240	12 924	3 171	8 314		8 314
Other equity	F.519							
Other UK equity	F.519N6	–1 345	–1 345	–	–			
UK shares and bonds issued by other UK residents	F.519N7	–	–	–	–	–		–
Shares and other equity issued by rest of the world	F.519N9							
Investment fund shares/units	F.52							
UK mutual funds' shares	F.52N1	8 482		8 482		8 482	8 482	
Rest of the world mutual funds' shares	F.52N9							
Total	F.5	57 975	25 546	32 429	9 220	21 395	8 482	12 913
Insurance, pensions and standardised guarantee schemes	F.6							
Non-life insurance technical reserves	F.61	–3 105		–3 105				
Life insurance and annuity entitlements	F.62	57 601		57 601				
Pension schemes[6]	F.6M	59 281	9 186	47 513	499	354	8	346
Provisions for calls under standardised guarantees	F.66	14						
Total	F.6	113 791	9 186	102 009	499	354	8	346
Financial derivatives and employee stock options	F.7	1 823	1 669	154	77	57	–	57
Of which: financial derivatives	F.71	–				–		
Other accounts payable	F.8	2 638	6 963	–17 945	1 112	–1 510	–712	–798
Total net acquisition of financial liabilities	**F.L**	1 037.00	68 776.00	–217 319	–112 123	–214 499	7 180	–221 679
Net lending(+) / net borrowing(-)	B.9							
Total net acquisition of financial assets	F.A	–89 855.0	49 253.0	–264 157	–92 147	–191 244	42 052	–233 296
less total net acquisition of financial liabilities	F.L	1 037.00	68 776.00	–217 319	–112 123	–214 499	7 180	–221 679
Net lending(+) / borrowing(-) from the financial account	B.9f	–90 891.00	–19 523.00	–46 838	19 976	23 255	34 872	–11 617
Statistical discrepancy between financial and non-financial accounts	dB.9	–9 232	–23 026	13 575	–20 118	–47 188		
Net lending (+) / borrowing (-) from non-financial accounts	**B.9n**	**–100 123**	**–42 549**	**–33 263**	**–142**	**–23 933**		

1.7.8 UK summary accounts
2015
continued   **Total economy: all sectors and the rest of the world. Unconsolidated**   £ million

		Insurance corporations and pension funds S.128+S.129	General govern -ment S.13	Central govern -ment S.1311	Local govern -ment S.1313	Households and NPISH[3] S.14+S.15	Households S.14	NPISH S.15	Not sectorised S.N	Rest of the world S.2
Financial account	III.2									
Net acquisition of financial liabilities	F.L									
Monetary gold and special drawing rights	F.1									
Special drawing rights	F.12		–	–						55
Total	F.1		–	–						55
Currency and deposits	F.2									
Currency	F.21		168	168						–23
Transferable deposits	F.22									
Deposits with UK MFIs[4]	F.22N1									
Deposits with rest of the world MFIs[4]	F.22N9									–120 279
Other deposits	F.29		10 689	10 689						
Total	F.2		10 857	10 857						–120 302
Debt securities	F.3									
Short-term	F.31									
Issued by UK central government	F.31N1		19 721	19 721						
Issued by UK local government	F.31N2		–		–					
Issued by UK MFIs[4]	F.31N5									
MMIs issued by other UK residents[5]	F.31N6					57		57		
MMIs issued by rest of the world[5]	F.31N9									3 642
Long-term	F.32									
Issued by UK central government	F.32N1		53 250	53 250						
Issued by UK local government	F.32N2		590		590					
Issued by UK MFIs and other UK residents[4]	F.32N5-6	3 110	–14 718	–14 718		314		314		
Bonds issued by rest of the world	F.32N9									9 640
Total	F.3	3 110	58 843	58 253	590	371		371		13 282
Loans	F.4									
Short-term	F.41									
By UK MFIs[4]	F.41N1	2 695	4 036	3 799	237	7 798	7 659	139		6 612
Of which: foreign currency loans by UK banks	F.41N12	78	4 411	4 411		21	34	–13		–797
By rest of the world	F.41N9	4 519	5 021	5 021	–	–803	–798	–5		
Long-term	F.42									
Direct investment	F.421	523								–24 328
Secured on dwellings	F.422					26 050	26 050	–		
Finance leasing	F.423		–25	–	–25					–
Other long-term loans	F.424									
Issued by other UK residents	F.424N1	13 013	465	–5	470	19 922	20 460	–538		8 214
Issued by rest of the world	F.424N9		829	449	380					
Total	F.4	20 750	10 326	9 264	1 062	52 967	53 371	–404		–9 502
Equity and investment fund shares/units	F.5									
Equity	F.51									
Listed UK shares	F.511N1	375								
Unlisted UK shares	F.512N1	1 439								
Other equity	F.519									
Other UK equity	F.519N6									
UK shares and bonds issued by other UK residents	F.519N7									
Shares and other equity issued by rest of the world	F.519N9									–43 059
Investment fund shares/units	F.52									
UK mutual funds' shares	F.52N1									
Rest of the world mutual funds' shares	F.52N9									6 164
Total	F.5	1 814								–36 895
Insurance, pensions and standardised guarantee schemes	F.6									
Non-life insurance technical reserves	F.61	–3 105								
Life insurance and annuity entitlements	F.62	57 601								
Pension schemes[6]	F.6M	46 660	1 980		1 980	602		602		–
Provisions for calls under standardised guarantees	F.66		14	14						
Total	F.6	101 156	1 994		1 980	602		602		–
Financial derivatives and employee stock options	F.7	20								–84 238
Of which: financial derivatives	F.71									–84 240
Other accounts payable	F.8	–17 547	5 914	–2 037	7 951	7 706	7 037	669		–867
Total net acquisition of financial liabilities	**F.L**	109 303	87 934	76 351	11 583	61 646	60 408	1 238		–238 467
Net lending(+)/ net borrowing(-)	B.9									
Total net acquisition of financial assets	F.A	19 234	6 034	–1 302	7 336	119 015	105 966	13 049		–147 575
less total net acquisition of financial liabilities	F.L	109 303	87 934	76 351	11 583	61 646	60 408	1 238		–238 467
Net lending(+) / borrowing(-) from the financial account	B.9f	–90 069	–81 900	–77 653	–4 247	57 370	45 558	11 812		90 892
Statistical discrepancy between financial and non-financial accounts	dB.9	80 881	941	547	394	–722	9 979	–10 701	–	9 231
Net lending (+) / borrowing (-) from non-financial accounts	**B.9n**	–9 188	–80 959	–77 106	–3 853	56 648	55 537	1 111	–	100 123

---

1 Monetary financial institutions and insurance corporation and pension funds
2 Monetary financial institutions, non-money market funds
3 Non-profit institutions serving households
4 Monetary Financial Institutions

5 Money Market Instruments
6 F.63 Pension entitlements, F.64 Claims on pension funds on pension managers, F.65 to non-pension benefits

1.7.9

UK summary accounts
2015

Total economy: all sectors and the rest of the world

£ million

		UK total economy	Non-financial corporations	Financial corporations	General government	Households and NPISH[1]	Rest of the world
		S.1	S.11	S.12	S.13	S.14+S.15	S.2
Other changes in assets account	**III.3**						
Other changes in volume of assets account	**III.3.1**						
Changes in net worth due to other changes in volume of assets	B.102						
Monetary gold and special drawing rights	F.1	–	–	–	–	–	–
Currency and deposits	F.2	26 927	–1 701	30 152	–382	–1 142	–26 927
Debt securities	F.3	11 481	–989	12 512	174	–216	–11 481
Loans	F.4	–42 556	–34 679	–17 604	2 233	7 494	42 556
Equity and investment fund shares	F.5	–	–	–	–	–	–
Insurance, pension and standardised guarantee schemes	F.6	–	–	–	–	–	–
Financial derivatives and employee stock options	F.7	–	–	–	–	–	–
Other accounts receivable/payable	F.8	6 247	383	10 315	–3 381	–1 070	–6 247
Total	B.102	2 099	–36 986	35 375	–1 356	5 066	–2 099

1 Non-profit institutions serving households

1.7.10 UK summary accounts 2015

Total economy: all sectors and the rest of the world

£ million

		UK total economy	Non-financial corporations	Financial corporations	General government	Households and NPISH[1]	Rest of the world
		S.1	S.11	S.12	S.13	S.14+S.15	S.2
Other changes in assets account	III.3						
Revaluation account	III.3.2						
Changes in net worth due to nominal holding gains and losses	B.103						
Monetary gold and special drawing rights	F.1	−587	–	–	−587	–	587
Currency and deposits	F.2	−25 496	−3 482	−18 535	−450	−3 029	25 496
Debt securities	F.3	−5 638	35 602	−84 104	38 518	4 346	5 638
Loans	F.4	11 059	−10 200	21 030	338	−109	−11 059
Equity and investment fund shares	F.5	173 238	80 498	21 575	536	70 629	−173 238
Insurance, pension and standardised guarantee schemes	F.6	−342	67 140	23 916	−4 286	−87 112	342
Financial derivatives and employee stock options	F.7	−1 620	1 825	−1 900	104	−1 649	1 620
Other accounts receivable/payable	F.8	−107	944	−2 963	757	1 155	107
Total	B.103	150 507	172 327	−40 981	34 930	−15 769	−150 507

1 Non-profit institutions serving households

1.7.11 UK summary accounts
2015
Total economy: all sectors and the rest of the world. Unconsolidated

£ billion

		UK total economy S.1	Non-financial corporations S.11	Financial corporations S.12	Monetary financial institutions (MFI) S.121+ S.122+ S.123	Financial corporations except MFI and ICPF[1] S.124+ S.125+ S.126+S.127	Non-money market funds S.124	Financial corporations except MFI, NMMF and ICPF[2] S.125+S.126+ S.127
Financial balance sheet at end of period	IV.3							
Total financial assets	AF.A							
Monetary gold and special drawing rights	AF.1							
Monetary gold	AF.11	7.1						
Special drawing rights	AF.12	9.1						
Total	AF.1	16.2						
Currency and deposits	AF.2							
Currency	AF.21	80.4	7.0	11.2	11.1	0.1	–	0.1
Transferable deposits	AF.22							
Deposits with UK MFIs[4]	AF.22N1	3 732.9	399.4	2 081.2	1 346.6	634.8	32.3	602.4
Deposits with rest of the world MFIs	AF.22N9	2 146.4	165.7	1 912.7	1 567.4	308.1	0.2	307.9
Other deposits	AF.29	180.0	6.9	8.2	–	8.2	4.7	3.5
Total	AF.2	6 139.7	579.1	4 013.3	2 925.1	951.2	37.3	913.9
Debt securities	AF.3							
Short-term	AF.31							
Issued by UK central government	AF.31N1	42.4	1.3	38.5	8.4	27.1		
Issued by UK local government	AF.31N2	–	–	–	–	–	–	–
Issued by MFIs	AF.31N5	72.4	12.4	51.0	5.2	36.5	4.9	31.5
MMIs issued by other UK residents[5]	AF.31N6	13.5	7.4	4.1	0.1	2.8		
MMIs issued by rest of the world	AF.31N9	96.7	7.2	85.5	50.2	30.4		
Long-term	AF.32							
Issued by UK central government	AF.32N1	1 210.6	2.7	1 200.9	549.4	179.4		
Issued by UK local government	AF.32N2	4.1	–	2.1	–	–		
Issued by UK MFIs and other UK residents	AF.32N5-6	900.0	37.9	854.0	286.7	291.5	61.7	229.8
Issued by rest of the world	AF.32N9	942.0	9.4	867.4	395.2	142.4	115.0	27.4
Total	AF.3	3 281.6	78.3	3 103.5	1 295.2	710.1	235.8	474.3
Loans	AF.4							
Short-term	AF.41							
By UK MFIs	AF.41N1	2 064.6		2 064.6	2 064.6			
By rest of the world MFIs	AF.41N9							
Long-term	AF.42							
Direct investment	AF.421	249.6	222.1	27.5	–	12.5		12.5
Outward direct investment	AF.421N1	180.8	163.8	17.0	–	5.5		5.5
Inward direct investment	AF.421N2	68.8	58.3	10.5	–	7.0		7.0
Secured on dwellings	AF.422	1 327.1	–	1 279.7	1 151.0	117.2		117.2
Finance leasing	AF.423	38.2	6.7	31.5	2.5	29.1		29.1
Other long-term loans	AF.424							
Issued by other UK residents	AF.424N1	967.1	39.6	746.6	9.6	589.6		589.6
Issued by rest of the world	AF.424N9							
Total	AF.4	4 646.7	268.4	4 149.9	3 227.7	748.4		748.4
Equity and investment fund shares/units	AF.5							
Equity	AF.51							
Listed UK shares	AF.511N1	767.4	33.2	452.7	23.5	272.6	264.8	7.8
Unlisted UK shares	AF.512N1	675.2	76.2	328.5	91.6	229.2	3.0	226.2
Other equity	AF.519							
Other UK equity	AF.519N6	128.8						
UK shares and bonds issued by other UK residents	AF.519N7	–	–	–	–	–	–	–
Shares and other equity issued by rest of the world	AF.519N9	2 138.4	804.9	1 167.2	150.9	546.6	335.4	211.2
Investment fund shares/units	AF.52							
UK mutual funds' shares	AF.52N1	1 010.4	0.8	742.6	2.3	90.7	85.5	5.3
Rest of the world mutual funds' shares	AF.52N9	252.2		252.1		39.3	39.3	–
Total	AF.5	4 972.5	915.1	2 943.1	268.2	1 178.4	728.0	450.4
Insurance, pensions and standardised guarantee schemes	AF.6							
Non-life insurance technical reserves	AF.61	45.8	3.8	0.4	0.1	0.1	–	0.1
Life insurance and annuity entitlements	AF.62	605.8						
Pension schemes[6]	AF.6M	3 423.2		792.1				
Provisions for calls under standardised guarantees	AF.66	–		–	–			
Total	AF.6	4 074.8	3.8	792.6	0.2	0.1	–	0.1
Financial derivatives and employee stock options	AF.7	4 577.5	31.0	4 538.6	2 911.4	1 523.2	12.7	1 510.5
Of which: financial derivatives	AF.71	4 572.2	31.0	4 538.6	2 911.4	1 523.2	12.7	1 510.5
Other accounts receivable	AF.8	468.4	131.5	59.1	0.1	27.9	4.6	23.3
Total financial assets	**AF.A**	28 177.3	2 007.2	19 600.1	10 627.8	5 139.2	1 018.4	4 120.8

UK summary accounts
2015

Total economy: all sectors and the rest of the world. Unconsolidated

£ billion

		Insurance corporations and pension funds S.128+S.129	General government S.13	Central government S.1311	Local government S.1313	Households and NPISH[3] S.14+S.15	Households S.14	NPISH S.15	Rest of the world S.2
Financial balance sheet at end of period	IV.3								
Total financial assets	AF.A								
Monetary gold and special drawing rights	AF.1								
Monetary gold	AF.11		7.1	7.1					
Special drawing rights	AF.12		9.1	9.1					9.5
Total	AF.1		16.2	16.2					9.5
Currency and deposits	AF.2								
Currency	AF.21					62.3	51.9	10.4	1.9
Transferable deposits	AF.22								
Deposits with UK MFIs[4]	AF.22N1	99.8	40.5	12.8	27.7	1 211.7	1 187.7	24.0	2 542.4
Deposits with rest of the world MFIs	AF.22N9	37.2	10.9	9.6	1.4	57.1	57.1	–	
Other deposits	AF.29	–	31.1	24.0	7.0	133.9	133.6	0.2	1.7
Total	AF.2	137.0	82.5	46.4	36.1	1 464.9	1 430.3	34.6	2 546.0
Debt securities	AF.3								
Short-term	AF.31								
Issued by UK central government	AF.31N1	3.0	2.6		2.6	–	–	–	40.0
Issued by UK local government	AF.31N2		–			–	–	–	
Issued by UK MFIs	AF.31N5	9.4	1.3	–	1.3	7.6	5.0	2.6	125.7
MMIs issued by other UK residents[5]	AF.31N6	1.2	1.8	0.2	1.6	0.2	0.2	0.1	30.8
MMIs issued by rest of the world	AF.31N9	4.9	4.1	4.1		–	–		
Long-term	AF.32								
Issued by UK central government	AF.32N1	472.1	0.5		0.5	6.4	2.7	3.7	467.6
Issued by UK local government	AF.32N2	2.1	–	–		1.9	1.8	0.1	–
Issued by UK MFIs and other UK residents	AF.32N5-6	275.8	1.0	0.8	0.2	7.0	4.9	2.1	1 070.5
Bonds issued by rest of the world	AF.32N9	329.8	62.7	62.7		2.6	1.6	0.9	
Total	AF.3	1 098.3	74.0	67.8	6.3	25.7	16.1	9.5	1 734.6
Loans	AF.4								
Short-term	AF.41								
By UK MFIs	AF.41N1								
By rest of the world MFIs	AF.41N9								680.9
Long-term	AF.42								
Direct investment	AF.421	15.0				–			419.4
Outward direct investment	AF.421N1	11.5				–			256.4
Inward direct investment	AF.421N2	3.4				–			163.0
Secured on dwellings	AF.422	11.5	47.4	37.4	10.0				
Finance leasing	AF.423								
Other long-term loans	AF.424								
Issued by other UK residents	AF.424N1	147.4	162.1	156.3	5.8	18.8	18.8	–	
Issued by rest of the world	AF.424N9								36.6
Total	AF.4	173.8	209.5	193.7	15.8	18.8	18.8	–	1 136.9
Equity and investment fund shares/units	AF.5								
Equity	AF.51								
Listed UK shares	AF.511N1	156.6	37.3	33.2	4.1	244.3	215.8	28.5	1 170.9
Unlisted UK shares	AF.512N1	7.8	16.4	15.7	0.7	254.1	224.4	29.7	900.3
Other equity	AF.519								
Other UK equity	AF.519N6		127.4	2.6	124.8	1.4	1.4	–	13.1
UK shares and bonds issued by other UK residents	AF.519N7	–	–	–	–	–	–	–	
Shares and other equity issued by rest of the world	AF.519N9	469.8	5.9	5.9		160.4	113.3	47.1	
Investment fund shares/units	AF.52								
UK mutual funds' shares	AF.52N1	649.6				267.1	246.7	20.4	2.3
Rest of the world mutual funds' shares	AF.52N9	212.8				0.1	0.1		
Total	AF.5	1 496.5	186.9	57.3	129.6	927.4	801.6	125.7	2 086.6
Insurance, pensions and standardised guarantee schemes	AF.6								
Non-life insurance technical reserves	AF.61	0.2	0.6		0.6	40.9	40.3	0.6	10.8
Life insurance and annuity entitlements	AF.62					605.8	605.8	–	10.7
Pension schemes[6]	AF.6M	792.1				2 631.1	2 631.1	–	
Provisions for calls under standardised guarantees	AF.66		–						
Total	AF.6	792.3	0.6		0.6	3 277.8	3 277.2	0.6	21.6
Financial derivatives and employee stock options	AF.7	104.1	2.1	2.1		5.8	5.6	0.2	2 391.4
Of which: financial derivatives	AF.71	104.1	2.1	2.1		0.5	0.3	0.2	2 391.4
Other accounts payable	AF.8	31.1	81.4	79.0	2.4	196.4	184.1	12.3	8.7
Total financial assets	**AF.A**	3 833.1	653.3	462.5	190.8	5 916.8	5 733.9	182.9	9 935.3

UK summary accounts
2015

Total economy: all sectors and the rest of the world. Unconsolidated £ billion

		UK total economy	Non-financial corporations	Financial corporations	Monetary financial institutions (MFI) S.121+ S.122+ S.123	Financial corporations except MFI and ICPF[1] S.124+ S.125+ S.126+S.127	Non-money market funds	Financial corporations except MFI, NMMF and ICPF[2] S.125+S.126+ S.127
		S.1	S.11	S.12			S.124	
Financial balance sheet at end of period	IV.3							
Total financial liabilities	AF.L							
Monetary gold and special drawing rights	AF.1							
Monetary gold	AF.11							
Special drawing rights	AF.12	9.5						
Total	AF.1	9.5						
Currency and deposits	AF.2							
Currency	AF.21	81.6		76.9	76.9			
Transferable deposits	AF.22							
Deposits with UK MFIs[4]	AF.22N1	6 275.3		6 275.3	6 275.3			
Deposits with rest of the MFIs[4]	AF.22N9							
Other deposits	AF.29	181.8	–	31.2		31.2		31.2
Total	AF.2	6 538.6	–	6 383.4	6 352.2	31.2		31.2
Debt securities	AF.3							
Short-term	AF.31							
Issued by UK central government	AF.31N1	82.3						
Issued by UK local government	AF.31N2	–						
Issued by MFIs[4]	AF.31N5	198.1		198.1	198.1			
MMIs issued by other UK residents[5]	AF.31N6	44.3	28.7	14.1		14.1	–	14.0
MMIs issued by rest of the world[5]	AF.31N9							
Long-term	AF.32							
Issued by UK central government	AF.32N1	1 678.1						
Issued by UK local government	AF.32N2	4.1						
Issued by UK MFIs and other UK residents[4]	AF.32N5-6	1 970.5	318.7	1 643.9	677.5	941.7	1.5	940.2
Issued by rest of the world	AF.32N9							
Total	AF.3	3 977.4	347.4	1 856.1	875.5	955.8	1.5	954.2
Loans	AF.4							
Short-term	AF.41							
By UK MFIs[4]	AF.41N1	1 143.6	337.2	639.8	–	622.2	3.4	618.9
By rest of the world MFIs[4]	AF.41N9	680.9	112.8	531.2		506.2	0.7	505.4
Long-term	AF.42							
Direct investment	AF.421	419.4	373.6	45.8	–	27.9	–	27.9
Outward direct investment	AF.421N1	256.4	228.6	27.8	–	15.4	–	15.4
Inward direct investment	AF.421N2	163.0	144.9	18.1	–	12.6	–	12.6
Secured on dwellings	AF.422	1 327.1	41.0					
Finance leasing	AF.423	38.2	27.1	5.1	2.8	2.3	–	2.3
Other long-term loans	AF.424							
Issued by other UK residents	AF.424N1	567.6	256.7	96.6	–	96.1	1.5	94.6
Issued by other UK residents	AF.424N9	36.6	0.8	29.1	–	29.1	0.2	28.8
Total	AF.4	4 213.5	1 149.2	1 347.5	2.8	1 283.9	5.8	1 278.0
Equity and investment fund shares/units	AF.5							
Equity	AF.51							
Listed UK shares	AF.511N1	1 938.3	1 475.0	463.3	1.5	362.3		362.3
Unlisted UK shares	AF.512N1	1 575.6	870.2	705.3	244.1	436.7		436.7
Other equity	AF.519							
Other UK equity	AF.519N6	141.9	141.9					
UK shares and bonds issued by other UK residents	AF.519N7	–	–	–				
Shares and other equity issued by rest of the world	AF.519N9							
Investment fund shares/units	AF.52							
UK mutual funds' shares	AF.52N1	1 012.7		1 012.7		1 012.7	1 012.7	
Rest of the world mutual funds' shares	AF.52N9							
Total	AF.5	4 668.5	2 487.1	2 181.4	245.6	1 811.6	1 012.7	798.9
Insurance, pensions and standardised guarantee schemes	AF.6							
Non-life insurance technical reserves	AF.61	56.6		56.6				
Life insurance and annuity entitlements	AF.62	616.6		616.6				
Pension schemes[6]	AF.6M	3 423.2	617.6	2 696.6	33.8	24.0	0.5	23.5
Provisions for calls under standardised guarantees	AF.66	–						
Total	AF.6	4 096.4	617.6	3 369.8	33.8	24.0	0.5	23.5
Financial derivatives and employee stock options	AF.7	4 558.7	55.4	4 499.3	2 899.1	1 497.5	14.4	1 483.1
Of which: financial derivatives	AF.71	4 553.4	50.6	4 498.9	2 898.9	1 497.3	14.4	1 483.0
Other accounts payable	AF.8	462.1	183.9	88.1	5.5	0.3	0.2	–
Total financial liabilities	AF.L	28 524.6	4 840.6	19 725.6	10 414.5	5 604.2	1 035.2	4 569.0
Financial net worth	BF.90							
Total financial assets	AF.A	28 177.3	2 007.2	19 600.1	10 627.8	5 139.2	1 018.4	4 120.8
less total financial liabilities	AF.L	28 524.6	4 840.6	19 725.6	10 414.5	5 604.2	1 035.2	4 569.0
Financial net worth	BF.90	–347.3	–2 833.4	–125.5	213.2	–465.0	–16.8	–448.2

1.7.11
continued

UK summary accounts
2015

Total economy: all sectors and the rest of the world. Unconsolidated

£ billion

		Insurance corporations and pension funds S.128+S.129	General government S.13	Central government S.1311	Local government S.1313	Households and NPISH[3] S.14+S.15	Households S.14	NPISH S.15	Rest of the world S.2
Financial balance sheet at end of period	IV.3								
Total financial liabilities	AF.L								
Monetary gold and special drawing rights	AF.1								
Monetary gold	AF.11								–
Special drawing rights	AF.12		9.5	9.5					9.1
Total	AF.1		9.5	9.5					9.1
Currency and deposits	AF.2								
Currency	AF.21		4.7	4.7					0.8
Transferable deposits	AF.22								2 146.4
Deposits with UK MFIs[4]	AF.22N1								
Deposits with rest of the world MFIs	AF.22N9								
Other deposits	AF.29		150.6	150.6					
Total	AF.2		155.3	155.3					2 147.1
Debt securities	AF.3								
Short-term	AF.31								
Issued by UK central government	AF.31N1		82.3	82.3					
Issued by UK local government	AF.31N2		–		–				
Issued by UK MFIs	AF.31N5								
MMIs issued by other UK residents[5]	AF.31N6						1.6	1.6	
MMIs issued by rest of the world	AF.31N9								96.7
Long-term	AF.32								
Issued by UK central government	AF.32N1		1 678.1	1 678.1					
Issued by UK local government	AF.32N2		4.1		4.1				
Issued by UK MFIs and other UK residents	AF.32N5-6	24.7	6.4	6.4	–		1.4	1.4	
Issued by rest of the world	AF.32N9								942.0
Total	AF.3	24.7	1 770.9	1 766.8	4.1	3.0		3.0	1 038.7
Loans	AF.4								
Short-term	AF.41								
By UK MFIs	AF.41N1	17.6	13.2	2.9	10.3	153.3	144.4	8.9	921.0
By rest of the world MFIs	AF.41N9	25.0	6.4	6.4	–	30.5	24.4	6.1	
Long-term	AF.42								
Direct investment	AF.421	17.9				–			249.6
Outward direct investment	AF.421N1	12.4				–			180.8
Inward direct investment	AF.421N2	5.5				–			68.8
Secured on dwellings	AF.422					1 286.2	1 286.2	–	
Finance leasing	AF.423		6.1	5.6	0.5				–
Other long-term loans	AF.424								
Issued by other UK residents	AF.424N1	0.5	71.5	0.4	71.1	142.8	135.2	7.6	399.5
Issued by rest of the world	AF.424N9		6.7	0.5	6.3				
Total loans	AF.4	60.9	104.0	15.8	88.2	1 612.7	1 590.1	22.6	1 570.1
Equity and investment fund shares/units	AF.5								
Equity	AF.51								
Listed UK shares	AF.511N1	99.6							
Unlisted UK shares	AF.512N1	24.6							
Other equity	AF.519								
Other UK equity	AF.519N6								
UK shares and bonds issued by other UK residents	AF.519N7	–							
Shares and other equity issued by rest of the world	AF.519N9								2 138.4
Investment fund shares/units	AF.52								
UK mutual funds' shares	AF.52N1								
Rest of the world mutual funds' shares	AF.52N9								252.2
Total	AF.5	124.2							2 390.6
Insurance, pensions and standardised guarantee schemes	AF.6								
Non-life insurance technical reserves	AF.61	56.6							
Life insurance and annuity entitlements	AF.62	616.6							
Pension schemes[6]	AF.6M	2 638.8	68.5		68.5	40.5		40.5	–
Provisions for calls under standardised guarantees	AF.66		–	–					
Total	AF.6	3 312.0	68.6		68.5	40.5		40.5	–
Financial derivatives and employee stock options	AF.7	102.7	2.2	2.2		1.8	1.5	0.3	2 410.1
Of which: financial derivatives	AF.71	102.7	2.2	2.2		1.8	1.5	0.3	2 410.1
Other accounts payable	AF.8	82.3	98.4	55.1	43.3	91.7	79.6	12.1	15.0
Total financial liabilities	**AF.L**	3 706.9	2 208.9	2 004.8	204.1	1 749.6	1 671.2	78.5	9 580.8
Financial net worth	BF.90						4 062.7	104.4	
Total financial assets	AF.A	3 833.1	653.3	462.5	190.8	5 916.8	5 733.9	182.9	9 935.3
less total financial liabilities	AF.L	3 706.9	2 208.9	2 004.8	204.1	1 749.6	1 671.2	78.5	9 580.8
Financial net worth	**BF.90**	126.3	-1 555.6	-1 542.3	-13.3	4 167.2	4 062.7	104.4	354.5

1 Monetary financial institutions and insurance corporation and pension funds
2 Monetary financial institutions, non-money market funds and insurance corporation and pension funds
3 Non-profit institutions serving households
4 Monetary Financial Institutions
5 Money Market Instruments

6 F.63 Pension entitlements, F.64 Claims on pension funds on pension managers, F.65 Entitlements to non-pension benefits

1.8A FISIM[1] impact on UK gross domestic product and national income
Current prices

£ million

			2009	2010	2011	2012	2013	2014	2015	2016
Impact of FISIM on gross domestic product										
Gross domestic product: output										
Output of services		P.1								
Financial intermediaries	D8NH		65 403	63 376	58 371	54 556	57 217	58 650	60 020	62 793
Non-market	D8N9		616	769	843	779	748	1 119	1 164	1 130
Intermediate consumption		P.2								
Non-financial corporations	G7VJ		12 386	12 185	12 214	11 553	11 098	11 240	11 474	12 502
Financial corporations	D8OO		1 700	819	927	827	604	930	905	460
General government	C5PR		268	377	401	363	361	549	567	533
Households and NPISH[2]	IV8A		26 125	27 084	22 255	20 709	24 332	18 741	17 034	16 785
Gross domestic product at market prices	C95M	**B.1g**	25 541	23 680	23 415	21 883	21 570	28 309	31 204	33 643
Gross domestic product: expenditure										
Total final consumption expenditure		P.3								
Households and NPISH	IV8B		21 946	17 519	17 351	16 381	15 269	23 066	25 772	27 209
General government	C5PR		268	377	401	363	361	549	567	533
Exports of services	C6FD	P.6	5 843	8 129	7 930	7 399	8 405	7 110	7 103	8 289
less imports of services	C6F7	P.7	2 516	2 345	2 268	2 260	2 465	2 416	2 238	2 388
Gross domestic product at market prices	C95M	**B.1g**	25 541	23 680	23 415	21 883	21 570	28 309	31 204	33 643
Gross domestic product: income										
Operating surplus, gross		B.2g								
Non-financial corporations	IV8H		−12 386	−12 185	−12 214	−11 553	−11 098	−11 240	−11 474	−12 502
Financial corporations	IV8I		63 703	62 556	57 442	53 729	56 613	57 720	59 115	62 333
Households	IV8J		−25 777	−26 692	−21 813	−20 293	−23 945	−18 171	−16 437	−16 188
Gross domestic product at market prices	C95M	**B.1g**	25 541	23 680	23 415	21 883	21 570	28 309	31 204	33 643
Impact of FISIM on gross national income										
Gross domestic product at market prices	C95M	B.1g	25 541	23 680	23 415	21 883	21 570	28 309	31 204	33 643
Property and entrepreneurial income		D.4								
Receipts from rest of the world	IV8E		−4 889	−5 139	−1 746	−2 562	−4 521	−3 691	−3 457	−4 781
less payments to rest of the world	IV8F		−1 562	646	3 916	2 577	1 506	1 170	1 466	1 120
Gross national income at market prices	IV8G	**B.5g**	22 214	17 897	17 754	16 744	15 630	23 615	26 339	27 742

1 Financial intermediation services indirectly measured
2 Non-profit institutions serving households

1.8B FISIM[1] impact on UK gross domestic product and national income
Chained volume measures (reference year 2015)

£ million

			2009	2010	2011	2012	2013	2014	2015	2016
Impact of FISIM on gross domestic product										
Gross domestic product: expenditure										
Total final consumption expenditure		P.3								
Households and NPISH[2]	IV8D		25 288	24 658	24 183	24 397	24 048	24 463	25 779	26 780
General government	C5Q9		775	647	518	526	555	563	567	558
Exports of services	C6FM	P.6	13 128	11 938	10 931	9 356	8 416	7 267	7 103	6 811
less imports of services	C6FL	P.7	1 976	1 838	2 278	2 506	2 592	2 459	2 275	2 124
Gross domestic product at market prices	DZ4H	**B.1g**	38 232	36 821	34 235	32 448	30 911	29 842	31 174	32 026

1 Financial intermediation services indirectly measured
2 Non-profit institutions serving households

1.8C FISIM[1] impact upon interest resources and uses by sector[2]
Current prices

£ million

			2009	2010	2011	2012	2013	2014	2015	2016
Public corporations										
Resources										
Unadjusted interest received	NENH		426	434	407	408	394	410	371	428
plus FISIM	C7RL		−8	2	4	11	13	30	24	14
Interest received	CPBV	D.41	418	436	411	419	407	440	395	442
Uses										
Unadjusted interest paid	NENG		4 329	3 633	3 546	3 539	3 905	3 904	4 423	4 414
less FISIM	D8KD		58	38	42	24	13	8	7	17
Interest paid	XAQZ	D.41	4 271	3 595	3 504	3 515	3 892	3 896	4 416	4 397
Private non-financial corporations										
Resources										
Unadjusted interest received	I69R		8 909	8 771	8 936	8 526	9 250	9 225	9 313	10 248
plus FISIM	IV87		3 313	2 662	3 745	3 574	3 034	4 805	5 490	5 739
Interest received	DSZR	D.41	12 222	11 433	12 681	12 100	12 284	14 030	14 803	15 987
Uses										
Unadjusted interest paid	I6A2		45 039	37 341	35 500	37 697	37 957	36 421	32 055	33 660
less FISIM	IV86		9 023	9 483	8 424	7 944	7 971	6 275	5 924	6 732
Interest paid	DSZV	D.41	36 016	27 858	27 076	29 753	29 986	30 146	26 131	26 928
Non-financial corporations										
Resources										
Unadjusted interest received	J4WQ		9 335	9 205	9 343	8 934	9 644	9 635	9 684	10 676
plus FISIM	IV89		3 305	2 664	3 749	3 585	3 047	4 835	5 514	5 753
Interest received	EABC	D.41	12 640	11 869	13 092	12 519	12 691	14 470	15 198	16 429
Uses										
Unadjusted interest paid	J4WS		49 368	40 974	39 046	41 236	41 862	40 325	36 478	38 074
less FISIM	IV88		9 081	9 521	8 466	7 968	7 984	6 283	5 931	6 749
Interest paid	EABG	D.41	40 287	31 453	30 580	33 268	33 878	34 042	30 547	31 325
Financial corporations										
Resources										
Unadjusted interest received	J4WU		290 594	247 667	253 859	236 945	219 598	208 188	198 062	201 120
plus FISIM	IV8Y		−56 981	−58 855	−47 087	−45 198	−51 019	−40 223	−37 816	−40 278
Interest received	NHCK	D.41	233 613	188 812	206 772	191 747	168 579	167 965	160 246	160 842
Uses										
Unadjusted interest paid	J4WW		209 764	168 869	172 009	162 787	141 780	127 700	118 296	114 985
plus FISIM	IV8Z		6 722	3 703	10 357	8 531	5 602	17 447	21 305	22 055
Interest paid	NHCM	D.41	216 486	172 572	182 366	171 318	147 382	145 147	139 601	137 040
Central government										
Resources										
Unadjusted interest received	I69N		7 874	7 338	7 370	9 073	7 586	7 465	8 010	7 715
plus FISIM	C6GA		86	−14	49	48	22	46	60	50
Interest received	NMCE	D.41	7 960	7 324	7 419	9 121	7 608	7 511	8 070	7 765
Uses										
Unadjusted interest paid	I69W		27 869	44 980	51 335	47 982	49 192	48 424	43 209	47 273
less FISIM	C6G9		26	63	38	26	4	−1	−5	14
Interest paid	NUHA	D.41	27 843	44 917	51 297	47 956	49 188	48 425	43 214	47 259
Local government										
Resources										
Unadjusted interest received	I69O		796	591	637	686	731	657	664	633
plus FISIM	C6FQ		−68	61	135	112	130	336	338	285
Interest received	NMKB	D.41	728	652	772	798	861	993	1 002	918
Uses										
Unadjusted interest paid	I69X		3 512	3 554	3 402	5 198	3 562	3 743	3 910	3 921
less FISIM	C6FP		224	267	182	177	205	175	174	184
Interest paid	NCBW	D.41	3 288	3 287	3 220	5 021	3 357	3 568	3 736	3 737

1.8C FISIM[1] impact upon interest resources and uses by sector[2]
Current prices

£ million

			2009	2010	2011	2012	2013	2014	2015	2016
Households and NPISH[3]										
Resources										
Unadjusted interest received	J4WY		19 663	18 800	20 494	21 948	19 715	15 922	14 650	13 526
plus FISIM	IV8W		3 015	−695	548	216	−624	8 386	10 594	11 199
Interest received	QWLZ	D.41	22 678	18 105	21 042	22 164	19 091	24 308	25 244	24 725
Uses										
Unadjusted interest paid	J4WZ		72 004	64 816	62 089	61 730	61 550	60 422	58 419	58 495
less FISIM	IV8X		44 708	44 908	38 619	36 458	39 826	32 749	31 592	32 198
Interest paid	QWMG	D.41	27 296	19 908	23 470	25 272	21 724	27 673	26 827	26 297
Rest of the world										
Resources										
Unadjusted interest received	I69V		125 377	111 399	117 344	109 272	100 996	92 123	82 260	88 358
FISIM on interest paid to rest of the world	IV8F		−1 562	646	3 916	2 577	1 506	1 170	1 466	1 120
Interest received	QYNG	D.41	123 815	112 045	121 260	111 849	102 502	93 293	83 726	89 478
Uses										
Unadjusted interest paid	I6A6		91 122	71 807	81 166	67 928	60 325	53 376	53 018	59 280
FISIM on interest received from rest of the world	IV8E		−4 889	−5 139	−1 746	−2 562	−4 521	−3 691	−3 457	−4 781
Interest paid	QYNJ	D.41	86 233	66 668	79 420	65 366	55 804	49 685	49 561	54 499

1 Financial intermediation services indirectly measured
2 Interest is recorded within the allocation of primary income account
3 Non-profit institutions serving households

United Kingdom National Accounts

The Blue Book
Chapter 02: The Industrial Analyses

2017 edition

Editors: Dean Goodway & Sarah Nightingale

Office for National Statistics

Chapter 2: Explanation of industrial analyses

The industrial analysis

Analysis of the 10 broad industrial groups shows that in 2015, the "government, health and education" and "distribution, transport, hotel and restaurant" industries provided the largest contributions to gross value added at current basic prices. These industries contributed 18.2% each to the total gross value added of £1,685 billion; with values of £306.7 billion and £306.1 billion respectively.

Of the remainder:

- production industries contributed 14%

- real estate industries contributed 13.9%

Figure 2.1: Breakdown of gross value added at basic prices, by industry, 2015, UK

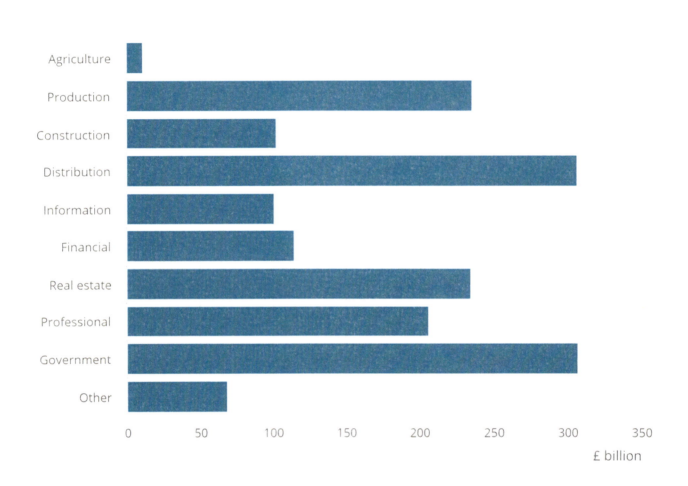

Source: Office for National Statistics

In 2015, of all goods and services entering into final demand:

- households consumed 48.5%

- 11.8% of goods and 9.4% of services were exported

- government, both central and local, consumed 14.8%

- gross capital formation, by all sectors of the economy, consumed 13.1%

- non-profit institutions serving households (NPISH) consumed 2.3%

Figure 2.2: Composition of final demand for 2015, UK

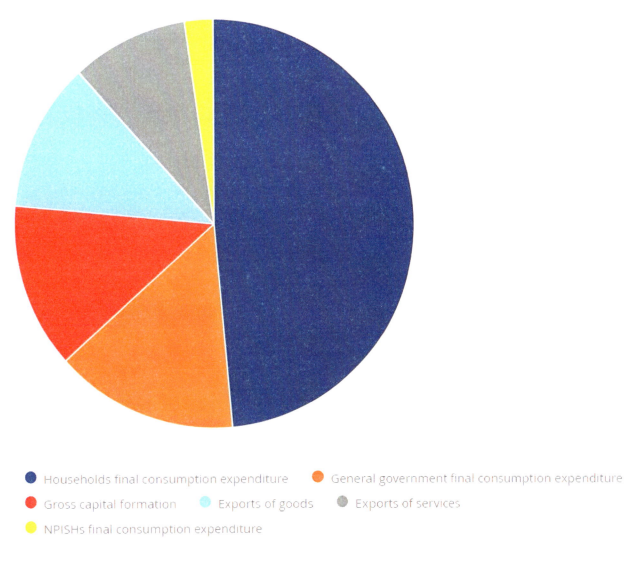

● Households final consumption expenditure   ● General government final consumption expenditure

● Gross capital formation   ● Exports of goods   ● Exports of services

● NPISHs final consumption expenditure

Source: Office for National Statistics

Source: Office for National Statistics

The government, health and education industries showed the highest level of compensation of employees in 2015 at £242.3 billion (26%). The second largest industries, in terms of their contribution to total compensation of employees, were the distribution, transport, hotel and restaurant industries at £198.5 billion (21.3%).

Figure 2.3: Compensation of employees, by industry, 2015, UK

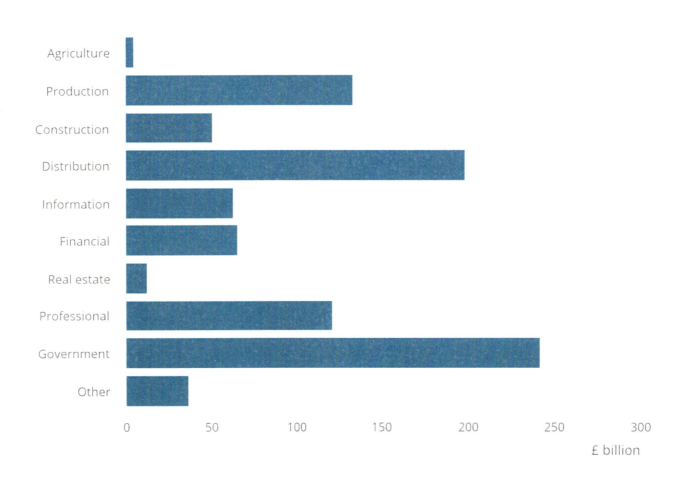

Source: Office for National Statistics

Input-output supply and use tables

The annual estimates included in the UK National Accounts, The Blue Book: 2017 edition incorporate the results of annual inquiries that become available in the first part of the year, although last year's estimates are largely based on quarterly information. Any newly-collected data are shown as revisions. In order to reassess these estimates, supply and use tables are prepared using all the available information on inputs, outputs, gross value added, income and expenditure. To produce consolidated sector and financial accounts requires preparation of "top-to-bottom" sector and sub-sector accounts to identify discrepancies in the estimates relating to each sector.

The latest annual supply and use tables provide estimates for the years 1997 to 2015, with data for 2015 balanced for the first time. Data for 2013 to 2014 have been fully re-balanced. Data from 1997 to 2012 have been revised to incorporate changes required under new international standards and guidelines, as well as to make sure the data are comparable and meet user needs.

Further general information regarding the supply and use framework and the balancing process is available.

Current price analysis (Tables 2.1, 2.1A and 2.2)

The analyses of gross value added and other variables by industry, shown in Tables 2.1, 2.1A and 2.2 reflect estimates based on Standard Industrial Classification 2007: SIC 2007. These tables are based on current price data reconciled through the input-output supply and use framework from 1997 to 2015.

Estimates of total output and gross value added are valued at basic prices, the method recommended by European System of Accounts 2010: ESA 2010. Therefore, the only taxes and subsidies included in the price will be those paid or received as part of the production process (such as business rates), rather than those associated with the production of a unit of output (such as Value Added Tax).

Chained volume indices (2015=100) analyses (Table 2.3)

Table 2.3 shows chained volume estimates of gross value added (GVA) at basic prices by industry. The output approach provides the lead indicator of economic change in the short-term. In the longer-term, the output measure of real gross domestic product (GDP) is required to follow the annual path indicated by the expenditure measure of real GDP (usually to within 0.2% of the average annual GVA growth). To achieve this, balancing adjustments are sometimes applied to the output-based gross value added estimates.

We have developed an automatic function for assigning the annual adjustments to GVA. This is designed to minimise changes to the quarterly path while adjusting the overall annual growth rate to align to the expenditure measure. For technical and other reasons the adjustments are not, at present, made to retail or the non-services industries for any years.

Workforce jobs by industry (Table 2.4)

Workforce jobs (WFJ) is the preferred measure of the change in jobs by industry. A person can have more than one job; therefore the number of jobs is not the same as the number of people employed.

Table 2.4 breaks down WFJ into 10 broad industry groupings on Standard Industrial Classification 2007: SIC 2007.

The main component of WFJ is employee jobs. Estimates for employee jobs are obtained mainly from surveys of businesses selected from the Inter-Departmental Business Register (IDBR). All other business surveys collecting economic data also use this register.

WFJ also includes Her Majesty's Forces (within industry section O) and government-supported trainees from administrative sources (split by industry using the Labour Force Survey).

The Labour Force Survey (LFS), a household survey, is used to collect self-employment jobs. It codes respondents according to their own view of the industry they work in; therefore the industry breakdown is less reliable than that for the business surveys.

Summary supply and use tables for the UK

Table 2.1a: Summary supply and use tables 2012

Table 2.1b: Summary supply and use tables 2013

Table 2.1c: Summary supply and use tables 2014

Table 2.1d: Summary supply and use tables 2015

Gross value added (GVA)

The UK National Accounts, The Blue Book provides a comprehensive industry breakdown of gross value added (GVA), with activities grouped into 20 broad sections in accordance with Standard Industrial Classification 2007: SIC 2007.

The Blue Book also includes supplementary information for the different components that make up GVA for each industry. Under the income approach, GVA is split into compensation of employees (CoE), taxes less subsidies, gross operating surplus (GOS) and mixed income. Estimates of each industry's intermediate consumption and total output are also published, with the difference between the two equalling GVA.

This additional information, available in The Blue Book, allows for more detailed analysis of national output to be conducted. For example, CoE can be used to calculate how much of an industry's production income is spent on wages and salaries and employers' social contributions, whereas GOS data can be used to estimate how much profit is generated by companies after considering labour costs and taxes less subsidies.

2.1 Output and capital formation: by industry[1,2]
Gross value added at current basic prices

£ million

			2009	2010	2011	2012	2013	2014	2015
Agriculture									
Output									
Compensation of employees	KLR2	D.1	4 152	4 234	4 301	4 459	4 718	4 747	4 832
Taxes less subsidies on production other than those on products	KLR3	D.29-D.39	−3 513	−2 606	−2 557	−2 158	−2 254	−2 119	−1 794
Operating surplus and mixed income, gross	KLR4	B.2g+B.3g	7 785	8 789	8 229	7 869	8 993	9 115	8 158
Gross value added at basic prices	KLR5	B.1g	8 424	10 417	9 973	10 170	11 457	11 743	11 196
Intermediate consumption at purchasers' prices	KLR6	P.2	15 667	14 871	15 948	16 188	16 946	17 073	17 051
Total output at basic prices	KLR7	P.1	24 091	25 288	25 921	26 358	28 403	28 816	28 247
Gross capital formation	KLR8	P.5	4 558	4 235	4 861	5 195	5 281	5 048	4 428
Production									
Output									
Compensation of employees	KLR9	D.1	115 554	118 570	121 935	124 046	130 060	129 932	133 336
Taxes less subsidies on production other than those on products	KLS4	D.29-D.39	3 929	3 855	3 812	3 973	4 433	4 680	4 807
Operating surplus and mixed income, gross	KLS3	B.2g+B.3g	78 824	81 174	83 999	86 788	92 617	95 289	96 940
Gross value added at basic prices	KLS5	B.1g	198 307	203 599	209 746	214 807	227 110	229 901	235 083
Intermediate consumption at purchasers' prices	KLS6	P.2	358 705	387 527	415 782	429 471	442 198	442 387	434 075
Total output at basic prices	KLS7	P.1	557 012	591 126	625 528	644 278	669 308	672 288	669 158
Gross capital formation	KLS8	P.5	33 948	36 914	46 965	50 127	53 510	54 087	54 487
Construction									
Output									
Compensation of employees	KLS9	D.1	44 792	45 110	46 542	47 641	49 183	50 240	50 793
Taxes less subsidies on production other than those on products	KLT3	D.29-D.39	1 028	1 069	1 030	1 325	1 181	1 087	1 280
Operating surplus and mixed income, gross	KLT2	B.2g+B.3g	31 278	34 507	37 821	38 261	40 685	46 316	49 950
Gross value added at basic prices	KLT4	B.1g	77 098	80 686	85 393	87 227	91 049	97 643	102 023
Intermediate consumption at purchasers' prices	KLT5	P.2	118 924	121 360	124 297	128 437	133 449	142 180	157 417
Total output at basic prices	KLT6	P.1	196 022	202 046	209 690	215 664	224 498	239 823	259 440
Gross capital formation	KLT7	P.5	12 967	18 190	18 006	20 927	19 055	26 773	27 484

2.1
continued

Output and capital formation: by industry[1,2]
Gross value added at current basic prices

£ million

			2009	2010	2011	2012	2013	2014	2015
Distribution, transport, hotels and restaurants									
Output									
Compensation of employees	KLT8	D.1	165 096	169 338	173 033	176 254	185 349	192 476	198 478
Taxes less subsidies on production other than		D.29-D.39							
those on products	KLU2		11 128	11 646	12 590	13 079	13 423	13 706	13 972
Operating surplus and mixed income, gross	KLT9	B.2g+B.3g	67 595	73 249	73 667	74 406	78 611	89 071	93 630
Gross value added at basic prices	KLU3	B.1g	243 819	254 233	259 290	263 739	277 383	295 253	306 080
Intermediate consumption at purchasers' prices	KLU4	P.2	239 065	241 611	246 817	258 994	270 450	279 422	288 359
Total output at basic prices	KLU5	P.1	482 884	495 844	506 107	522 733	547 833	574 675	594 439
Gross capital formation	KLU6	P.5	26 614	40 152	34 084	36 748	41 149	50 366	45 054
Information and communication									
Output									
Compensation of employees	KLU7	D.1	50 128	51 350	54 086	56 733	59 491	60 232	63 178
Taxes less subsidies on production other than		D.29-D.39							
those on products	KLU9		744	789	813	713	758	713	548
Operating surplus and mixed income, gross	KLU8	B.2g+B.3g	31 873	31 180	32 919	32 095	33 734	37 594	36 926
Gross value added at basic prices	KLV2	B.1g	82 745	83 319	87 818	89 541	93 983	98 539	100 652
Intermediate consumption at purchasers' prices	KLV3	P.2	63 634	68 432	68 172	69 736	73 821	72 892	73 907
Total output at basic prices	KLV4	P.1	146 379	151 751	155 990	159 277	167 804	171 431	174 559
Gross capital formation	KLV5	P.5	17 418	17 357	17 055	17 322	18 864	17 586	18 396
Financial and insurance									
Output									
Compensation of employees	KLV6	D.1	61 289	63 500	61 022	58 830	62 390	63 809	65 721
Taxes less subsidies on production other than									
those on products	KLV8	D.29-D.39	2 438	5 759	2 408	2 574	2 682	2 730	2 781
Operating surplus and mixed income, gross	KLV7	B.2g+B.3g	62 197	46 414	50 698	51 466	52 963	55 819	45 765
Gross value added at basic prices	KLV9	B.1g	125 924	115 673	114 128	112 870	118 035	122 358	114 267
Intermediate consumption at purchasers' prices	KLW2	P.2	122 121	116 578	129 406	127 322	136 292	136 034	137 613
Total output at basic prices	KLW3	P.1	248 045	232 251	243 534	240 192	254 327	258 392	251 880
Gross capital formation	KLW4	P.5	5 996	7 747	7 308	8 906	7 359	7 981	9 183

2.1 Output and capital formation: by industry[1,2]
Gross value added at current basic prices

£ million

			2009	2010	2011	2012	2013	2014	2015
Real estate									
Output									
Compensation of employees	KLW5	D.1	9 536	9 865	9 900	11 318	11 753	12 216	12 990
Taxes less subsidies on production other than those on products	KLW7	D.29-D.39	−995	−711	−258	−308	207	118	−20
Operating surplus and mixed income, gross	KLW6	B.2g+B.3g	164 312	166 094	175 320	191 059	194 175	208 339	221 548
Gross value added at basic prices	KLW8	B.1g	172 853	175 248	184 962	202 069	206 135	220 673	234 518
Intermediate consumption at purchasers' prices	KLW9	P.2	62 619	66 216	63 301	60 750	68 226	64 828	64 661
Total output at basic prices	KLX2	P.1	235 472	241 464	248 263	262 819	274 361	285 501	299 179
Gross capital formation	KLX3	P.5	−2 275	−2 544	−2 599	−2 674	−2 459	−3 251	−2 577
Professional and support									
Output									
Compensation of employees	KLX4	D.1	95 973	96 026	98 366	103 995	111 073	116 120	121 483
Taxes less subsidies on production other than those on products	KLX6	D.29-D.39	2 160	2 158	2 558	2 674	2 769	2 594	2 657
Operating surplus and mixed income, gross	KLX5	B.2g+B.3g	55 851	60 317	63 208	67 125	71 669	78 784	82 110
Gross value added at basic prices	KLX7	B.1g	153 984	158 501	164 132	173 794	185 511	197 498	206 250
Intermediate consumption at purchasers' prices	KLX8	P.2	115 741	119 375	123 171	128 557	132 716	138 470	142 674
Total output at basic prices	KLX9	P.1	269 725	277 876	287 303	302 351	318 227	335 968	348 924
Gross capital formation	KLY2	P.5	14 495	16 729	19 584	19 302	21 295	23 533	28 026
Government, health and education									
Output									
Compensation of employees	KLY3	D.1	220 067	227 498	227 518	231 629	234 169	236 554	242 278
Taxes less subsidies on production other than those on products	KLY5	D.29-D.39	460	582	548	662	651	755	766
Operating surplus and mixed income, gross	KLY4	B.2g+B.3g	55 693	55 398	58 161	58 703	57 239	63 046	63 630
Gross value added at basic prices	KLY6	B.1g	276 220	283 478	286 227	290 994	292 059	300 355	306 674
Intermediate consumption at purchasers' prices	KLY7	P.2	161 719	161 202	162 335	166 215	175 399	180 287	183 779
Total output at basic prices	KLY8	P.1	437 939	444 680	448 562	457 209	467 458	480 642	490 453
Gross capital formation	KLY9	P.5	38 562	38 757	36 383	35 515	36 425	38 970	39 420

2.1 **Output and capital formation: by industry[1,2]**
Gross value added at current basic prices
continued
£ million

			2009	2010	2011	2012	2013	2014	2015
Other services									
Output									
Compensation of employees	KLZ2	D.1	28 488	33 468	33 502	34 488	35 315	35 968	37 117
Taxes less subsidies on production other		D.29-D.39							
than those on products	KLZ4		1 058	958	858	1 110	1 114	1 077	1 069
Operating surplus and mixed income, gross	KLZ3	B.2g+B.3g	23 353	22 448	22 791	24 909	25 279	27 714	30 008
Gross value added at basic prices	KLZ5	B.1g	52 899	56 874	57 151	60 507	61 708	64 759	68 194
Intermediate consumption at purchasers' prices	KLZ6	P.2	31 464	29 882	32 414	34 489	36 178	36 486	36 427
Total output at basic prices	KLZ7	P.1	84 363	86 756	89 565	94 996	97 886	101 245	104 621
Gross capital formation	KLZ8	P.5	5 395	5 566	5 442	5 775	5 794	6 934	7 368
Not allocated to industries									
Gross capital formation[3]	KN28	P.5	63 009	64 614	67 313	68 406	80 409	86 308	89 294
All industries									
Output									
Compensation of employees	HAEA	D.1	795 075	818 959	830 205	849 393	883 501	902 294	930 206
Taxes less subsidies on production other		D.29-D.39							
than those on products	KN22		18 437	23 499	21 802	23 644	24 964	25 341	26 066
Operating surplus, gross	ABNF	B.2g	486 276	490 303	513 420	531 808	549 001	596 927	609 397
Mixed income, gross	QWLT	B.3g	92 485	89 267	93 393	100 873	106 964	114 160	119 268
Statistical discrepancy between income and GDP	RVFC	di	–	–	–	–	–	–	–
Gross value added at basic prices	ABML	B.1g	1 392 273	1 422 028	1 458 820	1 505 718	1 564 430	1 638 722	1 684 937
Intermediate consumption at purchasers' prices	KN25	P.2	1 289 659	1 327 054	1 381 643	1 420 159	1 485 675	1 510 059	1 535 963
Total output at basic prices	KN26	P.1	2 681 932	2 749 082	2 840 463	2 925 877	3 050 105	3 148 781	3 220 900
Gross capital formation										
Gross fixed capital formation	NPQX	P.51g	233 395	242 186	251 411	262 820	277 209	300 965	313 189
Changes in inventories	ABMP	P.52	−14 441	5 458	2 686	1 900	4 712	13 268	7 812
Acquisitions less disposals of valuables[4]	NPJO	P.53	1 733	73	305	829	4 761	102	−438
Total gross capital formation	NQFM	P.5	220 687	247 717	254 402	265 549	286 682	314 335	320 563

1 The contribution of each industry to the gross domestic product before providing for consumption of fixed capital. The industrial composition in this
table is consistent with the Supply-Use Tables in Table 2.1, which show data from 2010-2013.
2 Components may not sum to totals due to rounding.
3 Gross fixed capital formation of dwellings and costs associated with the
transfer of non-produced assets and acquisitions less disposals of valuable
4 Acquisitions less disposals of valuables can be a volatile series but any
volatility is likely to be GDP neutral as it is offset in UK trade figures

2.1A Gross value added at current basic prices analysed by industry[1,2,3,4]

Percentage

	2009	2010	2011	2012	2013	2014	2015
Agriculture	0.6	0.7	0.7	0.7	0.7	0.7	0.7
Production	14.2	14.3	14.4	14.3	14.5	14.0	14.0
Construction	5.5	5.7	5.9	5.8	5.8	6.0	6.1
Distribution, transport, hotels and restaurants	17.5	17.9	17.8	17.5	17.7	18.0	18.2
Information and communication	5.9	5.9	6.0	5.9	6.0	6.0	6.0
Financial and insurance	9.0	8.1	7.8	7.5	7.5	7.5	6.8
Real estate	12.4	12.3	12.7	13.4	13.2	13.5	13.9
Professional and support	11.1	11.1	11.3	11.5	11.9	12.1	12.2
Government, health and education	19.8	19.9	19.6	19.3	18.7	18.3	18.2
Other services[4]	3.8	4.0	3.9	4.0	3.9	4.0	4.0
Gross value added at basic prices	100.0	100.0	100.0	100.0	100.0	100.0	100.0

1 Based on table 2.1
2 The industrial composition in this table is consistent with the Supply-Use
  Tables in Table 2.1 which show data from 1997-2015
3 Components may not sum to totals due to rounding
4 Comprising sections R,S and T of the SIC2007.

2.2 Gross value added at current basic prices: by industry[1,2]

£ million

			2009	2010	2011	2012	2013	2014	2015
Agriculture	KKD5	A	8 424	10 417	9 973	10 170	11 457	11 743	11 196
Production and construction		B - F							
Production		B - E							
Mining and quarrying	KKD7	B	27 233	30 389	32 121	28 398	27 417	23 819	20 480
Manufacturing		C							
Food products, beverages and tobacco	KKE5	CA	24 522	22 543	22 792	23 928	25 890	26 237	26 914
Textiles, wearing apparel and leather products	KKE7	CB	3 412	4 607	4 729	4 877	5 820	5 871	6 308
Wood, paper products and printing	KKE9	CC	10 538	10 797	10 716	11 085	11 590	11 683	11 820
Coke and refined petroleum products	KKF3	CD	5 854	4 446	4 210	3 772	2 307	2 237	3 064
Chemicals and chemical products	KKF5	CE	7 686	8 780	7 294	8 043	8 962	9 486	11 646
Basic pharmaceutical products and preparations	KKF7	CF	13 404	14 036	13 964	12 818	12 619	12 220	12 019
Rubber, plastic and other non-metallic mineral products	KKF9	CG	11 203	11 430	11 528	12 009	12 565	12 758	13 747
Basic metals and metal products	KKG3	CH	13 549	14 959	16 026	17 523	18 880	19 595	20 604
Computer, electronic and optical products	KKG5	CI	7 049	7 570	7 385	7 922	7 817	8 019	7 761
Electrical equipment	KKG7	CJ	4 097	4 519	4 652	4 685	4 778	5 149	5 091
Machinery and equipment n.e.c.	KKG9	CK	6 694	9 263	10 996	11 018	11 501	11 571	10 354
Transport equipment	KKH3	CL	13 624	15 320	18 231	17 430	21 156	22 395	24 198
Other manufacturing and repair	KKH5	CM	11 796	12 843	13 243	13 296	14 721	15 459	15 844
Total manufacturing	KKE3	C	133 428	141 113	145 766	148 406	158 606	162 680	169 370
Electricity, gas, steam and air conditioning supply	KKH7	D	22 296	15 312	13 992	20 359	23 924	25 862	28 287
Water supply, sewerage, waste mgmt and remediation	KKH9	E	15 350	16 785	17 867	17 644	17 163	17 540	16 946
Total production	KKJ5	B - E	198 307	203 599	209 746	214 807	227 110	229 901	235 083
Construction	KKI3	F	77 098	80 686	85 393	87 227	91 049	97 643	102 023
Total production and construction	KKD9	B - F	275 405	284 285	295 139	302 034	318 159	327 544	337 106

1 Components may not sum to totals as a result of rounding.
2 Because of differences in the annual and monthly production inquiries, estimates of current price output and gross value added by industry derived from the current price Input-Output Supply and Use Tables are not consistent with the equivalent measures of chained volume measures growth given in 2.3. These differences do not affect GDP totals.

2.2 Gross value added at current basic prices: by industry[1,2]

continued

£ million

			2009	2010	2011	2012	2013	2014	2015
Services		G - T							
Distribution, transport, hotels and restaurants		G - I							
Wholesale, retail, repair of motor vehicles and m/cycles	KKI5	G	152 443	159 133	159 881	159 605	165 134	175 646	181 474
Transportation and storage	KKI9	H	56 457	60 071	62 602	63 050	67 297	71 988	75 174
Accommodation and food service activities	KKJ3	I	34 919	35 029	36 807	41 084	44 952	47 619	49 432
Total distribution, transport, hotels and restaurants	KKI7	G - I	243 819	254 233	259 290	263 739	277 383	295 253	306 080
Information and communication		J							
Publishing, audiovisual and broadcasting activities	KKK3	JA	23 089	24 018	24 347	25 616	26 288	27 038	27 030
Telecommunications	KKK5	JB	26 295	24 745	25 454	26 013	28 081	30 012	30 372
IT and other information service activities	KKK7	JC	33 361	34 556	38 017	37 912	39 614	41 489	43 250
Total information and communication	KKJ9	J	82 745	83 319	87 818	89 541	93 983	98 539	100 652
Financial and insurance	KKK9	K	125 924	115 673	114 128	112 870	118 035	122 358	114 267
Real estate	KKL3	L	172 853	175 248	184 962	202 069	206 135	220 673	234 518
Professional and support		M - N							
Professional, scientific and technical activities		M							
Legal, accounting, mgmt, architect, engineering etc	KKL9	MA	69 417	71 209	73 126	76 974	83 130	87 896	92 870
Scientific research and development	KKM3	MB	7 934	8 268	8 480	8 714	8 397	9 032	9 669
Other professional, scientific and technical activities	KKM5	MC	16 669	17 376	18 579	20 087	22 334	24 550	25 902
Total professional, scientific and technical activities	KKL5	M	94 020	96 853	100 185	105 775	113 861	121 478	128 441
Administrative and support service activities	KKM7	N	59 964	61 648	63 947	68 019	71 650	76 020	77 809
Total professional and support	KKL7	M - N	153 984	158 501	164 132	173 794	185 511	197 498	206 250
Government, health and education		O - Q							
Public admin, defence, compulsory social security	KKM9	O	75 851	78 275	77 930	78 734	79 080	78 954	79 724
Education	KKN5	P	93 028	95 241	96 675	97 228	98 321	101 796	102 992
Human health and social work activities		Q							
Human health activities	KKN9	QA	77 398	81 760	84 159	87 038	85 412	89 356	92 422
Residential care and social work activities	KKO3	QB	29 943	28 202	27 463	27 994	29 246	30 249	31 536
Total human health and social work activities	KKN7	Q	107 341	109 962	111 622	115 032	114 658	119 605	123 958
Total government, health and education	KKN3	O - Q	276 220	283 478	286 227	290 994	292 059	300 355	306 674
Other services		R - T							
Arts, entertainment and recreation	KKO5	R	19 955	19 712	20 363	22 624	22 034	23 351	25 593
Other service activities	KKO9	S	27 522	30 989	30 920	31 833	33 239	34 845	36 009
Activities of households as employers, undiff. goods	KKP3	T	5 422	6 173	5 868	6 050	6 435	6 563	6 592
Total other services	KKO7	R - T	52 899	56 874	57 151	60 507	61 708	64 759	68 194
Total service industries	KKJ7	G - T	1 108 444	1 127 326	1 153 708	1 193 514	1 234 814	1 299 435	1 336 635
All industries	ABML	B.1g	1 392 273	1 422 028	1 458 820	1 505 718	1 564 430	1 638 722	1 684 937

1 Components may not sum to totals as a result of rounding.
2 Because of differences in the annual and monthly production inquiries, estimates of current price output and gross value added by industry derived from the current price Input-Output Supply and Use Tables are not consistent with the equivalent measures of chained volume measures growth given in 2.3. These differences do not affect GDP totals.

2.3 Gross value added at basic prices: by industry[1,2,3]
Chained volume indices

Indices 2015=100

		Weight per 1000[1] 2015		2009	2010	2011	2012	2013	2014	2015	2016
Agriculture	A	6.6	L2KL	85.4	85.2	94.4	87.6	88.0	98.8	100.0	94.3
Production and construction	B-F										
Production	B-E										
Mining and quarrying	B	12.2	L2KR	128.2	123.9	106.3	94.6	91.9	92.5	100.0	99.0
Manufacturing	C										
Food products, beverages and tobacco	CA	16.0	KN3D	90.1	94.0	100.1	97.6	95.9	100.0	100.0	101.5
Textiles, wearing apparel and leather products	CB	3.7	KN3E	107.5	110.8	112.3	108.4	103.6	100.9	100.0	95.6
Wood, paper products and printing	CC	7.0	KN3F	106.6	107.5	101.4	96.0	98.2	99.3	100.0	99.7
Coke and refined petroleum products	CD	1.8	KN3G	121.8	119.8	121.5	109.2	107.1	97.5	100.0	98.4
Chemicals and chemical products	CE	6.9	KN3H	89.4	88.9	95.0	93.1	92.1	94.6	100.0	97.2
Basic pharmaceutical products and preparations	CF	7.1	KN3I	141.5	131.7	113.9	107.2	104.4	99.2	100.0	103.4
Rubber, plastic and other non-metallic mineral products	CG	8.2	KN3J	97.7	97.8	97.6	93.5	90.9	102.9	100.0	102.2
Basic metals and metal products	CH	12.2	KN3K	88.8	94.1	98.2	101.1	98.2	99.8	100.0	98.6
Computer, electronic and optical products	CI	4.6	KN3L	105.8	101.2	99.9	100.4	98.3	102.2	100.0	100.0
Electrical equipment	CJ	3.0	KN3M	90.8	101.2	97.4	108.0	103.0	99.7	100.0	95.1
Machinery and equipment n.e.c.	CK	6.1	KN3N	95.1	113.8	123.5	124.9	110.1	114.8	100.0	100.7
Transport equipment	CL	14.4	KN3O	60.2	73.9	81.4	84.9	91.4	94.5	100.0	103.6
Other manufacturing and repair	CM	9.4	KN3P	88.6	92.4	97.4	91.2	95.4	100.7	100.0	104.7
Total manufacturing	C	100.5	L2KX	93.2	97.4	99.6	98.1	97.2	100.0	100.0	100.9
Electricity, gas, steam and air conditioning supply	D	16.8	L2MW	108.7	113.2	106.3	105.3	105.1	99.0	100.0	102.6
Water supply, sewerage, waste mgmt and remediation	E	10.1	L2N2	86.0	87.3	92.3	92.2	96.1	96.7	100.0	105.3
Total production	B - E	139.5	L2KQ	98.3	101.4	100.8	98.0	97.3	98.8	100.0	101.3
Construction	F	60.6	L2N8	83.9	91.0	93.0	86.6	87.9	95.7	100.0	103.8
Total production and construction	B - F	200.1	L2KP	93.8	98.2	98.4	94.5	94.4	97.9	100.0	102.0

1 The weights shown are in proportion to total gross value added (GVA) in 2015 and are used to combine the industry output indices to calculate the totals. For 2014 and earlier, totals are calculated using the equivalent weights for the previous year (e.g. totals for 2009 use 2008 weights). Weights may not sum to totals due to rounding.

2 As GVA is expressed in index number form, it is inappropriate to show as a statistical adjustment any divergence from the other measures of GDP. Such an adjustment does, however, exist implicitly.

3 Because of differences in the annual and monthly production inquiries, estimates of current price output and gross value added by industry derived from the current price Input-Output Supply and Use Tables are not consistent with the equivalent measures of chained volume measures growth given in 2.3. These differences do not affect GDP totals.

2.3 Gross value added at basic prices: by industry[1,2,3]
Chained volume indices
continued

			Weight per 1000[1]									
			2015		2009	2010	2011	2012	2013	2014	2015	2016
Services	G-T											
Distribution, transport, hotels and restaurants	G-I											
Wholesale, retail, repair of motor vehicles and m/cycles	G	107.7	L2NE		83.8	84.5	85.7	86.6	90.9	95.6	100.0	105.0
Transportation and storage	H	44.6	L2NI		89.7	90.2	92.7	92.4	93.7	98.8	100.0	100.5
Accommodation and food service activities	I	29.3	L2NQ		87.0	89.0	91.1	94.9	92.5	95.2	100.0	105.2
Total distribution, transport, hotels and restaurants	G - I	181.7	L2ND		85.7	86.6	88.2	89.2	91.8	96.3	100.0	103.9
Information and communication	J											
Publishing, audiovisual and broadcasting activities	JA	16.0	L2NU		82.5	84.1	87.3	91.3	95.5	91.9	100.0	110.4
Telecommunications	JB	18.0	L2NZ		99.3	103.4	105.4	105.2	100.4	96.0	100.0	97.6
IT and other information service activities	JC	25.7	L2O3		71.9	78.7	79.5	84.6	88.3	94.7	100.0	110.8
Total information and communication	J	59.7	L2NT		81.9	86.6	88.4	92.0	93.7	94.3	100.0	106.7
Financial and insurance	K	67.8	L2O6		114.8	105.8	105.4	106.8	104.5	103.2	100.0	99.9
Real estate	L	139.2	L2OC		86.5	88.9	89.4	92.3	94.4	97.3	100.0	100.3
Professional and support	M-N											
Professional, scientific and technical activities	M											
Legal, accounting, management, architect, engineering etc	MA	55.1	L2OJ		76.6	77.1	79.9	82.9	88.7	94.7	100.0	103.7
Scientific research and development	MB	5.7	L2OQ		76.9	85.9	80.2	83.4	87.2	91.8	100.0	113.5
Other professional, scientific and technical activities	MC	15.4	L2OS		68.0	72.7	84.3	91.0	91.6	97.6	100.0	106.8
Total professional, scientific and technical activities	M	76.2	L2OI		74.9	76.9	80.8	84.4	89.2	95.1	100.0	105.1
Administrative and support service activities	N	46.2	L2OX		63.7	71.0	76.3	82.2	86.4	94.6	100.0	103.1
Total professional and support	M - N	122.4	L2OH		70.3	74.6	79.0	83.6	88.1	94.9	100.0	104.3
Government, health and education	O-Q											
Public admin, defence, compulsory social security	O	47.3	L2P8		113.7	112.1	107.2	105.8	103.4	101.8	100.0	98.6
Education	P	61.1	L2PA		93.5	92.2	92.7	95.7	96.5	98.3	100.0	100.0
Human health and social work activities	Q											
Human health activities	QA	54.9	L2PD		83.6	85.6	87.6	91.2	94.0	98.3	100.0	103.7
Residential care and social work activities	QB	18.7	L2PF		88.1	95.6	95.9	98.4	99.3	100.0	100.0	100.3
Total human health and social work activities	Q	73.6	L2PC		84.5	88.0	89.6	93.0	95.3	98.7	100.0	102.9
Total government, health and education	O - Q	182.0	L2P7		94.6	95.4	95.0	97.2	97.8	99.4	100.0	100.8
Other services	R-T											
Arts, entertainment and recreation	R	15.2	L2PJ		94.0	92.1	95.0	101.3	97.7	99.9	100.0	96.2
Other service activities	S	21.4	L2PP		86.7	83.9	89.1	86.0	86.3	95.9	100.0	106.2
Activities of households as employers, undiff. Goods	T	3.9	L2PT		94.8	105.5	99.4	104.8	107.1	101.4	100.0	118.9
Total other services	R - T	40.5	L2PI		89.7	88.6	92.0	93.0	92.1	97.9	100.0	103.7
Total service industries	G - T	793.3	L2NC		87.8	88.8	90.2	92.6	94.3	97.5	100.0	102.5
All industries	B.1g	1 000.0	CGCE		88.9	90.5	91.7	92.9	94.2	97.6	100.0	101.6

1 The weights shown are in proportion to total gross value added (GVA) in 2015 and are used to combine the industry output indices to calculate the totals. For 2014 and earlier, totals are calculated using the equivalent weights for the previous year (e.g. totals for 2009 use 2008 weights). Weights may not sum to totals due to rounding.

2 As GVA is expressed in index number form, it is inappropriate to show as a statistical adjustment any divergence from the other measures of GDP. Such an adjustment does, however, exist implicitly.

3 Because of differences in the annual and monthly production inquiries, estimates of current price output and gross value added by industry derived from the current price Input-Output Supply and Use Tables are not consistent with the equivalent measures of chained volume measures growth given in 2.3. These differences do not affect GDP totals.

2.4 Workforce jobs by Industry (SIC 2007)[1]

United Kingdom (thousands), not seasonally adjusted

			2009	2010	2011	2012	2013	2014	2015	2016
Agriculture, hunting and forestry; fishing		A								
Self-employment jobs	KI4P	ESE	175	190	199	199	165	200	163	169
Employee jobs and government supported trainees	KI4Q	EEM	213	227	204	225	203	219	205	199
Workforce jobs	KI4R	ETO	388	418	403	425	368	419	368	368
Production industries, including energy		B-E								
Self-employment jobs	KI4S	ESE	187	200	179	224	231	220	241	237
Employee jobs and government supported trainees	KI4T	EEM	2 806	2 743	2 757	2 775	2 709	2 779	2 805	2 825
Workforce jobs	KI4U	ETO	2 993	2 942	2 936	2 999	2 939	2 998	3 046	3 062
Construction		F								
Self-employment jobs	KI4V	ESE	775	775	803	814	804	835	785	872
Employee jobs and government supported trainees	KI4W	EEM	1 476	1 326	1 259	1 259	1 241	1 291	1 337	1 369
Workforce jobs	KI4X	ETO	2 252	2 100	2 062	2 073	2 045	2 125	2 122	2 241
Distribution		G								
Self-employment jobs	KI4Y	ESE	370	378	363	403	389	382	374	381
Employee jobs and government supported trainees	KI4Z	EEM	4 529	4 429	4 415	4 445	4 433	4 525	4 606	4 701
Workforce jobs	KI52	ETO	4 898	4 807	4 778	4 848	4 822	4 907	4 980	5 082
Transport, accommodation, information and communication		H-J								
Self-employment jobs	KI53	ESE	522	529	570	588	574	615	599	618
Employee jobs and government supported trainees	KI54	EEM	4 200	4 067	4 153	4 203	4 288	4 457	4 651	4 790
Workforce jobs	KI55	ETO	4 722	4 596	4 724	4 791	4 861	5 072	5 250	5 408
Financial and insurance activities		K								
Self-employment jobs	KI56	ESE	66	72	62	81	63	87	80	80
Employee jobs and government supported trainees	KI57	EEM	1 126	1 053	1 070	1 064	1 055	1 046	1 031	1 012
Workforce jobs	KI58	ETO	1 192	1 125	1 132	1 145	1 118	1 132	1 111	1 091
Real estate, professional and support		L-N								
Self-employment jobs	KI59	ESE	700	776	769	862	825	956	920	933
Employee jobs and government supported trainees	KI5A	EEM	4 541	4 552	4 563	4 793	4 934	5 230	5 422	5 576
Workforce jobs	KI5B	ETO	5 242	5 328	5 332	5 655	5 759	6 186	6 342	6 509
Public administration and defence, education and health		O-Q								
Self-employment jobs	KI5C	ESE	514	536	564	563	600	666	666	686
Employee jobs, HM forces and government supported trainees	KI5D	EEM	7 766	7 918	7 823	7 790	7 886	7 974	8 028	8 089
Workforce jobs	KI5E	ETO	8 280	8 453	8 387	8 352	8 486	8 640	8 693	8 775
Arts, entertainment and recreation and other services		R-T								
Self-employment jobs	KI5F	ESE	416	426	457	491	511	587	560	551
Employee jobs and government supported trainees	KI5G	EEM	1 344	1 346	1 332	1 298	1 307	1 351	1 393	1 424
Workforce jobs	KI5H	ETO	1 760	1 771	1 789	1 790	1 818	1 938	1 953	1 975
All industries		A-T								
Self-employment jobs	BCAG	ESE	3 726	3 881	3 966	4 225	4 161	4 547	4 389	4 526
Employee jobs, HM forces and government supported trainees	IK6H	EEM	28 001	27 660	27 576	27 852	28 056	28 870	29 477	29 986
Workforce jobs	YEJZ	ETO	31 727	31 541	31 543	32 078	32 217	33 417	33 865	34 511

1 Data sources are: Labour Force Survey for self-employment jobs; employer surveys for employee jobs; administrative sources for HM forces and government supported trainees. Figures as at June of each year.

United Kingdom National Accounts

The Blue Book
Chapter 03: Non-financial Corporations

2017 edition

Editors: Dean Goodway & Sarah Nightingale

Office for National Statistics

Chapter 3: Non-financial corporations

Non-financial corporations

Non-financial corporations produce goods and services for the market and do not, as a primary activity, deal in financial assets and liabilities.

This sector includes retailers, manufacturers, utilities, business service providers (such as accountancy and law firms), caterers, haulage companies, airlines, construction companies and farms, amongst others.

The non-financial sector is broken down into two sub-sectors:

- public sector non-financial corporations
- private sector non-financial corporations

Tables 3.1.1 to 3.1.11 relate to non-financial corporations as a whole. Tables 3.2.1 to 3.2.11 relate to public non-financial corporations, which are government-owned trading businesses. Tables 3.3.1 to 3.3.11 relate to private non-financial corporations, which are trading businesses in the private sector.

Further information on sector classifications and classification decisions can be found in the Economic statistics classifications pages.

3.1.1 Non-financial corporations
ESA 2010 sector S.11

			2009	2010	2011	2012	2013	2014	2015
Production account		I							
Resources									
Output		P.1							
Market output	FAIN	P.11	1 672 505	1 739 815	1 806 333	1 874 798	1 958 141	2 021 272	2 073 825
Output for own final use	FAIO	P.12	25 998	27 885	31 416	31 897	34 234	37 056	38 683
Total	FAFA	P.1	1 698 503	1 767 700	1 837 749	1 906 695	1 992 375	2 058 328	2 112 508
Total resources	FAFA	TR	1 698 503	1 767 700	1 837 749	1 906 695	1 992 375	2 058 328	2 112 508
Uses									
Intermediate consumption	FAIQ	P.2	897 830	936 414	976 089	1 015 994	1 056 699	1 080 050	1 101 827
Gross value added	FAIS	**B.1g**	**800 673**	**831 286**	**861 660**	**890 701**	**935 676**	**978 278**	**1 010 681**
Total uses	FAFA	T	1 698 503	1 767 700	1 837 749	1 906 695	1 992 375	2 058 328	2 112 508
Gross value added	FAIS	**B.1g**	**800 673**	**831 286**	**861 660**	**890 701**	**935 676**	**978 278**	**1 010 681**
less consumption of fixed capital	DBGF	P.51c	107 870	107 520	110 836	114 089	117 802	121 153	124 981
Value added, net	FAIT	B.1n	692 803	723 766	750 824	776 612	817 874	857 125	885 700

3.1.2 Non-financial corporations
ESA 2010 sector S.11

£ million

			2009	2010	2011	2012	2013	2014	2015
Distribution and use of income accounts		II							
Primary distribution of income account		II.1							
Generation of income account before deduction of fixed capital consumption		II.1.1							
Resources									
Total resources (gross value added)	FAIS	**B.1g**	**800 673**	**831 286**	**861 660**	**890 701**	**935 676**	**978 278**	**1 010 681**
Uses									
Compensation of employees		D.1							
Wages and salaries	FAKT	D.11	440 784	441 724	456 978	471 002	498 272	513 092	536 290
Employers' social contributions	FAKU	D.12	73 385	83 152	84 532	91 708	95 952	90 917	88 569
Total	FCFV	D.1	514 169	524 876	541 510	562 710	594 224	604 009	624 859
Taxes on production and imports, paid		D.2							
Production taxes other than on products	EACJ	D.29	22 040	22 522	23 711	25 146	26 431	27 021	27 890
less production subsidies other than on products	JQJV	D.39	3 069	2 228	1 693	1 993	2 140	2 595	3 115
Operating surplus, gross	NQBE	B.2g	267 533	286 116	298 132	304 838	317 161	349 843	361 047
Total uses (gross value added)	FAIS	**B.1g**	**800 673**	**831 286**	**861 660**	**890 701**	**935 676**	**978 278**	**1 010 681**
less consumption of fixed capital	DBGF	P.51c	107 870	107 520	110 836	114 089	117 802	121 153	124 981
Operating surplus, net	FAIR	B.2n	159 663	178 596	187 296	190 749	199 359	228 690	236 066

3.1.3 Non-financial corporations
ESA 2010 sector S.11

£ million

Allocation of primary income account		II.1.2	2009	2010	2011	2012	2013	2014	2015	2016
Resources										
Operating surplus, gross	NQBE	B.2g	267 533	286 116	298 132	304 838	317 161	349 843	361 047	370 689
Property income, received		D.4								
Interest		D.41								
Interest before FISIM allocation[1]	J4WQ	D.41g	9 335	9 205	9 343	8 934	9 644	9 635	9 684	10 676
plus FISIM[1]	IV89	P.119	3 305	2 664	3 749	3 585	3 047	4 835	5 514	5 753
Total	EABC	D.41	12 640	11 869	13 092	12 519	12 691	14 470	15 198	16 429
Distributed income of corporations	EABD	D.42	53 343	50 284	58 136	53 196	55 158	74 936	51 125	51 061
Reinvested earnings on foreign direct investment	WEYD	D.43	12 455	26 240	27 262	11 717	6 982	−19 005	−8 190	−7 594
Other investment income		D.44								
Attributable to insurance policy holders	L8GM	D.441	975	430	297	219	280	331	153	158
Attributable to collective investment fund shareholders		D.443								
Dividends	L8H9	D.4431	2	5	3	–	4	4	4	4
Retained earnings	L8HG	D.4432	4	8	4	4	4	4	4	5
Total	L8H2	D.443	6	13	7	4	8	8	8	9
Total other investment income	FAOF	D.44	981	443	304	223	288	339	161	167
Rent	FAOG	D.45	110	110	122	131	135	140	136	144
Total	FAKY	D.4	79 529	88 946	98 916	77 786	75 254	70 880	58 430	60 207
Total resources	FBXJ	TR	347 062	375 062	397 048	382 624	392 415	420 723	419 477	430 896
Uses										
Property income, paid		D.4								
Interest		D.41								
Interest before FISIM allocation[1]	J4WS	D.41g	49 368	40 974	39 046	41 236	41 862	40 325	36 478	38 074
less FISIM[1]	IV88	P.119	9 081	9 521	8 466	7 968	7 984	6 283	5 931	6 749
Total	EABG	D.41	40 287	31 453	30 580	33 268	33 878	34 042	30 547	31 325
Distributed income of corporations	NVCS	D.42	145 985	131 788	152 123	163 662	175 365	182 380	207 511	190 430
Of which: PNFCs dividends[2]	NETZ	D.421	118 078	100 660	121 222	132 857	141 453	147 856	171 166	154 369
Reinvested earnings on foreign direct investment	HDVB	D.43	−4 539	156	−5 971	−5 363	5 263	−1 055	−2 543	−99
Rent	FBXO	D.45	1 521	1 556	1 548	1 571	1 730	1 745	1 743	1 789
Total	FBXK	D.4	183 254	164 953	178 280	193 138	216 236	217 112	237 258	223 445
Balance of primary incomes, gross	NQBG	**B.5g**	**163 808**	**210 109**	**218 768**	**189 486**	**176 179**	**203 611**	**182 219**	**207 451**
Total uses	FBXJ	TU	347 062	375 062	397 048	382 624	392 415	420 723	419 477	430 896
less consumption of fixed capital	DBGF	P.51c	107 870	107 520	110 836	114 089	117 802	121 153	124 981	129 700
Balance of primary incomes, net	FBXQ	B.5n	55 938	102 589	107 932	75 397	58 377	82 458	57 238	77 751

1 Financial intermediation services indirectly measured.

3.1.4 Non-financial corporations
ESA 2010 sector S.11

£ million

			2009	2010	2011	2012	2013	2014	2015	2016
Secondary distribution of income account		II.2								
Resources										
Balance of primary incomes, gross	NQBG	**B.5g**	**163 808**	**210 109**	**218 768**	**189 486**	**176 179**	**203 611**	**182 219**	**207 451**
Net social contributions		D.61								
Employers' imputed social contributions	L8RD	D.612	4 293	3 337	3 025	3 459	3 457	3 506	3 568	3 198
Total	L8TP	D.61	4 293	3 337	3 025	3 459	3 457	3 506	3 568	3 198
Current transfers other than taxes,		D.7								
social contributions and benefits										
Non-life insurance claims	FCBP	D.72	5 578	5 775	3 745	3 523	6 458	5 700	4 923	5 623
Miscellaneous current transfers	CY8C	D.75	–	–	–	724	136	–	–	–
Total	NRJB	D.7	5 578	5 775	3 745	4 247	6 594	5 700	4 923	5 623
Total resources	FCBR	TR	173 679	219 221	225 538	197 192	186 230	212 817	190 710	216 272
Uses										
Current taxes on income, wealth etc.		D.5								
Taxes on income	FCBS	D.51	33 992	35 667	35 731	32 967	33 034	31 615	32 974	35 094
Social benefits other than social transfers in kind		D.62								
Other social insurance benefits	L8S3	D.622	4 293	3 337	3 025	3 459	3 457	3 506	3 568	3 198
Total	L8TD	D.62	4 293	3 337	3 025	3 459	3 457	3 506	3 568	3 198
Current transfers other than taxes,		D.7								
social contributions and benefits										
Net non-life insurance premiums	FCBY	D.71	5 578	5 775	3 745	3 523	6 458	5 700	4 923	5 623
Miscellaneous current transfers	CY8B	D.75	5 865	4 771	5 155	4 857	4 768	4 876	4 535	4 214
Total	FCBX	D.7	11 443	10 546	8 900	8 380	11 226	10 576	9 458	9 837
Gross disposable income	NRJD	**B.6g**	**123 951**	**169 671**	**177 882**	**152 386**	**138 513**	**167 120**	**144 710**	**168 143**
Total uses	FCBR	TU	173 679	219 221	225 538	197 192	186 230	212 817	190 710	216 272
less consumption of fixed capital	DBGF	P.51c	107 870	107 520	110 836	114 089	117 802	121 153	124 981	129 700
Disposable income, net	FCCF	B.6n	16 081	62 151	67 046	38 297	20 711	45 967	19 729	38 443

3.1.6 Non-financial corporations
ESA 2010 sector S.11

£ million

			2009	2010	2011	2012	2013	2014	2015	2016
Use of disposable income account		II.4.1								
Resources										
Total resources (gross disposable income)	NRJD	B.6g	**123 951**	**169 671**	**177 882**	**152 386**	**138 513**	**167 120**	**144 710**	**168 143**
Uses										
Total uses (gross saving)	NRJD	B.8g	**123 951**	**169 671**	**177 882**	**152 386**	**138 513**	**167 120**	**144 710**	**168 143**
less consumption of fixed capital	DBGF	P.51c	107 870	107 520	110 836	114 089	117 802	121 153	124 981	129 700
Saving, net	FCCF	B.8n	16 081	62 151	67 046	38 297	20 711	45 967	19 729	38 443

3.1.7 Non-financial corporations
ESA 2010 sector S.11

£ million

			2009	2010	2011	2012	2013	2014	2015	2016
Accumulation accounts		III								
Capital account		III.1								
Change in net worth due to saving and capital transfers account		III.1.1								
Changes in liabilities and net worth										
Gross saving	NRJD	**B.8g**	**123 951**	**169 671**	**177 882**	**152 386**	**138 513**	**167 120**	**144 710**	**168 143**
Capital transfers, receivable		D.9r								
Investment grants	FCCO	D.92r	7 517	6 749	5 276	3 927	4 858	4 451	4 402	4 073
Other capital transfers	LNZN	D.99r	4 074	−121	−153	−12	1	47	59	105
Total	FCCQ	D.9r	11 591	6 628	5 123	3 915	4 859	4 498	4 461	4 178
Capital transfers, payable		D.9p								
Capital taxes	QYKB	D.91p	–	–	–	–	–	–	–	–
Other capital transfers	JRWI	D.99p	843	773	887	861	1 512	1 483	1 481	1 629
Total	JRWJ	D.9p	843	773	887	861	1 512	1 483	1 481	1 629
Changes in net worth due to gross saving and capital transfers	FCCY	B.101g	134 699	175 526	182 118	155 440	141 860	170 135	147 690	170 692
Changes in assets										
Changes in net worth due to gross saving and capital transfers	FCCY	B.101g	134 699	175 526	182 118	155 440	141 860	170 135	147 690	170 692
less consumption of fixed capital	DBGF	P.51c	107 870	107 520	110 836	114 089	117 802	121 153	124 981	129 700
Changes in net worth due to net saving and capital transfers	FCCV	B.101n	26 829	68 006	71 282	41 351	24 058	48 982	22 709	40 992
Acquisition of non-financial assets account		III.1.2								
Changes in liabilities and net worth										
Changes in net worth due to net saving and capital transfers	FCCV	B.101n	26 829	68 006	71 282	41 351	24 058	48 982	22 709	40 992
Consumption of fixed capital	DBGF	P.51c	107 870	107 520	110 836	114 089	117 802	121 153	124 981	129 700
Changes in net worth due to gross saving and capital transfers	FCCY	B.101g	134 699	175 526	182 118	155 440	141 860	170 135	147 690	170 692
Changes in assets										
Gross capital formation		P.5								
Gross fixed capital formation	DBGP	P.51g	127 582	132 759	139 924	150 972	161 143	171 910	180 040	180 510
Changes in inventories	DBGM	P.52	−13 545	5 108	2 628	1 919	4 461	12 541	7 703	8 186
Acquisitions less disposals of valuables[1]	NPOV	P.53	427	55	−8	−107	276	−1 170	−404	576
Total	FCCZ	P.5	114 464	137 922	142 544	152 784	165 880	183 281	187 339	189 272
Acquisitions less disposals of non-produced non-financial assets	FCFY	NP	1 005	1 352	1 513	1 772	1 848	2 825	2 900	3 218
Net lending(+) / net borrowing(-)	EABO	**B.9n**	**19 230**	**36 252**	**38 061**	**884**	**−25 868**	**−15 971**	**−42 549**	**−21 798**
Total change in assets	FCCY	Total	134 699	175 526	182 118	155 440	141 860	170 135	147 690	170 692

1 Acquisitions less disposals of valuables can be a volatile series but any
  volatility is likely to be GDP neutral as it is offset in UK trade figures

3.1.8 Non-financial corporations
ESA 2010 sector S.11 Unconsolidated

£ million

			2009	2010	2011	2012	2013	2014	2015	2016
Financial account		III.2								
Net acquisition of financial assets		F.A								
Currency and deposits		F.2								
Currency	NGIJ	F.21	524	226	236	196	311	342	616	919
Transferable deposits		F.22								
Deposits with UK Monetary financial institutions	NGIL	F.22N1	19 425	16 249	−1 613	17 098	20 964	28 117	37 479	27 390
Of which: foreign currency deposits with UK banks	NGIN	F.22N12	9 612	11 929	−7 662	6 913	−3 676	482	2 086	10 554
Deposits with rest of the world Monetary financial institutions	NGIP	F.22N9	802	761	−4 130	−2 548	3 761	23 338	9 761	11 026
Other deposits	NGIQ	F.29	−1 236	−1 180	306	−584	−531	−461	−583	−358
Total	NGII	F.2	19 515	16 056	−5 201	14 162	24 505	51 336	47 273	38 977
Debt securities		F.3								
Short-term		F.31								
Issued by UK central government	NGIT	F.31N1	−245	17	33	386	214	38	289	−315
Issued by UK local government	NGIX	F.31N2								
Issued by UK Monetary financial institutions	NGIY	F.31N5	−63	−1 096	−2 801	133	361	537	2 642	1 360
Money market instruments issued by other UK residents	NGJD	F.31N6	−1 707	1 806	522	−120	202	−1 590	351	−2 580
Money market instruments issued by rest of the world	NGJE	F.31N9	1 615	1 936	1 800	−3 911	−1 001	1 615	4 519	1 425
Long-term		F.32								
Issued by UK central government	NGJG	F.32N1	674	774	152	−720	−314	45	−620	−23
Issued by UK local government	NGJJ	F.32N2	–	–	–	–	–	–	–	–
Issued by UK Monetary financial institutions and other UK residents	KVG8	F.32N5-6	−1 261	267	1 068	−22	4 649	7 446	5 684	3 770
Issued by rest of the world	NGJO	F.32N9	−1 285	4 522	−189	169	−146	7 284	−369	−608
Total	NGIR	F.3	−2 272	8 226	585	−4 085	3 965	15 375	12 496	3 029
Loans		F.4								
Long-term		F.42								
Direct investment	NGKB	F.421	−47 561	−15 893	−8 741	−12 698	11 118	28 107	−25 062	28 336
Secured on dwellings	NGKE	F.422	–	–	–	–	–	–	–	–
Finance leasing	NGKI	F.423	142	−1 526	−860	−199	−86	−78	−82	546
Other long-term loans		F.424								
By UK residents	NGKJ	F.424N1	5 834	10 658	7 739	631	−4 714	17 312	22 497	−8 625
Total	NGJT	F.4	−41 585	−6 761	−1 862	−12 266	6 318	45 341	−2 647	20 257
Equity and investment fund shares/units		F.5								
Equity		F.51								
Listed UK shares[1]	NGKQ	F.511N1	6 570	−233	9 674	634	−3 294	−8 140	−2	16 492
Unlisted UK shares[1]	NGKR	F.512N1	8 459	1 693	5 217	16 067	10 014	6 793	8 548	17 390
Other equity		F.519								
UK shares and bonds issued by other UK residents	NSQC	F.519N7	–	–	–	–	–	–	–	–
Shares and other equity issued by rest of the world	NGKV	F.519N9	−642	34 965	48 942	14 449	17 811	−84 909	−11 794	986
Investment fund shares/units		F.52								
UK mutual funds' shares	NGKZ	F.52N1	11	14	3	3	8	16	31	20
Total	NGKL	F.5	14 398	36 439	63 836	31 153	24 539	−86 240	−3 217	34 888
Insurance, pensions and standardised guarantee schemes		F.6								
Non-life insurance technical reserves	NGLE	F.61	−2 164	−4 031	−2 447	−568	−137	–	−209	63
Total	NPXB	F.6	−2 164	−4 031	−2 447	−568	−137	–	−209	63
Financial derivatives and employee stock options	MN5G	F.7	−2 928	−981	−8 096	4 419	3 393	−6 817	−3 120	−533
Of which: financial derivatives	NGJP	F.71	−2 928	−981	−8 096	4 419	3 393	−6 817	−3 120	−533
Other accounts receivable	NGLF	F.8	2 696	−13 087	554	13 017	−3 102	2 495	−1 323	6 839
Total net acquisition of financial assets	NRGP	F.A	−12 340	35 861	47 369	45 832	59 481	21 490	49 253	103 520

3.1.8 Non-financial corporations
ESA 2010 sector S.11 Unconsolidated
continued

£ million

			2009	2010	2011	2012	2013	2014	2015	2016
Financial account		III.2								
Net acquisition of financial liabilities		F.L								
Currency and deposits		F.2								
Other deposits	A4VS	F.29	–	–	–	–	–	–	–	–
Total	A4VR	F.2	–	–	–	–	–	–	–	–
Debt securities		F.3								
Short-term		F.31								
Money market instruments issued by other UK residents	NGMH	F.31N6	−5 808	3 934	8 082	−6 158	2 387	−1 689	−2 739	1 953
Long-term		F.32								
Issued by Monetary financial institutions and other UK residents	KVI4	F.32N5-6	29 802	8 889	19 895	12 201	23 495	14 003	25 706	25 879
Total	NGLV	F.3	23 994	12 823	27 977	6 043	25 882	12 314	22 967	27 832
Loans		F.4								
Short-term		F.41								
By UK Monetary financial institutions	NGMZ	F.41N1	−49 175	−28 595	−13 790	−17 246	−9 736	−3 946	5 681	15 491
By rest of the world	NGND	F.41N9	−6 171	−3 235	−12 992	−217	563	−5 899	5 167	3 002
Long-term		F.42								
Direct investment	NGNF	F.421	−34 838	−5 342	−3 703	310	−3 554	21 074	638	16 970
Secured on dwellings	G9JS	F.422	3 226	1 095	2 867	−234	486	−823	−1 120	−120
Finance leasing	NGNM	F.423	228	−1 330	−513	141	258	271	267	265
Other long-term loans		F.424								
By UK residents	NGNN	F.424N1	−355	8 026	4 123	21 665	39 097	26 987	−8 188	28 301
By rest of the world	NGNO	F.424N9	−4	–	–	–	−1	–	–	–
Total	NGMX	F.4	−87 089	−29 381	−24 008	4 419	27 113	37 664	2 445	63 909
Equity and investment fund shares/units		F.5								
Equity		F.51								
Listed UK shares	NGNU	F.511N1	32 864	11 623	3 272	1 027	5 849	−30 284	11 651	−97 353
Unlisted UK shares	NGNV	F.512N1	11 135	13 647	−1 693	15 533	12 152	9 993	15 240	123 919
Other equity		F.519								
Other UK equity	NGNW	F.519N6	−4 908	−528	189	−562	−740	−1 094	−1 345	−968
UK shares and bonds issued by other UK residents	NSQD	F.519N7	–	–	–	–	–	–	–	–
Total	NGNP	F.5	39 091	24 742	1 768	15 998	17 261	−21 385	25 546	25 598
Insurance, pensions and standardised guarantee schemes		F.6								
Pension schemes[1]	MA2M	F.6M	7 243	8 277	8 388	8 843	9 718	9 411	9 186	9 862
Total	NPXC	F.6	7 243	8 277	8 388	8 843	9 718	9 411	9 186	9 862
Financial derivatives and employee stock options	MN62	F.7	1 388	1 418	1 465	1 491	1 546	1 613	1 669	1 714
Other accounts payable	NGOJ	F.8	−1 534	1 255	6 809	4 772	1 306	2 997	6 963	8 362
Total net acquisition of financial liabilities	NRGR	F.L	−16 907	19 134	22 399	41 566	82 826	42 614	68 776	137 277
Net lending(+) / net borrowing(-)		B.9								
Total net acquisition of financial assets	NRGP	F.A	−12 340	35 861	47 369	45 832	59 481	21 490	49 253	103 520
less total net acquisition of financial liabilities	NRGR	F.L	−16 907	19 134	22 399	41 566	82 826	42 614	68 776	137 277
Net lending(+) / borrowing(-) from the financial account	NYNT	B.9f	4 567	16 727	24 970	4 266	−23 345	−21 124	−19 523	−33 757
Statistical discrepancy between financial and non-financial accounts	NYPF	dB.9	14 663	19 525	13 091	−3 382	−2 523	5 153	−23 026	11 959
Net lending (+) / borrowing (-) from non-financial accounts	EABO	B.9n	19 230	36 252	38 061	884	−25 868	−15 971	−42 549	−21 798

1 F.63 Pension entitlements, F.64 Claims on pension funds on pension managers, F.65 Entitlements to non-pension benefits

3.1.9 Non-financial corporations
ESA 2010 sector S.11

			2013	2014	2015	2016
Other changes in assets account		**III.3**				
Other changes in volume of assets account		**III.3.1**				
Changes in net worth due to other changes in volume of assets		**B.102**				
Monetary gold and special drawing rights	H286	AF.1	–	–	–	–
Currency and deposits	M9LX	AF.2	–961	432	–1 701	–1 897
Debt securities	M9ZG	AF.3	724	–1 846	–989	–5 519
Loans	N493	AF.4	52 883	28 196	–34 679	9 302
Equity and investment fund shares/units	N4B5	AF.5	–	–	–	–
Insurance, pensions and standardised guarantee schemes	N4D7	AF.6	–	–	–	–
Financial derivatives and employee stock options	N4F5	AF.7	–	–	–	–
Other accounts receivable/payable	N4H3	AF.8	1 221	–6 279	383	–2 775
Total	CWTE	**B.102**	53 867	20 503	–36 986	–889

3.1.10 Non-financial corporations
ESA 2010 sector S.11

£ million

			2013	2014	2015	2016
Other changes in assets account		III.3				
Revaluation account		III.3.2				
Changes in net worth due to nominal holding gains and losses		B.103				
Monetary gold and special drawing rights	H28B	AF.1	–	–	–	–
Currency and deposits	M9R2	AF.2	3 791	–13 396	–3 482	34 957
Debt securities	N482	AF.3	11 485	15 161	35 602	–2 213
Loans	N4A4	AF.4	18 928	25 859	–10 200	–24 107
Equity and investment fund shares/units	N4C6	AF.5	–184 692	–2 762	80 498	–118 656
Insurance, pensions and standardised guarantee schemes	N4E6	AF.6	136 233	–293 424	67 140	–48 804
Financial derivatives and employee stock options	N4G4	AF.7	1 391	1 898	1 825	1 501
Other accounts receivable/payable	N4I4	AF.8	–19	887	944	–6 159
Total	CWU6	**B.103**	–12 883	–265 777	172 327	–163 481

3.1.11 Non-financial corporations
ESA 2010 sector S.11 Unconsolidated

£ billion

			2009	2010	2011	2012	2013	2014	2015	2016
Financial balance sheet at end of period		IV.3								
Non-financial assets	NG2I	AN	2 268.1	2 413.3	2 499.8	2 544.8	2 678.4	2 883.7	3 002.2	3 125.7
Total financial assets		AF.A								
Currency and deposits		AF.2								
Currency	NNZG	AF.21	5.2	5.4	5.6	5.8	6.0	6.4	7.0	7.8
Transferable deposits		AF.22								
Deposits with UK Monetary financial institutions	NNZI	AF.22N1	281.0	301.8	296.8	315.2	334.2	363.0	399.4	436.1
Of which: foreign currency deposits	NNZK	AF.22N12	48.7	62.2	55.0	62.0	55.8	55.9	60.4	81.6
Deposits with rest of world Monetary financial institutions	NNZM	AF.22N9	123.9	129.3	127.8	142.5	150.9	160.5	165.7	200.3
Other deposits	NNZN	AF.29	9.0	8.3	8.2	7.8	7.4	7.1	6.9	6.9
Total	NNZF	AF.2	419.1	444.7	438.5	471.3	498.6	537.0	579.1	651.1
Debt securities		AF.3								
Short-term		AF.31								
Issued by UK central government	NNZQ	AF.31N1	0.3	0.3	0.4	0.8	1.0	1.0	1.3	1.0
Issued by UK local government	NNZU	AF.31N2	–	–	–	–	–	–	–	–
Issued by UK Monetary financial institutions	NNZV	AF.31N5	11.5	10.4	7.6	7.8	8.2	9.5	12.4	14.1
Issued by other UK residents	NOLO	AF.31N6	5.9	7.7	8.2	8.1	8.2	6.9	7.4	4.9
Issued by rest of the world	NOLP	AF.31N9	2.9	4.8	6.7	2.1	0.8	2.6	7.2	8.7
Long-term		AF.32								
Issued by UK central government	NOLR	AF.32N1	2.6	3.4	3.6	2.9	2.7	3.2	2.7	2.9
Issued by UK local government	NOLU	AF.32N2	–	–	–	–	–	–	–	–
Issued by UK Monetary financial institutions and other UK residents[1]	KVF9	AF.32N5-6	8.3	9.3	11.4	11.3	14.8	32.2	37.9	45.2
Issued by rest of the world	NOLZ	AF.32N9	18.0	22.9	27.7	26.7	25.6	9.7	9.4	13.1
Total	NNZO	AF.3	49.6	59.0	65.6	59.6	61.3	65.1	78.3	89.9
Loans		AF.4								
Long-term		AF.42								
Direct investment	NOMM	AF.421	243.2	243.0	220.3	242.3	257.4	272.0	222.1	230.2
Secured on dwellings	NOMP	AF.422	–	–	–	–	–	–	–	–
Finance leasing	NOMT	AF.423	8.3	7.1	6.2	6.0	6.0	6.3	6.7	7.3
Other long-term loans		AF.424								
By UK residents	NOMU	AF.424N1	11.3	40.1	39.5	39.5	38.8	39.2	39.6	39.8
Total	NOME	AF.4	262.8	290.1	266.0	287.8	302.2	317.5	268.4	277.3
Equity and investment fund shares/units		AF.5								
Equity		AF.51								
Listed UK shares[1]	NONB	AF.511N1	45.0	40.6	36.9	39.6	43.7	39.6	33.2	31.5
Unlisted UK shares[1]	NONC	AF.512N1	72.9	71.3	67.4	68.7	76.6	75.2	76.2	77.7
UK shares and bonds issued by other UK residents[1]	NSQW	AF.519N7	–	–	–	–	–	–	–	–
Shares and other equity issued by rest of the world	NONG	AF.519N9	694.1	750.3	786.4	770.9	784.4	759.5	804.9	886.6
Investment fund shares/units		AF.52								
UK mutual funds' shares	NONK	AF.52N1	0.4	0.5	0.4	0.5	0.6	0.7	0.8	0.8
Total	NOMW	AF.5	812.4	862.7	891.1	879.6	905.3	875.0	915.1	996.6
Insurance, pensions and standardised guarantee schemes		AF.6								
Non-life insurance technical reserves	NONP	AF.61	11.0	7.2	4.7	4.2	4.0	4.0	3.8	3.9
Total	NPYN	AF.6	11.0	7.2	4.7	4.2	4.0	4.0	3.8	3.9
Financial derivatives and employee stock options	MMU6	AF.7	24.3	25.3	29.7	28.6	25.6	30.0	31.0	37.0
Of which: financial derivatives	JX25	AF.71	24.3	25.3	29.7	28.6	25.6	30.0	31.0	37.0
Other accounts receivable	NONQ	AF.8	132.0	129.8	130.8	132.3	133.2	131.2	131.5	129.8
Total financial assets	NNZB	**AF.A**	1 711.2	1 818.8	1 826.4	1 863.4	1 930.2	1 959.8	2 007.2	2 185.7

3.1.11 Non-financial corporations
ESA 2010 sector S.11 Unconsolidated

continued

£ billion

			2009	2010	2011	2012	2013	2014	2015	2016
Financial balance sheet at end of period		IV.3								
Total financial liabilities		AF.L								
Currency and deposits		AF.2								
Other deposits	NOOF	AF.29	–	–	–	–	–	–	–	–
Total	NONX	AF.2	–	–	–	–	–	–	–	–
Debt securities		AF.3								
Short-term		AF.31								
Money market instruments issued by other UK residents	NOOS	AF.31N6	22.5	27.7	35.5	28.2	29.9	30.3	28.7	36.6
Long-term		AF.32								
Issued by UK Monetary financial institutions and other UK residents[1]	KVH6	AF.32N5-6	279.1	277.1	307.6	331.3	341.1	328.1	318.7	355.0
Total	NOOG	AF.3	301.6	304.8	343.1	359.6	371.0	358.4	347.4	391.6
Loans		AF.4								
Short-term		AF.41								
By UK Monetary financial institutions	NOPK	AF.41N1	476.5	434.6	400.9	377.1	356.1	340.1	337.2	355.8
By rest of the world	NOPO	AF.41N91	130.8	127.6	113.8	117.8	120.4	107.3	112.8	126.1
Long-term		AF.42								
Direct investment	NOPQ	AF.421	328.7	333.9	336.7	419.2	399.3	388.2	373.6	376.3
Secured on dwellings	G9JO	AF.422	43.5	40.7	43.6	42.9	43.1	42.1	41.0	41.4
Finance leasing	NOPX	AF.423	28.0	26.7	26.1	26.3	26.5	26.8	27.1	27.3
Other long-term loans		AF.424								
By UK residents	NOPY	AF.424N1	211.5	251.7	250.7	247.4	248.4	243.0	256.7	288.7
By rest of the world	NOPZ	AF.424N9	0.9	0.9	0.9	0.9	0.9	0.8	0.8	0.9
Total	NOPI	AF.4	1 219.8	1 216.0	1 172.7	1 231.4	1 194.7	1 148.3	1 149.2	1 216.5
Equity and investment fund shares/units		AF.5								
Equity		AF.51								
Listed UK shares[1]	NOQF	AF.511N1	1 200.3	1 361.3	1 275.5	1 308.5	1 470.7	1 452.1	1 475.0	1 506.7
Unlisted UK shares[1]	NOQG	AF.512N1	631.7	709.4	702.5	815.7	855.1	907.3	870.2	1 027.0
Other equity		AF.519								
Other UK equity	NOQH	AF.519N6	127.5	129.7	131.6	134.1	135.6	139.3	141.9	144.3
UK shares and bonds issued by other UK residents[1]	NSQX	AF.519N7	–	–	–	–	–	–	–	–
Total	NOQA	AF.5	1 959.5	2 200.4	2 109.6	2 258.3	2 461.4	2 498.7	2 487.1	2 678.0
Insurance, pensions and standardised guarantee schemes		AF.6								
Pension schemes[2]	M9VI	AF.6M	392.4	348.0	579.7	499.2	372.7	675.5	617.6	676.3
Total	NPYO	AF.6	392.4	348.0	579.7	499.2	372.7	675.5	617.6	676.3
Financial derivatives and employee stock options	MMX2	AF.7	36.9	39.9	52.0	46.8	40.6	51.5	55.4	62.3
Of which: financial derivatives	JX26	AF.71	32.7	35.7	47.7	42.4	36.1	46.8	50.6	57.3
Other accounts payable	NOQU	AF.8	158.4	159.9	166.5	168.5	172.7	176.6	183.9	192.6
Total financial liabilities	NONT	**AF.L**	4 068.7	4 269.0	4 423.6	4 563.9	4 613.1	4 909.0	4 840.6	5 217.3
Financial net worth		**BF.90**								
Total financial assets	NNZB	AF.A	1 711.2	1 818.8	1 826.4	1 863.4	1 930.2	1 959.8	2 007.2	2 185.7
less total financial liabilities	NONT	AF.L	4 068.7	4 269.0	4 423.6	4 563.9	4 613.1	4 909.0	4 840.6	5 217.3
Financial net worth	NYOM	**BF.90**	−2 357.4	−2 450.2	−2 597.2	−2 700.5	−2 682.8	−2 949.2	−2 833.4	−3 031.5
Net worth										
Non-financial assets	NG2I	AN	2 268.1	2 413.3	2 499.8	2 544.8	2 678.4	2 883.7	3 002.2	3 125.7
Financial net worth	NYOM	BF.90	−2 357.4	−2 450.2	−2 597.2	−2 700.5	−2 682.8	−2 949.2	−2 833.4	−3 031.5
Net worth	CGRV	**B.90**	−89.4	−36.9	−97.4	−155.6	−4.4	−65.5	168.8	94.1

1 Prior to 1990 it is not possible to distinguish some elements of AF.32N5-6, AF.511N1 and AF.512N1. These elements are shown combined as AF.519N7
2 F.63 Pension entitlements, F.64 Claims on pension funds on pension managers, F.65 Entitlements to non-pension benefits

3.2.1 Public non-financial corporations
ESA 2010 sector S.11001

			2009	2010	2011	2012	2013	2014	2015
Production account		I							
Resources									
Output		P.1							
Market output	FCZI	P.11	51 673	53 465	53 887	54 973	52 665	47 025	47 573
Output for own final use	GIRZ	P.12	–	–	–	–	–	–	–
Total	FCZG	P.1	51 673	53 465	53 887	54 973	52 665	47 025	47 573
Total resources	FCZG	TR	51 673	53 465	53 887	54 973	52 665	47 025	47 573
Uses									
Intermediate consumption	QZLQ	P.2	23 732	23 671	23 981	23 427	21 915	20 287	20 402
Gross value added	FACW	**B.1g**	**27 941**	**29 794**	**29 906**	**31 546**	**30 750**	**26 738**	**27 171**
Total uses	FCZG	TU	51 673	53 465	53 887	54 973	52 665	47 025	47 573
Gross value added	FACW	**B.1g**	**27 941**	**29 794**	**29 906**	**31 546**	**30 750**	**26 738**	**27 171**
less consumption of fixed capital	NSRM	P.51c	9 438	9 330	9 457	9 560	9 950	10 194	10 352
Value added, net	FACX	B.1n	18 503	20 464	20 449	21 986	20 800	16 544	16 819

3.2.2 Public non-financial corporations
ESA 2010 sector S.11001

			2009	2010	2011	2012	2013	2014	2015
Distribution and use of income accounts		II							
Primary distribution of income account		II.1							
Generation of income account before deduction of fixed capital consumption		II.1.1							
Resources									
Total resources (gross value added)	FACW	**B.1g**	**27 941**	**29 794**	**29 906**	**31 546**	**30 750**	**26 738**	**27 171**
Uses									
Compensation of employees		D.1							
Wages and salaries	FAIZ	D.11	14 242	14 230	13 670	14 499	13 264	9 945	9 993
Employers' social contributions	FAOH	D.12	2 513	2 511	2 412	2 558	2 340	1 754	1 764
Total	FDDI	D.1	16 755	16 741	16 082	17 057	15 604	11 699	11 757
Taxes on production and imports, paid		D.2							
Production taxes other than on products	FAOK	D.29	76	94	79	81	64	8	8
less production subsidies other than on products	ARDD	D.39	1 983	963	362	615	516	623	792
Operating surplus, gross	NRJT	B.2g	13 093	13 922	14 107	15 023	15 598	15 654	16 198
Total uses (gross value added)	FACW	**B.1g**	**27 941**	**29 794**	**29 906**	**31 546**	**30 750**	**26 738**	**27 171**
less consumption of fixed capital	NSRM	P.51c	9 438	9 330	9 457	9 560	9 950	10 194	10 352
Operating surplus, net	FAOO	B.2n	3 655	4 592	4 650	5 463	5 648	5 460	5 846

3.2.3 Public non-financial corporations
ESA 2010 sector S.11001

£ million

			2009	2010	2011	2012	2013	2014	2015	2016
Allocation of primary income account		II.1.2								
before deduction of fixed capital consumption										
Resources										
Operating surplus, gross	NRJT	B.2g	13 093	13 922	14 107	15 023	15 598	15 654	16 198	16 190
Property income, received		D.4								
Interest		D.41								
Interest before FISIM allocation[1]	NENH	D.41g	426	434	407	408	394	410	371	428
plus FISIM[1]	C7RL	P.119	−8	2	4	11	13	30	24	14
Total	CPBV	D.41	418	436	411	419	407	440	395	442
Distributed income of corporations	FACT	D.42	9	106	110	131	181	311	388	167
Reinvested earnings on foreign direct investment	WUHM	D.43	118	61	61	61	71	117	63	64
Other investment income		D.44								
Attributable to insurance policy holders	KZH8	D.441	−	−	−	−	−	−	−	−
Attributable to collective investment fund shareholders		D.443								
Dividends	KZI2	D.4431	−	−	−	−	−	−	−	−
Retained earnings	KZI3	D.4432	−	−	−	−	−	−	−	−
Total	L5TY	D.443	−	−	−	−	−	−	−	−
Total	FAOT	D.44	−	−	−	−	−	−	−	−
Total	FAOP	D.4	545	603	582	611	659	868	846	673
Total resources	FAOU	TR	13 638	14 525	14 689	15 634	16 257	16 522	17 044	16 863
Uses										
Property income, paid		D.4								
Interest		D.41								
Interest before FISIM allocation[1]	NENG	D.41g	4 329	3 633	3 546	3 539	3 905	3 904	4 423	4 414
less FISIM[1]	D8KD	P.119	58	38	42	24	13	8	7	17
Total	XAQZ	D.41	4 271	3 595	3 504	3 515	3 892	3 896	4 416	4 397
Distributed income of corporations	ZOYB	D.42	839	760	1 052	1 252	1 286	952	889	835
Rent	FAOZ	D.45	−	−	−	−	−	−	−	−
Total	FAOV	D.4	5 110	4 355	4 556	4 767	5 178	4 848	5 305	5 232
Balance of primary incomes, gross	NRJX	**B.5g**	**8 528**	**10 170**	**10 133**	**10 867**	**11 079**	**11 674**	**11 739**	**11 631**
Total uses	FAOU	T	13 638	14 525	14 689	15 634	16 257	16 522	17 044	16 863
less consumption of fixed capital	NSRM	P.51c	9 438	9 330	9 457	9 560	9 950	10 194	10 352	10 523
Balance of primary incomes, net	FARX	B.5n	−910	840	676	1 307	1 129	1 480	1 387	1 108

1 Financial intermediation services indirectly measured

3.2.4 Public non-financial corporations
ESA 2010 sector S.11001

£ million

			2009	2010	2011	2012	2013	2014	2015	2016
Secondary distribution of income account		II.2								
Resources										
Balance of primary incomes, gross	NRJX	**B.5g**	**8 528**	**10 170**	**10 133**	**10 867**	**11 079**	**11 674**	**11 739**	**11 631**
Net social contributions		D.61								
Employers' imputed social contributions	L8RH	D.612	186	152	127	150	120	96	99	90
Total	L8TT	D.61	186	152	127	150	120	96	99	90
Current transfers other than taxes, social contributions and benefits		D.7								
Net non-life insurance claims	FDDF	D.72	–	–	–	–	–	–	–	–
Miscellaneous current transfers	CY89	D.75	–	–	–	724	136	–	–	–
Total	FDEK	D.7	–	–	–	724	136	–	–	–
Total resources	FDDH	TR	8 714	10 322	10 260	11 741	11 335	11 770	11 838	11 721
Uses										
Current taxes on income, wealth etc.		D.5								
Taxes on income	FCCS	D.51	251	149	109	106	73	35	45	73
Social security benefits other than social transfers in kind		D.62								
Other social insurance benefits	L8S7	D.622	186	152	127	150	120	96	99	90
Total	L8TF	D.62	186	152	127	150	120	96	99	90
Current transfers other than taxes, social contributions and benefits		D.7								
Net non-life insurance premiums	FDDM	D.71	–	–	–	–	–	–	–	–
Miscellaneous current transfers	CY87	D.75	–	–	–	–	–	–	–	–
Total	FDDL	D.7	–	–	–	–	–	–	–	–
Gross disposable income	NRKD	**B.6g**	**8 277**	**10 021**	**10 024**	**11 485**	**11 142**	**11 639**	**11 694**	**11 558**
Total uses	FDDH	TU	8 714	10 322	10 260	11 741	11 335	11 770	11 838	11 721
less consumption of fixed capital	NSRM	P.51c	9 438	9 330	9 457	9 560	9 950	10 194	10 352	10 523
Disposable income, net	FDDP	B.6n	–1 161	691	567	1 925	1 192	1 445	1 342	1 035

3.2.6 Public non-financial corporations
ESA 2010 sector S.11001

£ million

			2009	2010	2011	2012	2013	2014	2015	2016
Use of disposable income account		II.4.1								
Resources										
Total resources (gross disposable income)	NRKD	**B.6g**	**8 277**	**10 021**	**10 024**	**11 485**	**11 142**	**11 639**	**11 694**	**11 558**
Uses										
Total uses (gross saving)	NRKD	**B.8g**	**8 277**	**10 021**	**10 024**	**11 485**	**11 142**	**11 639**	**11 694**	**11 558**
less consumption of fixed capital	NSRM	P.51c	9 438	9 330	9 457	9 560	9 950	10 194	10 352	10 523
Saving, net	FDDP	B.8n	−1 161	691	567	1 925	1 192	1 445	1 342	1 035

3.2.7 Public non-financial corporations
ESA 2010 sector S.11001

£ million

			2009	2010	2011	2012	2013	2014	2015	2016
Accumulation accounts		III								
Capital account		III.1								
Change in net worth due to saving and capital transfers account		III.1.1								
Changes in liabilities and net worth										
Gross saving	NRKD	**B.8g**	**8 277**	**10 021**	**10 024**	**11 485**	**11 142**	**11 639**	**11 694**	**11 558**
Capital transfers, receivable		D.9r								
Investment grants	FDBV	D.92r	4 615	4 500	3 567	2 268	2 893	2 218	1 898	1 478
Other capital transfers	NZGD	D.99r	4 258	84	47	63	54	61	64	55
Total	FDBU	D.9r	8 873	4 584	3 614	2 331	2 947	2 279	1 962	1 533
Other capital transfers	ZMLL	D.99p	83	73	80	97	118	111	100	110
Changes in net worth due to gross saving and capital transfers	FDEG	B.101g	17 067	14 532	13 558	13 719	13 971	13 807	13 556	12 981
Changes in assets										
Changes in net worth due to gross saving and capital transfers	FDEG	B.101g	17 067	14 532	13 558	13 719	13 971	13 807	13 556	12 981
less consumption of fixed capital	NSRM	P.51c	9 438	9 330	9 457	9 560	9 950	10 194	10 352	10 523
Changes in net worth due to net saving and capital transfers	FDED	B.101n	7 629	5 202	4 101	4 159	4 021	3 613	3 204	2 458
Acquisition of non-financial assets account		III.1.2								
Changes in liabilities and net worth										
Changes in net worth due to net saving and capital transfers	FDED	B.101n	7 629	5 202	4 101	4 159	4 021	3 613	3 204	2 458
Consumption of fixed capital	NSRM	P.51c	9 438	9 330	9 457	9 560	9 950	10 194	10 352	10 523
Changes in net worth due to gross saving and capital transfers	FDEG	B.101g	17 067	14 532	13 558	13 719	13 971	13 807	13 556	12 981
Changes in assets										
Gross capital formation		P.5								
Gross fixed capital formation	FCCJ	P.51g	14 262	13 718	12 831	12 245	11 844	13 319	13 260	13 593
Changes in inventories	DHHL	P.52	−73	48	22	1	31	81	41	1
Total	FDEH	P.5	14 189	13 766	12 853	12 246	11 875	13 400	13 301	13 594
Acquisitions less disposals of non-produced non-financial assets	FDEJ	NP	3 784	3 866	2 360	1 888	1 171	2 395	1 678	1 899
Net lending (+) / net borrowing (-)	CPCM	**B.9n**	**−906**	**−3 100**	**−1 655**	**−415**	**925**	**−1 988**	**−1 423**	**−2 512**
Total change in assets	FDEG	B.101g	17 067	14 532	13 558	13 719	13 971	13 807	13 556	12 981

3.2.8 Public non-financial corporations
ESA 2010 sector S.11001 Unconsolidated

£ million

			2009	2010	2011	2012	2013	2014	2015	2016
Financial account		III.2								
Net acquisition of financial assets		F.A								
Currency and deposits		F.2								
Currency	NCXV	F.21	13	29	1	−85	59	5	229	79
Transferable deposits		F.22								
Deposits with UK monetary financial institutions	NCXX	F.22N1	908	−294	1 018	−138	1 158	411	682	239
Of which: foreign currency deposits with UK MFIs[1]	NCXZ	F.22N12	191	−159	84	−125	68	58	−52	−20
Deposits with rest of the world MFIs[1]	NCYB	F.22N9	–	–	–	–	–	–	–	–
Other deposits	NCYC	F.29	−913	230	1 083	−8	−256	−637	3	−446
Total	NCXU	F.2	8	−35	2 102	−231	961	−221	914	−128
Debt securities		F.3								
Short-term		F.31								
Issued by UK central government	NCYF	F.31N1	−86	8	25	−40	−45	–	–	–
Issued by UK MFIs[1]	NCYK	F.31N5	–	–	–	–	–	–	–	–
MMIs issued by other UK residents[2]	NCYP	F.31N6	−93	−21	9	1	–	–	–	–
Long-term		F.32								
Issued by UK central government	NCYS	F.32N1	102	1	−46	−758	–	–	–	–
Issued by UK local government	NCYV	F.32N2	–	–	–	–	–	–	–	–
Issued by UK MFIs and other UK residents[1,3]	NCYZ	F.32N5-6	–	–	–	–	–	–	–	–
Issued by rest of the world	NCZA	F.32N9	−5	–	–	–	–	–	–	–
Total	NCYD	F.3	−82	−12	−12	−797	−45	–	–	–
Loans		F.4								
Long-term loans		F.42								
Direct investment	CFZI	F.421	–	−18	–	1	−4	–	–	–
Loans secured on dwellings	NCZQ	F.422	–	–	–	–	–	–	–	–
Other long-term loans		F.424								
By UK residents	NCZV	F.424N1	−178	59	−183	−110	−166	−88	−202	−174
Total	NCZF	F.4	−178	41	−183	−109	−170	−88	−202	−174
Equity and investment fund shares/units		F.5								
Equity		F.51								
Listed UK shares[3]	NEBC	F.511N1	–	–	–	–	–	–	–	–
Unlisted UK shares[3]	NEBD	F.512N1	–	–	–	–	–	−510	–	–
Other equity		F.519								
UK shares and bonds issued by other UK residents[3]	NSPN	F.519N7	–	–	–	–	–	–	–	–
Shares and other equity issued by rest of the world	NEBH	F.519N9	97	108	108	61	71	117	63	64
Total	NCZX	F.5	97	108	108	61	71	−393	63	64
Insurance, pensions and standardised guarantee schemes		F.6								
Non-life insurance technical reserves	NEBQ	F.61	–	–	–	–	–	–	–	–
Total	NPWL	F.6	–	–	–	–	–	–	–	–
Financial derivatives and employee stock options	MN5H	F.7	–	4	–	–	–	–	–	–
Of which: financial derivatives	NSUH	F.71	–	4	–	–	–	–	–	–
Other accounts receivable	NEBR	F.8	−1 309	−3 400	633	2 599	984	706	797	103
Total net acquisition of financial assets	NCXQ	F.A	−1 464	−3 294	2 648	1 523	1 801	4	1 572	−135

3.2.8 Public non-financial corporations
ESA 2010 sector S.11001 Unconsolidated
continued

£ million

			2009	2010	2011	2012	2013	2014	2015	2016
Financial account		III.2								
Net acquisition of financial liabilities		F.L								
Currency and deposits		F.2								
Other deposits	WUGZ	F.29	–	–	–	–	–	–	–	–
Total	A4FK	F.2	–	–	–	–	–	–	–	–
Debt securities		F.3								
Long-term		F.32								
Bonds issued by UK MFIs and other UK residents[1,3]	KLC4	F.32N5-6	248	384	447	3 231	3 355	3 673	2 228	1 107
Total	NENJ	F.3	248	384	447	3 231	3 355	3 673	2 228	1 107
Loans		F.4								
Short-term		F.41								
Loans by UK MFIs[1]	NEON	F.41N1	31	148	63	–23	–318	122	570	299
Long-term		F.42								
Direct investment	CFZJ	F.421	–6	–118	–136	–	–5	–4	–	–
Loans secured on dwellings	CPLJ	F.422	2 572	–818	1 194	93	–481	–1 254	–848	111
Finance leasing	NEPA	F.423	–117	–1 659	–837	–183	–67	–55	–57	–59
Other long-term loans		F.424								
By UK residents	NEPB	F.424N1	1 527	4 362	2 739	–265	–1 274	1 547	1 103	1 907
By rest of the world	NEPC	F.424N9	–4	–	–	–	–1	–	–	–
Total	NEOL	F.4	4 015	2 151	3 295	–378	–2 136	364	768	2 258
Equity and investment fund shares/units		F.5								
Equity		F.51								
Unlisted UK shares[3]	NEPJ	F.512N1	–	–	–	–	–	–510	–	–
Other equity		F.519								
Other UK equity	NEPK	F.519N6	–4 960	–582	–684	–895	–1 078	–1 400	–1 345	–1 691
UK shares and bonds issued by other UK residents	NSPO	F.519N9	–	–	–	–	–	–	–	–
Total	NEPD	F.5	–4 960	–582	–684	–895	–1 078	–1 910	–1 345	–1 691
Other accounts payable	NEPX	F.8	263	–1 507	830	84	872	651	1 029	393
Total net acquisition of financial liabilities	NEBU	F.L	–434	446	3 888	2 042	1 013	2 778	2 680	2 067
Net lending(+) / net borrowing(-)		B.9								
Total net acquisition of financial assets	NCXQ	F.A	–1 464	–3 294	2 648	1 523	1 801	4	1 572	–135
less total net acquisition of financial liabilities	NEBU	F.L	–434	446	3 888	2 042	1 013	2 778	2 680	2 067
Net lending(+) / borrowing(-) from the financial account	NZEC	B.9f	–1 030	–3 740	–1 240	–519	788	–2 774	–1 108	–2 202
Statistical discrepancy between financial and non-financial accounts	NYPI	dB.9	124	640	–415	104	137	786	–315	–310
Net lending (+) / borrowing (-) from non-financial accounts	CPCM	B.9n	**–906**	**–3 100**	**–1 655**	**–415**	**925**	**–1 988**	**–1 423**	**–2 512**

1 Monetary financial institutions
2 Money market instruments
3 Prior to 1990, it is not possible to distinguish some elements of F.32N5-6,
  F.511N1 and F.512N1. These elements are shown combined as F.519N7

3.2.11 Public non-financial corporations
ESA 2010 sector S.11001 Unconsolidated

£ billion

			2009	2010	2011	2012	2013	2014	2015	2016
Financial balance sheet at end of period		IV.3								
Non-financial assets[1]	NG2Q	AN	..	..	..	..	..	..	..	..
Total financial assets		AF.A								
Currency and deposits		AF.2								
Currency	NKDS	AF.21	0.6	0.6	0.6	0.5	0.6	0.6	0.8	0.9
Transferable deposits		AF.22								
Deposits with UK MFIs[2]	NKDU	AF.22N1	5.2	5.0	6.2	6.1	7.5	8.0	8.7	9.0
Of which: foreign currency deposits	NKDW	AF.22N12	0.3	0.1	0.2	0.1	0.1	0.2	0.2	0.2
Deposits with rest of the world MFIs[2]	NKDY	AF.22N9	–	–	–	–	–	–	–	–
Other deposits	NKDZ	AF.29	3.9	4.2	4.9	4.9	4.5	3.8	3.9	3.5
Total	NKDR	AF.2	9.7	9.9	11.8	11.6	12.7	12.5	13.5	13.4
Debt securities		AF.3								
Short-term		AF.31								
Issued by UK central government	NKEC	AF.31N1	0.3	0.3	0.4	0.3	0.3	0.3	0.3	0.3
Issued by UK MFIs[2]	NKEH	AF.31N5	0.4	0.4	0.4	0.4	0.4	0.4	0.4	0.4
Issued by other UK residents	NKEM	AF.31N6	0.2	0.2	0.2	0.1	0.1	0.1	0.1	0.1
Long-term		AF.32								
Issued by UK central government	NKEP	AF.32N1	1.3	1.3	1.3	0.5	0.5	0.5	0.5	0.5
Issued by UK local government	NKES	AF.32N2	–	–	–	–	–	–	–	–
Issued by UK MFIs[2] and other UK residents[3]	NKEW	AF.32N5-6	–	–	–	–	–	–	–	–
Bonds issued by rest of the world	NKIQ	AF.32N9	0.1	0.1	0.1	0.1	0.1	0.1	0.1	0.1
Total	NKEA	AF.3	2.3	2.3	2.3	1.5	1.4	1.4	1.4	1.4
Loans		AF.4								
Long-term loans		AF.42								
Direct investment loans	ZYBN	AF.421	–	–	–	–	0.1	–	–	0.043
Secured on dwellings	NKFN	AF.422	–	–	–	–	–	–	–	0.001
Other long-term loans		AF.424								
By UK residents	NKFS	AF.424N1	1.6	1.6	1.5	1.5	1.3	1.3	1.1	1.1
Total	NKFC	AF.4	1.6	1.6	1.5	1.5	1.4	1.4	1.2	1.1
Equity and investment fund shares/units		AF.5								
Equity		AF.51								
Listed UK shares[3]	NKFZ	AF.511N1	–	–	–	–	–	–	–	–
Unlisted UK shares[3]	NKGA	AF.512N1	0.3	0.3	0.3	0.3	0.8	0.3	0.3	0.3
Other equity		AF.519								
UK shares and bonds issued by other UK residents[3]	NSOL	AF.519N7	–	–	–	–	–	–	–	–
Shares and other equity issued by rest of the world	NKGE	AF.519N9	0.4	0.6	0.6	1.2	1.3	1.4	1.4	1.5
Total	NKFU	AF.5	0.8	0.9	0.9	1.5	2.2	1.7	1.7	1.8
Insurance, pensions and standardised guarantee schemes		AF.6								
Non-life insurance technical reserves	NKGN	AF.61	–	–	–	–	–	–	–	–
Total insurance, pensions and standardised guarantee schemes	NPYB	AF.6	–	–	–	–	–	–	–	–
Other accounts receivable	NKGO	AF.8	12.8	13.0	13.9	13.4	14.6	15.3	15.5	15.6
Total financial assets	NKFB	**AF.A**	27.2	27.7	30.4	29.5	32.2	32.3	33.3	33.5

3.2.11 Public non-financial corporations

ESA 2010 sector S.11001 Unconsolidated

continued

£ billion

Financial balance sheet at end of period		IV.3	2009	2010	2011	2012	2013	2014	2015	2016
Total financial liabilities		**AF.L**								
Currency and deposits		AF.2								
Other deposits	NKHD	AF.29	–	–	–	–	–	–	–	–
Total	NKGV	AF.2	–	–	–	–	–	–	–	–
Debt securities		AF.3								
Long-term		AF.32								
Issued by UK MFIs and other UK residents[2,3]	NKIA	AF.32N5-6	16.8	18.9	15.1	14.0	18.6	21.4	22.8	24.0
Total	NKHE	AF.3	16.8	18.9	15.1	14.0	18.6	21.4	22.8	24.0
Loans		AF.4								
Short-term		AF.41								
By UK MFIs[2]	NKII	AF.41N1	1.2	1.3	1.2	1.2	0.9	1.2	1.7	2.0
By rest of the world MFIs[2]	NKIM	AF.41N9	–	–	–	–	–	–	–	–
Long-term		AF.42								
Direct investment	ZYBO	AF.421	0.6	0.7	0.7	0.7	0.7	0.7	0.7	0.7
Secured on dwellings	CPLF	AF.422	38.5	37.7	38.9	39.0	38.5	38.0	37.1	37.2
Finance leasing	NKIV	AF.423	3.5	1.8	1.0	0.8	0.8	0.7	0.6	0.6
Other long-term		AF.424								
By UK residents	NKIW	AF.424N1	7.9	11.4	14.1	13.7	12.3	13.8	14.8	16.6
By rest of the world	NKIX	AF.424N9	0.4	0.4	0.4	0.4	0.4	0.4	0.4	0.4
Total	NKIG	AF.4	52.0	53.3	56.2	55.7	53.5	54.7	55.4	57.5
Equity and investment fund shares/units		AF.5								
Equity		AF.51								
Listed UK shares[3]	C308	AF.511N1	–	–	–	–	–	–	–	–
Unquoted UK shares[3]	NKJE	AF.512N1	1.7	1.7	1.7	1.5	2.0	1.5	1.5	1.5
Other equity		AF.519								
Other UK equity	H406	AF.519N6	117.5	118.8	120.1	122.2	123.2	125.7	127.4	128.5
UK shares and bonds issued by other UK residents[3]	NSOM	AF.519N7	–	–	–	–	–	–	–	–
Total	NKIY	AF.5	119.2	120.5	121.8	123.7	125.2	127.2	128.9	130.1
Other accounts payable	NKJS	AF.8	19.7	18.2	19.0	19.0	19.9	23.3	24.3	24.6
Total financial liabilities	NKIF	**AF.L**	207.7	210.9	212.1	212.5	217.2	226.6	231.4	236.2
Financial net worth		**BF.90**								
Total financial assets	NKFB	AF.A	27.2	27.7	30.4	29.5	32.2	32.3	33.3	33.5
less total financial liabilities	NKIF	AF.L	207.7	210.9	212.1	212.5	217.2	226.6	231.4	236.2
Financial net worth	NYOP	**BF.90**	−180.5	−183.2	−181.7	−183.0	−185.0	−194.3	−198.1	−202.8
Net worth										
Non-financial assets[1]	NG2Q	AN	..	..	..	..	..	..	..	..
Financial net worth	NYOP	BF.90	−180.5	−183.2	−181.7	−183.0	−185.0	−194.3	−198.1	−202.8
Net worth[1]	CGRW	**B.90**	..	..	..	..	..	..	..	..

1 .. indicates that data have been suppressed in this table. This is because the institutional sector and asset breakdown of non-financial corporations (S.11), into public corporations (S.11001) and private non-financial corporations (S.11002 and S.11003) is unavailable from the capital stocks dataset.

2 Monetary financial institutions

3 Prior to 1990 it is not possible to distinguish some elements of AF.32N5-6, AF.511N1 and AF.512N1. These elements are shown combined as AF.519N7

3.3.1 Private non-financial corporations
ESA 2010 sectors S.11002 and S.11003[1]

£ million

			2009	2010	2011	2012	2013	2014	2015
Production account		I							
Resources									
Output		P.1							
Market output	FBXS	P.11	1 620 832	1 686 350	1 752 446	1 819 825	1 905 476	1 974 247	2 026 252
Output for own final use	FDCG	P.12	25 998	27 885	31 416	31 897	34 234	37 056	38 683
Total	FBXR	P.1	1 646 830	1 714 235	1 783 862	1 851 722	1 939 710	2 011 303	2 064 935
Total resources	FBXR	TR	1 646 830	1 714 235	1 783 862	1 851 722	1 939 710	2 011 303	2 064 935
Uses									
Intermediate consumption	FARP	P.2	874 098	912 743	952 108	992 567	1 034 784	1 059 763	1 081 425
Gross value added	FARR	**B.1g**	**772 732**	**801 492**	**831 754**	**859 155**	**904 926**	**951 540**	**983 510**
Total uses	FBXR	TU	1 646 830	1 714 235	1 783 862	1 851 722	1 939 710	2 011 303	2 064 935
Gross value added	FARR	**B.1g**	**772 732**	**801 492**	**831 754**	**859 155**	**904 926**	**951 540**	**983 510**
less consumption of fixed capital	NSRK	P.51c	98 432	98 190	101 379	104 529	107 852	110 959	114 629
Value added, net	FARS	B.1n	674 300	703 302	730 375	754 626	797 074	840 581	868 881

1 S.11002 National controlled and S.11003 Foreign controlled

3.3.2 Private non-financial corporations
ESA 2010 sectors S.11002 and S.11003[1]

£ million

			2009	2010	2011	2012	2013	2014	2015
Distribution and use of income accounts		II							
Primary distribution of income account		II.1							
Generation of income account before deduction of fixed capital consumption		II.1.1							
Resources									
Total resources (gross value added)	FARR	**B.1g**	**772 732**	**801 492**	**831 754**	**859 155**	**904 926**	**951 540**	**983 510**
Uses									
Compensation of employees		D.1							
Wages and salaries	FAAX	D.11	426 542	427 494	443 308	456 503	485 008	503 147	526 297
Employers' social contributions	FABH	D.12	70 872	80 641	82 120	89 150	93 612	89 163	86 805
Total	FBDA	D.1	497 414	508 135	525 428	545 653	578 620	592 310	613 102
Taxes on production and imports, paid		D.2							
Production taxes other than on products	FACQ	D.29	21 964	22 428	23 632	25 065	26 367	27 013	27 882
less subsidies, received		D.3							
less production subsidies other than on products	JQJW	D.39	1 086	1 265	1 331	1 378	1 624	1 972	2 323
Operating surplus, gross	NRJK	B.2g	254 440	272 194	284 025	289 815	301 563	334 189	344 849
Total uses (gross value added)	FARR	**B.1g**	**772 732**	**801 492**	**831 754**	**859 155**	**904 926**	**951 540**	**983 510**
less consumption of fixed capital	NSRK	P.51c	98 432	98 190	101 379	104 529	107 852	110 959	114 629
Operating surplus, net	FACU	B.2n	156 008	174 004	182 646	185 286	193 711	223 230	230 220

1 S.11002 National controlled and S.11003 Foreign controlled

3.3.3 Private non-financial corporations
ESA 2010 sectors S.11002 and S.11003[1]

£ million

			2009	2010	2011	2012	2013	2014	2015	2016
Allocation of primary income account before deduction of fixed capital consumption		II.1.2								
Resources										
Operating surplus, gross	NRJK	B.2g	254 440	272 194	284 025	289 815	301 563	334 189	344 849	354 499
Property income, received		D.4								
Interest		D.41								
Interest before FISIM allocation[2]	I69R	D.41g	8 909	8 771	8 936	8 526	9 250	9 225	9 313	10 248
plus FISIM[2]	IV87	P.119	3 313	2 662	3 745	3 574	3 034	4 805	5 490	5 739
Total	DSZR	D.41	12 222	11 433	12 681	12 100	12 284	14 030	14 803	15 987
Distributed income of corporations	DSZS	D.42	53 334	50 178	58 026	53 065	54 977	74 625	50 737	50 894
Reinvested earnings on foreign direct investment	HDVR	D.43	12 337	26 179	27 201	11 656	6 911	−19 122	−8 253	−7 658
Other investment income		D.44								
Attributable to insurance policy holders	KZI4	D.441	975	430	297	219	280	331	153	158
Attributable to collective investment fund shares		D.443								
Dividends	KZI6	D.4431	2	5	3	–	4	4	4	4
Retained earnings	KZI7	D.4432	4	8	4	4	4	4	4	5
Total	L5U6	D.443	6	13	7	4	8	8	8	9
Total	FCFP	D.44	981	443	304	223	288	339	161	167
Rent	FAOL	D.45	110	110	122	131	135	140	136	144
Total	FACV	D.4	78 984	88 343	98 334	77 175	74 595	70 012	57 584	59 534
Total resources	FCFQ	TR	333 424	360 537	382 359	366 990	376 158	404 201	402 433	414 033
Uses										
Property income, paid		D.4								
Interest		D.41								
Interest before FISIM allocation[2]	I6A2	D.41g	45 039	37 341	35 500	37 697	37 957	36 421	32 055	33 660
less FISIM[2]	IV86	P.119	9 023	9 483	8 424	7 944	7 971	6 275	5 924	6 732
Total	DSZV	D.41	36 016	27 858	27 076	29 753	29 986	30 146	26 131	26 928
Distributed income of corporations	NVDC	D.42	145 146	131 028	151 071	162 410	174 079	181 428	206 622	189 595
Of which: dividend payments	NETZ	D.421	118 078	100 660	121 222	132 857	141 453	147 856	171 166	154 369
Reinvested earnings on foreign direct investment	HDVB	D.43	−4 539	156	−5 971	−5 363	5 263	−1 055	−2 543	−99
Rent	FCFU	D.45	1 521	1 556	1 548	1 571	1 730	1 745	1 743	1 789
Total	FCFR	D.4	178 144	160 598	173 724	188 371	211 058	212 264	231 953	218 213
Balance of primary incomes, gross	NRJM	**B.5g**	**155 280**	**199 939**	**208 635**	**178 619**	**165 100**	**191 937**	**170 480**	**195 820**
Total uses	FCFQ	TU	333 424	360 537	382 359	366 990	376 158	404 201	402 433	414 033
less consumption of fixed capital	NSRK	P.51c	98 432	98 190	101 379	104 529	107 852	110 959	114 629	119 177
Balance of primary incomes, net	FCFW	B.5n	56 848	101 749	107 256	74 090	57 248	80 978	55 851	76 643

1 S.11002 National controlled and S.11003 Foreign controlled
2 Financial intermediation services indirectly measured

3.3.4 Private non-financial corporations
ESA 2010 sectors S.11002 and S.11003[1]

£ million

			2009	2010	2011	2012	2013	2014	2015	2016
Secondary distribution of income account		II.2								
Resources										
Balance of primary incomes, gross	NRJM	**B.5g**	**155 280**	**199 939**	**208 635**	**178 619**	**165 100**	**191 937**	**170 480**	**195 820**
Net social contributions		D.61								
Employers' imputed social contributions	L8RJ	D.612	4 107	3 185	2 898	3 309	3 337	3 410	3 469	3 108
Total	L8TV	D.61	4 107	3 185	2 898	3 309	3 337	3 410	3 469	3 108
Other current transfers		D.7								
Net non-life insurance claims	FDBA	D.72	5 578	5 775	3 745	3 523	6 458	5 700	4 923	5 623
Total resources	FDBC	TR	164 965	208 899	215 278	185 451	174 895	201 047	178 872	204 551
Uses										
Current taxes on income, wealth etc.		D.5								
Taxes on income	FCCP	D.51	33 741	35 518	35 622	32 861	32 961	31 580	32 929	35 021
Social security benefits other than social transfers in kind		D.62								
Other social insurance benefits	L8S9	D.622	4 107	3 185	2 898	3 309	3 337	3 410	3 469	3 108
Total	L8TH	D.62	4 107	3 185	2 898	3 309	3 337	3 410	3 469	3 108
Current transfers other than taxes, social contributions and benefits		D.7								
Net non-life insurance premiums	FDBH	D.71	5 578	5 775	3 745	3 523	6 458	5 700	4 923	5 623
Miscellaneous current transfers	CY88	D.75	5 865	4 771	5 155	4 857	4 768	4 876	4 535	4 214
Total	FCCN	D.7	11 443	10 546	8 900	8 380	11 226	10 576	9 458	9 837
Disposable income, gross	NRJQ	**B.6g**	**115 674**	**159 650**	**167 858**	**140 901**	**127 371**	**155 481**	**133 016**	**156 585**
Total uses	FDBC	TU	164 965	208 899	215 278	185 451	174 895	201 047	178 872	204 551
less consumption of fixed capital	NSRK	P.51c	98 432	98 190	101 379	104 529	107 852	110 959	114 629	119 177
Disposable income, net	FDBK	B.6n	17 242	61 460	66 479	36 372	19 519	44 522	18 387	37 408

1 S.11002 National controlled and S.11003 Foreign controlled

3.3.6 Private non-financial corporations
ESA 2010 sectors S.11002 and S.11003[1]

£ million

			2009	2010	2011	2012	2013	2014	2015	2016
Use of disposable income account		II.4.1								
Resources										
Total resources (gross disposable income)	NRJQ	B.6g	**115 674**	**159 650**	**167 858**	**140 901**	**127 371**	**155 481**	**133 016**	**156 585**
Uses										
Total uses (gross saving)	NRJQ	B.8g	**115 674**	**159 650**	**167 858**	**140 901**	**127 371**	**155 481**	**133 016**	**156 585**
less consumption of fixed capital	NSRK	P.51c	98 432	98 190	101 379	104 529	107 852	110 959	114 629	119 177
Saving, net	FDBK	B.8n	17 242	61 460	66 479	36 372	19 519	44 522	18 387	37 408

1 S.11002 National controlled and S.11003 Foreign controlled

3.3.7 Private non-financial corporations
ESA 2010 sectors S.11002 and S.11003[1]

£ million

			2009	2010	2011	2012	2013	2014	2015	2016
Accumulation accounts		III								
Capital account		III.1								
Change in net worth due to saving and capital transfers account		III.1.1								
Changes in liabilities and net worth										
Gross saving	NRJQ	B.8g	115 674	159 650	167 858	140 901	127 371	155 481	133 016	156 585
Capital transfers, receivable		D.9r								
Investment grants	AIBR	D.92r	2 902	2 249	1 709	1 659	1 965	2 233	2 504	2 595
Other capital transfers	LNZM	D.99r	−184	−205	−200	−75	−53	−14	−5	50
Total	OEUV	D.9r	2 718	2 044	1 509	1 584	1 912	2 219	2 499	2 645
Capital transfers, payable		D.9p								
Capital taxes	QYKB	D.91p	–	–	–	–	–	–	–	–
Other capital transfers	CISB	D.99p	760	700	807	764	1 394	1 372	1 381	1 519
Total	FCFX	D.9p	760	700	807	764	1 394	1 372	1 381	1 519
Changes in net worth due to gross saving and capital transfers	NRMG	B.101g	117 632	160 994	168 560	141 721	127 889	156 328	134 134	157 711
Changes in assets										
Changes in net worth due to gross saving and capital transfers	NRMG	B.101g	117 632	160 994	168 560	141 721	127 889	156 328	134 134	157 711
less consumption of fixed capital	NSRK	P.51c	98 432	98 190	101 379	104 529	107 852	110 959	114 629	119 177
Changes in net worth due to net saving and capital transfers	FDCH	B.101n	19 200	62 804	67 181	37 192	20 037	45 369	19 505	38 534
Acquisition of non-financial assets account		III.1.2								
Changes in liabilities and net worth										
Changes in net worth due to net saving and capital transfers	FDCH	B.101n	19 200	62 804	67 181	37 192	20 037	45 369	19 505	38 534
Consumption of fixed capital	NSRK	P.51c	98 432	98 190	101 379	104 529	107 852	110 959	114 629	119 177
Changes in net worth due to gross saving and capital transfers	NRMG	B.101g	117 632	160 994	168 560	141 721	127 889	156 328	134 134	157 711
Changes in assets										
Gross capital formation		P.5								
Gross fixed capital formation	FDBM	P.51g	113 320	119 041	127 093	138 727	149 299	158 591	166 780	166 917
Changes in inventories	DLQX	P.52	−13 472	5 060	2 606	1 918	4 430	12 460	7 662	8 185
Acquisitions less disposals of valuables[2]	NPOV	P.53	427	55	−8	−107	276	−1 170	−404	576
Total	FDCL	P.5	100 275	124 156	129 691	140 538	154 005	169 881	174 038	175 678
Acquisitions less disposals of non-produced non-financial assets	FDCN	NP	−2 779	−2 514	−847	−116	677	430	1 222	1 319
Net lending(+) / net borrowing(-)	DTAL	B.9n	20 136	39 352	39 716	1 299	−26 793	−13 983	−41 126	−19 286
Total change in assets	NRMG	Total	117 632	160 994	168 560	141 721	127 889	156 328	134 134	157 711

1 S.11002 National controlled and S.11003 Foreign controlled
2 Acquisitions less disposals of valuables can be a volatile series but any
volatility is likely to be GDP neutral as it is offset in UK trade figures

3.3.8 Private non-financial corporations
ESA 2010 sectors S.11002 and S.11003[1] Unconsolidated

£ million

			2009	2010	2011	2012	2013	2014	2015	2016
Financial account		III.2								
Net acquisition of financial assets		F.A								
Currency and deposits		F.2								
Currency	NEQF	F.21	511	197	235	281	252	337	387	840
Transferable deposits		F.22								
Deposits with MFIs[2]	NEQH	F.22N1	18 517	16 543	−2 631	17 236	19 806	27 706	36 797	27 151
Of which: foreign currency deposits with UK MFIs[2]	NEQJ	F.22N12	9 421	12 088	−7 746	7 038	−3 744	424	2 138	10 574
Deposits with rest of the world MFIs[2]	NEQL	F.22N9	802	761	−4 130	−2 548	3 761	23 338	9 761	11 026
Other deposits	NEQM	F.29	−323	−1 410	−777	−576	−275	176	−586	88
Total	NEQE	F.2	19 507	16 091	−7 303	14 393	23 544	51 557	46 359	39 105
Debt securities		F.3								
Short-term		F.31								
Issued by UK central government	NEQP	F.31N1	−159	9	8	426	259	38	289	−315
Issued by UK MFIs[2]	NEQU	F.31N5	−63	−1 096	−2 801	133	361	537	2 642	1 360
Issued by other UK residents	NEQZ	F.31N6	−1 614	1 827	513	−121	202	−1 590	351	−2 580
Issued by rest of the world	NERA	F.31N9	1 615	1 936	1 800	−3 911	−1 001	1 615	4 519	1 425
Long-term		F.32								
Issued by UK central government	NERC	F.32N1	572	773	198	38	−314	45	−620	−23
Issued by UK MFIs and other UK residents[2,5]	KLG6	F.32N5-6	−1 261	267	1 068	−22	4 649	7 446	5 684	3 770
Bonds issued by rest of the world	NERK	F.32N9	−1 280	4 522	−189	169	−146	7 284	−369	−608
Total	NEQN	F.3	−2 190	8 238	597	−3 288	4 010	15 375	12 496	3 029
Loans		F.4								
Long-term		F.42								
Direct investment		F.421								
Outward direct investment	NERY	F.421N1	−36 862	−20 237	−15 043	−8 493	8 443	17 916	−32 045	9 280
Inward direct investment	NERZ	F.421N2	−10 699	4 362	6 302	−4 206	2 679	10 191	6 983	19 056
Finance leasing	F8Y9	F.423	142	−1 526	−860	−199	−86	−78	−82	546
Other long-term loans		F.424								
By UK residents	NESF	F.424N1	6 012	10 599	7 922	741	−4 548	17 400	22 699	−8 451
Total	NERP	F.4	−41 407	−6 802	−1 679	−12 157	6 488	45 429	−2 445	20 431
Equity and investment fund shares/units		F.5								
Equity		F.51								
Listed UK shares[5]	NESM	F.511N1	6 570	−233	9 674	634	−3 294	−8 140	−2	16 492
Unlisted UK shares[5]	NESN	F.512N1	8 459.0	1 693.0	5 217.0	16 067.0	10 014.0	7 303.0	8 548.0	17 390.0
Other equity		F.519								
UK shares and bonds issued by other UK residents[5]	NSPP	F.519N7	–	–	–	–	–	–	–	–
Shares and other equity issued by rest of the world	NESR	F.519N9	−739	34 857	48 834	14 388	17 740	−85 026	−11 857	922
UK mutual funds' shares	NESV	F.52N1	11	14	3	3	8	16	31	20
Total	NESH	F.5	14 301.0	36 331.0	63 728.0	31 092.0	24 468.0	−85 847.0	−3 280.0	34 824.0
Insurance, pensions and standardised guarantee schemes		F.6								
Non-life insurance technical reserves	NETA	F.61	−2 164	−4 031	−2 447	−568	−137	–	−209	63
Total	NPWN	F.6	−2 164	−4 031	−2 447	−568	−137	–	−209	63
Financial derivatives and employee stock options	MN5I	F.7	−2 928	−985	−8 096	4 419	3 393	−6 817	−3 120	−533
Of which: financial derivatives	J8XO	F.71	−2 928	−985	−8 096	4 419	3 393	−6 817	−3 120	−533
Other accounts receivable	NETB	F.8	4 005	−9 687	−79	10 418	−4 086	1 789	−2 120	6 736
Total net acquisition of financial assets	NEQA	F.A	−10 876.0	39 155.0	44 721.0	44 309.0	57 680.0	21 486.0	47 681.0	103 655.0

3.3.8 Private non-financial corporations
ESA 2010 sectors S.11002 and S.11003[1] Unconsolidated

continued

£ million

			2009	2010	2011	2012	2013	2014	2015	2016
Financial account		III.2								
Net acquisition of financial liabilities		F.L								
Debt securities		F.3								
Short-term		F.31								
MMIs issued by UK residents[3]	NEUD	F.31N6	−5 808	3 934	8 082	−6 158	2 387	−1 689	−2 739	1 953
Long-term		F.32								
Issued by UK MFIs and other UK residents[2,5]	KLC5	F.32N5-6	29 554	8 505	19 448	8 970	20 140	10 330	23 478	24 772
Total	NETR	F.3	23 746	12 439	27 530	2 812	22 527	8 641	20 739	26 725
Loans		F.4								
Short-term		F.41								
By UK MFIs[2]	NEUV	F.41N1	−49 206	−28 743	−13 853	−17 223	−9 418	−4 068	5 111	15 192
By rest of the world	NEUZ	F.41N9	−6 171	−3 235	−12 992	−217	563	−5 899	5 167	3 002
Long-term		F.42								
Direct investment		F.421								
Outward direct investment	NEVC	F.421N1	−41 057	−957	−15 077	−1 709	−1 246	15 224	9 112	19 835
Inward direct investment	NEVD	F.421N2	6 213	−4 503	11 238	2 019	−2 313	5 846	−8 474	−2 865
Secured on dwellings	G9JQ	F.422	654	1 913	1 673	−327	967	431	−272	−231
Finance leasing	NEVI	F.423	345	329	324	324	325	326	324	324
Other long-term loans		F.424								
By UK residents	NEVJ	F.424N1	−1 882	3 664	1 384	21 930	40 371	25 440	−9 291	26 394
By rest of the world	NEVK	F.424N9	–	–	–	–	–	–	–	–
Total	NEUT	F.4	−91 104	−31 532	−27 303	4 797	29 249	37 300	1 677	61 651
Equity and investment fund shares/units		F.5								
Equity		F.51								
Listed UK shares[5]	NEVQ	F.511N1	32 864	11 623	3 272	1 027	5 849	−30 284	11 651	−97 353
Unlisted UK shares[5]	NEVR	F.512N1	11 135	13 647	−1 693	15 533	12 152	10 503	15 240	123 919
Other equity		F.519								
Other UK equity	NEVS	F.519N6	52	54	873	333	338	306	–	723
UK shares and bonds issued by other UK residents[5]	NSPQ	F.519N7	–	–	–	–	–	–	–	–
Total	NEVL	F.5	44 051	25 324	2 452	16 893	18 339	−19 475	26 891	27 289
Insurance, pensions and standardised guarantee schemes		F.6								
Pension schemes[4]	MA2P	F.6M	7 243	8 277	8 388	8 843	9 718	9 411	9 186	9 862
Total	M9VY	F.6	7 243	8 277	8 388	8 843	9 718	9 411	9 186	9 862
Financial derivatives and employee stock options	MN64	F.7	1 388	1 418	1 465	1 491	1 546	1 613	1 669	1 714
Other accounts payable	NEWF	F.8	−1 797	2 762	5 979	4 688	434	2 346	5 934	7 969
Total net acquisition of financial liabilities	NETE	F.L	−16 473	18 688	18 511	39 524	81 813	39 836	66 096	135 210
Net lending(+) / net borrowing(-)		B.9n								
Total net acquisition of financial assets	NEQA	FA	−10 876	39 155	44721	44309	57680	21486	47681	103 655
less total net acquisition of financial liabilities	NETE	FL	−16 473	18 688	18 511	39 524	81 813	39 836	66 096	135 210
Net lending(+) / borrowing(-) from the financial account	NYOA	B.9f	5 597	20 467	26 210	4 785	−24 133	−18 350	−18 415	−31 555
Statistical discrepancy between financial and non-financial accounts	NYPM	dB.9	14 539	18 885	13 506	−3 486	−2 660	4 367	−22 711	12 269
Net lending (+) / borrowing (-) from non-financial accounts	DTAL	B.9n	20 136	39 352	39 716	1 299	−26 793	−13 983	−41 126	−19 286

1 S.11002 National controlled and S.11003 Foreign controlled
2 Monetary financial institutions
3 Money market instruments
4 F.63 pension entitlements, F.64 Claims on pension fund on pension
  managers, F.65 Entitlements to non-pension benefits
5 Prior to 1990, it is not possible to distinguish some elements of F.32N5-6,
  F.511N1 and F.512N1. These elements are shown combined as F.519N7

3.3.11 Private non-financial corporations
ESA 2010 sectors S.11002 and S.11003[1] Unconsolidated

£ billion

			2009	2010	2011	2012	2013	2014	2015	2016
Financial balance sheet at end of period		IV.3								
Non-financial assets[2]	NG2Y	**AN**	..	..	..	..	..	..	..	..
Total financial assets		**AF.A**								
Currency and deposits		AF.2								
Currency	NKKA	AF.21	4.6	4.8	5.0	5.2	5.4	5.8	6.2	6.8
Transferable deposits		AF.22								
With UK MFIs[3]	NKKC	AF.22N1	275.8	296.7	290.6	309.1	326.7	354.9	390.7	427.1
Of which: foreign currency deposits with UK MFIs[3]	NKKE	AF.22N12	48.5	62.1	54.8	62.0	55.6	55.7	60.3	81.4
Deposits with rest of the world MFIs[3]	NKKG	AF.22N9	123.9	129.3	127.8	142.5	150.9	160.5	165.7	200.3
Other deposits	NKKH	AF.29	5.1	4.0	3.3	2.9	2.9	3.3	3.0	3.4
Total	NKJZ	AF.2	409.4	434.8	426.7	459.7	485.9	524.5	565.6	637.7
Debt securities		AF.3								
Short-term		AF.31								
Issued by UK central government	NKKK	AF.31N1	–	–	–	0.5	0.7	0.7	1.0	0.7
Issued by UK MFIs[3]	NKKP	AF.31N5	11.1	10.0	7.2	7.4	7.8	9.1	12.0	13.7
MMIs issued by other UK residents[4]	NKKU	AF.31N6	5.7	7.5	8.1	7.9	8.1	6.8	7.3	4.8
MMIs issued by rest of the world[4]	NKKV	AF.31N9	2.9	4.8	6.7	2.1	0.8	2.6	7.2	8.7
Long-term		AF.32								
Issued by UK central government	NKKX	AF.32N1	1.3	2.1	2.3	2.4	2.2	2.7	2.2	2.4
Issued by UK local government	NKLA	AF.32N2	–	–	–	–	–	–	–	–
Issued by UK MFIs and other UK residents[3,6]	KLF8	AF.32N5-6	8.3	9.3	11.4	11.3	14.8	32.2	37.9	45.2
Issued by rest of the world	NKLF	AF.3N29	17.9	22.8	27.5	26.6	25.5	9.5	9.3	13.0
Total	NKKI	AF.3	47.3	56.6	63.3	58.2	59.9	63.7	76.9	88.5
Loans		AF.4								
Long-term		AF.42								
Direct investment		AF.421								
Outward direct investment	NKXH	AF.421N1	187.8	185.7	157.0	183.2	189.4	210.1	163.8	171.7
Inward direct investment	NKXI	AF.421N2	55.4	57.2	63.2	59.1	67.9	61.9	58.3	58.5
Finance leasing	F8YG	AF.423	8.3	7.1	6.2	6.0	6.0	6.3	6.7	7.3
Other long-term loans		AF.424								
By UK residents	NKXO	AF.424N1	9.6	38.5	38.0	38.0	37.4	37.8	38.4	38.7
Total	NKWY	AF.4	261.1	288.5	264.5	286.3	300.8	316.1	267.3	276.1
Equity and investment fund shares/units		AF.5								
Equity		AF.51								
Listed UK shares[6]	NKXV	AF.511N1	45.0	40.6	36.9	39.6	43.7	39.6	33.2	31.5
Unlisted UK shares[6]	NKXW	AF.512N1	72.6	71.0	67.1	68.4	75.8	74.9	75.9	77.4
Other equity		AF.519								
UK shares and bonds issued by other UK residents[6]	NSON	AF.519N7	–	–	–	–	–	–	–	–
Shares and other equity issued by rest of the world	NKYA	AF.519N9	693.7	749.7	785.8	769.6	783.1	758.1	803.5	885.1
Investment fund/units		AF.52								
UK mutual funds' shares	NKYE	AF.52N1	0.4	0.5	0.4	0.5	0.6	0.7	0.8	0.8
Total	NKXQ	AF.5	811.7	861.9	890.3	878.1	903.1	873.3	913.3	994.8
Insurance, pensions and standardised guarantee schemes		AF.6								
Non-life insurance technical reserves	NKYJ	AF.61	11.0	7.2	4.7	4.2	4.0	4.0	3.8	3.9
Total	NPYD	AF.6	11.0	7.2	4.7	4.2	4.0	4.0	3.8	3.9
Financial derivatives and employee stock options	MMU8	AF.7	24.3	25.3	29.7	28.6	25.6	30.0	31.0	37.0
Of which: financial derivatives	J8XH	AF.71	24.3	25.3	29.7	28.6	25.6	30.0	31.0	37.0
Other accounts receivable	NKYK	AF.8	119.2	116.8	116.9	118.8	118.6	115.9	116.0	114.2
Total financial assets	NKWX	**AF.A**	1 684.0	1 791.1	1 796.0	1 833.8	1 898.0	1 927.6	1 973.9	2 152.3

3.3.11 Private non-financial corporations

ESA 2010 sectors S.11002 and S.11003[1] Unconsolidated

continued

£ billion

			2009	2010	2011	2012	2013	2014	2015	2016
Financial balance sheet at end of period		IV.3								
Total financial liabilities		**AF.L**								
Debt securities		AF.3								
Short-term		AF.31								
MMIs issued by other UK residents[4]	NKZM	AF.31N6	22.5	27.7	35.5	28.2	29.9	30.3	28.7	36.6
Long-term		AF.32								
Issued by UK MFIs and other UK residents[3,6]	KLB6	AF.32N5-6	262.3	258.1	292.5	317.3	322.5	306.7	295.9	331.0
Total	NKZA	AF.3	284.8	285.9	328.0	345.6	352.4	337.0	324.6	367.6
Loans		AF.4								
Short-term		AF.41								
By MFIs[3]	NLBE	AF.41N1	475.3	433.3	399.7	375.9	355.2	338.9	335.5	353.7
Of which: foreign currency loans	NLBG	AF.41N12	59.9	54.4	46.7	40.0	36.0	39.9	42.0	55.3
By rest of the world	NLBI	AF.41N9	130.8	127.6	113.8	117.8	120.4	107.3	112.8	126.1
Long-term		AF.42								
Outward direct investment	NLBL	AF.421N1	185.1	201.1	177.2	230.7	220.0	209.1	228.0	246.4
Inward direct investment	NLBM	AF.421N2	143.0	132.1	158.9	187.7	178.6	178.5	144.9	129.2
Secured on dwellings	G9JM	AF.422	5.0	3.0	4.7	3.9	4.6	4.1	3.8	4.1
Finance leasing	NLBR	AF.423	24.5	24.8	25.1	25.5	25.8	26.1	26.4	26.8
Other long-term loans		AF.424								
By UK residents	NLBS	AF.424N1	203.6	240.2	236.6	233.7	236.1	229.1	241.8	272.1
By rest of the world	NLBT	AF.424N9	0.5	0.5	0.5	0.5	0.5	0.4	0.4	0.5
Total	NLBC	AF.4	1 167.8	1 162.7	1 116.4	1 175.6	1 141.1	1 093.5	1 093.8	1 159.0
Equity and investment fund shares/units		AF.5								
Equity		AF.51								
Listed UK shares[6]	NLBZ	AF.511N1	1 200.3	1 361.3	1 275.5	1 308.5	1 470.7	1 452.1	1 475.0	1 506.7
Unlisted UK shares[6]	NLCA	AF.512N1	630.0	707.7	700.8	814.1	853.0	905.8	868.7	1 025.5
Other equity		AF.519								
Other UK equity (including direct investment in property)	NLCB	AF.519N6	10.0	10.9	11.6	11.9	12.4	13.6	14.5	15.8
UK shares and bonds issued by other UK residents[6]	NSOO	AF.519N7	–	–	–	–	–	–	–	–
Total	NLBU	AF.5	1 840.3	2 079.9	1 987.9	2 134.6	2 336.2	2 371.5	2 358.1	2 547.9
Insurance, pensions and standardised guarantee schemes		AF.6								
Pension schemes[5]	M9VL	AF.6M	392.4	348.0	579.7	499.2	372.7	675.5	617.6	676.3
Total	M9RJ	AF.6	392.4	348.0	579.7	499.2	372.7	675.5	617.6	676.3
Financial derivatives and employee stock options	MMX4	AF.7	36.9	39.9	52.0	46.8	40.6	51.5	55.4	62.3
Of which: financial derivatives	J8XI	AF.71	32.7	35.7	47.7	42.4	36.1	46.8	50.6	57.3
Other accounts payable	NLCO	AF.8	138.7	141.7	147.5	149.5	152.8	153.3	159.6	168.0
Total financial liabilities	NLBB	**AF.L**	3 860.9	4 058.1	4 211.5	4 351.3	4 395.8	4 682.4	4 609.2	4 981.0
Financial net worth		**BF.90**								
Total financial assets	NKWX	AF.A	1 684.0	1 791.1	1 796.0	1 833.8	1 898.0	1 927.6	1 973.9	2 152.3
less total financial liabilities	NLBB	AF.L	3 860.9	4 058.1	4 211.5	4 351.3	4 395.8	4 682.4	4 609.2	4 981.0
Financial net worth	NYOT	**BF.90**	−2 176.9	−2 267.1	−2 415.5	−2 517.5	−2 497.8	−2 754.9	−2 635.3	−2 828.8
Net worth										
Non-financial assets	NG2Y	AN	..	..	..	..	..	..	..	..
Financial net worth	NYOT	BF.90	−2 176.9	−2 267.1	−2 415.5	−2 517.5	−2 497.8	−2 754.9	−2 635.3	−2 828.8
Net worth	TMPN	**B.90**	..	..	..	..	..	..	..	..

1 S.11002 National controlled and S.11003 Foreign controlled
2 .. indicates that data have been suppressed in this table. This is because the institutional sector and asset breakdown of non-financial corporations (S.11), into public corporations (S.11001) and private non-financial corporations (S.11PR) is unavailable from the capital stocks dataset.
3 Monetary financial institutions
4 Money market instruments
5 AF.63 Pension entitlements, AF.64 Claims on pension funds on pension managers, AF.65 Entitlements to non-pension benefits

6 Prior to 1990 it is not possible to distinguish some elements of AF.32N5-6, AF.511N1 and AF.512N1. These elements are shown combined as AF.519N7

United Kingdom National Accounts

The Blue Book
Chapter 04: Financial Corporations

2017 edition

Editors: Dean Goodway & Sarah Nightingale

Office for National Statistics

Chapter 4: Financial corporations

The financial corporations sector (S.12) consists of institutional units that are independent legal entities and market producers, and whose principal activity is the production of financial services. Such institutional units comprise all corporations and quasi-corporations that are principally engaged in:

- financial intermediation (financial intermediaries) and/or

- auxiliary financial activities (financial auxiliaries)

Also included are institutional units providing financial services, where most of either their assets or their liabilities are not transacted on open markets.

Financial intermediation is the activity in which an institutional unit acquires financial assets and incurs liabilities on its own account by engaging in financial transactions on the market. The assets and liabilities of financial intermediaries are transformed or repackaged in relation to – for example – maturity, scale, risk in the financial intermediation process.

Auxiliary financial activities are activities related to financial intermediation but which do not involve financial intermediation themselves.

Financial corporations are presented in the following groupings:

- monetary financial institutions (MFIs)
- financial corporations except MFI and ICPF
- insurance corporations and pension funds (ICPFs)

Further information on sector classifications and classification decisions can be found in Economic statistics classifications.

4.1.1 Financial corporations[1]
ESA 2010 sector S.12

£ million

			2009	2010	2011	2012	2013	2014	2015
Production account		I							
Resources									
Output		P.1							
Market output	NHCV	P.11	243 229	227 491	238 729	235 482	249 559	253 406	246 725
Output for own final use	NHCW	P.12	4 376	4 368	4 422	4 363	4 338	4 463	4 624
Other non-market output	MM6Y	P.13	184	173	192	223	209	332	360
Total	NHCT	P.1	247 789	232 032	243 343	240 068	254 106	258 201	251 709
Total resources	NHCT	TR	247 789	232 032	243 343	240 068	254 106	258 201	251 709
Uses									
Intermediate consumption	NHCX	P.2	122 092	116 551	129 378	127 296	136 285	136 028	137 606
Gross value added	NHDB	**B.1g**	**125 697**	**115 481**	**113 965**	**112 772**	**117 821**	**122 173**	**114 103**
Total uses	NHCT	TU	247 789	232 032	243 343	240 068	254 106	258 201	251 709
Gross value added	NHDB	**B.1g**	**125 697**	**115 481**	**113 965**	**112 772**	**117 821**	**122 173**	**114 103**
less consumption of fixed capital	NHCE	P.51c	6 281	6 382	6 675	7 065	7 188	7 699	8 199
Value added, net of fixed capital consumption	NHDC	B.1n	119 416	109 099	107 290	105 707	110 633	114 474	105 904

1 The sector includes public monetary financial institutions

4.1.2 Financial corporations[1]
ESA 2010 sector S.12

£ million

			2009	2010	2011	2012	2013	2014	2015
Distribution and use of income accounts		II							
Primary distribution of income account		II.1							
Generation of income account		II.1.1							
Resources									
Total resources (gross value added)	NHDB	**B.1g**	**125 697**	**115 481**	**113 965**	**112 772**	**117 821**	**122 173**	**114 103**
Uses									
Compensation of employees		D.1							
Wages and salaries	NHCC	D.11	50 244	50 276	47 520	45 268	48 246	50 206	52 332
Employers' social contributions	NHCD	D.12	11 046	13 224	13 503	13 560	14 144	13 602	13 389
Total	NHCR	D.1	61 290	63 500	61 023	58 828	62 390	63 808	65 721
Taxes on production and imports, paid		D.2							
Production taxes other than on products	NHCS	D.29	2 466	5 786	2 435	2 602	2 689	2 737	2 788
less subsidies, received		D.3							
Production subsidies other than on products	NHCA	D.39	–	–	–	–	–	–	–
Operating surplus, gross	NQNV	B.2g	61 941	46 195	50 507	51 342	52 742	55 628	45 594
Total uses (gross value added)	NHDB	**B.1g**	**125 697**	**115 481**	**113 965**	**112 772**	**117 821**	**122 173**	**114 103**
less consumption of fixed capital	NHCE	P.51c	6 281	6 382	6 675	7 065	7 188	7 699	8 199
Operating surplus, net	NHDA	B.2n	55 660	39 813	43 832	44 277	45 554	47 929	37 395

1 The sector includes public monetary financial institutions

4.1.3 Financial corporations[1]
ESA 2010 sector S.12

£ million

			2009	2010	2011	2012	2013	2014	2015	2016
Allocation of primary income account		II.1.2								
Resources										
Operating surplus, gross	NQNV	B.2g	61 941	46 195	50 507	51 342	52 742	55 628	45 594	46 092
Property income, received		D.4								
Interest		D.41								
Interest before FISIM allocation[2,3]	J4WU	D.41g	290 594	247 667	253 859	236 945	219 598	208 188	198 062	201 120
plus FISIM[3]	IV8Y	P.119	−56 981	−58 855	−47 087	−45 198	−51 019	−40 223	−37 816	−40 278
Total[3]	NHCK	D.41	233 613	188 812	206 772	191 747	168 579	167 965	160 246	160 842
Distributed income of corporations	NHCL	D.42	81 780	73 809	85 833	87 461	86 281	83 480	100 920	85 299
Reinvested earnings on foreign direct investment	NHEM	D.43	−1 469	1 329	2 302	8 800	2 853	5 542	8 695	2 287
Other investment income		D.44								
Attributable to insurance policy holders	L8GJ	D.441	16 895	13 039	11 928	13 381	14 532	21 316	4 391	4 020
Attributable to collective investment fund shareholders		D.443								
Dividends	L8H6	D.4431	2 665	6 113	3 249	3 635	4 204	4 170	4 369	4 851
Retained earnings	L8HD	D.4432	4 170	9 559	5 081	5 680	6 576	6 523	6 835	7 584
Total	L8GX	D.443	6 835	15 672	8 330	9 315	10 780	10 693	11 204	12 435
Total	NHDG	D.44	23 730	28 711	20 258	22 696	25 312	32 009	15 595	16 455
Rent	NHDH	D.45	31	33	35	36	36	36	36	36
Total	NHDF	D.4	337 685	292 694	315 200	310 740	283 061	289 032	285 492	264 919
Total resources	NQNW	TR	399 626	338 889	365 707	362 082	335 803	344 660	331 086	311 011
Uses										
Property income, paid		D.4								
Interest		D.41								
Interest before FISIM allocation[2]	J4WW	D.41g	209 764	168 869	172 009	162 787	141 780	127 700	118 296	114 985
plus FISIM[2]	IV8Z	P.119	6 722	3 703	10 357	8 531	5 602	17 447	21 305	22 055
Total	NHCM	D.41	216 486	172 572	182 366	171 318	147 382	145 147	139 601	137 040
Distributed income of corporations	NHCN	D.42	49 487	42 443	49 338	50 014	59 094	52 518	71 140	60 622
Reinvested earnings on foreign direct investment	NHEO	D.43	11 417	4 683	3 603	4 478	9 528	6 052	9 897	11 676
Other investment income		D.44								
Attributable to insurance policy holders	L8GO	D.441	43 608	39 480	37 891	36 905	38 158	43 743	29 518	27 714
Payable on pension entitlements	L8GV	D.442	67 817	77 856	74 956	65 918	63 132	77 972	71 412	73 681
Attributable to collective investment fund shareholders		D.443								
Dividends	L8HB	D.4431	3 218	6 694	3 412	3 666	4 127	4 213	4 461	4 916
Retained earnings	L8HI	D.4432	5 035	10 468	5 330	5 729	6 451	6 596	6 980	7 686
Total	L8H4	D.443	8 253	17 162	8 742	9 395	10 578	10 809	11 441	12 602
Total	NQCG	D.44	119 678	134 498	121 589	112 218	111 868	132 524	112 371	113 997
Rent	NHDK	D.45	–	–	–	–	–	–	–	–
Total	NHDI	D.4	397 068	354 196	356 896	338 028	327 872	336 241	333 009	323 335
Balance of primary incomes, gross	NQNY	B.5g	**2 558**	**−15 307**	**8 811**	**24 054**	**7 931**	**8 419**	**−1 923**	**−12 324**
Total uses	NQNW	TU	399 626	338 889	365 707	362 082	335 803	344 660	331 086	311 011
less consumption of fixed capital	NHCE	P.51c	6 281	6 382	6 675	7 065	7 188	7 699	8 199	8 634
Balance of primary incomes, net	NHDL	B.5n	−3 723	−21 689	2 136	16 989	743	720	−10 122	−20 958

1 The sector includes public monetary financial institutions
2 Financial intermediation services indirectly measured
3 For years 1987 to 1996 the FISIM and non-FISIM components do not sum to the
total interest received by financial corporations. The components will be reviewed when this period is next open for revision in Blue Book 2018, all else being equal total interest received by financial corporations will be unrevised

4.1.4 Financial corporations[1]
ESA 2010 sector S.12

£ million

			2009	2010	2011	2012	2013	2014	2015	2016
Secondary distribution of income account		**II.2**								
Resources										
Balance of primary incomes, gross	NQNY	**B.5g**	**2 558**	**−15 307**	**8 811**	**24 054**	**7 931**	**8 419**	**−1 923**	**−12 324**
Net social contributions		D.61								
Employers' actual social contributions	L8N7	D.611	43 239	55 536	55 078	59 446	62 430	55 557	51 009	53 479
Employers' imputed social contributions	M9WV	D.612	10 515	12 268	12 464	12 917	14 019	13 620	13 362	14 314
Households' actual social contributions	L8PD	D.613	10 257	10 896	10 257	11 002	12 094	13 948	11 933	13 488
Households' social contribution supplements	L8PZ	D.614	67 817	77 856	74 956	65 918	63 132	77 972	71 412	73 681
Social insurance scheme service charges	L8LP	D.61SC	−11 101	−12 568	−14 740	−17 046	−18 324	−18 819	−19 620	−20 318
Total	NQNZ	D.61	120 727	143 988	138 015	132 237	133 351	142 278	128 096	134 644
Other current transfers		D.7								
Net non-life insurance premiums	NQOF	D.71	37 750	47 996	45 636	44 589	47 631	41 805	43 123	42 813
Non-life insurance claims	NHDN	D.72	2 435	2 873	1 986	2 112	1 966	1 986	2 181	2 149
Miscellaneous current transfers	NQOG	D.75	182	173	193	212	229	243	240	240
Total	NQOE	D.7	40 367	51 042	47 815	46 913	49 826	44 034	45 544	45 202
Total resources	NQOH	TR	163 652	179 723	194 641	203 204	191 108	194 731	171 717	167 522
Uses										
Current taxes on income and wealth		D.5								
Taxes on income	NHDO	D.51	5 135	10 072	11 657	12 241	11 123	12 597	13 674	14 168
Other current taxes	MTF7	D.59	–	–	1 899	1 641	2 352	2 853	3 363	3 111
Total	NHCP	D.5	5 135	10 072	13 556	13 882	13 475	15 450	17 037	17 279
Other social insurance benefits	L8R3	D.622	65 286	71 162	71 946	78 077	79 189	75 162	81 550	84 970
Other current transfers		D.7								
Net non-life insurance premiums	NHDU	D.71	2 435	2 873	1 986	2 112	1 966	1 988	2 187	2 157
Non-life insurance claims	NQOI	D.72	37 750	47 996	45 636	44 589	47 631	41 805	43 123	42 813
Miscellaneous current transfers	NHEK	D.75	262	253	2 592	7 559	6 118	6 330	5 697	4 052
Total	NHDT	D.7	40 447	51 122	50 214	54 260	55 715	50 123	51 007	49 022
Gross disposable income	NQOJ	**B.6g**	**52 784**	**47 367**	**58 925**	**56 985**	**42 729**	**53 996**	**22 123**	**16 251**
Total uses	NQOH	TU	163 652	179 723	194 641	203 204	191 108	194 731	171 717	167 522
less consumption of fixed capital	NHCE	P.51c	6 281	6 382	6 675	7 065	7 188	7 699	8 199	8 634
Disposable income, net	NHDV	B.6n	46 503	40 985	52 250	49 920	35 541	46 297	13 924	7 617

1 The sector includes public monetary financial institutions

4.1.6 Financial corporations[1]
ESA 2010 sector S.12

£ million

Use of disposable income account		II.4.1	2009	2010	2011	2012	2013	2014	2015	2016
Resources											
Total resources (gross disposable income)	NQOJ	**B.6g**	**52 784**	**47 367**	**58 925**	**56 985**	**42 729**	**53 996**	**22 123**	**16 251**
Uses											
Adjustment for the change in pension entitlements	NQOK	D.8	55 441	72 826	66 069	54 160	54 162	67 116	46 546	49 674
Gross saving	NQOL	**B.8g**	**−2 657**	**−25 459**	**−7 144**	**2 825**	**−11 433**	**−13 120**	**−24 423**	**−33 423**
Total uses (gross disposable income)	NQOJ	**B.6g**	**52 784**	**47 367**	**58 925**	**56 985**	**42 729**	**53 996**	**22 123**	**16 251**
less consumption of fixed capital	NHCE	P.51c	6 281	6 382	6 675	7 065	7 188	7 699	8 199	8 634
Saving, net	NQOM	B.8n	−8 938	−31 841	−13 819	−4 240	−18 621	−20 819	−32 622	−42 057

1 The sector includes public monetary financial institutions

4.1.7 Financial corporations[1]
ESA 2010 sector S.12

£ million

			2009	2010	2011	2012	2013	2014	2015	2016
Accumulation accounts		III								
Capital account		III.1								
Change in net worth due to saving and capital transfers account		III.1.1								
Changes in liabilities and net worth										
Gross saving	NQOL	**B.8g**	**−2 657**	**−25 459**	**−7 144**	**2 825**	**−11 433**	**−13 120**	**−24 423**	**−33 423**
Capital transfers, receivable		D.9r								
Other capital transfers	NHEB	D.99r	10 120	67	22	8 922	755	436	1 079	186
Total	NHDZ	D.9r	10 120	67	22	8 922	755	436	1 079	186
Capital transfers, payable		D.9p								
Capital taxes	NHBW	D.91p	1 805	–	–	–	–	–	–	–
Other capital transfers	NHCB	D.99p	176	67	22	48	755	436	1 079	186
Total	NHEC	D.9p	1 981	67	22	48	755	436	1 079	186
Changes in net worth due to gross saving and capital transfers	NQON	B.101g	5 482	−25 459	−7 144	11 699	−11 433	−13 120	−24 423	−33 423
Changes in assets										
Changes in net worth due to gross saving and capital transfers	NQON	B.101g	5 482	−25 459	−7 144	11 699	−11 433	−13 120	−24 423	−33 423
less consumption of fixed capital	NHCE	P.51c	6 281	6 382	6 675	7 065	7 188	7 699	8 199	8 634
Changes in net worth due to net saving and capital transfers	NHEF	B.101n	−799	−31 841	−13 819	4 634	−18 621	−20 819	−32 622	−42 057
Acquisition of non-financial assets account		III.1.2								
Changes in liabilities and net worth										
Changes in net worth due to net saving and capital transfers	NHEF	B.101n	−799	−31 841	−13 819	4 634	−18 621	−20 819	−32 622	−42 057
Consumption of fixed capital	NHCE	P.51c	6 281	6 382	6 675	7 065	7 188	7 699	8 199	8 634
Total change in liabilities and net worth	NQON	B.101g	5 482	−25 459	−7 144	11 699	−11 433	−13 120	−24 423	−33 423
Changes in assets										
Gross capital formation		P.5								
Gross fixed capital formation	NHCJ	P.51g	5 701	6 544	7 454	9 059	7 451	8 081	9 450	9 891
Changes in inventories	NHCI	P.52	−6	1	4	1	3	8	4	–
Acquisitions less disposals of valuables[2]	NPQI	P.53	746	102	−14	−184	1 586	−626	−618	−78
Total	NHEG	P.5	6 441	6 647	7 444	8 876	9 040	7 463	8 836	9 813
Acquisitions less disposals of non-produced non-financial assets	NHEI	NP	4	4	4	4	4	4	4	4
Net lending(+) / net borrowing(-)	NHCQ	**B.9n**	**−963**	**−32 110**	**−14 592**	**2 819**	**−20 477**	**−20 587**	**−33 263**	**−43 240**
Total change in assets	NQON	B.101g	5 482	−25 459	−7 144	11 699	−11 433	−13 120	−24 423	−33 423

1 The sector includes public monetary financial institutions
2 Acquisitions less disposals of valuables can be a volatile series but any volatility is likely to be GDP neutral as it is offset in UK trade figures

4.1.8 Financial corporations[1]
ESA 2010 sector S.12. Unconsolidated

£ million

			2009	2010	2011	2012	2013	2014	2015	2016
Financial account		III.2								
Net acquisition of financial assets		F.A								
Currency and deposits		F.2								
Currency	NFCV	F.21	2 476	−181	431	541	−438	545	−327	663
Transferable deposits		F.22								
With UK MFIs[2]	NFCX	F.22N1	535 802	−61 735	36 932	206 112	−21 611	−196 233	−69 521	171 216
With rest of the world MFIs	NFDB	F.22N9	−208 510	191 533	94 840	−183 548	−233 648	23 697	−125 569	97 911
Other deposits	NFDC	F.29	5 372	−6 330	4 566	−587	−7 587	10 479	−9 235	8 251
Total	NFCU	F.2	335 140	123 287	136 769	22 518	−263 284	−161 512	−204 652	278 041
Debt securities		F.3								
Short-term		F.31								
Issued by UK central government	NFDF	F.31N1	25 565	−11 251	10 705	−10 660	−6 927	13 095	5 592	9 595
Issued by UK local government	NFDJ	F.31N2	–	–	–	–	–	–	–	–
Issued by UK MFIs	NFDK	F.31N5	−61 787	−14 790	−8 840	−2 039	−1 848	3 610	356	10 501
Issued by other UK residents[3]	NFDP	F.31N6	−925	−2 369	1 365	−371	−529	2 374	−483	2 113
Issued by rest of the world	NFDQ	F.31N9	7 679	−11 869	−4 860	9 659	−18 969	3 710	−1 785	−23 228
Long-term		F.32								
Issued by UK central government	NFDS	F.32N1	169 651	93 418	81 295	97 593	64 365	67 099	−2 325	12 984
Issued by UK local government	NFDV	F.32N2	−139	−29	505	964	58	−209	185	128
Issued by UK MFIs and other UK residents[4]	KVG3	F.32N5-6	144 421	−702	−40 052	−53 671	−9 340	−18 667	−45 709	−10 684
Issued by rest of the world	NFEA	F.32N9	32 113	−9 509	−47 577	32 775	−23 074	40 148	−6 137	−95 883
Total	NFDD	F.3	316 578	42 899	−7 459	74 250	3 736	111 160	−50 306	−94 474
Loans		F.4								
Short-term		F.41								
By UK MFIs[5]	NFEH	F.41N1	−208 015	−20 477	−52 628	−27 683	−50 656	−103 483	18 474	73 021
Long-term		F.42								
Direct investment	NFEN	F.421	1 189	−759	1 369	843	−1 537	−17 641	734	3 391
Secured on dwellings	NFEQ	F.422	9 862	7 070	19 278	16 043	18 824	27 388	41 405	42 901
Finance leasing	NFEU	F.423	486	473	468	468	469	470	468	468
Other by UK residents[6]	NFEV	F.424N1	25 361	62 491	2 407	−21 232	42 192	13 309	12 110	31 083
Total	NFEF	F.4	−171 117	48 798	−29 106	−31 561	9 292	−79 957	73 191	150 864
Equity and investment fund shares/units		F.5								
Equity		F.51								
Listed UK shares[4]	NFFC	F.511N1	20 110	10 965	−3 170	−2 915	−11 509	−24 496	−12 108	−21 812
Unlisted UK shares[4]	NFFD	F.512N1	59 667	6 386	26 021	−45 046	−19 812	−1 031	−1 816	−7 406
Other equity		F.519								
UK shares and bonds issued by other UK residents[4]	NSPS	F.519N7	–	–	–	–	–	–	–	–
Shares and other equity issued by rest of the world	NFFH	F.519N9	33 787	−4 475	−64 378	55 605	−9 839	27 590	−41 834	−56 220
Investment fund shares/units		F.52								
UK mutual funds' shares	NFFL	F.52N1	22 927	30 989	2 950	16 796	1 904	23 851	35 997	20 805
Rest of the world mutual funds' shares	NFFM	F.52N9	10 565	26 441	13 225	19 029	10 213	7 485	6 164	2 910
Total	NFEX	F.5	147 056	70 306	−25 352	43 469	−29 043	33 399	−13 597	−61 723
Insurance, pensions and standardised guarantee schemes		F.6								
Non-life insurance technical reserves	NFFQ	F.61	−227	−416	−253	−64	−16	–	−25	8
Pension schemes[7]	MA2A	F.6M	9 910	11 645	11 845	12 304	13 469	13 045	12 735	13 686
Provisions for calls under standardised guarantees	M9ZL	F.66	–	–	–	–	–	27	14	–
Total	NPWR	F.6	9 683	11 229	11 592	12 240	13 453	13 072	12 724	13 694
Financial derivatives and employee stock options	MN5J	F.7	−26 876	−44 107	13 390	−46 557	36 534	27 303	−79 798	20 687
Of which: financial derivatives	NFEB	F.71	−26 876	−44 107	13 390	−46 557	36 534	27 303	−79 798	20 687
Other accounts receivable	NFFR	F.8	−8 653	−9 826	6 194	8 524	2 878	−46	−1 719	9 222
Total net acquisition of financial assets	NFCQ	F.A	601 811	242 586	106 028	82 883	−226 434	−56 581	−264 157	316 311

4.1.8 Financial corporations[1]

ESA 2010 sector S.12. Unconsolidated

continued

£ million

			2009	2010	2011	2012	2013	2014	2015	2016
Financial account		III.2								
Net acquisition of financial liabilities		F.L								
Currency and deposits		F.2								
Currency	NFFZ	F.21	6 330	1 988	3 220	3 313	2 236	3 637	3 849	7 363
Transferable deposits		F.22								
With UK MFIs	NFGB	F.22N1	203 231	37 738	140 592	161 331	−237 016	−130 732	−111 973	285 587
Other deposits	NFGG	F.29	7 920	−9 173	9 884	−166	9 604	5 248	−4 704	3 188
Total	NFFY	F.2	217 481	30 553	153 696	164 478	−225 176	−121 847	−112 828	296 138
Debt securities		F.3								
Short-term		F.31								
Issued by UK MFIs	NFGO	F.31N5	22 398	−85 918	−91 548	4 869	−11 755	22 015	−4 207	20 237
MMIs issued by other UK residents	NFGT	F.31N6	−1 738	−62	252	249	554	1 505	347	978
Long-term		F.32								
Issued by UK MFIs and other UK residents[4]	KVH8	F.32N5-6	179 318	104 864	31 169	−169 773	34 183	−564	−58 846	7 438
Total	NFGH	F.3	199 978	18 884	−60 127	−164 655	22 982	22 956	−62 706	28 653
Loans		F.4								
Short-term		F.41								
By UK MFIs	NFHL	F.41N1	−11 062	−4 805	−51 334	27 159	−28 975	−146 304	−5 653	11 227
By rest of the world MFIs	NFHP	F.41N9	−53 507	101 253	−30 026	20 728	−30 760	108 347	−188 786	−49 027
Long-term		F.42								
Direct investment	NFHR	F.421	−62	−941	−1 385	−561	2 564	−2 853	4 175	8 032
Finance leasing	NFHY	F.423	141	144	144	144	144	144	144	144
Other long-term loans		F.424								
By UK residents	NFHZ	F.424N1	2 185	12 385	8 031	3 018	−2 939	7 976	26 934	−19 278
By rest of the world	NFIA	F.424N9	−17 774	−338	1 488	−1 155	1 505	2 103	4 754	312
Total	NFHJ	F.4	−80 079	107 698	−73 082	49 333	−58 461	−30 587	−158 432	−48 590
Equity and investment fund shares/units		F.5								
Equity		F.51								
Listed UK shares[4]	NFIG	F.511N1	87 172	9 175	1 731	3 952	8 273	5 049	11 023	2 509
Unlisted UK shares[4]	NFIH	F.512N1	93 499	4 820	11 582	−30 152	−13 666	9 073	12 924	15 838
Other equity		F.519								
Other UK equity	NFII	F.519N6	–	–	–	–	–	–	–	–
UK shares and bonds issued by other UK residents[4]	NSPT	F.519N7	–	–	–	–	–	–	–	–
Investment fund shares/units		F.52								
UK mutual funds' shares	NFIP	F.52N1	26 271	43 235	19 580	18 375	17 723	25 256	8 482	2 031
Total	NFIB	F.5	206 942	57 230	32 893	−7 825	12 330	39 378	32 429	20 378
Insurance, pensions and standardised guarantee schemes		F.6								
Non-life insurance technical reserves	NFIU	F.61	−1 953	−12 463	−945	4 232	−2 033	6	−3 105	936
Life insurance and annuity entitlements	M9WL	F.62	4 204	4 950	7 835	436	−8 600	−14 194	57 601	20 437
Pension schemes[7]	MA2N	F.6M	56 136	73 871	67 036	55 126	55 189	68 106	47 513	50 730
Total	NPWS	F.6	58 387	66 358	73 926	59 794	44 556	53 918	102 009	72 103
Financial derivatives and employee stock options	MN65	F.7	173	180	169	163	157	156	154	166
Other accounts payable	NFIV	F.8	−14 539	−21 566	−5 892	−23 926	−3 912	−199	−17 945	6 062
Total net acquisition of financial liabilities	NFFU	F.L	588 343	259 337	121 583	77 362	−207 524	−36 225	−217 319	374 910
Net lending(+) / net borrowing(-)		B.9								
Total net acquisition of financial assets	NFCQ	F.A	601 811	242 586	106 028	82 883	−226 434	−56 581	−264 157	316 311
less total net acquisition of financial liabilities	NFFU	F.L	588 343	259 337	121 583	77 362	−207 524	−36 225	−217 319	374 910
Net lending(+) / borrowing(-) from the financial account	NYNL	B.9f	13 468	−16 751	−15 555	5 521	−18 910	−20 356	−46 838	−58 599
Statistical discrepancy between the financial and non-financial accounts	NYOX	dB.9	−14 431	−15 359	963	−2 702	−1 567	−231	13 575	15 359
Net lending (+) / borrowing (-) from non-financial accounts	NHCQ	B.9n	−963	−32 110	−14 592	2 819	−20 477	−20 587	−33 263	−43 240

1 The sector includes public monetary financial institutions
2 Monetary financial institutions
3 Money market instruments
4 Prior to 1990, it is not possible to distinguish some elements of F.32N5-6, F.511N1 and F.512N1. These elements are shown combined as F.519N7.
5 All loans secured on dwellings and all finance leasing are treated as long-term loans
6 Other than direct investment loans, loans secured on dwellings and loans for finance leasing
7 F.63 pension entitlements, F.64 Claims on pension fund on pension managers, F.65 Entitlements to non-pension benefits

4.1.9 Financial corporations[1]
ESA 2010 sector S.12

£ million

			2013	2014	2015	2016
Other changes in assets account		**III.3**				
Other changes in volume of assets account		**III.3.1**				
Changes in net worth due to other changes in volume of assets		**B.102**				
Monetary gold and special drawing rights	H287	AF.1	–	–	–	–
Currency and deposits	M9NJ	AF.2	1 874	3 165	30 152	24 367
Debt securities	N474	AF.3	–5 349	–32 930	12 512	–18 344
Loans	N496	AF.4	–37 209	–43 683	–17 604	–119 426
Equity and investment fund shares/units	N4B8	AF.5	–	–	–	–
Insurance, pensions and standardised guarantee schemes	N4DA	AF.6	–	–	–	–
Financial derivatives and employee stock options	N4F7	AF.7	–	–	–	–
Other accounts receivable/payable	N4H6	AF.8	–7 283	–21 515	10 315	–15 598
Total	CWTH	**B.102**	–47 967	–94 963	35 375	–129 001

1 The sector includes public monetary financial institutions

4.1.10 Financial corporations[1]
ESA 2010 sector S.12

£ million

			2013	2014	2015	2016
Other changes in assets account		III.3				
Revaluation account		III.3.2				
Changes in net worth due to nominal holding gains and losses		B.103				
Monetary gold and special drawing rights	H28C	AF.1	–	–	–	–
Currency and deposits	M9R5	AF.2	2 258	–16 636	–18 535	–63 957
Debt securities	N485	AF.3	129 117	137 479	–84 104	341 485
Loans	N4A7	AF.4	–38 600	55 948	21 030	210 114
Equity and investment fund shares/units	N4C9	AF.5	126 214	–61 499	21 575	220 708
Insurance, pensions and standardised guarantee schemes	N4E9	AF.6	–57 984	–63 389	23 916	–223 376
Financial derivatives and employee stock options	N4G6	AF.7	5 796	–23 480	–1 900	11 298
Other accounts receivable/payable	N4I7	AF.8	57	–2 787	–2 963	19 336
Total	CWU9	**B.103**	166 858	25 636	–40 981	515 608

1 The sector includes public monetary financial institutions

4.1.11 Financial corporations[1]
ESA 2010 sector S.12. Unconsolidated

£ billion

			2009	2010	2011	2012	2013	2014	2015	2016
Financial balance sheet at end of period		IV.3								
Non-financial assets	NG38	**AN**	114.6	124.0	128.5	129.9	133.8	141.7	143.2	145.8
Total financial assets		**AF.A**								
Currency and deposits		AF.2								
Currency	NLJE	AF.21	12.8	10.4	10.9	11.4	10.9	11.5	11.2	12.1
Deposits with UK MFIs[2]	NLJG	AF.22N1	2 363.8	2 248.0	2 363.8	2 555.1	2 562.1	2 147.9	2 081.2	2 345.4
Deposits with rest of the world MFIs[2]	NLJK	AF.22N9	2 115.7	2 287.4	2 540.9	2 285.1	2 037.1	2 042.4	1 912.7	2 335.7
Other deposits	NLJL	AF.29	16.9	10.6	15.1	14.6	7.0	17.4	8.2	16.5
Total	NLJD	AF.2	4 509.2	4 556.3	4 930.7	4 866.0	4 617.1	4 219.2	4 013.3	4 709.7
Debt securities		AF.3								
Short-term		AF.31								
Issued by UK central government	NLJO	AF.31N1	37.6	26.2	37.1	26.6	19.2	32.2	38.5	48.5
Issued by UK local government	NLJS	AF.31N2	–	–	–	–	–	–	–	–
Issued by UK MFIs	NLJT	AF.31N5	73.5	57.4	45.3	43.6	43.2	49.2	51.0	62.7
MMIs issued by other UK residents[3]	NLJY	AF.31N6	4.3	2.7	3.3	3.0	2.3	5.0	4.1	6.3
MMIs issued by rest of the world	NLJZ	AF.31N9	109.3	102.9	93.9	99.9	78.5	83.5	85.5	79.8
Long-term		AF.32								
Issued by UK central government	NLKB	AF.32N1	576.6	689.9	864.0	942.1	978.4	1 230.0	1 200.9	1 382.3
Issued by UK local government	NLKE	AF.32N2	0.5	0.6	1.4	2.0	2.1	3.2	2.1	2.7
Issued by UK MFIs and other UK residents[4]	KVF4	AF.32N5-6	878.3	909.1	894.3	893.6	873.6	890.1	854.0	927.7
Issued by rest of the world	NLKJ	AF.32N9	845.1	845.2	820.4	859.0	818.6	881.4	867.4	915.3
Total	NLJM	AF.3	2 525.2	2 633.9	2 759.7	2 869.7	2 816.0	3 174.6	3 103.5	3 425.3
Loans		AF.4								
Short-term		AF.41								
By UK MFIs[5]	NLKQ	AF.41N1	2 503.5	2 468.2	2 372.7	2 285.0	2 179.0	2 079.1	2 064.6	2 331.8
Long-term		AF.42								
Direct investment	NLKW	AF.421	6.9	6.6	6.6	49.6	54.5	28.0	27.5	23.1
Loans secured on dwellings	NLKZ	AF.422	1 230.9	1 147.0	1 162.7	1 190.6	1 208.4	1 237.3	1 279.7	1 323.5
Finance leasing	NLLD	AF.423	28.7	29.2	29.6	30.1	30.6	31.0	31.5	32.0
Other by UK residents[6]	NLLE	AF.424N1	627.2	767.7	761.9	758.1	779.1	729.5	746.6	849.7
Total	NLKO	AF.4	4 397.1	4 418.7	4 333.5	4 313.4	4 251.6	4 105.0	4 149.9	4 560.2
Equity and investment fund shares/units		AF.5								
Equity		AF.51								
Listed UK shares[4]	NLLL	AF.511N1	572.0	639.5	490.7	451.9	490.8	460.7	452.7	448.4
Unlisted UK shares[4]	NLLM	AF.512N1	324.1	362.1	373.4	380.4	383.0	328.2	328.5	325.7
Other equity		AF.519								
UK shares and bonds issued by other UK residents[4]	NSQL	AF.519N7	–	–	–	–	–	–	–	–
Shares and other equity issued by rest of the world	NLLQ	AF.519N9	872.1	969.3	862.6	989.3	1 092.5	1 198.5	1 167.2	1 363.4
Investment fund shares/units		AF.52								
UK mutual funds' shares	NLLU	AF.52N1	385.2	502.1	488.7	574.4	661.2	718.5	742.6	788.7
Rest of the world mutual funds' shares	NLLV	AF.52N9	118.3	155.9	168.9	209.4	227.7	224.2	252.1	287.0
Total	NLLG	AF.5	2 271.6	2 628.8	2 384.3	2 605.4	2 855.2	2 930.1	2 943.1	3 213.2
Insurance, pensions and standardised guarantee schemes		AF.6								
Non-life insurance technical reserves	NLLZ	AF.61	1.2	0.8	0.6	0.5	0.5	0.5	0.4	0.5
Pension schemes[6]	M9V6	AF.6M	562.5	494.5	777.0	657.8	504.1	853.2	792.1	862.5
Provisions for calls under standardised guarantees	M9UK	AF.66	–	–	–	–	–	–	–	0.041
Total	NPYH	AF.6	563.7	495.3	777.6	658.3	504.5	853.7	792.6	863.0
Financial derivatives and employee stock options	MMU9	AF.7	5 248.5	6 387.1	8 124.2	6 921.7	5 562.9	6 212.2	4 538.6	5 368.3
Of which: financial derivatives	NLKK	AF.71	5 248.5	6 387.1	8 124.2	6 921.7	5 562.9	6 212.2	4 538.6	5 368.3
Other accounts receivable	NLMA	AF.8	68.3	56.3	53.2	58.6	62.0	55.6	59.1	73.4
Total financial assets	NLIZ	**AF.A**	19 583.6	21 176.5	23 363.2	22 293.2	20 669.3	21 550.3	19 600.1	22 213.0

4.1.11 Financial corporations[1]
ESA 2010 sector S.12. Unconsolidated

£ billion

			2009	2010	2011	2012	2013	2014	2015	2016
Financial balance sheet at end of period		IV.3								
Total financial liabilities		AF.L								
Currency and deposits		AF.2								
Currency	NLMI	AF.21	58.7	60.7	63.9	67.2	69.4	73.1	76.9	84.3
Transferable deposits		AF.22								
With UK MFIs	NLMK	AF.22N1	6 601.9	6 610.2	6 953.6	6 980.7	6 754.0	6 400.3	6 275.3	7 018.9
Other deposits	NLMP	AF.29	25.2	11.1	21.0	20.9	30.4	35.8	31.2	34.3
Total	NLMH	AF.2	6 685.8	6 681.9	7 038.5	7 068.8	6 853.9	6 509.1	6 383.4	7 137.4
Debt securities		AF.3								
Short-term		AF.31								
Issued by UK MFIs	NLMX	AF.31N5	360.1	278.3	180.8	185.4	173.6	196.4	198.1	236.2
MMIs issued by other UK residents	NLNC	AF.31N6	10.5	10.7	11.4	11.7	12.2	13.7	14.1	15.0
Long-term		AF.32								
Issued by UK MFIs and other UK residents[4]	KVH2	AF.32N5-6	1 701.6	1 682.9	1 718.3	1 663.3	1 516.2	1 657.9	1 643.9	1 726.7
Total	NLMQ	AF.3	2 072.2	1 971.9	1 910.6	1 860.3	1 702.1	1 867.9	1 856.1	1 977.8
Loans		AF.4								
Short-term		AF.41								
By UK MFIs	NLNU	AF.41N1	925.0	873.4	790.3	820.2	769.9	643.6	639.8	705.7
By rest of the world MFIs	NLNY	AF.41N9	579.2	682.8	650.4	677.3	644.8	717.7	531.2	587.3
Long-term		AF.42								
Direct investment	NLOA	AF.421	8.7	7.6	5.6	50.6	53.3	43.3	45.8	33.0
Finance leasing	NLOH	AF.423	4.2	4.3	4.5	4.6	4.8	4.9	5.1	5.2
Other by UK residents	NLOI	AF.424N1	36.0	97.5	102.8	109.5	124.0	95.2	96.6	105.5
By rest of the world	NLOJ	AF.424N9	42.2	39.1	37.2	38.5	50.4	33.0	29.1	31.0
Total	NLNS	AF.4	1 595.4	1 704.7	1 590.9	1 700.9	1 647.2	1 537.6	1 347.5	1 467.7
Equity and investment fund shares/units		AF.5								
Equity		AF.51								
Listed UK shares[4]	NLOP	AF.511N1	373.3	415.9	289.2	391.4	460.7	480.9	463.3	454.3
Unlisted UK shares[4]	NLOQ	AF.512N1	595.9	619.1	654.1	667.3	657.1	699.9	705.3	770.1
Other equity		AF.519								
UK shares and bonds issued by other UK residents[4]	NSQM	AF.519N7	–	–	–	–	–	–	–	–
Investment fund shares/units		AF.52								
UK mutual funds' shares	NLOY	AF.52N1	566.4	694.0	678.8	777.9	883.7	963.1	1 012.7	1 088.5
Total	NLOK	AF.5	1 535.6	1 729.0	1 622.1	1 836.6	2 001.5	2 143.9	2 181.4	2 312.9
Insurance, pensions and standardised guarantee schemes		AF.6								
Non-life insurance technical reserves	NLPD	AF.61	70.9	58.5	57.5	61.8	59.7	59.7	56.6	57.6
Life insurance and annuity entitlements	M9S4	AF.62	549.8	572.3	547.3	554.3	574.2	575.7	616.6	641.0
Pension schemes[6]	M9VJ	AF.6M	1 836.8	1 923.4	2 340.6	2 360.8	2 278.2	2 730.1	2 696.6	3 023.5
Total	NPYI	AF.6	2 457.6	2 554.1	2 945.4	2 976.8	2 912.1	3 365.5	3 369.8	3 722.0
Financial derivatives and employee stock options	MMX5	AF.7	5 159.2	6 308.1	8 021.7	6 846.4	5 445.4	6 091.0	4 499.3	5 297.1
Of which: financial derivatives	NLNO	AF.71	5 158.7	6 307.6	8 021.2	6 845.9	5 444.9	6 090.5	4 498.9	5 296.7
Other accounts payable	NLPE	AF.8	100.8	82.2	80.5	86.6	90.5	108.2	88.1	95.5
Total financial liabilities	NLMD	**AF.L**	19 606.6	21 032.0	23 209.7	22 376.5	20 652.7	21 623.3	19 725.6	22 010.5
Financial net worth		**BF.90**								
Total financial assets	NLIZ	AF.A	19 583.6	21 176.5	23 363.2	22 293.2	20 669.3	21 550.3	19 600.1	22 213.0
less total financial liabilities	NLMD	AF.L	19 606.6	21 032.0	23 209.7	22 376.5	20 652.7	21 623.3	19 725.6	22 010.5
Financial net worth	NYOE	**BF.90**	−23.0	144.4	153.5	−83.3	16.6	−73.1	−125.5	202.5
Net worth										
Non-financial assets	NG38	AN	114.6	124.0	128.5	129.9	133.8	141.7	143.2	145.8
Financial net worth	NYOE	BF.90	−23.0	144.4	153.5	−83.3	16.6	−73.1	−125.5	202.5
Net worth	CGRU	**B.90**	91.6	268.4	282.0	46.6	150.4	68.6	17.7	348.3

1 The sector includes public monetary financial institutions
2 Monetary financial institutions
3 Money market instruments
4 Prior to 1990 it is not possible to distinguish some elements of AF.32N5-6, AF.511N1 and AF.512N1. These elements are shown combined as AF.519N7
5 All loans secured on dwellings and all finance leasing are treated as long-long-term loans

6 Other than direct investment loans, loans secured on dwellings and loans for finance leasing
7 AF.63 Pension entitlements, AF.64 Claims on pension funds on pension managers, AF.65 to non-pension benefits

4.2.2 Monetary financial institutions
ESA 2010 sectors S.121, S.122 and S.123[1]

£ million

			2009	2010	2011	2012	2013	2014	2015
Distribution and use of income accounts		II							
Primary distribution of income account		II.1							
Generation of income account before deduction of fixed capital consumption		II.1.1							
Resources									
Total resources (gross value added)	NHJN	**B.1g**	**67 971**	**65 434**	**58 290**	**53 443**	**53 275**	**53 750**	**54 724**
Uses									
Compensation of employees		D.1							
Wages and salaries	NHDJ	D.11	27 977	27 990	26 769	25 659	25 030	25 645	26 256
Employers' social contributions	NHDM	D.12	6 150	7 364	7 606	7 687	7 338	6 948	6 717
Total	NHFL	D.1	34 127	35 354	34 375	33 346	32 368	32 593	32 973
Taxes on production and imports, paid		D.2							
Production taxes other than on products	NHJE	D.29	1 155	4 413	1 015	1 118	1 148	1 168	1 189
less subsidies, received		D.3							
Production subsidies other than on products	NHET	D.39	–	–	–	–	–	–	–
Operating surplus, gross	NHBX	B.2g	32 689	25 667	22 900	18 979	19 759	19 989	20 562
Total uses (gross value added)	NHJN	**B.1g**	**67 971**	**65 434**	**58 290**	**53 443**	**53 275**	**53 750**	**54 724**

1 S.121 Central Bank, S.122 Deposit-taking corporations except the central
bank, S.123 Other monetary financial institutions

4.2.3 Monetary financial institutions
ESA 2010 sectors S.121, S.122 and S.123[1]

£ million

			2009	2010	2011	2012	2013	2014	2015	2016
Allocation of primary income account		II.1.2								
Resources										
Operating surplus, gross	NHBX	B.2g	32 689	25 667	22 900	18 979	19 759	19 989	20 562	21 974
Property income, received		D.4								
Interest	NHFE	D.41	148 121	113 182	128 462	114 655	92 971	92 909	88 793	88 686
Distributed income of corporations	NHFF	D.42	21 707	13 597	18 061	16 416	14 695	14 680	24 753	15 811
Reinvested earnings on foreign direct investment	NHKY	D.43	−1 680	−1 641	1 458	1 562	1 451	1 956	91	−994
Other investment income		D.44								
Attributable to insurance policy holders	KZJ8	D.441	28	12	8	6	8	11	5	5
Attributable to collective investment fund shareholders		D.443								
Dividends	KZK2	D.4431	8	16	8	8	8	8	9	12
Retained earnings	KZK3	D.4432	11	23	11	8	13	16	16	17
Total	L5UO	D.443	19	39	19	16	21	24	25	29
Total	NHJS	D.44	47	51	27	22	29	35	30	34
Rent	NHJT	D.45	–	–	–	–	–	–	–	–
Total	NHJR	D.4	168 195	125 189	148 008	132 655	109 146	109 580	113 667	103 537
Total resources	NRKH	TR	200 884	150 856	170 908	151 634	128 905	129 569	134 229	125 511
Uses										
Property income, paid		D.4								
Interest	NHFG	D.41	141 400	111 126	124 924	115 153	93 082	92 575	88 182	86 703
Distributed income of corporations	NHFH	D.42	18 683	13 932	16 776	14 457	32 502	18 350	30 217	25 774
Reinvested earnings on foreign direct investment	NHLB	D.43	4 450	3 986	4 438	2 912	2 341	2 853	1 918	1 299
Rent	NHJW	D.45	–	–	–	–	–	–	–	–
Total	NHJU	D.4	164 533	129 044	146 138	132 522	127 925	113 778	120 317	113 776
Balance of primary incomes, gross	NRKI	**B.5g**	**36 351**	**21 812**	**24 770**	**19 112**	**980**	**15 791**	**13 912**	**11 735**
Total uses	NRKH	TU	200 884	150 856	170 908	151 634	128 905	129 569	134 229	125 511

1 S.121 Central Bank, S.122 Deposit-taking corporations except the central
bank, S.123 Other monetary financial institutions

4.2.4 Monetary financial institutions
ESA 2010 sectors S.121, S.122 and S.123[1]

£ million

			2009	2010	2011	2012	2013	2014	2015	2016
Secondary distribution of income account		II.2								
Resources										
Balance of primary incomes, gross	NRKI	**B.5g**	**36 351**	**21 812**	**24 770**	**19 112**	**980**	**15 791**	**13 912**	**11 735**
Net social contributions		D.61								
Employers' imputed social contributions	L8RL	D.612	337	348	348	348	286	294	315	332
Total	L8TX	D.61	337	348	348	348	286	294	315	332
Other current transfers		D.7								
Non-life insurance claims	DMGE	D.72	153	154	102	82	89	77	79	78
Miscellaneous current transfers	CY8D	D.75	121	113	137	150	163	173	172	172
Total	NRKN	D.7	274	267	239	232	252	250	251	250
Total resources	NRKP	TR	36 962	22 427	25 357	19 692	1 518	16 335	14 478	12 317
Uses										
Current taxes on income, wealth etc.		D.5								
Taxes on income	NHKA	D.51	1 841	2 172	1 421	1 063	911	1 096	1 177	1 406
Other current taxes	MTF8	D.59	–	–	1 899	1 641	2 352	2 853	3 363	3 111
Total	NHFJ	D.5	1 841	2 172	3 320	2 704	3 263	3 949	4 540	4 517
Social benefits other than social transfers in kind		D.62								
Other social insurance benefits	L8SB	D.622	337	348	348	348	286	294	315	332
Total	L8TJ	D.62	337	348	348	348	286	294	315	332
Other current transfers		D.7								
Net non-life insurance premiums	DM9W	D.71	153	154	102	82	89	79	85	86
Miscellaneous current transfers	NHKW	D.75	238	229	2 104	6 226	5 023	5 398	4 764	3 297
Total	NHKF	D.7	391	383	2 206	6 308	5 112	5 477	4 849	3 383
Gross disposable income	NRKQ	**B.6g**	**34 393**	**19 524**	**19 483**	**10 332**	**−7 143**	**6 615**	**4 774**	**4 085**
Total uses	NRKP	TU	36 962	22 427	25 357	19 692	1 518	16 335	14 478	12 317

1 S.121 Central Bank, S.122 Deposit-taking corporations except the central
bank, S.123 Other monetary financial institutions

4.2.6 Monetary financial institutions
ESA 2010 sectors S.121, S.122 and S.123[1]

£ million

			2009	2010	2011	2012	2013	2014	2015	2016
Use of disposable income account		II.4.1								
Resources										
Total resources (gross disposable income)	NRKQ	**B.6g**	**34 393**	**19 524**	**19 483**	**10 332**	**−7 143**	**6 615**	**4 774**	**4 085**
Uses										
Total uses (gross saving)	NRKT	**B.8g**	**34 393**	**19 524**	**19 483**	**10 332**	**−7 143**	**6 615**	**4 774**	**4 085**

1 S.121 Central Bank, S.122 Deposit-taking corporations except the central
bank, S.123 Other monetary financial institutions

4.2.7 Monetary financial institutions
ESA 2010 sectors S.121, S.122 and S.123[1]

£ million

			2009	2010	2011	2012	2013	2014	2015	2016
Accumulation accounts		III								
Capital account		III.1								
Change in net worth due to saving and capital transfers account		III.1.1								
Changes in liabilities and net worth										
Gross saving	NRKT	B.8g	34 393	19 524	19 483	10 332	−7 143	6 615	4 774	4 085
Capital transfers, receivable		D.9r								
Other capital transfers	J97X	D.99r	9 944	–	–	–	–	–	–	–
Total	J97Y	D.9r	9 944	–	–	–	–	–	–	–
Capital transfers, payable		D.9p								
Capital taxes	NRXX	D.91p	1 805	–	–	–	–	–	–	–
Other capital transfers	NHEV	D.99p	–	–	–	–	–	–	–	–
Total	NHKP	D.9p	1 805	–	–	–	–	–	–	–
Changes in net worth due to gross saving and capital transfers	NRMH	B.101g	42 532	19 524	19 483	10 332	−7 143	6 615	4 774	4 085
Changes in assets										
Changes in net worth due to gross saving and capital transfers	NRMH	B.101g	42 532	19 524	19 483	10 332	−7 143	6 615	4 774	4 085
Acquisition of non-financial assets account		III.1.2								
Changes in net worth due to gross saving and capital transfers	NRMH	B.101g	42 532	19 524	19 483	10 332	−7 143	6 615	4 774	4 085
Changes in assets										
Gross capital formation		P.5								
Gross fixed capital formation	NHFD	P.51g	3 490	3 919	4 883	5 030	4 827	4 626	4 916	5 192
Changes in inventories	NHFC	P.52	–	–	–	–	–	–	–	–
Acquisitions less disposals of valuables[2]	NHKT	P.53	–	–	–	–	–	–	–	–
Total	NHKS	P.5	3 490	3 919	4 883	5 030	4 827	4 626	4 916	5 192
Acquisitions less disposals of non-produced non-financial assets	NHKU	NP	–	–	–	–	–	–	–	–
Net lending(+) / net borrowing(-)	NHFK	B.9n	39 042	15 605	14 600	5 302	−11 970	1 989	−142	−1 107
Changes in net worth due to gross saving and capital transfers	NRMH	B.101g	42 532	19 524	19 483	10 332	−7 143	6 615	4 774	4 085

1 S.121 Central Bank, S.122 Deposit-taking corporations except the central bank, S.123 Other monetary financial institutions
2 Acquisitions less disposals of valuables can be a volatile series but any volatility is likely to be GDP neutral as it is offset in UK trade figures

4.2.8 Monetary financial institutions
ESA 2010 sectors S.121, S.122 and S.123[1] Unconsolidated

£ million

			2009	2010	2011	2012	2013	2014	2015	2016
Financial account		III.2								
Net acquisition of financial assets		F.A								
Currency and deposits		F.2								
Currency	NGCB	F.21	2 476	−181	431	541	−438	545	−327	663
Transferable deposits		F.22								
With UK MFIs[2]	NGCD	F.22N1	442 679	11 253	139 182	250 634	38 912	−61 117	−8 638	111 218
With rest of the world MFIs	NGCH	F.22N9	−147 423	123 070	34 863	−122 631	−259 125	21 697	−61 393	99 983
Other deposits	NGCI	F.29	–	–	–	–	–	–	–	–
Total	NGCA	F.2	297 732	134 142	174 476	128 544	−220 651	−38 875	−70 358	211 864
Debt securities		F.3								
Short-term		F.31								
Issued by UK central government	NGCL	F.31N1	19 749	−11 760	2 432	−5 431	−2 588	1 653	246	−1 553
Issued by UK local government	NGCP	F.31N2					−1			
Issued by UK MFIs	NGCQ	F.31N5	−40 882	−11 494	−6 727	−5 253	264	−4 416	−342	−167
MMIs issued by other UK residents[3]	NGCV	F.31N6	−469	−36	−12	31	109	−14	39	32
MMIs issued by rest of the world	NGCW	F.31N9	10 690	−401	−10 141	4 185	−10 843	−2 726	5 950	−17 353
Long-term		F.32								
Issued by UK central government	NGCY	F.32N1	209 739	50 712	68 237	107 588	37 999	5 255	266	51 581
Issued by UK local government	NGDB	F.32N2	–	−3	–	–	–	–	–	–
Issued by UK MFIs and other UK residents[4]	KVG7	F.32N5-6	77 328	−27 071	−52 768	−52 452	−17 376	−16 697	−34 896	−17 757
Issued by rest of the world	NGDG	F.32N9	−5 939	−26 880	−31 108	−3 190	−55 345	18 757	−19 813	−84 817
Total	NGCJ	F.3	270 216	−26 933	−30 087	45 478	−47 781	1 812	−48 550	−70 034
Loans		F.4								
Short-term		F.41								
By UK MFIs[5]	NGDN	F.41N1	−208 015	−20 477	−52 628	−27 683	−50 656	−103 483	18 474	73 021
Long-term		F.42								
Direct investment	NGDT	F.421	–	–	–	–	–	–	–	–
Secured on dwellings	NGDW	F.422	35 765	15 148	14 079	10 244	13 552	24 307	32 386	40 694
Finance leasing	NGEA	F.423	–	−19	−24	−24	−23	−22	−24	−24
Other long-term loans		F.424								
By UK residents	NGEB	F.424N1	885	3 620	1 649	−232	−2 184	108	−266	724
Total	NGDL	F.4	−171 365	−1 728	−36 924	−17 695	−39 311	−79 090	50 570	114 415
Equity and investment fund shares/units		F.5								
Equity		F.51								
Listed UK shares[4]	NGEI	F.511N1	10 151	1 022	−11 110	5 705	5 867	−713	503	−263
Unlisted UK shares[4]	NGEJ	F.512N1	62 641	−11 384	−5 113	−49 918	−19 881	−2 988	−9 184	−4 220
Other equity										
UK shares and bonds issued by other UK residents[4]	NSQA	F.519N7	–	–	–	–	–	–	–	–
Shares and other equity issued by rest of the world	NGEN	F.519N9	9 570	16 321	−2 264	26 481	−13 026	7 809	−26 212	−45
Investment fund shares/units		F.52								
UK mutual funds' shares	NGER	F.52N1	35	44	9	11	27	51	91	59
Total	NGED	F.5	82 397	6 003	−18 478	−17 721	−27 013	4 159	−34 802	−4 469
Insurance, pensions and standardised guarantee schemes		F.6								
Non-life insurance technical reserves	NGEW	F.61	−59	−106	−66	−15	−4	–	−6	2
Provisions for calls under standardised guarantees	M9ZM	F.66	–	–	–	–	–	27	14	–
Total	NPWZ	F.6	−59	−106	−66	−15	−4	27	8	2
Financial derivatives and employee stock options	MN5K	F.7	−38 072	−27 480	−14 579	−6 816	11 956	2 360	10 967	19 474
Of which: financial derivatives	NGDH	F.71	−38 072	−27 480	−14 579	−6 816	11 956	2 360	10 967	19 474
Other accounts receivable	NGEX	F.8	−43	−5	26	10	−19	57	18	45
Total net acquisition of financial assets	NGBW	F.A	440 806	83 893	74 368	131 785	−322 823	−109 550	−92 147	271 297

4.2.8 Monetary financial institutions
ESA 2010 sectors S.121, S.122 and S.123[1] Unconsolidated

continued

£ million

			2009	2010	2011	2012	2013	2014	2015	2016
Financial account		III.2								
Net acquisition of financial liabilities		**F.L**								
Currency and deposits		F.2								
Currency	NGFF	F.21	6 330	1 988	3 220	3 313	2 236	3 637	3 849	7 363
Transferable deposits		F.22								
With UK MFIs	NGFH	F.22N1	203 231	37 738	140 592	161 331	−237 016	−130 732	−111 973	285 587
Total	NGFE	F.2	209 561	39 726	143 812	164 644	−234 780	−127 095	−108 124	292 950
Debt securities		F.3								
Short-term		F.31								
Issued by UK MFIs[2]	NGFU	F.31N5	22 398	−85 918	−91 548	4 869	−11 755	22 015	−4 207	20 237
Long-term		F.32								
Issued by UK MFIs and other UK residents[4]	KVI3	F.32N5-6	79 227	47 519	−38 524	−100 636	−53 219	−12 090	−10 784	−1 472
Total	NGFN	F.3	101 625	−38 399	−130 072	−95 767	−64 974	9 925	−14 991	18 765
Loans		F.4								
Long-term		F.42								
Finance leasing	NGHE	F.423	81	84	84	84	84	84	84	84
Other long-term loans		F.424								
By rest of the world	NGHG	F.424N9	82	68	44	−34	–	–	–	–
Total	NGGP	F.4	163	152	128	50	84	84	84	84
Equity and investment fund shares/units		F.5								
Equity		F.51								
Listed UK shares[4]	NGHM	F.511N1	–	–	–	−3	–	74	6 049	76
Unlisted UK shares[4]	NGHN	F.512N1	4 434	3 986	5 674	11 726	−7 892	1 697	3 171	−167
Other UK equity	NGHO	F.519N6	–	–	–	–	–	–	–	–
UK shares and bonds issued by other UK residents[4]	NSQB	F.519N7	–	–	–	–	–	–	–	–
Total	NGHH	F.5	4 434	3 986	5 674	11 723	−7 892	1 771	9 220	−91
Insurance, pensions and standardised guarantee schemes		F.6								
Pension schemes[6]	MA2Q	F.6M	343	545	541	531	535	507	499	528
Total	NPXA	F.6	343	545	541	531	535	507	499	528
Financial derivatives and employee stock options	MN66	F.7	93	94	88	90	85	85	77	84
Other accounts payable	NGIB	F.8	−3 531	216	726	−41	−413	−97	1 112	95
Total net acquisition of financial liabilities	NGFA	**F.L**	312 688	6 320	20 897	81 230	−307 355	−114 820	−112 123	312 415
Net lending(+) / borrowing(-) from the financial account		**B.9f**								
Total net acquisition of financial assets	NGBW	F.A	440 806	83 893	74 368	131 785	−322 823	−109 550	−92 147	271 297
less total net acquisition of financial liabilities	NGFA	F.L	312 688	6 320	20 897	81 230	−307 355	−114 820	−112 123	312 415
Net lending(+) / borrowing(-) from the financial account	NYNS	B.9f	128 118	77 573	53 471	50 555	−15 468	5 270	19 976	−41 118
Statistical discrepancy between the financial and non-financial accounts	NYPE	dB.9	−89 076	−61 968	−38 871	−45 253	3 498	−3 281	−20 118	40 011
Net lending (+) / borrowing (-) from non-financial accounts	NHFK	**B.9n**	**39 042**	**15 605**	**14 600**	**5 302**	**−11 970**	**1 989**	**−142**	**−1 107**

1 S.121 Central Bank, S.122 Deposit-taking corporations except the central
  bank, S.123 Other monetary financial institutions
2 Monetary financial institutions
3 Money market instruments
4 Prior to 1990, it is not possible to distinguish some elements of F.32N5-6,
  F.511N1 and F.512N1. These elements are shown combined as F.519N7
5 All loans secured on dwellings and all finance leasing are treated as
  long-term loans
6 F.63 pension entitlements, F.64 Claims on pension fund on pension
  managers, F.65 Entitlements to non-pension benefits

4.2.11 Monetary financial institutions
ESA 2010 sectors S.121, S.122 and S.123[1] Unconsolidated

£ billion

			2009	2010	2011	2012	2013	2014	2015	2016
Financial balance sheet at end of period		IV.3								
Total financial assets		AF.A								
Currency and deposits		AF.2								
Currency	NNSY	AF.21	12.7	10.3	10.8	11.3	10.9	11.4	11.1	12.0
Transferable deposits		AF.22								
With UK MFIs[2]	NNTA	AF.22N1	1 364.5	1 186.0	1 381.1	1 611.4	1 655.9	1 355.1	1 346.6	1 498.0
With rest of the MFIs	NNTE	AF.22N9	1 779.3	1 876.3	2 072.0	1 860.7	1 585.8	1 620.5	1 567.4	1 923.1
Other deposits	NNTF	AF.29	-	-	-	-	-	-	-	0.028
Total	NNSX	AF.2	3 156.6	3 072.5	3 463.9	3 483.4	3 252.6	2 987.0	2 925.1	3 433.2
Debt securities		AF.3								
Short-term		AF.31								
Issued by UK central government	NNTI	AF.31N1	22.8	10.7	13.7	8.4	5.0	6.7	8.4	7.6
Issued by UK local government	NNTM	AF.31N2	–	–	–	–	–	–	–	–
Issued by UK MFIs	NNTN	AF.31N5	32.0	21.0	14.2	8.9	9.7	5.2	5.2	5.3
MMIs issued by other UK residents[3]	NNTS	AF.31N6	–	–	–	–	0.1	0.1	0.1	0.2
MMIs issued by rest of the world	NNTT	AF.31N9	65.4	65.5	57.5	59.8	48.6	43.8	50.2	41.2
Long-term		AF.32								
Issued by UK central government	NNTV	AF.32N1	234.6	295.1	400.9	498.8	507.7	562.8	549.4	636.0
Issued by UK local government	NNTY	AF.32N2	–	–	–	–	–	–	–	–
Issued by UK MFIs and other UK residents[4]	KVF8	AF.32N5-6	367.3	374.9	334.3	312.0	332.6	311.3	286.7	330.9
Issued by rest of the world	NNUD	AF.32N9	504.0	489.0	474.7	461.0	402.0	416.5	395.2	375.1
Total	NNTG	AF.3	1 226.1	1 256.1	1 295.2	1 348.9	1 305.7	1 346.5	1 295.2	1 396.3
Loans		AF.4								
Short-term		AF.41								
By UK MFIs[5]	NNUK	AF.41N1	2 503.5	2 468.2	2 372.7	2 285.0	2 179.0	2 079.1	2 064.6	2 331.8
Long-term		AF.42								
Direct investment	NNUQ	AF.421	–	–	–	–	–	–	–	–
Secured on dwellings	NNUT	AF.422	922.0	1 045.8	1 057.2	1 077.3	1 091.4	1 116.5	1 151.0	1 197.1
Finance leasing	NNUX	AF.423	2.6	2.6	2.5	2.5	2.5	2.5	2.5	2.4
Other long-term loans		AF.424								
By UK residents	NNUY	AF.424N1	6.7	10.4	12.0	11.7	9.5	9.8	9.6	10.7
Total	NNUI	AF.4	3 434.7	3 527.0	3 444.5	3 376.5	3 282.4	3 207.9	3 227.7	3 542.0
Equity and investment fund shares/units		AF.5								
Equity		AF.51								
Listed UK shares[4]	NNVF	AF.511N1	22.4	22.0	14.5	15.8	22.5	23.2	23.5	23.2
Unlisted UK shares[4]	NNVG	AF.512N1	113.3	135.6	145.9	156.1	150.9	94.4	91.6	85.7
Other equity		AF.519								
UK shares and bonds issued by other UK residents[4]	NSQU	AF.519N7	–	–	–	–	–	–	–	–
Shares and other equity issued by rest of the world	NNVK	AF.519N9	117.8	130.5	130.7	161.2	169.1	176.4	150.9	174.8
Investment fund shares/units		AF.52								
UK mutual funds' shares	NNVO	AF.52N1	1.3	1.6	1.3	1.4	1.8	2.1	2.3	2.5
Total	NNVA	AF.5	254.8	289.7	292.5	334.4	344.3	296.2	268.2	286.2
Insurance, pensions and standardised guarantee schemes		AF.6								
Non-life insurance technical reserves	NNVT	AF.61	0.3	0.2	0.1	0.1	0.1	0.1	0.1	0.1
Provisions for calls under standardised guarantees	M9UL	AF.66	–	–	–	–	–	–	–	0.041
Total	NPYR	AF.6	0.3	0.2	0.1	0.1	0.1	0.1	0.2	0.2
Financial derivatives and employee stock options	MMV2	AF.7	4 079.8	4 242.0	5 412.7	4 650.6	3 406.2	3 778.5	2 911.4	3 339.4
Of which: financial derivatives	NNUE	AF.71	4 079.8	4 242.0	5 412.7	4 650.6	3 406.2	3 778.5	2 911.4	3 339.4
Other accounts receivable	NNVU	AF.8	0.2	0.2	0.1	0.1	0.1	0.1	0.1	0.1
Total financial assets	NNST	**AF.A**	12 152.5	12 387.8	13 909.1	13 194.0	11 591.5	11 616.4	10 627.8	11 997.2

4.2.11 Monetary financial institutions
ESA 2010 sectors S.121, S.122 and S.123[1] Unconsolidated

continued

£ billion

			2009	2010	2011	2012	2013	2014	2015	2016
Financial balance sheet at end of period		IV.3								
Total financial liabilities		**AF.L**								
Currency and deposits		AF.2								
Currency	NNWC	AF.21	58.7	60.7	63.9	67.2	69.4	73.1	76.9	84.3
Transferable deposits		AF.22								
With UK MFIs	NNWE	AF.22N1	6 601.9	6 610.2	6 953.6	6 980.7	6 754.0	6 400.3	6 275.3	7 018.9
Total	NNWB	AF.2	6 660.6	6 670.8	7 017.5	7 047.9	6 823.4	6 473.3	6 352.2	7 103.2
Debt securities		AF.3								
Short-term		AF.31								
Issued by UK MFIs	NNWR	AF.31N5	360.1	278.3	180.8	185.4	173.6	196.4	198.1	236.2
Long-term		AF.32								
Issued by UK MFIs and other UK residents[4]	KVH5	AF.32N5-6	793.9	832.6	843.4	781.3	668.5	688.9	677.5	742.8
Total	NNWK	AF.3	1 154.0	1 110.9	1 024.2	966.7	842.2	885.3	875.5	979.0
Loans		AF.4								
Short-term		AF.41								
By UK MFIs	NNXO	AF.41N1	–	–	–	–	–	–	–	–
Long-term		AF.42								
Direct investment	NNXU	AF.421	–	–	–	–	–	–	–	–
Finance leasing	NNYB	AF.423	2.3	2.3	2.4	2.5	2.6	2.7	2.8	2.8
Other long-term loans		AF.424								
By UK residents[6]	NNYC	AF.424N1	–	–	–	–	–	–	–	–
By rest of the world	NNYD	AF.424N9	1.0	1.0	0.9	1.0	1.0	–	–	–
Total	NNXM	AF.4	3.3	3.3	3.3	3.5	3.5	2.7	2.8	2.8
Equity and investment fund shares/units		AF.5								
Equity		AF.51								
Listed UK shares[4]	NNYJ	AF.511N1	0.1	0.2	0.1	0.8	1.4	1.3	1.5	1.1
Unlisted UK shares[4]	NNYK	AF.512N1	162.9	174.2	210.7	228.2	222.6	235.1	244.1	255.5
UK shares and bonds issued by other UK residents[4]	NSQV	AF.519N7	–	–	–	–	–	–	–	–
Total	NNYE	AF.5	163.0	174.4	210.7	229.0	224.0	236.5	245.6	256.5
Insurance, pensions and standardised guarantee schemes		AF.6								
Pension schemes[7]	M9VM	AF.6M	27.0	24.7	37.7	29.7	20.5	36.4	33.8	36.5
Total	NPYS	AF.6	27.0	24.7	37.7	29.7	20.5	36.4	33.8	36.5
Financial derivatives and employee stock options	MMX6	AF.7	4 027.0	4 204.4	5 387.8	4 641.6	3 379.5	3 774.2	2 899.1	3 286.8
Of which: financial derivatives	NNXI	AF.71	4 026.8	4 204.2	5 387.5	4 641.4	3 379.2	3 773.9	2 898.9	3 286.6
Other accounts payable	NNYY	AF.8	25.4	12.4	7.5	6.6	5.7	5.1	5.5	6.1
Total financial liabilities	NNVX	**AF.L**	12 060.4	12 200.9	13 688.8	12 925.0	11 298.8	11 413.5	10 414.5	11 671.0
Financial net worth		**BF.90**								
Total financial assets	NNST	AF.A	12 152.5	12 387.8	13 909.1	13 194.0	11 591.5	11 616.4	10 627.8	11 997.2
less total financial liabilities	NNVX	AF.L	12 060.4	12 200.9	13 688.8	12 925.0	11 298.8	11 413.5	10 414.5	11 671.0
Net worth	NYOL	**B.90**	92.1	186.9	220.4	269.1	292.7	202.9	213.2	326.2

1 S.121 Central Bank, S.122 Deposit-taking corporations except the central bank, S.123 Other monetary financial institutions
2 Monetary financial institutions
3 Money market instruments
4 Prior to 1990 it is not possible to distinguish some elements of AF.32N5-6, AF.511N1 and AF.512N1. These elements are shown combined as AF.519N7
5 All loans secured on dwellings and all finance leasing are treated as long-term loans
6 Other than direct investment loans, loans secured on dwellings and loans for finance leasing

7 AF.63 Pension entitlements, AF.64 Claims on pension funds on pension managers, AF.65 Entitlements to non-pension benefits

4.3.2 Financial corporations except MFI & ICPF[1]
ESA 2010 sectors S.124, S.125, S.126 & S.127[2]

£ million

			2009	2010	2011	2012	2013	2014	2015
Distribution and use of income accounts		II							
Primary distribution of income account		II.1							
Generation of income account		II.1.1							
before deduction of fixed capital consumption									
Resources									
Total resources (gross value added)	NHMH	B.1g	**33 793**	**29 862**	**33 440**	**32 251**	**34 612**	**32 464**	**34 409**
Uses									
Compensation of employees		D.1							
Wages and salaries	NHED	D.11	16 254	15 849	14 908	13 815	17 485	18 394	20 077
Employers' social contributions	NHEE	D.12	3 574	4 168	4 236	4 138	5 126	4 984	5 136
Total	NHLX	D.1	19 828	20 017	19 144	17 953	22 611	23 378	25 213
Taxes on production and imports, paid		D.2							
Production taxes other than on products	NHLY	D.29	874	931	957	1 000	1 035	1 050	1 069
less subsidies, received		D.3							
Production subsidies other than on products	NHLF	D.39	–	–	–	–	–	–	–
Operating surplus, gross	NHBY	B.2g	13 091	8 914	13 339	13 298	10 966	8 036	8 127
Total uses (gross value added)	NHMH	B.1g	**33 793**	**29 862**	**33 440**	**32 251**	**34 612**	**32 464**	**34 409**

1 Monetary financial institutions & insurance corporations and pension funds
2 S.124 Non-MMF investment funds, S.125 Other financial intermediaries, except insurance corporations and pension funds, S.126 Financial auxiliaries & S.127 Captive financial institutions and money lenders

4.3.3 Financial corporations except MFI & ICPF[1]
ESA 2010 sectors S.124, S.125, S.126 & S.127[2]

£ million

			2009	2010	2011	2012	2013	2014	2015	2016
Allocation of primary income account		II.1.2								
Resources										
Operating surplus, gross	NHBY	B.2g	13 091	8 914	13 339	13 298	10 966	8 036	8 127	6 998
Property income, received		D.4								
Interest	NHLQ	D.41	52 155	43 919	46 131	44 024	40 894	41 212	38 809	40 474
Distributed income of corporations	NHLR	D.42	27 877	34 607	36 514	39 652	43 700	39 642	40 518	38 898
Reinvested earnings on foreign direct investment	NHNS	D.43	1 403	2 398	3 245	7 187	7 072	6 105	6 401	2 989
Other investment income		D.44								
Attributable to insurance policy holders	KZI8	D.441	19	10	7	5	7	8	4	4
Attributable to collective investment fund shareholders		D.443								
Dividends	MN7C	D.4431	275	598	323	389	497	523	559	655
Retained earnings	MN7G	D.4432	434	934	508	608	778	815	872	1 023
Total	L5UC	D.443	709	1 532	831	997	1 275	1 338	1 431	1 678
Total	NHMM	D.44	728	1 542	838	1 002	1 282	1 346	1 435	1 682
Rent	NHMN	D.45	–	–	–	–	–	–	–	–
Total	NHML	D.4	82 163	82 466	86 728	91 865	92 948	88 305	87 163	84 043
Total resources	NRKX	TR	95 254	91 380	100 067	105 163	103 914	96 341	95 290	91 041
Uses										
Property income		D.4								
Interest	NHLS	D.41	73 049	59 806	55 933	54 435	52 713	50 748	49 856	48 377
Distributed income of corporations	NHLT	D.42	28 423	24 747	27 436	30 631	20 217	27 781	36 223	30 042
Reinvested earnings on foreign direct investment	NHNU	D.43	6 699	1 020	–680	1 008	6 224	2 455	6 543	9 077
Other investment income		D.44								
Attributable to collective investment fund shareholders		D.443								
Dividends	L5YG	D.4431	3 218	6 694	3 412	3 666	4 127	4 213	4 461	4 916
Retained earnings	L5YH	D.4432	5 035	10 468	5 330	5 729	6 451	6 596	6 980	7 686
Total	L5YI	D.443	8 253	17 162	8 742	9 395	10 578	10 809	11 441	12 602
Total	L6RB	D.44	8 253	17 162	8 742	9 395	10 578	10 809	11 441	12 602
Rent	NHMQ	D.45	–	–	–	–	–	–	–	–
Total	NHMO	D.4	116 424	102 735	91 431	95 469	89 732	91 793	104 063	100 098
Balance of primary incomes, gross	NRKZ	B.5g	**–21 170**	**–11 355**	**8 636**	**9 694**	**14 182**	**4 548**	**–8 773**	**–9 057**
Total uses	NRKX	TU	95 254	91 380	100 067	105 163	103 914	96 341	95 290	91 041

1 Monetary financial institutions & insurance corporations and pension funds
2 S.124 Non-MMF investment funds, S.125 Other financial intermediaries, except insurance corporations and pension funds, S.126 Financial auxiliaries & S.127 Captive financial institutions and money lenders

4.3.4 Financial corporations except MFI & ICPF[1]
ESA 2010 sectors S.124, S.125, S.126 & S.127[2]

£ million

			2009	2010	2011	2012	2013	2014	2015	2016
Secondary distribution of income account		II.2								
Resources										
Balance of primary incomes, gross	NRKZ	**B.5g**	−21 170	−11 355	8 636	9 694	14 182	4 548	−8 773	−9 057
Net social contributions		D.61								
Employers' imputed social contributions	L8RN	D.612	197	197	194	187	200	209	242	256
Total	L8TZ	D.61	197	197	194	187	200	209	242	256
Other current transfers		D.7								
Non-life insurance claims	NHMT	D.72	2 155	2 588	1 795	1 960	1 802	1 843	2 035	2 005
Miscellaneous current transfers	NRLD	D.75	61	60	56	62	66	70	68	68
Total	NRLE	D.7	2 216	2 648	1 851	2 022	1 868	1 913	2 103	2 073
Total resources	NRLF	TR	−18 757	−8 510	10 681	11 903	16 250	6 670	−6 428	−6 728
Uses										
Current taxes on income, wealth etc.		D.5								
Taxes on income	NHMU	D.51	498	5 733	8 811	8 519	8 011	7 915	10 435	8 976
Social benefits other than social transfers in kind		D.62								
Other social insurance benefits	L8SD	D.622	197	197	194	187	200	209	242	256
Total	L8TL	D.62	197	197	194	187	200	209	242	256
Other current transfers		D.7								
Net non-life insurance premiums	NHNA	D.71	2 155	2 588	1 795	1 960	1 802	1 843	2 035	2 005
Miscellaneous current transfers	NHNQ	D.75	24	24	488	1 333	1 095	932	933	755
Total	NHMZ	D.7	2 179	2 612	2 283	3 293	2 897	2 775	2 968	2 760
Gross disposable income	NRLG	**B.6g**	−21 631	−17 052	−607	−96	5 142	−4 229	−20 073	−18 720
Total uses	NRLF	TU	−18 757	−8 510	10 681	11 903	16 250	6 670	−6 428	−6 728

1 Monetary financial institutions & insurance corporations and pension funds
2 S.124 Non-MMF investment funds, S.125 Other financial intermediaries, except insurance corporations and pension funds, S.126 Financial auxiliaries
  & S.127 Captive financial institutions and money lenders

4.3.6 Financial corporations except MFI & ICPF[1]
ESA 2010 sectors S.124, S.125, S.126 & S.127[2]

£ million

			2009	2010	2011	2012	2013	2014	2015	2016
Use of disposable income account		II.4.1								
Resources										
Total resources (gross disposable income)	NRLG	**B.6g**	−21 631	−17 052	−607	−96	5 142	−4 229	−20 073	−18 720
Uses										
Total uses (gross saving)	NRLJ	**B.8g**	−21 631	−17 052	−607	−96	5 142	−4 229	−20 073	−18 720

1 Monetary financial institutions & insurance corporations and pension funds
2 S.124 Non-MMF investment funds, S.125 Other financial intermediaries, except insurance corporations and pension funds, S.126 Financial auxiliaries
  & S.127 Captive financial institutions and money lenders

4.3.7 Financial corporations except MFI & ICPF[1]
ESA 2010 sectors S.124, S.125, S.126 & S.127[2]

£ million

			2009	2010	2011	2012	2013	2014	2015	2016
Accumulation accounts		III								
Capital account		III.1								
Change in net worth due to saving and capital transfers account		III.1.1								
Changes in liabilities and net worth										
Gross saving	NRLJ	B.8g	**−21 631**	**−17 052**	**−607**	**−96**	**5 142**	**−4 229**	**−20 073**	**−18 720**
Changes in net worth due to gross saving and capital transfers	NRMI	B.101g	−21 631	−17 052	−607	−96	5 142	−4 229	−20 073	−18 720
Changes in assets										
Change in net worth due to gross saving and capital transfers	NRMI	B.101g	−21 631	−17 052	−607	−96	5 142	−4 229	−20 073	−18 720
Acquisition of non-financial assets account		III.1.2								
Changes in net worth due to gross saving and capital transfers	NRMI	B.101g	**−21 631**	**−17 052**	**−607**	**−96**	**5 142**	**−4 229**	**−20 073**	**−18 720**
Changes in assets										
Gross capital formation		P.5								
Gross fixed capital formation	NHLP	P.51g	1 965	2 291	2 294	3 555	2 422	3 257	3 844	4 049
Changes in inventories	NHLO	P.52	−	−	−	−	−	−	−	−
Acquisitions less disposals of valuables[3]	NHNN	P.53	−	−	−	−	−	−	−	−
Total	NHNM	P.5	1 965	2 291	2 294	3 555	2 422	3 257	3 844	4 049
Acquisitions less disposals of non-produced non-financial assets	NHNO	NP	16	16	16	16	16	16	16	16
Net lending(+) / net borrowing(-)	NHLW	B.9n	**−23 612**	**−19 359**	**−2 917**	**−3 667**	**2 704**	**−7 502**	**−23 933**	**−22 785**
Total change in assets	NRMI	B.101g	−21 631	−17 052	−607	−96	5 142	−4 229	−20 073	−18 720

1 Monetary financial institutions & insurance corporations and pension funds
2 S.124 Non-MMF investment funds, S.125 Other financial intermediaries, except insurance corporations and pension funds, S.126 Financial auxiliaries & S.127 Captive financial institutions and money lenders
3 Acquisitions less disposals of valuables can be a volatile series but any volatility is likely to be GDP neutral as it is offset in UK trade figures

4.3.8 Financial corporations except MFI & ICPF[1]

ESA 2010 sectors S.124, S.125, S.126 & S.127[2] Unconsolidated

£ million

			2009	2010	2011	2012	2013	2014	2015	2016
Financial account		III.2								
Net acquisition of financial assets		F.A								
Currency and deposits		F.2								
Currency	NFJD	F.21	–	–	–	–	–	–	–	–
Transferable deposits		F.22								
With UK MFIs[3]	NFJF	F.22N1	95 565	−61 167	−103 545	−43 523	−51 535	−136 313	−56 380	61 152
Of which: foreign currency deposits	NFJH	F.22N12	−20 527	−4 549	−30 566	42 001	305	−28 074	14 823	30 277
With rest of the world MFIs[3]	NFJJ	F.22N9	−55 351	59 968	48 109	−58 786	20 466	−1 459	−53 068	2 408
Other deposits	NFJK	F.29	5 372	−6 330	4 566	−587	−7 587	10 479	−9 235	8 251
Total	NFJC	F.2	45 586	−7 529	−50 870	−102 896	−38 656	−127 293	−118 683	71 811
Debt securities		F.3								
Short-term		F.31								
Issued by UK central government	NFJN	F.31N1	3 706	2 485	7 853	−5 356	−5 167	9 223	7 158	9 523
Issued by UK local government	NFJR	F.31N2	–	–	–	–	1	–	–	–
Issued by UK MFIs[3]	NFJS	F.31N5	−7 697	−2 500	−3 960	7 652	−1 060	6 943	413	13 792
Issued by other UK residents	NFJX	F.31N6	−53	−308	1 270	−439	55	2 634	−580	2 267
Issued by rest of the world	NFJY	F.31N9	−2 710	−10 472	3 587	6 717	−8 841	3 600	−5 679	−7 645
Long-term		F.32								
Issued by UK central government	NFKA	F.32N1	−54 570	17 362	14 268	−3 060	18 364	61 334	−1 778	−52 774
Issued by UK local government	NFKD	F.32N2	–	–	–	–	–	–	4	7
Issued by UK MFIs and other UK residents[3,5]	KLG9	F.32N5-6	58 587	30 595	11 840	−5 994	4 914	6 650	−2 943	11 142
Issued by rest of the world	NFKI	F.32N9	21 949	7 885	−22 579	21 217	26 307	30 659	5 541	1 422
Total	NFJL	F.3	19 212	45 047	12 279	20 737	34 573	121 043	2 136	−22 266
Loans		F.4								
Long-term		F.42								
Direct investment	NFKV	F.421	–	–	–	1 066	−807	−7 409	1 849	1 672
Secured on dwellings	NFKY	F.422	−26 743	−7 640	4 714	2 529	1 824	2 992	6 757	1 217
Finance leasing	NFLC	F.423	486	492	492	492	492	492	492	492
Other long-term loans		F.424								
By UK residents	NFLD	F.424N1	27 838	57 251	−10 114	−23 136	44 013	9 692	4 302	30 983
Total	NFKN	F.4	1 581	50 103	−4 908	−19 049	45 522	5 767	13 400	34 364
Equity and investment fund shares/units		F.5								
Equity		F.51								
Listed UK shares[5]	NFLK	F.511N1	28 926	32 452	38 316	19 283	11 942	−85	3 849	−5 805
Unlisted UK shares[5]	NFLL	F.512N1	−2 861	17 631	32 625	5 697	480	2 019	6 891	−344
Other equity		F.519								
UK shares and bonds issued by other UK residents[5]	NSPJ	F.519N7	–	–	–	–	–	–	–	–
Shares and other equity issued by rest of the world	NFLP	F.519N9	21 242	−22 311	−50 006	29 423	26 234	35 779	−12 436	−29 457
Investment fund shares/units		F.52								
UK mutual funds' shares	NFLT	F.52N1	94	114	34	49	75	175	248	166
Issued by rest of the world	MDN2	F.52N9	1 726	4 385	1 595	2 557	1 770	626	2 877	2 603
Total	NFLF	F.5	49 127	32 271	22 564	57 009	40 501	38 514	1 429	−32 837
Insurance, pensions and standardised guarantee schemes		F.6								
Non-life insurance technical reserves	NFLY	F.61	−48	−86	−54	−16	−3	–	−6	2
Total	NPWT	F.6	−48	−86	−54	−16	−3	–	−6	2
Financial derivatives and employee stock options	MN5N	F.7	10 305	−18 256	25 636	−34 769	25 318	25 246	−89 935	152
Of which: financial derivatives	NFKJ	F.71	10 305	−18 256	25 636	−34 769	25 318	25 246	−89 935	152
Other accounts receivable	NFLZ	F.8	644	−725	7 042	608	806	576	415	483
Total net acquisition of financial assets	NFIY	F.A	126 407	100 825	11 689	−78 376	108 061	63 853	−191 244	51 709

4.3.8 Financial corporations except MFI & ICPF[1]
ESA 2010 sectors S.124, S.125, S.126 & S.127[2] Unconsolidated

£ million

			2009	2010	2011	2012	2013	2014	2015	2016
Financial account		III.2								
Net acquisition of financial liabilities		F.L								
Currency and deposits	NFMG	F.2	7 920	−9 173	9 884	−166	9 604	5 248	−4 704	3 188
Debt securities		F.3								
Short-term		F.31								
Issued by other UK residents	NFNB	F.31N6	−1 738	−62	252	249	554	1 505	347	978
Long-term		F.32								
Issued by UK MFIs and other UK residents[3,5]	KLC8	F.32N5-6	97 451	57 084	68 533	−69 362	85 911	9 094	−51 172	5 742
Total	NFMP	F.3	95 713	57 022	68 785	−69 113	86 465	10 599	−50 825	6 720
Loans		F.4								
Short-term		F.41								
By UK MFIs[3]	NFNT	F.41N1	−9 188	−2 818	−53 201	23 609	−36 919	−144 084	−8 348	6 849
Of which: foreign currency loans by UK banks	NFNV	F.41N12	−8 600	37 637	−23 727	3 618	8 023	−46 361	−14 149	−19 839
By rest of the world	NFNX	F.41N9	−51 717	101 521	−37 373	24 560	−26 858	109 558	−193 305	−52 836
Long-term		F.42								
Direct investment	NFNZ	F.421	–	–	–	1 137	1 940	4 322	3 652	6 384
Finance leasing	NFOG	F.423	60	60	60	60	60	60	60	60
Other long-term loans		F.424								
By UK residents	NFOH	F.424N1	8 488	14 034	10 829	−1 614	−2 354	−2 688	13 921	−17 183
By rest of the world	NFOI	F.424N9	−17 856	−406	1 444	−1 121	1 505	2 103	4 754	312
Total	NFNR	F.4	−70 213	112 391	−78 241	46 631	−62 626	−30 729	−179 266	−56 414
Equity and investment fund shares/units		F.5								
Equity		F.51								
Listed UK shares[5]	NFOO	F.511N1	86 657	8 733	1 682	3 131	7 274	2 231	4 599	2 330
Unlisted UK shares[5]	NFOP	F.512N1	88 271	1 109	5 378	−42 441	−7 945	6 925	8 314	9 199
Other equity		F.519								
UK shares and bonds issued by other UK residents[5]	NSPK	F.519N7	–	–	–	–	–	–	–	–
Investment fund shares/units		F.52								
UK mutual funds' shares	NFOX	F.52N1	26 271	43 235	19 580	18 375	17 723	25 256	8 482	2 031
Total	NFOJ	F.5	201 199	53 077	26 640	−20 935	17 052	34 412	21 395	13 560
Insurance, pensions and standardised guarantee schemes		F.6								
Pension schemes[4]	MA2S	F.6M	240	366	279	313	369	361	354	410
Total	NPWU	F.6	240	366	279	313	369	361	354	410
Financial derivatives and employee stock options	MN69	F.7	53	65	61	53	53	55	57	61
Of which: financial derivatives	NFNN	F.71	–	–	–	–	–	–	–	–
Other accounts payable	NFPD	F.8	−12 090	−16 964	−10 939	−37 570	−4 904	−7 529	−1 510	−1 858
Total net acquisition of financial liabilities	NFMC	**F.L**	222 822	196 784	16 469	−80 787	46 013	12 417	−214 499	−34 333
Net lending(+) / net borrowing(-)		**B.9**								
Total net acquisition of financial assets	NFIY	F.A	126 407	100 825	11 689	−78 376	108 061	63 853	−191 244	51 709
less total net acquisition of financial liabilities	NFMC	F.L	222 822	196 784	16 469	−80 787	46 013	12 417	−214 499	−34 333
Net lending(+) / borrowing(-) from the financial account	NYNM	B.9f	−96 415	−95 959	−4 780	2 411	62 048	51 436	23 255	86 042
Statistical discrepancy between the financial and non-financial account	NYOY	dB.9	72 803	76 600	1 863	−6 078	−59 344	−58 938	−47 188	−108 827
Net lending (+) / borrowing (-) from non-financial accounts	NHLW	**B.9n**	**−23 612**	**−19 359**	**−2 917**	**−3 667**	**2 704**	**−7 502**	**−23 933**	**−22 785**

1 Monetary financial institutions & insurance corporations and pension funds
2 S.124 Non-MMF investment funds, S.125 Other financial intermediaries, except insurance corporations and pension funds, S.126 Financial auxiliaries & S.127 Captive financial institutions and money lenders
3 Monetary financial institutions
4 F.63 pension entitlements, F.64 Claims on pension fund on pension managers, F.65 Entitlements to non-pension benefits
5 Prior to 1990, it is not possible to distinguish some elements of F.32N5-6, F.511N1 and F.512N1. These elements are shown combined as F.519N7

4.3.8A
Non-money market fund investment funds
Not seasonally adjusted
ESA 2010 sector S.124

£ million

			2009	2010	2011	2012	2013	2014	2015	2016
Financial account		III.2								
Net acquisition of financial assets		F.A								
Currency and deposits		F.2								
Currency	CER2	F.21	–	–	–	–	–	–	–	–
Transferable deposits		F.22								
With UK MFIs[1]	CER6	F.22N1	−2 392	3 124	311	1 604	5 414	1 253	4 637	2 128
Of which: foreign currency deposits	CER8	F.22N12	−1 381	867	−655	997	868	1 045	1 008	247
With rest of the world MFIs	CES2	F.22N9	42	305	−848	−37	52	136	−28	51
Other deposits	CES4	F.29	−118	702	520	−236	2 413	1 207	−314	878
Total	CEQ8	F.2	−2 468	4 131	−17	1 331	7 879	2 596	4 295	3 057
Debt securities		F.3								
Short-term		F.31								
Issued by UK central government	CES6	F.31N1	−221	679	592	381	−777	−260	−528	101
Issued by UK local government	CES8	F.31N2	–	–	–	–	–	–	–	–
Issued by UK MFIs	CET2	F.31N5	−1 452	1 768	918	2 228	1 162	2 867	−4 755	6 195
MMIs[2] issued by other UK residents	CET4	F.31N6	54	−112	749	−53	−707	453	264	527
MMIs issued by rest of the world	CET6	F.31N9	49	−4	−366	221	−160	231	8 386	−5 401
Long-term		F.32								
Issued by UK central government	CET8	F.32N1	−631	3 857	348	−681	100 728	8 891	−185	3 108
Issued by UK local government	CEU2	F.32N2	–	–	–	–	–	−4	1	15
Issued by UK MFIs and other UK residents	CEU4	F.32N5-6	7 306	6 886	4 448	6 662	1 088	4 388	−1 602	3 910
Issued by rest of the world	CEU6	F.32N9	9 591	9 233	6 412	22 257	10 969	20 175	9 808	2 922
Total	C5N7	F.3	14 696	22 307	13 101	31 015	112 299	36 746	11 389	11 377
Equity and investment fund shares/units		F.5								
Equity		F.51								
Listed UK shares	CEX2	F.511N1	24 639	733	270	5 607	4 159	5 764	6 039	119 515
Unlisted UK shares	CEX6	F.512N1	263	−128	524	−68	234	122	−2	−262
Other equity		F.519								
UK shares and bonds issued by other UK residents[5]	CEY2	F.519N7	–	–	–	–	–	–	–	–
Shares and other equity issued by rest of the world	CEY4	F.519N9	12 833	6 973	7 932	10 776	16 074	217	4 870	−8 746
Investment fund shares/units		F.52								
UK mutual funds' shares	CEY8	F.52N1	3 388	4 088	6 308	5 777	3 092	3 320	2 485	2 728
Rest of the world mutual funds' shares	CEZ2	F.52N9	1 881	2 452	2 102	−1 981	1 770	−18 634	19 866	−31 486
Total	CEW4	F.5	43 004	14 118	17 136	20 111	25 329	−9 211	33 258	81 749
Insurance, pensions and standardised guarantee schemes		F.6								
Non-life insurance technical reserves	CEZ6	F.61	−1	−1	−1	–	–	–	–	–
Total	CEZ4	F.6	−1	−1	−1	–	–	–	–	–
Financial derivatives and employee stock options	CF2C	F.7	2 315	3 261	1 537	7 962	3 257	−2 476	−6 775	−4 544
Of which: financial derivatives	CF2E	F.71	2 315	3 261	1 537	7 962	3 257	−2 476	−6 775	−4 544
Other accounts receivable	CF2I	F.8	–	−685	3 200	−18	82	−34	−115	−81
Total net acquisition of financial assets	CEP8	**F.A**	57 546	43 131	34 956	60 401	148 846	27 621	42 052	91 558

Non-money market fund investment funds
Not seasonally adjusted
ESA 2010 sector S.124

£ million

			2009	2010	2011	2012	2013	2014	2015	2016
Financial account		III.2								
Net acquisition of financial liabilities		F.L								
Debt securities		F.3								
Short-term		F.31								
Issued MMIs by other UK residents	CK4T	F.31N6	1	–	–29	19	–16	62	–56	–14
Long-term		F.32								
Issued by UK MFIs and other UK residents	CK74	F.32N5-6	126	–25	–243	–842	–199	–39	261	–213
Total	CAPF	F.3	127	–25	–272	–823	–215	23	205	–227
Loans		F.4								
Short-term		F.41								
Issued by UK MFIs	CK76	F.41N1	–1 876	–769	1 043	1 164	150	–615	–665	989
Of which: Foreign currency loans by UK MFIs	CK78	F.41N12	–220	–275	81	503	–124	37	–16	454
Issued by rest of the world MFIs	CK7A	F.41N9	–140	–21	139	–24	68	299	–107	–217
Long-term		F.42								
Direct investment	CK7C	F.421	–	–	–	–	–	–	–	–
Finance leasing	CK7E	F.423	–	–	–	–	–	–	–	–
Other long-term loans		F.424								
Issued by UK residents[4]	CK7L	F.424N1	–188	405	508	–48	324	–302	–75	413
Issued by rest of the world	CK88	F.424N9	–36	–10	–55	–13	–87	100	44	12
Total	CAPL	F.4	–2 240	–395	1 635	1 079	455	–518	–803	1 197
Equity and investment fund shares/units		F.5								
Investment fund shares/units		F.52								
UK mutual funds' shares	CKBQ	F.52N1	26 271	43 235	19 580	18 375	17 723	25 256	8 482	2 031
Total	CK8C	F.5	26 271	43 235	19 580	18 375	17 723	25 256	8 482	2 031
Insurance, pensions and standardised guarantee schemes		F.6								
Pension schemes[5]	CKEZ	F.6M	4	8	5	6	8	8	8	8
Total	CKBS	F.6	4	8	5	6	8	8	8	8
Financial derivatives and employee stock options	CKFI	F.7	–	–	–	–	–	–	–	–
Other accounts payable	CKR7	F.8	–6 028	–8 496	–5 481	–18 802	–2 490	–3 736	–712	–958
Total net acquisition of financial liabilities	CJQI	F.L	18 134	34 327	15 467	–165	15 481	21 033	7 180	2 051
Net lending(+) / net borrowing(-)		B.9								
Total net acquisition of financial assets	CEP8	F.A	57 546	43 131	34 956	60 401	148 846	27 621	42 052	91 558
less total net acquisition of financial liabilities	CJQI	F.L	18 134	34 327	15 467	–165	15 481	21 033	7 180	2 051
Net lending(+) / borrowing(-) from the financial account	CORK	B.9f	39 412	8 804	19 489	60 566	133 365	6 588	34 872	89 507

1 Monetary financial institutions
2 Money market instruments
3 All loans secured on dwellings and all finance leasing are
   treated as long term loans
4 Other than direct investment loans, loans secured on dwellings
   and loans for finance leasing
5 F.63 Pension entitlements, F.64 Claims of pension funds on pension
   managers, F.65 Entitlements to non-pension benefits

4.3.11 Financial corporations except MFI & ICPF[1]
ESA 2010 sectors S.124, S.125, S.126 & S.127[2] Unconsolidated

£ billion

			2009	2010	2011	2012	2013	2014	2015	2016
Financial balance sheet at end of period		IV.3								
Total financial assets		AF.A								
Currency and deposits		AF.2								
Currency	NLPM	AF.21	0.1	0.1	0.1	0.1	0.1	0.1	0.1	0.1
Deposits with UK MFIs[3]	NLPO	AF.22N1	909.5	982.7	900.3	860.9	810.8	695.3	634.8	742.8
Of which: foreign currency deposits with UK MFIs[3]	NLPQ	AF.221N2	273.8	267.8	264.4	293.3	304.1	271.3	284.0	367.5
Deposits with rest of the world MFIs[3]	NLPS	AF.22N9	301.0	370.4	420.6	376.5	400.6	372.9	308.1	371.9
Other deposits	NLPT	AF.29	16.9	10.5	15.1	14.5	6.9	17.4	8.2	16.4
Total	NLPL	AF.2	1 227.5	1 363.7	1 336.1	1 252.0	1 218.4	1 085.7	951.2	1 131.2
Debt securities		AF.3								
Short-term		AF.31								
Issued by UK central government	NLPW	AF.31N1	11.6	14.3	21.9	16.4	11.7	20.7	27.1	36.2
Issued by UK local government	NLQA	AF.31N2	–	–	–	–	–	–	–	–
Issued by UK MFIs[3]	NLQB	AF.31N5	29.1	24.8	17.7	25.7	25.5	34.8	36.5	51.2
Issued by other UK residents	NLQG	AF.31N6	0.3	0.7	1.2	0.8	0.8	3.7	2.8	5.1
Issued by rest of the world	NLQH	AF.31N9	40.0	34.4	31.8	36.7	25.8	32.7	30.4	31.9
Long-term		AF.32								
Issued by UK central government	NLQJ	AF.32N1	44.6	72.8	72.5	39.4	53.1	205.1	179.4	182.0
Issued by UK local government	NLQM	AF.32N2	–	–	–	–	–	–	–	0.02
Issued by UK MFIs and other UK residents[3]	KLG3	AF.32N5-6	257.4	288.7	307.6	310.1	281.3	297.8	291.5	308.0
Issued by rest of the world	NLQR	AF.32N9	90.9	88.4	65.3	89.7	109.6	136.7	142.4	170.6
Total	NLPU	AF.3	473.9	524.1	518.0	518.7	507.7	731.6	710.1	785.0
Loans		AF.4								
Long-term		AF.42								
Direct investment	NLRE	AF.421	–	–	–	22.1	27.6	11.4	12.5	11.7
Secured on dwellings	NLRH	AF.422	306.4	99.2	103.1	107.6	107.8	111.6	117.2	114.0
Finance leasing	NLRL	AF.423	26.1	26.6	27.1	27.6	28.1	28.6	29.1	29.5
Other long-term loans by UK residents	NLRM	AF.424N1	543.3	637.8	614.0	603.1	599.8	577.6	589.6	678.7
Total	NLQW	AF.4	875.8	763.6	744.2	760.4	763.2	729.2	748.4	833.9
Equity and investment fund shares/units		AF.5								
Equity		AF.51								
Listed UK shares	NLRT	AF.511N1	251.9	360.7	277.2	250.6	282.9	265.3	272.6	276.3
Unlisted UK shares	NLRU	AF.512N1	205.8	219.6	220.2	217.3	225.0	226.7	229.2	233.9
Other equity		AF.519								
UK shares and bonds issued by other UK residents	NSOH	AF.519N7	–	–	–	–	–	–	–	–
Shares and other equity issued by rest of the world	NLRY	AF.519N9	363.5	413.6	347.5	403.7	481.9	543.7	546.6	633.9
Investment fund shares/units		AF.52								
UK mutual funds' shares	NLSC	AF.52N1	39.2	46.7	49.8	63.1	83.2	83.5	90.7	102.7
Issued by rest of the world	MDM8	AF.52N9	10.9	17.1	18.3	23.8	28.3	32.9	39.3	47.1
Total	NLRO	AF.5	871.4	1 057.8	912.9	958.5	1 101.3	1 152.0	1 178.4	1 294.0
Insurance, pensions and standardised guarantee scheme		AF.6								
Non-life insurance technical reserves	NLSH	AF.61	0.2	0.2	0.1	0.1	0.1	0.1	0.1	0.1
Total	NPYP	AF.6	0.2	0.2	0.1	0.1	0.1	0.1	0.1	0.1
Financial derivatives and employee stock options	MMV5	AF.7	1 072.1	2 049.9	2 570.4	2 144.9	2 030.5	2 282.6	1 523.2	1 893.0
Of which: financial derivatives	NLQS	AF.71	1 072.1	2 049.9	2 570.4	2 144.9	2 030.5	2 282.6	1 523.2	1 893.0
Other accounts receivable	NLSI	AF.8	18.1	19.1	22.1	27.2	27.6	21.1	27.9	32.6
Total financial assets	NLPH	**AF.A**	4 539.0	5 778.5	6 103.8	5 661.8	5 649.0	6 002.2	5 139.2	5 969.8

4.3.11 Financial corporations except MFI & ICPF[1]

ESA 2010 sectors S.124, S.125, S.126 & S.127[2] Unconsolidated

continued

£ billion

			2009	2010	2011	2012	2013	2014	2015	2016
Financial balance sheet at end of period		IV.3								
Total financial liabilities		AF.L								
Currency and deposits	NLSP	AF.2	25.2	11.1	21.0	20.9	30.4	35.8	31.2	34.3
Debt securities		AF.3								
Short-term		AF.31								
MMIs issued by other UK residents[4]	NLTK	AF.31N6	10.5	10.7	11.4	11.7	12.2	13.7	14.1	15.0
Long-term		AF.32								
Issued by UK MFIs and other UK residents[3]	KLB9	AF.32N5-6	881.6	826.2	850.9	855.8	823.8	940.3	941.7	953.7
Total	NLSY	AF.3	892.1	836.9	862.3	867.5	836.0	954.0	955.8	968.7
Loans		AF.4								
Short-term		AF.41								
By UK MFIs[3,6]	NLUC	AF.41N1	919.3	869.7	784.7	811.1	752.8	628.7	622.2	683.6
Of which: foreign currency loans by UK banks	NLUE	AF.41N12	376.8	408.9	353.2	351.0	344.5	295.1	280.1	310.6
By rest of the world MFIs[3]	NLUG	AF.41N9	556.5	661.2	621.7	649.3	619.1	697.4	506.2	552.8
Long-term		AF.42								
Direct investment	NLUI	AF.421	–	–	–	26.2	28.2	25.5	27.9	17.6
Finance leasing	NLUP	AF.423	1.9	2.0	2.1	2.1	2.2	2.2	2.3	2.4
Other by UK residents[5]	NLUQ	AF.424N1	35.5	97.0	102.4	109.1	123.5	94.7	96.1	105.0
Other by rest of the world	NLUR	AF.424N9	41.2	38.1	36.3	37.6	49.4	33.0	29.1	31.0
Total	NLUA	AF.4	1 554.5	1 668.0	1 547.1	1 635.3	1 575.3	1 481.6	1 283.9	1 392.6
Equity and investment fund shares/units		AF.5								
Equity		AF.51								
Listed UK shares	NLUX	AF.511N1	329.3	367.8	249.0	335.2	389.6	392.2	362.3	353.5
Unlisted UK shares	NLUY	AF.512N1	418.4	428.2	428.1	420.3	408.3	437.7	436.7	489.3
Other equity		AF.519								
UK shares and bonds issued by other UK residents	NSOI	AF.519N7	–	–	–	–	–	–	–	–
Investment fund shares/units		AF.52								
UK mutual funds' shares	NLVG	AF.52N1	566.4	694.0	678.8	777.9	883.7	963.1	1 012.7	1 088.5
Total	NLUS	AF.5	1 314.1	1 490.0	1 355.9	1 533.3	1 681.6	1 793.0	1 811.6	1 931.3
Insurance, pensions and standardised guarantee schemes		AF.6								
Pension schemes[7]	M9VO	AF.6M	15.7	14.0	21.0	16.0	14.2	26.0	24.0	28.3
Total	NPYQ	AF.6	15.7	14.0	21.0	16.0	14.2	26.0	24.0	28.3
Financial derivatives and employee stock options	MMX9	AF.7	1 038.6	2 011.6	2 498.0	2 079.6	1 940.5	2 167.6	1 497.5	1 876.4
Of which: financial derivatives	NLTW	AF.71	1 038.4	2 011.4	2 497.8	2 079.4	1 940.3	2 167.4	1 497.3	1 876.2
Other accounts payable	NLVM	AF.8	2.5	0.2	0.1	−0.2	1.8	4.6	0.3	1.7
Total financial liabilities	NLSL	**AF.L**	4 842.7	6 031.7	6 305.4	6 152.4	6 079.8	6 462.5	5 604.2	6 233.3
Financial net worth		**BF.90**								
Total financial assets	NLPH	AF.A	4 539.0	5 778.5	6 103.8	5 661.8	5 649.0	6 002.2	5 139.2	5 969.8
less total financial liabilities	NLSL	AF.L	4 842.7	6 031.7	6 305.4	6 152.4	6 079.8	6 462.5	5 604.2	6 233.3
Financial net worth	NYOF	**BF.90**	−303.7	−253.3	−201.6	−490.6	−430.8	−460.3	−465.0	−263.5

1 Monetary financial institutions & insurance corporations and pension funds
2 S.124 Non-MMF investment funds, S.125 Other financial intermediaries, except insurance corporations and pension funds, S.126 Financial auxiliaries & S.127 Captive financial institutions and money lenders
3 Monetary financial institutions
4 Money market instruments
5 All loans secured on dwellings and all finance leasing are treated as long-term loans
6 Other than direct investment loans, loans secured on dwellings and loans for finance leasing
7 AF.63 Pension entitlements, AF.64 Claims on pension funds on pension managers, AF.65 Entitlements to non-pension benefits

171

4.3.11A
Non-money market fund investment funds
Not seasonally adjusted
ESA 2010 sector S.124

£ billion

			2009	2010	2011	2012	2013	2014	2015	2016
Financial balance sheet at end of period		IV.3								
Total financial assets		**AF.A**								
Currency and deposits		AF.2								
Currency	CF97	AF.21	–	–	–	–	–	–	–	–
Deposits with UK MFIs[1]	CF9B	AF.22N1	16.2	19.4	19.7	21.1	26.4	27.7	32.3	35.6
Of which: foreign currency deposits	CF9D	AF.221N2	3.0	4.0	3.3	4.1	4.9	5.9	7.0	8.4
Deposits with rest of the world MFIs	CF9F	AF.22N9	0.6	0.9	0.1	–	0.1	0.2	0.2	0.3
Other deposits	CF9H	AF.29	0.4	1.1	1.6	1.4	3.8	5.0	4.7	5.6
Total	CF95	AF.2	17.2	21.4	21.4	22.6	30.3	32.9	37.3	41.5
Debt securities		AF.3								
Short-term		AF.31								
Issued by UK central government		AF.31N1								
Issued by UK local government	CF9L	AF.31N2								
Issued by UK MFIs	CF9N	AF.31N5	0.8	2.5	3.5	5.7	6.8	9.7	4.9	11.2
MMIs[2] issued by other UK residents		AF.31N6								
MMIs[2] issued by rest of the world		AF.31N9								
Long-term		AF.32								
Issued by UK central government		AF.32N1								
Issued by UK local government		AF.32N2								
Issued by UK MFIs and other UK residents[2]	CF9X	AF.32N5-6	36.6	52.5	52.3	62.5	59.7	64.3	61.7	70.0
Issued by rest of the world	CF9Z	AF.32N9	50.3	60.1	64.8	83.9	89.0	102.6	115.0	136.6
Total	CADV	AF.3	120.0	152.0	163.1	181.0	196.6	226.0	235.8	274.0
Equity and investment fund shares/units		AF.5								
Equity		AF.51								
Listed UK shares	CFC5	AF.511N1	180.8	217.8	194.5	217.5	246.8	257.3	264.8	69.1
Unlisted UK shares	CFC9	AF.512N1	1.5	2.5	1.8	1.6	4.6	2.3	3.0	3.1
Other equity		AF.519								
UK shares and bonds issued by other UK residents	CFD5	AF.519N7	–	–	–	–	–	–	–	–
Shares and other equity issued by rest of the world	CFD7	AF.519N9	174.7	229.4	216.8	246.5	297.1	319.6	335.4	416.6
Investment fund shares/units		AF.52								
UK mutual funds' shares	CFE2	AF.52N1	36.7	43.7	47.3	60.0	78.9	79.5	85.5	96.9
Rest of the world's mutual funds' shares	CFE4	AF.52N9	10.9	17.1	18.3	23.8	28.3	32.9	39.3	47.1
Total	CFB7	AF.5	404.6	510.4	478.6	549.4	655.8	691.6	728.0	632.8
Insurance, pensions and standardised guarantee scheme		AF.6								
Non-life insurance technical reserves	CFE8	AF.61	–	–	–	–	–	–	–	0.002
Total	CFE6	AF.6	–	–	–	–	–	–	–	0.002
Financial derivatives and employee stock options	CFG3	AF.7	17.3	26.2	18.3	25.7	28.1	13.5	12.7	12.4
Of which: financial derivatives	CFG5	AF.71	17.3	26.2	18.3	25.7	28.1	13.5	12.7	12.4
Other accounts receivable	CFG9	AF.8	1.7	1.9	3.1	5.3	5.2	1.5	4.6	6.7
Total financial assets	CF8V	**AF.A**	560.8	711.9	684.4	784.0	916.1	965.5	1 018.4	967.4

4.3.11A

Non-money market fund investment funds
Not seasonally adjusted

continued

ESA 2010 sector S.124

£ billion

			2009	2010	2011	2012	2013	2014	2015	2016
Financial balance sheet at end of period		IV.3								
Total financial liabilities		**AF.L**								
Debt securities		AF.3								
Short-term		AF.31								
MMIs issued by other UK residents	COLA	AF.31N6	–	–	–	–	–	0.1	–	0.017
Long-term		AF.32								
Issued by UK MFIs and other UK residents	COLE	AF.32N5-6	1.7	1.6	1.7	1.5	1.5	1.3	1.5	1.5
Total	CCBF	AF.3	1.7	1.7	1.7	1.5	1.5	1.4	1.5	1.5
Loans		AF.4								
Short-term		AF.41								
Issued by UK MFIs[1]	COLG	AF.41N1	3.1	2.4	3.4	4.5	4.7	4.0	3.4	4.7
Of which: foreign currency loans by UK	COLI	AF.41N12	1.3	1.1	1.2	1.6	1.5	1.5	1.5	2.3
Issued by rest of the world	COLK	AF.41N9	0.4	0.4	0.5	0.5	0.6	0.9	0.7	0.6
Long-term[3]		AF.42								
Direct investment	COLM	AF.421	–	–	–	–	–	–	–	–
Finance leasing	COLO	AF.423	–	–	–	–	–	–	–	–
Other, issued by UK residents[4]	COLS	AF.424N1	0.7	1.1	1.6	1.6	1.9	1.6	1.5	2.1
Other, issued by rest of the world	COLU	AF.424N9	0.2	0.2	0.2	0.2	0.1	0.2	0.2	0.2
Total	CCWP	AF.4	4.5	4.1	5.8	6.7	7.2	6.6	5.8	7.6
Equity and investment fund shares/units		AF.5								
Investment fund shares/units		AF.52								
UK mutual funds' shares	COMT	AF.52N1	566.4	694.0	678.8	777.9	883.7	963.1	1 012.7	1 088.5
Total	COLW	AF.5	566.4	694.0	678.8	777.9	883.7	963.1	1 012.7	1 088.5
Insurance, pensions and standardised guarantee schemes		AF.6								
Pension schemes[5]	CONJ	AF.6M	0.3	0.3	0.4	0.3	0.3	0.5	0.5	0.6
Total	COMV	AF.6	0.3	0.3	0.4	0.3	0.3	0.5	0.5	0.6
Financial derivatives and employee stock options	CONL	AF.7	15.4	23.8	17.5	22.9	26.4	12.2	14.4	15.6
Of which: financial derivatives	CONN	AF.71	15.4	23.8	17.5	22.9	26.4	12.2	14.4	15.6
Other accounts payable	CONR	AF.8	0.1	0.1	0.2	0.2	0.2	0.2	0.2	0.3
Total financial liabilities	COKK	**AF.L**	588.4	724.0	704.3	809.6	919.2	984.1	1 035.2	1 114.0
Financial net worth		**BF.90**								
Total financial assets	CF8V	AF.A	560.8	711.9	684.4	784.0	916.1	965.5	1 018.4	967.4
less total financial liabilities	COKK	AF.L	588.4	724.0	704.3	809.6	919.2	984.1	1 035.2	1 114.0
Financial net worth	COSR	**BF.90**	−27.5	−12.1	−19.9	−25.6	−3.1	−18.5	−16.8	−146.6

1 Monetary financial institutions
2 Money market instruments
3 All loans secured on dwellings and all finance leasing
  are treated as long term loans
4 Other than direct investment loans, loans secured on dwellings
  and loans for finance leasing
5 F.63 Pension entitlements, F.64 Claims on pension funds on pension
  managers, F.65 Entitlements to non-pension benefits
6 The following asset series are not available as publishing them would
  disclose commercially sensitive information. AF.31N1, AF.31N6, AF.31N9,
  AF.32N1 and AF.32N2, for full description of codes see confidentiality
  section in notes.

4.4.2 Insurance corporations and pension funds
ESA 2010 sectors S.128 and S.129[1]

£ million

			2009	2010	2011	2012	2013	2014	2015
Distribution and use of income accounts		II							
Primary distribution of income account		II.1							
Generation of income account		II.1.1							
Resources									
Total resources (gross value added)	NRHH	**B.1g**	**23 933**	**20 185**	**22 235**	**27 078**	**29 934**	**35 959**	**24 970**
Uses									
Compensation of employees		D.1							
Wages and salaries	NHEJ	D.11	6 013	6 437	5 843	5 794	5 731	6 167	5 999
Employers' social contributions	NHEL	D.12	1 322	1 692	1 661	1 735	1 680	1 670	1 536
Total	NSCV	D.1	7 335	8 129	7 504	7 529	7 411	7 837	7 535
Taxes on production and imports, paid		D.2							
Production taxes other than on products	NHOS	D.29	437	442	463	484	506	519	530
less subsidies, received		D.3							
Production subsidies other than on products	NHNZ	D.39	–	–	–	–	–	–	–
Operating surplus, gross	NHBZ	B.2g	16 161	11 614	14 268	19 065	22 017	27 603	16 905
Total uses (gross value added)	NRHH	**B.1g**	**23 933**	**20 185**	**22 235**	**27 078**	**29 934**	**35 959**	**24 970**

1 S.128 Insurance corporations and S.129 Pension funds

4.4.3 Insurance corporations and pension funds
ESA 2010 sectors S.128 and S.129[1]

£ million

			2009	2010	2011	2012	2013	2014	2015	2016
Allocation of primary income account		II.1.2								
Resources										
Operating surplus, gross	NHBZ	B.2g	16 161	11 614	14 268	19 065	22 017	27 603	16 905	17 120
Property income, received		D.4								
Interest	NHOK	D.41	33 337	31 711	32 179	33 068	34 714	33 844	32 644	31 682
Distributed income of corporations	NHOL	D.42	32 196	25 605	31 258	31 393	27 886	29 158	35 649	30 590
Reinvested earnings on foreign direct investment	NHQM	D.43	−1 192	572	−2 401	51	−5 670	−2 519	2 203	292
Other investment income		D.44								
Attributable to insurance policy holders	KZJ4	D.441	16 848	13 017	11 913	13 370	14 517	21 297	4 382	4 011
Attributable to collective investment fund shareholders		D.443								
Dividends	MN7B	D.4431	2 382	5 499	2 918	3 238	3 699	3 639	3 801	4 184
Retained earnings	MN7F	D.4432	3 725	8 602	4 562	5 064	5 785	5 692	5 947	6 544
Total	L5UN	D.443	6 107	14 101	7 480	8 302	9 484	9 331	9 748	10 728
Total	NHPG	D.44	22 955	27 118	19 393	21 672	24 001	30 628	14 130	14 739
Rent	NHPH	D.45	31	33	35	36	36	36	36	36
Total	NHPF	D.4	87 327	85 039	80 464	86 220	80 967	91 147	84 662	77 339
Total resources	NRMN	TR	103 488	96 653	94 732	105 285	102 984	118 750	101 567	94 459
Uses										
Property income		D.4								
Interest	NHOM	D.41	2 037	1 640	1 509	1 730	1 587	1 824	1 563	1 960
Distributed income of corporations	NHON	D.42	2 381	3 764	5 126	4 926	6 375	6 387	4 700	4 806
Reinvested earnings on foreign direct investment	NHQO	D.43	268	−323	−155	558	963	744	1 436	1 300
Other investment income		D.44								
Attributable to insurance policy holders	L5VG	D.441	43 608	39 480	37 891	36 905	38 158	43 743	29 518	27 714
Payable on pension entitlements	L5VH	D.442	67 817	77 856	74 956	65 918	63 132	77 972	71 412	73 681
Total	L6RD	D.44	111 425	117 336	112 847	102 823	101 290	121 715	100 930	101 395
Rent	NHPK	D.45	–	–	–	–	–	–	–	–
Total	NHPI	D.4	116 111	122 417	119 327	110 037	110 215	130 670	108 629	109 461
Balance of primary incomes, gross	NRMO	**B.5g**	**−12 623**	**−25 764**	**−24 595**	**−4 752**	**−7 231**	**−11 920**	**−7 062**	**−15 002**
Total uses	NRMN	TU	103 488	96 653	94 732	105 285	102 984	118 750	101 567	94 459

1 S.128 Insurance corporations and S.129 Pension funds

4.4.4 Insurance corporations and pension funds
ESA 2010 sectors S.128 and S.129[1]

£ million

			2009	2010	2011	2012	2013	2014	2015	2016
Secondary distribution of income account		II.2								
Resources										
Balance of primary incomes, gross	NRMO	B.5g	−12 623	−25 764	−24 595	−4 752	−7 231	−11 920	−7 062	−15 002
Net social contributions		D.61								
Employers' actual social contributions	L8NF	D.611	43 239	55 536	55 078	59 446	62 430	55 557	51 009	53 479
Employers' imputed social contributions	M9WX	D.612	9 981	11 723	11 922	12 382	13 533	13 117	12 805	13 726
Households' actual social contributions	L8PL	D.613	10 257	10 896	10 257	11 002	12 094	13 948	11 933	13 488
Households' social contribution supplements	L8Q3	D.614	67 817	77 856	74 956	65 918	63 132	77 972	71 412	73 681
Social insurance scheme service charge	M92S	D.61SC	−11 101	−12 568	−14 740	−17 046	−18 324	−18 819	−19 620	−20 318
Total	NRMP	D.61	120 193	143 443	137 473	131 702	132 865	141 775	127 539	134 056
Other current transfers		D.7								
Net non-life insurance premiums	NSCT	D.71	37 750	47 996	45 636	44 589	47 631	41 805	43 123	42 813
Non-life insurance claims	NHPN	D.72	127	131	89	70	75	66	67	66
Total	NRMR	D.7	37 877	48 127	45 725	44 659	47 706	41 871	43 190	42 879
Total resources	NRMS	TR	145 447	165 806	158 603	171 609	173 340	171 726	163 667	161 933
Uses										
Current taxes on income, wealth, etc.		D.5								
Taxes on income	NHPO	D.51	2 796	2 167	1 425	2 659	2 201	3 586	2 062	3 786
Other social insurance benefits	L8R7	D.622	64 752	70 617	71 404	77 542	78 703	74 659	80 993	84 382
Other current transfers		D.7								
Net non-life insurance premiums	NHPU	D.71	127	131	89	70	75	66	67	66
Non-life insurance claims	NSCS	D.72	37 750	47 996	45 636	44 589	47 631	41 805	43 123	42 813
Miscellaneous current transfers	NHQK	D.75	−	−	−	−	−	−	−	−
Total	NHPT	D.7	37 877	48 127	45 725	44 659	47 706	41 871	43 190	42 879
Gross disposable income	NRMT	B.6g	40 022	44 895	40 049	46 749	44 730	51 610	37 422	30 886
Total uses	NRMS	TU	145 447	165 806	158 603	171 609	173 340	171 726	163 667	161 933

1 S.128 Insurance corporations and S.129 Pension funds

4.4.6 Insurance corporations and pension funds
ESA 2010 sectors S.128 and S.129[1]

£ million

			2009	2010	2011	2012	2013	2014	2015	2016
Use of disposable income account		II.4.1								
Resources										
Total resources (gross disposable income)	NRMT	B.6g	40 022	44 895	40 049	46 749	44 730	51 610	37 422	30 886
Uses										
Adjustment for the change in pension entitlements	NRYH	D.8	55 441	72 826	66 069	54 160	54 162	67 116	46 546	49 674
Gross saving	NRMV	B.8g	−15 419	−27 931	−26 020	−7 411	−9 432	−15 506	−9 124	−18 788
Total uses (gross disposable income)	NRMT	B.6g	40 022	44 895	40 049	46 749	44 730	51 610	37 422	30 886

1 S.128 Insurance corporations and S.129 Pension funds

4.4.7 Insurance corporations and pension funds
ESA 2010 sectors S.128 and S.129[1]

£ million

			2009	2010	2011	2012	2013	2014	2015	2016
Accumulation accounts		III								
Capital account		III.1								
Change in net worth due to saving and capital transfers account		III.1.1								
Changes in liabilities and net worth										
Gross saving	NRMV	**B.8g**	**−15 419**	**−27 931**	**−26 020**	**−7 411**	**−9 432**	**−15 506**	**−9 124**	**−18 788**
Capital transfers, receivable		D.9r								
Other capital transfers	NHQB	D.99r	176	67	22	8 922	755	436	1 079	186
Total	NHPZ	D.9r	176	67	22	8 922	755	436	1 079	186
Capital transfers, payable		D.9p								
Other capital transfers	NHOB	D.99p	176	67	22	48	755	436	1 079	186
Total	NHQD	D.9p	176	67	22	48	755	436	1 079	186
Changes in net worth due to gross saving and capital transfers	NRYI	B.101g	−15 419	−27 931	−26 020	1 463	−9 432	−15 506	−9 124	−18 788
Changes in assets										
Changes in net worth due to gross saving and capital transfers	NRYI	B.101g	−15 419	−27 931	−26 020	1 463	−9 432	−15 506	−9 124	−18 788
Acquisition of non-financial assets account		III.1.2								
Changes in net worth due to gross saving and capital transfers	NRYI	B.101g	−15 419	−27 931	−26 020	1 463	−9 432	−15 506	−9 124	−18 788
Changes in assets										
Gross capital formation		P.5								
Gross fixed capital formation	NHOJ	P.51g	246	334	277	474	202	198	690	650
Changes in inventories	NHOI	P.52	−6	1	4	1	3	8	4	–
Acquisitions less disposals of valuables[2]	NHQH	P.53	746	102	−14	−184	1 586	−626	−618	−78
Total	NHQG	P.5	986	437	267	291	1 791	−420	76	572
Acquisitions less disposals of non-produced non-financial assets	NHQI	NP	−12	−12	−12	−12	−12	−12	−12	−12
Net lending(+) / net borrowing(-)	NHOQ	**B.9n**	**−16 393**	**−28 356**	**−26 275**	**1 184**	**−11 211**	**−15 074**	**−9 188**	**−19 348**
Total change in assets	NRYI	B.101g	−15 419	−27 931	−26 020	1 463	−9 432	−15 506	−9 124	−18 788

1 S.128 Insurance corporations and S.129 Pension funds
2 Acquisitions less disposals of valuables can be a volatile series but any volatility is likely to be GDP neutral as it is offset in UK trade figures

4.4.8 Insurance corporations and pension funds
ESA 2010 sectors S.128 and S.129[1] Unconsolidated

£ million

			2009	2010	2011	2012	2013	2014	2015	2016
Financial account		III.2								
Net acquisition of financial assets		F.A								
Currency and deposits		F.2								
Transferable deposits		F.22								
With UK MFIs[2]	NBSJ	F.22N1	−2 442	−11 821	1 295	−999	−8 988	1 197	−4 503	−1 154
Of which: foreign currency deposits with UK banks	IE2X	F.22N12	−823	−1 242	522	−390	1 374	−226	1 339	−655
With rest of the world MFIs[2]	NBSN	F.229	−5 736	8 495	11 868	−2 131	5 011	3 459	−11 108	−4 480
Other deposits	NBSO	F.29	–	–	–	–	–	–	–	–
Total	NBSG	F.2	−8 178	−3 326	13 163	−3 130	−3 977	4 656	−15 611	−5 634
Debt securities		F.3								
Short-term		F.31								
Issued by UK central government	NBSR	F.31N1	2 110	−1 976	420	127	828	2 219	−1 812	1 625
Issued by UK MFIs[2]	NBSW	F.31N5	−13 208	−796	1 847	−4 438	−1 052	1 083	285	−3 124
MMIs by other UK residents[3]	NBTB	F.31N6	−403	−2 025	107	37	−693	−246	58	−186
MMIs by rest of the world[3]	NBTC	F.31N9	−301	−996	1 694	−1 243	715	2 836	−2 056	1 770
Long-term		F.32								
Issued by UK central government	NBTE	F.32N1	14 482	25 344	−1 210	−6 935	8 002	510	−813	14 177
Issued by UK local government	NBTH	F.32N2	−139	−26	505	964	58	−209	181	121
Issued by UK MFIs and other UK residents[2]	KLH2	F.32N5-6	8 506	−4 226	876	4 775	3 122	−8 620	−7 870	−4 069
Issued by rest of the world	NBTM	F.32N9	16 103	9 486	6 110	14 748	5 964	−9 268	8 135	−12 488
Total	NBSP	F.3	27 150	24 785	10 349	8 035	16 944	−11 695	−3 892	−2 174
Loans		F.4								
Long-term		F.42								
Direct investment	NBTZ	F.421	1 189	−759	1 369	−223	−730	−10 232	−1 115	1 719
Secured on dwellings	NBUC	F.422	840	−438	485	3 270	3 448	89	2 262	990
Other by UK residents[4]	NBUH	F.424N1	−3 362	1 620	10 872	2 136	363	3 509	8 074	−624
Total	NBTR	F.4	−1 333	423	12 726	5 183	3 081	−6 634	9 221	2 085
Equity and investment fund shares/units		F.5								
Equity		F.51								
Listed UK shares	NBUO	F.511N1	−18 967	−22 509	−30 376	−27 903	−29 318	−23 698	−16 460	−15 744
Unlisted UK shares	NBUP	F.512N1	−113	139	−1 491	−825	−411	−62	477	−2 842
Other equity		F.519								
UK shares and bonds issued by other UK residents	NSPC	F.519N7	–	–	–	–	–	–	–	–
Shares and other equity issued by rest of the world	NBUT	F.519N9	2 975	1 515	−12 108	−299	−23 047	−15 998	−3 186	−26 718
Investment fund shares/units		F.52								
UK mutual funds' shares	NBUX	F.52N1	22 798	30 831	2 907	16 736	1 802	23 625	35 658	20 580
Issued by rest of the world	MDN3	F.52N9	8 839	22 056	11 630	16 472	8 443	6 859	3 287	307
Total	NBUJ	F.5	15 532	32 032	−29 438	4 181	−42 531	−9 274	19 776	−24 417
Insurance, pensions and standardised guarantee schemes		F.6								
Non-life insurance technical reserves	NBVC	F.61	−120	−224	−133	−33	−9	–	−13	4
Pension schemes[5]	MA2F	F.6M	9 910	11 645	11 845	12 304	13 469	13 045	12 735	13 686
Total	NPWB	F.6	9 790	11 421	11 712	12 271	13 460	13 045	12 722	13 690
Financial derivatives and employee stock options	MN5Q	F.7	891	1 629	2 333	−4 972	−740	−303	−830	1 061
Of which: financial derivatives	J8XQ	F.71	891	1 629	2 333	−4 972	−740	−303	−830	1 061
Other accounts receivable	NBVD	F.8	−9 254	−9 096	−874	7 906	2 091	−679	−2 152	8 694
Total net acquisition of financial assets	NBSC	F.A	34 598	57 868	19 971	29 474	−11 672	−10 884	19 234	−6 695

4.4.8 Insurance corporations and pension funds

ESA 2010 sectors S.128 and S.129[1] Unconsolidated

continued

£ million

			2009	2010	2011	2012	2013	2014	2015	2016
Financial account		III.2								
Net acquisition of financial liabilities		F.L								
Debt securities		F.3								
Bonds issued by UK MFIs and other UK residents[2]	KLC9	F.32N5-6	2 640	261	1 160	225	1 491	2 432	3 110	3 168
Total	NBVT	F.3	2 640	261	1 160	225	1 491	2 432	3 110	3 168
Loans		F.4								
Short-term		F.41								
By UK MFIs[2]	NBWX	F.41N1	−1 874	−1 987	1 867	3 550	7 944	−2 220	2 695	4 378
By rest of the world MFIs[2]	NBXB	F.41N9	−1 790	−268	7 347	−3 832	−3 902	−1 211	4 519	3 809
Long-term		F.42								
Direct investment	NBXD	F.421	−62	−941	−1 385	−1 698	624	−7 175	523	1 648
Other long-term loans by UK residents	NBXL	F.424N1	−6 303	−1 649	−2 798	4 632	−585	10 664	13 013	−2 095
Total	NBWV	F.4	−10 029	−4 845	5 031	2 652	4 081	58	20 750	7 740
Equity and investment fund shares/units		F.5								
Equity		F.51								
Listed UK shares	NBXS	F.511N1	515	442	49	824	999	2 744	375	103
Unlisted UK shares	NBXT	F.512N1	794	−275	530	563	2 171	451	1 439	6 806
Total	NBXN	F.5	1 309	167	579	1 387	3 170	3 195	1 814	6 909
Insurance, pensions and standardised guarantee schemes		F.6								
Non-life insurance technical reserves	NBYG	F.61	−1 953	−12 463	−945	4 232	−2 033	6	−3 105	936
Life insurance and annuity entitlements	M9WQ	F.62	4 204	4 950	7 835	436	−8 600	−14 194	57 601	20 437
Pension schemes[5]	MA2V	F.6M	55 553	72 960	66 216	54 282	54 285	67 238	46 660	49 792
Total	NPWC	F.6	57 804	65 447	73 106	58 950	43 652	53 050	101 156	71 165
Financial derivatives and employee stock options	MN6C	F.7	27	21	20	20	19	16	20	21
Other accounts payable	NBYH	F.8	1 082	−4 818	4 321	13 685	1 405	7 427	−17 547	7 825
Total net acquisition of financial liabilities	NBVG	F.L	52 833	56 233	84 217	76 919	53 818	66 178	109 303	96 828
Net lending(+) / net borrowing(-)		B.9								
Total net acquisition of financial assets	NBSC	F.A	34 598	57 868	19 971	29 474	−11 672	−10 884	19 234	−6 695
less total net acquisition of financial liabilities	NBVG	F.L	52 833	56 233	84 217	76 919	53 818	66 178	109 303	96 828
Net lending(+) / borrowing(-) from the financial account	NYNN	B.9f	−18 235	1 635	−64 246	−47 445	−65 490	−77 062	−90 069	−103 523
Statistical discrepancy between the financial and capital accounts	NYPB	dB.9	1 842	−29 991	37 971	48 629	54 279	61 988	80 881	84 175
Net lending (+) / borrowing (-) from non-financial accounts	NHOQ	B.9n	−16 393	−28 356	−26 275	1 184	−11 211	−15 074	−9 188	−19 348

1 S.128 Insurance corporations and S.129 Pension funds
2 Monetary financial institutions
3 Money market instruments
4 Other than direct investment loans, loans secured on dwellings
 and loans for finance leasing
5 F.63 pension entitlements, F.64 Claims on pension fund on pension
 managers, F.65 Entitlements to non-pension benefits

4.4.11 Insurance corporations and pension funds
ESA 2010 sectors S.128 and S.129[1] Unconsolidated

£ billion

			2009	2010	2011	2012	2013	2014	2015	2016
Financial balance sheet at end of period		IV.3								
Total financial assets		AF.A								
Currency and deposits		AF.2								
Transferable deposits		AF.22								
With UK MFIs[2]	NIYG	AF.22N1	89.7	79.3	82.4	82.8	95.4	97.5	99.8	104.6
Of which: foreign currency deposits with UK banks	IE2Y	AF.22N12	7.8	6.6	7.1	6.7	8.1	7.8	9.2	8.5
With rest of the world MFIs[2]	NIYK	AF.22N9	35.4	40.8	48.3	47.9	50.7	48.9	37.2	40.7
Other deposits	NIYL	AF.29	–	–	–	–	–	–	–	–
Total	NIYD	AF.2	125.1	120.1	130.7	130.7	146.1	146.5	137.0	145.2
Debt securities		AF.3								
Short-term		AF.31								
Issued by UK central government	NIYO	AF.31N1	3.2	1.2	1.6	1.7	2.6	4.8	3.0	4.6
Issued by UK MFIs[2]	NIYT	AF.31N5	12.4	11.7	13.5	9.1	8.0	9.1	9.4	6.3
MMIs issued by other UK residents[3]	NIYY	AF.31N6	4.0	2.0	2.1	2.1	1.4	1.2	1.2	1.0
MMIs issued by rest of the world[3]	NIYZ	AF.31N9	4.0	3.0	4.7	3.4	4.1	7.0	4.9	6.7
Long-term		AF.32								
Issued by UK central government	NIZB	AF.32N1	297.4	321.9	390.6	403.9	417.6	462.0	472.1	564.3
Issued by UK local government	NIZE	AF.32N2	0.5	0.6	1.4	2.0	2.1	3.2	2.1	2.6
Issued by UK MFIs and other UK residents[2,6]	KLG4	AF.32N5-6	253.5	245.6	252.4	271.5	259.6	281.0	275.8	288.9
Issued by rest of the world	NIZJ	AF.32N9	250.1	267.8	280.3	308.4	307.1	328.2	329.8	369.7
Total	NIYM	AF.3	825.2	853.6	946.5	1 002.1	1 002.5	1 096.5	1 098.3	1 244.1
Loans		AF.4								
Long-term[4]		AF.42								
Direct investment	NIZW	AF.421	6.9	6.6	6.6	27.5	26.9	16.6	15.0	11.5
Secured on dwellings	NIZZ	AF.422	2.4	2.0	2.4	5.7	9.2	9.2	11.5	12.5
Other long-term loans by UK residents	NJAE	AF.424N1	77.2	119.5	135.8	143.3	169.8	142.0	147.4	160.3
Total	NIZO	AF.4	86.5	128.1	144.8	176.5	205.9	167.9	173.8	184.3
Equity and investment fund shares/units		AF.5								
Equity		AF.51								
Listed UK shares[6]	NJAL	AF.511N1	297.8	256.7	199.0	185.5	185.4	172.2	156.6	148.9
Unlisted UK shares[6]	NJAM	AF.512N1	4.9	6.8	7.2	7.0	7.1	7.1	7.8	6.1
UK shares and bonds issued by other UK residents[6]	NSOC	AF.519N7	–	–	–	–	–	–	–	–
Shares and other equity issued by rest of the world	NJAQ	AF.519N9	390.8	425.2	384.4	424.5	441.6	478.4	469.8	554.7
Investment fund shares/units		AF.52								
UK mutual funds' shares	NJAU	AF.52N1	344.6	453.8	437.6	509.9	576.2	632.9	649.6	683.5
Issued by rest of the world	MDM9	AF.52N9	107.4	138.8	150.6	185.6	199.4	191.3	212.8	239.9
Total	NJAG	AF.5	1 145.4	1 281.3	1 178.9	1 312.5	1 409.6	1 481.8	1 496.5	1 633.0
Insurance, pensions and standardised guarantee schemes		AF.6								
Non-life insurance technical reserves	NJAZ	AF.61	0.6	0.4	0.3	0.3	0.3	0.3	0.2	0.2
Pension schemes[5]	M9VB	AF.6M	562.5	494.5	777.0	657.8	504.1	853.2	792.1	862.5
Total	NPXR	AF.6	563.1	494.9	777.3	658.1	504.3	853.4	792.3	862.8
Financial derivatives and employee stock options	MMV8	AF.7	96.6	95.1	141.1	126.3	126.1	151.1	104.1	135.9
Of which: financial derivatives	J8XL	AF.71	96.6	95.1	141.1	126.3	126.1	151.1	104.1	135.9
Other accounts receivable	NJBA	AF.8	50.1	37.0	31.0	31.3	34.3	34.4	31.1	40.7
Total financial assets	NIZN	**AF.A**	2 892.1	3 010.2	3 350.4	3 437.4	3 428.8	3 931.7	3 833.1	4 246.0

4.4.11 Insurance corporations and pension funds
ESA 2010 sectors S.128 and S.129[1] Unconsolidated

continued

£ billion

			2009	2010	2011	2012	2013	2014	2015	2016
Financial balance sheet at end of period		IV.3								
Total financial liabilities		AF.L								
Debt securities		AF.3								
Long-term		AF.32								
Issued by UK MFIs and other UK residents[2,6]	KLC2	AF.32N5-6	26.1	24.1	24.1	26.2	23.9	28.7	24.7	30.1
Total	NJBQ	AF.3	26.1	24.1	24.1	26.2	23.9	28.7	24.7	30.1
Loans		AF.4								
Short-term		AF.41								
By UK MFIs[2]	NJCU	AF.41N1	5.7	3.7	5.6	9.2	17.1	14.9	17.6	21.9
By rest of the world MFIs[2]	C657	AF.41N9	22.7	21.6	28.7	28.0	25.7	20.3	25.0	34.4
Long-term		AF.42								
Direct investment	NJDA	AF.421	8.7	7.6	5.6	24.5	25.1	17.7	17.9	15.4
Other long-term loans by UK residents	NJDI	AF.424N1	0.5	0.5	0.5	0.5	0.5	0.5	0.5	0.5
Total	NJCS	AF.4	37.6	33.4	40.4	62.1	68.3	53.3	60.9	72.2
Equity and investment fund shares/units		AF.5								
Equity		AF.51								
Listed UK shares[6]	NJDP	AF.511N1	43.9	47.9	40.2	55.4	69.7	87.3	99.6	99.7
Unlisted UK shares[6]	NJDQ	AF.512N1	14.6	16.7	15.3	18.9	26.3	27.0	24.6	25.3
UK shares and bonds issued by other UK residents[6]	NSOD	AF.519N7	–	–	–	–	–	–	–	–
Total	NJDK	AF.5	58.5	64.6	55.5	74.3	95.9	114.4	124.2	125.0
Insurance, pensions and standardised guarantee schemes		AF.6								
Non-life insurance technical reserves	NJED	AF.61	70.9	58.5	57.5	61.8	59.7	59.7	56.6	57.6
Life insurance and annuity entitlements	M9S9	AF.62	549.8	572.3	547.3	554.3	574.2	575.7	616.6	641.0
Pension schemes[5]	M9VR	AF.6M	1 794.1	1 884.7	2 281.9	2 315.1	2 243.5	2 667.7	2 638.8	2 958.7
Total	NPXS	AF.6	2 414.8	2 515.5	2 886.8	2 931.1	2 877.4	3 303.2	3 312.0	3 657.2
Financial derivatives and employee stock options	MMY4	AF.7	93.6	92.1	135.9	125.2	125.4	149.3	102.7	133.9
Of which: financial derivatives	J8XM	AF.71	93.6	92.0	135.8	125.2	125.4	149.2	102.7	133.9
Other accounts payable	NJEE	AF.8	72.8	69.6	72.9	80.2	83.1	98.5	82.3	87.7
Total financial liabilities	NJCR	**AF.L**	2 703.5	2 799.4	3 215.6	3 299.2	3 274.1	3 747.3	3 706.9	4 106.2
Financial net worth		**BF.90**								
Total financial assets	NIZN	AF.A	2 892.1	3 010.2	3 350.4	3 437.4	3 428.1	3 931.7	3 833.1	4 246.0
less total financial liabilities	NJCR	AF.L	2 703.5	2 799.4	3 215.6	3 299.2	3 274.1	3 747.3	3 706.9	4 106.2
Financial net worth	NYOI	**BF.90**	188.6	210.8	134.8	138.2	154.7	184.4	126.3	139.8

1 S.128 Insurance corporations and S.129 Pension funds
2 Monetary financial institutions
3 Money market instruments
4 Other than direct investment loans, loans secured on dwellings
 and loans for finance leasing
5 AF.63 Pension entitlements, AF.64 Claims on pension funds on pension
 managers, AF.65 Entitlements to non-pension benefits

6 Prior to 1990 it is not possible to distinguish some elements of AF.32N5-6,
 AF.511N1 and AF.512N1. These elements are shown combined as AF.519N7

United Kingdom National Accounts

The Blue Book
Chapter 05: General Government

2017 edition

Editors: Dean Goodway & Sarah Nightingale

Office for National Statistics

Chapter 5: General government

The general government sector is made up of units providing services for collective or individual consumption that are not sold at market prices. These units are usually funded by compulsory payments from units in other sectors (taxes) and may be involved in the redistribution of national income (for example, benefits and State Pension).

The sector includes government departments and agencies, local authorities, the devolved administrations in Northern Ireland, Scotland and Wales, the state education system, the National Health Service, the armed forces and the police. Non-departmental public bodies are also included in the general government sector.

The UK National Accounts, The Blue Book presents estimates for the general government sector and sub-sector breakdowns for:

- central government
- local government

Further information on sector classifications and classification decisions can be found in Economic statistics classifications.

5.1.1 General government
ESA 2010 sector S.13 Unconsolidated

£ million

			2009	2010	2011	2012	2013	2014	2015
Production account		I							
Resources									
Output		P.1							
Market output	NMXJ	P.11	876	756	741	774	808	837	1 038
Output for own final use	NMXK	P.12	2 982	4 095	3 669	3 683	3 603	3 606	3 379
Other non-market output		P.13							
Payments for non-market output	DPKE	P.131	40 364	39 883	38 081	36 103	38 705	40 288	42 150
Non-market output, other	DPKF	P.132	292 626	298 159	298 221	304 372	306 657	314 158	318 103
Total	NMYK	P.13	332 990	338 042	336 302	340 475	345 362	354 446	360 253
Total	NMXL	P.1	336 848	342 893	340 712	344 932	349 773	358 889	364 670
Total resources	NMXL	TR	336 848	342 893	340 712	344 932	349 773	358 889	364 670
Uses									
Intermediate consumption	NMXM	P.2	148 604	147 711	145 525	147 849	155 211	159 230	162 302
Gross value added	NMXN	**B.1g**	**188 244**	**195 182**	**195 187**	**197 083**	**194 562**	**199 659**	**202 368**
Total uses	NMXL	TU	336 848	342 893	340 712	344 932	349 773	358 889	364 670
Gross value added	NMXN	**B.1g**	**188 244**	**195 182**	**195 187**	**197 083**	**194 562**	**199 659**	**202 368**
less consumption of fixed capital	NMXO	P.51c	22 694	23 892	25 321	26 549	27 441	28 304	29 182
Value added, net of fixed capital consumption	NMXP	B.1n	165 550	171 290	169 866	170 534	167 121	171 355	173 186

5.1.2 General government
ESA 2010 sector S.13 Unconsolidated

£ million

			2009	2010	2011	2012	2013	2014	2015
Distribution and use of income accounts		II							
Primary distribution of income account		II.1							
Generation of income account		II.1.1							
Resources									
Total resources (gross value added)	NMXN	**B.1g**	**188 244**	**195 182**	**195 187**	**197 083**	**194 562**	**199 659**	**202 368**
Uses									
Compensation of employees		D.1							
Wages and salaries	NMXQ	D.11	128 179	132 342	131 333	133 740	129 372	132 784	132 792
Employers' social contributions	NMXR	D.12	37 371	38 948	38 533	36 794	37 749	38 571	40 394
Total	NMXS	D.1	165 550	171 290	169 866	170 534	167 121	171 355	173 186
Taxes on production and imports, paid		D.2							
Production taxes other than on products	NMXT	D.29	–	–	–	–	–	–	–
less subsidies, received		D.3							
Production subsidies other than on products	NMXU	D.39	–	–	–	–	–	–	–
Operating surplus, gross	NMXV	B.2g	22 694	23 892	25 321	26 549	27 441	28 304	29 182
Total uses (gross value added)	NMXN	**B.1g**	**188 244**	**195 182**	**195 187**	**197 083**	**194 562**	**199 659**	**202 368**
less consumption of fixed capital	NMXO	P.51c	22 694	23 892	25 321	26 549	27 441	28 304	29 182
Operating surplus, net	NMXW	B.2n	–	–	–	–	–	–	–

5.1.3 General government
ESA 2010 sector S.13 Unconsolidated

£ million

			2009	2010	2011	2012	2013	2014	2015	2016
Allocation of primary income account		II.1.2								
Resources										
Operating surplus, gross	NMXV	B.2g	22 694	23 892	25 321	26 549	27 441	28 304	29 182	29 763
Taxes on production and imports, received		D.2								
Taxes on products		D.21								
Value added tax (VAT)	NZGF	D.211	79 900	95 865	111 437	113 859	118 234	124 211	129 177	133 671
Taxes and duties on imports excluding VAT		D.212								
Import duties	NMXZ	D.2121	–	–	–	–	–	–	–	–
Taxes on imports excluding VAT and import duties	NMBT	D.2122	–	–	–	–	–	–	–	–
Taxes on products excluding VAT and import duties	NMYB	D.214	61 193	65 976	68 163	69 819	73 734	78 465	80 062	85 922
Total	NVCC	D.21	141 093	161 841	179 600	183 678	191 968	202 676	209 239	219 593
Other taxes on production	NMYD	D.29	24 917	28 786	26 661	28 262	29 559	30 242	31 142	32 220
Total	NMYE	D.2	166 010	190 627	206 261	211 940	221 527	232 918	240 381	251 813
less subsidies, paid		D.3								
Subsidies on products	NMYF	D.31	6 485	6 937	6 295	7 069	6 770	7 296	8 526	9 442
Other subsidies on production	LIUF	D.39	3 069	2 228	1 693	1 993	2 140	2 595	3 115	3 735
Total	NMRL	D.3	9 554	9 165	7 988	9 062	8 910	9 891	11 641	13 177
Property income		D.4								
Total interest	NMYL	D.41	8 688	7 976	8 191	9 919	8 469	8 504	9 072	8 683
Distributed income of corporations	NMYM	D.42	2 140	1 480	1 743	4 180	20 661	10 402	10 406	11 511
Other investment income		D.44								
Attributable to insurance policy holders	L8GK	D.441	65	43	42	36	47	55	27	27
Attributable to collective investment fund shareholders		D.443								
Dividends	L8H7	D.4431	–	–	–	–	–	–	–	–
Retained earnings	L8HE	D.4432	–	–	–	–	–	–	–	–
Total	L8GY	D.443	–	–	–	–	–	–	–	–
Total	NMYO	D.44	65	43	42	36	47	55	27	27
Rent from sectors other than general government	NMYR	D.45	1 317	1 310	1 302	1 314	1 432	1 423	1 409	1 416
Total	NMYU	D.4	12 210	10 809	11 278	15 449	30 609	20 384	20 914	21 637
Total resources	NMYV	TR	191 360	216 163	234 872	244 876	270 667	271 715	278 836	290 036
Uses										
Property income, paid		D.4								
Total interest	NRKB	D.41	31 131	48 204	54 517	52 977	52 545	51 993	46 950	50 996
Total	NMYY	D.4	31 131	48 204	54 517	52 977	52 545	51 993	46 950	50 996
Balance of primary incomes, gross	NMZH	**B.5g**	**160 229**	**167 959**	**180 355**	**191 899**	**218 122**	**219 722**	**231 886**	**239 040**
Total uses	NMYV	TU	191 360	216 163	234 872	244 876	270 667	271 715	278 836	290 036
less consumption of fixed capital	NMXO	P.51c	22 694	23 892	25 321	26 549	27 441	28 304	29 182	29 763
Balance of primary incomes, net	NMZI	B.5n	137 535	144 067	155 034	165 350	190 681	191 418	202 704	209 277

5.1.4 General government
ESA 2010 sector S.13 Unconsolidated

£ million

			2009	2010	2011	2012	2013	2014	2015	2016
Secondary distribution of income account		II.2								
Resources										
Balance of primary incomes, gross	NMZH	B.5g	160 229	167 959	180 355	191 899	218 122	219 722	231 886	239 040
Current taxes on income, wealth, etc.		D.5								
Taxes on income	NMZJ	D.51	190 532	197 652	204 706	198 737	203 077	206 879	217 794	228 095
Other current taxes	NVCM	D.59	34 443	35 294	37 436	37 566	39 590	40 958	42 255	42 884
Total	NMZL	D.5	224 975	232 946	242 142	236 303	242 667	247 837	260 049	270 979
Net social contributions		D.61								
Employers' actual social contributions	L8N9	D.611	70 351	73 170	75 075	75 714	78 015	80 453	84 741	90 359
Employers' imputed social contributions	M9WW	D.612	2 064	1 516	1 313	1 323	1 261	1 416	1 548	1 307
Households' actual social contributions	L8PF	D.613	46 919	47 772	50 144	52 359	52 762	53 261	56 584	59 582
Total	NMZR	D.61	119 334	122 458	126 532	129 396	132 038	135 130	142 873	151 248
Other current transfers		D.7								
Net non-life insurance premiums	DNKQ	D.71	–	–	–	–	–	2	6	8
Non-life insurance claims	NMZS	D.72	376	530	512	471	507	438	447	444
Current transfers within general government	NMZT	D.73	124 708	132 310	126 922	128 448	121 658	124 073	121 126	113 778
Current international cooperation	NMZU	D.74	208	223	−87	172	137	150	60	157
Miscellaneous current transfers from sectors other than general government	NMZX	D.75	943	977	984	1 944	2 783	4 328	3 479	2 977
Total	NNAA	D.7	126 235	134 040	128 331	131 035	125 085	128 991	125 118	117 364
Total resources	NNAB	TR	630 773	657 403	677 360	688 633	717 912	731 680	759 926	778 631
Uses										
Other current taxes	EBFQ	D.59	1 189	1 236	1 356	1 389	1 389	1 389	1 389	1 389
Social benefits other than social transfers in kind		D.62								
Social security benefits in cash	L8QN	D.621	82 873	84 277	86 113	91 472	93 708	96 232	99 140	101 772
Other social insurance benefits	L8R5	D.622	29 653	30 717	32 512	34 826	36 173	38 364	40 001	40 826
Social assistance benefits in cash	ZOXY	D.623	105 153	112 257	115 624	118 922	119 646	120 613	121 463	120 963
Total	NNAD	D.62	217 679	227 251	234 249	245 220	249 527	255 209	260 604	263 561
Other current transfers		D.7								
Net non-life insurance premiums	NNAE	D.71	376	530	512	471	507	438	447	444
Non-life insurance claims	DNKR	D.72	–	–	–	–	–	–	–	–
Current transfers within general government	NNAF	D.73	124 708	132 310	126 922	128 448	121 658	124 073	121 126	113 778
Current international cooperation	NNAG	D.74	5 021	5 668	6 274	6 122	8 060	7 198	6 823	7 620
Miscellaneous current transfers to sectors other than general government	NNAI	D.75	27 715	28 963	25 263	25 173	22 578	20 389	19 068	18 916
VAT and GNI based EU own resources		D.76								
VAT-based third EU own resource	M9LI	D.761	1 593	2 253	2 197	2 282	2 154	2 388	2 715	2 675
GNI-based fourth EU own resource	M9LJ	D.762	5 163	7 773	7 814	8 190	10 637	9 346	8 877	7 764
Total	M9LE	D.76	6 756	10 026	10 011	10 472	12 791	11 734	11 592	10 439
Total	NNAN	D.7	164 576	177 497	168 982	170 686	165 594	163 832	159 056	151 197
Gross disposable income	NNAO	**B.6g**	**247 329**	**251 419**	**272 773**	**271 338**	**301 402**	**311 250**	**338 877**	**362 484**
Total uses	NNAB	TU	630 773	657 403	677 360	688 633	717 912	731 680	759 926	778 631
less consumption of fixed capital	NMXO	P.51c	22 694	23 892	25 321	26 549	27 441	28 304	29 182	29 763
Disposable income, net	NNAP	B.6n	224 635	227 527	247 452	244 789	273 961	282 946	309 695	332 721

5.1.5 General government
ESA 2010 sector S.13 Unconsolidated

£ million

			2009	2010	2011	2012	2013	2014	2015	2016
Redistribution of income in kind account		II.3								
Resources										
Total resources (gross disposable income)	NNAO	**B.6g**	**247 329**	**251 419**	**272 773**	**271 338**	**301 402**	**311 250**	**338 877**	**362 484**
Uses										
Social transfers in kind		D.63								
Non-market produced	DPRP	D.631	167 710	171 318	171 951	175 933	179 875	183 816	189 748	191 148
Purchased market production	NSZE	D.632	38 138	39 279	40 557	41 341	41 419	44 856	43 959	48 321
Total	NSZA	D.63	205 848	210 597	212 508	217 274	221 294	228 672	233 707	239 469
Adjusted disposable income, gross	NSZI	B.7g	41 481	40 822	60 265	54 064	80 108	82 578	105 170	123 015
Total uses (gross disposable income)	NNAO	**B.6g**	**247 329**	**251 419**	**272 773**	**271 338**	**301 402**	**311 250**	**338 877**	**362 484**

5.1.6 General government
ESA 2010 sector S.13 Unconsolidated

£ million

			2009	2010	2011	2012	2013	2014	2015	2016
Use of income account		II.4								
Use of disposable income account		II.4.1								
Resources										
Total resources (gross disposable income)	NNAO	**B.6g**	**247 329**	**251 419**	**272 773**	**271 338**	**301 402**	**311 250**	**338 877**	**362 484**
Uses										
Final consumption expenditure		P.3								
Individual consumption expenditure	NNAQ	P.31	205 848	210 597	212 508	217 274	221 294	228 672	233 707	239 469
Collective consumption expenditure	NQEP	P.32	124 916	126 841	126 270	128 439	126 782	130 342	128 355	130 498
Total	NMRK	P.3	330 764	337 438	338 778	345 713	348 076	359 014	362 062	369 967
Gross saving	NNAU	**B.8g**	**−83 435**	**−86 019**	**−66 005**	**−74 375**	**−46 674**	**−47 764**	**−23 185**	**−7 483**
Total uses (gross disposable income)	NNAO	**B.6g**	**247 329**	**251 419**	**272 773**	**271 338**	**301 402**	**311 250**	**338 877**	**362 484**
less consumption of fixed capital	NMXO	P.51c	22 694	23 892	25 321	26 549	27 441	28 304	29 182	29 763
Saving, net	NNAV	B.8n	−106 129	−109 911	−91 326	−100 924	−74 115	−76 068	−52 367	−37 246
Use of adjusted disposable income account		II.4.2								
Resources										
Total resources, adjusted disposable income, gross	NSZI	B.7g	41 481	40 822	60 265	54 064	80 108	82 578	105 170	123 015
Uses										
Actual final consumption		P.4								
Actual collective consumption	NRMZ	P.42	124 916	126 841	126 270	128 439	126 782	130 342	128 355	130 498
Gross saving	NNAU	**B.8g**	**−83 435**	**−86 019**	**−66 005**	**−74 375**	**−46 674**	**−47 764**	**−23 185**	**−7 483**
Total uses	NSZI	TU	41 481	40 822	60 265	54 064	80 108	82 578	105 170	123 015

5.1.7 General government
ESA 2010 sector S.13 Unconsolidated

£ million

			2009	2010	2011	2012	2013	2014	2015	2016
Accumulation accounts		III								
Capital account		III.1								
Change in net worth due to saving and capital transfers account		III.1.1								
Changes in liabilities and net worth										
Gross saving	NNAU	B.8g	−83 435	−86 019	−66 005	−74 375	−46 674	−47 764	−23 185	−7 483
Capital transfers, receivable		D.9r								
Capital taxes	NMGI	D.91r	4 206	2 642	2 936	3 129	4 255	3 886	4 442	4 801
from sectors other than general government										
Investment grants	NSZF	D.92r	13 284	12 998	13 601	13 172	11 563	12 269	13 084	11 916
Other capital transfers	NNAX	D.99r	1 346	769	845	20 012	2 833	3 589	3 924	2 476
Total	NNAY	D.9r	18 836	16 409	17 382	36 313	18 651	19 744	21 450	19 193
Capital transfers, payable		D.9p								
Investment grants	NNAW	D.92p	29 813	29 596	26 316	26 325	23 754	25 547	28 489	25 983
Other capital transfers	NNBB	D.99p	15 677	1 996	1 846	29 774	1 957	1 715	3 157	1 690
Total	NNBC	D.9p	45 490	31 592	28 162	56 099	25 711	27 262	31 646	27 673
Changes in net worth due to gross saving and capital transfers	NMWG	B.101g	−110 089	−101 202	−76 785	−94 161	−53 734	−55 282	−33 381	−15 963
Changes in assets										
Changes in net worth due to gross saving and capital transfers	NMWG	B.101g	−110 089	−101 202	−76 785	−94 161	−53 734	−55 282	−33 381	−15 963
less consumption of fixed capital	NMXO	P.51c	22 694	23 892	25 321	26 549	27 441	28 304	29 182	29 763
Changes in net worth due to net saving and capital transfers	NNBD	B.101n	−132 783	−125 094	−102 106	−120 710	−81 175	−83 586	−62 563	−45 726
Acquisition of non-financial assets account		III.1.2								
Changes in liabilities and net worth										
Changes in net worth due to net saving										
and capital transfers	NNBD	B.101n	−132 783	−125 094	−102 106	−120 710	−81 175	−83 586	−62 563	−45 726
Consumption of fixed capital	NMXO	P.51c	22 694	23 892	25 321	26 549	27 441	28 304	29 182	29 763
Changes in net worth due to gross saving and capital transfers	NMWG	B.101g	−110 089	−101 202	−76 785	−94 161	−53 734	−55 282	−33 381	−15 963
Changes in assets										
Gross capital formation		P.5								
Gross fixed capital formation	NNBF	P.51g	50 553	50 220	48 275	46 223	45 718	50 954	50 288	51 763
Changes in inventories	NNBG	P.52	83	−14	−126	−132	−41	−38	−277	−261
Acquisitions less disposals of valuables[1]	NPOZ	P.53	−18	46	95	97	73	65	72	53
Total	NNBI	P.5	50 618	50 252	48 244	46 188	45 750	50 981	50 083	51 555
Acquisitions less disposals of non-produced										
Non-financial assets	NNBJ	NP	−1 136	−1 168	−1 474	−1 876	−1 838	−2 316	−2 505	−3 225
Net lending(+) / net borrowing(-)	NNBK	**B.9n**	**−159 571**	**−150 286**	**−123 555**	**−138 473**	**−97 646**	**−103 947**	**−80 959**	**−64 293**
Total change in assets	NMWG	B.101g	−110 089	−101 202	−76 785	−94 161	−53 734	−55 282	−33 381	−15 963

1 Acquisitions less disposals of valuables can be a volatile series but any
volatility is likely to be GDP neutral as it is offset in UK trade figures

5.1.8 General government
ESA 2010 sector S.13 Unconsolidated

£ million

			2009	2010	2011	2012	2013	2014	2015	2016
Financial account		III.2								
Net acquisition of financial assets		F.A								
Monetary gold and special drawing rights		F.1								
Monetary gold	NFPI	F.11	–	–	–	–	–	–	–	–
Special drawing rights	NFPJ	F.12	8 522	18	333	111	43	−14	55	−1 397
Total	NFPH	F.1	8 522	18	333	111	43	−14	55	−1 397
Currency and deposits		F.2								
Transferable deposits		F.22								
Deposits with UK MFIs[1]	NFPN	F.22N1	636	−4 363	3 178	8 168	−2 740	624	−969	−4 589
Of which: foreign currency deposits with UK MFIs[1]	NFPP	F.22N12	−736	37	1 711	−295	926	−1 102	−842	100
With rest of the world MFIs[1]	NFPR	F.22N9	−250	449	189	834	277	945	3 361	3 059
Other deposits	NFPS	F.29	9 148	−11 064	9 982	597	7 037	4 576	−6 880	2 744
Total	NFPK	F.2	9 534	−14 978	13 349	9 599	4 574	6 145	−4 488	1 214
Debt securities		F.3								
Short-term		F.31								
Issued by UK central government	NFPV	F.31N1	82	856	−430	787	226	744	321	−1 726
Issued by UK MFIs[1]	NFQA	F.31N5	−2 330	−574	−311	−5	78	832	121	−657
Money market instruments										
Issued by other UK residents	NFQF	F.31N6	−15	1 348	3 452	−3 610	1 863	−517	−2 277	895
Issued by rest of the world	NFQG	F.31N9	471	466	315	−967	−2 314	363	908	2 309
Long-term		F.32								
Issued by UK central government	NFQI	F.32N1	22	−19	209	−49	1 275	−534	−582	−114
Issued by UK MFIs and other UK residents[1,6]	KVG5	F.32N5-6	−5 236	–	–	1 152	−327	–	–	–
Issued by rest of the world	NFQQ	F.32N9	−820	5 439	4 099	5 182	−2 863	5 566	17 583	3 701
Total	NFPT	F.3	−7 826	7 516	7 334	2 490	−2 062	6 454	16 074	4 408
Loans		F.4								
Long-term		F.42								
Secured on dwellings	NFRG	F.422	1 214	−6 162	−8 587	−4 789	−6 082	−7 915	−16 475	−4 533
Other loans by UK residents[3]	NFRL	F.424N1	4 442	9 577	6 331	17 658	7 851	14 482	16 180	22 469
Other by rest of the world	NFRM	F.424N9	–	–	–	–	–	–	–	–
Total	NFQV	F.4	5 656	3 415	−2 256	12 869	1 769	6 567	−295	17 936
Equity and investment fund shares/units		F.5								
Equity		F.51								
Listed UK shares[6]	NFRS	F.511N1	40 496	−689	−774	1 973	−7 933	−4 727	−12 112	−3 001
Unlisted UK shares[6]	NFRT	F.512N1	−277	482	–	7	−21 957	−2 375	−758	−3
Other equity		F.519								
Other UK equity	NFRU	F.519N6	−4 960	−582	−684	−895	−1 078	−1 400	−1 345	−1 691
UK shares and bonds issued by other UK residents[6]	NSPW	F.519N7	–	–	–	–	–	–	–	–
Shares and other equity issued by rest of the world	NFRX	F.519N9	300	77	337	178	1 497	285	93	277
Total	NFRN	F.5	35 559	−712	−1 121	1 263	−29 471	−8 217	−14 122	−4 418
Insurance, pensions and standardised guarantee schemes		F.6								
Non-life insurance technical reserves	NFSG	F.61	−144	−65	−17	13	−23	–	−35	11
Total	NPWV	F.6	−144	−65	−17	13	−23	–	−35	11
Financial derivatives and employee stock options	MN5S	F.7	619	−271	−133	587	−11	−855	−1 219	894
Of which: financial derivatives	NFQR	F.71	619	−271	−133	587	−11	−855	−1 219	894
Other accounts receivable	NFSH	F.8	−1 272	3 136	302	2 098	4 921	5 343	10 064	8 804
Total net acquisition of financial assets	NFPG	**F.A**	50 648	−1 941	17 791	29 030	−20 260	15 423	6 034	27 452

5.1.8 General government
ESA 2010 sector S.13 Unconsolidated

continued

£ million

			2009	2010	2011	2012	2013	2014	2015	2016
Financial account		III.2								
Net acquisition of financial liabilities		F.L								
Special drawing rights	NFSN	F.12	8 654	–	–	–	–	–	–	–
Currency and deposits		F.2								
Currency	NFSP	F.21	48	82	30	158	30	191	168	140
Other deposits	NFSW	F.29	9 228	–8 090	9 186	–2 254	–7 912	17 852	10 689	17 856
Total	NFSO	F.2	9 276	–8 008	9 216	–2 096	–7 882	18 043	10 857	17 996
Debt securities		F.3								
Short-term		F.31								
Issued by UK central government	NFSZ	F.31N1	25 975	–2 077	14 454	–18 706	–14 315	25 809	19 721	12 524
Issued by UK local government	NFTD	F.31N2	–	–	–	–	–	–	–	–
Long-term		F.32								
Issued by UK central government	NFTM	F.32N1	194 266	171 851	124 826	133 873	106 136	64 601	53 250	56 083
Issued by UK local government	NFTP	F.32N2	–83	–17	595	676	717	496	590	362
Issued by UK MFIs and other UK residents[1,6]	MS5Y	F.32N5-6	–	–5 416	–10 967	–5 296	–11 682	–3 738	–14 718	–6 613
Total	NFSX	F.3	220 158	164 341	128 908	110 547	80 856	87 168	58 843	62 356
Loans		F.4								
Short-term		F.41								
By UK MFIs[1,4]	NFUB	F.41N1	–27 842	–1 430	694	–642	862	–1 186	4 036	46
By rest of the world	NFUF	F.41N9	–1 731	–44	–208	911	–825	1 228	5 021	–2 398
Long-term		F.42								
Finance leasing	NFUO	F.423	259	133	–23	–16	–19	–23	–25	605
Other loans by UK residents	NFUP	F.424N1	–1 873	2 406	1 051	9 246	696	1 089	465	2 174
Other loans by rest of the world	NFUQ	F.424N9	499	–403	–1 625	1 180	669	1 231	829	249
Total	NFTZ	F.4	–30 688	662	–111	10 679	1 383	2 339	10 326	676
Insurance, pensions and standardised guarantee schemes		F.6								
Pension schemes[5]	MA2W	F.6M	1 540	1 809	1 841	1 912	2 093	2 027	1 980	2 121
Provisions for calls under standardised guarantees	MA25	F.66	–	–	–	–	–	27	14	–
Total	NMQL	F.6	1 540	1 809	1 841	1 912	2 093	2 054	1 994	2 121
Other accounts payable	NFVL	F.8	2 124	–10 573	1 915	47 036	1 302	8 851	5 914	8 691
Total net acquisition of financial liabilities	NFSK	F.L	211 064	148 231	141 769	168 078	77 752	118 455	87 934	91 840
Net lending(+) / net borrowing(-)		B.9								
Total net acquisition of financial assets	NFPG	F.A	50 648	–1 941	17 791	29 030	–20 260	15 423	6 034	27 452
less total net acquisition of financial liabilities	NFSK	F.L	211 064	148 231	141 769	168 078	77 752	118 455	87 934	91 840
Net lending(+) / borrowing(-) from the financial account	NYNO	B.9f	–160 416	–150 172	–123 978	–139 048	–98 012	–103 032	–81 900	–64 388
Statistical discrepancy between the financial and non-financial accounts	NYOZ	dB.9	845	–114	423	575	366	–915	941	95
Net lending (+) / borrowing (-) from non-financial accounts	NNBK	B.9n	–159 571	–150 286	–123 555	–138 473	–97 646	–103 947	–80 959	–64 293

1 Monetary financial institutions
2 Money market instruments
3 Other than direct investment loans, loans secured on dwellings
  and loans for finance leasing
4 All loans secured on dwellings and all finance leasing are treated as
  long-term loans
5 F.63 Pension entitlements, F.64 Claims of pension funds on pension
  managers, F.65 Entitlements to non-pension benefits
6 Prior to 1990, it is not possible to distinguish some elements of F.32N5-6,
  F.511N1 and F.512N1. These elements are shown combined as F.519N7

5.1.9 General Government
ESA 2010 sector S.13

£ million

			2013	2014	2015	2016
Other changes in assets account		III.3				
Other changes in volume of assets account		III.3.1				
Changes in net worth due to other changes in volume of assets		B.102				
Monetary gold and special drawing rights	M9K4	AF.1	–	–	–	–
Currency and deposits	M9QM	AF.2	–2 404	–4 512	–382	1 767
Debt securities	N47N	AF.3	–141	–70	174	–133
Loans	N49P	AF.4	–3 110	–3 656	2 233	–4 089
Equity and investment fund shares/units	N4BR	AF.5	–	–	–	–
Insurance, pensions and standardised guarantee schemes	N4DS	AF.6	–	–	–	–
Financial derivatives and employee stock options	N4FQ	AF.7	–	–	–	–
Other accounts receivable/payable	N4HP	AF.8	–1 794	6 757	–3 381	12 897
Total	CWTV	**B.102**	–7 449	–1 481	–1 356	10 442

5.1.10 General Government
ESA 2010 sector S.13

£ million

			2013	2014	2015	2016
Other changes in assets account		III.3				
Revaluation account		III.3.2				
Changes in net worth due to nominal holding gains and losses		B.103				
Monetary gold and special drawing rights	M9L8	AF.1	−2 931	468	−587	1 844
Currency and deposits	M9TU	AF.2	−664	−974	−450	1 607
Debt securities	N48O	AF.3	71 688	−175 651	38 518	−189 472
Loans	N4AQ	AF.4	468	1 016	338	−1 241
Equity and investment fund shares/units	N4CS	AF.5	11 395	13 384	536	−666
Insurance, pensions and standardised guarantee schemes	N4ER	AF.6	7 739	7 515	−4 286	1 934
Financial derivatives and employee stock options	N4GP	AF.7	796	194	104	−8 901
Other accounts receivable/payable	N4IQ	AF.8	−16	710	757	−4 931
Total	CWUN	**B.103**	88 475	−153 338	34 930	−199 826

5.1.11 General government
ESA 2010 S.13 Unconsolidated

£ billion

			2009	2010	2011	2012	2013	2014	2015	2016
Financial balance sheet at end of period		IV.3								
Non-financial assets	NG3I	AN	676.8	749.3	777.1	779.2	812.7	906.5	942.0	964.8
Total financial assets		AF.A								
Monetary gold and special drawing rights		AF.1								
Monetary gold	NLVR	AF.11	6.8	9.1	9.8	10.2	7.3	7.7	7.1	9.4
Special drawing rights	NLVS	AF.12	8.9	9.1	9.4	9.1	9.0	9.0	9.1	8.9
Total	NIFC	AF.1	15.7	18.2	19.2	19.3	16.3	16.7	16.2	18.3
Currency and deposits		AF.2								
Transferable deposits		AF.22								
Deposits With UK MFIs[1]	NLVW	AF.22N1	59.4	43.1	43.6	51.2	46.0	41.9	40.5	38.2
Of which: foreign currency deposits with UK MFIs[1]	NLVY	AF.22N12	1.3	1.2	3.0	2.3	3.4	3.4	2.5	2.8
Deposits with rest of the world MFIs[1]	NLWA	AF.22N9	5.3	6.4	8.5	8.4	8.0	8.0	10.9	15.2
Other deposits	NLWB	AF.29	26.8	15.7	25.7	26.3	33.4	38.0	31.1	33.8
Total	NLUT	AF.2	91.5	65.2	77.8	85.9	87.4	87.9	82.5	87.2
Debt securities		AF.3								
Short-term		AF.31								
Issued by UK central government	NLWE	AF.31N1	0.1	0.9	0.5	1.3	1.5	2.3	2.6	0.9
Issued by UK MFIs[1]	NLWJ	AF.31N5	1.6	1.0	0.7	0.7	0.4	1.2	1.3	0.7
MMIs by other UK residents[2]	NLWO	AF.31N6	1.4	2.8	6.3	2.8	4.5	3.9	1.8	2.6
Issued by rest of the world	NLWP	AF.31N9	5.6	6.1	6.4	5.3	2.9	3.2	4.1	6.8
Long-term		AF.32								
Issued by UK central government	NLWR	AF.32N1	0.2	0.2	0.4	0.4	1.7	1.1	0.5	0.4
Issued by UK local government	NLWU	AF.32N2	–	–	–	–	–	–	–	–
Issued by UK MFIs and other UK residents[1,5]	KVF6	AF.32N5-6	0.2	0.2	0.2	1.4	1.0	1.0	1.0	1.0
Issued by rest of the world	NLWZ	AF.32N9	21.1	36.7	40.3	43.9	40.0	45.3	62.7	77.3
Total	NLWC	AF.3	30.3	48.0	54.8	55.8	52.0	58.0	74.0	89.6
Loans		AF.4								
Long-term		AF.42								
Secured on dwellings	NLXP	AF.422	4.4	91.3	82.7	77.9	71.8	63.9	47.4	42.9
Other loans by UK residents[3]	NLXU	AF.424N1	93.6	102.5	109.1	127.3	133.8	146.8	162.1	181.9
Total	NLXE	AF.4	98.0	193.8	191.8	205.2	205.7	210.8	209.5	224.8
Equity and investment fund shares/units		AF.5								
Equity		AF.51								
Listed UK shares[5]	NLYB	AF.511N1	41.3	54.6	26.9	46.9	54.3	55.4	37.3	28.2
Unlisted UK shares[5]	NLYC	AF.512N1	12.5	20.7	28.7	40.2	12.3	13.7	16.4	18.9
Other equity		AF.519								
Other UK equity	H4O9	AF.519N6	117.5	118.8	120.1	122.2	123.2	125.7	127.4	128.5
UK shares and bonds issued by other UK residents[5]	NSQP	AF.519N7	–	–	–	–	–	–	–	–
Shares and other equity issued by rest of the world	NLYG	AF.519N9	3.5	3.6	3.9	4.1	5.5	5.8	5.9	6.1
Total[2]	NLXW	AF.5	174.8	197.7	179.6	213.4	195.3	200.5	186.9	181.8
Insurance, pensions and standardised guarantee schemes		AF.6								
Non-life insurance technical reserves	NLYP	AF.61	0.7	0.7	0.7	0.7	0.7	0.7	0.6	0.6
Total	NPYJ	AF.6	0.7	0.7	0.7	0.7	0.7	0.7	0.6	0.6
Financial derivatives and employee stock options	MMW2	AF.7	−0.3	2.0	2.7	3.3	2.9	2.1	2.1	−6.5
Of which: financial derivatives	NLXA	AF.71	−0.3	2.0	2.7	3.3	2.9	2.1	2.1	−6.5
Other accounts receivable	NLYQ	AF.8	71.3	61.3	61.3	62.6	67.2	72.2	81.4	90.7
Total financial assets	NPUP	**AF.A**	482.1	586.9	588.1	646.2	627.4	648.8	653.3	686.6

5.1.11 General government
ESA 2010 S.13 Unconsolidated
continued

£ billion

			2009	2010	2011	2012	2013	2014	2015	2016
Financial balance sheet at end of period		IV.3								
Total financial liabilities		AF.L								
Special drawing rights	NLYW	AF.12	9.8	10.1	10.1	9.6	9.4	9.4	9.5	11.1
Currency and deposits		AF.2								
Currency	NLYY	AF.21	4.0	4.1	4.1	4.3	4.3	4.5	4.7	4.8
Other deposits	NLZF	AF.29	126.9	123.8	132.5	130.2	122.3	139.9	150.6	168.6
Total	NLYX	AF.2	130.9	127.8	136.6	134.5	126.5	144.4	155.3	173.4
Debt securities		AF.3								
Short-term		AF.31								
Issued by UK central government	NLZI	AF.31N1	57.5	55.4	69.8	51.1	36.8	62.6	82.3	94.9
Issued by UK local government	NLZM	AF.31N2	–	–	–	–	–	–	–	–
Long-term		AF.32								
Issued by UK central government	NLZV	AF.32N1	822.0	1 021.9	1 280.4	1 392.5	1 422.6	1 663.1	1 678.1	1 934.6
Issued by UK local government	NLZY	AF.32N2	1.0	1.0	1.6	2.3	3.0	3.5	4.1	4.4
Issued by UK MFIs and other UK residents[1,5]	MNR8	AF.32N5-6	–	52.3	41.1	34.9	26.0	21.7	6.4	0.2
Total	NLZG	AF.3	880.5	1 130.5	1 392.9	1 480.8	1 488.3	1 750.9	1 770.9	2 034.1
Loans		AF.4								
Short-term		AF.41								
By UK monetary financial institutions[1]	NNKY	AF.41N1	17.3	15.5	16.7	14.3	15.1	14.1	13.2	13.8
By rest of the world monetary financial institutions	NNLC	AF.41N9	0.4	0.2	0.1	1.0	0.1	1.2	6.4	5.2
Long-term		AF.42								
Finance leasing	NNLL	AF.423	4.8	5.3	5.2	5.2	5.2	5.6	6.1	6.7
Other long-term loans		AF.424								
By UK residents	NNLM	AF.424N1	51.8	55.0	55.7	64.6	67.3	70.0	71.5	74.7
By rest of the world	NNLN	AF.424N9	4.3	4.4	4.7	5.8	6.0	6.4	6.7	6.9
Total	NNKW	AF.4	78.6	80.5	82.4	91.0	93.7	97.2	104.0	107.4
Insurance, pensions and standardised guarantee schemes		AF.6								
Pension schemes[4]	M9VS	AF.6M	92.0	74.2	85.0	73.4	67.7	62.2	68.5	68.7
Provisions for calls under standardised guarantees	M9UZ	AF.66	–	–	–	–	–	–	–	0.041
Total	NNBZ	AF.6	92.0	74.2	85.0	73.4	67.7	62.3	68.6	68.7
Financial derivatives and employee stock options	MMY6	AF.7	0.7	2.7	3.3	2.4	1.3	1.1	2.2	1.7
Of which: financial derivatives	NNKS	AF.71	0.7	2.7	3.3	2.4	1.3	1.1	2.2	–
Other accounts payable	NNMI	AF.8	46.1	48.3	48.5	86.9	89.7	90.7	98.4	99.6
Total financial liabilities	NPVQ	**AF.L**	1 238.5	1 474.1	1 758.8	1 878.6	1 876.8	2 156.0	2 208.9	2 495.9
Total financial assets	NPUP	AF.A	482.1	586.9	588.1	646.2	627.4	648.8	653.3	686.6
less total financial liabilities	NPVQ	AF.L	1 238.5	1 474.1	1 758.8	1 878.6	1 876.8	2 156.0	2 208.9	2 495.9
Financial net worth	NYOG	**BF.90**	−756.4	−887.2	−1 170.8	−1 232.4	−1 249.4	−1 507.3	−1 555.6	−1 809.4
Net worth										
Non-financial assets	NG3I	AN	676.8	749.3	777.1	779.2	812.7	906.5	942.0	964.8
Financial net worth	NYOG	BF.90	−756.4	−887.2	−1 170.8	−1 232.4	−1 249.4	−1 507.3	−1 555.6	−1 809.4
Net worth	CGRX	**B.90**	−79.7	−138.0	−393.7	−453.3	−436.7	−600.7	−613.6	−844.6

1 Monetary financial institutions
2 Money market instruments
3 Other than direct investment loans, loans secured on dwellings
  and loans for finance leasing
4 AF.63 Pension entitlements, AF.64 Claims of pension funds on
  pension mangers, AF.65 Entitlements to non-pension benefits

5 Prior to 1990 it is not possible to distinguish some elements of AF.32N5-6,
  AF.511N1 and AF.512N1. These elements are shown combined as AF.519N7

5.2.1 Central government
ESA 2010 sector S.1311

£ million

Production account		I	2009	2010	2011	2012	2013	2014	2015
Resources									
Output		P.1							
Market output	NMIW	P.11	233	125	121	155	177	196	370
Output for own final use	QYJV	P.12	2 623	3 742	3 303	3 318	3 251	3 247	3 006
Other non-market output		P.13							
Payments for non-market output	C3F5	P.131	15 869	14 969	14 350	12 755	14 907	15 509	16 698
Non-market output, other	DPKH	P.132	174 854	180 303	183 992	193 799	197 010	204 913	209 336
Total	DPS2	P.13	190 723	195 272	198 342	206 554	211 917	220 422	226 034
Total	NMAE	P.1	193 579	199 139	201 766	210 027	215 345	223 865	229 410
Total resources	NMAE	TR	193 579	199 139	201 766	210 027	215 345	223 865	229 410
Uses									
Intermediate consumption	NMAF	P.2	89 398	90 548	89 970	93 122	98 362	100 509	103 083
Gross value added	NMBR	B.1g	**104 181**	**108 591**	**111 796**	**116 905**	**116 983**	**123 356**	**126 327**
Total uses	NMAE	T	193 579	199 139	201 766	210 027	215 345	223 865	229 410
Gross value added	NMBR	B.1g	**104 181**	**108 591**	**111 796**	**116 905**	**116 983**	**123 356**	**126 327**
less consumption of fixed capital	NSRN	P.51c	14 804	15 515	16 417	17 135	17 497	17 843	18 220
Value added, net of fixed capital consumption	NMAH	B.1n	89 377	93 076	95 379	99 770	99 486	105 513	108 107

5.2.2 Central government
ESA 2010 sector S.1311

£ million

			2009	2010	2011	2012	2013	2014	2015
Distribution and use of income accounts		II							
Primary distribution of income account		II.1							
Generation of income account		II.1.1							
Resources									
Total resources (gross value added)	NMBR	B.1g	**104 181**	**108 591**	**111 796**	**116 905**	**116 983**	**123 356**	**126 327**
Uses									
Compensation of employees		D.1							
Wages and salaries	NMAI	D.11	71 046	73 684	76 233	82 074	80 737	85 733	86 599
Employers' social contributions	NMAL	D.12	18 331	19 392	19 146	17 696	18 749	19 780	21 508
Total	NMBG	D.1	89 377	93 076	95 379	99 770	99 486	105 513	108 107
Taxes on production and imports, paid		D.2							
Production taxes other than on products	NMAN	D.29	–	–	–	–	–	–	–
less subsidies, received		D.3							
Production subsidies other than on products	NMAO	D.39	–	–	–	–	–	–	–
Operating surplus, gross	NRLN	B.2g	14 804	15 515	16 417	17 135	17 497	17 843	18 220
Total uses (gross value added)	NMBR	B.1g	**104 181**	**108 591**	**111 796**	**116 905**	**116 983**	**123 356**	**126 327**
less consumption of fixed capital	NSRN	P.51c	14 804	15 515	16 417	17 135	17 497	17 843	18 220
Operating surplus, net	NMAP	B.2n	–	–	–	–	–	–	–

5.2.3 Central government
ESA 2010 sector S.1311

£ million

			2009	2010	2011	2012	2013	2014	2015	2016
Allocation of primary income account		II.1.2								
Resources										
Operating surplus, gross	NRLN	B.2g	14 804	15 515	16 417	17 135	17 497	17 843	18 220	18 289
Taxes on production and imports, received		D.2								
Taxes on products		D.21								
Value added tax (VAT)	NZGF	D.211	79 900	95 865	111 437	113 859	118 234	124 211	129 177	133 671
Taxes and duties on imports excluding VAT		D.212								
Import duties	NMXZ	D.2121	–	–	–	–	–	–	–	–
Taxes on imports excluding VAT and import duties	NMBT	D.2122	–	–	–	–	–	–	–	–
Taxes on products excluding VAT and import duties	NMBV	D.214	61 193	65 976	68 163	69 815	73 698	78 361	79 915	85 663
Total	NMYC	D.21	141 093	161 841	179 600	183 674	191 932	202 572	209 092	219 334
Other taxes on production	NMBX	D.29	24 600	28 289	26 097	27 685	28 992	29 671	30 542	31 591
Total	NMBY	D.2	165 693	190 130	205 697	211 359	220 924	232 243	239 634	250 925
less subsidies, paid		D.3								
Subsidies on products	NMCB	D.31	4 508	5 157	4 722	5 771	5 531	6 091	7 358	8 346
Other subsidies on production	NMCC	D.39	1 551	964	828	1 426	1 848	2 123	2 497	2 904
Total	NMCD	D.3	6 059	6 121	5 550	7 197	7 379	8 214	9 855	11 250
Property income		D.4								
Interest		D.41								
Interest before FISIM[1] allocation	I69N	D.41g	7 874	7 338	7 370	9 073	7 586	7 465	8 010	7 715
plus FISIM	C6GA	P.119	86	−14	49	48	22	46	60	50
Total	NMCE	D.41	7 960	7 324	7 419	9 121	7 608	7 511	8 070	7 765
Distributed income of corporations	NMCH	D.42	1 306	752	766	2 913	19 291	9 403	9 428	10 615
Rent from sectors other than general government	NMCK	D.45	1 317	1 310	1 302	1 314	1 432	1 423	1 409	1 416
Total	NMCL	D.4	10 583	9 386	9 487	13 348	28 331	18 337	18 907	19 796
Total resources	NMCM	TR	185 021	208 910	226 051	234 645	259 373	260 209	266 906	277 760
Uses										
Property income		D.4								
Interest		D.41								
Interest before FISIM allocation	I69W	D.41g	27 869	44 980	51 335	47 982	49 192	48 424	43 209	47 273
less FISIM	C6G9	P.119	26	63	38	26	4	−1	−5	14
Total	RVFK	D.41	27 843	44 917	51 297	47 956	49 188	48 425	43 214	47 259
Total	NUHA	D.4	27 843	44 917	51 297	47 956	49 188	48 425	43 214	47 259
Balance of primary incomes, gross	NRLP	**B.5g**	**157 178**	**163 993**	**174 754**	**186 689**	**210 185**	**211 784**	**223 692**	**230 501**
Total uses	NMCM	TU	185 021	208 910	226 051	234 645	259 373	260 209	266 906	277 760
less consumption of fixed capital	NSRN	P.51c	14 804	15 515	16 417	17 135	17 497	17 843	18 220	18 289
Balance of primary incomes, net	NMCT	B.5n	142 374	148 478	158 337	169 554	192 688	193 941	205 472	212 212

1 Financial intermediation services indirectly measured.

5.2.4 Central government
ESA 2010 sector S.1311

£ million

			2009	2010	2011	2012	2013	2014	2015	2016
Secondary distribution of income account		II.2								
Resources										
Balance of primary incomes, gross	NRLP	B.5g	**157 178**	**163 993**	**174 754**	**186 689**	**210 185**	**211 784**	**223 692**	**230 501**
Current taxes on income, wealth, etc.		D.5								
Taxes on income	NMCU	D.51	190 532	197 652	204 706	198 737	203 077	206 879	217 794	228 095
Other current taxes	NMCV	D.59	9 386	9 710	11 555	11 347	12 347	12 820	13 276	12 658
Total	NMCP	D.5	199 918	207 362	216 261	210 084	215 424	219 699	231 070	240 753
Net social contributions		D.61								
Employers' actual social contributions	L8NB	D.611	68 795	71 563	73 449	74 067	76 489	78 964	83 240	88 858
Employers' imputed social contributions	M9WU	D.612	1 003	751	655	648	630	722	834	719
Households' actual social contributions	L8PH	D.613	46 193	47 029	49 399	51 602	52 053	52 554	55 863	58 859
Total	NMCW	D.61	115 991	119 343	123 503	126 317	129 172	132 240	139 937	148 436
Other current transfers		D.7								
Net non-life insurance premiums	MW4L	D.71	–	–	–	–	–	2	6	8
Non-life insurance claims	NMDJ	D.72	–	–	–	–	–	–	–	–
Current transfers within general government	NMDK	D.73	–	–	–	–	–	–	–	–
Current international cooperation	NMDL	D.74	38	38	45	121	105	123	47	157
Miscellaneous current transfers	NMEZ	D.75	610	656	650	1 595	2 436	3 997	3 100	2 517
from sectors other than general government										
Total	NMDI	D.7	648	694	695	1 716	2 541	4 122	3 153	2 682
Total resources	NMDN	TR	473 735	491 392	515 213	524 806	557 322	567 845	597 852	622 372
Uses										
Social benefits other than social transfers in kind		D.62								
Social security benefits in cash	L8QP	D.621	82 873	84 277	86 113	91 472	93 708	96 232	99 140	101 772
Other social insurance benefits	L8R9	D.622	25 160	26 379	28 085	30 154	31 811	33 940	35 323	36 121
Social assistance benefits in cash	NZGO	D.623	84 386	89 499	91 507	93 470	93 274	93 702	94 260	93 829
Total	NMDR	D.62	192 419	200 155	205 705	215 096	218 793	223 874	228 723	231 722
Other current transfers		D.7								
Net non-life insurance premiums	NMDX	D.71	–	–	–	–	–	–	–	–
Non-life insurance claims	MW4K	D.72	–	–	–	–	–	–	–	–
Current transfers within general government	QYJR	D.73	124 708	132 310	126 922	128 448	121 658	124 073	121 126	113 778
Current international cooperation	NMDZ	D.74	5 021	5 668	6 274	6 122	8 060	7 198	6 823	7 620
Miscellaneous current transfers		D.75								
to sectors other than general government										
Current transfers to non-profit institutions serving households	DFT8	D.751	26 259	27 931	24 116	23 835	21 077	19 049	17 555	17 118
Other Miscellaneous current transfers	MJTI	D.759	1 427	1 006	1 115	1 308	1 423	1 245	1 411	1 692
Total	NMFC	D.75	27 686	28 937	25 231	25 143	22 500	20 294	18 966	18 810
VAT and GNI based EU own resources		D.76								
VAT-based third EU own resource	M9LI	D.761	1 593	2 253	2 197	2 282	2 154	2 388	2 715	2 675
GNI-based fourth EU own resource	M9LJ	D.762	5 163	7 773	7 814	8 190	10 637	9 346	8 877	7 764
Total	M9LH	D.76	6 756	10 026	10 011	10 472	12 791	11 734	11 592	10 439
Other current transfers	NMDW	D.7	164 171	176 941	168 438	170 185	165 009	163 299	158 507	150 647
Gross disposable income	NRLR	B.6g	**117 145**	**114 296**	**141 070**	**139 525**	**173 520**	**180 672**	**210 622**	**240 003**
Total uses	NMDN	TU	473 735	491 392	515 213	524 806	557 322	567 845	597 852	622 372
less consumption of fixed capital	NSRN	P.51c	14 804	15 515	16 417	17 135	17 497	17 843	18 220	18 289
Disposable income, net	NMEB	B.6n	102 341	98 781	124 653	122 390	156 023	162 829	192 402	221 714

5.2.4S Central government
Social contributions and benefits
ESA 2010 sector S.1311

£ million

Secondary distribution of income (further detail of certain items)		Part	2009	2010	2011	2012	2013	2014	2015	2016
Resources										
Net social contributions		D.61								
Employers' actual social contributions	L8NB	D.611	68 795	71 563	73 449	74 067	76 489	78 964	83 240	88 858
Employers' actual pension contributions	L67D	D.6111	62 398	65 437	67 493	68 674	71 906	74 869	79 068	84 395
Employers' actual non-pension contributions	L67E	D.6112	6 397	6 126	5 956	5 393	4 583	4 095	4 172	4 463
Employers' imputed social contributions	M9WU	D.612	1 003	751	655	648	630	722	834	719
Employers' imputed pension contributions	L67A	D.6121	–	–	–	–	–	–	–	–
Employers' imputed non-pension contributions	EWRO	D.6122	1 003	751	655	648	630	722	834	719
Households' actual social contributions	L8PH	D.613	46 193	47 029	49 399	51 602	52 053	52 554	55 863	58 859
Households' actual pension contributions	L67H	D.6131	41 478	42 482	44 967	47 709	48 794	49 656	52 879	55 709
Households' actual non-pension contributions	L67J	D.6132	4 715	4 547	4 432	3 893	3 259	2 898	2 984	3 150
Total	NMCW	D.61	115 991	119 343	123 503	126 317	129 172	132 240	139 937	148 436
National insurance contributions (NICs)										
Compulsory employers' actual social contributions	M976	D.611C	54 411	55 887	58 174	60 600	62 019	63 892	66 491	71 407
Compulsory households' actual social contributions	L8OB	D.613c	40 095	41 488	43 292	43 742	44 085	45 243	47 587	50 407
Compulsory employees' actual social contributions	M97A	D.613ce	37 245	38 732	40 651	41 182	41 500	42 571	44 465	47 218
Compulsory actual social contributions by the self-employed	M97C	D.613cs	2 793	2 711	2 603	2 512	2 536	2 624	3 089	3 158
Compulsory actual social contributions by the non-employed	M97E	D.613cn	57	45	38	48	49	48	33	31
Pension schemes[1]										
Voluntary employers' actual social contributions	M977	D.611V	14 384	15 676	15 275	13 467	14 470	15 072	16 749	17 451
Employers' imputed pension contributions	L67A	D.6121	–	–	–	–	–	–	–	–
Employees' voluntary social contribution	CX3X	D.613V	6 098	5 541	6 107	7 860	7 968	7 311	8 276	8 452
Uses										
Social benefits other than social transfers in kind		D.62								
Social security pension benefits in cash	L8LV	D.6211	68 459	69 697	73 068	78 787	82 430	85 707	88 486	91 241
Non pension social security benefits in cash	L8LX	D.6212	14 414	14 580	13 045	12 685	11 278	10 525	10 654	10 531
National insurance fund										
Widows' and guardians' allowances	CSDH		650	620	604	594	590	575	573	566
Unemployment benefit	CSDI		–	–	–	–	–	–	–	–
Jobseeker's allowance	CJTJ		1 223	819	735	677	563	407	314	277
Incapacity benefit	CUNL		6 657	6 546	6 391	5 819	4 880	4 316	4 457	4 668
Maternity benefit	CSDL		336	341	360	387	401	411	433	439
Payment in lieu of benefits foregone	GTKV		–	–	–	–	–	–	–	–
Statutory sick pay	CSDQ		96	24	72	135	109	96	96	96
Redundancy fund benefit	GTKN		522	439	342	419	52	489	271	239
Maternity fund benefit	GTKO		–	–	–	–	–	–	–	–
Statutory maternity pay	GTKZ		1 655	2 107	2 160	2 195	2 371	2 089	2 410	2 151
Social fund benefit	GTLQ		3 275	3 684	2 381	2 459	2 312	2 142	2 100	2 095
Total	L8QP	D.621	82 873	84 277	86 113	91 472	93 708	96 232	99 140	101 772
Other social insurance benefits	L8R9	D.622	25 160	26 379	28 085	30 154	31 811	33 940	35 323	36 121
Other social insurance pension benefits	L677	D.6221	24 157	25 628	27 430	29 506	31 181	33 218	34 489	35 402
Other social insurance non-pension benefits	EWRO	D.6222	1 003	751	655	648	630	722	834	719
Social assistance benefits in cash		D.623								
War pensions and allowances	CSDD		1 020	953	944	1 000	1 000	887	807	775
Income support	CSDE		16 574	16 164	15 157	13 260	10 984	9 513	8 675	8 108
Income tax credits and reliefs	RYCQ		26 964	28 735	29 626	29 941	29 840	29 577	28 975	27 774
Child benefit	EKY3		11 882	12 041	12 257	12 107	11 671	11 511	11 640	11 577
Non-contributory jobseeker's allowance	EKY4		3 513	3 851	4 067	4 496	4 034	2 940	2 117	1 699
Care allowances	EKY5		7 724	7 998	8 154	8 517	8 526	8 684	8 578	8 402
Disability benefits	EKY6		12 010	12 751	13 167	14 231	14 681	14 726	14 449	13 081
Other benefits	EKY7		4 648	7 006	8 135	9 918	12 538	15 864	19 019	22 413
Benefits paid to overseas residents	RNNF		51	–	–	–	–	–	–	–
Total	NZGO	D.623	84 386	89 499	91 507	93 470	93 274	93 702	94 260	93 829
Total	NMDR	D.62	192 419	200 155	205 705	215 096	218 793	223 874	228 723	231 722

1 Mainly civil service, armed forces', teachers' and NHS pension schemes.

5.2.5 Central government
ESA 2010 sector S.1311

£ million

Redistribution of income in kind account		II.3	2009	2010	2011	2012	2013	2014	2015	2016
Resources											
Total resources (gross disposable income)	NRLR	B.6g	117 145	114 296	141 070	139 525	173 520	180 672	210 622	240 003
Uses											
Social transfers in kind		D.63								
Non-market produced	DPKR	D.631	95 875	98 956	103 166	109 211	112 325	116 271	122 661	124 929
Purchased market production	C3FK	D.632	24 082	23 881	25 238	25 760	25 464	28 838	27 592	31 464
Total	NMED	D.63	119 957	122 837	128 404	134 971	137 789	145 109	150 253	156 393
Adjusted disposable income, gross	NSVS	B.7g	−2 812	−8 541	12 666	4 554	35 731	35 563	60 369	83 610
Total uses (gross disposable income)	NRLR	B.6g	117 145	114 296	141 070	139 525	173 520	180 672	210 622	240 003

5.2.6 Central government
ESA 2010 sector S.1311

£ million

			2009	2010	2011	2012	2013	2014	2015	2016
Use of income account		II.4								
Use of disposable income account		II.4.1								
Resources											
Total resources (gross disposable income)	NRLR	B.6g	117 145	114 296	141 070	139 525	173 520	180 672	210 622	240 003
Uses											
Final consumption expenditure		P.3								
Individual consumption expenditure	NMED	P.31	119 957	122 837	128 404	134 971	137 789	145 109	150 253	156 393
Collective consumption expenditure	NMEE	P.32	78 979	81 347	80 826	84 588	84 685	88 642	86 675	88 400
Total	NMBJ	P.3	198 936	204 184	209 230	219 559	222 474	233 751	236 928	244 793
Gross saving	NRLS	B.8g	**−81 791**	**−89 888**	**−68 160**	**−80 034**	**−48 954**	**−53 079**	**−26 306**	**−4 790**
Total uses (gross disposable income)	NRLR	B.6g	117 145	114 296	141 070	139 525	173 520	180 672	210 622	240 003
less consumption of fixed capital	NSRN	P.51c	14 804	15 515	16 417	17 135	17 497	17 843	18 220	18 289
Saving, net	NMEG	B.8n	−96 595	−105 403	−84 577	−97 169	−66 451	−70 922	−44 526	−23 079
Use of adjusted disposable income account		II.4.2								
Resources											
Total resources, adjusted disposable income, gross	NSVS	B.7g	−2 812	−8 541	12 666	4 554	35 731	35 563	60 369	83 610
Uses											
Actual final consumption		P.4								
Actual collective consumption	NMEE	P.42	78 979	81 347	80 826	84 588	84 685	88 642	86 675	88 400
Gross saving	NRLS	B.8g	**−81 791**	**−89 888**	**−68 160**	**−80 034**	**−48 954**	**−53 079**	**−26 306**	**−4 790**
Total uses	NSVS	TU	−2 812	−8 541	12 666	4 554	35 731	35 563	60 369	83 610

5.2.7 Central government
ESA 2010 sector S.1311

£ million

			2009	2010	2011	2012	2013	2014	2015	2016
Accumulation accounts		III								
Capital account		III.1								
Change in net worth due to saving and capital transfers account		III.1.1								
Changes in liabilities and net worth										
Gross saving	NRLS	B.8g	−81 791	−89 888	−68 160	−80 034	−48 954	−53 079	−26 306	−4 790
Capital transfers, receivable		D.9r								
Capital taxes	NMGI	D.91r	4 206	2 642	2 936	3 129	4 255	3 886	4 442	4 801
from sectors other than general government										
Investment grants	GCMT	D.92r	–	–	–	–	–	–	–	–
Other capital transfers	NMEK	D.99r	359	215	276	13 888	2 025	2 750	2 806	1 197
Total	NMEH	D.9r	4 565	2 857	3 212	17 017	6 280	6 636	7 248	5 998
Capital transfers, payable		D.9p								
Investment grants	NMEN	D.92p	27 453	27 187	23 515	22 444	20 515	23 025	24 937	23 451
Other capital transfers	NMEO	D.99p	15 226	1 741	1 576	16 176	1 679	1 411	2 012	1 488
Total	NMEL	D.9p	42 679	28 928	25 091	38 620	22 194	24 436	26 949	24 939
Changes in net worth due to gross saving and capital transfers	NMEP	B.101g	−119 905	−115 959	−90 039	−101 637	−64 868	−70 879	−46 007	−23 731
Changes in assets										
Changes in net worth due to gross saving and capital transfers	NMEP	B.101g	−119 905	−115 959	−90 039	−101 637	−64 868	−70 879	−46 007	−23 731
less consumption of fixed capital	NSRN	P.51c	14 804	15 515	16 417	17 135	17 497	17 843	18 220	18 289
Changes in net worth due to net saving and capital transfers	NMEQ	B.101n	−134 709	−131 474	−106 456	−118 772	−82 365	−88 722	−64 227	−42 020
Acquisition of non-financial assets account		III.1.2								
Changes in liabilities and net worth										
Changes in net worth due to saving and capital transfers	NMEQ	B.101n	−134 709	−131 474	−106 456	−118 772	−82 365	−88 722	−64 227	−42 020
Consumption of fixed capital	NSRN	P.51c	14 804	15 515	16 417	17 135	17 497	17 843	18 220	18 289
Changes in net worth due to gross saving and capital transfers	NMEP	B.101g	−119 905	−115 959	−90 039	−101 637	−64 868	−70 879	−46 007	−23 731
Changes in assets										
Gross capital formation		P.5								
Gross fixed capital formation	NMES	P.51g	31 515	31 341	29 152	28 381	28 848	33 090	31 788	32 177
Changes in inventories	NMFE	P.52	83	−14	−126	−132	−41	−38	−277	−261
Acquisitions less disposals of valuables[1]	NPPD	P.53	−18	46	95	97	73	65	72	53
Total	NMER	P.5	31 580	31 373	29 121	28 346	28 880	33 117	31 583	31 969
Acquisitions less disposals of non-produced Non-financial assets	NMFG	NP	−165	−86	−219	−399	−419	−702	−484	−877
Net lending(+) / net borrowing(-)	NMFJ	B.9n	**−151 320**	**−147 246**	**−118 941**	**−129 584**	**−93 329**	**−103 294**	**−77 106**	**−54 823**
Total change in assets	NMEP	B.101g	−119 905	−115 959	−90 039	−101 637	−64 868	−70 879	−46 007	−23 731

1 Acquisitions less disposals of valuables can be a volatile series but any volatility is likely to be GDP neutral as it is offset in UK trade figures

5.2.8 Central government
ESA 2010 sector S.1311

£ million

			2009	2010	2011	2012	2013	2014	2015	2016
Financial account		III.2								
Net acquisition of financial assets		F.A								
Monetary gold and special drawing rights		F.1								
Monetary gold	NARO	F.11	–	–	–	–	–	–	–	–
Special drawing rights	NARP	F.12	8 522	18	333	111	43	–14	55	–1 397
Total	NWXM	F.1	8 522	18	333	111	43	–14	55	–1 397
Currency and deposits		F.2								
Transferable deposits		F.22								
With UK monetary financial institutions	NART	F.22N1	7 554	–5 318	4 798	5 222	–3 186	1 026	–2 527	–2 007
Of which: foreign currency deposits with UK MFIs[1]	NARV	F.22N12	–782	28	1 737	–271	901	–1 117	–850	75
With rest of the world monetary financial institutions	NARX	F.22N9	540	423	140	935	142	463	2 997	2 958
Other deposits	RYWO	F.29	7 075	–9 754	7 583	–898	9 862	4 152	–8 782	1 251
Total	NARQ	F.2	15 169	–14 649	12 521	5 259	6 818	5 641	–8 312	2 202
Debt securities		F.3								
Short-term		F.31								
Issued by UK monetary financial institutions	NSUN	F.31N5	–2 144	–400	–	–	–	–	–	–
Money market instruments										
Issued by other UK residents	NSRI	F.31N6	882	1 349	3 336	–3 404	1 459	–1 137	–2 348	487
Issued by rest of the world	NASM	F.31N9	471	466	315	–967	–2 314	363	908	2 309
Long-term		F.32								
Issued by UK monetary financial institutions[2] and other UK residents	NASV	F.32N5-6	–5 236	–	–	1 152	–327	–	–	–
Issued by rest of the world	NASW	F.32N9	–820	5 439	4 099	5 182	–2 863	5 566	17 583	3 701
Total	NARZ	F.3	–6 847	6 854	7 750	1 963	–4 045	4 792	16 143	6 497
Loans		F.4								
Long-term		F.42								
Secured on dwellings	NATM	F.422	–	–6 616	–9 162	–6 649	–6 500	–9 030	–17 678	–5 417
Other loans by UK residents	NATR	F.424N1	3 751	8 707	5 513	16 889	6 140	12 407	13 752	18 744
Other loans by rest of the world	NATS	F.424N9	–	–	–	–	–	–	–	–
Total	NATB	F.4	3 751	2 091	–3 649	10 240	–360	3 377	–3 926	13 327
Equity and investment fund shares/units		F.5								
Equity		F.51								
Listed UK shares[2]	NATY	F.511N1	40 574	–903	–1 242	1 832	–9 222	–5 559	–12 731	–2 485
Unlisted UK shares[2]	NATZ	F.512N1	–277	482	–	7	–21 957	–2 375	–758	–3
Other equity		F.519								
Other UK equity	NAUA	F.519N6	–4 421	–	–	–	–10	–40	–1	–
UK shares and bonds issued by other UK residents[2]	NSOX	F.519N7	–	–	–	–	–	–	–	–
Shares and other equity issued by rest of the world	NAUD	F.519N9	300	77	337	178	1 497	285	93	277
Total	NATT	F.5	36 176	–344	–905	2 017	–29 692	–7 689	–13 397	–2 211
Financial derivatives and employee stock options	MN5T	F.7	619	–271	–133	587	–11	–855	–1 219	894
Of which: financial derivatives	CFZG	F.71	619	–271	–133	587	–11	–855	–1 219	894
Other accounts receivable	NAUN	F.8	–796	3 180	746	2 137	4 927	4 469	9 354	8 582
Total net acquisition of financial assets	NARM	F.A	56 594	–3 121	16 663	22 314	–22 320	9 721	–1 302	27 894

5.2.8 Central government
ESA 2010 sector S.1311

continued

£ million

			2009	2010	2011	2012	2013	2014	2015	2016
Financial account		III.2								
Net acquisition of financial liabilities		F.L								
Special drawing rights	M98C	F.12	8 654	–	–	–	–	–	–	–
Currency and deposits		F.2								
Currency	NAUV	F.21	48	82	30	158	30	191	168	140
Other deposits	NAVC	F.29	9 228	−8 090	9 186	−2 254	−7 912	17 852	10 689	17 856
Total	NAUU	F.2	9 276	−8 008	9 216	−2 096	−7 882	18 043	10 857	17 996
Debt securities		F.3								
Short-term		F.31								
Issued by UK central government	NAVF	F.31N1	25 975	−2 077	14 454	−18 706	−14 315	25 809	19 721	12 524
Long-term		F.32								
UK central government securities	NAVT	F.32N11	195 725	170 951	121 587	129 283	103 137	64 402	58 475	57 276
Other UK central government bonds	NAVU	F.32N12	−1 459	900	3 239	4 590	2 999	199	−5 225	−1 193
Bonds issued by UK MFIs[1] and other UK residents[2]	MNR7	F.32N5-6	–	−5 416	−10 967	−5 296	−11 682	−3 738	−14 718	−6 613
Total	NAVD	F.3	220 241	164 358	128 313	109 871	80 139	86 672	58 253	61 994
Loans		F.4								
Short-term		F.41								
By UK monetary financial institutions	NAWH	F.41N1	−28 068	−1 794	238	−601	848	−1 423	3 799	−81
By rest of the world	NAWL	F.41N9	−1 731	−44	−208	911	−825	1 228	5 021	−2 398
Long-term		F.42								
Finance leasing	NAWU	F.423	50	145	–	–	–	–	–	632
Other loans by UK residents	NAWV	F.424N1	−18	−9	−9	193	194	41	−5	−8
Other loans by rest of the world	NAWW	F.424N9	−21	−561	−2 055	−256	293	797	449	41
Total	NAWF	F.4	−29 788	−2 263	−2 034	247	510	643	9 264	−1 814
Insurance, pensions and standardised guarantee schemes		F.6								
Provisions for calls under standardised guarantees	MW4E	F.66	–	–	–	–	–	27	14	–
Total	DM53	F.6	–	–	–	–	–	27	14	–
Other accounts payable	NAXR	F.8	355	−10 916	133	44 432	−888	6 887	−2 037	4 788
Total net acquisition of financial liabilities	NAUQ	**F.L**	208 738	143 171	135 628	152 454	71 879	112 272	76 351	82 964
Net lending(+) / net borrowing(-)		**B.9**								
Total net acquisition of financial assets	NARM	F.A	56 594	−3 121	16 663	22 314	−22 320	9 721	−1 302	27 894
less total net acquisition of financial liabilities	NAUQ	F.L	208 738	143 171	135 628	152 454	71 879	112 272	76 351	82 964
Net lending(+) / borrowing(-) from the financial account	NZDX	B.9f	−152 144	−146 292	−118 965	−130 140	−94 199	−102 551	−77 653	−55 070
Statistical discrepancy between the financial and non-financial accounts	NZDW	dB.9	824	−954	24	556	870	−743	547	247
Net lending (+) / borrowing (-) from non-financial accounts	NMFJ	**B.9n**	**−151 320**	**−147 246**	**−118 941**	**−129 584**	**−93 329**	**−103 294**	**−77 106**	**−54 823**

1 Monetary financial institutions.
2 Prior to 1990, it is not possible to distinguish some elements of F.32N5-6, F.511N1 and F.512N1. These elements are shown combined as F.519N7

5.2.11 Central government
ESA 2010 sector S.1311

£ billion

Financial balance sheet at end of period		IV.3	2009	2010	2011	2012	2013	2014	2015	2016
Non-financial assets	NG3S	AN	409.3	449.5	464.7	468.1	489.9	556.7	577.1	587.0
Total financial assets		AF.A								
Monetary gold and special drawing rights		AF.1								
Monetary gold	NIFD	AF.11	6.8	9.1	9.8	10.2	7.3	7.7	7.1	9.4
Special drawing rights	NIFE	AF.12	8.9	9.1	9.4	9.1	9.0	9.0	9.1	8.9
Total	NIFC	AF.1	15.7	18.2	19.2	19.3	16.3	16.7	16.2	18.3
Currency and deposits		AF.2								
Transferable deposits		AF.22								
With UK MFIs[1]	NIFI	AF.22N1	37.4	20.1	22.0	25.1	20.2	15.9	12.8	12.8
Of which: foreign currency deposits with UK MFIs[1]	NIFK	AF.22N12	1.2	1.1	2.9	2.3	3.4	3.3	2.4	2.7
With rest of the world MFIs[1]	NIFM	AF.22N9	4.9	6.0	8.0	8.0	7.5	7.0	9.6	13.7
Other deposits	NIFN	AF.29	21.9	12.1	19.7	18.8	28.7	32.8	24.0	25.3
Total	NIFF	AF.2	64.1	38.2	49.7	51.9	56.4	55.8	46.4	51.8
Debt securities		AF.3								
Short-term		AF.31								
Issued by UK MFIs[1]	NSUO	AF.31N5	0.4	–	–	–	–	–	–	0.01
Money market instruments										
Issued by other UK residents	NSRH	AF.31N6	1.0	2.3	5.6	2.2	3.7	2.6	0.2	0.7
Issued by rest of the world	NIGB	AF.31N9	5.6	6.1	6.4	5.3	2.9	3.2	4.1	6.8
Long-term		AF.32								
Issued by UK local government	NIGG	AF.32N2	–	–	–	–	–	–	–	–
Issued by UK MFIs[1,5]	NIGK	AF.32N5-6	–	–	–	1.2	0.8	0.8	0.8	0.8
and other UK residents										
Issued by rest of the world	NIGL	AF.32N9	21.1	36.7	40.3	43.9	40.0	45.3	62.7	77.3
Total	NIFO	AF.3	28.1	45.1	52.3	52.7	47.4	51.9	67.8	85.6
Loans		AF.4								
Long-term		AF.42								
Secured on dwellings	NIHB	AF.422	0.1	86.5	77.3	70.7	64.2	55.1	37.4	32.0
Other loans by UK residents[3]	NIHG	AF.424N1	91.3	99.8	105.7	123.2	129.2	141.8	156.3	175.4
Total	NIGQ	AF.4	91.4	186.3	183.0	193.8	193.4	197.0	193.7	207.5
Equity and investment fund shares/units		AF.5								
Equity		AF.51								
Listed UK shares[5]	NIHN	AF.511N1	40.8	53.9	25.8	45.7	51.7	51.8	33.2	24.6
Unlisted UK shares[5]	NIHO	AF.512N1	11.7	20.0	28.0	39.5	11.6	13.0	15.7	18.2
Other equity		AF.519								
Other UK equity	H4O7	AF.519N6	3.6	2.6	2.4	2.5	2.4	2.5	2.6	2.6
UK shares and bonds issued by other UK residents[5]	NSNX	AF.519N7	–	–	–	–	–	–	–	–
Shares and other equity issued by rest of the world	NIHS	AF.519N9	3.5	3.6	3.9	4.1	5.5	5.8	5.9	6.1
Total[2]	NIHI	AF.5	59.7	80.0	60.0	91.7	71.2	73.0	57.3	51.5
Financial derivatives and employee stock options	MMW3	AF.7	−0.3	2.0	2.7	3.3	2.9	2.1	2.1	−6.5
Of which: financial derivatives	ZYBQ	AF.71	−0.3	2.0	2.7	3.3	2.9	2.1	2.1	−6.5
Other accounts receivable	NIIC	AF.8	69.9	60.0	60.4	61.7	66.3	70.4	79.0	88.0
Total financial assets	NIGP	**AF.A**	328.6	429.7	427.5	474.3	453.8	466.9	462.5	496.2

5.2.11 Central government
ESA 2010 sector S.1311
continued

£ billion

			2009	2010	2011	2012	2013	2014	2015	2016
Financial balance sheet at end of period		IV.3								
Total financial liabilities		**AF.L**								
Special drawing rights	M98F	AF.12	9.8	10.1	10.1	9.6	9.4	9.4	9.5	11.1
Currency and deposits		AF.2								
Currency	NIIK	AF.21	4.0	4.1	4.1	4.3	4.3	4.5	4.7	4.8
Other deposits	NIIR	AF.29	126.9	123.8	132.5	130.2	122.3	139.9	150.6	168.6
Total	NIIJ	AF.2	130.9	127.8	136.6	134.5	126.5	144.4	155.3	173.4
Debt securities		AF.3								
Short-term		AF.31								
Sterling treasury bills	NIIV	AF.31N11	57.5	55.4	69.8	51.1	36.6	62.6	82.3	94.9
Euro treasury bills	NIIW	AF.31N12	–	–	–	–	–	–	–	–
Other government short-term bonds	MW8O	AF.31N14	–	–	–	–	0.2	0.1	–	–
Long-term		AF.32								
UK central government securities	NIJI	AF.32N11	796.3	994.7	1 246.5	1 354.0	1 383.1	1 619.1	1 641.3	1 895.1
Other UK central government bonds	NIJJ	AF.32N12	25.7	27.1	33.9	38.5	39.5	44.0	36.8	39.5
Bonds issued by UK MFIs and other UK residents[1,5]	MNR8	AF.32N5-6	–	52.3	41.1	34.9	26.0	21.7	6.4	0.2
Total	NIIS	AF.3	879.5	1 129.5	1 391.3	1 478.5	1 485.3	1 747.4	1 766.8	2 029.7
Loans		AF.4								
Short-term		AF.41								
By UK MFIs[1,4]	NIJW	AF.41N1	6.2	3.9	4.9	3.1	4.4	3.5	2.9	3.5
By rest of the world MFIs[1]	NIKA	AF.41N9	0.4	0.2	0.1	1.0	0.1	1.2	6.4	5.2
Long-term		AF.42								
Finance leasing	NIKJ	AF.423	4.5	4.7	4.7	4.7	4.7	5.1	5.6	6.2
By UK residents	NIKK	AF.424N1	–	–	–	0.2	0.4	0.4	0.4	0.4
By rest of the world	NIKL	AF.424N9	1.3	1.3	1.0	0.7	0.6	0.5	0.5	0.5
Total	NIJU	AF.4	12.5	10.1	10.7	9.7	10.1	10.7	15.8	15.9
Insurance, pensions and standardised guarantee schemes		AF.6								
Provisions for calls under standardised guarantees	MW4H	AF.66	–	–	–	–	–	–	–	0.041
Total	DM55	AF.6	–	–	–	–	–	–	–	0.041
Financial derivatives and employee stock options	MMY7	AF.7	0.7	2.7	3.3	2.4	1.3	1.1	2.2	1.7
Of which: financial derivatives	KN2H	AF.71	0.7	2.7	3.3	2.4	1.3	1.1	2.2	1.7
Other accounts payable	NILG	AF.8	19.7	21.6	20.0	55.9	56.5	55.5	55.1	52.6
Total financial liabilities	NIJT	**AF.L**	1 053.0	1 301.8	1 572.1	1 690.6	1 689.3	1 968.6	2 004.8	2 284.2
Financial net worth		**BF.90**								
Total financial assets	NIGP	AF.A	328.6	429.7	427.5	474.3	453.8	466.9	462.5	496.2
less total financial liabilities	NIJT	AF.L	1 053.0	1 301.8	1 572.1	1 690.6	1 689.3	1 968.6	2 004.8	2 284.2
Financial net worth	NZDZ	**BF.90**	−724.4	−872.1	−1 144.6	−1 216.3	−1 235.5	−1 501.7	−1 542.3	−1 788.1
Net worth										
Non-financial assets	NG3S	AN	409.3	449.5	464.7	468.1	489.9	556.7	577.1	587.0
Financial net worth	NZDZ	BF.90	−724.4	−872.1	−1 144.6	−1 216.3	−1 235.5	−1 501.7	−1 542.3	−1 788.1
Net worth	CGRY	**B.90**	−315.1	−422.6	−679.8	−748.2	−745.5	−945.0	−965.2	−1 201.1

1 Monetary financial institutions.
2 Money market instruments
3 Other than direct investment loans, loans secured on dwellings
  and loans for finance leasing
4 All loans secured on dwellings and all finance leasing are treated
  as long-term loans

5 Prior to 1990 it is not possible to distinguish some elements of AF.32N5-6,
  AF.511N1 and AF.512N1. These elements are shown combined as AF.519N7

5.3.1 Local government
ESA 2010 sector S.1313

£ million

			2009	2010	2011	2012	2013	2014	2015
Production account		I							
Resources									
Output		P.1							
Market output	NMIX	P.11	643	631	620	619	631	641	668
Output for own final use	QYJW	P.12	359	353	366	365	352	359	373
Other non-market output		P.13							
Payments for non-market output	DM4V	P.131	24 495	24 914	23 731	23 348	23 798	24 779	25 452
Non-market output, other	DPKK	P.132	117 772	117 856	114 229	110 573	109 647	109 245	108 767
Total	DPS3	P.13	142 267	142 770	137 960	133 921	133 445	134 024	134 219
Total	NMIZ	P.1	143 269	143 754	138 946	134 905	134 428	135 024	135 260
Total resources	NMIZ	TR	143 269	143 754	138 946	134 905	134 428	135 024	135 260
Uses									
Intermediate consumption	NMJA	P.2	59 206	57 163	55 555	54 727	56 849	58 721	59 219
Gross value added	NMJB	**B.1g**	**84 063**	**86 591**	**83 391**	**80 178**	**77 579**	**76 303**	**76 041**
Total uses	NMIZ	TU	143 269	143 754	138 946	134 905	134 428	135 024	135 260
Gross value added	NMJB	**B.1g**	**84 063**	**86 591**	**83 391**	**80 178**	**77 579**	**76 303**	**76 041**
less consumption of fixed capital	NSRO	P.51c	7 890	8 377	8 904	9 414	9 944	10 461	10 962
Value added, net of fixed capital consumption	NMJD	B.1n	76 173	78 214	74 487	70 764	67 635	65 842	65 079

5.3.2 Local government
ESA 2010 sector S.1313

£ million

			2009	2010	2011	2012	2013	2014	2015
Distribution and use of income accounts		II							
Primary distribution of income account		II.1							
Generation of income account		II.1.1							
Resources									
Total resources (gross value added)	NMJB	**B.1g**	**84 063**	**86 591**	**83 391**	**80 178**	**77 579**	**76 303**	**76 041**
Uses									
Compensation of employees		D.1							
Wages and salaries	NMJF	D.11	57 133	58 658	55 100	51 666	48 635	47 051	46 193
Employers' social contributions	NMJG	D.12	19 040	19 556	19 387	19 098	19 000	18 791	18 886
Total	NMJE	D.1	76 173	78 214	74 487	70 764	67 635	65 842	65 079
Taxes on production and imports, paid		D.2							
Production taxes other than on products	NMHY	D.29	–	–	–	–	–	–	–
less subsidies, received		D.3							
Production subsidies other than on products	NMJL	D.39	–	–	–	–	–	–	–
Operating surplus, gross	NRLT	B.2g	7 890	8 377	8 904	9 414	9 944	10 461	10 962
Total uses (gross valued added)	NMJB	**B.1g**	**84 063**	**86 591**	**83 391**	**80 178**	**77 579**	**76 303**	**76 041**
less consumption of fixed capital	NSRO	P.51c	7 890	8 377	8 904	9 414	9 944	10 461	10 962
Operating surplus, net	NMJM	B.2n	–	–	–	–	–	–	–

5.3.3 Local government
ESA 2010 sector S.1313

£ million

			2009	2010	2011	2012	2013	2014	2015	2016
Allocation of primary income account		II.1.2								
Resources										
Operating surplus, gross	NRLT	B.2g	7 890	8 377	8 904	9 414	9 944	10 461	10 962	11 474
Taxes on production and imports, received		D.2								
Taxes on products	CPPM	D.214	–	–	–	4	36	104	147	259
Taxes on production other than on products	NMYH	D.29	317	497	564	577	567	571	600	629
Total	DMHD	D.2	317	497	564	581	603	675	747	888
less subsidies, paid		D.3								
Subsidies on products	LIUA	D.31	1 977	1 780	1 573	1 298	1 239	1 205	1 168	1 096
Other subsidies on production	LIUC	D.39	1 518	1 264	865	567	292	472	618	831
Total	ADAK	D.3	3 495	3 044	2 438	1 865	1 531	1 677	1 786	1 927
Property income		D.4								
Interest		D.41								
Interest before FISIM[1] allocation	I690	D.41g	796	591	637	686	731	657	664	633
plus FISIM	C6FQ	P.119	–68	61	135	112	130	336	338	285
Total	NMKB	D.41	728	652	772	798	861	993	1 002	918
Distributed income of corporations	FDDA	D.42	834	728	977	1 267	1 370	999	978	896
Other investment income		D.44								
Attributable to insurance policy holders	KZK4	D.441	65	43	42	36	47	55	27	27
Attributable to collective investment fund shareholders		D.443								
Dividends	KZK6	D.4431	–	–	–	–	–	–	–	–
Retained earnings	KZK7	D.4432	–	–	–	–	–	–	–	–
Total	L5UU	D.443	–	–	–	–	–	–	–	–
Total	NMKK	D.44	65	43	42	36	47	55	27	27
Rent from sectors other than general government	NMKM	D.45	–	–	–	–	–	–	–	–
Total	NMJZ	D.4	1 627	1 423	1 791	2 101	2 278	2 047	2 007	1 841
Total resources	NMKN	TR	6 339	7 253	8 821	10 231	11 294	11 506	11 930	12 276
Uses										
Property income		D.4								
Interest		D.41								
Interest before FISIM allocation	I69X	D.41g	3 512	3 554	3 402	5 198	3 562	3 743	3 910	3 921
less FISIM	C6FP	P.119	224	267	182	177	205	175	174	184
Total	NCBW	D.41	3 288	3 287	3 220	5 021	3 357	3 568	3 736	3 737
Total	NUHI	D.4	3 288	3 287	3 220	5 021	3 357	3 568	3 736	3 737
Balance of primary incomes, gross	**NRLU**	**B.5g**	**3 051**	**3 966**	**5 601**	**5 210**	**7 937**	**7 938**	**8 194**	**8 539**
Total uses	NMKN	TU	6 339	7 253	8 821	10 231	11 294	11 506	11 930	12 276
less consumption of fixed capital	NSRO	P.51c	7 890	8 377	8 904	9 414	9 944	10 461	10 962	11 474
Balance of primary incomes, net	NMKZ	B.5n	–4 839	–4 411	–3 303	–4 204	–2 007	–2 523	–2 768	–2 935

1 Financial intermediation services indirectly measured.

5.3.4 Local government
ESA 2010 sector S.1313

£ million

			2009	2010	2011	2012	2013	2014	2015	2016
Secondary distribution of income account		II.2								
Resources										
Balance of primary incomes, gross	NRLU	**B.5g**	**3 051**	**3 966**	**5 601**	**5 210**	**7 937**	**7 938**	**8 194**	**8 539**
Current taxes on income, wealth etc.		D.5								
Current taxes other than on income	NMIS	D.59	25 057	25 584	25 881	26 219	27 243	28 138	28 979	30 226
Net social contributions		D.61								
Employers' actual social contributions[1]	L8ND	D.611	1 556	1 607	1 626	1 647	1 526	1 489	1 501	1 501
Employers' imputed social contributions[1]	M9WY	D.612	1 061	765	658	675	631	694	714	588
Households' actual social contributions	L8PJ	D.613	726	743	745	757	709	707	721	723
Total	NSMM	D.61	3 343	3 115	3 029	3 079	2 866	2 890	2 936	2 812
Other current transfers		D.7								
Non-life insurance claims	NMLR	D.72	376	530	512	471	507	438	447	444
Current transfers within general government	QYJR	D.73	124 708	132 310	126 922	128 448	121 658	124 073	121 126	113 778
Current international cooperation	GNK9	D.74	170	185	−132	51	32	27	13	–
Miscellaneous current transfers to sectors other than general government	AWTO	D.75	333	321	334	349	347	331	379	460
Total	NMLO	D.7	125 587	133 346	127 636	129 319	122 544	124 869	121 965	114 682
Total resources	NMLX	TR	157 038	166 011	162 147	163 827	160 590	163 835	162 074	156 259
Uses										
Other current taxes	EBFS	D.59	1 189	1 236	1 356	1 389	1 389	1 389	1 389	1 389
Social benefits other than social transfers in kind		D.62								
Other social insurance benefits	L8RB	D.622	4 493	4 338	4 427	4 672	4 362	4 424	4 678	4 705
Social assistance benefits in cash	ADAL	D.623	20 767	22 758	24 117	25 452	26 372	26 911	27 203	27 134
Total	NSMN	D.62	25 260	27 096	28 544	30 124	30 734	31 335	31 881	31 839
Other current transfers		D.7								
Net non-life insurance premiums	NMMI	D.71	376	530	512	471	507	438	447	444
Current transfers within general government	NMDK	D.73	–	–	–	–	–	–	–	–
Miscellaneous current transfers	EBFE	D.75	29	26	32	30	78	95	102	106
Total	NMMF	D.7	405	556	544	501	585	533	549	550
Gross disposable income	NRLW	**B.6g**	**130 184**	**137 123**	**131 703**	**131 813**	**127 882**	**130 578**	**128 255**	**122 481**
Total uses	NMLX	TU	157 038	166 011	162 147	163 827	160 590	163 835	162 074	156 259
less consumption of fixed capital	NSRO	P.51c	7 890	8 377	8 904	9 414	9 944	10 461	10 962	11 474
Disposable income, net	NMMQ	B.6n	122 294	128 746	122 799	122 399	117 938	120 117	117 293	111 007

1 Data for 1987 to 1996 do not reflect the updated treatment of unfunded
  public sector pension schemes. This will be reflected at Blue Book 2018.

5.3.4S Local government
Social contributions and benefits
ESA 2010 sector S.1313

£ million

Secondary distribution of income (further detail of certain items)		Part	2009	2010	2011	2012	2013	2014	2015	2016
Resources										
Net social contributions		D.61								
Unfunded pension schemes[1]										
Employers' actual social contributions[2]	L8ND	D.611	1 556	1 607	1 626	1 647	1 526	1 489	1 501	1 501
Employers' actual pension contributions[2]	M93U	D.6111	1 556	1 607	1 626	1 647	1 526	1 489	1 501	1 501
Employers' imputed social contributions[2]	M9WY	D.612	1 061	765	658	675	631	694	714	588
Employers' imputed pension contributions[2]	M93O	D.6121	–	–	–	–	–	–	–	–
Employers' imputed non-pension contributions	EWRN	D.6122	1 061	765	658	675	631	694	714	588
Households' actual social contributions	L8PJ	D.613	726	743	745	757	709	707	721	723
Households' actual pension contributions	M93Q	D.6131	726	743	745	757	709	707	721	723
Total	NSMM	D.61	3 343	3 115	3 029	3 079	2 866	2 890	2 936	2 812
Uses										
Social benefits other than social transfers in kind		D.62								
Other social insurance benefits	L8RB	D.622	4 493	4 338	4 427	4 672	4 362	4 424	4 678	4 705
Other social insurance pension benefits	M93S	D.6221	3 432	3 573	3 769	3 997	3 731	3 730	3 964	4 117
Other social insurance non-pension benefits	EWRN	D.6222	1 061	765	658	675	631	694	714	588
Social assistance benefits in cash		D.623								
Student grants	GCSI		1 488	1 687	1 948	2 234	2 582	2 975	3 407	3 906
Rent rebates	CTML		5 449	5 418	5 441	5 673	5 829	5 881	5 853	5 714
Rent allowances	GCSR		13 830	15 653	16 728	17 545	17 961	18 055	17 943	17 514
Total other transfers	ZXHZ		–	–	–	–	–	–	–	–
Total social assistance benefits in cash	ADAL	D.623	20 767	22 758	24 117	25 452	26 372	26 911	27 203	27 134
Total social benefits	NSMN	D.62	25 260	27 096	28 544	30 124	30 734	31 335	31 881	31 839

1 Mainly schemes covering police and firefighters.
2 Data for 1987 to 1996 do not reflect the updated treatment of unfunded public sector pension schemes. This will be reflected at Blue Book 2018.

5.3.5 Local government
ESA 2010 sector S.1313

£ million

			2009	2010	2011	2012	2013	2014	2015	2016
Redistribution of income in kind account		II.3								
Resources										
Total resources (gross disposable income)	NRLW	B.6g	130 184	137 123	131 703	131 813	127 882	130 578	128 255	122 481
Uses										
Social transfers in kind		D.63								
Non-market produced	DPLV	D.631	71 835	72 362	68 785	66 722	67 550	67 545	67 087	66 219
Purchased market production	DM4A	D.632	14 056	15 398	15 319	15 581	15 955	16 018	16 367	16 857
Total	NMMU	D.63	85 891	87 760	84 104	82 303	83 505	83 563	83 454	83 076
Adjusted disposable income, gross	NSXL	B.7g	44 293	49 363	47 599	49 510	44 377	47 015	44 801	39 405
Total uses (gross disposable income)	NRLW	B.6g	130 184	137 123	131 703	131 813	127 882	130 578	128 255	122 481

5.3.6 Local government
ESA 2010 sector S.1313

£ million

			2009	2010	2011	2012	2013	2014	2015	2016
Use of income account		II.4								
Use of disposable income account		II.4.1								
Resources										
Total resources (gross disposable income)	NRLW	B.6g	130 184	137 123	131 703	131 813	127 882	130 578	128 255	122 481
Uses										
Final consumption expenditure		P.3								
Individual consumption expenditure	NMMU	P.31	85 891	87 760	84 104	82 303	83 505	83 563	83 454	83 076
Collective consumption expenditure	NMMV	P.32	45 937	45 494	45 444	43 851	42 097	41 700	41 680	42 098
Total	NMMT	P.3	131 828	133 254	129 548	126 154	125 602	125 263	125 134	125 174
Gross saving	NRLX	**B.8g**	**−1 644**	**3 869**	**2 155**	**5 659**	**2 280**	**5 315**	**3 121**	**−2 693**
Total uses (gross disposable income)	NRLW	B.6g	130 184	137 123	131 703	131 813	127 882	130 578	128 255	122 481
less consumption of fixed capital	NSRO	P.51c	7 890	8 377	8 904	9 414	9 944	10 461	10 962	11 474
Saving, net	NMMX	B.8n	−9 534	−4 508	−6 749	−3 755	−7 664	−5 146	−7 841	−14 167
Use of adjusted disposable income account		II.4.2								
Resources										
Total resources, adjusted disposable income, gross	NSXL	B.7g	44 293	49 363	47 599	49 510	44 377	47 015	44 801	39 405
Uses										
Actual final consumption		P.4								
Actual collective consumption	NMMV	P.42	45 937	45 494	45 444	43 851	42 097	41 700	41 680	42 098
Gross saving	NRLX	**B.8g**	**−1 644**	**3 869**	**2 155**	**5 659**	**2 280**	**5 315**	**3 121**	**−2 693**
Total uses	NSXL	TU	44 293	49 363	47 599	49 510	44 377	47 015	44 801	39 405

5.3.7 Local government
ESA 2010 sector S.1313

£ million

			2009	2010	2011	2012	2013	2014	2015	2016
Accumulation accounts		III								
Capital account		III.1								
Change in net worth due to savings and capital transfers account		III.1.1								
Changes in liabilities and net worth										
Gross saving	NRLX	**B.8g**	−1 644	3 869	2 155	5 659	2 280	5 315	3 121	−2 693
Capital transfers, receivable		D.9r								
Investment grants	NMNE	D.92r	13 284	12 998	13 601	13 172	11 563	12 269	13 084	11 916
Other capital transfers	NMNH	D.99r	987	554	569	6 124	808	839	1 118	1 279
Total	NMMY	D.9r	14 271	13 552	14 170	19 296	12 371	13 108	14 202	13 195
Capital transfers, payable		D.9p								
Investment grants	NMNR	D.92p	2 360	2 409	2 801	3 881	3 239	2 522	3 552	2 532
Other capital transfers	NMNU	D.99p	451	255	270	13 598	278	304	1 145	202
Total	NMNL	D.9p	2 811	2 664	3 071	17 479	3 517	2 826	4 697	2 734
Changes in net worth due to gross saving and capital transfers	NRMJ	B.101g	9 816	14 757	13 254	7 476	11 134	15 597	12 626	7 768
Changes in assets										
Changes in net worth due to gross saving and capital transfers	NRMJ	B.101g	9 816	14 757	13 254	7 476	11 134	15 597	12 626	7 768
less consumption of fixed capital	NSRO	P.51c	7 890	8 377	8 904	9 414	9 944	10 461	10 962	11 474
Changes in net worth due to net saving and capital transfers	NMNX	B.101n	1 926	6 380	4 350	−1 938	1 190	5 136	1 664	−3 706
Acquisition of non-financial assets account		III.1.2								
Changes in liabilities and net worth										
Changes in net worth due to saving and capital transfers	NMNX	B.101n	1 926	6 380	4 350	−1 938	1 190	5 136	1 664	−3 706
Consumption of fixed capital	NSRO	P.51c	7 890	8 377	8 904	9 414	9 944	10 461	10 962	11 474
Changes in net worth due to gross saving and capital transfers	NRMJ	B.101g	9 816	14 757	13 254	7 476	11 134	15 597	12 626	7 768
Changes in assets										
Gross capital formation		P.5								
Gross fixed capital formation	NMOA	P.51g	19 038	18 879	19 123	17 842	16 870	17 864	18 500	19 586
Changes in inventories	NMOB	P.52	–	–	–	–	–	–	–	–
Total	NMNZ	P.5	19 038	18 879	19 123	17 842	16 870	17 864	18 500	19 586
Acquisitions less disposals of non-produced non-financial assets	NMOD	NP	−971	−1 082	−1 255	−1 477	−1 419	−1 614	−2 021	−2 348
Net lending(+) / net borrowing(-)	NMOE	**B.9n**	**−8 251**	**−3 040**	**−4 614**	**−8 889**	**−4 317**	**−653**	**−3 853**	**−9 470**
Total change in assets	NRMJ	B.101g	9 816	14 757	13 254	7 476	11 134	15 597	12 626	7 768

5.3.8 Local government
ESA 2010 sector S.1313

£ million

			2009	2010	2011	2012	2013	2014	2015	2016
Financial account		III.2								
Net acquisition of financial assets		F.A								
Currency and deposits		F.2								
Transferable deposits		F.22								
With UK MFIs[1]	NBYR	F.22N1	−6 918	955	−1 620	2 946	446	−402	1 558	−2 582
Of which: foreign currency deposits with UK MFIs[1]	NBYT	F.22N12	46	9	−26	−24	25	15	8	25
With rest of the world MFIs[1]	GO56	F.22N9	−790	26	49	−101	135	482	364	101
Other deposits	NBYW	F.29	2 073	−1 310	2 399	1 495	−2 825	424	1 902	1 493
Total	NBYO	F.2	−5 635	−329	828	4 340	−2 244	504	3 824	−988
Debt securities		F.3								
Short-term		F.31								
Issued by UK central government	NBYZ	F.31N1	82	856	−430	787	226	744	321	−1 726
Issued by UK MFIs[1]	NBZE	F.31N5	−186	−174	−311	−5	78	832	121	−657
MMIs issued by other UK residents[2]	NBZJ	F.31N6	−897	−1	116	−206	404	620	71	408
Long-term		F.32								
Issued by UK central government	NBZM	F.32N1	22	−19	209	−49	1 275	−534	−582	−114
Issued by UK monetary financial institutions[1,6] and other UK residents	E55E	F.32N5-6	–	–	–	–	–	–	–	–
Total	NBYX	F.3	−979	662	−416	527	1 983	1 662	−69	−2 089
Loans		F.4								
Long-term		F.42								
Secured on dwellings	NCAK	F.422	1 214	454	575	1 860	418	1 115	1 203	884
Other loans by UK residents[3]	NCAP	F.424N1	691	870	818	769	1 711	2 075	2 428	3 725
Total	NBZZ	F.4	1 905	1 324	1 393	2 629	2 129	3 190	3 631	4 609
Equity and investment fund shares/units		F.5								
Equity		F.51								
Listed UK shares[6]	NCAW	F.511N1	−78	214	468	141	1 289	832	619	−516
Unlisted UK shares[6]	NCAX	F.512N1	–	–	–	–	–	–	–	–
Other UK equity	HN68	F.519N6	−539	−582	−684	−895	−1 068	−1 360	−1 344	−1 691
UK shares and bonds issued by other UK residents[6]	NSPE	F.519N7	–	–	–	–	–	–	–	–
Total	NCAR	F.5	−617	−368	−216	−754	221	−528	−725	−2 207
Insurance, pensions and standardised guarantee schemes		F.6								
Non-life insurance technical reserves	NCBK	F.61	−144	−65	−17	13	−23	–	−35	11
Total	NPWD	F.6	−144	−65	−17	13	−23	–	−35	11
Other accounts receivable	NCBL	F.8	−476	−44	−444	−39	−6	874	710	222
Total net acquisition of financial assets	NBYK	F.A	−5 946	1 180	1 128	6 716	2 060	5 702	7 336	−442

5.3.8 Local government
ESA 2010 sector S.1313

continued

£ million

			2009	2010	2011	2012	2013	2014	2015	2016
Financial account		III.2								
Net acquisition of financial liabilities		F.L								
Debt securities		F.3								
Short-term		F.31								
Issued by UK local government	NCCH	F.31N2	–	–	–	–	–	–	–	–
Long-term		F.32								
Issued by UK local government	NCCT	F.32N2	–83	–17	595	676	717	496	590	362
Issued by UK monetary financial institutions[1,6] and other UK residents	IH3H	F.32N5-6	–	–	–	–	–	–	–	–
Total	NCCB	F.3	–83	–17	595	676	717	496	590	362
Loans		F.4								
Short-term		F.41								
By UK MFIs[1,4]	NCDF	F.41N1	226	364	456	–41	14	237	237	127
By rest of the world MFIs[1]	NCDJ	F.41N9	–	–	–	–	–	–	–	–
Long-term		F.42								
Finance leasing	NCDS	F.423	209	–12	–23	–16	–19	–23	–25	–27
Other loans by UK residents	NCDT	F.424N1	–1 855	2 415	1 060	9 053	502	1 048	470	2 182
Other loans by rest of the world	NCDU	F.424N9	520	158	430	1 436	376	434	380	208
Total	NCDD	F.4	–900	2 925	1 923	10 432	873	1 696	1 062	2 490
Insurance, pensions and standardised guarantee schemes		F.6								
Pension schemes[5]	MA2X	F.6M	1 540	1 809	1 841	1 912	2 093	2 027	1 980	2 121
Total	M9W2	F.6	1 540	1 809	1 841	1 912	2 093	2 027	1 980	2 121
Other accounts payable	NCEP	F.8	1 769	343	1 782	2 604	2 190	1 964	7 951	3 903
Total net acquisition of financial liabilities	NCBO	F.L	2 326	5 060	6 141	15 624	5 873	6 183	11 583	8 876
Net lending(+) / net borrowing(-)		B.9								
Total net acquisition of financial assets	NBYK	F.A	–5 946	1 180	1 128	6 716	2 060	5 702	7 336	–442
less total net acquisition of financial liabilities	NCBO	F.L	2 326	5 060	6 141	15 624	5 873	6 183	11 583	8 876
Net lending(+) / borrowing(-) from the financial account	NYNQ	B.9f	–8 272	–3 880	–5 013	–8 908	–3 813	–481	–4 247	–9 318
Statistical discrepancy between the financial and non-financial accounts	NYPC	dB.9	21	840	399	19	–504	–172	394	–152
Net lending (+) / borrowing (-) from non-financial accounts	NMOE	B.9n	**–8 251**	**–3 040**	**–4 614**	**–8 889**	**–4 317**	**–653**	**–3 853**	**–9 470**

1 Monetary financial institutions
2 Money market instruments
3 Other than direct investment loans, loans secured on dwellings
  and loans for finance leasing
4 All loans secured on dwellings and all finance leasing
  are treated as long-term loans
5 F.63 Pension entitlements, F.64 Claims of pension funds on pension
  managers, F.65 Entitlements to non-pension benefits
6 Prior to 1990, it is not possible to distinguish some elements of F.32N5-6,
  F.511N1 and F.512N1. These elements are shown combined as F.519N7

5.3.11 Local government
ESA 2010 sector S.1313

£ billion

Financial balance sheet at end of period		IV.3	2009	2010	2011	2012	2013	2014	2015	2016
Non-financial assets	NG42	**AN**	267.5	299.8	312.4	311.1	322.7	349.9	364.9	377.8
Total financial assets		**AF.A**								
Currency and deposits		AF.2								
Transferable deposits		AF.22								
With UK MFIs[1]	NJEO	AF.22N1	22.0	23.0	21.6	26.1	25.8	25.9	27.7	25.4
Of which: foreign currency deposits with UK MFIs[1]	NJEQ	AF.22N12	0.1	0.1	0.1	–	–	0.1	0.1	0.1
With rest of the world MFIs[1]	GO55	AF.22N9	0.4	0.4	0.5	0.4	0.5	1.0	1.4	1.5
Other deposits	NJET	AF.29	4.9	3.6	6.0	7.5	4.7	5.1	7.0	8.5
Total	NJEL	AF.2	27.3	27.0	28.1	34.1	31.0	32.1	36.1	35.4
Debt securities		AF.3								
Short-term		AF.31								
Issued by UK central government	NJEW	AF.31N1	0.1	0.9	0.5	1.3	1.5	2.3	2.6	0.9
Issued by UK MFIs[1]	NJFB	AF.31N5	1.2	1.0	0.7	0.7	0.4	1.2	1.3	0.7
MMIs issued by other UK residents[20]	NJFG	AF.31N6	0.5	0.5	0.6	0.5	0.8	1.3	1.6	1.9
Long-term		AF.32								
Issued by UK central government	NJFJ	AF.32N1	0.2	0.2	0.4	0.4	1.7	1.1	0.5	0.4
Issued by UK MFIs[1,6] and other UK residents	E55D	AF.32N5-6	0.2	0.2	0.2	0.2	0.2	0.2	0.2	0.2
Total	NJEU	AF.3	2.2	2.9	2.5	3.1	4.6	6.2	6.3	4.1
Loans		AF.4								
Long-term		AF.42								
Secured on dwellings	NJGH	AF.422	4.4	4.8	5.4	7.3	7.7	8.8	10.0	10.9
Other long-term loans by UK residents[3]	NJGM	AF.424N1	2.3	2.7	3.4	4.1	4.6	5.0	5.8	6.4
Total	NJFW	AF.4	6.7	7.5	8.8	11.4	12.3	13.8	15.8	17.3
Equity and investment fund shares/units		AF.5								
Equity		AF.51								
Listed UK shares[6]	NJGT	AF.511N1	0.5	0.8	1.2	1.3	2.7	3.6	4.1	3.6
Unlisted UK shares[6]	NJGU	AF.512N1	0.7	0.7	0.7	0.7	0.7	0.7	0.7	0.7
Other UK equity	HN69	AF.519N6	113.9	116.2	117.7	119.7	120.8	123.2	124.8	125.9
UK shares and bonds issued by other UK residents[6]	NSOE	AF.519N7	–	–	–	–	–	–	–	–
Total	NJGO	AF.5	115.1	117.7	119.6	121.7	124.2	127.5	129.6	130.3
Insurance, pensions and standardised guarantee schemes		AF.6								
Non-life insurance technical reserves	NJHH	AF.61	0.7	0.7	0.7	0.7	0.7	0.7	0.6	0.6
Total	NPXT	AF.6	0.7	0.7	0.7	0.7	0.7	0.7	0.6	0.6
Other accounts receivable	NJHI	AF.8	1.4	1.4	0.9	0.9	0.9	1.7	2.4	2.7
Total financial assets	NJFV	**AF.A**	153.4	157.2	160.5	171.8	173.6	181.9	190.8	190.4

5.3.11 Local government
ESA 2010 sector S.1313
continued

£ billion

			2009	2010	2011	2012	2013	2014	2015	2016
Financial balance sheet at end of period		IV.3								
Total financial liabilities		**AF.L**								
Debt securities		AF.3								
Short-term		AF.31								
Issued by UK local government	NJIE	AF.31N2	–	–	–	–	–	–	–	–
Long-term		AF.32								
Issued by UK local government	NJIQ	AF.32N2	1.0	1.0	1.6	2.3	3.0	3.5	4.1	4.4
Issued by UK monetary institutions[1,6] and other UK residents	IH3I	AF.32N5-6	–	–	–	–	–	–	–	–
Total	NJHY	AF.3	1.0	1.0	1.6	2.3	3.0	3.5	4.1	4.4
Loans		AF.4								
Short-term		AF.41								
By UK MFIs[4]	NJJC	AF.41N1	11.0	11.7	11.8	11.2	10.7	10.6	10.3	10.3
By rest of the world MFIs[4]	NJJG	AF.41N9	–	–	–	–	–	–	–	–
Long-term		AF.42								
Finance leasing	NJJP	AF.423	0.3	0.6	0.6	0.6	0.5	0.5	0.5	0.5
By UK residents	NJJQ	AF.424N1	51.8	55.0	55.7	64.4	66.9	69.5	71.1	74.3
By rest of the world	NJJR	AF.424N9	3.0	3.2	3.6	5.1	5.4	5.9	6.3	6.5
Total	NJJA	AF.4	66.1	70.5	71.7	81.3	83.6	86.5	88.2	91.5
Insurance, pensions and standardised guarantee schemes		AF.6								
Pension schemes[5]	M9VT	AF.6M	92.0	74.2	85.0	73.4	67.7	62.2	68.5	68.7
Total	M9RL	AF.6	92.0	74.2	85.0	73.4	67.7	62.2	68.5	68.7
Other accounts payable	NJKM	AF.8	26.3	26.7	28.5	31.1	33.2	35.2	43.3	47.1
Total financial liabilities	NJIZ	**AF.L**	185.5	172.3	186.8	188.0	187.5	187.5	204.1	211.7
Financial net worth		**BF.90**								
Total financial assets	NJFV	AF.A	153.4	157.2	160.5	171.8	173.6	181.9	190.8	190.4
less total financial liabilities	NJIZ	AF.L	185.5	172.3	186.8	188.0	187.5	187.5	204.1	211.7
Financial net worth	NYOJ	**BF.90**	−32.1	−15.2	−26.2	−16.2	−14.0	−5.6	−13.3	−21.3
Net worth										
Non-financial assets	NG42	AN	267.5	299.8	312.4	311.1	322.7	349.9	364.9	377.8
Financial net worth	NYOJ	BF.90	−32.1	−15.2	−26.2	−16.2	−14.0	−5.6	−13.3	−21.3
Net worth	CGRZ	**B.90**	235.4	284.6	286.1	294.9	308.8	344.3	351.6	356.5

1 Monetary financial institutions
2 Money market instruments
3 Other than direct investment loans, loans secured on dwellings and loans for finance leasing
4 All loans secured on dwellings and all finance leasing are treated as long-term loans
5 F.63 Pension entitlements, F.64 Claims of pension funds on pension managers, F.65 Entitlements to non-pension benefits

6 Prior to 1990 it is not possible to distinguish some elements of AF.32N5-6, AF.511N1 and AF.512N1. These elements are shown combined as AF.519N7

United Kingdom National Accounts

The Blue Book

Chapter 06: Households and Non-Profit Institutions Serving Households

2017 edition

Editors: Dean Goodway & Sarah Nightingale

Office for National Statistics

Chapter 6: Households and non-profit institutions serving households

The households sector covers both consumers and producers. Households as consumers is made up of groups of people sharing the same living accommodation who share some or all of their income and collectively consume certain types of goods and services, such as food, electricity or housing. This sector also includes the self-employed who are treated as producers. A smaller group of units within the households sector is made up of those living permanently in institutions with little economic autonomy, such as prison populations and members of religious orders living in monasteries.

Non-profit institutions serving households (NPISH) are institutions that:

- provide goods and services, either free or below the market prices
- mainly derive their income from grants and donations
- are not controlled by government

In the UK the NPISH sector includes:

- most charities
- trade unions
- religious organisations
- political parties
- the majority of universities

For the first time, the UK National Accounts, The Blue Book: 2017 edition presents estimates for the households and NPISH sectors separately. To allow comparison with previous Blue Book publications, estimates for the combined households and NPISH sectors are also presented.

Further information on sector classifications and classification decisions can be found in Economic statistics classifications.

6.1.1 Households and non-profit institutions serving households
ESA 2010 sector S.14, not seasonally adjusted

£ million

			2009	2010	2011	2012	2013	2014	2015
Production account		I							
Resources									
Output		P.1							
Market output	QWLF	P.11	159 516	164 284	172 794	180 222	193 777	204 697	212 366
Output for own final use	QWLG	P.12	183 575	185 504	187 141	193 969	200 630	207 303	216 582
Other non-market output	QWLH	P.13	55 701	56 669	58 724	59 991	59 444	61 363	63 065
Total	QWLI	P.1	398 792	406 457	418 659	434 182	453 851	473 363	492 013
Total resources	QWLI	TR	398 792	406 457	418 659	434 182	453 851	473 363	492 013
Uses									
Intermediate consumption	QWLJ	P.2	121 133	126 378	130 651	129 020	137 480	134 751	134 228
Gross value added	QWLK	**B.1g**	**277 659**	**280 079**	**288 008**	**305 162**	**316 371**	**338 612**	**357 785**
Total uses	QWLI	TU	398 792	406 457	418 659	434 182	453 851	473 363	492 013
Gross value added	QWLK	**B.1g**	**277 659**	**280 079**	**288 008**	**305 162**	**316 371**	**338 612**	**357 785**
less consumption of fixed capital	QWLL	P.51c	53 931	55 577	57 581	59 488	63 504	67 703	69 168
Value added, net	QWLM	B.1n	223 728	224 502	230 427	245 674	252 867	270 909	288 617

6.1.2 Households and non-profit institutions serving households
ESA 2010 sectors S.14 and S.15

£ million

			2009	2010	2011	2012	2013	2014	2015
Distribution and use of income accounts		II							
Primary distribution of income account		II.1							
Generation of income account before deduction of fixed capital consumption		II.1.1							
Resources									
Total resources (gross value added)	QWLK	**B.1g**	277 659	280 079	288 008	305 162	316 371	338 612	357 785
Uses									
Compensation of employees		D.1							
Wages and salaries	QWLN	D.11	44 640	48 186	46 884	45 978	47 880	51 056	53 914
Employers' social contributions	QWLO	D.12	9 426	11 107	10 922	11 343	11 886	12 066	12 526
Total	QWLP	D.1	54 066	59 293	57 806	57 321	59 766	63 122	66 440
Taxes on production and imports, paid		D.2							
Production taxes other than on products	QWLQ	D.29	411	478	515	514	439	484	464
less subsidies received		D.3							
Production subsidies other than on products	QWLR	D.39	3 411	3 059	3 166	2 625	2 455	2 306	1 961
Operating surplus, gross	QWLS	B.2g	134 108	134 100	139 460	149 079	151 657	163 152	173 574
Mixed income, gross	QWLT	B.3g	92 485	89 267	93 393	100 873	106 964	114 160	119 268
Total uses (gross value added)	QWLK	**B.1g**	277 659	280 079	288 008	305 162	316 371	338 612	357 785
less consumption of fixed capital[1]	QWLL	P.51c	53 931	55 577	57 581	59 488	63 504	67 703	69 168
Operating surplus, net	QWLU	B.2n	91 117	90 297	93 944	101 865	101 925	111 269	120 747
Mixed income, net	QWLV	B.3n	81 545	77 493	81 328	88 599	93 192	98 340	102 927

1 Consumption of fixed capital is made up of
 P.51c1 - Consumption of fixed capital on gross operating surplus
 plus P.51c2 - Consumption of fixed capital on gross mixed income

6.1.3 Households and non-profit institutions serving households
ESA 2010 sectors S.14 and S.15

£ million

			2009	2010	2011	2012	2013	2014	2015	2016
Allocation of primary income account		II.1.2								
before deduction of fixed capital consumption										
Resources										
Gross operating surplus and gross mixed income		B.2g+B.3g								
Operating surplus, gross	QWLS	B.2g	134 108	134 100	139 460	149 079	151 657	163 152	173 574	177 299
Mixed income, gross	QWLT	B.3g	92 485	89 267	93 393	100 873	106 964	114 160	119 268	127 546
Total	RVGJ	B.2g+B.3g	226 593	223 367	232 853	249 952	258 621	277 312	292 842	304 845
Compensation of employees		D.1								
Wages and salaries	QWLW	D.11	663 588	672 139	682 542	695 840	723 444	746 669	775 239	804 241
Employers' social contributions	QWLX	D.12	131 228	146 431	147 490	153 405	159 731	155 156	154 878	163 154
Total	QWLY	D.1	794 816	818 570	830 032	849 245	883 175	901 825	930 117	967 395
Property income, received		D.4								
Interest		D.41								
Interest before FISIM[1] allocation	J4WY	D.41g	19 663	18 800	20 494	21 948	19 715	15 922	14 650	13 526
plus FISIM	IV8W	P.119	3 015	−695	548	216	−624	8 386	10 594	11 199
Total	QWLZ	D.41	22 678	18 105	21 042	22 164	19 091	24 308	25 244	24 725
Distributed income of corporations		D.42								
Dividends	CRWE	D.421	50 454	37 908	39 752	44 179	52 498	55 170	76 068	65 810
Withdrawals from the income of quasi-corporations	CRWG	D.422	28 038	31 247	30 649	30 421	33 939	34 940	37 006	36 925
Earnings on property investment	CRWI	D.423	977	953	880	812	817	778	750	882
Total	QWMA	D.42	79 469	70 108	71 281	75 412	87 254	90 888	113 824	103 617
Other investment income		D.44								
Attributable to insurance policy holders	L8GL	D.441	24 219	24 936	24 480	21 982	21 670	19 987	23 871	22 565
Payable on pension entitlements	L8GS	D.442	67 817	77 856	74 956	65 918	63 132	77 972	71 412	73 681
Attributable to collective investment fund shareholders		D.443								
Dividends	L8H8	D.4431	1 192	1 972	944	982	1 008	1 064	1 160	1 312
Retained earnings	L8HF	D.4432	1 863	3 083	1 472	1 538	1 576	1 667	1 813	2 055
Total	L8GZ	D.443	3 055	5 055	2 416	2 520	2 584	2 731	2 973	3 367
Total	QWMC	D.44	95 091	107 847	101 852	90 420	87 386	100 690	98 256	99 613
Rent	QWMD	D.45	75	117	112	109	145	163	180	208
Total	QWME	D.4	197 313	196 177	194 287	188 105	193 876	216 049	237 504	228 163
Total resources	QWMF	TR	1 218 722	1 238 114	1 257 172	1 287 302	1 335 672	1 395 186	1 460 463	1 500 403
Uses										
Property income, paid		D.4								
Interest		D.41								
Interest before FISIM allocation	J4WZ	D.41g	72 004	64 816	62 089	61 730	61 550	60 422	58 419	58 495
less FISIM	IV8X	P.119	44 708	44 908	38 619	36 458	39 826	32 749	31 592	32 198
Interest	QWMG	D.41	27 296	19 908	23 470	25 272	21 724	27 673	26 827	26 297
Rent	QWMH	D.45	12	14	23	19	18	17	18	15
Total	QWMI	D.4	27 308	19 922	23 493	25 291	21 742	27 690	26 845	26 312
Balance of primary incomes, gross	QWMJ	B.5g	**1 191 414**	**1 218 192**	**1 233 679**	**1 262 011**	**1 313 930**	**1 367 496**	**1 433 618**	**1 474 091**
Total uses	QWMF	TU	1 218 722	1 238 114	1 257 172	1 287 302	1 335 672	1 395 186	1 460 463	1 500 403
less consumption of fixed capital	QWLL	P.51c	53 931	55 577	57 581	59 488	63 504	67 703	69 168	72 158
Balance of primary incomes, net	QWMK	B.5n	1 137 483	1 162 615	1 176 098	1 202 523	1 250 426	1 299 793	1 364 450	1 401 933
Sector share of gross national income	RVGG		78.5	77.1	75.2	75.7	76.6	76.0	77.7	77.2

1 Financial intermediation services indirectly measured

6.1.4 Households and non-profit institutions serving households
ESA 2010 sectors S.14 and S.15

£ million

			2009	2010	2011	2012	2013	2014	2015	2016
Secondary distribution of income account		II.2								
Resources										
Balance of primary incomes, gross	QWMJ	B.5g	1 191 414	1 218 192	1 233 679	1 262 011	1 313 930	1 367 496	1 433 618	1 474 091
Net social contributions		D.61								
Employers' imputed social contributions	L8RF	D.612	764	603	535	546	549	604	650	497
Total	L8TR	D.61	764	603	535	546	549	604	650	497
Social benefits other than social transfers in kind		D.62								
Social security benefits in cash	L8QF	D.621	80 825	82 117	83 826	89 187	91 231	93 650	96 461	98 992
Other social insurance benefits	L8QT	D.622	99 996	105 819	108 018	116 908	119 368	117 636	125 769	129 491
Social assistance benefits in cash	MT3B	D.623R	105 102	112 257	115 624	118 922	119 646	120 613	121 463	120 963
Total	QWML	D.62	285 923	300 193	307 468	325 017	330 245	331 899	343 693	349 446
Other current transfers		D.7								
Non-life insurance claims	QWMM	D.72	21 975	30 811	32 085	30 112	32 375	28 017	28 626	28 422
Miscellaneous current transfers	QWMN	D.75	58 269	58 034	57 750	63 273	59 235	57 506	58 061	58 616
Total	QWMO	D.7	80 244	88 845	89 835	93 385	91 610	85 523	86 687	87 038
Total resources	QWMP	TR	1 558 345	1 607 833	1 631 517	1 680 959	1 736 334	1 785 522	1 864 648	1 911 072
Uses										
Current taxes on income, wealth, etc		D.5								
Taxes on income	QWMQ	D.51	151 348	152 424	157 598	153 734	158 990	162 612	171 393	178 961
Of which:										
Taxes on employment	DBBO	D.511pt	121 479	126 872	129 821	128 622	131 084	136 201	141 848	145 758
Taxes on self-employment and other	ZAFG	D.511pt	22 161	23 184	24 253	20 844	24 130	22 671	24 017	26 295
Other current taxes	NVCO	D.59	33 254	34 058	34 181	34 536	35 849	36 716	37 503	38 384
Total	QWMS	D.5	184 602	186 482	191 779	188 270	194 839	199 328	208 896	217 345
Net social contributions		D.61								
Employers' actual social contributions	L8NJ	D.611	113 590	128 706	130 153	135 160	140 445	136 010	135 750	143 838
Employers' imputed social contributions	M9X2	D.612	17 636	17 724	17 337	18 245	19 286	19 146	19 128	19 316
Households' actual social contributions	L8PR	D.613	57 115	58 639	60 376	63 338	64 837	67 194	68 506	73 056
Households' social contribution supplements	L8Q7	D.614	67 817	77 856	74 956	65 918	63 132	77 972	71 412	73 681
Social insurance scheme service charge	L8LT	D.61SC	−11 101	−12 568	−14 740	−17 046	−18 324	−18 819	−19 620	−20 318
Total	QWMY	D.61	245 057	270 357	268 082	265 615	269 376	281 503	275 176	289 573
Social benefits other than social transfers in kind		D.62								
Other social insurance benefits	L8S5	D.622	764	603	535	546	549	604	650	497
Total	QWMZ	D.62	764	603	535	546	549	604	650	497
Other current transfers		D.7								
Net non-life insurance premiums	QWNA	D.71	21 975	30 811	32 085	30 112	32 375	28 017	28 626	28 422
Miscellaneous current transfers	QWNB	D.75	26 787	26 680	27 274	30 124	30 957	32 583	34 048	35 880
Total	QWNC	D.7	48 762	57 491	59 359	60 236	63 332	60 600	62 674	64 302
Gross disposable income	QWND	B.6g	1 079 160	1 092 900	1 111 762	1 166 292	1 208 238	1 243 487	1 317 252	1 339 355
Total uses	QWMP	TU	1 558 345	1 607 833	1 631 517	1 680 959	1 736 334	1 785 522	1 864 648	1 911 072
Real households' & NPISH expenditure implied deflator (reference year 2015)	CRXB		88.4	89.9	93.3	95.3	97.5	99.4	100.0	101.4
Real households' & NPISH disposable income: (Chained volume measures)										
£ Million (reference year 2015)[1]	RVGK		1 221 480	1 215 781	1 191 981	1 224 261	1 238 947	1 250 788	1 317 251	1 321 342
Index (2015=100)	OSXR		92.7	92.3	90.5	92.9	94.1	95.0	100.0	100.3

1 Gross household disposable income deflated by the households and NPISH final consumption deflator

6.1.5 Households and non-profit institutions serving households
ESA 2010 sectors S.14 and S.15

£ million

			2009	2010	2011	2012	2013	2014	2015	2016
Redistribution of income in kind account		II.3								
Resources										
Gross disposable income	QWND	**B.6g**	**1 079 160**	**1 092 900**	**1 111 762**	**1 166 292**	**1 208 238**	**1 243 487**	**1 317 252**	**1 339 355**
Social transfers in kind		D.63								
Non-market produced	QWNH	D.631	218 394	222 594	225 598	229 597	234 303	240 441	246 362	248 153
Purchased market production	NSSA	D.632	38 138	39 279	40 557	41 341	41 419	44 856	43 959	48 321
Total	NSSB	D.63	256 532	261 873	266 155	270 938	275 722	285 297	290 321	296 474
Total resources	NSSC	TR	1 335 692	1 354 773	1 377 917	1 437 230	1 483 960	1 528 784	1 607 573	1 635 829
Uses										
Social transfers in kind		D.63								
Non-market produced	DPSD	D.631	50 684	51 276	53 647	53 664	54 428	56 625	56 614	57 005
Total	HAEK	D.63	50 684	51 276	53 647	53 664	54 428	56 625	56 614	57 005
Adjusted disposable income, gross	NSSD	B.7g	1 285 008	1 303 497	1 324 270	1 383 566	1 429 532	1 472 159	1 550 959	1 578 824
Total uses	NSSC	TU	1 335 692	1 354 773	1 377 917	1 437 230	1 483 960	1 528 784	1 607 573	1 635 829

6.1.6 Households and non-profit institutions serving households
ESA 2010 sectors S.14 and S.15

£ million

			2009	2010	2011	2012	2013	2014	2015	2016
Use of income account		II.4								
Use of disposable income account		II.4.1								
Resources										
Households' gross disposable income	QWND	B.6g	1 079 160	1 092 900	1 111 762	1 166 292	1 208 238	1 243 487	1 317 252	1 339 355
Adjustment for the change in pension entitlements	NSSE	D.8	55 441	72 826	66 069	54 160	54 162	67 116	46 546	49 674
Total resources	NSSF	TR	1 134 601	1 165 726	1 177 831	1 220 452	1 262 400	1 310 603	1 363 798	1 389 029
Uses										
Final consumption expenditure		P.3								
Individual consumption expenditure	NSSG	P.31	1 011 538	1 035 890	1 067 053	1 107 327	1 153 163	1 200 544	1 238 482	1 290 332
Gross saving	NSSH	B.8g	**123 063**	**129 836**	**110 778**	**113 125**	**109 237**	**110 059**	**125 316**	**98 697**
Total uses	NSSF	TU	1 134 601	1 165 726	1 177 831	1 220 452	1 262 400	1 310 603	1 363 798	1 389 029
less consumption of fixed capital	QWLL	P.51c	53 931	55 577	57 581	59 488	63 504	67 703	69 168	72 158
Saving, net	NSSI	B.8n	69 132	74 259	53 197	53 637	45 733	42 356	56 148	26 539
Use of adjusted disposable income account		II.4.2								
Resources										
Adjusted disposable income, gross	NSSD	B.7g	1 285 008	1 303 497	1 324 270	1 383 566	1 429 532	1 472 159	1 550 959	1 578 824
Adjustment for the change in pension entitlements	NSSE	D.8	55 441	72 826	66 069	54 160	54 162	67 116	46 546	49 674
Total resources	NSSJ	TR	1 340 449	1 376 323	1 390 339	1 437 726	1 483 694	1 539 275	1 597 505	1 628 498
Uses										
Actual final consumption		P.4								
Actual individual consumption	ABRE	P.41	1 217 386	1 246 487	1 279 561	1 324 601	1 374 457	1 429 216	1 472 189	1 529 801
Gross saving	NSSH	B.8g	**123 063**	**129 836**	**110 778**	**113 125**	**109 237**	**110 059**	**125 316**	**98 697**
Total uses	NSSJ	TU	1 340 449	1 376 323	1 390 339	1 437 726	1 483 694	1 539 275	1 597 505	1 628 498
Households & NPISH saving ratio (per cent)	RVGL		10.8	11.1	9.4	9.3	8.6	8.4	9.2	7.1

6.1.7 Households and non-profit institutions serving households
ESA 2010 sectors S.14 and S.15

£ million

			2009	2010	2011	2012	2013	2014	2015	2016
Accumulation accounts		III								
Capital account		III.1								
Change in net worth due to saving and capital transfers account		III.1.1								
Changes in liabilities and net worth										
Gross saving	NSSH	B.8g	123 063	129 836	110 778	113 125	109 237	110 059	125 316	98 697
Capital transfers, receivable		D.9r								
Investment grants	NSSL	D.92r	9 452	10 046	7 578	9 044	7 017	8 380	10 485	9 504
Other capital transfers	NSSM	D.99r	5 562	3 490	3 635	4 434	3 908	3 306	3 680	3 299
Total	NSSN	D.9r	15 014	13 536	11 213	13 478	10 925	11 686	14 165	12 803
less capital transfers, payable		D.9p								
Capital taxes	NSSO	D.91p	2 401	2 642	2 936	3 129	4 255	3 886	4 442	4 801
Other capital transfers	NSSQ	D.99p	4 976	2 344	2 693	3 441	4 357	4 924	4 276	3 575
Total	NSSR	D.9p	7 377	4 986	5 629	6 570	8 612	8 810	8 718	8 376
Changes in net worth due to gross saving and capital transfers	NSSS	B.101g	130 700	138 386	116 362	120 033	111 550	112 935	130 763	103 124
Changes in assets										
Changes in net worth due to gross saving and capital transfers	NSSS	B.101g	130 700	138 386	116 362	120 033	111 550	112 935	130 763	103 124
less consumption of fixed capital	QWLL	P.51c	53 931	55 577	57 581	59 488	63 504	67 703	69 168	72 158
Changes in net worth due to saving and capital transfers	NSST	B.101n	76 769	82 809	58 781	60 545	48 046	45 232	61 595	30 966
Acquisition of non-financial assets account		III.1.2								
Changes in liabilities and net worth										
Changes in net worth due to net saving and capital transfers	NSST	B.101n	76 769	82 809	58 781	60 545	48 046	45 232	61 595	30 966
Consumption of fixed capital	QWLL	P.51c	53 931	55 577	57 581	59 488	63 504	67 703	69 168	72 158
Changes in net worth due to gross saving and capital transfers	NSSS	B.101g	130 700	138 386	116 362	120 033	111 550	112 935	130 763	103 124
Changes in assets										
Gross capital formation		P.5								
Gross fixed capital formation	NSSU	P.51g	49 559	52 663	55 758	56 566	62 897	70 020	73 411	80 266
Changes in inventories	NSSV	P.52	−973	363	180	112	289	757	382	12
Acquisitions less disposals of valuables[1]	NSSW	P.53	578	−130	232	1 023	2 826	1 833	512	1 760
Total gross capital formation	NSSX	P.5	49 164	52 896	56 170	57 701	66 012	72 610	74 305	82 038
Acquisitions less disposals of non-produced non-financial assets	NSSY	NP	−246	−241	−239	−261	−233	−213	−190	−157
Net lending(+) / net borrowing(-)	NSSZ	**B.9n**	81 782	85 731	60 431	62 593	45 771	40 538	56 648	21 243
Total change in assets	NSSS	B.101g	130 700	138 386	116 362	120 033	111 550	112 935	130 763	103 124

1 Acquisitions less disposals of valuables can be a volatile series but any volatility is likely to be GDP neutral as it is offset in UK trade figures

6.1.8 Households and non-profit institutions serving households
ESA 2010 sectors S.14 and S.15 Unconsolidated

£ million

			2009	2010	2011	2012	2013	2014	2015	2016
Financial account		III.2								
Net acquisition of financial assets		F.A								
Currency and deposits		F.2								
Currency	NFVT	F.21	3 450	1 835	2 482	2 704	2 371	2 993	3 477	5 926
Transferable deposits		F.22								
Deposits with UK MFIs[1]	NFVV	F.22N1	21 387	25 434	27 394	48 879	43 744	45 499	43 064	71 446
Of which: foreign currency deposits with UK MFIs[1]	NFVX	F.22N12	−42	−153	67	−126	1 407	447	931	602
Deposits with rest of the world MFIs[1]	NFVZ	F.22N9	−13 285	3 090	6 494	−5 334	2 950	4 778	−7 832	−93
Other deposits	NFWA	F.29	3 663	1 018	3 650	−1 327	3 608	7 736	22 258	9 683
Total	NFVS	F.2	15 215	31 377	40 020	44 922	52 673	61 006	60 967	86 962
Debt securities		F.3								
Short-term		F.31								
Issued by UK central government	NFWD	F.31N1	–	–	–	–	–	−1	–	–
Issued by UK local government	NFWH	F.31N2	–	–	–	–	–	–	–	–
Issued by UK MFIs[1]	NFWI	F.31N5	587	−1 912	−1 180	−1 973	697	116	−1 112	2 564
MMIs issued by other UK residents[2]	NFWN	F.31N6	−155	−16	−118	−21	27	55	−59	2
MMIs issued by rest of world	NFWO	F.31N9	–	–	–	–	–	–	–	–
Long-term		F.32								
Issued by UK central government	NFWQ	F.32N1	1 266	−1 292	980	3 447	−1 717	130	−326	388
Issued by UK local government	NFWT	F.32N2	56	12	90	−288	659	705	405	234
Issued by UK MFIs and other UK residents[1,6]	KV2O	F.32N5-6	510	185	449	554	419	−99	276	317
Bonds issued by rest of the world	NFWY	F.32N9	1 910	470	−1 195	−550	−551	1 815	−1 437	628
Total	NFWB	F.3	4 174	−2 553	−974	1 169	−466	2 721	−2 253	4 133
Loans		F.4								
Long-term		F.42								
By UK residents[3]	NFXT	F.424N1	−3 035	2 083	−2 064	258	−1 457	−9 049	−3 440	−7 915
Total	NFXD	F.4	−3 035	2 083	−2 064	258	−1 457	−9 049	−3 440	−7 915
Equity and investment fund shares/units		F.5								
Equity		F.51								
Listed UK shares[6]	NFYA	F.511N1	25 004	2 080	−1 000	498	1 743	−1 224	−2 734	−9 484
Unlisted UK shares[6]	NFYB	F.512N1	−3 327	−16 596	−32 322	−18 298	−7 122	−6 585	−12 650	−10 776
Other equity		F.519								
Other UK equity	NFYC	F.519N6	–	*	–	–	–	–	–	–
UK shares and bonds issued by other UK residents[6]	NSPY	F.519N7	–	–	–	–	–	–	–	–
Shares and other equity issued by rest of the world	NFYF	F.519N9	−10 760	−4 214	13 246	−4 918	−18 344	−5 425	10 476	−5 269
Investment fund shares/units		F.52								
UK mutual funds' shares	NFYJ	F.52N1	3 298	12 188	16 618	1 565	15 784	1 338	−27 637	−18 853
Rest of the world mutual funds' shares	NFYK	F.52N9	−1 544	−185	−58	−118	−23	–	–	–
Total	NFXV	F.5	12 671	−6 727	−3 516	−21 271	−7 962	−11 896	−32 545	−44 382
Insurance, pensions and standardised guarantee schemes		F.6								
Non-life insurance technical reserves	NFYO	F.61	2 304	−4 047	2 079	1 777	−1 468	5	−2 242	675
Life insurance and annuity entitlements	M9WF	F.62	4 165	4 917	7 786	430	−8 471	−13 963	56 599	19 617
Pension schemes[4]	MA2H	F.6M	55 441	72 826	66 069	54 160	54 162	67 116	46 546	49 674
Total	NPWX	F.6	61 910	73 696	75 934	56 367	44 223	53 158	100 903	69 966
Financial derivatives and employee stock options	MN5V	F.7	1 551	2 060	963	1 570	2 496	1 223	1 719	2 447
Of which: financial derivatives	NFWZ	F.71	−9	463	−670	−83	794	−545	−103	568
Other accounts receivable	NFYP	F.8	−17 362	−17 171	−6 312	12 301	−6 308	−387	−6 336	4 554
Total net acquisition of financial assets	NFVO	F.A	75 124	82 765	104 051	95 316	83 199	96 776	119 015	115 765

6.1.8 Households and non-profit institutions serving households

ESA 2010 sectors S.14 and S.15 Unconsolidated

continued

£ million

			2009	2010	2011	2012	2013	2014	2015	2016
Financial account		III.2								
Net acquisition of financial liabilities		F.L								
Debt securities		F.3								
Short-term		F.31								
MMIs issued by other UK residents[2]	NFZR	F.31N6	−676	203	531	−50	404	516	57	11
Long-term		F.32								
Issued by UK MFIs and other UK residents[1,6]	KV2I	F.32N5-6	184	−27	−	20	44	254	314	−
Total	NFZF	F.3	−492	176	531	−30	448	770	371	11
Loans		F.4								
Short-term		F.41								
By UK MFIs[1]	NGAJ	F.41N1	−2 536	−2 736	−2 237	−3 016	2 153	5 683	7 798	9 151
Of which foreign currency loans by UK banks	NGAL	F.41N12	−162	−161	−99	−357	−69	618	21	114
By rest of the world	NGAN	F.41N9	701	625	8 928	−866	−2 063	2 728	−803	3 960
Long-term[5]		F.42								
Secured on dwellings	NGAS	F.422	7 850	−187	7 824	11 488	12 256	20 296	26 050	38 488
By UK residents	NGAX	F.424N1	−1 242	12 108	6 440	7 872	13 436	14 280	19 922	19 690
Total	NGAH	F.4	4 773	9 810	20 955	15 478	25 782	42 987	52 967	71 289
Insurance, pensions and standardised guarantee schemes		F.6								
Pension schemes[4]	MA2Y	F.6M	432	514	649	583	631	617	602	647
Total	NPWY	F.6	432	514	649	583	631	617	602	647
Other accounts payable	NGBT	F.8	−10 996	−5 248	−2 628	8 602	754	−2 205	7 706	6 636
Total net acquisition of financial liabilities	NFYS	F.L	−6 283	5 252	19 507	24 633	27 615	42 169	61 646	78 583
Net lending(+) / net borrowing(-)		B.9								
Total net acquisition of financial assets	NFVO	F.A	75 124	82 765	104 051	95 316	83 199	96 776	119 015	115 765
less total net acquisition of financial liabilities	NFYS	F.L	−6 283	5 252	19 507	24 633	27 615	42 169	61 646	78 583
Net lending(+) / borrowing(-) from the financial account	NZDY	B.9f	81 406	77 513	84 544	70 683	55 584	54 607	57 370	37 182
Statistical discrepancy between the financial and non-financial accounts	NZDV	dB.9	376	8 218	−24 113	−8 090	−9 813	−14 069	−722	−15 939
Net lending(+) / net borrowing(-)	NSSZ	B.9n	81 782	85 731	60 431	62 593	45 771	40 538	56 648	21 243

1 Monetary financial institutions
2 Money market instruments
3 Other than direct investment loans, loans secured on dwellings and loans for finance leasing
4 F.63 pension entitlements, F.64 Claims on pension fund on pension managers, F.65 entitlements to non-pension benefits
5 All loans secured on dwellings and all finance leasing are treated as long term loans
6 Prior to 1990, it is not possible to distinguish some elements of F.32N5-6, F.511N1 and F.512N1. These elements are shown combined as F.519N7

6.1.9 Households and non-profit institutions serving households
ESA 2010 sector S.14 and S.15

			2013	2014	2015	2016
Other changes in assets account		**III.3**				
Other changes in volume of assets account		**III.3.1**				
Changes in net worth due to other changes in volume of assets		**B.102**				
Currency and deposits	M9QS	AF.2	−2 497	−97	−1 142	−1 136
Debt securities	N47S	AF.3	96	−25	−216	−202
Loans	N49U	AF.4	12 728	8 127	7 494	8 769
Equity and investment fund shares/units	N4BW	AF.5	–	–	–	–
Insurance, pensions and standardised guarantee schemes	N4DW	AF.6	–	–	–	–
Financial derivatives and employee stock options	N4FU	AF.7	–	–	–	–
Other accounts receivable/payable	N4HU	AF.8	6 959	13 812	−1 070	8 719
Total	CWU2	**B.102**	17 286	21 817	5 066	16 150

6.1.10 Households and non-profit institutions serving households
ESA 2010 sector S.14 and S.15

£ million

			2013	2014	2015	2016
Other changes in assets account		**III.3**				
Revaluation account		**III.3.2**				
Changes in net worth due to nominal holding gains and losses		**B.103**				
Currency and deposits	M9XL	AF.2	797	−5 327	−3 029	7 546
Debt securities	N48T	AF.3	−1 314	489	4 346	−2 168
Loans	N4AV	AF.4	−1 277	4 192	−109	−3 477
Equity and investment fund shares/units	N4CX	AF.5	80 458	105 525	70 629	129 295
Insurance, pensions and standardised guarantee schemes	N4EV	AF.6	−86 804	348 296	−87 112	274 679
Financial derivatives and employee stock options	N4GT	AF.7	−1 598	−1 612	−1 649	−1 721
Other accounts receivable/payable	N4IV	AF.8	−20	1 089	1 155	−7 542
Total	CWUR	**B.103**	−9 758	452 652	−15 769	396 612

6.1.11 Households and non-profit institutions serving households
ESA 2010 sectors S.14 and S.15   Unconsolidated

£ billion

			2009	2010	2011	2012	2013	2014	2015	2016
Financial balance sheet at end of period		IV.3								
Non-financial assets	NG4A	AN	4 016.7	4 085.0	4 081.3	4 190.0	4 461.9	4 843.0	5 258.6	5 586.5
Total financial assets		AF.A								
Currency and deposits		AF.2								
Currency	NNMQ	AF.21	44.1	48.2	50.7	53.4	55.8	58.8	62.3	67.9
Transferable deposits		AF.22								
Deposits with UK MFIs[1]	NNMS	AF.22N1	971.5	998.7	1 024.8	1 082.3	1 123.7	1 169.3	1 211.7	1 284.0
Of which: foreign currency deposits with UK MFIs[1]	NNMU	AF.22N12	5.7	5.6	5.7	5.6	6.7	6.6	8.3	10.0
Deposits with rest of the world MFIs[1]	NNMW	AF.22N9	58.0	60.8	66.3	64.8	68.6	68.1	57.1	63.1
Other deposits	NNMX	AF.29	98.3	98.9	102.5	101.1	104.4	111.9	133.9	143.2
Total	NNMP	AF.2	1 171.8	1 206.7	1 244.4	1 301.5	1 352.5	1 408.1	1 464.9	1 558.2
Debt securities		AF.3								
Short-term		AF.31								
Issued by UK central government	NNNA	AF.31N1	–	–	–	–	–	–	–	0.01
Issued by UK local government	NNNE	AF.31N2	–	–	–	–	–	–	–	–
Issued by UK MFIs[1]	NNNF	AF.31N5	5.6	4.6	3.1	4.6	4.3	6.0	7.6	9.8
MMIs[2] issued by other UK residents	NNNK	AF.31N6	0.3	0.3	0.2	0.2	0.2	0.3	0.2	0.3
MMIs issued by the rest of the world	NNNL	AF.31N9	–	–	–	–	–	–	–	–
Long-term		AF.32								
Issued by UK central government	NNNN	AF.32N1	7.0	4.8	5.3	8.9	7.0	7.0	6.4	6.1
Issued by UK local government	NNNQ	AF.32N2	0.5	0.4	0.2	0.3	0.9	0.3	1.9	1.8
Issued by UK MFIs and other UK residents[1,3]	KV2L	AF.32N5-6	5.8	6.1	6.2	6.4	6.6	6.8	7.0	7.2
Bonds issued by rest of the world	NNNV	AF.32N9	2.6	2.9	2.5	1.8	1.4	3.3	2.6	2.6
Total	NNMY	AF.3	22.0	19.2	17.4	22.3	20.4	23.7	25.7	27.8
Loans		AF.4								
Long-term		AF.42								
Other long-term loans by UK residents[4]	NNOQ	AF.424N1	18.3	18.4	18.4	18.5	18.7	18.7	18.8	18.7
Total	NNOA	AF.4	18.3	18.4	18.4	18.5	18.7	18.7	18.8	18.7
Equity and investment fund shares/units		AF.5								
Equity		AF.51								
Listed UK shares[3]	NNOX	AF.511N1	173.2	190.4	168.8	179.9	220.4	240.1	244.3	253.5
Unlisted UK shares[3]	NNOY	AF.512N1	242.4	254.1	228.6	181.1	202.6	256.8	254.1	272.8
Other equity		AF.519								
Other UK equity	NNOZ	AF.519N6	1.4	1.4	1.4	1.4	1.4	1.4	1.4	1.4
UK shares and bonds issued by other UK residents[3]	NSQR	AF.519N7	–	–	–	–	–	–	–	–
Shares and other equity issued by rest of the world	NNPC	AF.519N9	160.8	155.3	164.1	158.7	151.1	149.2	160.4	188.2
Investment fund shares/units		AF.52								
UK mutual funds' shares	NNPG	AF.52N1	179.5	189.7	188.3	201.7	220.1	241.8	267.1	296.4
Rest of the world mutual funds' shares	NNPH	AF.52N9	0.8	0.7	0.5	0.4	0.1	0.1	0.1	–
Total	NNOS	AF.5	758.1	791.6	751.7	723.2	795.6	889.3	927.4	1 012.3
Insurance, pensions and standardised guarantee schemes		AF.6								
Non-life insurance technical reserves	NNPL	AF.61	49.3	40.7	42.8	44.6	43.1	43.1	40.9	41.6
Life insurance and annuity entitlements	M9RW	AF.62	544.8	568.4	543.8	546.4	565.6	566.3	605.8	633.9
Pension schemes[5]	M9VD	AF.6M	1 788.3	1 879.1	2 273.7	2 308.3	2 238.8	2 658.9	2 631.1	2 950.2
Total	NPYL	AF.6	2 382.3	2 488.2	2 860.3	2 899.3	2 847.5	3 268.4	3 277.8	3 625.7
Financial derivatives and employee stock options	MMW5	AF.7	7.4	7.5	9.2	5.3	8.6	6.8	5.8	5.9
Of which: financial derivatives	NNNW	AF.71	2.6	2.7	4.4	0.4	3.6	1.7	0.5	0.4
Other accounts receivable	NNPM	AF.8	138.8	139.5	143.5	189.5	188.6	200.1	196.4	201.5
Total financial assets	NNML	**AF.A**	4 498.8	4 671.1	5 044.8	5 159.5	5 232.0	5 815.1	5 916.8	6 450.0

6.1.11 Households and non-profit institutions serving households
ESA 2010 sectors S.14 and S.15   Unconsolidated

£ billion

			2009	2010	2011	2012	2013	2014	2015	2016
Financial balance sheet at end of period		IV.3								
Total financial liabilities		AF.L								
Debt securities		AF.3								
Short-term		AF.31								
MMIs[2] issued by other UK residents	NNQO	AF.31N6	0.4	0.5	0.5	0.5	0.8	1.3	1.6	1.8
Long-term		AF.32								
Issued by UK MFIs[1] and other UK residents	KV2E	AF.33N5-6	0.9	0.8	0.9	0.9	0.9	1.2	1.4	1.5
Total	NNQC	AF.3	1.3	1.3	1.4	1.4	1.7	2.5	3.0	3.3
Loans		AF.4								
Short-term		AF.41								
By UK MFIs[1]	NNRG	AF.41N1	181.2	173.4	163.2	150.3	142.3	148.9	153.3	159.5
Of which: foreign currency										
Loans by UK banks	NGAL	AF.1N12	−0.2	−0.2	−0.1	−0.4	−0.1	0.6	−	0.1
By rest of the world MFIs	NNRK	AF.41N9	22.6	22.5	31.2	33.3	32.6	31.2	30.5	37.7
Long-term loans [6]		AF.42								
Secured on dwellings	NNRP	AF.422	1 191.8	1 197.6	1 201.9	1 225.6	1 237.1	1 259.1	1 286.2	1 325.1
By UK residents	NNRU	AF.424N1	76.9	85.1	89.1	98.6	111.8	124.4	142.8	164.2
Total	NNRE	AF.4	1 472.5	1 478.6	1 485.3	1 507.8	1 523.8	1 563.6	1 612.7	1 686.4
Insurance, pensions and standardised guarantee schemes		AF.6								
Pensions schemes[5]	M9VU	AF.6M	29.5	28.0	45.5	32.8	24.2	44.3	40.5	44.4
Total	NPYM	AF.6	29.5	28.0	45.5	32.8	24.2	44.3	40.5	44.4
Financial derivatives and employee stock options	MMY9	AF.7	3.5	3.1	5.5	1.8	4.2	2.8	1.8	1.1
Of which: financial derivatives	NNRA	AF.71	3.5	3.1	5.5	1.8	4.2	2.8	1.8	1.1
Other accounts payable	NNSQ	AF.8	98.1	91.2	83.9	87.4	86.6	81.4	91.7	97.7
Total financial liabilities	NNPP	**AF.L**	1 604.9	1 602.3	1 621.5	1 631.2	1 640.5	1 694.6	1 749.6	1 832.9
Financial net worth		**BF.90**								
Total financial assets	NNML	AF.A	4 498.8	4 671.1	5 044.8	5 159.5	5 232.0	5 815.1	5 916.8	6 450.0
less total financial liabilities	NNPP	AF.L	1 604.9	1 602.3	1 621.5	1 631.2	1 640.5	1 694.6	1 749.6	1 832.9
Financial net worth	NZEA	**BF.90**	2 893.9	3 068.8	3 423.3	3 528.3	3 591.4	4 120.5	4 167.2	4 617.1

1 Monetary financial institutions
2 Money market instruments

3 Prior to 1990 it is not possible to distinguish some elements of
AF.32N5-6, AF.511N1 and AF.512N1. These elements are shown combined
as AF.519N7
4 Other than direct investment loans, loans secured on dwellings
and loans for finance leasing
5 AF.63 Pension entitlements, AF.64 Claims on pension funds on pension
managers, AF.65 to non-pension benefits
6 All loans secured on dwellings and all finance leasing are treated as
long-term loans
7 Reflects Housing Association reclassification in line with revisions policy
back to 2005q1

6.2.1 Households
ESA 2010 sector S.14, not seasonally adjusted

£ million

			2009	2010	2011	2012	2013	2014	2015
Production account		I							
Resources									
Output		P.1							
Market output	CRRV	P.11	143 884	149 238	157 268	164 636	176 706	187 284	193 604
Output for own final use	CRRX	P.12	177 202	178 971	180 719	187 054	193 479	200 721	209 471
Other non-market output	CRRZ	P.13	–	–	–	–	–	–	–
Total	CRRT	P.1	321 086	328 209	337 987	351 690	370 185	388 005	403 075
Total resources	CRRT	TR	321 086	328 209	337 987	351 690	370 185	388 005	403 075
Uses									
Intermediate consumption	CRSB	P.2	88 620	94 782	96 448	91 832	100 547	97 069	95 097
Gross value added	HAXE	**B.1g**	232 466	233 427	241 539	259 858	269 638	290 936	307 978
Total uses	CRRT	TU	321 086	328 209	337 987	351 690	370 185	388 005	403 075
Gross value added	HAXE	**B.1g**	232 466	233 427	241 539	259 858	269 638	290 936	307 978
less consumption of fixed capital	HAZH	P.51c	46 709	47 991	49 395	51 426	54 450	58 305	59 549
Value added, net	HAXF	B.1n	185 757	185 436	192 144	208 432	215 188	232 631	248 429

6.2.2 Households
ESA 2010 sector S.14

£ million

			2009	2010	2011	2012	2013	2014	2015
Distribution and use of income accounts		II							
Primary distribution of income account		II.1							
Generation of income account before deduction of fixed capital consumption		II.1.1							
Resources									
Total resources (gross value added)	HAXE	**B.1g**	232 466	233 427	241 539	259 858	269 638	290 936	307 978
Uses									
Compensation of employees		D.1							
Wages and salaries	HAXN	D.11	13 325	16 174	15 340	15 580	17 163	19 667	21 033
Employers' social contributions	HAXO	D.12	2 931	4 260	4 359	4 670	5 031	5 323	5 381
Total	HAXM	D.1	16 256	20 434	19 699	20 250	22 194	24 990	26 414
Taxes on production and imports, paid		D.2							
Production taxes other than on products	LITX	D.29	249	273	339	356	332	338	302
less subsidies received		D.3							
Production subsidies other than on products	EO9S	D.39	3 411	3 059	3 166	2 625	2 455	2 306	1 961
Operating surplus, gross	HABM	B.2g	126 887	126 512	131 274	141 004	142 603	153 754	163 955
Mixed income, gross	HAXH	B.3g	92 485	89 267	93 393	100 873	106 964	114 160	119 268
Total uses (gross value added)	HAXE	**B.1g**	232 466	233 427	241 539	259 858	269 638	290 936	307 978
less consumption of fixed capital[1]	HAZH	P.51c	46 709	47 991	49 395	51 426	54 450	58 305	59 549
Operating surplus, net	HAXG	B.2n	91 118	90 295	93 944	101 852	101 925	111 269	120 747
Mixed income, net	EAWX	B.3n	81 545	77 493	81 328	88 599	93 192	98 340	102 927

1 Consumption of fixed capital is made up of
  P.51c1 - Consumption of fixed capital on gross operating surplus
  plus P.51c2 - Consumption of fixed capital on gross mixed income

6.2.3 Households
ESA 2010 sector S.14

£ million

			2009	2010	2011	2012	2013	2014	2015	2016
Allocation of primary income account before deduction of fixed capital consumption		**II.1.2**								
Resources										
Gross operating surplus and gross mixed income		B.2g+B.3g								
Operating surplus, gross	HABM	B.2g	126 887	126 512	131 274	141 004	142 603	153 754	163 955	167 434
Mixed income, gross	HAXH	B.3g	92 485	89 267	93 393	100 873	106 964	114 160	119 268	127 546
Total	CRTY	B.2g+B.3g	219 372	215 779	224 667	241 877	249 567	267 914	283 223	294 980
Compensation of employees		D.1								
Wages and salaries	HAEC	D.11	663 588	672 139	682 542	695 840	723 444	746 669	775 239	804 241
Employers' social contributions	HAED	D.12	131 228	146 431	147 490	153 405	159 731	155 156	154 878	163 154
Total	HAEB	D.1	794 816	818 570	830 032	849 245	883 175	901 825	930 117	967 395
Property income, received		D.4								
Interest		D.41								
Interest before FISIM[1] allocation	I69P	D.41g	18 897	18 313	20 001	21 462	19 245	15 513	14 242	13 025
plus FISIM	CRNC	P.119	2 926	−909	291	−13	−808	7 977	10 143	10 759
Total	HAXV	D.41	21 823	17 404	20 292	21 449	18 437	23 490	24 385	23 784
Distributed income of corporations		D.42								
Dividends	C3ZT	D.421	48 404	35 826	37 438	41 895	50 244	52 925	73 863	61 737
Withdrawals from the income of quasi-corporations	HAXY	D.422	28 038	31 247	30 649	30 421	33 939	34 940	37 006	36 925
Earnings on property investment	HHLI	D.423	977	953	880	812	817	778	750	882
Total	HAXW	D.42	77 419	68 026	68 967	73 128	85 000	88 643	111 619	99 544
Other investment income		D.44								
Attributable to insurance policy holders	KZK8	D.441	24 167	24 902	24 445	21 951	21 630	19 938	23 848	22 542
Payable on pension entitlements	KZK9	D.442	67 817	77 856	74 956	65 918	63 132	77 972	71 412	73 681
Attributable to collective investment fund shareholders		D.443								
Dividends	MN7A	D.4431	1 080	1 813	883	907	926	995	1 078	1 206
Retained earnings	MN7E	D.4432	1 688	2 834	1 378	1 422	1 448	1 558	1 685	1 887
Total	L5V2	D.443	2 768	4 647	2 261	2 329	2 374	2 553	2 763	3 093
Total	NRVN	D.44	94 752	107 405	101 662	90 198	87 136	100 463	98 023	99 316
Rent	M8MD	D.45	17	18	22	19	22	23	25	23
Total	HAXU	D.4	194 011	192 853	190 943	184 794	190 595	212 619	234 052	222 667
Total resources	HABQ	TR	1 208 199	1 227 202	1 245 642	1 275 916	1 323 337	1 382 358	1 447 392	1 485 042
Uses										
Property income, paid		D.4								
Interest		D.41								
Interest before FISIM[1] allocation	AE7P	D.41g	71 112	63 999	61 287	60 906	60 727	59 640	57 639	57 712
less FISIM	CRNB	P.119	44 449	44 728	38 435	36 271	39 623	32 582	31 446	32 041
Interest	HACY	D.41	26 663	19 271	22 852	24 635	21 104	27 058	26 193	25 671
Rent	HACZ	D.45	12	14	23	19	18	17	18	15
Total	HACX	D.4	26 675	19 285	22 875	24 654	21 122	27 075	26 211	25 686
Balance of primary incomes, gross	HABL	**B.5g**	1 181 524	1 207 917	1 222 767	1 251 262	1 302 215	1 355 283	1 421 181	1 459 356
Total uses	HABQ	TU	1 208 199	1 227 202	1 245 642	1 275 916	1 323 337	1 382 358	1 447 392	1 485 042
less consumption of fixed capital	HAZH	P.51c	46 709	47 991	49 395	51 426	54 450	58 305	59 549	62 293
Balance of net primary income	HAXI	B.5n	1 134 815	1 159 926	1 173 372	1 199 836	1 247 765	1 296 978	1 361 632	1 397 063
Sector share of gross national income	ADIV		77.9	76.4	74.5	75.1	75.9	75.3	77.0	76.4

1 Financial intermediation services indirectly measured

6.2.4 Households

ESA 2010 sector S.14

£ million

			2009	2010	2011	2012	2013	2014	2015	2016
Secondary distribution of income account		II.2								
Resources										
Balance of primary incomes, gross	HABL	B.5g	1 181 524	1 207 917	1 222 767	1 251 262	1 302 215	1 355 283	1 421 181	1 459 356
Social contributions and benefits		D.6								
Employers' imputed social contributions	L8RP	D.612	367	284	253	275	270	283	313	183
Total	L8U4	D.61	367	284	253	275	270	283	313	183
Social benefits other than social transfers in kind		D.62								
Social security benefits in cash	L8QH	D.621	80 825	82 117	83 826	89 187	91 231	93 650	96 461	98 992
Other social insurance benefits	L8QV	D.622	99 996	105 819	108 018	116 908	119 368	117 636	125 769	129 491
Social assistance benefits in cash	HAYU	D.623R	105 102	112 257	115 624	118 922	119 646	120 613	121 463	120 963
Total	HAYP	D.62	285 923	300 193	307 468	325 017	330 245	331 899	343 693	349 446
Other current transfers		D.7								
Non-life insurance claims	HAYY	D.72	21 630	30 373	31 658	29 699	31 930	27 633	28 234	28 032
Miscellaneous current transfers	HAYZ	D.75	6 017	3 563	6 563	10 973	9 278	8 221	8 465	7 969
Total	HAYV	D.7	27 647	33 936	38 221	40 672	41 208	35 854	36 699	36 001
Total resources	HAXD	TR	1 495 461	1 542 330	1 568 709	1 617 226	1 673 938	1 723 319	1 801 886	1 844 986
Uses										
Current taxes on income, wealth, etc		D.5								
Taxes on income	HAYD	D.51	151 348	152 424	157 598	153 734	158 990	162 612	171 393	178 961
Of which:										
Taxes on employment	DBBO	D.511pt	121 479	126 872	129 821	128 622	131 084	136 201	141 848	145 758
Taxes on self-employment and other	ZAFG	D.511pt	22 161	23 184	24 253	20 844	24 130	22 671	24 017	26 295
Other current taxes	NMZK	D.59	33 020	33 813	33 900	34 216	35 507	36 353	37 119	37 989
Total	HAYC	D.5	184 368	186 237	191 498	187 950	194 497	198 965	208 512	216 950
Net social contributions		D.61								
Employers' actual social contributions	L8NL	D.611	113 590	128 706	130 153	135 160	140 445	136 010	135 750	143 838
Employers' imputed social contributions	MA4A	D.612	17 636	17 724	17 337	18 245	19 286	19 146	19 128	19 316
Households' actual social contributions	L8PT	D.613	57 115	58 639	60 376	63 338	64 837	67 194	68 506	73 056
Households' social contribution supplements	L8Q9	D.614	67 817	77 856	74 956	65 918	63 132	77 972	71 412	73 681
Social insurance scheme service charge	M92I	D.61SC	−11 101	−12 568	−14 740	−17 046	−18 324	−18 819	−19 620	−20 318
Total	HADI	D.61	245 057	270 357	268 082	265 615	269 376	281 503	275 176	289 573
Social benefits other than social transfers in kind		D.62								
Other social insurance benefits	L8SF	D.622	367	284	253	275	270	283	313	183
Total	L8TN	D.62	367	284	253	275	270	283	313	183
Other current transfers		D.7								
Net non-life insurance premiums	HAYX	D.71	21 630	30 373	31 658	29 699	31 930	27 633	28 234	28 032
Miscellaneous current transfers	HADP	D.75	23 542	25 389	25 366	28 168	29 718	31 345	32 770	34 550
Total	HADO	D.7	45 172	55 762	57 024	57 867	61 648	58 978	61 004	62 582
Gross disposable income	HABN	B.6g	1 020 497	1 029 690	1 051 852	1 105 519	1 148 147	1 183 590	1 256 881	1 275 698
Total uses	HAXD	TU	1 495 461	1 542 330	1 568 709	1 617 226	1 673 938	1 723 319	1 801 886	1 844 986
Real households' expenditure implied deflator (reference year 2015)	CRXA		88.3	89.8	93.3	95.3	97.6	99.4	100.0	101.4
Real households disposable income: (Chained volume measures)										
£ Million (reference year 2015)[1]	DG2V		1 156 187	1 146 658	1 127 087	1 159 707	1 176 905	1 190 413	1 256 881	1 257 784
Index (2015=100)	DG2Z		92.0	91.2	89.7	92.3	93.6	94.7	100.0	100.1

1 Gross household disposable income deflated by the households and NPISH final consumption deflator

234

6.2.4S Households
Social benefits and contributions
ESA 2010 sector S.14

£ million

			2009	2010	2011	2012	2013	2014	2015	2016
Secondary distribution of income (Further detail of certain items)										
Benefits										
Resources										
Social benefits other than social transfers in kind		D.62								
Social security benefits in cash[1]		D.621								
Social security pension benefits in cash	L8DK	D.6211	66 449	67 575	70 819	76 539	79 992	83 165	85 847	88 501
Social security non-pension benefits in cash	L8DH	D.6212	14 376	14 542	13 007	12 648	11 239	10 485	10 614	10 491
Total social security benefits in cash	L8QH	D.621	80 825	82 117	83 826	89 187	91 231	93 650	96 461	98 992
Other social insurance benefits		D.622								
Other social insurance pension benefits	L8MZ	D.6221	92 674	100 147	102 962	111 403	113 987	111 971	119 812	124 262
Other social insurance non-pension benefits	M8XD	D.6222	7 322	5 672	5 056	5 505	5 381	5 665	5 957	5 229
Total other social benefits	L8QV	D.622	99 996	105 819	108 018	116 908	119 368	117 636	125 769	129 491
Social assistance benefits in cash		D.623								
Received from central government	LNJT		84 335	89 499	91 507	93 470	93 274	93 702	94 260	93 829
Received from local government	ADAL		20 767	22 758	24 117	25 452	26 372	26 911	27 203	27 134
Total social assistance benefits in cash	HAYU	D.623	105 102	112 257	115 624	118 922	119 646	120 613	121 463	120 963
Total social security benefits other than social transfers in kind	HAYP	D.62	285 923	300 193	307 468	325 017	330 245	331 899	343 693	349 446
Uses										
Total	L8TN	D.62	367	284	253	275	270	283	313	183
Contributions										
Resources										
Employers' imputed social contributions		D.612								
Employers' imputed pension contributions	CRXL	D.6121	–	–	–	–	–	–	–	–
Employers' imputed non-pension contributions	M8WP	D.6122	367	284	253	275	270	283	313	183
Total employers' imputed social contributions	L8RP	D.612	367	284	253	275	270	283	313	183
Uses										
Net social contributions		D.61								
Employers' actual social contributions		D.611								
Employers' actual pension contributions	L8JR	D.6111	107 193	122 580	124 197	129 767	135 862	131 915	131 578	139 375
Employers' actual non-pension contributions	L8JV	D.6112	6 397	6 126	5 956	5 393	4 583	4 095	4 172	4 463
Total employers' actual contributions	L8NL	D.611	113 590	128 706	130 153	135 160	140 445	136 010	135 750	143 838
Employers' imputed social contributions		D.612								
Employers' imputed pension contributions	L8KJ	D.6121	10 314	12 052	12 281	12 740	13 905	13 481	13 171	14 087
Employers' imputed non-pension contributions	M8XD	D.6122	7 322	5 672	5 056	5 505	5 381	5 665	5 957	5 229
Total employers' imputed social contributions	MA4A	D.612	17 636	17 724	17 337	18 245	19 286	19 146	19 128	19 316
Households' actual social contributions		D.613								
Households' actual pension contributions	L8KX	D.6131	52 408	54 094	55 946	59 447	61 579	64 296	65 522	69 906
Households' actual non-pension contributions	L8J6	D.6132	4 707	4 545	4 430	3 891	3 258	2 898	2 984	3 150
Total households' actual social contributions	L8PT	D.613	57 115	58 639	60 376	63 338	64 837	67 194	68 506	73 056
Households' social contribution supplements	L8Q9	D.614	67 817	77 856	74 956	65 918	63 132	77 972	71 412	73 681
Social insurance scheme service charge	M92I	D.61SC	−11 101	−12 568	−14 740	−17 046	−18 324	−18 819	−19 620	−20 318
Total social contributions	QWMY	D.61	245 057	270 357	268 082	265 615	269 376	281 503	275 176	289 573

1 For a more detailed analysis see table 5.2.4S
2 Non-profit institutions serving households.

6.2.5 Households
ESA 2010 sector S.14

£ million

			2009	2010	2011	2012	2013	2014	2015	2016
Redistribution of income in kind account		II.3								
Resources										
Households' gross disposable income	HABN	**B.6g**	1 020 497	1 029 690	1 051 852	1 105 519	1 148 147	1 183 590	1 256 881	1 275 698
Social transfers in kind		D.63								
Non-market production	DPRN	D.631	218 394	222 594	225 598	229 597	234 303	240 441	246 362	248 153
Purchased market production	DPRO	D.632	38 138	39 279	40 557	41 341	41 419	44 856	43 959	48 321
Total	HACL	D.63	256 532	261 873	266 155	270 938	275 722	285 297	290 321	296 474
Total resources	HAYT	TR	1 277 029	1 291 563	1 318 007	1 376 457	1 423 869	1 468 887	1 547 202	1 572 172
Uses										
Households' adjusted disposable income, gross	HAYT	B.7g	1 277 029	1 291 563	1 318 007	1 376 457	1 423 869	1 468 887	1 547 202	1 572 172
Total uses	HAYT	TU	1 277 029	1 291 563	1 318 007	1 376 457	1 423 869	1 468 887	1 547 202	1 572 172

6.2.6 Households
ESA 2010 sector S.14

£ million

			2009	2010	2011	2012	2013	2014	2015	2016
Use of income account		II.4								
Use of disposable income account		II.4.1								
Resources										
Households' gross disposable income	HABN	B.6g	1 020 497	1 029 690	1 051 852	1 105 519	1 148 147	1 183 590	1 256 881	1 275 698
Adjustment for the change in pension entitlements	HAZA	D.8	55 441	72 826	66 069	54 160	54 162	67 116	46 546	49 674
Total resources	HAYW	TR	1 075 938	1 102 516	1 117 921	1 159 679	1 202 309	1 250 706	1 303 427	1 325 372
Uses										
Final consumption expenditure		P.3								
Individual consumption expenditure	ABPB	P.31	960 854	984 614	1 013 406	1 053 663	1 098 735	1 143 919	1 181 868	1 233 327
Gross saving	HADA	**B.8g**	115 084	117 902	104 515	106 016	103 574	106 787	121 559	92 045
Total uses	HAYW	TU	1 075 938	1 102 516	1 117 921	1 159 679	1 202 309	1 250 706	1 303 427	1 325 372
less consumption of fixed capital	HAZH	P.51c	46 709	47 991	49 395	51 426	54 450	58 305	59 549	62 293
Net saving	HAXK	B.8n	68 375	69 911	55 120	54 590	49 124	48 482	62 010	29 752
Use of adjusted disposable income account		II.4.2								
Resources										
Households' adjusted disposable income, gross	HAYT	B.7g	1 277 029	1 291 563	1 318 007	1 376 457	1 423 869	1 468 887	1 547 202	1 572 172
Adjustment for the change in pension entitlements	HAZA	D.8	55 441	72 826	66 069	54 160	54 162	67 116	46 546	49 674
Total resources	HACR	TR	1 332 470	1 364 389	1 384 076	1 430 617	1 478 031	1 536 003	1 593 748	1 621 846
Uses										
Actual final consumption		P.4								
Actual individual consumption	ABRE	P.41	1 217 386	1 246 487	1 279 561	1 324 601	1 374 457	1 429 216	1 472 189	1 529 801
Gross saving	HADA	**B.8g**	115 084	117 902	104 515	106 016	103 574	106 787	121 559	92 045
Total uses	HACR	TU	1 332 470	1 364 389	1 384 076	1 430 617	1 478 031	1 536 003	1 593 748	1 621 846
Households saving ratio (per cent)	DG5H		10.7	10.7	9.3	9.1	8.6	8.5	9.3	7.0

6.2.7 Households
ESA 2010 sector S.14

£ million

			2009	2010	2011	2012	2013	2014	2015	2016
Accumulation accounts		III								
Capital account		III.1								
Change in net worth due to saving and capital transfers account		III.1.1								
Changes in liabilities and net worth										
Gross saving	HADA	**B.8g**	115 084	117 902	104 515	106 016	103 574	106 787	121 559	92 045
Capital transfers, receivable		D.9r								
Investment grants	HAZF	D.92r	1 738	1 553	1 710	3 337	1 457	1 872	2 644	1 816
Other capital transfers	HAZG	D.99r	2 607	1 254	1 010	1 311	1 308	873	1 076	570
Total	HAZC	D.9r	4 345	2 807	2 720	4 648	2 765	2 745	3 720	2 386
less capital transfers, payable		D.9p								
Capital taxes	QYKC	D.91p	2 401	2 642	2 936	3 129	4 255	3 886	4 442	4 801
Other capital transfers	HADS	D.99p	4 976	2 343	2 661	3 344	4 151	4 406	4 254	3 291
Total	HADR	D.9p	7 377	4 985	5 597	6 473	8 406	8 292	8 696	8 092
Changes in net worth due to gross saving and capital transfers	HABD	B.101g	112 052	115 724	101 638	104 191	97 933	101 240	116 583	86 339
Changes in assets										
Gross capital formation		P.5								
Gross fixed capital formation	AAA4	P.51g	39 745	42 473	45 253	45 250	50 693	57 387	60 206	66 657
Changes in inventories	HAZU	P.52	−944	354	177	109	282	736	372	12
Acquisitions less disposals of valuables[1]	NPPH	P.53	152	−187	240	1 129	1 927	2 193	866	1 806
Total	NRLK	P.5	38 953	42 640	45 670	46 488	52 902	60 316	61 444	68 475
Acquisitions less disposals of non-produced non-financial assets	HAZJ	NP	−454	−449	−447	−469	−441	−421	−398	−365
Net lending(+) / net borrowing(-)	A99R	**B.9n**	73 553	73 533	56 415	58 172	45 472	41 345	55 537	18 229
Total change in assets	HABD	B.101g	112 052	115 724	101 638	104 191	97 933	101 240	116 583	86 339

1 Acquisitions less disposals of valuables can be a volatile series but any
  volatility is likely to be GDP neutral as it is offset in UK trade figures

6.2.8 Households
ESA 2010 sector S.14, not seasonally adjusted

£ million

			2009	2010	2011	2012	2013	2014	2015	2016
Financial account		III.2								
Net acquisition of financial assets		F.A								
Currency and deposits		F.2								
Currency	NBLZ	F.21	2 863	2 570	2 735	1 782	1 997	2 457	2 576	4 719
Transferable deposits		F.22								
Deposits with UK MFIs[1]	NBMB	F.22N1	20 498	25 295	26 937	48 212	42 956	44 798	42 616	70 401
Of which: foreign currency deposits with UK MFIs[1]	NBMD	F.22N12	375	−98	−3	−268	1 208	229	896	491
Deposits with rest of the world MFIs[1]	NBMF	F.22N9	−13 285	3 090	6 494	−5 334	2 950	4 778	−7 832	−93
Other deposits	NBMG	F.29	3 623	1 314	3 848	−1 939	4 220	7 952	22 170	9 663
Total	NBLY	F.2	13 699	32 269	40 014	42 721	52 123	59 985	59 530	84 690
Debt securities		F.3								
Short-term		F.31								
Issued by UK central government	NBMJ	F.31N1	1	–	1	1	−1	–	2	−3
Issued by UK local government	C46U	F.31N2	–	–	–	–	–	–	–	–
Issued by UK MFIs[1]	NBMO	F.31N5	527	−1 942	−1 449	−71	482	29	−807	1 678
MMIs issued by other UK residents[2]	NBMT	F.31N6	−114	48	−106	1	−7	53	−28	4
MMIs issued by rest of world	C46X	F.31N9	–	–	–	–	–	–	–	–
Long-term		F.32								
Issued by UK central government	NBMW	F.32N1	907	−1 508	832	3 040	−1 914	−262	−481	93
Issued by UK local government	NBMZ	F.32N2	47	−42	−121	−256	279	−317	1 598	−572
Issued by UK MFIs and other UK residents[1,3]	KVG6	F.32N5-6	817	113	471	1 022	−737	659	874	530
Bonds issued by rest of the world	NBNE	F.32N9	1 329	222	−575	−228	−490	1 075	−964	451
Total	NBMH	F.3	3 514	−3 109	−947	3 509	−2 388	1 237	194	2 181
Loans		F.4								
Long-term		F.42								
By UK residents[4]	NBNZ	F.424N1	−3 035	2 083	−2 064	258	−1 457	−9 049	−3 440	−7 915
Total	NBNJ	F.4	−3 035	2 083	−2 064	258	−1 457	−9 049	−3 440	−7 915
Equity and investment fund shares/units		F.5								
Equity		F.51								
Listed UK shares[6]	NBOG	F.511N1	24 563	2 000	−1 019	483	1 672	−1 138	−2 850	−8 844
Unlisted UK shares[6]	NBOH	F.512N1	−2 530	−16 552	−32 374	−18 372	−7 073	−6 282	−12 056	−9 368
Other equity		F.519								
Other UK equity	NBOI	F.519N6	–	–	–	–	–	–	–	–
UK shares and bonds issued by other UK residents[6]	NSPA	F.519N7	–	–	–	–	–	–	–	–
Shares and other equity issued by rest of the world	NBOL	F.519N9	−7 364	−8 161	1 088	367	−11 176	−8 262	−866	−3 629
Investment fund shares/units		F.52								
UK mutual funds' shares	NBOP	F.52N1	3 439	14 045	16 443	−291	16 425	931	−29 758	−20 807
Rest of the world mutual funds' shares	NBOQ	F.52N9	−1 544	−185	−58	−118	−23	–	–	–
Total	NBOB	F.5	16 564	−8 853	−15 920	−17 931	−175	−14 751	−45 530	−42 648
Insurance, pensions and standardised guarantee schemes		F.6								
Non-life insurance technical reserves	NBOU	F.61	2 424	−3 923	2 088	1 735	−1 448	5	−2 211	666
Life insurance and annuity entitlements	M9WG	F.62	4 165	4 917	7 786	430	−8 471	−13 963	56 599	19 617
Pension schemes[5]	MA2I	F.6M	55 441	72 826	66 069	54 160	54 162	67 116	46 546	49 674
Total	NPVZ	F.6	62 030	73 820	75 943	56 325	44 243	53 158	100 934	69 957
Financial derivatives and employee stock options	MN5W	F.7	−655	1 554	1 258	1 862	2 127	1 372	2 275	3 009
Of which: financial derivatives	J8XX	F.71	−2 215	−43	−375	209	425	−396	453	1 130
Other accounts receivable	NBOV	F.8	−18 064	−16 188	−6 272	10 800	−7 064	−1 580	−7 997	2 556
Total net acquisition of financial assets	NBLU	F.A	74 053	81 576	92 012	97 544	87 409	90 372	105 966	111 830

6.2.8 Households

ESA 2010 sector S.14, not seasonally adjusted

continued

£ million

			2009	2010	2011	2012	2013	2014	2015	2016
Financial account		III.2								
Net acquisition of financial liabilities		F.L								
Loans		F.4								
Short-term		F.41								
By UK MFIs[1]	NBQP	F.41N1	−3 255	−2 937	−2 507	−2 733	2 437	5 382	7 659	9 336
Of which foreign currency loans by UK banks	NBQR	F.41N12	−148	−175	−92	−367	−38	603	34	124
By rest of the world	ZMFQ	F.41N9	691	536	7 256	−749	−1 459	2 134	−798	2 950
Long-term[6]		F.42								
Secured on dwellings	NBQY	F.422	7 850	−187	7 824	11 488	12 256	20 296	26 050	38 488
By UK residents	NBRD	F.424N1	−819	12 063	6 502	8 516	13 347	14 506	20 460	19 080
Total	NBQN	F.4	4 467	9 475	19 075	16 522	26 581	42 318	53 371	69 854
Other accounts payable	NBRZ	F.8	−11 498	−5 162	−2 708	7 788	816	−2 453	7 037	5 858
Total net acquisition of financial liabilities	NBOY	**F.L**	**−7 031**	**4 313**	**16 367**	**24 310**	**27 397**	**39 865**	**60 408**	**75 712**
Net lending(+) / net borrowing(-)		**B.9**								
Total net acquisition of financial assets	NBLU	F.A	74 053	81 576	92 012	97 544	87 409	90 372	105 966	111 830
less total net acquisition of financial liabilities	NBOY	F.L	−7 031	4 313	16 367	24 310	27 397	39 865	60 408	75 712
Net lending(+) / borrowing(-) from the financial account	NYNP	B.9f	81 084	77 264	75 644	73 234	60 012	50 506	45 558	36 118
Statistical discrepancy between the financial and non-financial accounts	NYPA	dB.9	−7 531	−3 731	−19 229	−15 062	−14 540	−9 161	9 979	−17 889
Net lending(+) / net borrowing(-)	A99R	**B.9**	**73 553**	**73 533**	**56 415**	**58 172**	**45 472**	**41 345**	**55 537**	**18 229**

1 Monetary financial institutions
2 Money market instruments
3 Prior to 1990, it is not possible to distinguish some elements of F.32N5-6,
  F.511N1 and F.512N1. These elements are shown combined as F.519N7
4 Other than direct investment loans, loans secured on dwellings and loans
  for finance leasing
5 F.63 pension entitlements, F.64 Claims on pension fund on pension
  managers, F.65 to non-pension benefits
6 All loans secured on dwellings and all finance leasing are treated as long
  term loans

6.2.11 Households
ESA 2010 sectors S.14   Unconsolidated

£ billion

			2009	2010	2011	2012	2013	2014	2015	2016
Financial balance sheet at end of period		IV.3								
Non-financial assets	E45Y	AN	3 930.3	3 995.9	3 996.0	4 108.5	4 379.9	4 756.8	5 159.7	5 482.7
Total financial assets		AF.A								
Currency and deposits		AF.2								
Currency	NIRW	AF.21	35.5	40.3	43.1	44.9	46.9	49.3	51.9	56.4
Transferable deposits		AF.22								
Deposits with UK MFIs[1]	NIRY	AF.22N1	953.8	980.5	1 006.5	1 063.9	1 102.4	1 146.1	1 187.7	1 258.2
Of which: foreign currency deposits with UK MFIs[1]	NISA	AF.22N12	4.8	4.8	4.8	4.6	5.5	5.2	6.8	8.2
Deposits with rest of the world MFIs[1]	NISC	AF.22N9	58.0	60.8	66.3	64.8	68.6	68.1	57.1	63.1
Other deposits	NISD	AF.29	97.4	98.4	102.2	100.1	104.1	111.8	133.6	143.0
Total	NIRV	AF.2	1 144.6	1 180.1	1 218.1	1 273.7	1 321.9	1 375.3	1 430.3	1 520.7
Debt securities		AF.3								
Short-term		AF.31								
Issued by UK central government	NISG	AF.31N1	–	–	–	–	–	–	–	0.006
Issued by UK local government	DNCT	AF.31N2	–	–	–	–	–	–	–	–
Issued by UK MFIs[1]	NISL	AF.31N5	3.5	2.8	2.1	3.5	2.7	4.1	5.0	6.3
MMIs[2] issued by other UK residents	NISQ	AF.31N6	0.2	0.2	0.1	0.1	0.1	0.2	0.2	0.2
MMIs issued by the rest of the world	DPHV	AF.31N9	–	–	–	–	–	–	–	–
Long-term		AF.32								
Issued by UK central government	NIST	AF.32N1	3.1	1.5	2.2	5.2	3.7	3.1	2.7	2.6
Issued by UK local government	NISW	AF.32N2	0.3	0.2	0.1	0.2	0.5	0.2	1.8	1.4
Issued by UK MFIs and other UK residents[1,3]	KVF7	AF.32N5-6	3.7	3.7	4.2	4.8	4.3	4.5	4.9	4.5
Bonds issued by rest of the world	NITB	AF.32N9	1.4	1.5	1.7	1.4	1.0	2.0	1.6	1.6
Total	NISE	AF.3	12.3	10.0	10.4	15.3	12.4	14.1	16.1	16.6
Loans		AF.4								
Long-term		AF.42								
Other long-term loans by UK residents[4]	NITW	AF.424N1	18.3	18.4	18.4	18.5	18.7	18.7	18.8	18.7
Total	NITG	AF.4	18.3	18.4	18.4	18.5	18.7	18.7	18.8	18.7
Equity and investment fund shares/units		AF.5								
Equity		AF.51								
Listed UK shares[3]	NIUD	AF.511N1	161.8	175.5	156.3	169.9	204.7	218.2	215.8	219.1
Unlisted UK shares[3]	DHWT	AF.512N1	226.5	234.2	211.8	171.1	188.1	233.3	224.4	235.7
Other equity		AF.519								
Other UK equity	NIUF	AF.519N6	1.4	1.4	1.4	1.4	1.4	1.4	1.4	1.4
UK shares and bonds issued by other UK residents[3]	NSOA	AF.519N7	–	–	–	–	–	–	–	–
Shares and other equity issued by rest of the world	NIUI	AF.519N9	137.9	128.9	126.3	124.7	119.9	114.0	113.3	133.8
Investment fund shares/units		AF.52								
UK mutual funds' shares	NIUM	AF.52N1	163.2	177.1	175.4	185.0	204.7	225.6	246.7	272.1
Rest of the world mutual funds' shares	NIUN	AF.52N9	0.8	0.7	0.5	0.4	0.1	0.1	0.1	–
Total	NITY	AF.5	691.6	717.7	671.7	652.5	718.9	792.6	801.6	862.1
Insurance, pensions and standardised guarantee schemes		AF.6								
Non-life insurance technical reserves	NIUR	AF.61	48.6	40.2	42.2	44.0	42.5	42.5	40.3	41.0
Life insurance and annuity entitlements	M9RX	AF.62	544.8	568.4	543.8	546.4	565.6	566.3	605.8	633.9
Pension schemes[5]	M9VE	AF.6M	1 788.3	1 879.1	2 273.7	2 308.3	2 238.8	2 658.9	2 631.1	2 950.2
Total	NPXP	AF.6	2 381.7	2 487.6	2 859.7	2 898.7	2 846.9	3 267.8	3 277.2	3 625.1
Financial derivatives and employee stock options	MMW6	AF.7	7.4	7.5	9.1	5.2	8.2	6.4	5.6	5.7
Of which: financial derivatives	JS3J	AF.71	2.6	2.7	4.4	0.4	3.2	1.2	0.3	0.2
Other accounts receivable	NIUS	AF.8	130.7	132.3	136.3	180.9	179.2	189.5	184.1	187.2
Total financial assets	NITF	**AF.A**	4 386.5	4 553.6	4 923.7	5 044.7	5 106.2	5 664.4	5 733.9	6 236.0

6.2.11 Households
ESA 2010 sectors S.14 Unconsolidated
continued

£ billion

			2009	2010	2011	2012	2013	2014	2015	2016
Financial balance sheet at end of period		IV.3								
Total financial liabilities		AF.L								
Loans		AF.4								
Short-term		AF.41								
By UK MFIs[1]	NIWM	AF.41N1	171.6	164.1	153.5	141.0	133.7	140.1	144.4	150.7
Of which: Foreign currency loans	NIWO	AF.1N12	1.7	1.4	1.3	0.9	0.9	1.5	1.5	1.1
Loans by UK banks										
By rest of the world MFIs	ZMFD	AF.41N9	19.4	19.2	26.0	26.8	26.4	25.1	24.4	29.5
Long-term loans [6]		AF.42								
Secured on dwellings	NIWV	AF.422	1 191.8	1 197.6	1 201.9	1 225.6	1 237.1	1 259.1	1 286.2	1 325.1
By UK residents	NIXA	AF.424N1	70.6	78.9	82.8	91.7	105.0	117.4	135.2	156.0
Total	NIWK	AF.4	1 453.5	1 459.8	1 464.2	1 485.1	1 502.2	1 541.6	1 590.1	1 661.3
Financial derivatives and employee stock options	MMZ2	AF.7	3.5	3.1	5.4	1.6	4.0	2.7	1.5	0.7
Of which: financial derivatives	JS3K	AF.71	3.5	3.1	5.4	1.6	4.0	2.7	1.5	0.7
Other accounts payable	NIXW	AF.8	88.0	81.2	73.8	76.3	75.6	70.2	79.6	84.6
Total financial liabilities	NIWJ	**AF.L**	1 545.0	1 544.1	1 543.4	1 563.1	1 581.8	1 614.6	1 671.2	1 746.6
Financial net worth		**BF.90**								
Total financial assets	NITF	AF.A	4 386.5	4 553.6	4 923.7	5 044.7	5 106.2	5 664.4	5 733.9	6 236.0
less total financial liabilities	NIWJ	AF.L	1 545.0	1 544.1	1 543.4	1 563.1	1 581.8	1 614.6	1 671.2	1 746.6
Financial net worth	NYOH	**BF.90**	2 841.5	3 009.5	3 380.3	3 481.6	3 524.4	4 049.9	4 062.7	4 489.4

1 Monetary financial institutions
2 Money market instruments

3 Prior to 1990 it is not possible to distinguish some elements of
AF.32N5-6, AF.511N1 and AF.512N1. These elements are shown combined
as AF.519N7
4 Other than direct investment loans, loans secured on dwellings
and loans for finance leasing
5 AF.63 Pension entitlements, AF.64 Claims on pension funds on pension
managers, AF.65 to non-pension benefits
6 All loans secured on dwellings and all finance leasing are treated as
long-term loans
7 Reflects Housing Association reclassification in line with revisions policy
back to 2005q1

6.2.12 Household final consumption expenditure: classified by purpose
At current market prices

£ million

			2009	2010	2011	2012	2013	2014	2015	2016
Final consumption expenditure of households		P.31								
Durable goods										
Furnishings, household equipment and routine maintenance of the house	LLIJ	05	20 418	20 774	21 598	21 426	21 709	23 887	25 765	27 929
Health	LLIK	06	3 166	2 978	2 962	3 092	3 625	3 648	3 551	3 618
Transport	LLIL	07	35 069	35 423	35 932	38 719	41 303	45 081	47 967	50 545
Communication	LLIM	08	868	759	754	919	994	780	876	993
Recreation and culture	LLIN	09	23 210	23 698	22 528	21 794	22 986	23 961	25 908	26 938
Miscellaneous goods and services	LLIO	12	5 314	5 678	6 558	7 505	7 316	8 300	8 600	9 219
Total durable goods	UTIA	D	88 045	89 310	90 332	93 455	97 933	105 657	112 667	119 242
Semi-durable goods										
Clothing and footwear	LLJL	03	48 336	50 245	53 266	54 869	57 135	60 750	64 138	66 752
Furnishings, household equipment and routine maintenance of the house	LLJM	05	13 859	14 340	13 954	14 692	15 718	16 087	17 171	17 468
Transport	LLJN	07	4 121	3 929	3 831	4 283	4 679	4 718	4 654	4 783
Recreation and culture	LLJO	09	28 279	28 245	26 790	27 712	26 841	27 180	28 257	30 923
Miscellaneous goods and services	LLJP	12	3 555	5 505	5 767	5 824	7 087	6 692	6 908	6 922
Total semi-durable goods	UTIQ	SD	98 150	102 264	103 608	107 380	111 460	115 427	121 128	126 848
Non-durable goods										
Food and drink	ABZV	01	80 529	83 607	86 955	91 415	96 358	97 740	97 641	98 443
Alcoholic beverages, tobacco and narcotics	ADFL	02	37 598	37 866	41 662	41 445	41 915	42 548	43 227	43 809
Housing, water, electricity, gas and other fuels	LLIX	04	34 207	35 518	34 633	38 430	41 062	37 489	37 424	37 214
Furnishings, household equipment and routine maintenance of the house	LLIY	05	4 276	4 286	4 146	4 184	4 383	4 436	4 575	4 636
Health	LLIZ	06	4 693	4 880	4 965	4 966	6 620	7 153	6 794	6 654
Transport	LLJA	07	26 621	30 820	35 415	35 513	34 259	33 067	28 297	27 604
Recreation and culture	LLJB	09	15 296	15 220	15 184	15 216	15 865	16 146	16 456	16 768
Miscellaneous goods and services	LLJC	12	15 983	16 080	16 845	17 485	18 445	19 742	20 933	22 370
Total non-durable goods	UTII	ND	219 203	228 277	239 805	248 654	258 907	258 321	255 347	257 498
Total goods	UTIE		405 398	419 851	433 745	449 489	468 300	479 405	489 142	503 588
Services										
Clothing and footwear	LLJD	03	1 199	1 129	1 010	1 029	1 015	1 065	926	945
Housing, water, electricity, gas and other fuels	LLJE	04	225 858	231 247	236 793	247 948	259 339	270 252	282 165	292 661
Furnishings, household equipment and routine maintenance of the house	LLJF	05	5 962	6 759	6 591	6 744	7 136	7 274	7 350	8 702
Health	LLJG	06	7 094	8 009	8 419	8 357	8 472	8 432	10 391	11 558
Transport	LLJH	07	55 996	58 097	61 049	64 535	70 117	74 214	77 500	80 598
Communication	LLJI	08	17 613	18 634	18 860	18 969	20 195	20 204	21 579	23 050
Recreation and culture	LLJJ	09	33 337	34 264	35 956	37 868	37 589	38 954	40 239	41 475
Education	ADIE	10	14 622	14 837	14 786	15 751	17 739	18 808	20 233	21 652
Restaurants and hotels	ADIF	11	82 284	86 510	92 332	97 185	102 267	106 771	110 372	116 195
Miscellaneous goods and services	LLJK	12	98 680	94 070	95 036	97 556	99 564	112 020	113 888	118 813
Total services	UTIM	S	542 645	553 556	570 832	595 942	623 433	657 994	684 643	715 649
Final consumption expenditure in the UK by resident and non-resident households (domestic concept)		0								
	ABQI		948 043	973 407	1 004 577	1 045 431	1 091 733	1 137 399	1 173 785	1 219 237
Final consumption expenditure outside the UK by UK resident households	ABTA	P.33	33 572	34 002	33 024	33 773	35 733	37 088	40 132	44 923
Final consumption expenditure in the UK by households resident in rest of the world	CDFD	P.34	−20 761	−22 795	−24 195	−25 541	−28 731	−30 568	−32 049	−30 833
Final consumption expenditure by UK resident households in the UK and abroad (national concept)	ABPB	P.31	960 854	984 614	1 013 406	1 053 663	1 098 735	1 143 919	1 181 868	1 233 327

6.2.13 Household final consumption expenditure: classified by purpose
Chained volume measures (reference year 2015)

£ million

			2009	2010	2011	2012	2013	2014	2015	2016
Final consumption expenditure of households	P.31									
Durable goods										
Furnishings, household equipment and routine maintenance of the house	LLME	05	22 413	22 109	22 272	21 559	21 703	23 817	25 765	27 737
Health	LLMF	06	3 311	3 082	3 048	3 167	3 738	3 684	3 551	3 605
Transport	LLMG	07	40 016	36 961	36 033	38 760	41 835	45 032	47 967	49 445
Communication	LLMH	08	1 026	858	820	968	1 018	791	876	964
Recreation and culture	LLMI	09	16 282	17 369	18 189	19 095	21 118	22 584	25 908	28 225
Miscellaneous goods and services	LLMJ	12	6 636	6 649	7 137	7 619	7 264	8 252	8 600	9 100
Total durable goods	UTIC	D	88 306	86 545	87 253	90 969	96 593	104 076	112 667	119 076
Semi-durable goods										
Clothing and footwear	LLNG	03	50 071	52 539	54 484	55 721	57 510	60 910	64 138	66 823
Furnishings, household equipment and routine maintenance of the house	LLNH	05	15 755	15 888	14 510	14 841	15 843	16 096	17 171	17 804
Transport	LLNI	07	4 551	4 164	3 906	4 326	4 683	4 668	4 654	4 746
Recreation and culture	LLNJ	09	27 247	27 313	26 645	27 661	26 555	26 800	28 257	30 982
Miscellaneous goods and services	LLNK	12	3 671	5 726	5 971	5 942	7 092	6 687	6 908	7 060
Total semi-durable goods	UTIS	SD	101 292	105 636	105 550	108 539	111 700	115 164	121 128	127 415
Non-durable goods										
Food and drink	ADIP	01	91 187	91 712	90 351	92 113	93 632	95 212	97 641	100 887
Alcoholic beverages, tobacco and narcotics	ADIS	02	48 882	48 644	46 835	45 434	44 736	43 862	43 227	42 422
Housing, water, electricity, gas and other fuels	LLMS	04	41 812	44 454	39 879	41 147	41 399	36 424	37 424	38 203
Furnishings, household equipment and routine maintenance of the house	LLMT	05	4 791	4 656	4 232	4 155	4 297	4 316	4 575	4 857
Health	LLMU	06	5 115	5 237	5 263	5 179	6 826	7 260	6 794	6 571
Transport	LLMV	07	29 526	28 474	29 206	29 031	28 287	28 732	28 297	27 980
Recreation and culture	LLMW	09	18 026	17 184	16 473	16 132	16 436	16 268	16 456	16 526
Miscellaneous goods and services	LLMX	12	16 518	16 216	16 549	17 034	18 012	19 469	20 933	22 714
Total non-durable goods	UTIK	ND	255 063	255 620	248 702	250 116	253 344	251 565	255 347	260 160
Total goods	UTIG		444 065	447 277	441 386	449 673	461 792	470 889	489 142	506 651
Services										
Clothing and footwear	LLMY	03	1 367	1 265	1 090	1 091	1 060	1 089	926	927
Housing, water, electricity, gas and other fuels	LLMZ	04	259 267	265 330	265 241	269 577	275 199	279 228	282 165	284 465
Furnishings, household equipment and routine maintenance of the house	LLNA	05	6 705	7 451	7 135	7 197	7 504	7 481	7 350	8 418
Health	LLNB	06	8 361	9 115	9 300	9 031	8 878	8 629	10 391	11 624
Transport	LLNC	07	67 764	68 438	68 148	69 725	71 880	75 475	77 500	79 651
Communication	LLND	08	21 039	21 221	20 685	20 023	20 712	20 482	21 579	22 443
Recreation and culture	LLNE	09	40 845	40 421	40 443	41 375	39 697	40 015	40 239	39 945
Education	ADMJ	10	24 659	23 759	22 518	22 091	21 220	20 429	20 233	20 671
Restaurants and hotels	ADMK	11	99 531	102 047	103 387	104 804	107 794	109 377	110 372	113 444
Miscellaneous goods and services	LLNF	12	108 962	106 819	106 234	108 971	110 533	114 841	113 888	116 766
Total services	UTIO	S	637 386	644 976	643 568	653 440	664 350	676 997	684 643	698 354
Final consumption expenditure in the UK by resident and non-resident households (domestic concept)	ABQJ	0	1 081 124	1 091 836	1 084 277	1 102 519	1 125 788	1 147 539	1 173 785	1 205 005
Final consumption expenditure outside the UK by UK resident households	ABTC	P.33	33 228	32 309	30 122	31 679	31 611	34 697	40 132	41 175
Final consumption expenditure in the UK by households resident in rest of the world	CCHX		−25 218	−27 088	−27 626	−28 181	−30 414	−31 383	−32 049	−30 172
Final consumption expenditure by UK resident households in the UK and abroad (national concept)	ABPF	P.3	1 088 615	1 096 462	1 085 891	1 105 308	1 126 255	1 150 513	1 181 868	1 216 008

Notes

1 ESA 2010 Classification of Individual consumption by Purpose (COICOP).

6.2.14 Individual consumption expenditure at current market prices by households, non-profit institutions serving households and general government

Classified by function (COICOP/COPNI/COFOG)[1]

£ million

			2009	2010	2011	2012	2013	2014	2015	2016
Final consumption expenditure of households	P.31									
Food and non-alcoholic beverages	ABZV	01	80 529	83 607	86 955	91 415	96 358	97 740	97 641	98 443
Food	ABZW	01.1	71 188	73 909	76 359	80 435	84 957	86 210	86 081	86 885
Non-alcoholic beverages	ADFK	01.2	9 341	9 698	10 596	10 980	11 401	11 530	11 560	11 558
Alcoholic beverages, tobacco and narcotics	ADFL	02	37 598	37 866	41 662	41 445	41 915	42 548	43 227	43 809
Alcoholic beverages	ADFM	02.1	14 577	15 389	16 197	16 998	17 593	18 137	18 542	19 391
Tobacco	ADFN	02.2	16 211	17 292	18 205	18 699	19 138	19 905	20 176	20 120
Narcotics	MNC2	02.3	6 810	5 185	7 260	5 748	5 184	4 506	4 509	4 298
Clothing and footwear	ADFP	03	49 535	51 374	54 276	55 898	58 150	61 815	65 064	67 697
Clothing	ADFQ	03.1	42 022	43 719	46 611	47 729	49 895	52 653	54 842	56 334
Footwear	ADFR	03.2	7 513	7 655	7 665	8 169	8 255	9 162	10 222	11 363
Housing, water, electricity, gas and other fuels	ADFS	04	260 065	266 765	271 426	286 378	300 401	307 741	319 589	329 875
Actual rentals for housing	ADFT	04.1	52 312	55 749	59 631	64 548	69 353	73 684	77 833	81 914
Imputed rentals for housing	ADFU	04.2	167 868	169 784	171 302	177 172	183 414	189 939	197 523	203 601
Maintenance and repair of the dwelling	ADFV	04.3	2 356	2 231	2 249	2 454	2 667	2 952	3 078	3 026
Water supply and miscellaneous dwelling services	ADFW	04.4	8 194	8 523	8 807	9 141	9 568	9 846	9 705	9 976
Electricity, gas and other fuels	ADFX	04.5	29 335	30 478	29 437	33 063	35 399	31 320	31 450	31 358
Furnishings, household equipment and routine		05								
maintenance of the house	ADFY		44 515	46 159	46 289	47 046	48 946	51 684	54 861	58 735
Furniture, furnishings, carpets and other floor coverings	ADFZ	05.1	15 698	15 740	16 783	16 399	16 764	18 376	20 188	21 137
Household textiles	ADGG	05.2	5 718	6 305	4 926	5 250	5 927	6 194	6 702	6 735
Household appliances	ADGL	05.3	5 693	6 079	6 222	6 331	6 191	6 927	7 026	8 152
Glassware, tableware and household utensils	ADGM	05.4	4 222	4 132	4 684	4 813	5 067	5 106	5 351	5 415
Tools and equipment for house and garden	ADGN	05.5	3 407	3 366	3 570	3 918	4 058	3 979	4 290	4 675
Goods and services for routine household maintenance	ADGO	05.6	9 777	10 537	10 104	10 335	10 939	11 102	11 304	12 621
Health	ADGP	06	14 953	15 867	16 346	16 415	18 717	19 233	20 736	21 830
Medical products, appliances and equipment	ADGQ	06.1	7 859	7 858	7 927	8 058	10 245	10 801	10 345	10 272
Out-patient services	ADGR	06.2	3 978	4 875	5 339	5 190	5 458	5 282	7 018	8 066
Hospital services	ADGS	06.3	3 116	3 134	3 080	3 167	3 014	3 150	3 373	3 492
Transport	ADGT	07	121 807	128 269	136 227	143 050	150 358	157 080	158 418	163 530
Purchase of vehicles	ADGU	07.1	35 069	35 423	35 932	38 719	41 303	45 081	47 967	50 545
Operation of personal transport equipment	ADGV	07.2	53 694	58 859	63 469	64 855	65 242	66 186	63 244	63 636
Transport services	ADGW	07.3	33 044	33 987	36 826	39 476	43 813	45 813	47 207	49 349
Communication	ADGX	08	18 481	19 393	19 614	19 888	21 189	20 984	22 455	24 043
Postal services	CDEF	08.1	1 054	909	755	588	793	732	784	1 135
Telephone and telefax equipment	ADWO	08.2	868	759	754	919	994	780	876	993
Telephone and telefax services	ADWP	08.3	16 559	17 725	18 105	18 381	19 402	19 472	20 795	21 915
Recreation and culture	ADGY	09	100 122	101 427	100 458	102 590	103 281	106 241	110 860	116 104
Audio-visual, photographic and information processing equipment	ADGZ	09.1	21 301	21 052	20 079	19 101	18 698	17 909	17 528	17 708
Other major durables for recreation and culture	ADHL	09.2	7 378	7 728	7 206	7 618	8 702	10 530	12 709	13 870
Other recreational items and equipment; flowers, garden and pets	ADHZ	09.3	29 174	30 036	28 666	29 602	29 752	31 046	32 610	35 571
Recreational and cultural services	ADIA	09.4	30 584	31 206	33 087	34 722	34 264	35 492	36 723	37 586
Newspapers, books and stationery	ADIC	09.5	11 685	11 405	11 420	11 547	11 865	11 264	11 290	11 369
Package holidays[2]	ADID	09.6	–	–	–	–	–	–	–	–
Education		10								
Education services	ADIE	10	14 622	14 837	14 786	15 751	17 739	18 808	20 233	21 652
Restaurants and hotels	ADIF	11	82 284	86 510	92 332	97 185	102 267	106 771	110 372	116 195
Catering services	ADIG	11.1	65 344	68 455	73 107	76 242	80 381	83 151	85 404	89 533
Accommodation services	ADIH	11.2	16 940	18 055	19 225	20 943	21 886	23 620	24 968	26 662
Miscellaneous goods and services	ADII	12	123 532	121 333	124 206	128 370	132 412	146 754	150 329	157 324
Personal care	ADIJ	12.1	22 771	23 561	24 173	24 829	26 038	27 695	29 077	30 915
Prostitution	MNC8	12.2	4 190	4 336	4 459	4 575	4 680	4 839	5 044	4 783
Personal effects n.e.c.	ADIK	12.3	7 702	9 824	10 939	11 989	12 964	13 507	14 144	14 701
Social protection	ADIL	12.4	13 243	13 374	13 183	13 650	14 845	15 683	18 632	19 814
Insurance	ADIM	12.5	21 449	20 242	21 291	23 737	23 621	26 389	21 365	21 165
Financial services n.e.c.	ADIN	12.6	44 886	41 236	41 325	39 452	39 938	48 280	51 514	54 405
Other services n.e.c.	ADIO	12.7	9 291	8 760	8 836	10 138	10 326	10 361	10 553	11 541
Final consumption expenditure in the UK by resident and non-resident households(domestic concept)	ABQI	0	948 043	973 407	1 004 577	1 045 431	1 091 733	1 137 399	1 173 785	1 219 237
Final consumption expenditure outside the UK by UK resident households	ABTA	P.33	33 572	34 002	33 024	33 773	35 733	37 088	40 132	44 923
Final consumption expenditure in the UK by households resident in rest of the world	CDFD	P.34	−20 761	−22 795	−24 195	−25 541	−28 731	−30 568	−32 049	−30 833
Final consumption expenditure by UK resident households in the UK and abroad (national concept)	ABPB	P.31	960 854	984 614	1 013 406	1 053 663	1 098 735	1 143 919	1 181 868	1 233 327

6.2.14
continued

Individual consumption expenditure at current market prices by households, non-profit institutions serving households and general government

Classified by function (COICOP/COPNI/COFOG)[1]

£ million

			2009	2010	2011	2012	2013	2014	2015	2016
Consumption expenditure of UK resident households		P.31								
Final consumption expenditure of UK resident households in theUK and abroad	ABPB	P.31	960 854	984 614	1 013 406	1 053 663	1 098 735	1 143 919	1 181 868	1 233 327
Final individual consumption expenditure of NPISH		13								
Final individual consumption expenditure of NPISH	ABNV	P.31	50 684	51 276	53 647	53 664	54 428	56 625	56 614	57 005
Final individual consumption expenditure of general government		14								
Health	IWX5	14.1	109 096	111 872	115 251	117 284	120 297	126 089	130 178	134 890
Recreation and culture	IWX6	14.2	6 290	6 193	6 254	6 477	5 866	5 821	5 925	5 426
Education	IWX7	14.3	58 888	60 823	59 978	60 131	61 120	61 962	62 405	63 329
Social protection	IWX8	14.4	31 574	31 709	31 025	33 382	34 011	34 800	35 199	35 824
Final individual consumption expenditure of general government	NNAQ	P.31	205 848	210 597	212 508	217 274	221 294	228 672	233 707	239 469
Total, individual consumption expenditure/ actual individual consumption	ABRE	P.31 P.41	1 217 386	1 246 487	1 279 561	1 324 601	1 374 457	1 429 216	1 472 189	1 529 801

1 "Purpose" or "function" classifications are designed to indicate the "socio-economic objectives" that institutional units aim to achieve through various kinds of outlays. COICOP is the Classification of Individual Consumption by Purpose and applies to households. COPNI is the Classification of the Purposes of Non-profit Institutions Serving Households and COFOG is the Classification of the Functions of Government.

2 Package holidays data are dispersed between components (transport etc).

6.2.15 Individual consumption expenditure by households, NPISH and general government Chained volume measures (reference year 2015)

Classified by function (COICOP/COPNI/COFOG)[1]

£ million

			2009	2010	2011	2012	2013	2014	2015	2016
Final consumption expenditure of households		P.31								
Food and non-alcoholic beverages	ADIP	01	91 187	91 712	90 351	92 113	93 632	95 212	97 641	100 887
Food	ADIQ	01.1	79 970	80 717	79 311	81 119	82 377	83 838	86 081	89 069
Non-alcoholic beverages	ADIR	01.2	11 233	10 991	11 043	10 998	11 258	11 376	11 560	11 818
Alcoholic beverages, tobacco and narcotics	ADIS	02	48 882	48 644	46 835	45 434	44 736	43 862	43 227	42 422
Alcoholic beverages	ADIT	02.1	17 779	18 262	17 786	17 942	17 747	18 137	18 542	19 327
Tobacco	ADIU	02.2	24 979	24 848	23 665	22 583	21 612	20 816	20 176	19 212
Narcotics	MNC4	02.3	6 261	5 807	5 601	5 172	5 489	4 959	4 509	3 883
Clothing and footwear	ADIW	03	51 403	53 782	55 566	56 805	58 566	61 995	65 064	67 750
Clothing	ADIX	03.1	44 302	46 505	48 048	48 760	50 359	52 898	54 842	56 354
Footwear	ADIY	03.2	7 108	7 300	7 543	8 053	8 219	9 104	10 222	11 396
Housing, water, electricity, gas and other fuels	ADIZ	04	301 072	309 687	305 355	310 948	316 818	315 618	319 589	322 668
Actual rentals for housing	ADJA	04.1	72 388	74 694	75 962	77 067	78 898	79 048	77 833	78 650
Imputed rentals for housing	ADJB	04.2	180 124	183 967	182 857	185 941	189 673	193 593	197 523	198 780
Maintenance and repair of the dwelling	ADJC	04.3	2 537	2 325	2 253	2 429	2 658	2 945	3 078	2 986
Water supply and miscellaneous dwelling services	ADJD	04.4	9 759	10 035	10 029	9 865	9 851	9 856	9 705	9 895
Electricity, gas and other fuels	ADJE	04.5	36 138	38 798	34 240	35 618	35 722	30 320	31 450	32 357
Furnishings, household equipment and routine maintenance of the house	ADJF	05	49 622	50 048	48 131	47 725	49 313	51 693	54 861	58 816
Furniture, furnishings, carpets and other floor coverings	ADJG	05.1	17 338	16 908	17 446	16 542	16 805	18 325	20 188	21 017
Household textiles	ADJH	05.2	6 150	6 701	4 960	5 195	5 837	6 186	6 702	6 865
Household appliances	ADJI	05.3	6 027	6 184	6 188	6 276	6 111	6 898	7 026	8 068
Glassware, tableware and household utensils	ADJJ	05.4	4 781	4 500	4 866	4 923	5 143	5 081	5 351	5 562
Tools and equipment for house and garden	ADJK	05.5	4 378	4 187	3 960	4 050	4 239	4 028	4 290	4 732
Goods and services for routine household maintenance	ADJL	05.6	11 053	11 626	10 758	10 780	11 223	11 180	11 304	12 572
Health	ADJM	06	16 797	17 394	17 563	17 341	19 448	19 584	20 736	21 800
Medical products, appliances and equipment	ADJN	06.1	8 436	8 321	8 311	8 350	10 563	10 944	10 345	10 176
Out-patient services	ADJO	06.2	4 378	5 273	5 680	5 488	5 647	5 425	7 018	8 228
Hospital services	ADJP	06.3	4 121	3 891	3 625	3 551	3 224	3 199	3 373	3 396
Transport	ADJQ	07	142 814	138 806	138 170	142 564	147 058	154 088	158 418	161 822
Purchase of vehicles	ADJR	07.1	40 016	36 961	36 033	38 760	41 835	45 032	47 967	49 445
Operation of personal transport equipment	ADJS	07.2	61 249	60 090	59 723	60 371	60 594	62 486	63 244	63 332
Transport services	ADJT	07.3	40 986	41 326	42 131	43 188	44 498	46 524	47 207	49 045
Communication	ADJU	08	22 065	22 078	21 504	20 990	21 730	21 273	22 455	23 407
Postal services	CCGZ	08.1	1 702	1 384	1 054	694	840	745	784	1 121
Telephone and telefax equipment	ADQF	08.2	1 026	858	820	968	1 019	791	876	964
Telephone and telefax services	ADQG	08.3	19 567	19 980	19 694	19 318	19 874	19 737	20 795	21 322
Recreation and culture	ADJV	09	100 505	101 065	100 881	103 553	103 504	105 488	110 860	115 678
Audio-visual, photographic and information processing equipment	ADJW	09.1	13 004	13 747	14 833	15 519	16 081	16 184	17 528	19 056
Other major durables for recreation and culture	ADJX	09.2	8 708	8 711	7 811	7 990	9 024	10 705	12 709	13 739
Other recreational items and equipment; flowers, gardens and pets	ADJY	09.3	29 002	29 587	28 530	29 505	29 551	30 683	32 610	35 773
Recreational and cultural services	ADJZ	09.4	37 629	36 971	37 384	38 076	36 280	36 530	36 723	36 065
Newspapers, books and stationery	ADKM	09.5	14 115	13 251	12 872	12 845	12 696	11 480	11 290	11 045
Package holidays[2]	ADMI	09.6	–	–	–	–	–	–	–	–
Education		10								
Education services	ADMJ	10	24 659	23 759	22 518	22 091	21 220	20 429	20 233	20 671
Restaurants and hotels	ADMK	11	99 531	102 047	103 387	104 804	107 794	109 377	110 372	113 444
Catering services	ADML	11.1	79 735	81 253	81 907	82 037	84 455	84 849	85 404	87 611
Accommodation services	ADMM	11.2	19 818	20 796	21 470	22 753	23 324	24 525	24 968	25 833
Miscellaneous goods and services	ADMN	12	135 373	135 119	135 639	139 305	142 756	149 184	150 329	155 640
Personal care	ADMO	12.1	24 017	24 236	24 178	24 587	25 756	27 510	29 077	31 131
Prostitution	MND2	12.2	4 664	4 733	4 784	4 833	4 862	4 930	5 044	4 695
Personal effects n.e.c.	ADMP	12.3	8 884	11 010	11 747	12 257	12 943	13 474	14 144	14 709
Social protection	ADMQ	12.4	15 684	15 349	14 698	14 835	15 815	16 228	18 632	19 266
Insurance	ADMR	12.5	27 169	24 149	24 066	26 635	26 027	27 944	21 365	20 435
Financial services n.e.c.	ADMS	12.6	44 882	45 980	46 747	45 640	46 913	48 769	51 514	54 049
Other services n.e.c.	ADMT	12.7	10 971	10 056	9 788	10 907	10 736	10 618	10 553	11 355
Final consumption expenditure in the UK by resident and non-resident households (domestic concept)	ABQJ	0	1 081 124	1 091 836	1 084 277	1 102 519	1 125 788	1 147 539	1 173 785	1 205 005
Final consumption expenditure outside the UK by UK resident households	ABTC	P.33	33 228	32 309	30 122	31 679	31 611	34 697	40 132	41 175
Final consumption expenditure in the UK by households resident in rest of the world	CCHX	P.34	−25 218	−27 088	−27 626	−28 181	−30 414	−31 383	−32 049	−30 172
Final consumption expenditure by UK resident households in the UK and abroad (national concept)	ABPF	P.31	1 088 615	1 096 462	1 085 891	1 105 308	1 126 255	1 150 513	1 181 868	1 216 008

6.2.15
continued

Individual consumption expenditure by households, NPISH and general government Chained volume measures (reference year 2015)
Classified by function (COICOP/COPNI/COFOG)[1]

£ million

			2009	2010	2011	2012	2013	2014	2015	2016
Consumption expenditure of UK resident households		P.31								
Final consumption expenditure of UK resident households in the UK and abroad	ABPF	P.31	1 088 615	1 096 462	1 085 891	1 105 308	1 126 255	1 150 513	1 181 868	1 216 008
Final individual consumption expenditure of NPISH		13								
Final individual consumption expenditure of NPISH	ABNU	P.31	56 325	55 899	58 155	57 057	56 218	57 081	56 614	56 970
Final individual consumption expenditure of general government		14								
Health	K4CP	14.1	111 520	113 850	116 360	118 656	121 786	127 580	130 178	133 265
Recreation and culture	K4CQ	14.2	6 846	6 628	6 594	6 709	5 985	5 861	5 925	5 356
Education	K4CR	14.3	55 117	55 718	56 498	57 971	59 086	59 641	62 405	63 671
Social protection	K4CS	14.4	37 904	37 789	36 877	36 546	36 168	35 979	35 199	35 031
Final individual consumption expenditure of general government	NSZK	P.31	208 601	211 501	213 967	218 262	222 841	229 143	233 707	237 323
Total, individual consumption expenditure/ actual individual consumption	YBIO	P.31 P.41	1 352 849	1 363 299	1 357 866	1 380 548	1 405 287	1 436 736	1 472 189	1 510 301

1 "Purpose" or "function" classifications are designed to indicate the "soci-economic objectives" that institutional units aim to achieve through various kinds of outlays. COICOP is the Classification of Individual Consumption by Purpose and applies to households. COPNI is the Classification of the Purposes of Non-profit Institutions Serving Households and COFOG is the Classification of the Functions of Government
2 Package holidays data are dispersed between components (transport etc).

6.3.1 Non profit making institutions serving households
ESA 2010 sector S.15, not seasonally adjusted

£ million

			2009	2010	2011	2012	2013	2014	2015
Production account		I							
Resources									
Output		P.1							
Market output	CRRW	P.11	15 632	15 046	15 526	15 586	17 071	17 413	18 762
Output for own final use	CRRY	P.12	6 373	6 533	6 422	6 915	7 151	6 582	7 111
Other non-market output	CRSA	P.13	55 701	56 669	58 724	59 991	59 444	61 363	63 065
Total	CRRU	P.1	77 706	78 248	80 672	82 492	83 666	85 358	88 938
Total resources	CRRU	TR	77 706	78 248	80 672	82 492	83 666	85 358	88 938
Uses									
Intermediate consumption	CRSC	P.2	32 513	31 596	34 203	37 188	36 933	37 682	39 131
Gross value added	HAZX	**B.1g**	45 193	46 652	46 469	45 304	46 733	47 676	49 807
Total uses	CRRU	TU	77 706	78 248	80 672	82 492	83 666	85 358	88 938
Gross value added	HAZX	**B.1g**	45 193	46 652	46 469	45 304	46 733	47 676	49 807
less consumption of fixed capital	HACB	P.51c	7 222	7 586	8 186	8 062	9 054	9 398	9 619
Value added, net	HAZY	B.1n	37 971	39 066	38 283	37 242	37 679	38 278	40 188

249

6.3.2 Non profit making organisations serving households
ESA 2010 sector S.15

£ million

			2009	2010	2011	2012	2013	2014	2015
Distribution and use of income accounts		II							
Primary distribution of income account		II.1							
Generation of income account before deduction of fixed capital consumption		II.1.1							
Resources									
Total resources (gross value added)	HAZX	**B.1g**	45 193	46 652	46 469	45 304	46 733	47 676	49 807
Uses									
Compensation of employees		D.1							
Wages and salaries	HAAH	D.11	31 315	32 012	31 544	30 398	30 717	31 389	32 881
Employers' social contributions	HAAI	D.12	6 495	6 847	6 563	6 673	6 855	6 743	7 145
Total	HAAG	D.1	37 810	38 859	38 107	37 071	37 572	38 132	40 026
Taxes on production and imports, paid		D.2							
Production taxes other than on products	QYQM	D.29	162	205	176	158	107	146	162
less subsidies received		D.3							
Production subsidies other than on products	HAAN	D.39	–	–	–	–	–	–	–
Operating surplus, gross	HABV	B.2g	7 221	7 588	8 186	8 075	9 054	9 398	9 619
Total uses (gross value added)	HAZX	**B.1g**	45 193	46 652	46 469	45 304	46 733	47 676	49 807
less consumption of fixed capital[1]	HACB	P.51c	7 222	7 586	8 186	8 062	9 054	9 398	9 619
Operating surplus, net	HAZZ	B.2n	−1	2	–	13	–	–	–

1 Consumption of fixed capital is made up of
   P.51c1 - Consumption of fixed capital on gross operating surplus
   plus P.51c2 - Consumption of fixed capital on gross mixed income

6.3.3 Non profit making institutions serving households
ESA 2010 sector S.15

			2009	2010	2011	2012	2013	2014	2015	2016
Allocation of primary income account		II.1.2								
before deduction of fixed capital consumption										
Resources										
Gross operating surplus and gross mixed income		B.2g+B.3g								
Operating surplus, gross	HABV	B.2g	7 221	7 588	8 186	8 075	9 054	9 398	9 619	9 865
Property income, received		D.4								
Interest		D.41								
Interest before FISIM[1] allocation	I69Q	D.41g	766	487	493	486	470	409	408	501
plus FISIM	TGQB	P.119	89	214	257	229	184	409	451	440
Total	HAAP	D.41	855	701	750	715	654	818	859	941
Distributed income of corporations		D.42								
Dividends	C3ZU	D.421	2 050	2 082	2 314	2 284	2 254	2 245	2 205	4 073
Total	CPMA	D.42	2 050	2 082	2 314	2 284	2 254	2 245	2 205	4 073
Other investment income		D.44								
Attributable to insurance policy holders	KZL8	D.441	52	34	35	31	40	49	23	23
Attributable to collective investment fund shareholders		D.443								
Dividends	M8K9	D.4431	112	159	61	75	82	69	82	106
Retained earnings	M8LB	D.4432	175	249	94	116	128	109	128	168
Total	L5V4	D.443	287	408	155	191	210	178	210	274
Total	HAAU	D.44	339	442	190	222	250	227	233	297
Rent	M8OQ	D.45	58	99	90	90	123	140	155	185
Total	HAAO	D.4	3 302	3 324	3 344	3 311	3 281	3 430	3 452	5 496
Total resources	HACQ	TR	10 523	10 912	11 530	11 386	12 335	12 828	13 071	15 361
Uses										
Property income, paid		D.4								
Interest		D.41								
Interest before FISIM[1] allocation	I69Z	D.41g	892	817	802	824	823	782	780	783
less FISIM	TGPQ	P.119	259	180	184	187	203	167	146	157
Interest	HADC	D.41	633	637	618	637	620	615	634	626
Rent	M8QZ	D.45	–	–	–	–	–	–	–	–
Total	HADB	D.4	633	637	618	637	620	615	634	626
Balance of primary incomes, gross	HACC	**B.5g**	9 890	10 275	10 912	10 749	11 715	12 213	12 437	14 735
Total uses	HACQ	TU	10 523	10 912	11 530	11 386	12 335	12 828	13 071	15 361
less consumption of fixed capital	HACB	P.51c	7 222	7 586	8 186	8 062	9 054	9 398	9 619	9 865
Balance of net primary income	HACC	B.5n	9 890	10 275	10 912	10 749	11 715	12 213	12 437	14 735
Sector share of gross national income	ADSY		0.7	0.7	0.7	0.6	0.7	0.7	0.7	0.8

1 Financial intermediation services indirectly measured

6.3.4 Non-profit making institutions serving households
ESA 2010 sector S.15

£ million

			2009	2010	2011	2012	2013	2014	2015	2016
Secondary distribution of income account		**II.2**								
Resources										
Balance of primary incomes, gross	HACC	**B.5g**	9 890	10 275	10 912	10 749	11 715	12 213	12 437	14 735
Social contributions and benefits		D.6								
Employers' imputed social contributions	L8RR	D.612	397	319	282	271	279	321	337	314
Total	L8U6	D.61	397	319	282	271	279	321	337	314
Other current transfers		D.7								
Non-life insurance claims	HABS	D.72	345	438	427	413	445	384	392	390
Miscellaneous current transfers	HABT	D.75	52 252	54 471	51 187	52 300	49 957	49 285	49 596	50 647
Total	HABP	D.7	52 597	54 909	51 614	52 713	50 402	49 669	49 988	51 037
Total resources	HAXL	TR	62 884	65 503	62 808	63 733	62 396	62 203	62 762	66 086
Uses										
Current taxes on income, wealth, etc		D.5								
Taxes on income	M8YS	D.51	–	–	–	–	–	–	–	–
Other current taxes	UFIH	D.59	234	245	281	320	342	363	384	395
Total	HAAW	D.5	234	245	281	320	342	363	384	395
Social benefits other than social transfers in kind		D.62								
Other social insurance benefits	L8SH	D.622	397	319	282	271	279	321	337	314
Total	RVFI	D.62	397	319	282	271	279	321	337	314
Other current transfers		D.7								
Net non-life insurance premiums	HABR	D.71	345	438	427	413	445	384	392	390
Miscellaneous current transfers	EAXO	D.75	3 245	1 291	1 908	1 956	1 239	1 238	1 278	1 330
Total	HADT	D.7	3 590	1 729	2 335	2 369	1 684	1 622	1 670	1 720
Gross disposable income	HAAJ	**B.6g**	58 663	63 210	59 910	60 773	60 091	59 897	60 371	63 657
Total uses	HAXL	TU	62 884	65 503	62 808	63 733	62 396	62 203	62 762	66 086

1 Gross household disposable income deflated by the households and NPISH final consumption deflator

6.3.5 Non-profit making institutions serving households
ESA 2010 sector S.15

£ million

			2009	2010	2011	2012	2013	2014	2015	2016
Redistribution of income in kind account		II.3								
Resources										
Households' gross disposable income	HAAJ	**B.6g**	58 663	63 210	59 910	60 773	60 091	59 897	60 371	63 657
Total resources	HAAJ	TR	58 663	63 210	59 910	60 773	60 091	59 897	60 371	63 657
Uses										
Social transfers in kind	M8YY	D.63	50 684	51 276	53 647	53 664	54 428	56 625	56 614	57 005
Social transfers in kind - non-market production	RVFL	D.631	50 684	51 276	53 647	53 664	54 428	56 625	56 614	57 005
Households' adjusted gross disposable income	HABX	B.7g	7 979	11 934	6 263	7 109	5 663	3 272	3 757	6 652
Total uses	HAAJ	TU	58 663	63 210	59 910	60 773	60 091	59 897	60 371	63 657

6.3.6 Non-profit making institutions serving households
ESA 2010 sector S.15

£ million

			2009	2010	2011	2012	2013	2014	2015	2016
Use of income account		II.4								
Use of disposable income account		II.4.1								
Resources										
Total resources, gross disposable income	HAAJ	B.6g	58 663	63 210	59 910	60 773	60 091	59 897	60 371	63 657
Uses										
Final consumption expenditure		P.3								
Individual consumption expenditure	ABNV	P.31	50 684	51 276	53 647	53 664	54 428	56 625	56 614	57 005
Gross saving	HAZI	**B.8g**	7 979	11 934	6 263	7 109	5 663	3 272	3 757	6 652
Total uses	HAAJ	TU	58 663	63 210	59 910	60 773	60 091	59 897	60 371	63 657
less consumption of fixed capital	HACB	P.51c	7 222	7 586	8 186	8 062	9 054	9 398	9 619	9 865
Net saving	HAAE	B.8n	757	4 348	−1 923	−953	−3 391	−6 126	−5 862	−3 213
Use of adjusted disposable income account		II.4.2								
Resources										
Households' adjusted disposable income, gross	HABX	B.7g	7 979	11 934	6 263	7 109	5 663	3 272	3 757	6 652
Uses										
Gross saving	HAZI	B.8g	7 979	11 934	6 263	7 109	5 663	3 272	3 757	6 652
Total uses	HABX	TU	7 979	11 934	6 263	7 109	5 663	3 272	3 757	6 652

6.3.7 Non-profit making institutions serving households
ESA 2010 sector S.15

£ million

			2009	2010	2011	2012	2013	2014	2015	2016
Accumulation accounts		III								
Capital account		III.1								
Change in net worth due to saving and capital transfers account		III.1.1								
Changes in liabilities and net worth										
Gross saving	HAZI	**B.8g**	7 979	11 934	6 263	7 109	5 663	3 272	3 757	6 652
Capital transfers, receivable		D.9r								
Investment grants	HABZ	D.92r	7 714	8 493	5 868	5 707	5 560	6 508	7 841	7 688
Other capital transfers	IZXY	D.99r	2 955	2 236	2 625	3 123	2 600	2 433	2 604	2 729
Total	HABW	D.9r	10 669	10 729	8 493	8 830	8 160	8 941	10 445	10 417
less capital transfers, payable		D.9p								
Capital taxes	ACBB	D.91p	–	–	–	–	–	–	–	–
Other capital transfers	ACBE	D.99p	–	1	32	97	206	518	22	284
Total	CRXD	D.9p	–	1	32	97	206	518	22	284
Changes in net worth due to gross saving and capital transfers	HABU	B.101g	18 648	22 662	14 724	15 842	13 617	11 695	14 180	16 785
Changes in assets										
Gross capital formation		P.5								
Gross fixed capital formation	ABV8	P.51g	9 814	10 190	10 505	11 316	12 204	12 633	13 205	13 609
Changes in inventories	HACO	P.52	−29	9	3	3	7	21	10	–
Acquisitions less disposals of valuables[1]	NPPX	P.53	426	57	−8	−106	899	−360	−354	−46
Total	EP8C	P.5	10 211	10 256	10 500	11 213	13 110	12 294	12 861	13 563
Acquisitions less disposals of non-produced non-financial assets	HACD	NP	208	208	208	208	208	208	208	208
Net lending(+) / net borrowing(-)	AA7W	**B.9n**	8 229	12 198	4 016	4 421	299	−807	1 111	3 014
Total change in assets	HABU	B.101g	18 648	22 662	14 724	15 842	13 617	11 695	14 180	16 785

1 Acquisitions less disposals of valuables can be a volatile series but any
  volatility is likely to be GDP neutral as it is offset in UK trade figures

6.3.8 Non-profit making institutions serving households
ESA 2010 sector S.15, not seasonally adjusted

£ million

			2009	2010	2011	2012	2013	2014	2015	2016
Financial account		III.2								
Net acquisition of financial assets		F.A								
Currency and deposits		F.2								
Currency	NCEX	F.21	587	−735	−253	922	374	536	901	1 207
Transferable deposits		F.22								
Deposits with UK MFIs[1]	NCEZ	F.22N1	889	139	457	667	788	701	448	1 045
Of which: foreign currency deposits with UK MFIs[1]	NCFB	F.22N12	−417	−55	70	142	199	218	35	111
Deposits with rest of the world MFIs[1]	NCFD	F.22N9	–	–	–	–	–	–	–	–
Other deposits	NCFE	F.29	40	−296	−198	612	−612	−216	88	20
Total	NCEW	F.2	1 516	−892	6	2 201	550	1 021	1 437	2 272
Debt securities		F.3								
Short-term		F.31								
Issued by UK central government	NCFH	F.31N1	−1	–	−1	−1	1	−1	−2	3
Issued by UK local government	NCFL	F.31N2	–	–	–	–	–	–	–	–
Issued by UK MFIs[1]	NCFM	F.31N5	60	30	269	−1 902	215	87	−305	886
MMIs issued by other UK residents[2]	NCFR	F.31N6	−41	−64	−12	−22	34	2	−31	−2
MMIs issued by the rest of the world	NCIW	F.31N9	–	–	–	–	–	–	–	–
Long-term		F.32								
Issued by UK central government	NCFU	F.32N1	359	216	148	407	197	392	155	295
Issued by UK local government	NCFX	F.32N2	9	54	211	−32	380	1 022	−1 193	806
Issued by UK MFIs and other UK residents[1,3]	KV2X	F.32N5-6	−307	72	−22	−468	1 156	−758	−598	−213
Bonds issued by rest of the world	NCGC	F.32N9	581	248	−620	−322	−61	740	−473	177
Total	NCFF	F.3	660	556	−27	−2 340	1 922	1 484	−2 447	1 952
Loans		F.4								
Long-term		F.42								
By UK residents[4]	NCGX	F.424N1	–	–	–	–	–	–	–	–
Total	NCGH	F.4	–	–	–	–	–	–	–	–
Equity and investment fund shares/units		F.5								
Equity		F.51								
Listed UK shares[3]	NCHE	F.511N1	441	80	19	15	71	−86	116	−640
Unlisted UK shares[3]	NCHF	F.512N1	−797	−44	52	74	−49	−303	−594	−1 408
Other equity		F.519								
Other UK equity	NCHG	F.519N6	–	–	–	–	–	–	–	–
UK shares and bonds issued by other UK residents[3]	NSPF	F.519N7	–	–	–	–	–	–	–	–
Shares and other equity issued by rest of the world	NCHJ	F.519N9	−3 396	3 947	12 158	−5 285	−7 168	2 837	11 342	−1 640
Investment fund shares/units		F.52								
UK mutual funds' shares	NCHN	F.52N1	−141	−1 857	175	1 856	−641	407	2 121	1 954
Rest of the world mutual funds' shares	NCHO	F.52N9	–	–	–	–	–	–	–	–
Total	NCGZ	F.5	−3 893	2 126	12 404	−3 340	−7 787	2 855	12 985	−1 734
Insurance, pensions and standardised guarantee schemes		F.6								
Non-life insurance technical reserves	NCHS	F.61	−120	−124	−9	42	−20	–	−31	9
Life insurance and annuity entitlements	M9WH	F.62	–	–	–	–	–	–	–	–
Pension schemes[5]	MA2J	F.6M	–	–	–	–	–	–	–	–
Total	NPWF	F.6	−120	−124	−9	42	−20	–	−31	9
Financial derivatives and employee stock options	MN5X	F.7	2 206	506	−295	−292	369	−149	−556	−562
Of which: financial derivatives	NCGD	F.71	2 206	506	−295	−292	369	−149	−556	−562
Other accounts receivable	NCHT	F.8	702	−983	−40	1 501	756	1 193	1 661	1 998
Total net acquisition of financial assets	NCES	F.A	1 071	1 189	12 039	−2 228	−4 210	6 404	13 049	3 935

6.3.8 Non-profit making institutions serving households
ESA 2010 sector S.15, not seasonally adjusted

continued

£ million

			2009	2010	2011	2012	2013	2014	2015	2016
Financial account		**III.2**								
Net acquisition of financial liabilities		**F.L**								
Debt securities		F.3								
MMIs issued by other UK residents	NCIV	F.31N6	−676	203	531	−50	404	516	57	11
Bonds issued by UK MFIs and other UK residents[1,3]	KV2S	F.32N5-6	184	−27	–	20	44	254	314	–
Total	NCIJ	F.3	−492	176	531	−30	448	770	371	11
Loans		F.4								
Short-term		F.41								
By UK MFIs[1]	NCJN	F.41N1	719	201	270	−283	−284	301	139	−185
Of which foreign currency loans by UK banks	NCJP	F.41N12	−14	14	−7	10	−31	15	−13	−10
By rest of the world	ZMFM	F.41N9	10	89	1 672	−117	−604	594	−5	1 010
Long-term[6]		F.42								
Secured on dwellings	NCJW	F.422	–	–	–	–	–	–	–	–
By UK residents	NCKB	F.424N1	−423	45	−62	−644	89	−226	−538	610
Total	NCJL	F.4	306	335	1 880	−1 044	−799	669	−404	1 435
Pension schemes[5]	MA2Z	F.6M	432	514	649	583	631	617	602	647
Other accounts payable	NCKX	F.8	502	−86	80	814	−62	248	669	778
Total net acquisition of financial liabilities	NCHW	**F.L**	748	939	3 140	323	218	2 304	1 238	2 871
Net lending(+) / net borrowing(-)		**B.9**								
Total net acquisition of financial assets	NCES	F.A	1 071	1 189	12 039	−2 228	−4 210	6 404	13 049	3 935
less total net acquisition of financial liabilities	NCHW	F.L	748	939	3 140	323	218	2 304	1 238	2 871
Net lending(+) / borrowing(-) from the financial account	NYNW	B.9f	322	249	8 900	−2 551	−4 428	4 101	11 812	1 064
Statistical discrepancy between the financial and non-financial accounts	NYPH	dB.9	7 907	11 949	−4 884	6 972	4 727	−4 908	−10 701	1 950
Net lending(+) / net borrowing(-)	AA7W	**B.9n**	8 229	12 198	4 016	4 421	299	−807	1 111	3 014

1 Monetary financial institutions
2 Money market instruments
3 Prior to 1990, it is not possible to distinguish some elements of F.32N5-6, F.511N1 and F.512N1. These elements are shown combined as F.519N7
4 Other than direct investment loans, loans secured on dwellings and loans for finance leasing
5 F.63 pension entitlements, F.64 Claims on pension fund on pension managers, F.65 to non-pension benefits
6 All loans secured on dwellings and all finance leasing are treated as long term loans

6.3.11 Non-profit making institutions serving households
ESA 2010 sectors S.15 Unconsolidated

£ billion

Financial balance sheet at end of period		IV.3	2009	2010	2011	2012	2013	2014	2015	2016
Non-financial assets	E45Z	AN	86.3	89.1	85.3	81.5	82.1	86.3	98.9	103.8
Total financial assets		AF.A								
Currency and deposits		AF.2								
Currency	NJKU	AF.21	8.6	7.9	7.6	8.5	8.9	9.5	10.4	11.6
Transferable deposits		AF.22								
Deposits with UK MFIs[1]	NJKW	AF.22N1	17.7	18.2	18.3	18.3	21.3	23.2	24.0	25.7
Of which: foreign currency deposits with UK MFIs[1]	NJKY	AF.22N12	0.9	0.8	0.9	1.0	1.2	1.4	1.4	1.8
Deposits with rest of the world MFIs[1]	NJLA	AF.22N9	–	–	–	–	–	–	–	–
Other deposits	NJLB	AF.29	0.8	0.5	0.3	1.0	0.3	0.1	0.2	0.2
Total	NJKT	AF.2	27.2	26.6	26.3	27.8	30.6	32.8	34.6	37.5
Debt securities		AF.3								
Short-term		AF.31								
Issued by UK central government	NJLE	AF.31N1	–	–	–	–	–	–	–	0.004
Issued by UK local government	NIMC	AF.31N2	–	–	–	–	–	–	–	–
Issued by UK MFIs[1]	NJLJ	AF.31N5	2.1	1.8	1.0	1.1	1.6	1.8	2.6	3.5
MMIs[2] issued by other UK residents	NJLO	AF.31N6	0.1	0.1	0.1	–	0.1	0.1	0.1	0.1
MMIs issued by the rest of the world	NJLP	AF.31N9	–	–	–	–	–	–	–	–
Long-term		AF.32								
Issued by UK central government	NJLR	AF.32N1	3.9	3.3	3.1	3.7	3.4	4.0	3.7	3.5
Issued by UK local government	NJLU	AF.32N2	0.2	0.2	0.1	0.1	0.3	0.1	0.1	0.3
Issued by UK MFIs and other UK residents[1,3]	KV2W	AF.32N5-6	2.2	2.4	2.0	1.6	2.3	2.3	2.1	2.7
Bonds issued by rest of the world	NJLZ	AF.32N9	1.2	1.5	0.8	0.4	0.4	1.3	0.9	1.0
Total	NJLC	AF.3	9.8	9.2	7.1	7.0	8.0	9.5	9.5	11.2
Loans		AF.4								
Long-term		AF.42								
Other long-term loans by UK residents[4]	NJMU	AF.424N1	–	–	–	–	–	–	–	–
Total	NJME	AF.4	–	–	–	–	–	–	–	–
Equity and investment fund shares/units		AF.5								
Equity		AF.51								
Listed UK shares[3]	NJNB	AF.511N1	11.4	14.9	12.4	10.0	15.8	21.9	28.5	34.4
Unlisted UK shares[3]	NJNC	AF.512N1	15.9	19.9	16.8	10.1	14.5	23.4	29.7	37.0
Other equity		AF.519								
Other UK equity	NJND	AF.519N6	–	–	–	–	–	–	–	–
UK shares and bonds issued by other UK residents[3]	NSOF	AF.519N7	–	–	–	–	–	–	–	–
Shares and other equity issued by rest of the world	NJNG	AF.519N9	22.9	26.4	37.8	34.0	31.1	35.2	47.1	54.5
Investment fund shares/units		AF.52								
UK mutual funds' shares	NJNK	AF.52N1	16.3	12.6	13.0	16.7	15.4	16.2	20.4	24.3
Rest of the world mutual funds' shares	NJNL	AF.52N9	–	–	–	–	–	–	–	–
Total	NJMW	AF.5	66.5	73.9	80.0	70.7	76.8	96.7	125.7	150.2
Insurance, pensions and standardised guarantee schemes		AF.6								
Non-life insurance technical reserves	NJNP	AF.61	0.6	0.6	0.6	0.6	0.6	0.6	0.6	0.6
Life insurance and annuity entitlements	M9RY	AF.62	–	–	–	–	–	–	–	–
Pension schemes[5]	M9VF	AF.6M	–	–	–	–	–	–	–	–
Total	NPXV	AF.6	0.6	0.6	0.6	0.6	0.6	0.6	0.6	0.6
Financial derivatives and employee stock options	MMW7	AF.7	–	–	–	0.1	0.4	0.5	0.2	0.2
Of which: financial derivatives	NJMA	AF.71	–	–	–	0.1	0.4	0.5	0.2	0.2
Other accounts receivable	NJNQ	AF.8	8.2	7.2	7.1	8.6	9.4	10.6	12.3	14.2
Total financial assets	NJKP	**AF.A**	112.2	117.5	121.1	114.8	125.7	150.7	182.9	214.0

6.3.11 Non-profit making institutions serving households
ESA 2010 sectors S.15 Unconsolidated

£ billion

			2009	2010	2011	2012	2013	2014	2015	2016
Financial balance sheet at end of period		IV.3								
Total financial liabilities		**AF.L**								
Debt securities		AF.3								
Short-term MMIs by other UK residents	NJOS	AF.31N6	0.4	0.5	0.5	0.5	0.8	1.3	1.6	1.8
Long-term bonds issued by UK MFIs and other UK residents[1,3]	KV2V	AF.32N5-6	0.9	0.8	0.9	0.9	0.9	1.2	1.4	1.5
Total	NJOG	AF.3	1.3	1.3	1.4	1.4	1.7	2.5	3.0	3.3
Loans		AF.4								
Short-term		AF.41								
By UK MFIs[1]	NJPK	AF.41N1	9.5	9.3	9.6	9.3	8.6	8.8	8.9	8.7
Of which: Foreign currency loans by UK banks	NJPM	AF.41N12	0.1	0.1	0.1	0.1	–	0.1	0.1	0.1
By rest of the world MFIs	ZMFA	AF.41N9	3.2	3.3	5.2	6.5	6.2	6.1	6.1	8.2
Long-term loans[6]		AF.42								
Secured on dwellings	NJPT	AF.422	–	–	–	–	–	–	–	–
By UK residents	NJPY	AF.424N1	6.3	6.2	6.3	6.9	6.8	7.1	7.6	8.2
Total	NJPI	AF.4	19.0	18.8	21.1	22.7	21.6	22.0	22.6	25.1
Pension schemes[5]	M9VV	AF.6M	29.5	28.0	45.5	32.8	24.2	44.3	40.5	44.4
Financial derivatives and employee stock options	MMZ3	AF.7	–	–	–	0.2	0.3	0.1	0.3	0.4
Of which: financial derivatives	NJPE	AF.71	–	–	–	0.2	0.3	0.1	0.3	0.4
Other accounts payable	NJQU	AF.8	10.1	10.0	10.1	11.1	11.0	11.3	12.1	13.1
Total financial liabilities	NJNT	**AF.L**	59.9	58.2	78.1	68.2	58.7	80.1	78.5	86.3
Financial net worth		**BF.90**								
Total financial assets	NJKP	AF.A	112.2	117.5	121.1	114.8	125.7	150.7	182.9	214.0
less total financial liabilities	NJNT	AF.L	59.9	58.2	78.1	68.2	58.7	80.1	78.5	86.3
Financial net worth	NYOO	**BF.90**	52.3	59.3	43.1	46.7	67.0	70.6	104.4	127.7

1 Monetary financial institutions
2 Money market instruments

3 Prior to 1990 it is not possible to distinguish some elements of
AF.32N5-6, AF.511N1 and AF.512N1. These elements are shown combined
as AF.519N7
4 Other than direct investment loans, loans secured on dwellings
and loans for finance leasing
5 AF.63 Pension entitlements, AF.64 Claims on pension funds on pension
managers, AF.65 to non-pension benefits
6 All loans secured on dwellings and all finance leasing are treated as
long-term loans
7 Reflects Housing Association reclassification in line with revisions policy
back to 2005q1

United Kingdom National Accounts

The Blue Book
Chapter 07: Rest of the World

2017 edition

Editors: Dean Goodway & Sarah Nightingale

Office for National Statistics

Chapter 7: Rest of the world

The rest of the world sector includes all those institutions or individuals not resident in the UK that have economic interactions with resident units. It can include overseas corporations, charities, governments or private individuals. The sector also includes foreign embassies and consulates on UK soil.

Further information on sector classifications and classification decisions can be found in Economic statistics classifications.

7.1.0 Rest of the world
ESA 2010 sector S.2

£ million

			2009	2010	2011	2012	2013	2014	2015	2016
External account of goods and services		V.I								
Resources										
Imports of goods and services		P.7								
Imports of goods	LQBL	P.71	315 521	367 376	402 950	410 308	421 952	420 428	407 396	437 458
Imports of services	KTMR	P.72	117 581	119 540	121 083	124 111	133 328	135 328	142 135	153 028
Of which: imports of FISIM[1]	C6F7	P72F	2 516	2 345	2 268	2 260	2 465	2 416	2 238	2 388
Total resources, total imports	KTMX	P.7	433 102	486 916	524 033	534 419	555 280	555 756	549 531	590 486
Uses										
Exports of goods and services		P.6								
Exports of goods	LQAD	P.61	229 107	270 196	308 171	301 621	302 169	297 306	288 770	302 067
Exports of services	KTMQ	P.62	170 542	175 552	190 691	199 434	217 744	221 619	228 391	245 406
Of which: exports of FISIM[1]	C6FD	P.62F	5 843	8 129	7 930	7 399	8 405	7 110	7 103	8 289
Total exports	KTMW	P.6	399 649	445 748	498 862	501 055	519 913	518 925	517 161	547 473
External balance of goods and services	KTMY	**B.11**	−33 453	−41 168	−25 171	−33 364	−35 367	−36 831	−32 370	−43 013
Total uses, total imports	KTMX	P.7	433 102	486 916	524 033	534 419	555 280	555 756	549 531	590 486

1 Financial intermediation services indirectly measured

7.1.2 Rest of the world
ESA 2010 sector S.2

			2009	2010	2011	2012	2013	2014	2015	2016
External account of primary and secondary incomes		V.II								
Resources										
External balance of goods and services	KTMY	**B.11**	−33 453	−41 168	−25 171	−33 364	−35 367	−36 831	−32 370	−43 013
Compensation of employees		D.1								
Wages and salaries	KTMO	D.11	1 435	1 486	1 294	1 272	1 420	1 551	1 384	1 735
Taxes on production and imports, received		D.2								
Taxes on products		D.21								
Taxes and duties on imports excluding VAT		D.212								
Import duties	FJWE	D.2121	2 645	2 933	2 925	2 885	2 914	2 949	3 077	3 318
Taxes on imports excluding VAT and duties	FJWF	D.2122	−	−	−	−	−	−	−	−
Taxes on products excluding VAT and import duties	FJWG	D.214	10	12	12	13	12	11	10	9
Total	FJWB	D.2	2 655	2 945	2 937	2 898	2 926	2 960	3 087	3 327
less subsidies, paid		D.3								
Subsidies on products	FJWJ	D.31	−	−	−	−	−	−	−	−
Other subsidies on production	NHQR	D.39	3 411	3 059	3 166	2 625	2 455	2 306	1 961	2 431
Total	FJWI	D.3	3 411	3 059	3 166	2 625	2 455	2 306	1 961	2 431
Property income, received		D.4								
Interest		D.41								
Interest before FISIM[1] allocation	I69V	D.41g	125 377	111 399	117 344	109 272	100 996	92 123	82 260	88 358
FISIM[1]	IV8F	P.119	−1 562	646	3 916	2 577	1 506	1 170	1 466	1 120
Total	QYNG	D.41	123 815	112 045	121 260	111 849	102 502	93 293	83 726	89 478
Distributed income of corporations	QYNH	D.42	55 896	55 196	73 983	76 233	74 410	78 786	81 394	80 088
Reinvested earnings on foreign direct investment	QYNI	D.43	6 878	4 839	−2 368	−885	14 791	4 997	7 354	11 577
Other investment income		D.44								
Attributable to insurance policy holders	KZM4	D.441	1 454	1 032	1 144	1 287	1 629	2 054	1 076	944
Payable on pension entitlements	KZM5	D.442	−	−	−	−	−	−	−	−
Attributable to collective investment fund shareholders		D.443								
Dividends	KZM6	D.4431	8	16	8	8	8	8	9	12
Retained earnings	KZM7	D.4432	11	23	11	8	13	16	16	17
Total	L5VA	D.443	19	39	19	16	21	24	25	29
Total	NHRM	D.44	1 473	1 071	1 163	1 303	1 650	2 078	1 101	973
Rent	MC25	D.45	−	−	−	−	−	−	−	−
Total	HMBO	D.4	188 062	173 151	194 038	188 500	193 353	179 154	173 575	182 116
Current taxes on income, wealth etc		D.5								
Taxes on income	FJWM	D.51	565	1 068	746	640	565	476	726	728
Net social contributions		D.61								
Employers' actual social contributions	L8NN	D.611	−	−	−	−	−	−	−	−
Households' actual social contributions	L8PN	D.613	−	−	−	−	−	−	−	−
Total	FJWN	D.61	−	−	−	−	−	−	−	−
Social benefits other than social transfers in kind		D.62								
Social security benefits in cash	L8QJ	D.621	2 048	2 160	2 287	2 285	2 477	2 582	2 679	2 780
Other social insurance benefits	L8QX	D.622	−	−	−	−	−	−	−	−
Social assistance benefits in cash	RNNF	D.623	51	−	−	−	−	−	−	−
Total	FJKO	D.62	2 099	2 160	2 287	2 285	2 477	2 582	2 679	2 780
Other current transfers		D.7								
Net non-life insurance premiums	FJKS	D.71	77	345	197	711	3 433	3 082	2 249	2 969
Non-life insurance claims	NHRR	D.72	7 463	8 352	7 505	9 082	9 758	8 746	9 195	9 144
Current international cooperation	FJWT	D.74	5 021	5 668	6 274	6 122	8 060	7 198	6 823	7 620
Miscellaneous current transfers	FJWU	D.75	5 336	5 539	5 744	5 947	6 150	6 320	6 462	6 647
VAT and GNI based EU own resources	M9LD	D.76	6 756	10 026	10 011	10 472	12 791	11 734	11 592	10 439
Total	FJWR	D.7	24 653	29 930	29 731	32 334	40 192	37 080	36 321	36 819
Adjustment for the change in pension entitlement	QZEP	D.8	−	−	−	−	−	−	−	−
Total resources	NSUK	TR	249 511	248 849	253 038	258 668	273 845	258 328	248 181	268 087

1 Financial intermediation services indirectly measured

7.1.2 Rest of the world
ESA 2010 sector S.2

continued

£ million

			2009	2010	2011	2012	2013	2014	2015	2016
External account of primary incomes and secondary incomes		V.II								
Uses										
Compensation of employees		D.1								
Wages and salaries	KTMN	D.11	1 176	1 097	1 121	1 124	1 094	1 082	1 295	1 376
Taxes on production and imports, paid		D.2								
Taxes on products		D.21								
Taxes and duties on imports excluding VAT		D.212								
Import duties	FJVQ	D.2121	–	–	–	–	–	–	–	–
Taxes on imports excluding VAT and duties	FJVR	D.2122	–	–	–	–	–	–	–	–
Taxes on products excluding VAT and import duties	FJVS	D.214	–	–	–	–	–	–	–	–
Total	FJVN	D.21	–	–	–	–	–	–	–	–
Total	FJVM	D.2	–	–	–	–	–	–	–	–
Property income, paid		D.4								
Interest		D.41								
Interest before FISIM[1] allocation	I6A6	D.41g	91 122	71 807	81 166	67 928	60 325	53 376	53 018	59 280
FISIM	IV8E	P.119	–4 889	–5 139	–1 746	–2 562	–4 521	–3 691	–3 457	–4 781
Total	QYNJ	D.41	86 233	66 668	79 420	65 366	55 804	49 685	49 561	54 499
Distributed income of corporations	QYNK	D.42	77 156	76 646	89 515	82 806	89 305	103 594	79 018	80 524
Reinvested earnings on foreign direct investment	QYNL	D.43	10 986	27 569	29 564	20 517	9 835	–13 463	505	–5 307
Other investment income		D.44								
Attributable to collective investment fund shareholders		D.443								
Dividends	MN7D	D.4431	649	1 412	792	959	1 097	1 033	1 081	1 263
Retained earnings	MN7H	D.4432	1 013	2 205	1 238	1 501	1 718	1 614	1 688	1 975
Total	MN79	D.443	1 662	3 617	2 030	2 460	2 815	2 647	2 769	3 238
Total	MNQ9	D.44	1 662	3 617	2 030	2 460	2 815	2 647	2 769	3 238
Total	HMBN	D.4	176 037	174 500	200 529	171 149	157 759	142 463	131 853	132 954
Current taxes on income, wealth etc		D.5								
Taxes on income	NHRS	D.51	622	557	466	435	495	531	479	600
Net social contributions		D.61								
Households' actual social contributions	L8PV	D.613	61	29	25	23	19	15	11	14
Other current transfers		D.7								
Net non-life insurance premiums	NHRX	D.71	7 463	8 352	7 505	9 082	9 758	8 746	9 195	9 144
Non-life insurance claims	FJTT	D.72	77	345	197	711	3 433	3 082	2 249	2 969
Current international cooperation	FJWA	D.74	208	223	–87	172	137	150	60	157
Miscellaneous current transfers	NHSI	D.75	4 101	4 056	4 387	4 387	4 112	4 219	4 894	5 418
Total	NHRW	D.7	11 849	12 976	12 002	14 352	17 440	16 197	16 398	17 688
Current external balance	HBOG	**B.12**	–59 766	–59 690	–38 895	–71 585	–97 038	–98 040	–98 145	–115 455
Total uses	NSUK	TU	249 511	248 849	253 038	258 668	273 845	258 328	248 181	268 087

1 Financial intermediation services indirectly measured

7.1.7 Rest of the World
ESA 2010 sector S.2

£ million

			2009	2010	2011	2012	2013	2014	2015	2016
Accumulation accounts		V.III								
Capital account		V.III.1								
Changes in liabilities and net worth										
Current external balance	HBOG	**B.12**	−59 766	−59 690	−38 895	−71 585	−97 038	−98 040	−98 145	−115 455
Capital transfers, receivable		D.9r								
Investment grants	NHSA	D.92r	415	1 000	883	911	1 233	2 068	1 433	1 249
Other capital transfers	NHSB	D.99r	570	975	1 099	768	1 084	1 180	1 251	1 014
Total	NHRZ	D.9r	985	1 975	1 982	1 679	2 317	3 248	2 684	2 263
Capital transfers, payable		D.9p								
Investment grants	NHQQ	D.92p	855	1 197	1 022	729	917	1 621	915	759
Other capital transfers	NHQS	D.99p	−	−	−	−	−	−	−	−
Total	NHSC	D.9	855	1 197	1 022	729	917	1 621	915	759
Changes in net worth due to current external balance and capital transfers	NHSD	B.101g	59 896	60 468	39 855	72 535	98 438	99 667	99 914	116 959
Changes in assets										
Acquisitions less disposals of non-produced non-financial assets	NHSG	NP	373	53	196	361	219	−300	−209	160
Net lending(+) / net borrowing(-)	NHRB	**B.9n**	**59 523**	**60 415**	**39 659**	**72 174**	**98 219**	**99 967**	**100 123**	**116 799**
Total change in assets	NHSD	B.101g	59 896	60 468	39 855	72 535	98 438	99 667	99 914	116 959

7.1.8 Rest of the world
ESA 2010 sector S.2 Unconsolidated

£ million

			2009	2010	2011	2012	2013	2014	2015	2016
Financial account		III.2								
Net acquisition of financial assets		F.A								
Monetary gold and special drawing rights		F.1								
Monetary gold	NEWK	F.11	–	–	–	–	–	–	–	–
Special drawing rights	M98B	F.12	8 654	–	–	–	–	–	–	–
Total	NEWJ	F.1	8 654	–	–	–	–	–	–	–
Currency and deposits		F.2								
Currency	NEWN	F.21	−133	51	17	71	63	81	228	286
Transferable deposits		F.22								
Deposits with UK MFIs[1]	NEWP	F.22N1	−374 019	62 153	74 701	−118 926	−277 373	−8 739	−122 026	20 124
Of which: foreign currency deposits with UK banks	NFAS	F.22N12	−315 252	90 035	124 469	−161 294	−254 510	2 713	−145 395	15 741
Other deposits	NEWU	F.29	201	293	566	−519	−835	770	425	724
Total	NEWM	F.2	−373 951	62 497	75 284	−119 374	−278 145	−7 888	−121 373	21 134
Debt securities		F.3								
Short-term		F.31								
Issued by UK central government	NEWX	F.31N1	573	8 301	4 146	−9 219	−7 828	11 933	13 519	4 970
Issued by UK MFIs[1]	NEXC	F.31N5	85 991	−67 546	−78 416	8 753	−11 043	16 920	−6 214	6 469
MMIs issued by other UK residents[2]	NEXH	F.31N6	−5 420	3 306	3 644	−1 837	1 782	10	133	2 512
Long-term		F.32								
Issued by UK central government	NEXK	F.32N1	22 653	78 970	42 190	33 602	42 527	−2 139	57 103	42 848
Issued by UK local government	NEXN	F.32N2	–	–	–	–	–	–	–	–
Issued by UK MFIs and other UK residents[1,4]	KV3C	F.32N5-6	70 870	108 560	78 632	−110 861	50 639	21 275	−7 795	33 301
Total	NEWV	F.3	174 667	131 591	50 196	−79 562	76 077	47 999	56 746	90 100
Loans		F.4								
Short-term		F.41								
By rest of the world MFIs[1]	NEYD	F.41N91	−35 654	40 749	66 987	4 491	−26 325	38 717	7 330	34 212
Other short-term loans by rest of the world	ZMDZ	F.41N92	−25 054	57 850	−101 285	16 065	−6 760	67 687	−186 731	−78 675
Long-term		F.42								
Direct investment		F.421								
Outward direct investment	NEYG	F.421N1	−41 310	−668	−15 907	−1 250	1 057	12 409	9 273	27 411
Inward direct investment	NEYH	F.421N2	6 410	−5 615	10 819	999	−2 047	5 812	−4 460	−2 409
By rest of the world	QYLT	F.424N9	−17 279	−741	−137	25	2 173	3 334	5 583	561
Total	NEXX	F.4	−112 887	91 575	−39 523	20 330	−31 902	127 959	−169 005	−18 900
Equity and investment fund shares/units		F.5								
Equity		F.51								
Listed UK shares[4]	NEYU	F.511N1	27 856	8 675	273	4 789	35 115	13 352	49 630	−77 039
Unlisted UK shares[4]	NEYV	F.512N1	40 112	26 502	10 973	32 651	37 363	22 264	34 840	140 552
Other UK equity		F.519								
Other UK equity	NEYW	F.519N6	52	54	873	333	338	306	–	723
UK shares and bonds issued by other UK residents[4]	NSPR	F.519N7	–	–	–	–	–	–	–	–
Investment fund shares/units		F.52								
UK mutual funds' shares	NEZD	F.52N1	35	44	9	11	27	51	91	59
Total	NEYP	F.5	68 055	35 275	12 128	37 784	72 843	35 973	84 561	64 295
Insurance, pensions and standardised guarantee schemes		F.6								
Non-life insurance technical reserves	NEZI	F.61	−1 722	−3 904	−307	3 074	−389	1	−594	179
Life insurance and annuity entitlements	M9WI	F.62	39	33	49	6	−129	−231	1 002	820
Pension schemes[3]	MA2K	F.6M	–	–	–	–	–	–	–	–
Total	NPWP	F.6	−1 683	−3 871	−258	3 080	−518	−230	408	999
Financial derivatives and employee stock options	MN5Y	F.7	3	3	3	3	3	3	3	4
Of which: financial derivatives	JWC2	F.71	–	–	–	–	–	–	–	–
Other accounts receivable	NEZJ	F.8	108	814	305	373	1 172	1 626	1 085	−25
Total net acquisition of financial assets	NEWI	F.A	−237 034	317 884	98 135	−137 366	−160 470	205 442	−147 575	157 607

7.1.8 Rest of the world
ESA 2010 sector S.2 Unconsolidated

£ million

			2009	2010	2011	2012	2013	2014	2015	2016
Financial account		III.2								
Net acquisition of financial liabilities		F.L								
Monetary gold and special drawing rights		F.1								
Monetary gold	MT5R	F.11	–	–	–	–	–	–	–	–
Special drawing rights	M98A	F.12	8 522	18	333	111	43	–14	55	–1 397
Total	M9MJ	F.1	8 522	18	333	111	43	–14	55	–1 397
Currency and deposits		F.2								
Currency	NEZR	F.21	–61	–139	–84	41	41	133	–23	291
Transferable deposits		F.22								
Deposits with rest of the world MFIs[1]	NEZX	F.22N9	–221 243	195 833	97 393	–190 596	–226 660	52 758	–120 279	111 903
Total	NEZQ	F.2	–221 304	195 694	97 309	–190 555	–226 619	52 891	–120 302	112 194
Debt securities		F.3								
Short-term MMIs		F.31								
Issued by rest of the world[2]	NFAM	F.31N9	9 765	–9 467	–2 745	4 781	–22 284	5 688	3 642	–19 494
Long-term		F.32								
Bonds issued by rest of the world	NFAW	F.32N9	31 918	922	–44 862	37 576	–26 634	54 813	9 640	–92 162
Total	NEZZ	F.3	41 683	–8 545	–47 607	42 357	–48 918	60 501	13 282	–111 656
Loans		F.4								
Short-term		F.41								
By UK MFIs[1]	NFBD	F.41N1	–117 400	17 089	14 039	–33 938	–14 960	42 270	6 612	37 106
Of which: foreign currency loans by UK banks	NFBF	F.41N12	–98 828	15 333	12 975	–25 980	–18 750	33 059	–797	13 460
Long-term		F.42								
Direct investment		F.421								
Outward direct investment loans	NFBK	F.421N1	–36 313	–21 964	–13 577	–7 663	7 923	1 453	–31 795	13 237
Inward direct investment loans	NFBL	F.421N2	–10 059	5 312	6 205	–4 192	1 658	9 013	7 467	18 490
Finance leasing	NFBQ	F.423	–	–	–	–	–	–	–	–
Other long-term loans		F.424								
By UK residents	NSRT	F.424N1	33 887	49 884	–5 232	–44 486	–6 418	–14 278	8 214	6 125
Total	NFBB	F.4	–129 885	50 321	1 435	–90 279	–11 797	38 458	–9 502	74 958
Equity and investment fund shares/units		F.5								
Equity		F.51								
Shares and other equity issued by rest of the world	NFCD	F.519N9	22 685	26 353	–1 853	65 314	–8 875	–62 459	–43 059	–60 226
Investment fund shares/units		F.52								
Rest of the world mutual funds' shares	NFCI	F.52N9	9 021	26 256	13 167	18 911	10 190	7 485	6 164	2 910
Total	NFBT	F.5	31 706	52 609	11 314	84 225	1 315	–54 974	–36 895	–57 316
Insurance, pensions and standardised guarantee schemes		F.6								
Pension schemes[3]	MA32	F.6M	–	–	–	–	–	–	–	–
Total	M9W4	F.6	–	–	–	–	–	–	–	–
Financial derivatives and employee stock options	MN6K	F.7	–29 192	–44 894	4 493	–41 632	40 712	19 088	–84 238	21 619
Of which: financial derivatives	NSUL	F.71	–29 194	–44 896	4 491	–41 634	40 710	19 086	–84 240	21 616
Other accounts payable	NFCN	F.8	462	–2	839	–171	111	–413	–867	–357
Total net acquisition of financial liabilities	NEZM	F.L	–298 008	245 201	68 116	–195 944	–245 153	115 537	–238 467	38 045
Net lending(+) / net borrowing(-)		B.9								
Total net acquisition of financial assets	NEWI	F.A	–237 034	317 884	98 135	–137 366	–160 470	205 442	–147 575	157 607
less total net acquisition of financial liabilities	NEZM	F.L	–298 008	245 201	68 116	–195 944	–245 153	115 537	–238 467	38 045
Net lending(+) / borrowing(-) from the financial account	NYOD	B.9f	60 974	72 683	30 019	58 578	84 683	89 905	90 892	119 562
Statistical discrepancy between the financial and non-financial accounts	NYPO	dB.9	–1 451	–12 268	9 640	13 596	13 536	10 062	9 231	–2 763
Net lending (+) / borrowing (-) from non-financial accounts	NHRB	B.9n	**59 523**	**60 415**	**39 659**	**72 174**	**98 219**	**99 967**	**100 123**	**116 799**

1 Monetary financial institutions
2 Money market instruments
3 F.63 Pension entitlements, F.64 Claims of pension funds on pension
  managers, F.65 Entitlements to non-pension benefits
4 Prior to 1990, it is not possible to distinguish some elements of F.32N5-6,
  F.511N1 and F.512N1. These elements are shown combined as F.519N7

7.1.9 Rest of the world
ESA 2010 sector S.2

£ million

			2013	2014	2015	2016
Other changes in assets account		**III.3**				
Other changes in volume of assets account		**III.3.1**				
Changes in net worth due to other changes in volume of assets		**B.102**				
Monetary gold and special drawing rights	M9K6	AF.1	–	–	–	–
Currency and deposits	M9QX	AF.2	3 988	1 012	–26 927	–23 101
Debt securities	N47X	AF.3	4 670	34 871	–11 481	24 198
Loans	N49Z	AF.4	–25 292	11 016	42 556	105 444
Equity and investment fund shares/units	N4C3	AF.5	–	–	–	–
Insurance, pensions and standardised guarantee schemes	N4E3	AF.6	–	–	–	–
Financial derivatives and employee stock options	N4FZ	AF.7	–	–	–	–
Other accounts receivable/payable	N4HZ	AF.8	897	7 225	–6 247	–3 243
Total	CWU4	**B.102**	–15 737	54 124	–2 099	103 298

7.1.10 Rest of the world
ESA 2010 sector S.2

£ million

			2013	2014	2015	2016
Other changes in assets account		III.3				
Revaluation account		III.3.2				
Changes in net worth due to nominal holding gains and losses		B.103				
Monetary gold and special drawing rights	M9LU	AF.1	2 931	−468	587	−1 844
Currency and deposits	M9YV	AF.2	−6 182	36 333	25 496	19 847
Debt securities	N48Y	AF.3	−210 976	22 522	5 638	−147 632
Loans	N4B2	AF.4	20 481	−87 015	−11 059	−181 289
Equity and investment fund shares/units	N4D4	AF.5	−33 375	−54 648	−173 238	−230 681
Insurance, pensions and standardised guarantee schemes	N4F2	AF.6	816	1 002	342	−4 433
Financial derivatives and employee stock options	N4GY	AF.7	−6 385	23 000	1 620	−2 177
Other accounts receivable/payable	N4J2	AF.8	−2	101	107	−704
Total	CWUT	**B.103**	−232 692	−59 173	−150 507	−548 913

7.1.11 Rest of the world
ESA 2010 sector S.2 Unconsolidated

£ billion

Financial balance sheet at end of period		IV.3	2009	2010	2011	2012	2013	2014	2015	2016
Total financial assets		**AF.A**								
Special drawing rights	M98E	AF.12	9.8	10.1	10.1	9.6	9.4	9.4	9.5	11.1
Currency and deposits		AF.2								
Currency	NLCW	AF.21	1.4	1.4	1.5	1.5	1.6	1.7	1.9	2.2
Transferable deposits		AF.22								
Deposits with UK MFIs[1]	NLCY	AF.22N1	2 926.3	3 018.6	3 224.5	2 977.0	2 688.0	2 678.2	2 542.4	2 915.2
Of which: foreign currency deposits with UK MFIs[1]	NLDA	AF.22N12	2 425.1	2 534.9	2 796.3	2 511.8	2 256.8	2 258.5	2 101.0	2 465.8
Other deposits	NLDD	AF.29	1.0	1.3	1.9	1.4	0.5	1.3	1.7	2.5
Total	NLCV	AF.2	2 928.7	3 021.4	3 227.9	2 979.9	2 690.2	2 681.2	2 546.0	2 919.8
Debt securities		AF.3								
Short-term		AF.31								
Issued by UK central government	NLDG	AF.31N1	19.4	27.9	31.8	22.5	15.1	27.2	40.0	44.5
Issued by UK MFIs[1]	NLDL	AF.31N5	267.8	205.0	124.1	128.7	117.6	130.5	125.7	148.9
MMIs issued by other UK residents[2]	NLDQ	AF.31N6	21.5	25.4	29.5	26.4	27.6	29.2	30.8	39.4
Long-term		AF.32								
Issued by UK central government	NLDT	AF.32N1	235.5	323.5	407.2	438.1	432.7	421.7	467.6	542.8
Issued by UK local government	NLDW	AF.32N2	–	–	–	–	–	–	–	–
Issued by UK MFIs[1,4] and other UK residents	KV39	AF.32N5-6	1 088.9	1 088.3	1 155.8	1 117.7	988.3	1 078.8	1 070.5	1 102.3
Total	NLDE	AF.3	1 633.1	1 670.1	1 748.3	1 733.4	1 581.2	1 687.3	1 734.6	1 877.8
Loans		AF.4								
Short-term		AF.41								
By rest of the world MFIs[1]	NLEM	AF.41N91	438.7	479.1	542.8	564.4	549.2	545.2	554.7	651.5
Other short-term loans by rest of the world	ZMEA	AF.41N92	294.3	354.0	252.6	265.0	248.7	312.1	126.2	104.9
Long-term		AF.42								
Direct investment		AF.421								
Outward direct investment loans	NLEP	AF.421N1	191.0	206.8	181.9	260.7	252.7	237.3	256.4	266.6
Inward direct investment loans	NLEQ	AF.421N2	146.4	134.7	160.5	209.1	199.9	194.1	163.0	142.8
Other long-term loans		AF.429								
By rest of the world	NLEX	AF.429N9	47.5	44.4	42.8	45.2	57.3	40.2	36.6	38.9
Total	NLEG	AF.4	1 117.9	1 219.0	1 180.6	1 344.3	1 307.7	1 329.0	1 136.9	1 204.6
Equity and investment fund shares/units		AF.5								
Equity		AF.51								
Listed UK shares[4]	NLFD	AF.511N1	742.2	852.2	841.4	981.6	1 122.1	1 137.2	1 170.9	1 199.2
Unlisted UK shares[4]	NLFE	AF.512N1	575.8	620.3	658.5	812.6	837.7	933.3	900.3	1 102.1
Other equity										
Other UK equity	NLFF	AF.519N6	8.6	9.5	10.2	10.6	11.1	12.3	13.1	14.4
UK shares and bonds issued by other UK residents[2,4]	NSOP	AF.519N7	–	–	–	–	–	–	–	–
Investment fund shares/units		AF.52								
UK mutual funds' shares	NLFM	AF.52N1	1.3	1.6	1.3	1.4	1.8	2.1	2.3	2.5
Total	NLEY	AF.5	1 327.9	1 483.6	1 511.4	1 806.1	1 972.8	2 085.0	2 086.6	2 318.2
Insurance, pensions and standardised guarantee schemes		AF.6								
Non-life insurance technical reserves	NLFR	AF.61	8.8	9.1	8.8	11.8	11.4	11.4	10.8	11.0
Life insurance and annuity entitlements	M9RZ	AF.62	5.0	3.9	3.5	7.9	8.6	9.4	10.7	7.1
Pension schemes[3]	M9VG	AF.6M	–	–	–	–	–	–	–	–
Total	NPYF	AF.6	13.8	12.9	12.3	19.8	20.0	20.8	21.6	18.1
Financial derivatives and employee stock options	MMW8	AF.7	2 096.8	2 895.0	3 554.9	3 032.2	2 376.7	2 806.4	2 391.4	2 607.4
Of which: financial derivatives	J8XN	AF.71	2 096.8	2 895.0	3 554.9	3 032.2	2 376.7	2 806.4	2 391.4	2 607.4
Other accounts receivable	NLFS	AF.8	2.6	3.5	3.8	4.1	5.9	7.6	8.7	8.9
Total financial assets	NLEF	**AF.A**	9 130.6	10 315.7	11 249.2	10 929.4	9 964.0	10 626.7	9 935.3	10 966.0

7.1.11 Rest of the world
ESA 2010 sector S.2 Unconsolidated

continued

£ billion

			2009	2010	2011	2012	2013	2014	2015	2016
Financial balance sheet at end of period		IV.3								
Total financial liabilities		**AF.L**								
Monetary gold and special drawing rights		AF.1								
Monetary gold	MT5Q	AF.11	–	–	–	–	–	–	–	–
Special drawing rights	M98D	AF.12	8.9	9.1	9.4	9.1	9.0	9.0	9.1	8.9
Total	M9ML	AF.1	8.9	9.1	9.4	9.1	9.0	9.0	9.1	8.9
Currency and deposits		AF.2								
Currency	NLGA	AF.21	0.8	0.7	0.6	0.6	0.6	0.8	0.8	0.9
Transferable deposits		AF.22								
Deposits with rest of the world MFIs[1]	NLGG	AF.22N9	2 302.8	2 483.9	2 743.5	2 500.7	2 264.7	2 279.1	2 146.4	2 614.3
Total	NLFZ	AF.2	2 303.6	2 484.6	2 744.1	2 501.3	2 265.3	2 279.8	2 147.1	2 615.3
Debt securities		AF.3								
Short-term		AF.31								
MMIs issued by rest of the world[2]	NLGV	AF.31N9	117.9	113.8	107.0	107.2	82.2	89.3	96.7	95.2
Long-term		AF.32								
Bonds issued by rest of the world	NLHF	AF.32N9	886.8	907.8	890.8	931.5	885.7	939.8	942.0	1 008.4
Total	NLGI	AF.3	1 004.7	1 021.6	997.8	1 038.7	967.9	1 029.1	1 038.7	1 103.6
Loans		AF.4								
Short-term		AF.41								
By UK MFIs[1]	NLHM	AF.41N1	903.5	971.2	1 001.6	923.0	895.6	932.5	921.0	1 097.1
Of which: foreign currency loans by UK banks	NLHO	AF.41N12	806.9	867.9	895.3	824.1	796.7	826.7	809.5	962.2
Long-term loans		AF.42								
Direct investment		AF.421								
Outward direct investment loans	NLHT	AF.421N1	193.5	190.5	163.3	214.5	217.7	226.9	180.8	186.5
Inward direct investment loans	NLHU	AF.421N2	56.5	59.0	63.6	77.4	94.1	73.1	68.8	66.9
Finance leasing	NLHZ	AF.423	–	–	–	–	–	–	–	–
Other long-term loans										
By UK residents	NROS	AF.424N1	374.2	439.4	430.6	423.2	418.9	401.7	399.5	457.0
Total	NLHK	AF.4	1 527.8	1 660.2	1 659.0	1 638.1	1 626.4	1 634.2	1 570.1	1 807.5
Equity and investment fund shares/units		AF.5								
Equity		AF.51								
Shares and other equity issued by rest of the world	NLIM	AF.519N9	1 730.6	1 878.6	1 817.0	1 922.9	2 033.5	2 112.9	2 138.4	2 444.3
Investment fund shares/units		AF.52								
Rest of the world mutual funds' shares	NLIR	AF.52N9	119.1	156.5	169.4	209.8	227.8	224.3	252.2	287.0
Total	NLIC	AF.5	1 849.7	2 035.1	1 986.4	2 132.8	2 261.3	2 337.2	2 390.6	2 731.3
Insurance pensions and standardised guarantees		AF.6								
Pension schemes[3]	M9VW	AF.6M	–	–	–	–	–	–	–	–
Total	M9RN	AF.6	–	–	–	–	–	–	–	–
Financial derivatives and employee stock options	MMZ4	AF.7	2 176.4	2 963.0	3 638.2	3 093.7	2 485.3	2 911.0	2 410.1	2 649.9
Of which: financial derivatives	NLEC	AF.71	2 176.4	2 962.9	3 638.2	3 093.6	2 485.3	2 911.0	2 410.1	2 649.9
Other accounts payable	NLIW	AF.8	9.7	8.8	13.2	17.5	17.4	9.7	15.0	18.9
Total financial liabilities	NLHJ	**AF.L**	8 880.8	10 182.4	11 048.2	10 431.3	9 632.6	10 209.9	9 580.8	10 935.4
Financial net worth		**BF.90**								
Total financial assets	NLEF	AF.A	9 130.6	10 315.7	11 249.2	10 929.4	9 964.0	10 626.7	9 935.3	10 966.0
less total liabilities	NLHJ	AF.L	8 880.8	10 182.4	11 048.2	10 431.3	9 632.6	10 209.9	9 580.8	10 935.4
Financial net worth	NLFK	**BF.90**	249.8	133.3	201.0	498.1	331.5	416.8	354.5	30.6

1 Monetary financial institutions
2 Money marker instruments
3 AF.63 Pension entitlements, AF.64 Claims on pension funds on pension managers, AF.65 Entitlements to non-pension benefits

4 Prior to 1990 it is not possible to distinguish some elements of AF.32N5-6, AF.511N1 and AF.512N1. These elements are shown combined as AF.519N7

United Kingdom National Accounts

The Blue Book

Chapter 08: Gross Fixed Capital Formation Supplementary Tables

2017 edition

Editors: Dean Goodway & Sarah Nightingale

Office for National Statistics

Chapter 8: Gross fixed capital formation supplementary tables

Gross fixed capital formation (GFCF) is the estimate of net capital expenditure (acquisitions less the proceeds from disposals) on fixed assets by both the public and private sectors. Fixed assets are purchased assets used in production processes for more than one year.

Examples of capital expenditure include: spending on machinery and equipment, transport equipment, software, artistic originals, new dwellings and major improvements to dwellings, other buildings and major improvements to buildings, and structures such as roads. Additional assets consisting of research and development and military weapons systems were introduced into the definition of GFCF in the UK National Accounts, The Blue Book 2014.

Following a quality review after Blue Book 2016, it was identified that the methodology used to estimate elements of purchased software within GFCF had led to some double-counting from 1997 onwards. This issue has now been resolved and has reduced the level of GFCF across the period by around 1.1% per year. The average impact on quarter-on-quarter GFCF growth is negative 0.02% and the average impact on quarter-on-quarter gross domestic product (GDP) growth is 0.00%.

In Blue Book 2017, we have also introduced a number of other methodology changes to the estimates of GFCF and business investment. These include:

- the final integration of the new GFCF estimation system, first used for the Quarter 4 (Oct to Dec) 2016 provisional publication

- changes to methodology affecting the transfer costs asset, including:

  - the addition of transfer costs associated with the buying and selling of players in the sports industries, that is, club and agents' fees and any taxes associated with the buying and selling of players from one sports club to another; it is important to distinguish this from the transfer fee itself (that is, the monies paid from one sports club (the buyer) to another sports club (the seller))

  - the inclusion of Office for National Statistics's (ONS's) updated House Price Index methodology, used by GFCF in part for the calculation of current price transfer costs data

  - a new method to estimate the breakdown of transfer costs by institutional sector, replacing the previous method, which was based on historical proportions

- the separation of households and non-profit institutions serving households within Blue Book, as elsewhere in the UK National Accounts; this is in line with recommendations in the European System of National Accounts: ESA 2010 (Eurostat, 2013), which requires their presentation as separate entities

- reclassification of private registered providers of social housing (PRPs) in England, following a review in October 2015, which concluded that PRPs are public, market producers and should be reclassified to the public non-financial corporations' sector for the purpose of national accounts and our other economic statistics; this has impacted sectoral estimates of GFCF for public corporations and private non-financial corporations but not total GFCF

- additionally, new data has been introduced for investment in aircraft, which is included in transport equipment

Detailed explanations of these changes can be found in the Annual improvements to gross fixed capital formation source data for Blue Book 2017 article published on 16 February 2017.

8.1 Gross fixed capital formation at current purchasers' prices[1]
Analysis by type of asset and sector

Total economy

£ million

			2009	2010	2011	2012	2013	2014	2015	2016
Dwellings, excluding land		AN.111								
Public non-financial corporations	L5YQ	S.11001	8 024	7 721	7 246	6 640	6 357	7 617	7 523	7 698
Private non-financial corporations	L5YR	S.11PR	4 547	5 170	5 786	6 167	7 713	8 419	9 542	7 494
Financial corporations	L5YS	S.12	–	–	–	–	–	–	–	–
Central government	L5YT	S.1311	1	−5	−8	115	–	–	–	53
Local government	L5YU	S.1313	–	–	–	–	–	–	–	–
Households	CRGO	S.14	33 957	35 983	38 722	38 645	42 484	47 659	50 377	55 959
NPISH[2]	CRGP	S.15	38	40	44	43	48	54	58	96
Total	DFDK	S.1	46 567	48 909	51 790	51 611	56 601	63 750	67 501	71 300
Other buildings and structures		AN.112								
Public non-financial corporations	DEES	S.11001	1 907	1 957	1 710	1 449	1 339	1 519	1 399	1 243
Private non-financial corporations	L5YW	S.11PR	33 193	31 909	37 234	44 386	47 312	46 674	50 673	50 275
Financial corporations	L5YX	S.12	1 060	1 015	1 061	1 232	877	1 056	1 271	1 503
Central government	L5YY	S.1311	16 270	14 013	12 527	13 197	13 553	16 202	15 214	15 273
Local government	L5YZ	S.1313	14 103	13 539	14 129	13 062	11 917	12 245	12 879	13 486
Households	CRGQ	S.14	350	336	391	467	497	492	461	460
NPISH	CRGR	S.15	1 398	1 344	1 566	1 869	1 992	1 965	1 844	1 840
Total	DLWS	S.1	68 280	64 115	68 619	75 662	77 490	80 152	83 740	84 077
Transport equipment		AN.1131								
Public non-financial corporations	DEEP	S.11001	340	196	156	510	461	400	552	628
Private non-financial corporations	L5Z4	S.11PR	8 929	12 312	7 639	9 295	10 275	14 212	18 539	21 701
Financial corporations	L5Z5	S.12	6	59	90	41	29	609	1 433	1 806
Central government	L5Z6	S.1311	73	163	76	34	32	39	35	35
Local government	L5Z7	S.1313	532	539	526	426	406	428	442	464
Households	CRGS	S.14	95	130	81	98	109	149	195	228
NPISH	CRGT	S.15	376	518	321	391	433	599	781	914
Total	DLWZ	S.1	10 348	13 917	8 887	10 795	11 742	16 435	21 977	25 775
ICT[3] equipment, other machinery and equipment, cultivated biological resources, weapons[4]		AN.1132+AN.1139+ AN.115+AN.114								
Public non-financial corporations	DEEQ	S.11001	1 156	902	935	913	888	859	840	1 039
Private non-financial corporations	L5ZA	S.11PR	26 952	28 619	33 523	33 821	35 729	40 592	40 944	38 680
Financial corporations	L5ZB	S.12	1 814	2 577	3 334	4 551	3 334	2 949	3 369	3 247
Central government	L5ZC	S.1311	8 635	9 517	9 605	8 089	8 231	8 914	8 583	9 124
Local government	L5ZD	S.1313	1 583	1 633	1 426	1 268	1 197	1 267	1 311	1 375
Households	CRGU	S.14	283	301	353	356	376	426	504	474
NPISH	CRGV	S.15	1 135	1 205	1 411	1 425	1 503	1 709	2 014	1 896
Total	DLXI	S.1	41 559	44 755	50 587	50 423	51 258	56 716	57 565	55 834
Intellectual property products		AN.117								
Public non-financial corporations	DLXJ	S.11001	2 245	2 317	2 287	2 286	2 277	2 269	2 259	2 260
Private non-financial corporations	L5ZG	S.11PR	36 157	37 423	38 990	40 387	42 547	42 356	40 849	41 723
Financial corporations	L5ZH	S.12	2 704	2 772	2 852	3 098	3 101	3 325	3 204	3 130
Central government	L5ZI	S.1311	3 644	4 945	4 680	4 663	4 609	4 892	5 060	5 069
Local government	L5ZJ	S.1313	230	214	228	227	208	218	237	311
Households	CRGW	S.14	218	225	235	253	262	260	237	238
NPISH	CRGX	S.15	6 734	6 961	7 038	7 449	8 068	8 135	8 330	8 669
Total	DLXP	S.1	51 931	54 857	56 310	58 362	61 071	61 455	60 176	61 400
Costs associated with the transfer of ownership of non-produced assets		AN.116								
Public non-financial corporations	L5ZL	S.11001	590	626	496	447	522	655	687	725
Private non-financial corporations	L5ZM	S.11PR	3 543	3 608	3 922	4 670	5 724	6 338	6 234	7 045
Financial corporations	L5ZN	S.12	117	120	118	136	111	144	171	206
Central government	L5ZO	S.1311	2 892	2 708	2 272	2 283	2 423	3 043	2 896	2 623
Local government	L5ZP	S.1313	2 590	2 954	2 814	2 859	3 142	3 706	3 631	3 950
Households	CRGY	S.14	4 843	5 497	5 471	5 431	6 965	8 402	8 432	9 298
NPISH	CRGZ	S.15	133	121	125	139	159	171	179	197
Total	DFBH	S.1	14 709	15 632	15 218	15 966	19 045	22 459	22 231	24 044
Gross fixed capital formation		P.51g								
Public non-financial corporations	FCCJ	S.11001	14 262	13 718	12 831	12 245	11 844	13 319	13 260	13 593
Private non-financial corporations	FDBM	S.11PR	113 320	119 041	127 093	138 727	149 299	158 591	166 780	166 917
Financial corporations	NHCJ	S.12	5 701	6 544	7 454	9 059	7 451	8 081	9 450	9 891
Central government	NMES	S.1311	31 515	31 341	29 152	28 381	28 848	33 090	31 788	32 177
Local government	NMOA	S.1313	19 038	18 879	19 123	17 842	16 870	17 864	18 500	19 586
Households	CRHA	S.14	39 745	42 473	45 253	45 250	50 693	57 387	60 206	66 657
NPISH	CRHB	S.15	9 814	10 190	10 505	11 316	12 204	12 633	13 205	13 609
Total gross fixed capital formation	NPQX	P.51g, S1	233 395	242 186	251 411	262 820	277 209	300 965	313 189	322 430

1 Components may not sum to totals due to rounding
2 Non-profit institutions serving households
3 Information Communication Technology
4 Weapons data are central government only.

8.2 Gross fixed capital formation at current purchasers' prices[1]
Analysis by broad sector and type of asset
Total economy

£ million

			2009	2010	2011	2012	2013	2014	2015	2016
Private sector		S.1PT								
New dwellings, excluding land	L5ZQ	AN.111	38 540	41 193	44 552	44 856	50 244	56 133	59 978	63 549
Other buildings and structures	EQBU	AN.112	36 002	34 605	40 251	47 955	50 681	50 186	54 248	54 076
Transport equipment	EQBV	AN.1131	9 403	13 019	8 129	9 826	10 843	15 567	20 948	24 648
ICT[2] equipment and other machinery and equipment and cultivated biological resources	EQBW	AN.1132+AN.1139+ AN.115	30 185	32 703	38 621	40 153	40 942	45 677	46 831	44 296
Intellectual property products	EQBX	AN.117	45 813	47 381	49 114	51 185	53 977	54 077	52 620	53 759
Costs associated with the transfer of ownership of non-produced assets	L5ZR	AN.116	8 635	9 345	9 637	10 377	12 959	15 054	15 018	16 746
Total	EQBZ	P.51g, S.1PT	168 580	178 248	190 305	204 352	219 647	236 692	249 642	257 074
Public non-financial corporations		S.11001								
New dwellings, excluding land	L5YQ	AN.111	8 024	7 721	7 246	6 640	6 357	7 617	7 523	7 698
Other buildings and structures	DEES	AN.112	1 907	1 957	1 710	1 449	1 339	1 519	1 399	1 243
Transport equipment	DEEP	AN.1131	340	196	156	510	461	400	552	628
ICT equipment and other machinery and equipment and cultivated biological resources	DEEQ	AN.1132+AN.1139+ AN.115	1 156	902	935	913	888	859	840	1 039
Intellectual property products	DLXJ	AN.116	2 245	2 317	2 287	2 286	2 277	2 269	2 259	2 260
Costs associated with the transfer of ownership of non-produced assets	L5ZL	N116G	590	626	496	447	522	655	687	725
Total	FCCJ	P.51g, S.11001	14 262	13 718	12 831	12 245	11 844	13 319	13 260	13 593
General government		S.13								
New dwellings, excluding land	L5ZU	AN.111	1	−5	−8	115	–	–	–	53
Other buildings and structures	EQCH	AN.112	30 371	27 552	26 657	26 259	25 470	28 447	28 093	28 759
Transport equipment	EQCI	AN.1131	605	702	602	460	438	467	477	499
ICT equipment, other machinery and equipment, Cultivated biological resources, weapons	EQCJ	AN.1132+AN.1139+ AN.115+AN.114	10 218	11 150	11 031	9 357	9 428	10 181	9 894	10 499
Intellectual property products	EQCK	AN.117	3 874	5 159	4 908	4 890	4 817	5 110	5 297	5 380
Costs associated with the transfer of ownership of non-produced assets	L5ZV	AN.116	5 484	5 662	5 085	5 142	5 564	6 749	6 527	6 573
Total	NNBF	P.51g, S.13	50 553	50 220	48 275	46 223	45 718	50 954	50 288	51 763
Total gross fixed capital formation	NPQX	P.51g, S.1	233 395	242 186	251 411	262 820	277 209	300 965	313 189	322 430

1 Components may not sum to totals due to rounding
2 Information Communication Technology.

8.3 Gross fixed capital formation at current purchasers' prices[1]
Analysis by type of asset
Total economy

£ million

			2009	2010	2011	2012	2013	2014	2015	2016
Tangible fixed assets		AN.11								
New dwellings, excluding land	DFDK	AN.111	46 567	48 909	51 790	51 611	56 601	63 750	67 501	71 300
Other buildings and structures	DLWS	AN.112	68 280	64 115	68 619	75 662	77 490	80 152	83 740	84 077
Transport equipment	DLWZ	AN.1131	10 348	13 917	8 887	10 795	11 742	16 435	21 977	25 775
ICT[2] equipment, other machinery and equipment, cultivated biological resources, weapons[3]	DLXI	AN.1132+AN.1139+ AN.115+AN.114	41 559	44 755	50 587	50 423	51 258	56 716	57 565	55 834
Total	EQCQ	AN.11, S.1	166 754	171 696	179 884	188 492	197 093	217 051	230 783	236 985
Intellectual property products	DLXP	AN.117	51 931	54 857	56 310	58 362	61 071	61 455	60 176	61 400
Costs associated with the transfer of ownership of non-produced assets	DFBH	AN.116	14 709	15 632	15 218	15 966	19 045	22 459	22 231	24 044
Total gross fixed capital formation	NPQX	P.51g, S.1	233 395	242 186	251 411	262 820	277 209	300 965	313 189	322 430

1 Components may not sum to totals due to rounding
2 Information Communication Technology
3 Weapons data are central government only.

8.4 Gross fixed capital formation[1,2]
Chained volume measures (reference year 2015)
Total economy: Analysis by broad sector and type of asset

£ million

			2009	2010	2011	2012	2013	2014	2015	2016
Private sector		S.1PT								
New dwellings, excluding land	L62K	AN.111	43 715	46 496	49 303	47 758	51 886	56 235	59 978	62 516
Other buildings and structures	EQCU	AN.112	38 861	39 427	45 516	52 027	53 050	50 695	54 247	52 777
Transport equipment	EQCV	AN.1131	9 300	12 811	7 765	9 418	10 386	15 453	20 949	25 330
ICT[3] equipment and other machinery and equipment and cultivated biological resources	EQCW	AN.1132+AN.1139+ AN.115	32 542	34 764	40 536	41 459	42 119	47 506	46 832	42 802
Intellectual property products	EQCX	AN.117	48 606	49 820	50 725	52 514	54 689	54 511	52 620	52 899
Costs associated with the transfer of ownership of non-produced assets	L62L	AN.116	9 272	10 011	10 146	10 747	13 292	15 237	15 018	16 604
Total	EQCZ	P.51g, S.1PT	182 390	193 668	203 271	213 363	225 137	239 642	249 641	252 927
Public non-financial corporations		S.11001								
New dwellings, excluding land	L62M	AN.111	8 322	8 159	7 642	6 894	6 493	7 624	7 523	7 575
Other buildings and structures	DEEX	AN.112	2 037	2 216	1 939	1 579	1 405	1 533	1 400	1 218
Transport equipment	DEEU	AN.1131	325	189	145	480	434	394	552	655
ICT equipment and other machinery and equipment and cultivated biological resources	DEEV	AN.1132+AN.1139+ AN.115	1 257	953	973	936	902	895	840	998
Intellectual property products	EQDE	AN.117	2 096	2 170	2 151	2 176	2 161	2 241	2 260	2 273
Costs associated with the transfer of ownership of non-produced assets	L62N	AN.116	631	668	521	462	535	663	687	720
Total	EQDG	P.51g, S.11001	14 556	14 244	13 293	12 527	11 943	13 346	13 260	13 438
General government		S.13								
New dwellings, excluding land costs	L62O	AN.111	59	4	7	215	4	–	–	53
Other buildings and structures	EQDI	AN.112	34 010	31 976	30 425	28 620	26 715	28 752	28 093	28 326
Transport equipment	EQDJ	AN.1131	578	676	563	434	413	463	477	524
ICT equipment, other machinery and equipment, Cultivated biological resources, weapons	EQDK	AN.1132+AN.1139+ AN.115+AN.114	11 061	11 914	11 666	9 772	9 838	10 506	9 894	10 321
Intellectual property services	EQDL	AN.117	4 265	5 637	5 196	5 140	4 977	5 199	5 297	5 277
Costs associated with the transfer of ownership of non-produced assets	L62P	AN.116	5 870	6 048	5 341	5 320	5 705	6 830	6 526	6 520
Total	EQDN	P.51g, S.13	55 739	56 217	53 177	49 349	47 638	51 747	50 287	51 020
Total gross fixed capital formation	NPQR	P.51g	252 432	263 858	269 573	275 163	284 562	304 735	313 189	317 386

1 For the years before the reference year (2015), totals differ from the sum of
   their components
2 Components may not sum to totals due to rounding
3 Information Communication Technology.

8.5 Gross fixed capital formation[1,2]
Chained volume measures (reference year 2015)
Total economy: Analysis by type of asset

£ million

			2009	2010	2011	2012	2013	2014	2015	2016
Tangible fixed assets		AN.11								
New dwellings, excluding land	DFDV	AN.111	52 180	54 740	56 907	54 788	58 376	63 859	67 501	70 143
Other buildings and structures	EQDP	AN.112	74 796	73 527	77 840	82 223	81 179	80 982	83 740	82 321
Transport equipment	DLWJ	AN.1131	10 213	13 679	8 477	10 335	11 234	16 312	21 977	26 508
ICT[3] equipment, other machinery and equipment, cultivated biological resources, weapons[4]	DLWM	AN.1132+AN.1139+ AN.115, AN.114	44 763	47 537	53 097	52 094	52 793	58 896	57 566	54 122
Total	EQDS	AN.11, S.1	181 591	189 450	195 451	198 755	203 137	220 041	230 783	233 096
Intellectual property products	EQDT	AN.117	55 066	57 666	58 120	59 892	61 824	61 951	60 176	60 450
Costs associated with the transfer of ownership of non-produced assets	DFDW	AN.116	15 776	16 731	16 008	16 529	19 531	22 730	22 231	23 842
Total gross fixed capital formation	NPQR	P.51g, S.1	252 432	263 858	269 573	275 163	284 562	304 735	313 189	317 386

1 For the years before the reference year (2015), totals differ from the sum of
   their components
2 Components may not sum to totals due to rounding
3 Information Communication Technology
4 Weapons data are central government only.

United Kingdom National Accounts

The Blue Book
Chapter 09: National Balance Sheet

2017 edition

Editors: Dean Goodway & Sarah Nightingale

Office for National Statistics

Chapter 9: National balance sheet

The national balance sheet is a measure of the national wealth, or total net worth, of the UK. It shows the estimated market value of financial assets, for example, shares and deposits at banks and non-financial assets like dwellings and machinery. Market value is an estimate of how much these assets would sell for, if sold on the market.

The estimates are used for international comparisons, to monitor economic performance and inform monetary and fiscal policy decisions.

Financial assets and liabilities include:
- means of payment, such as currency
- financial claims, such as loans
- economic assets, which are close to financial claims in nature, such as shares

Non-financial assets include:

Produced non-financial assets:
- buildings and other structures
- machinery and equipment
- certain farming stocks, mainly dairy cattle and orchards
- intellectual property products, such as computer software and databases, and research and development
- inventories
- valuables, such as works of art and precious stones

Non-produced assets:
- contracts, leases and licences
- natural resources

Data sources include:
- Office for National Statistics's (ONS's) National Balance Sheet Survey
- Chartered Institute of Public Finance and Accountancy report on local authority assets
- annual reports of public corporations and major businesses
- industry publications
- other government departments and agencies

Where non-financial asset market valuations are not readily available, we use a proxy based on the UK net capital stocks data, modelled in the perpetual inventory method (PIM).

For central government, data are taken from returns made by government departments to HM Treasury.

Local authority housing is shown in the public non-financial corporations sector. This is because government-owned market activities are always treated as being carried out by public corporations, either in their own right or via quasi-corporations.

9.1 National balance sheet: by sector
At current prices[1]

billion at end year

			2009	2010	2011	2012	2013	2014	2015	2016
Non-financial corporations[2]										
Public[3]	CGRW	S.11001	..	..	..	..	..	..	..	..
Private[2]	TMPN	S.11002+S.11003	..	..	..	..	..	..	..	..
Total	CGRV	S.11	−89.4	−36.9	−97.4	−155.6	−4.4	−65.5	168.8	94.1
Financial corporations	CGRU	S.12	91.6	268.4	282.0	46.6	150.4	68.6	17.7	348.3
General government[3]										
Central government	CGRY	S.1311	−315.1	−422.6	−679.8	−748.2	−745.5	−945.0	−965.2	−1 201.1
Local government	CGRZ	S.1313	235.4	284.6	286.1	294.9	308.8	344.3	351.6	356.5
Total	CGRX	S.13	−79.7	−138.0	−393.7	−453.3	−436.7	−600.7	−613.6	−844.6
Households and NPISH[4]										
Households	E45V	S.14	6 771.9	7 005.3	7 376.3	7 590.1	7 904.3	8 806.6	9 222.4	9 972.2
NPISH[4]	E45W	S.15	138.7	148.4	128.3	128.1	149.0	156.9	203.3	231.5
Total	CGRC	S.14+S.15	6 910.5	7 153.8	7 504.6	7 718.3	8 053.3	8 963.5	9 425.7	10 203.6
Total net worth	CGDA	S.1	6 833.1	7 247.3	7 295.5	7 155.9	7 762.6	8 365.9	8 998.6	9 801.5

1 .. indicates that data have been suppressed in this table. This is because the institutional sector and asset breakdown of public non-financial corporations (S.11), into public non-financial corporations (S.11001) and private non-financial corporations (S.11002 and S.11003) is unavailable from the capital stocks dataset.
2 Including quasi-corporations.
3 Public sector (general government plus public non-financial corporations) is shown in table 9.13.
4 Non-profit institutions serving households.

9.2 National balance sheet: by asset
At current prices

			2011	2012	2013	2014	2015	2016
Non-financial assets								
Produced non-financial assets								
Fixed assets		AN.11						
Dwellings[1]	E46Y	AN.111	1 538.9	1 591.3	1 652.0	1 687.6	1 719.0	1 777.8
Other buildings and structures[1]		AN.112						
Buildings other than dwellings[1]	E497	AN.1121	687.3	691.3	733.2	795.9	788.4	809.3
Other structures[1]	E49R	AN.1122	715.8	782.6	808.5	819.1	883.3	931.1
Total	E47J	AN.112	1 403.1	1 473.9	1 541.7	1 615.0	1 671.6	1 740.4
Machinery, equipment and weapons systems		AN.113+114						
Transport equipment	E4AC	AN.1131	90.1	89.0	92.3	100.2	110.7	123.8
ICT equipment	MU7W	AN.1132	31.1	33.3	33.6	38.5	42.1	47.2
Other machinery, equipment and weapons systems	CGRA	AN.1139+114	538.9	550.4	560.2	564.3	582.9	624.0
Total	NG26	AN.113+114	660.1	672.6	686.1	702.9	735.7	795.0
Cultivated biological resources[1]	E4BE	AN.115	6.9	7.0	7.0	7.4	7.5	7.6
Intellectual property products	NG27	AN.117	175.1	177.4	181.4	181.3	184.2	178.6
Total	NG23	AN.11	3 784.1	3 922.2	4 068.1	4 194.2	4 318.1	4 499.4
Inventories	CGRD	AN.12	256.7	261.5	269.9	284.5	287.2	302.3
Total produced non-financial assets	NG22	AN.1	4 040.8	4 183.7	4 338.0	4 478.7	4 605.3	4 801.7
Non-produced non-financial assets								
Natural resources		AN.21						
Land	E44R	AN.211	3 443.7	3 458.0	3 746.4	4 293.7	4 738.0	5 018.2
Total	MHQ3	AN.21	3 443.7	3 458.0	3 746.4	4 293.7	4 738.0	5 018.2
Contracts, leases and licences[2]		AN.22						
Permits to undertake specific activities[2]	MHQ8	AN.223	2.2	2.3	2.4	2.5	2.7	2.9
Total	MHQ5	AN.22	2.2	2.3	2.4	2.5	2.7	2.9
Total non-produced non-financial assets	NG28	AN.2	3 445.9	3 460.2	3 748.7	4 296.2	4 740.6	5 021.1
Total non-financial assets	NG2A	AN	7 486.7	7 643.9	8 086.8	8 775.0	9 345.9	9 822.8
Financial assets and liabilities								
Financial assets								
Monetary gold and special drawing rights	NYVN	AF.1	19.2	19.3	16.3	16.7	16.2	18.3
Currency and deposits	NYVT	AF.2	6 691.3	6 724.8	6 555.6	6 252.1	6 139.7	7 006.2
Debt securities	NYWL	AF.3	2 897.5	3 007.4	2 949.7	3 321.5	3 281.6	3 632.7
Loans	NYYP	AF.4	4 809.7	4 824.9	4 778.1	4 652.0	4 646.7	5 080.9
Equity and investment fund shares/units	NYZZ	AF.5	4 206.8	4 421.6	4 751.4	4 894.8	4 972.5	5 403.9
Insurance, pension and standardised guarantee schemes	NZBF	AF.6	3 643.3	3 582.5	3 356.8	4 126.8	4 074.8	4 493.2
Financial derivatives and employee stock options	MMU5	AF.7	8 165.8	6 958.9	5 600.1	6 251.1	4 577.5	5 404.7
Other accounts receivable/payable	NZBP	AF.8	388.8	443.0	451.0	459.1	468.4	495.4
Total financial assets	NZBV	AF.A	30 822.5	29 962.3	28 458.9	29 974.0	28 177.3	31 535.3
Financial liabilities								
Monetary gold and special drawing rights	NYVO	AF.1	10.1	9.6	9.4	9.4	9.5	11.1
Currency and deposits	NYVU	AF.2	7 175.1	7 203.3	6 980.4	6 653.5	6 538.6	7 310.8
Debt securities	NYWM	AF.3	3 648.0	3 702.1	3 563.1	3 979.7	3 977.4	4 406.9
Loans	NYYQ	AF.4	4 331.3	4 531.1	4 459.4	4 346.8	4 213.5	4 478.0
Equity and investment fund shares/units	NZAA	AF.5	3 731.8	4 094.9	4 462.9	4 642.6	4 668.5	4 990.9
Insurance, pension and standardised guarantee schemes	NZBG	AF.6	3 655.5	3 582.2	3 376.8	4 147.6	4 096.4	4 511.4
Financial derivatives and employee stock options	MMW9	AF.7	8 082.5	6 897.5	5 491.5	6 146.5	4 558.7	5 362.2
Other accounts receivable/payable	NZBQ	AF.8	379.4	429.5	439.5	457.0	462.1	485.5
Total financial liabilities	NZBW	AF.L	31 013.7	30 450.2	28 783.1	30 383.0	28 524.6	31 556.6
Financial net worth	NQFT	BF.90	−191.1	−487.9	−324.2	−409.0	−347.3	−21.3
Net worth	CGDA	B.90	7 295.5	7 155.9	7 762.6	8 365.9	8 998.6	9 801.5

1 Excludes the value of the land underneath the assets.
2 Includes cherished or personalised vehicle registration plates.

9.3 Non-financial corporations
At current prices

£ billion at end year

			2011	2012	2013	2014	2015	2016
Non-financial assets								
Produced non-financial assets								
Fixed assets		AN.11						
Dwellings[1]	E46D	AN.111	190.8	197.6	205.4	212.9	219.7	226.5
Other buildings and structures[1]		AN.112						
Buildings other than dwellings[1]	E47L	AN.1121	418.2	427.1	457.1	490.1	484.0	498.8
Other structures[1]	E498	AN.1122	435.6	483.4	504.0	504.3	542.2	573.9
Total	E46Z	AN.112	853.9	910.5	961.0	994.4	1 026.2	1 072.8
Machinery and equipment		AN.113						
Transport equipment	E49U	AN.1131	56.1	53.9	52.5	54.6	60.8	69.2
ICT equipment	MU7X	AN.1132	13.7	13.9	14.2	17.6	20.2	23.7
Other machinery and equipment	CGUX	AN.1139	340.1	339.9	343.6	342.7	349.6	376.0
Total	NG2G	AN.113	409.8	407.7	410.3	414.8	430.6	469.0
Cultivated biological resources[1]	E4AM	AN.115	6.5	6.6	6.6	7.0	7.2	7.2
Intellectual property products	NG2H	AN.117	131.5	134.5	137.7	139.1	143.0	140.8
Total	NG2D	AN.11	1 592.6	1 656.9	1 721.0	1 768.3	1 826.7	1 916.3
Inventories	CGUZ	AN.12	232.0	236.6	244.6	258.4	260.9	275.5
Total produced non-financial assets	NG2C	AN.1	1 824.6	1 893.5	1 965.6	2 026.7	2 087.6	2 191.8
Non-produced non-financial assets								
Natural resources		AN.21						
Land	E43B	AN.211	675.2	651.3	712.8	857.1	914.5	933.8
Total	L683	AN.21	675.2	651.3	712.8	857.1	914.5	933.8
Total non-produced non-financial assets	L684	AN.2	675.2	651.3	712.8	857.1	914.5	933.8
Total non-financial assets	NG2I	AN	2 499.8	2 544.8	2 678.4	2 883.7	3 002.2	3 125.7
Financial assets and liabilities								
Financial assets								
Currency and deposits	NNZF	AF.2	438.5	471.3	498.6	537.0	579.1	651.1
Debt securities	NNZO	AF.3	65.6	59.6	61.3	65.1	78.3	89.9
Loans	NOME	AF.4	266.0	287.8	302.2	317.5	268.4	277.3
Equity and investment fund shares/units	NOMW	AF.5	891.1	879.6	905.3	875.0	915.1	996.6
Insurance, pension and standardised guarantee schemes	NPYN	AF.6	4.7	4.2	4.0	4.0	3.8	3.9
Financial derivatives and employee stock options	MMU6	AF.7	29.7	28.6	25.6	30.0	31.0	37.0
Other accounts receivable/payable	NONQ	AF.8	130.8	132.3	133.2	131.2	131.5	129.8
Total financial assets	NNZB	AF.A	1 826.4	1 863.4	1 930.2	1 959.8	2 007.2	2 185.7
Financial liabilities								
Currency and deposits	NONX	AF.2	–	–	–	–	–	–
Debt securities	NOOG	AF.3	343.1	359.6	371.0	358.4	347.4	391.6
Loans	NOPI	AF.4	1 172.7	1 231.4	1 194.7	1 148.3	1 149.2	1 216.5
Equity and investment fund shares/units	NOQA	AF.5	2 109.6	2 258.3	2 461.4	2 498.7	2 487.1	2 678.0
Insurance, pension and standardised guarantee schemes	NPYO	AF.6	579.7	499.2	372.7	675.5	617.6	676.3
Financial derivatives and employee stock options	MMX2	AF.7	52.0	46.8	40.6	51.5	55.4	62.3
Other accounts receivable/payable	NOQU	AF.8	166.5	168.5	172.7	176.6	183.9	192.6
Total financial liabilities	NONT	AF.L	4 423.6	4 563.9	4 613.1	4 909.0	4 840.6	5 217.3
Financial net worth	NYOM	BF.90	−2 597.2	−2 700.5	−2 682.8	−2 949.2	−2 833.4	−3 031.5
Net worth	CGRV	B.90	−97.4	−155.6	−4.4	−65.5	168.8	94.1

1 Excludes the value of the land underneath the assets.

9.4 Public non-financial corporations
At current prices[1]

			2011	2012	2013	2014	2015	2016
Non-financial assets								
Produced non-financial assets								
Fixed assets		AN.11						
Dwellings[2]	E46E	AN.111	..	..	..	..	..	..
Other buildings and structures[2]		AN.112						
Buildings other than dwellings[2]	E47M	AN.1121	..	..	..	..	..	..
Other structures[2]	E499	AN.1122	..	..	..	..	..	..
Total	E472	AN.112	..	..	..	..	..	..
Machinery and equipment		AN.113						
Transport equipment	E49V	AN.1131	..	..	..	..	..	..
ICT equipment	MU7Y	AN.1132	..	..	..	..	..	..
Other machinery and equipment	CGVJ	AN.1139	..	..	..	..	..	..
Total	NG2O	AN.113	..	..	..	..	..	..
Cultivated biological resources[2]	E4AN	AN.115	..	..	..	..	..	..
Intellectual property products	NG2P	AN.117	..	..	..	..	..	..
Total	NG2L	AN.11	..	..	..	..	..	..
Inventories	CGVL	AN.12	5.6	5.7	5.8	5.9	5.9	6.0
Total produced non-financial assets	NG2K	AN.1	..	..	..	..	..	..
Non-produced non-financial assets								
Natural resources		AN.21						
Land	E43E	AN.211	309.9	316.8	344.6	401.4	457.1	490.0
Total	E423	AN.21	309.9	316.8	344.6	401.4	457.1	490.0
Total non-produced non-financial assets	E3T5	AN.2	309.9	316.8	344.6	401.4	457.1	490.0
Total non-financial assets	NG2Q	AN	..	..	..	..	..	..
Financial assets and liabilities								
Financial assets								
Currency and deposits	NKDR	AF.2	11.8	11.6	12.7	12.5	13.5	13.4
Debt securities	NKEA	AF.3	2.3	1.5	1.4	1.4	1.4	1.4
Loans	NKFC	AF.4	1.5	1.5	1.4	1.4	1.2	1.1
Equity and investment fund shares/units	NKFU	AF.5	0.9	1.5	2.2	1.7	1.7	1.8
Insurance, pension and standardised guarantee schemes	NPYB	AF.6	–	–	–	–	–	–
Other accounts receivable/payable	NKGO	AF.8	13.9	13.4	14.6	15.3	15.5	15.6
Total financial assets	NKFB	AF.A	30.4	29.5	32.2	32.3	33.3	33.5
Financial liabilities								
Currency and deposits	NKGV	AF.2	–	–	–	–	–	–
Debt securities	NKHE	AF.3	15.1	14.0	18.6	21.4	22.8	24.0
Loans	NKIG	AF.4	56.2	55.7	53.5	54.7	55.4	57.5
Equity and investment fund shares/units	NKIY	AF.5	121.8	123.7	125.2	127.2	128.9	130.1
Insurance, pension and standardised guarantee schemes	M9VK	AF.6	–	–	–	–	–	–
Other accounts receivable/payable	NKJS	AF.8	19.0	19.0	19.9	23.3	24.3	24.6
Total financial liabilities	NKIF	AF.L	212.1	212.5	217.2	226.6	231.4	236.2
Financial net worth	NYOP	BF.90	−181.7	−183.0	−185.0	−194.3	−198.1	−202.8
Net worth	CGRW	B.90	..	..	..	..	..	..

1 .. indicates that data have been suppressed in this table. This is because
the institutional sector and asset breakdown of public non-financial
corporations (S.11), into public non-financial corporations (S.11001) and
private non-financial corporations (S.11002 and S.11003) is unavailable
from the capital stocks dataset.
2 Excludes the value of the land underneath the assets.

9.5 Private non-financial corporations
At current prices[1]

			2011	2012	2013	2014	2015	2016
Non-financial assets								
Produced non-financial assets								
Fixed assets		AN.11						
Dwellings[2]	E46F	AN.111	..	..	..	..	..	..
Other buildings and structures[2]		AN.112						
Buildings other than dwellings[2]	E47N	AN.1121	..	..	..	..	..	..
Other structures[2]	E49B	AN.1122	..	..	..	..	..	..
Total	E473	AN.112	..	..	..	..	..	..
Machinery and equipment		AN.113						
Transport equipment	E49W	AN.1131	..	..	..	..	..	..
ICT equipment	MU7Z	AN.1132	..	..	..	..	..	..
Other machinery and equipment	TMPF	AN.1139	..	..	..	..	..	..
Total	NG2W	AN.113	..	..	..	..	..	..
Cultivated biological resources[2]	E4AP	AN.115	..	..	..	..	..	..
Intellectual property products	NG2X	AN.117	..	..	..	..	..	..
Total	NG2T	AN.11	..	..	..	..	..	..
Inventories	TMPG	AN.12	226.3	230.9	238.8	252.5	255.0	269.5
Total produced non-financial assets	NG2S	AN.1	..	..	..	..	..	..
Non-produced non-financial assets								
Natural resources		AN.21						
Land	E43J	AN.211	365.3	334.5	368.1	455.7	457.4	443.8
Total	L686	AN.21	365.3	334.5	368.1	455.7	457.4	443.8
Total non-produced non-financial assets	L687	AN.2	365.3	334.5	368.1	455.7	457.4	443.8
Total non-financial assets	NG2Y	AN	..	..	..	..	..	..
Financial assets and liabilities								
Financial assets								
Currency and deposits	NKJZ	AF.2	426.7	459.7	485.9	524.5	565.6	637.7
Debt securities	NKKI	AF.3	63.3	58.2	59.9	63.7	76.9	88.5
Loans	NKWY	AF.4	264.5	286.3	300.8	316.1	267.3	276.1
Equity and investment fund shares/units	NKXQ	AF.5	890.3	878.1	903.1	873.3	913.3	994.8
Insurance, pension and standardised guarantee schemes	NPYD	AF.6	4.7	4.2	4.0	4.0	3.8	3.9
Financial derivatives and employee stock options	MMU8	AF.7	29.7	28.6	25.6	30.0	31.0	37.0
Other accounts receivable/payable	NKYK	AF.8	116.9	118.8	118.6	115.9	116.0	114.2
Total financial assets	NKWX	AF.A	1 796.0	1 833.8	1 898.0	1 927.6	1 973.9	2 152.3
Financial liabilities								
Debt securities	NKZA	AF.3	328.0	345.6	352.4	337.0	324.6	367.6
Loans	NLBC	AF.4	1 116.4	1 175.6	1 141.1	1 093.5	1 093.8	1 159.0
Equity and investment fund shares/units	NLBU	AF.5	1 987.9	2 134.6	2 336.2	2 371.5	2 358.1	2 547.9
Insurance, pension and standardised guarantee schemes	M9RJ	AF.6	579.7	499.2	372.7	675.5	617.6	676.3
Financial derivatives and employee stock options	MMX4	AF.7	52.0	46.8	40.6	51.5	55.4	62.3
Other accounts receivable/payable	NLCO	AF.8	147.5	149.5	152.8	153.3	159.6	168.0
Total financial liabilities	NLBB	AF.L	4 211.5	4 351.3	4 395.8	4 682.4	4 609.2	4 981.0
Financial net worth	NYOT	BF.90	−2 415.5	−2 517.5	−2 497.8	−2 754.9	−2 635.3	−2 828.8
Net worth	TMPN	B.90	..	..	..	..	..	..

1 .. indicates that data have been suppressed in this table. This is because
the institutional sector and asset breakdown of public non-financial
corporations (S.11), into public non-financial corporations (S.11001) and
private non-financial corporations (S.11002 and S.11003) is unavailable
from the capital stocks dataset.
2 Excludes the value of the land underneath the assets.

9.6 Financial corporations
At current prices

			2011	2012	2013	2014	2015	2016
Non-financial assets								
Produced non-financial assets								
Fixed assets		AN.11						
Dwellings[1]	E46G	AN.111	1.2	1.1	0.9	0.7	0.3	0.3
Other buildings and structures[1]		AN.112						
Buildings other than dwellings[1]	E47O	AN.1121	40.4	40.4	42.0	44.0	42.6	42.6
Other structures[1]	E49D	AN.1122	42.1	45.8	46.3	45.2	47.7	49.1
Total	E474	AN.112	82.6	86.2	88.3	89.2	90.3	91.7
Machinery and equipment		AN.113						
Transport equipment	E49Y	AN.1131	0.3	0.3	0.3	0.7	1.9	3.2
ICT equipment	MU82	AN.1132	3.1	3.9	3.9	4.7	4.6	4.7
Other machinery and equipment	CGUH	AN.1139	13.5	14.9	15.8	15.9	16.6	18.6
Total	NG36	AN.113	17.0	19.1	20.0	21.3	23.1	26.5
Cultivated biological resources[1]	E4AS	AN.115	–	–	–	–	–	–
Intellectual property products	NG37	AN.117	7.1	7.2	7.6	7.4	7.7	7.3
Total	NG33	AN.11	107.8	113.6	116.8	118.6	121.4	125.8
Inventories	CGUO	AN.12	0.4	0.4	0.4	0.5	0.5	0.6
Total produced non-financial assets	NG32	AN.1	108.2	114.0	117.3	119.0	121.9	126.4
Non-produced non-financial assets								
Natural resources		AN.21						
Land	E43K	AN.211	20.3	15.9	16.5	22.6	21.2	19.4
Total	E42E	AN.21	20.3	15.9	16.5	22.6	21.2	19.4
Total non-produced non-financial assets	E3TA	AN.2	20.3	15.9	16.5	22.6	21.2	19.4
Total non-financial assets	NG38	AN	128.5	129.9	133.8	141.7	143.2	145.8
Financial assets and liabilities								
Financial assets								
Currency and deposits	NLJD	AF.2	4 930.7	4 866.0	4 617.1	4 219.2	4 013.3	4 709.7
Debt securities	NLJM	AF.3	2 759.7	2 869.7	2 816.0	3 174.6	3 103.5	3 425.3
Loans	NLKO	AF.4	4 333.5	4 313.4	4 251.6	4 105.0	4 149.9	4 560.2
Equity and investment fund shares/units	NLLG	AF.5	2 384.3	2 605.4	2 855.2	2 930.1	2 943.1	3 213.2
Insurance, pension and standardised guarantee schemes	NPYH	AF.6	777.6	658.3	504.5	853.7	792.6	863.0
Financial derivatives and employee stock options	MMU9	AF.7	8 124.2	6 921.7	5 562.9	6 212.2	4 538.6	5 368.3
Other accounts receivable/payable	NLMA	AF.8	53.2	58.6	62.0	55.6	59.1	73.4
Total financial assets	NLIZ	AF.A	23 363.2	22 293.2	20 669.3	21 550.3	19 600.1	22 213.0
Financial liabilities								
Currency and deposits	NLMH	AF.2	7 038.5	7 068.8	6 853.9	6 509.1	6 383.4	7 137.4
Debt securities	NLMQ	AF.3	1 910.6	1 860.3	1 702.1	1 867.9	1 856.1	1 977.8
Loans	NLNS	AF.4	1 590.9	1 700.9	1 647.2	1 537.6	1 347.5	1 467.7
Equity and investment fund shares/units	NLOK	AF.5	1 622.1	1 836.6	2 001.5	2 143.9	2 181.4	2 312.9
Insurance, pension and standardised guarantee schemes	NPYI	AF.6	2 945.4	2 976.8	2 912.1	3 365.5	3 369.8	3 722.0
Financial derivatives and employee stock options	MMX5	AF.7	8 021.7	6 846.4	5 445.4	6 091.0	4 499.3	5 297.1
Other accounts receivable/payable	NLPE	AF.8	80.5	86.6	90.5	108.2	88.1	95.5
Total financial liabilities	NLMD	AF.L	23 209.7	22 376.5	20 652.7	21 623.3	19 725.6	22 010.5
Financial net worth	NYOE	BF.90	153.5	−83.3	16.6	−73.1	−125.5	202.5
Net worth	CGRU	B.90	282.0	46.6	150.4	68.6	17.7	348.3

1 Excludes the value of the land underneath the assets.

9.7 General government
At current prices

Non-financial assets			2011	2012	2013	2014	2015	2016
Produced non-financial assets								
Fixed assets		AN.11						
Dwellings[1]	E46I	AN.111	9.6	10.2	10.4	11.3	12.1	12.8
Other buildings and structures[1]		AN.112						
Buildings other than dwellings[1]	E47P	AN.1121	205.7	202.6	213.0	240.4	239.7	245.1
Other structures[1]	E49E	AN.1122	214.3	229.3	234.9	247.4	268.6	282.0
Total	E475	AN.112	420.0	431.9	447.9	487.8	508.3	527.0
Machinery, equipment and weapons systems		AN.113+114						
Transport equipment	E49Z	AN.1131	28.7	29.7	34.3	39.3	41.5	43.8
ICT equipment	MU83	AN.1132	11.2	12.3	12.3	12.2	13.1	14.0
Other machinery, equipment and weapons systems	CGVU	AN.1139+114	160.1	170.1	174.5	178.7	188.1	197.6
Total	NG3E	AN.113+114	200.0	212.1	221.0	230.1	242.6	255.5
Cultivated biological resources[1]	E4AT	AN.115	–	–	–	–	–	–
Intellectual property products	NG3F	AN.117	25.5	24.4	24.5	22.8	21.0	17.6
Total	NG3B	AN.11	655.1	678.6	703.9	752.1	784.0	812.9
Inventories	CGVW	AN.12	0.9	0.8	0.7	0.7	0.6	0.4
Total produced non-financial assets	NG3A	AN.1	656.0	679.4	704.6	752.7	784.6	813.3
Non-produced non-financial assets								
Natural resources		AN.21						
Land	E43Z	AN.211	121.1	99.8	108.0	153.8	157.4	151.5
Total	E42F	AN.21	121.1	99.8	108.0	153.8	157.4	151.5
Total non-produced non-financial assets	NG3G	AN.2	121.1	99.8	108.0	153.8	157.4	151.5
Total non-financial assets	NG3I	AN	777.1	779.2	812.7	906.5	942.0	964.8
Financial assets and liabilities								
Financial assets								
Monetary gold and special drawing rights	NIFC	AF.1	19.2	19.3	16.3	16.7	16.2	18.3
Currency and deposits	NLUT	AF.2	77.8	85.9	87.4	87.9	82.5	87.2
Debt securities	NLWC	AF.3	54.8	55.8	52.0	58.0	74.0	89.6
Loans	NLXE	AF.4	191.8	205.2	205.7	210.8	209.5	224.8
Equity and investment fund shares/units	NLXW	AF.5	179.6	213.4	195.3	200.5	186.9	181.8
Insurance, pension and standardised guarantee schemes	NPYJ	AF.6	0.7	0.7	0.7	0.7	0.6	0.6
Financial derivatives and employee stock options	MMW2	AF.7	2.7	3.3	2.9	2.1	2.1	−6.5
Other accounts receivable/payable	NLYQ	AF.8	61.3	62.6	67.2	72.2	81.4	90.7
Total financial assets	NPUP	AF.A	588.1	646.2	627.4	648.8	653.3	686.6
Financial liabilities								
Monetary gold and special drawing rights	NLYU	AF.1	10.1	9.6	9.4	9.4	9.5	11.1
Currency and deposits	NLYX	AF.2	136.6	134.5	126.5	144.4	155.3	173.4
Debt securities	NLZG	AF.3	1 392.9	1 480.8	1 488.3	1 750.9	1 770.9	2 034.1
Loans	NNKW	AF.4	82.4	91.0	93.7	97.2	104.0	107.4
Insurance, pension and standardised guarantee schemes	NNBZ	AF.6	85.0	73.4	67.7	62.3	68.6	68.7
Financial derivatives and employee stock options	MMY6	AF.7	3.3	2.4	1.3	1.1	2.2	1.7
Other accounts receivable/payable	NNMI	AF.8	48.5	86.9	89.7	90.7	98.4	99.6
Total financial liabilities	NPVQ	AF.L	1 758.8	1 878.6	1 876.8	2 156.0	2 208.9	2 495.9
Financial net worth	NYOG	BF.90	−1 170.8	−1 232.4	−1 249.4	−1 507.3	−1 555.6	−1 809.4
Net worth	CGRX	B.90	−393.7	−453.3	−436.7	−600.7	−613.6	−844.6

1 Excludes the value of the land underneath the assets.

9.8 Central government
At current prices

Non-financial assets			2011	2012	2013	2014	2015	2016
Produced non-financial assets								
Fixed assets		AN.11						
Dwellings[1]	E46K	AN.111	9.6	10.2	10.4	11.3	12.1	12.8
Other buildings and structures[1]		AN.112						
Buildings other than dwellings[1]	E47U	AN.1121	112.7	111.6	117.7	138.2	137.6	139.9
Other structures[1]	E49F	AN.1122	117.4	126.3	129.8	142.2	154.2	161.0
Total	E476	AN.112	230.1	237.8	247.6	280.5	291.8	300.9
Machinery, equipment and weapons systems		AN.113+114						
Transport equipment	E4A2	AN.1131	13.9	14.3	15.0	15.0	15.5	16.0
ICT equipment	MU84	AN.1132	0.5	0.5	0.5	0.5	0.6	0.6
Other machinery, equipment and weapons systems	CGWF	AN.1139+114	113.5	119.0	123.2	127.2	132.3	137.3
Total	NG3O	AN.113+114	127.9	133.8	138.7	142.7	148.4	153.9
Cultivated biological resources[1]	E4AU	AN.115	–	–	–	–	–	–
Intellectual property products	NG3P	AN.117	16.8	16.9	17.9	17.0	16.1	13.5
Total	NG3L	AN.11	384.4	398.7	414.6	451.5	468.4	481.1
Inventories	CGWH	AN.12	0.9	0.8	0.7	0.7	0.6	0.4
Total produced non-financial assets	NG3K	AN.1	385.3	399.5	415.3	452.2	469.0	481.5
Non-produced non-financial assets								
Natural resources		AN.21						
Land	E447	AN.211	79.4	68.6	74.6	104.5	108.2	105.5
Total	E42G	AN.21	79.4	68.6	74.6	104.5	108.2	105.5
Total non-produced non-financial assets	NG3Q	AN.2	79.4	68.6	74.6	104.5	108.2	105.5
Total non-financial assets	NG3S	AN	464.7	468.1	489.9	556.7	577.1	587.0
Financial assets and liabilities								
Financial assets								
Monetary gold and special drawing rights	NIFC	AF.1	19.2	19.3	16.3	16.7	16.2	18.3
Currency and deposits	NIFF	AF.2	49.7	51.9	56.4	55.8	46.4	51.8
Debt securities	NIFO	AF.3	52.3	52.7	47.4	51.9	67.8	85.6
Loans	NIGQ	AF.4	183.0	193.8	193.4	197.0	193.7	207.5
Equity and investment fund shares/units	NIHI	AF.5	60.0	91.7	71.2	73.0	57.3	51.5
Financial derivatives and employee stock options	MMW3	AF.7	2.7	3.3	2.9	2.1	2.1	−6.5
Other accounts receivable/payable	NIIC	AF.8	60.4	61.7	66.3	70.4	79.0	88.0
Total financial assets	NIGP	AF.A	427.5	474.3	453.8	466.9	462.5	496.2
Financial liabilities								
Monetary gold and special drawing rights	M9MM	AF.1	10.1	9.6	9.4	9.4	9.5	11.1
Currency and deposits	NIIJ	AF.2	136.6	134.5	126.5	144.4	155.3	173.4
Debt securities	NIIS	AF.3	1 391.3	1 478.5	1 485.3	1 747.4	1 766.8	2 029.7
Loans	NIJU	AF.4	10.7	9.7	10.1	10.7	15.8	15.9
Insurance, pension and standardised guarantee schemes	DM55	AF.6	–	–	–	–	–	0.041
Financial derivatives and employee stock options	MMY7	AF.7	3.3	2.4	1.3	1.1	2.2	1.7
Other accounts receivable/payable	NILG	AF.8	20.0	55.9	56.5	55.5	55.1	52.6
Total financial liabilities	NIJT	AF.L	1 572.1	1 690.6	1 689.3	1 968.6	2 004.8	2 284.2
Financial net worth	NZDZ	BF.90	−1 144.6	−1 216.3	−1 235.5	−1 501.7	−1 542.3	−1 788.1
Net worth	CGRY	B.90	−679.8	−748.2	−745.5	−945.0	−965.2	−1 201.1

1 Excludes the value of the land underneath the assets.

9.9 Local government
At current prices

£ billion at end year

			2011	2012	2013	2014	2015	2016
Non-financial assets								
Produced non-financial assets								
Fixed assets		AN.11						
Dwellings[1]	E46L	AN.111	–	–	–	–	–	–
Other buildings and structures[1]		AN.112						
Buildings other than dwellings[1]	E47V	AN.1121	93.0	91.0	95.3	102.2	102.1	105.1
Other structures[1]	E49G	AN.1122	96.9	103.0	105.1	105.2	114.4	121.0
Total	E477	AN.112	189.9	194.0	200.4	207.4	216.5	226.1
Machinery and equipment		AN.113						
Transport equipment	E4A3	AN.1131	14.8	15.4	19.3	24.2	26.0	27.9
ICT equipment	MU85	AN.1132	10.7	11.8	11.7	11.7	12.5	13.4
Other machinery and equipment	CGWQ	AN.1139	46.6	51.1	51.3	51.5	55.7	60.3
Total	NG3Y	AN.113	72.1	78.3	82.4	87.4	94.2	101.6
Cultivated biological resources[1]	E4AV	AN.115	–	–	–	–	–	–
Intellectual property products	NG3Z	AN.117	8.7	7.5	6.6	5.8	4.9	4.1
Total	NG3V	AN.11	270.7	279.9	289.3	300.6	315.6	331.8
Inventories	CGWS	AN.12	–	–	–	–	–	–
Total produced non-financial assets	NG3U	AN.1	270.7	279.9	289.3	300.6	315.6	331.8
Non-produced non-financial assets								
Natural resources		AN.21						
Land	E44C	AN.211	41.7	31.2	33.4	49.3	49.2	46.0
Total	E42N	AN.21	41.7	31.2	33.4	49.3	49.2	46.0
Total non-produced non-financial assets	E3TN	AN.2	41.7	31.2	33.4	49.3	49.2	46.0
Total non-financial assets	NG42	AN	312.4	311.1	322.7	349.9	364.9	377.8
Financial assets and liabilities								
Financial assets								
Currency and deposits	NJEL	AF.2	28.1	34.1	31.0	32.1	36.1	35.4
Debt securities	NJEU	AF.3	2.5	3.1	4.6	6.2	6.3	4.1
Loans	NJFW	AF.4	8.8	11.4	12.3	13.8	15.8	17.3
Equity and investment fund shares/units	NJGO	AF.5	119.6	121.7	124.2	127.5	129.6	130.3
Insurance, pension and standardised guarantee schemes	NPXT	AF.6	0.7	0.7	0.7	0.7	0.6	0.6
Other accounts receivable/payable	NJHI	AF.8	0.9	0.9	0.9	1.7	2.4	2.7
Total financial assets	NJFV	AF.A	160.5	171.8	173.6	181.9	190.8	190.4
Financial liabilities								
Debt securities	NJHY	AF.3	1.6	2.3	3.0	3.5	4.1	4.4
Loans	NJJA	AF.4	71.7	81.3	83.6	86.5	88.2	91.5
Insurance, pension and standardised guarantee schemes	M9RL	AF.6	85.0	73.4	67.7	62.2	68.5	68.7
Other accounts receivable/payable	NJKM	AF.8	28.5	31.1	33.2	35.2	43.3	47.1
Total financial liabilities	NJIZ	AF.L	186.8	188.0	187.5	187.5	204.1	211.7
Financial net worth	NYOJ	BF.90	−26.2	−16.2	−14.0	−5.6	−13.3	−21.3
Net worth	CGRZ	B.90	286.1	294.9	308.8	344.3	351.6	356.5

1 Excludes the value of land underneath the assets.

9.10 Households & non-profit institutions serving households (NPISH)
At current prices

£ billion at end year

			2011	2012	2013	2014	2015	2016
Non-financial assets								
Produced non-financial assets								
Fixed assets		AN.11						
Dwellings[1]	E46M	AN.111	1 337.4	1 382.5	1 435.2	1 462.7	1 486.9	1 538.2
Other buildings and structures[1]		AN.112						
Buildings other than dwellings[1]	E47X	AN.1121	22.8	21.3	21.1	21.5	22.1	22.7
Other structures[1]	E49J	AN.1122	23.8	24.1	23.3	22.1	24.8	26.2
Total	E479	AN.112	46.6	45.3	44.4	43.6	46.9	48.9
Machinery and equipment		AN.113						
Transport equipment	E4A4	AN.1131	5.0	5.1	5.2	5.6	6.4	7.5
ICT equipment	MU86	AN.1132	3.1	3.2	3.3	4.0	4.3	4.8
Other machinery and equipment	CGRM	AN.1139	25.1	25.4	26.3	27.1	28.7	31.7
Total	NG48	AN.113	33.3	33.7	34.8	36.6	39.4	44.1
Cultivated biological resources[1]	E4AX	AN.115	0.3	0.3	0.3	0.4	0.4	0.4
Intellectual property products	NG49	AN.117	11.0	11.2	11.7	12.0	12.4	12.8
Total	NG45	AN.11	1 428.6	1 473.1	1 526.4	1 555.3	1 585.9	1 644.3
Inventories	CGRO	AN.12	23.4	23.7	24.2	25.0	25.2	25.9
Total produced non-financial assets	NG44	AN.1	1 452.0	1 496.8	1 550.5	1 580.3	1 611.1	1 670.2
Non-produced non-financial assets								
Natural resources		AN.21						
Land	E44D	AN.211	2 627.2	2 690.9	2 909.0	3 260.2	3 644.8	3 913.4
Total	E42X	AN.21	2 627.2	2 690.9	2 909.0	3 260.2	3 644.8	3 913.4
Contracts, leases and licences[2]		AN.22						
Permits to undertake specific activities[2]	L688	AN.223	2.2	2.3	2.4	2.5	2.7	2.9
Total	L689	AN.22	2.2	2.3	2.4	2.5	2.7	2.9
Total non-produced non-financial assets	L68A	AN.2	2 629.3	2 693.2	2 911.4	3 262.7	3 647.5	3 916.3
Total non-financial assets	NG4A	AN	4 081.3	4 190.0	4 461.9	4 843.0	5 258.6	5 586.5
Financial assets and liabilities								
Financial assets								
Currency and deposits	NNMP	AF.2	1 244.4	1 301.5	1 352.5	1 408.1	1 464.9	1 558.2
Debt securities	NNMY	AF.3	17.4	22.3	20.4	23.7	25.7	27.8
Loans	NNOA	AF.4	18.4	18.5	18.7	18.7	18.8	18.7
Equity and investment fund shares/units	NNOS	AF.5	751.7	723.2	795.6	889.3	927.4	1 012.3
Insurance, pension and standardised guarantee schemes	NPYL	AF.6	2 860.3	2 899.3	2 847.5	3 268.4	3 277.8	3 625.7
Financial derivatives and employee stock options	MMW5	AF.7	9.2	5.3	8.6	6.8	5.8	5.9
Other accounts receivable/payable	NNPM	AF.8	143.5	189.5	188.6	200.1	196.4	201.5
Total financial assets	NNML	AF.A	5 044.8	5 159.5	5 232.0	5 815.1	5 916.8	6 450.0
Financial liabilities								
Debt securities	NNQC	AF.3	1.4	1.4	1.7	2.5	3.0	3.3
Loans	NNRE	AF.4	1 485.3	1 507.8	1 523.8	1 563.6	1 612.7	1 686.4
Insurance, pension and standardised guarantee schemes	NPYM	AF.6	45.5	32.8	24.2	44.3	40.5	44.4
Financial derivatives and employee stock options	MMY9	AF.7	5.5	1.8	4.2	2.8	1.8	1.1
Other accounts receivable/payable	NNSQ	AF.8	83.9	87.4	86.6	81.4	91.7	97.7
Total financial liabilities	NNPP	AF.L	1 621.5	1 631.2	1 640.5	1 694.6	1 749.6	1 832.9
Financial net worth	NZEA	BF.90	3 423.3	3 528.3	3 591.4	4 120.5	4 167.2	4 617.1
Net worth	CGRC	B.90	7 504.6	7 718.3	8 053.3	8 963.5	9 425.7	10 203.6

1 Excludes the value of the land underneath the assets.
2 Includes cherished or personalised vehicle registration plates.

9.11 Households
At current prices

			2011	2012	2013	2014	2015	2016
Non-financial assets								
Produced non-financial assets		AN.11						
Fixed assets		AN.11						
Dwellings[1]	E46V	AN.111	1 324.0	1 368.7	1 420.9	1 447.9	1 470.3	1 520.9
Other buildings and structures[1]		AN.112						
Buildings other than dwellings[1]	E48G	AN.1121	9.8	10.0	10.7	11.5	11.4	11.7
Other structures[1]	E49K	AN.1122	10.2	11.3	11.8	11.8	12.7	13.5
Total	E47C	AN.112	20.0	21.4	22.4	23.2	24.1	25.2
Machinery and equipment		AN.113						
Transport equipment	E4A5	AN.1131	5.0	5.1	5.2	5.6	6.4	7.5
ICT equipment	E4AD	AN.1132	2.6	2.8	3.0	3.7	4.0	4.5
Other machinery and equipment	E4AG	AN.1139	23.6	24.3	25.3	26.1	27.7	30.7
Total	E49S	AN.113	31.2	32.2	33.4	35.5	38.1	42.7
Cultivated biological resources[1]	E4AZ	AN.115	0.3	0.3	0.3	0.4	0.4	0.4
Intellectual property products	E4BF	AN.117	0.4	0.5	0.5	0.5	0.5	0.5
Total	E468	AN.11	1 376.0	1 423.0	1 477.6	1 507.5	1 533.4	1 589.7
Inventories	E4BK	AN.12	22.2	22.5	23.0	23.8	23.9	24.6
Total produced non-financial assets	E462	AN.1	1 398.2	1 445.5	1 500.6	1 531.2	1 557.3	1 614.4
Non-produced non-financial assets		AN.21						
Natural resources		AN.21						
Land	E44N	AN.211	2 595.6	2 660.7	2 876.9	3 223.0	3 599.7	3 865.5
Total	E42Y	AN.21	2 595.6	2 660.7	2 876.9	3 223.0	3 599.7	3 865.5
Contracts, leases and licences[2]		AN.22						
Permits to undertake specific activities[2]	J5B8	AN.223	2.2	2.3	2.4	2.5	2.7	2.9
Total	E3TU	AN.22	2.2	2.3	2.4	2.5	2.7	2.9
Total non-produced non-financial assets	E3VW	AN.2	2 597.8	2 663.0	2 879.3	3 225.5	3 602.4	3 868.4
Total non-financial assets	E45Y	AN	3 996.0	4 108.5	4 379.9	4 756.8	5 159.7	5 482.7
Financial assets and liabilities								
Financial assets								
Currency and deposits	NIRV	AF.2	1 218.1	1 273.7	1 321.9	1 375.3	1 430.3	1 520.7
Debt securities	NISE	AF.3	10.4	15.3	12.4	14.1	16.1	16.6
Loans	NITG	AF.4	18.4	18.5	18.7	18.7	18.8	18.7
Equity and investment fund shares/units	NITY	AF.5	671.7	652.5	718.9	792.6	801.6	862.1
Insurance, pension and standardised guarantee schemes	NPXP	AF.6	2 859.7	2 898.7	2 846.9	3 267.8	3 277.2	3 625.1
Financial derivatives and employee stock options	MMW6	AF.7	9.1	5.2	8.2	6.4	5.6	5.7
Other accounts receivable/payable	NIUS	AF.8	136.3	180.9	179.2	189.5	184.1	187.2
Total financial assets	NITF	AF.A	4 923.7	5 044.7	5 106.2	5 664.4	5 733.9	6 236.0
Financial liabilities								
Debt securities	NIVI	AF.3	–	–	–	–	–	–
Loans	NIWK	AF.4	1 464.2	1 485.1	1 502.2	1 541.6	1 590.1	1 661.3
Financial derivatives and employee stock options	MMZ2	AF.7	5.4	1.6	4.0	2.7	1.5	0.7
Other accounts receivable/payable	NIXW	AF.8	73.8	76.3	75.6	70.2	79.6	84.6
Total financial liabilities	NIWJ	AF.L	1 543.4	1 563.1	1 581.8	1 614.6	1 671.2	1 746.6
Financial net worth	NYOH	BF.90	3 380.3	3 481.6	3 524.4	4 049.9	4 062.7	4 489.4
Net worth	E45V	B.90	7 376.3	7 590.1	7 904.3	8 806.6	9 222.4	9 972.2

1 Excludes the value of the land underneath the assets.
2 Includes cherished or personalised vehicle registration plates.

9.12 Non-profit institutions serving households (NPISH)
At current prices

			2011	2012	2013	2014	2015	2016
Non-financial assets								
Produced non-financial assets								
Fixed assets		AN.11						
Dwellings[1]	E46W	AN.111	13.3	13.8	14.3	14.8	16.6	17.2
Other buildings and structures[1]		AN.112						
Buildings other than dwellings[1]	E48S	AN.1121	13.0	11.2	10.4	10.0	10.7	11.0
Other structures[1]	E49O	AN.1122	13.6	12.7	11.5	10.3	12.0	12.7
Total	E47D	AN.112	26.6	23.9	22.0	20.3	22.7	23.6
Machinery and equipment		AN.113						
Transport equipment	E4A6	AN.1131	–	–	–	–	–	–
ICT equipment	E4AF	AN.1132	0.5	0.4	0.3	0.2	0.3	0.3
Other machinery and equipment	E4AH	AN.1139	1.6	1.2	1.0	0.9	1.0	1.1
Total	E49T	AN.113	2.1	1.6	1.3	1.2	1.3	1.4
Cultivated biological resources[1]	E4B3	AN.115	–	–	–	–	–	–
Intellectual property products	E4BG	AN.117	10.5	10.8	11.2	11.5	11.9	12.3
Total	E46A	AN.11	52.6	50.1	48.8	47.8	52.6	54.6
Inventories	E4BL	AN.12	1.2	1.2	1.2	1.3	1.3	1.3
Total produced non-financial assets	E467	AN.1	53.7	51.2	50.0	49.1	53.8	55.9
Non-produced non-financial assets								
Natural resources		AN.21						
Land	E44O	AN.211	31.5	30.2	32.1	37.2	45.1	47.9
Total	E433	AN.21	31.5	30.2	32.1	37.2	45.1	47.9
Total non-produced non-financial assets	E422	AN.2	31.5	30.2	32.1	37.2	45.1	47.9
Total non-financial assets	E45Z	AN	85.3	81.5	82.1	86.3	98.9	103.8
Financial assets and liabilities								
Financial assets								
Currency and deposits	NJKT	AF.2	26.3	27.8	30.6	32.8	34.6	37.5
Debt securities	NJLC	AF.3	7.1	7.0	8.0	9.5	9.5	11.2
Loans	NJME	AF.4	–	–	–	–	–	–
Equity and investment fund shares/units	NJMW	AF.5	80.0	70.7	76.8	96.7	125.7	150.2
Insurance, pension and standardised guarantee schemes	NPXV	AF.6	0.6	0.6	0.6	0.6	0.6	0.6
Financial derivatives and employee stock options	MMW7	AF.7	–	0.1	0.4	0.5	0.2	0.2
Other accounts receivable/payable	NJNQ	AF.8	7.1	8.6	9.4	10.6	12.3	14.2
Total financial assets	NJKP	AF.A	121.1	114.8	125.7	150.7	182.9	214.0
Financial liabilities								
Debt securities	NJOG	AF.3	1.4	1.4	1.7	2.5	3.0	3.3
Loans	NJPI	AF.4	21.1	22.7	21.6	22.0	22.6	25.1
Insurance, pension and standardised guarantee schemes	NPXW	AF.6	45.5	32.8	24.2	44.3	40.5	44.4
Financial derivatives and employee stock options	MMZ3	AF.7	–	0.2	0.3	0.1	0.3	0.4
Other accounts receivable/payable	NJQU	AF.8	10.1	11.1	11.0	11.3	12.1	13.1
Total financial liabilities	NJNT	AF.L	78.1	68.2	58.7	80.1	78.5	86.3
Financial net worth	NYOO	BF.90	43.1	46.7	67.0	70.6	104.4	127.7
Net worth	E45W	B.90	128.3	128.1	149.0	156.9	203.3	231.5

1 Excludes the value of the land underneath the assets.

9.13 Public sector[1]
At current prices[2]

£ billion at end year

Non-financial assets			2011	2012	2013	2014	2015	2016
Produced non-financial assets								
Fixed assets		AN.11						
Dwellings[3]	E46X	AN.111	..	..	..	..	..	..
Other buildings and structures[3]		AN.112						
Buildings other than dwellings[3]	E494	AN.1121	..	..	..	..	..	..
Other structures[3]	E49P	AN.1122	..	..	..	..	..	..
Total	E47I	AN.112	..	..	..	..	..	..
Machinery, equipment and weapons systems		AN.113+114						
Transport equipment	E4A7	AN.1131	..	..	..	..	..	..
ICT equipment	MU87	AN.1132	..	..	..	..	..	..
Other machinery, equipment and weapons systems	CGXB	AN.1139+114	..	..	..	..	..	..
Total	NG4G	AN.113+114	..	..	..	..	..	..
Cultivated biological resources[3]	E4BD	AN.115	..	..	..	..	..	..
Intellectual property products	NG4H	AN.117	..	..	..	..	..	..
Total	NG4D	AN.11	..	..	..	..	..	..
Inventories	CGXD	AN.12	6.6	6.5	6.5	6.5	6.5	6.4
Total produced non-financial assets	NG4C	AN.1	..	..	..	..	..	..
Non-produced non-financial assets								
Natural resources		AN.21						
Land	E44Q	AN.211	431.0	416.6	452.7	555.2	614.5	641.5
Total	E435	AN.21	431.0	416.6	452.7	555.2	614.5	641.5
Total non-produced non-financial assets	NG4I	AN.2	431.0	416.6	452.7	555.2	614.5	641.5
Total non-financial assets	NG4K	AN	..	..	..	..	..	..
Financial assets and liabilities								
Financial assets								
Monetary gold and special drawing rights	NG4L	AF.1	19.2	19.3	16.3	16.7	16.2	18.3
Currency and deposits	NG4M	AF.2	89.6	97.5	100.1	100.3	96.0	100.7
Debt securities	NG4N	AF.3	57.1	57.2	53.4	59.5	75.4	91.1
Loans	NG4O	AF.4	193.4	206.7	207.1	212.1	210.7	225.9
Equity and investment fund shares/units	NG4P	AF.5	180.5	215.0	197.5	202.2	188.7	183.6
Insurance, pension and standardised guarantee schemes	NG4Q	AF.6	0.7	0.7	0.7	0.7	0.6	0.6
Financial derivatives and employee stock options	MUM8	AF.7	2.7	3.3	2.9	2.1	2.1	−6.5
Other accounts receivable/payable	NG4R	AF.8	75.2	76.0	81.8	87.5	96.9	106.3
Total financial assets	KQ8D	AF.A	618.4	675.7	659.6	681.0	686.6	720.0
Financial liabilities								
Monetary gold and special drawing rights	MUV2	AF.1	10.1	9.6	9.4	9.4	9.5	11.1
Currency and deposits	NG4S	AF.2	136.6	134.5	126.5	144.4	155.3	173.4
Debt securities	NG4T	AF.3	1 408.0	1 494.8	1 507.0	1 772.3	1 793.7	2 058.1
Loans	NG4U	AF.4	138.7	146.7	147.2	152.0	159.4	164.9
Equity and investment fund shares/units	NG4V	AF.5	121.8	123.7	125.2	127.2	128.9	130.1
Insurance, pension and standardised guarantee schemes	MUU6	AF.6	85.0	73.4	67.7	62.3	68.6	68.7
Financial derivatives and employee stock options	MUM9	AF.7	3.3	2.4	1.3	1.1	2.2	1.7
Other accounts receivable/payable	NG4X	AF.8	67.5	106.0	109.6	114.0	122.7	124.3
Total financial liabilities	NG4Y	AF.L	1 970.9	2 091.1	2 094.1	2 382.6	2 440.3	2 732.1
Financial net worth	CGSA	BF.90	−1 352.5	−1 415.4	−1 434.4	−1 701.6	−1 753.7	−2 012.1
Net worth	CGTY	B.90	..	..	..	..	..	..

1 Public sector is general government plus public non-financial corporations.
2 .. indicates that data have been suppressed in this table. This is because
  the institutional sector and asset breakdown of public non-financial
  corporations (S.11), into public non-financial corporations (S.11001) and
  private non-financial corporations (S.11002 and S.11003) is unavailable
  from the capital stocks dataset.
3 Excludes the value of the land underneath the assets.

United Kingdom National Accounts

The Blue Book
Chapter 10: Public Sector Supplementary Tables

2017 edition

Editors: Dean Goodway & Sarah Nightingale

Office for National Statistics

Chapter 10: Public sector supplementary tables

The majority of government income is provided by taxes and social contributions. Table 10.1 provides a breakdown of the main taxes and social contributions payable by UK residents to both the government (both central and local government) and to the European Union.

Taxes and social contributions payable by UK residents

Taxes on production are included in gross domestic product (GDP) at market prices.

Other taxes on production include taxes levied on inputs to production. This includes national non-domestic rates, also known as business rates, and a range of compulsory unrequited levies that producers have to pay.

Taxes on products are taxes levied on the sale of goods and services, this includes Value Added Tax (VAT) and Fuel Duty.

Taxes on income and wealth include Income Tax and Corporation Tax. Income Tax is the largest single source of tax revenue paid by UK residents. This category also includes a number of other charges payable by households including Council Tax, the BBC licence fee and taxes such as Vehicle Excise Duty, which, when paid by businesses, are classified as taxes on production. The totals include tax credits and reliefs recorded as expenditure in the national accounts, such as Working Tax Credit and Child Tax Credit.

The European System of Accounts 2010: ESA 2010 has a specific category of payments to government called compulsory social contributions. These are payments associated with social security schemes, such as unemployment benefit and pensions. In the UK accounts this category includes all National Insurance contributions. Details of total social contributions and benefits are shown in Tables 5.2.4S and 5.3.4S.

Capital taxes are taxes levied at irregular or infrequent intervals on the values of assets, gifts or legacies. In the UK the main capital tax is Inheritance Tax.

Some UK taxes are recorded as the resources of the European Union (EU). These include taxes on imports, which are payable to the EU under the EU treaties.

10.1 Taxes paid by UK residents to general government and the European Union

Total economy sector S.1

£ million

			2009	2010	2011	2012	2013	2014	2015	2016
Generation of income										
Uses										
Taxes on production and imports		D.2								
Taxes on products and imports		D.21								
Value added tax (VAT)		D.211								
Paid to central government	NZGF		79 900	95 865	111 437	113 859	118 234	124 211	129 177	133 671
Total	QYRC	D.211	79 900	95 865	111 437	113 859	118 234	124 211	129 177	133 671
Taxes and duties on imports excluding VAT		D.212								
Paid to central government: import duties[1]	NMXZ	D.2121	–	–	–	–	–	–	–	–
Paid to EU: import duties	FJWE	D.2121	2 645	2 933	2 925	2 885	2 914	2 949	3 077	3 318
Total	QYRB	D.212	2 645	2 933	2 925	2 885	2 914	2 949	3 077	3 318
Taxes on products excluding VAT and import duties		D.214								
Paid to central government										
Customs and excise revenue										
Beer	GTAM		3 189	3 278	3 429	3 425	3 337	3 337	3 294	3 288
Wines, cider, perry and spirits	GTAN		5 728	6 075	6 439	6 775	7 063	7 246	7 385	7 578
Tobacco	GTAO		9 056	9 076	9 361	9 897	9 479	9 436	9 190	9 087
Hydrocarbon oils	GTAP		25 894	27 013	26 923	26 703	26 698	27 095	27 416	27 989
Car tax	GTAT		–	–	–	–	–	–	–	–
Betting, gaming and lottery	CJQY		1 013	1 092	1 206	1 207	1 538	1 708	2 053	2 329
Air passenger duty	CWAA		1 800	2 094	2 605	2 766	2 960	3 154	3 119	3 150
Insurance premium tax	CWAD		2 259	2 401	2 942	3 022	3 018	2 964	3 294	4 827
Landfill tax	BKOF		842	1 065	1 090	1 094	1 191	1 143	1 028	1 024
Other	ACDN		–	–	–	–	–	–	–	–
Fossil fuel levy	CIQY		–	–	–	–	–	–	–	–
Gas levy	GTAZ		–	–	–	–	–	–	–	–
Stamp duties	GTBC		7 141	9 098	8 831	8 918	11 542	14 069	13 791	16 025
Levies on exports (third country trade)	CUDF		–	–	–	–	–	–	–	–
Camelot payments to national lottery										
Distribution fund	LIYH		1 553	1 625	1 793	1 832	1 644	1 721	1 713	1 713
Hydro-benefit	LITN		–	–	–	–	–	–	–	–
Aggregates levy	MDUQ		275	290	290	264	282	342	354	405
Milk super levy	DFT3		–	–	–	–	–	–	–	–
Climate change levy	LSNT		693	666	675	624	1 098	1 506	1 752	1 881
Channel 4 funding formula	EG9G		–	–	–	–	–	–	–	–
Renewable energy obligations	EP89		1 099	1 243	1 423	1 842	2 391	2 931	3 691	4 479
Rail franchise premia	LITT		496	792	993	1 275	1 275	1 501	1 611	1 656
Other taxes and levies	GCSP		–	–	–	–	–	–	–	–
Vehicle registration tax	MVPC		122	123	120	125	138	151	169	171
Air travel organisers' licensing protection contribution	N3DV		33	45	43	46	44	57	55	61
Total paid to central government[6]	NMBV		61 193	65 976	68 163	69 815	73 698	78 361	79 915	85 663
Paid to local government										
Community infrastructure levy	DMHG		–	–	–	4	36	104	147	259
Total paid to local government	CPPM		–	–	–	4	36	104	147	259
Paid to the european union										
Sugar levy	GTBA		10	12	12	13	12	11	10	9
European coal and steel community levy	GTBB		–	–	–	–	–	–	–	–
Total paid to the european union	FJWG		10	12	12	13	12	11	10	9
Total taxes on products excluding VAT and import duties[6]	QYRA	D.214	61 203	65 988	68 175	69 832	73 746	78 476	80 072	85 931
Total taxes on products and imports	NZGW	D.21	143 748	164 786	182 537	186 576	194 894	205 636	212 326	222 920
Production taxes other than on products		D.29								
Paid to central government										
Consumer credit act fees	CUDB		435	480	480	480	480	480	480	480
National non-domestic rates	CUKY		21 361	21 509	22 444	23 514	24 599	25 173	25 834	26 607
Northern Ireland non-domestic rates	NSEZ		325	361	368	366	373	378	398	410
Levies paid to central government levy-funded bodies	LITK		746	569	508	600	585	630	621	657
London regional transport levy	GTBE		–	–	–	–	–	–	–	–
IBA levy	GTAL		–	–	–	–	–	–	–	–
Motor vehicle duties paid by businesses	EKED		1 416	1 466	1 683	1 804	1 704	1 707	1 746	2 234
Regulator fees	GCSQ		72	90	78	81	84	93	87	75
Northern Ireland driver vehicle agency	IY9N		4	4	4	4	4	4	4	4
Bank payroll tax: accrued receipts	JT2Q		–	3 413	–	–	–	–	–	–
Emissions trading scheme	M98G		45	192	315	278	339	418	493	386
Carbon reduction commitment	L8UA		–	–	–	346	607	569	659	520
Light dues	DPIH		71	80	89	87	89	86	78	73
Payments under police service agreement	CY6Z		125	125	128	125	128	133	142	145
Total	NMBX		24 600	28 289	26 097	27 685	28 992	29 671	30 542	31 591
Paid to local government										
Non-domestic rates[2]	DM9L		317	329	336	344	350	353	376	398
Crossrail business rates supplement	MHG4		–	168	228	233	217	218	224	231
Total	NMYH		317	497	564	577	567	571	600	629
Total production taxes other than on products	NMYD	D.29	24 917	28 786	26 661	28 262	29 559	30 242	31 142	32 220
Total taxes on production and imports, paid		D.2								
Paid to central government	NMBY		165 693	190 130	205 697	211 359	220 924	232 243	239 634	250 925
Paid to local government	DMHD		317	497	564	581	603	675	747	888
Paid to the European Union	FJWB		2 655	2 945	2 937	2 898	2 926	2 960	3 087	3 327
Total	NZGX	D.2	168 665	193 572	209 198	214 838	224 453	235 878	243 468	255 140

10.1

Taxes paid by UK residents to general government and the European Union

continued **Total economy sector S.1**

£ million

			2009	2010	2011	2012	2013	2014	2015	2016
Secondary distribution of income										
Uses										
Current taxes on income, wealth etc.		D.5								
Taxes on income		D.51								
Paid to central government										
Households income taxes	DRWH		143 620	150 038	154 055	149 449	155 198	158 855	165 841	172 021
Corporation tax	ACCD		35 458	41 206	42 263	39 857	39 438	40 635	44 131	46 708
Petroleum revenue tax	DBHA		1 047	1 349	1 775	2 106	1 296	568	−552	−768
Windfall tax	EYNK		–	–	–	–	–	–	–	–
Other taxes on income	BMNX		10 407	5 059	6 613	7 325	7 145	6 821	8 374	10 134
Total	NMCU	D.51	190 532	197 652	204 706	198 737	203 077	206 879	217 794	228 095
Other current taxes		D.59								
Paid to central government										
Motor vehicle duty paid by households	CDDZ		4 214	4 374	4 137	4 069	4 397	4 268	4 153	3 755
Northern Ireland domestic rates	NSFA		355	335	391	416	409	404	384	372
Boat licences	NSNP		–	–	–	–	–	–	–	–
Fishing licences	NRQB		20	20	23	21	21	21	21	21
National non-domestic rates paid by Non-market sectors[3]	BMNY		1 423	1 481	1 637	1 709	1 731	1 752	1 773	1 784
Passport fees	E8A6		351	400	368	362	343	386	439	447
Television licence fee	DH7A		3 009	3 088	3 088	3 117	3 082	3 124	3 131	3 156
Northern Ireland driver vehicle agency	IY9O		14	12	12	12	12	12	12	12
Bank levy	KIH3		–	–	1 899	1 641	2 352	2 853	3 363	3 111
Total	NMCV		9 386	9 710	11 555	11 347	12 347	12 820	13 276	12 658
Paid to local government										
Domestic rates[2]	NMHK		131	146	157	164	170	176	195	208
Community charge	NMHL		–	–	–	–	–	–	–	–
Council tax	NMHM		24 926	25 438	25 724	26 055	27 073	27 962	28 784	30 018
Total	NMIS		25 057	25 584	25 881	26 219	27 243	28 138	28 979	30 226
Total	NVCM	D.59	34 443	35 294	37 436	37 566	39 590	40 958	42 255	42 884
Total current taxes on income, wealth etc		D.5								
Paid to central government	NMCP		199 918	207 362	216 261	210 084	215 424	219 699	231 070	240 753
Paid to local government	NMIS		25 057	25 584	25 881	26 219	27 243	28 138	28 979	30 226
Total	NMZL	D.5	224 975	232 946	242 142	236 303	242 667	247 837	260 049	270 979
Social contributions		D.61								
Actual social contributions										
Paid to central government										
(National insurance contributions)										
Employers' compulsory contributions	CEAN		54 411	55 887	58 174	60 600	62 019	63 892	66 491	71 407
Employees' compulsory contributions	GCSE		37 184	38 703	40 626	41 159	41 481	42 556	44 454	47 204
Self- and non-employed persons' Compulsory contributions	NMDE		2 850	2 756	2 641	2 560	2 585	2 672	3 122	3 189
Total	AIIH		94 445	97 346	101 441	104 319	106 085	109 120	114 067	121 800
Capital account		Part								
Changes in liabilities and net worth										
Other capital taxes		D.91								
Paid to central government										
Inheritance tax	GILF		2 305	2 592	2 856	3 041	3 293	3 702	4 359	4 703
Tax on other capital transfers	GILG		50	50	50	50	50	50	50	50
Tax on swiss bank accounts[4]	KW69		–	–	–	–	876	–	–	–
Development land tax and other	GCSV		–	–	–	–	–	–	–	–
Tax paid on local government equal pay settlements	C625		46	–	30	38	36	134	33	48
FSCS levies on private sector[5]	HZQ4		1 805	–	–	–	–	–	–	–
Total	NMGI	D.91	4 206	2 642	2 936	3 129	4 255	3 886	4 442	4 801
Total taxes and **Compulsory social contributions**										
Paid to central government	GCSS		464 262	497 480	526 335	528 891	546 688	564 948	589 213	618 279
Paid to local government	GCST		25 374	26 081	26 445	26 796	27 810	28 709	29 579	30 855
Paid to the European Union	FJWB		2 655	2 945	2 937	2 898	2 926	2 960	3 087	3 327
Total	GCSU		492 291	526 506	555 717	558 585	577 424	596 617	621 879	652 461

1 These taxes existed before the UKs entry into the EEC in 1973.
2 From 1990/1991 onwards these series only contain rates paid in Northern Ireland.
3 Up until 1995/96 these payments are included in national non-domestic rates under production taxes other than on products.
4 Tax liable from banking deposits of UK residents held in Swiss banks.

5 Financial Services Compensation Scheme.
6 Total taxes for D.214 will not necessarily equal the sum of its components

United Kingdom National Accounts

The Blue Book
Chapter 11: Statistics for European Purposes

2017 edition

Editors: Dean Goodway & Sarah Nightingale

Office for National Statistics

Chapter 11: How our statistics are used by the European Union

The European Union (EU) uses national accounts data for a number of administrative and economic purposes. Gross national income (GNI) is one of the four measures used by the EU and is calculated in accordance with the European System of Accounts. GNI is used to set the EU budget and to calculate part of member states' contributions to the EU budget and is based on the European System of Accounts 2010: ESA 2010.

UK transactions with the institutions of the European Union

Table 11.1 shows payments flowing between the EU and the UK. The first part of the table shows the payments flowing into the UK in the form of EU expenditure. The second part of the table shows the UK contribution to the EU budget, which depends on UK GNI. An explanatory note detailing GDP, GNI and the UK's contribution to the EU budget was published on 8 September 2015.

Data to monitor government deficit and debt

The convergence criteria for Economic and Monetary Union (EMU) are set out in the 1992 Treaty on European Union (The Maastricht Treaty). The Treaty, plus the Stability and Growth Pact, requires member states to avoid excessive government deficits – defined as general government net borrowing and gross debt as a percentage of gross domestic product (GDP). The Treaty does not determine what constitutes "excessive". This is agreed by the Economic and Finance Council (ECOFIN).

Member states report their planned and actual deficits and the levels of their debt to the European Commission. Data to monitor excessive deficits are supplied in accordance with EU legislation.

The UK submitted the estimates in Table 11.a to the European Commission in October 2017.

Table 11.a: UK government deficit and debt, 2010/11 to 2016/17, UK

	2010 to 2011	2011 to 2012	2012 to 2013	2013 to 2014	2014 to 2015	2015 to 2016	2016 to 2017
General government deficit							
Net borrowing (£ billion)	142.0	123.8	124.2	100.1	91.0	75.8	45.5
As a percentage of GDP	8.9	7.5	7.3	5.6	4.9	4.0	2.3
General government debt							
Debt at nominal value (£ billion)	1,214.5	1,349.7	1,425.6	1,522.5	1,604.0	1,652.0	1,720.0
As a percentage of GDP	75.9	82.3	83.8	85.8	86.7	86.8	86.8

Source: Office for National Statistics

11.1 UK official transactions with institutions of the EU
UK transactions with ESA 2010 sector S.212

£ million

			2009	2010	2011	2012	2013	2014	2015	2016
UK resources										
Exports of services		P.62								
UK charge for collecting duties and levies(net)[1,2]	QWUE		664	737	735	724	731	741	772	788
Subsidies on products		D.31								
Agricultural guarantee fund	EBGL		3 411	3 059	3 166	2 625	2 455	2 306	1 961	2 431
European coal and steel community grants	FJKP		–	–	–	–	–	–	–	–
Social assistance		D.75								
European social fund	HDIZ		609	642	388	585	247	263	556	309
Current international co-operation		D.74								
Grants to research councils and Miscellaneous[2]	GCSD		104	105	89	153	105	123	47	157
Capital transfers		D.92								
Agricultural guidance fund	FJXL		215	439	419	291	620	567	461	400
European regional development fund	HBZA		640	758	603	438	297	1 054	454	359
Agricultural compensation scheme payments[3]	EBGO	D.99	–	–	–	–	–	–	–	–
Total identified UK resources	GCSL		5 643	5 740	5 400	4 816	4 455	5 054	4 251	4 444
UK uses										
Taxes on products		D.21								
Import duties	FJWD	D.212	2 645	2 933	2 925	2 885	2 914	2 949	3 077	3 318
Sugar levy	GTBA	D.214	10	12	12	13	12	11	10	9
European coal and steel community levy	GTBB	D.214	–	–	–	–	–	–	–	–
Other current transfers		D.74								
Jet contributions and miscellaneous[4]	GVEG		−14	−18	−17	−39	−15	−3	125	119
Inter-government agreements[4]	HCBW		–	–	–	–	–	–	–	–
EU non-budget (miscellaneous)[4]	HRTM		–	–	–	–	–	–	–	–
VAT and GNI based EU own resources[5]		D.76								
VAT-based third EU own resource	M9LI	D.761	1 593	2 253	2 197	2 282	2 154	2 388	2 715	2 675
GNI-based fourth EU own resource	M9LJ	D.762	5 163	7 773	7 814	8 190	10 637	9 346	8 877	7 764
Of which: Fontainebleau abatement[8]	-FKKL		−5 392	−3 046	−3 144	−3 110	−3 675	−4 416	−4 913	−5 026
Total	M9MC	D.76	6 756	10 026	10 011	10 472	12 791	11 734	11 592	10 439
Total identified UK uses	GCSM		9 397	12 953	12 931	13 331	15 702	14 691	14 804	13 885
Balance, UK net contribution to the EU[6,7]	BLZS		−3 754	−7 213	−7 531	−8 515	−11 247	−9 637	−10 553	−9 441

1 Before 1989 this is netted off the VAT contribution but cannot be identified separately.
2 UK central government resources.
3 Before 1999 these have been included in Agricultural guarantee fund payments (series EBGL).
4 UK central government uses.
5 Gross National Income.
6 As defined in pre-ESA95 Blue Books.
7 A negative balance means the UK pays more to the EU than it receives.
8 Previously recorded as positive D.74R, now recorded as negative D.76U

United Kingdom National Accounts

The Blue Book
Chapter 12: Environmental Accounts

2017 edition

Editors: Dean Goodway & Sarah Nightingale

Office for National Statistics

Chapter 12: UK Environmental Accounts

1. Environmental accounts

Environmental accounts are:

- "satellite accounts" to the main national accounts
- compiled in accordance with the System of Environmental-Economic Accounting (SEEA), which closely follows the United Nations System of National Accounts (SNA)

Environmental accounts measure:

- the impact the economy has on the environment
- how the environment contributes to the economy
- how society responds to environmental issues by using the accounting framework and concepts of the national accounts

Environmental accounts are used to:

- inform sustainable development policy
- model impacts of fiscal or monetary measures
- evaluate the environmental impacts of different sectors of the economy

Environmental accounts data:

- are mostly provided in units of physical measurement (mass or volume)
- can be provided in monetary units, where this is the most relevant or only data available

Tables 12.1 to 12.5 show estimates of oil and gas reserves, energy consumption, atmospheric emissions and material flows. More data, information and other environmental accounts (including fuel use, environmental goods and services sector, waste, environmental taxes, environmental protection expenditure, low carbon and renewable energy economy and experimental natural capital accounts) can be found on the UK Environmental Accounts release page.

2. Temperature

Figure 12.1 shows the change in mean air temperature between 1990 and 2015. This measure helps to contextualise some of the changes observed across the environmental accounts. For example, the average temperature fell to 8.0 degrees Celsius (°C) in 2010 from 9.2°C in 2009, which contributed to the increases in energy consumption and greenhouse gas emissions observed during that year. At the same time, gross domestic product (GDP) started to recover following the economic downturn, which may also explain the increases in consumption and emissions. Between 2014 and 2015, the average air temperature fell by 0.7°C (from a record high of 9.9°C to 9.2°C). Despite this fall, the average air temperature in 2015 was above usual levels.

Figure 12.1: Mean air temperature
UK, 1990 to 2015

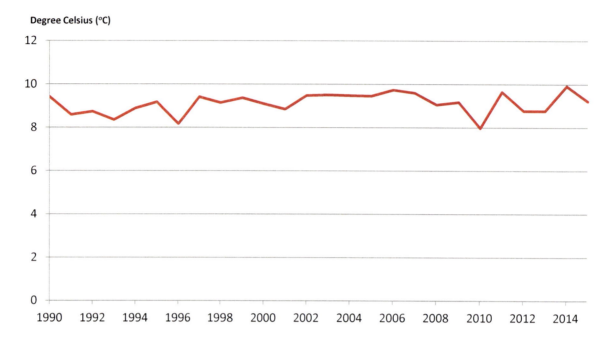

Degree Celsius (°C)

Source: Met Office

3. Oil and gas reserves

Table 12.1 presents non-monetary estimates of the oil and gas reserves and resources in the UK. "Resources" are minerals that are potentially valuable and could eventually be extracted, whereas "reserves" refer to discovered minerals that are recoverable and commercially viable.

Reserves can be proven, probable or possible depending on the confidence level:

- proven reserves (based on the available evidence) are virtually certain to be technically and commercially producible, that is, have a better than 90% chance of being produced
- probable reserves are not yet proven but have a more than 50% chance of being produced
- possible reserves cannot be regarded as probable at present, but are estimated to have a significant (but less than 50%) chance of being technically and commercially producible

This year the Oil and Gas Authority has developed a new category of oil and gas reserves, known as "contingent resources". Contingent resources are defined as "significant discoveries where development plans are under discussion". In the past these would have been included as "probable reserves".

Oil is defined as both oil and the liquids that can be obtained from gas fields. Shale oil is not included in the estimates. Total (discovered; proven and probable, plus possible reserve, contingent resources and undiscovered) oil reserves and resources for 2015 were estimated to be between 1,387 million tonnes and 2,287 million tonnes. The upper range for total oil reserves decreased between 2014 and 2015 by 4.9%, whilst the lower range decreased by 7.8%.

Gas includes gas expected to be available for sale from dry gas fields, gas condensate fields, oil fields associated with gas and a small amount from coal bed methane projects. Shale gas is not included in these estimates. These reserves include onshore and offshore discoveries, but not flared gas or gas consumed in production operations. Total gas reserves and resources were estimated between 872 billion cubic metres (bcm) and 1,507 bcm in 2015. The upper range for total gas reserves and resources had fallen by 5.5% between 2014 and 2015, and the lower range had fallen by 9.1%.

4. Energy consumption

Table 12.2 presents energy consumption by industry for the UK. Energy consumption is defined as the use of energy for power generation, heating and transport. This is essential to most economic activities, for example, as input for production processes. "Direct use of energy" refers to the energy content of fuel for energy at the point of use, allocated to the original purchasers and consumers of fuels. For "reallocated use of energy", the losses incurred during transformation[1] and distribution[2] are allocated to the final consumer of the energy rather than incorporating it all in the electricity generation sector.

Total energy consumption of primary fuels and equivalent was 202.4 million tonnes of oil equivalent (Mtoe) in 2015, which was 0.6% higher than in 2014. Fossil fuels remained the dominant source of energy supply. Energy consumption from fossil fuels in 2015 was at the lowest level since 1990 at 167.7 Mtoe. This represented 82.9% of total energy consumption.

Although fossil fuels are the main source of energy for consumption, other sources (including nuclear, net imports, and renewable and waste sources) are becoming increasingly important. Total energy consumption from other sources was 34.7 Mtoe in 2015, which was 15.7% higher than in 2014. This is the second largest year-on-year increase across the time series. The largest increase occurred between 2008 and 2009, when energy consumption from other sources rose by 17.1%.

5. Atmospheric emissions

Tables 12.3 and 12.4 show emissions of greenhouse gases, acid rain precursors (ARP) and other pollutants by industry for the UK.

Atmospheric emissions of greenhouse gases are widely believed to contribute to global warming and climate change. In 2015, emissions of greenhouse gases were estimated to be 595.2 million tonnes of carbon dioxide equivalent (Mt CO2e), the lowest level since 1990. Across the time series, the largest annual fall in emissions of greenhouse gases occurred in 2009, following the onset of the economic downturn in 2008, when emissions decreased by 8.3%. Between 2014 and 2015, emissions decreased by 12.1 Mt CO2e (2.0%). This was due primarily to reductions in carbon dioxide and methane emissions from the "energy supply, water and waste" sector.

Unlike the majority of other sectors the "transport, storage and communications sector"[3] has seen an increase in greenhouse gas (GHG) emissions. Between 2014 and 2015, this increase was due largely to increases in emissions from fuel oil used in shipping.

Carbon dioxide (CO2) was the dominant greenhouse gas, accounting for 84.7% of the UK's total greenhouse gas emissions in 2015. The remainder of greenhouse gas emissions comprised methane (8.8%), nitrous oxide (3.7%) and fluorinated gases (2.8%).

Acid rain can have harmful effects on the environment and is caused primarily by emissions of sulphur dioxide (SO2), nitrogen oxide (NOX) and ammonia (NH3). For comparability, all figures are weighted according to their acidifying potential and presented as sulphur dioxide equivalents (SO2e). Since 1990, acid rain precursors (ARP) emissions have decreased sharply, falling by 73.9%, from 6.9 million tonnes of sulphur dioxide equivalent (Mt SO2e) to 1.8 Mt SO2e in 2015.

The reduction in ARPs was due largely to a reduction in sulphur dioxide (SO2) emissions, which fell by over 90% between 1990 and 2015. This change can be linked to policy initiatives[4] to discourage the use of high sulphur fuels, control the sulphur content of those fuels and encourage the adoption of cleaner technologies and in particular to the switch from coal to gas in electricity generation.

6. Material flows

Table 12.5 presents economy-wide material flow accounts, which estimate the physical flow of materials[5] through the UK economy. The quantity of materials extracted in the UK has been gradually declining and fell to 419 million tonnes in 2013, the lowest point since 2000. However, in the last two years, we have observed a rise in domestic extraction. Between 2014 and 2015, total domestic extraction increased by 1.6% to 450 million tonnes.

Domestic extraction is divided into four categories: biomass, non-metallic minerals, fossil energy materials or carriers and metal ores. Biomass includes material of biological origin that is not from fossil, such as crops, wood and wild fish catch. In 2015, there were 135 million tonnes of biomass extracted, 8 million tonnes less than in 2014 (143 million tonnes). Of this, crop residues, fodder crops and grazed biomass accounted for 62.6% (85 million tonnes).

Non-metallic minerals are mainly construction and industrial minerals, including limestone and gypsum, sand and gravel, and clays. There has been an overall fall in extraction of non-metallic minerals since 2000. However, extraction of non-metallic minerals has been increasing since 2012. In 2015, there was a 4.7% increase in the extraction of non-metallic minerals (from 211 million tonnes to 221 million tonnes).

Fossil energy materials and carriers include coal, peat, crude oil and natural gas. The extraction of these increased by 6.0% between 2014 and 2015, to 94 million tones. This was the first increase since 2000 and can be attributed to an increase in the production of crude oil and natural gas liquids from the North Sea due to the opening of new fields. Prior to this increase, extraction of fossil energy materials had fallen 66.7% between 2000 and 2014.

Physical imports increased by 32.4% between 2000 and 2015, rising from 210 million tonnes to 278 million tonnes. Contrary to this, physical exports have gradually decreased, peaking at 197 million tonnes in 2002 and falling to 152 million tonnes in 2015 – the lowest point since 2000. The rise in imports partly offsets the decline in domestic extraction.

The physical trade balance (PTB) shows the relationship between imports and exports and is calculated by subtracting the weight of exports from the weight of imports[6]. The UK has a positive PTB, meaning that more materials and products are imported than are exported.

In 2000, the PTB was relatively small at 16 million tonnes. It generally increased until 2007, but then fell between 2008 and 2010 during the economic downturn. Since 2010, the PTB has increased, peaking at 148 million tonnes in 2013. However, the PTB decreased by 11.9% in 2015 (to 127 million tonnes). Despite this, the amount of materials and products that were imported (278 million tonnes) was almost twice the amount of materials and products that were exported (152 million tonnes), suggesting that the UK may be becoming more reliant on the production of materials in other countries.

Direct material input (DMI) (domestic extraction plus imports) measures the total amount of materials that are available for use in the economy.

Domestic material consumption (DMC) (domestic extraction plus imports minus exports) measures the amount of materials used in the economy and is calculated by subtracting exports from DMI.

In 2015, the UK consumed 576 million tonnes of material, consisting of 230 million tonnes of non-metallic minerals (40.0%), 173 million tonnes of biomass (30.1%), 159 million tonnes of fossil fuels (27.6%) and 14 million tonnes of metal ores (2.4%).

Between 2000 and 2015, DMI and DMC decreased by 21.5% and 22.0% respectively. DMI and DMC have gradually declined since the start of the economic downturn in 2008. This indicates that fewer material resources were being used and consumed in the UK economy. DMI and DMC fell most sharply between 2008 and 2009 (decreasing by 11.4% and 12.2%, respectively). Between 2014 and 2015, DMI decreased by 1.5%, from 739 million tonnes to 728 million tonnes and DMC decreased by 2.5%, from 591 million tonnes to 576 million tonnes.

7. More information

There is more information about environmental accounts on the UK Environmental Accounts release page.

Notes

1. Transformation losses are the differences between the energy content of the input and output product, arising from the transformation of one energy product to another.
2. Distribution losses are losses of energy product during transmission (for example, losses of electricity in the grid) between the supplier and the user of the energy.
3. To enable a consistent time series the following SICs have been combined: "transport and storage" and "information and communication" into "transport, storage and communications sector".
4. Policies include UK National Air Quality Strategy Directive on Integrated Pollution Prevention and Control (IPPC) (Directive 2008/1/EC); Directive on industrial emissions 2010/75/EU (IED); UK Pollution Prevention and Control (PPC) regulations; Large combustion plant directive (LCPD, 2001/80/EC); Limiting sulphur emissions from the combustion of certain liquid fuels by controlling the sulphur contents of certain liquid fuels (Directive 1999/32/EC); Annex VI of the MARPOL agreement for ship emissions, augmented by the Sulphur Content of Marine Fuels Directive 2005/33/EC and the introduction of Sulphur Emission Control Areas.
5. Provisional figures for 2014 have been revised and data gaps addressed, resulting in an increase in domestic extraction in the previously reported 2014 figures. Data on minerals and crops are not available for 2015, so estimates have been used in the calculations of the material flow accounts.
6. The physical trade balance (imports minus exports) is defined in reverse to the monetary trade balance (exports minus imports). Physical estimates can differ quite significantly from monetary estimates.

12.1 Estimates of remaining recoverable oil and gas reserves[1]

		2009	2010	2011	2012	2013	2014	2015
Oil (million tonnes)								
Reserves								
Proven	K7MI	378	374	413	405	404	374	349
Probable	K7MJ	390	377	374	405	342	342	217
Proven plus probable	K7MK	769	751	788	811	746	716	566
Possible	K7ML	343	342	319	253	338	344	161
Maximum[2]	K7MM	1 112	1 093	1 106	1 064	1 084	1 060	943
Range of undiscovered resources								
Lower	K7MN	397	475	422	455	453	444	444
Upper	K7MO	1 477	1 374	1 321	1 344	1 331	1 344	1 344
Range of total reserves and resources								
Lower[3]	K7MP	1 509	1 568	1 528	1 519	1 537	1 504	1 387
Upper[4]	K7MQ	2 589	2 467	2 427	2 408	2 415	2 404	2 287
Expected level of reserves[5]								
Opening stocks	K7MR	770	769	751	788	811	746	716
Extraction[6]	K7MS	−68	−63	−52	−45	−41	−40	−45
Other volume changes	K7MT	67	45	89	68	−24	10	−105
Closing stocks	K7MU	769	751	788	811	746	716	566
Gas (billion cubic metres)								
Reserves								
Proven	K7MV	256	253	246	244	241	205	207
Probable	K7MW	308	267	246	217	211	201	126
Proven plus probable	K7MX	564	520	493	461	452	407	333
Possible	K7MY	276	261	216	238	198	187	113
Maximum[2]	K7MZ	840	781	709	699	650	594	507
Range of undiscovered resources								
Lower	K7N2	300	363	353	370	357	365	365
Upper	K7N3	949	1 021	977	1 011	997	1 000	1 000
Range of total reserves and resources								
Lower[3]	K7N4	1 140	1 144	1 062	1 069	1 007	959	872
Upper[4]	K7N5	1 789	1 802	1 686	1 710	1 647	1 594	1 507
Expected level of reserves[5]								
Opening stocks	K7N6	601	564	520	493	461	452	407
Extraction[6]	K7N7	−57	−55	−43	−37	−34	−35	−38
Other volume changes	K7N8	20	10	16	5	25	−10	−36
Closing stocks	K7N9	564	520	493	461	452	407	333

1 All data refer to end of year.
  Components may not sum to totals due to rounding.
2 Maximum reserves for 2015 include central estimates for contingent resource
  which for oil are estimated at 216 million tonnes and for gas are estimated
  at 62 million cubic metres. For further details see
  https://www.ogauthority.co.uk/data-centre/data-downloads-and-publications/
  reserves-and-resources/
3 The lower end of the range of total reserves and resources has been
  calculated as the sum of maximum and the lower end of the range of
  undiscovered resources. Estimates for 2015 are the same as estimates for
  2014. The OGA is currently revising the method of producing undiscovered
  resources estimates (due to be published later this year), but expect
  estimates for 2015 to be very similar to those produced for 2014.
4 The upper end of the range of total reserves and resources has been
  calculated as the sum of maximum and the upper end of the range of
  undiscovered resources. Estimates for 2015 are the same as estimates
  2014, for the same reason given above.
5 Expected reserves are the sum of proven and probable reserves.
6 The negative of extraction is shown here for the purposes of the
  calculation only. Of itself, extraction should be considered as a positive
  value.

Source: ONS and Department for Business, Energy and Industrial Strategy

12.2 Energy Consumption[1]

		2009	2010	2011	2012	2013	2014	2015
Direct use of energy from fossil fuels								
Agriculture, forestry and fishing	K7YT	1.8	1.9	1.8	1.8	1.8	1.8	1.8
Mining and quarrying	K7YU	6.6	6.7	5.8	5.4	5.2	5.2	5.6
Manufacturing	K7YV	29.5	30.2	29.2	27.9	27.8	27.1	26.3
Electricity, gas, steam and air conditioning supply, water supply, sewerage, waste management activities and remediation services	K7YW	55.0	57.2	51.4	51.6	48.3	42.1	36.2
Construction	K7YX	3.7	3.8	3.7	3.8	3.7	3.9	3.9
Wholesale and retail trade; repair of motor vehicles and motorcycles	K7YY	4.8	4.9	4.7	4.8	4.7	4.5	4.7
Transport and storage; information and communication	K7YZ	28.1	28.3	29.3	27.6	26.6	27.6	28.6
Accommodation and food services	K7Z5	1.5	1.6	1.5	1.5	1.6	1.3	1.4
Financial and insurance activities	K8BZ	–	–	–	–	–	–	–
Real estate activities; professional scientific and technical activities; administrative and support service activities	K8C2	2.1	2.2	2.2	2.2	2.2	2.0	2.1
Public administration and defence; compulsory social security	K7Z3	2.6	2.5	2.5	2.6	2.4	2.1	2.1
Education	K7Z4	1.5	1.7	1.5	1.3	1.3	1.1	1.1
Human health and social work activities	K8C3	2.0	2.1	2.0	2.1	2.3	2.1	2.0
Arts, entertainment and recreation; other service activities	K8C4	1.2	1.2	1.2	1.2	1.2	1.1	1.1
Activities of households as employers, undifferentiated goods and services-producing activities of households for own use	K8C5	0.1	0.1	0.1	0.1	0.1	0.1	0.1
Consumer expenditure	K7Z7	56.4	60.0	50.7	55.1	55.1	49.1	50.7
Total use of energy from fossil fuels	K7Z8	196.9	204.3	187.6	189.3	184.3	171.1	167.7
Energy from other sources[2]	K7Z9	23.3	22.9	25.6	26.7	29.0	30.0	34.7
Total energy consumption of primary fuels and equivalents	K7ZA	220.2	227.2	213.2	215.9	213.4	201.1	202.4
Direct use of energy including other sources								
Agriculture, forestry and fishing	K7ZB	2.3	2.4	2.3	2.4	2.4	2.5	2.5
Mining and quarrying	K7ZC	6.8	6.9	6.0	5.6	5.4	5.3	5.8
Manufacturing	K7ZD	36.0	37.2	36.2	34.6	34.7	33.9	33.4
Electricity, gas, steam and air conditioning supply; water supply, sewerage, waste management activities and remediation services	K7ZE	50.5	50.9	49.0	50.2	48.7	44.5	43.4
Of which: transformation losses by major producers	K7ZF	40.9	41.4	39.5	40.8	39.2	34.6	32.2
Distribution losses of electricity supply	K7ZG	2.4	2.3	2.4	2.5	2.4	2.5	2.4
Construction	K7ZH	4.6	4.7	4.6	4.7	4.5	4.7	4.8
Wholesale and retail trade; repair of motor vehicles and motorcycles	K7ZI	7.5	7.7	7.5	7.4	7.4	7.2	7.2
Transport and storage; information and communication	K7ZJ	29.7	30.0	30.9	29.2	28.3	29.2	30.0
Accommodation and food services	K7ZN	2.0	2.2	2.1	2.1	2.1	1.9	1.9
Financial and insurance activities	K8C7	1.0	1.0	1.1	1.1	1.0	1.0	1.0
Real estate activities; professional scientific and technical activities; administrative and support service activities	K8C8	2.9	3.0	2.9	3.0	3.0	2.8	2.8
Public administration and defence; compulsory social security	K7ZL	3.0	2.9	2.8	2.9	2.7	2.2	2.1
Education	K7ZM	1.8	1.9	1.7	1.5	1.5	1.3	1.2
Human health and social work activities	K8C9	2.4	2.5	2.3	2.5	2.6	2.3	2.1
Arts, entertainment and recreation, other service activities	K8CA	1.6	1.6	1.5	1.6	1.6	1.4	1.4
Activities of households as employers; undifferentiated goods and services-producing activities of households for own use	K8CB	0.1	0.1	0.1	0.1	0.1	0.1	0.1
Consumer expenditure	K7ZP	68.2	72.3	62.2	67.2	67.4	61.0	62.6
Total energy consumption of primary fuels and equivalents	K7ZA	220.2	227.2	213.2	215.9	213.4	201.1	202.4
Reallocated use of energy								
Energy industry electricity transformation losses and Distribution losses allocated to final consumer								
Agriculture, forestry and fishing	K7ZR	2.8	3.0	2.9	2.9	2.9	2.9	3.0
Mining and quarrying	K7ZS	7.1	7.1	6.3	5.8	5.7	5.6	6.0
Manufacturing	K7ZT	45.3	47.2	45.8	44.1	44.1	42.3	41.5
Electricity, gas, steam and air conditioning supply; water supply, sewerage, waste management activities and remediation services	K7ZU	10.8	10.7	10.5	10.6	10.7	10.5	11.7
Construction	K7ZV	5.9	6.0	5.9	5.9	5.7	5.8	5.8
Wholesale and retail trade; repair of motor vehicles and motorcycles	K7ZW	11.6	11.9	11.6	11.6	11.6	10.9	10.7
Transport and storage; information and communication	K7ZX	31.7	32.2	33.2	31.5	30.5	31.1	31.9
Accommodation and food services	K823	2.9	3.0	2.9	3.0	3.0	2.7	2.7
Financial and insurance activities	K8CD	2.4	2.5	2.7	2.7	2.4	2.4	2.3
Real estate activities; professional scientific and technical activities administration and support service activities	K8CE	4.2	4.2	4.1	4.2	4.1	3.9	3.9
Public administration and defence compulsory social security	K7ZZ	3.6	3.4	3.3	3.3	3.0	2.4	2.1
Education	K822	2.1	2.3	2.0	1.9	1.8	1.5	1.2
Human health and social work activities	K8CF	3.1	3.2	2.9	3.1	3.2	2.6	2.2
Arts, entertainment and recreation; other service activities	K8CG	2.2	2.2	2.0	2.1	2.1	1.8	1.7
Activities of households as employers; undifferentiated goods and services-producing activities of households for own use	K8CH	0.1	0.1	0.1	0.1	0.1	0.1	0.1
Consumer expenditure	K825	84.3	88.3	77.2	83.1	82.5	74.7	75.6
Total energy consumption of primary fuels and equivalents	K7ZA	220.2	227.2	213.2	215.9	213.4	201.1	202.4
Energy from renewable and waste sources[3]	K827	7.8	8.7	9.5	10.4	12.4	14.4	17.4
Percentage from renewable and waste sources[3]	K828	3.5	3.8	4.5	4.8	5.8	7.2	8.6

1 Components may not sum to totals due to rounding.
2 Nuclear power, imports of electricity and renewable & waste sources.
3 Renewable sources include solar power and energy from wind, wave and tide,
   hydroelectricity, wood, straw, liquid biofuels and sewage gas.
   Landfill gas, poultry litter and municipal solid waste combustion
   have also been included within this definition.

Sources: Ricardo Energy & Environment Department for Business, Energy and Industrial ; Strategy, ONS

12.3 Atmospheric emissions[1]
2015

	Total greenhouse gas emissions	Carbon Dioxide (CO2)	Methane (CH4)	Nitrous Oxide (N2O)	Hydrofluoro-carbons (HFCs)	Perfluoro-carbons (PFCs)	Sulphur hexafluoride (SF6)
Thousand tonnes CO2 equivalent							
Agriculture, forestry and fishing	51 546	7 519	27 657	16 321	48	–	–
Mining and quarrying	20 495	17 473	2 659	354	9	–	–
Manufacturing	88 529	85 368	223	585	1 887	327	139
Electricity, gas, steam and air conditioning supply; water supply, sewerage, waste management activities and remediation services	149 500	126 913	20 142	2 015	231	–	199
Construction	11 905	11 207	21	372	305	–	–
Wholesale and retail trade; repair of motor vehicles and motorcycles	17 883	12 555	36	167	5 126	–	–
Transport and storage; information and communication	85 727	83 049	86	898	1 693	–	–
Accommodation and food services	3 742	3 077	9	18	638	–	–
Financial and insurance activities	226	98	–	10	118	–	–
Real estate activities; professional scientific and technical activities; administration and support service activities	6 158	5 239	7	34	877	–	1
Public administration and defence; compulsory social security	5 661	5 298	7	49	189	–	118
Education	2 916	2 588	6	10	312	–	–
Human health and social work activities	5 550	4 465	9	598	476	–	1
Arts, entertainment and recreation; other service activities	2 897	2 659	5	14	220	–	–
Activities of households as employers; undifferentiated goods and services-producing activities of households for own use	240	238	1	1	–	–	–
Consumer expenditure	142 223	136 581	1 311	627	3 705	–	–
Total	595 197	504 327	52 179	22 072	15 833	327	457
Of which: emissions from road transport[2]	115 394	114 267	107	1 020	..	..	..

	Total acid rain precursors	Sulphur Dioxide (SO2)	Nitrogen Oxides (NOx)	Ammonia (NH3)
Thousand tonnes SO2 equivalent				
Agriculture, forestry and fishing	497	–	20	477
Mining and quarrying	55	6	49	–
Manufacturing	215	103	104	8
Electricity, gas, steam and air conditioning supply; water supply, sewerage, waste management activities and remediation services	249	91	143	15
Construction	37	–	36	–
Wholesale and retail trade; repair of motor vehicles and motorcycles	27	–	27	–
Transport and storage; information and communication	466	108	357	1
Accommodation and food services	4	–	4	–
Financial and insurance activities	–	–	–	–
Real estate activities; professional scientific and technical activities; administrative and support service activities	12	–	11	1
Public administration and defence; compulsory social security	24	1	17	6
Education	5	2	3	–
Human health and social work activities	5	–	5	–
Arts, entertainment and recreation; other service activities	12	–	4	7
Activities of households as employers; undifferentiated goods and services-producing activities of households for own use	–	–	–	–
Consumer expenditure	187	27	124	35
Total (excluding natural world)	1 794	341	903	550
Of which: emissions from road transport[2]	229	–	218	10

	Thousand tonnes						Tonnes		
	PM10[3]	PM2.5[3]	CO	NMVOC	Benzene	Butadiene	Lead	Cadmium	Mercury
Agriculture, forestry and fishing	18.98	7.56	52.69	180.43	0.11	0.04	0.42	0.04	0.02
Mining and quarrying	7.97	2.00	36.96	99.79	0.30	–	0.36	0.05	0.02
Manufacturing	32.49	24.36	415.25	264.61	2.13	0.19	52.14	1.76	2.02
Electricity, gas, steam and air conditioning supply; water supply, sewerage, waste management activities and remediation services	5.89	3.80	72.66	31.06	1.19	–	3.33	0.18	1.61
Construction	8.68	3.42	185.47	50.68	0.54	0.14	0.36	0.05	0.02
Wholesale and retail trade; repair of motor vehicles and motorcycles	2.35	1.61	15.45	36.49	0.08	0.02	1.33	0.03	0.02
Transport and storage; information and communication	34.50	31.66	92.40	27.89	2.26	0.19	3.12	1.29	0.13
Accommodation and food services	0.18	0.16	2.51	0.53	0.02	–	0.02	–	–
Financial and insurance activities	0.05	0.05	0.41	0.12	–	–	0.01	–	–
Real estate activities; professional scientific and technical activities; administration and support service activities	0.66	0.50	15.77	1.07	0.04	0.01	0.05	0.01	0.01
Public administration and defence: compulsory social security	0.81	0.72	18.73	1.87	0.11	0.02	0.12	0.02	0.01
Education	0.49	0.45	4.74	0.20	0.01	–	0.66	0.01	0.06
Human health and social work activities	0.15	0.13	2.94	0.98	0.02	–	0.01	–	–
Arts, entertainment and recreation; other service activities	0.30	0.24	4.84	1.92	0.01	–	0.09	0.01	0.60
Activities of households as employers; undifferentiated goods and services-producing activities of households for own use	–	–	50.70	0.98	0.07	0.01	–	–	–
Consumer expenditure	59.98	54.65	738.10	219.58	6.73	1.26	5.51	1.21	0.34
Total (excluding natural world)	173.48	131.31	1 709.62	918.20	13.61	1.89	67.52	4.67	4.84
Of which: emissions from road transport[2]	20.53	13.88	334.26	26.26	0.92	0.24	1.67	0.36	0.23

1 Components may not sum to totals due to rounding.
2 Includes emissions from fuel sources which are used by road vehicles (eg HGVs, LGVs, cars and motorcycles) across all industries.
3 PM10 and PM2.5 is particulate matter arising from various sources including fuel combustion, quarrying and construction, and formation of 'secondary' particles in the atmosphere from reactions involving other pollutants - sulphur dioxide, nitrogen oxides, ammonia and NMVOCs.

Source: Ricardo Energy & Environment, ONS

12.4 Greenhouse gas and acid rain precursor emissions[1]

		2009	2010	2011	2012	2013	2014	2015
Thousand tonnes CO2 equivalent								
Greenhouse gases - CO2,CH4,N2O,HFC,PFCs,NF3 and SF6[2]								
Agriculture, forestry and fishing	K8AQ	49 974	50 710	50 340	49 998	50 434	51 504	51 546
Mining and quarrying	K8AR	24 771	24 646	22 423	21 111	20 036	19 884	20 495
Manufacturing	K8AS	93 115	96 854	92 193	89 376	90 655	91 119	88 529
Electricity, gas, steam and air conditioning supply; water supply, sewerage, waste management activities and remediation services	K8AT	204 926	207 706	192 742	204 144	191 304	167 050	149 500
Construction	K8AU	11 051	11 392	11 008	11 503	11 131	11 677	11 905
Wholesale and retail trade; repair of motor vehicles and motorcycles	K8AV	18 823	19 641	17 932	18 132	18 075	17 801	17 883
Transport and storage; information and communication	K8AW	84 283	84 979	87 794	82 529	79 653	82 934	85 727
Accommodation and food services	K8AX	4 286	4 504	4 129	4 186	4 195	3 711	3 742
Financial and insurance activities	K8B2	227	238	224	249	212	221	226
Real estate activities; professional, scientific and technical activities; administration and support service activities	KI4H	6 103	6 342	6 285	6 362	6 266	6 035	6 158
Public administration and defence; compulsory social security	K8AY	7 144	6 877	6 806	6 923	6 503	5 689	5 661
Education	K8AZ	3 698	4 069	3 758	3 290	3 295	2 952	2 916
Human health and social work activities	KI4I	5 216	5 572	5 339	5 593	5 952	5 552	5 550
Arts, entertainment and recreation; other service activities	KI4J	3 064	3 080	3 023	3 074	3 081	2 814	2 897
Activities of households as employers; undifferentiated goods and services - producing activities of households for own use	KI4K	225	227	228	230	233	236	240
Consumer expenditure	K8B4	151 180	160 583	138 959	149 784	151 545	138 108	142 223
Total greenhouse gas emissions	K8B5	668 087	687 421	643 181	656 483	642 569	607 287	595 197
Of which: road transport emissions from all industries[3]	K8B6	115 711	114 899	113 199	112 466	112 012	113 899	115 394

		2009	2010	2011	2012	2013	2014	2015
Thousand tonnes SO2 equivalent								
Acid rain precursor emissions - SO2,NOx,NH3[4]								
Agriculture, forestry and fishing	K8B9	473	476	475	468	464	487	497
Mining and quarrying	K8BA	67	68	59	55	52	53	55
Manufacturing	K8BB	309	326	303	285	272	249	215
Electricity, gas, steam and air conditioning supply; water supply, sewerage, waste management activities and remediation services	K8BC	372	377	359	454	391	302	249
Construction	K8BD	41	40	36	38	34	35	37
Wholesale and retail trade; repair of motor vehicles and motorcycles	K8BE	40	38	35	33	30	29	27
Transport and storage; information and communication	K8BF	553	553	552	472	381	436	466
Accommodation and food services	K8BG	5	5	4	4	4	4	4
Financial and insurance activities	K8BJ	1	1	1	1	–	–	–
Real estate activities; professional, scientific and technical activities; administrative and support service activities	KI4L	12	12	11	11	11	11	12
Public administration and defence; compulsory social security	KI4M	37	36	33	31	29	26	24
Education	KI4N	7	7	7	6	6	5	5
Human health and social work activities	KI4O	5	5	5	5	5	5	5
Arts, entertainment and recreation; other service activities	K8BH	14	13	12	12	12	12	12
Activities of households as employers; undifferentiated goods and services - producing activities of households for own use	K8BI	–	–	–	–	–	–	–
Consumer expenditure	K8BL	207	202	191	194	194	185	187
Total acid rain precursor emissions (excluding natural world)	K8BM	2 142	2 159	2 083	2 070	1 886	1 839	1 794
Of which: road transport emissions from all industries[3]	K8BN	304	286	268	255	244	237	229

1 Components may not sum to totals due to rounding.
2 Carbon dioxide, methane, nitrous oxide, hydrofluorocarbons, perfluorocarbon, nitrogen trifluoride and sulphur hexafluoride expressed as thousand tonnes of carbon dioxide equivalent.
3 Includes emissions from all fuel sources which are used by road vehicles (eg HGVs, LGVs, cars and motorcycles) across all industries.
4 Sulphur dioxide, nitrogen oxides and ammonia expressed as thousand tonnes of sulphur dioxide equivalent.

Source: Ricardo Energy & Environment, ONS

12.5 Material flows[1,2]

		2009	2010	2011	2012	2013	2014	2015
Domestic extraction								
Biomass								
Crops[3]	MU44	42	40	43	37	40	46	44
Crop residues (used), fodder crops and grazed biomass	MU45	86	85	87	85	85	90	85
Wood	MU46	5	6	6	6	6	7	6
Wild fish catch and aquatic plants/animals	MU47	1	1	1	1	1	1	1
Total biomass	MU48	134	131	136	129	132	143	135
Metal ores								
Total metal ores	MU49	–	–	–	–	–	–	–
Non-metallic minerals[4]								
Limestone and gypsum	MU4A	61	58	59	56	58	68	71
Clays and kaolin	MU4B	7	8	9	7	8	9	9
Sand and gravel	MU4C	127	122	124	112	114	121	126
Other non-metallic minerals	MU4D	15	16	16	16	16	14	14
Total non-metallic minerals	MU4E	210	205	208	192	196	211	221
Fossil fuels								
Coal	MU4F	19	19	19	17	14	12	9
Crude oil	MU4G	68	63	52	45	41	40	45
Natural gas	MU4H	59	56	45	38	36	36	39
Total fossil fuels	MU4I	146	139	116	100	90	88	94
Total domestic extraction	MU4J	490	474	460	421	419	443	450
Imports								
Biomass	MU4K	49	51	50	52	58	60	59
Metal ores	MU4L	27	33	33	34	38	41	38
Non-metallic minerals	MU4M	13	15	16	14	15	18	18
Fossil fuels	MU4N	149	148	165	180	175	162	148
Other products	MU4O	15	17	16	15	16	17	16
Total imports	MU4P	253	264	281	295	302	297	278
Exports								
Biomass	MU4Q	20	22	22	22	21	22	23
Metal ores	MU4R	21	24	25	24	25	26	24
Non-metallic minerals	MU4S	17	17	17	14	15	14	12
Fossil fuels	MU4T	88	96	92	89	85	82	85
Other products	MU4U	8	8	8	8	8	8	8
Total exports	MU4V	154	166	163	157	154	153	152
Indicators								
Domestic material consumption[5] (Domestic extraction + imports - exports)	MU4W	593	577	582	563	570	591	576
Of which:								
Biomass	MU4X	166	163	167	161	172	183	173
Metal ores	MU4Y	6	10	9	10	13	15	14
Non-metallic minerals	MU4Z	208	206	209	194	198	218	230
Fossil fuels	MU52	213	198	197	198	187	175	159
Direct material input (Domestic extraction + imports)	MU53	743	739	741	716	721	739	728
Physical trade balance[5] (Imports - exports)	MU54	99	98	118	138	148	144	127

1 Components may not sum to totals due to rounding.
2 Estimates for indirect flows are currently under development. It has not therefore been possible to include these or estimates for Total Material Requirement (direct material input plus indirect flows).
3 2015 crops data estimated based on the Eurostat method of estimation.
4 2015 data estimated due to unavailable data source
5 Domestic material consumption may not equal domestic extraction plus imports minus exports, as it has not been possible to proportion all of the residence adjustment to imports.
6 A positive physical trade balance (PTB) indicates a net import of material into the UK. This calculation of the PTB differs from the National Accounts formula (exports minus imports) because flows of materials and products are considered the inverse of the flows of money recorded in the National Accounts.

Sources: Department for Environment, Food and Rural Affairs; ;
Food and Agriculture Organization of the United Nations;;
Eurostat; ;
Kentish Cobnuts Association;;
British Geological Survey;;
HM Revenue & Customs; ;
Office for National Statistics.

United Kingdom
National Accounts

The Blue Book
Chapter 13: Flow of Funds

2017 edition

Editors: Dean Goodway & Sarah Nightingale

Office for National Statistics

Chapter 13: Flow of funds

The tables in this chapter present estimates of stocks and flows of financial assets and liabilities by institutional sector and financial instrument.

Of these tables:

- Table 13.1 presents flows (or transactions) of financial assets and liabilities for each institutional sector and lower-level financial instrument (financial account)

- Table 13.2 presents levels (or stocks) of financial assets and liabilities for each institutional sector and lower-level financial instrument (balance sheet)

- Tables 13.3.1 to 13.3.8 present both financial flows and stocks by institutional sector and financial instrument

Estimates for all the institutional sectors are brought together in this chapter, to allow changes in assets and liabilities to be compared across the sectors. Estimates for each individual sector are also published in the appropriate sector chapters in this publication.

These financial statistics are important for identifying the build-up of risks in the financial sector and for understanding financial connections among the institutional sectors and sub-sectors within the economy.

What is flow of funds?

"Flow of funds" are the financial flows across sectors of the UK economy and the rest of the world. Information can be presented on debtor and creditor relationships and the changes in financial assets and liabilities in the economy. Flow of funds is based on the principle that the movement of all funds must be accounted for. Across the total economy (UK and the rest of the world), the total sources of funds must equal the total uses of funds and every financial asset transaction must have a counterpart liability transaction.

Since the recent global financial crisis, the international community has had an increased focus on the analysis of financial stability and the development of improvements to the data, which support that analysis. This is particularly important for those countries, like the UK, which have a significant financial sector. An important area identified internationally for improvement is the development of flow of funds counterpart statistics. These improve our understanding of how each individual sector may be exposed to the risk that may build up in other sectors. These statistics support macro-economic analysis and financial stability policy.

Counterpart statistics are not currently presented in this chapter. However, in response to the need for counterpart statistics, Office for National Statistics and the Bank of England started the joint Flow of Funds Project in 2014. More information on the project and experimental counterpart statistics is available based on last year's figures. Updated figures will be published on 17 November 2017.

13.1 Flow of funds
2016
Total economy: all sectors and the rest of the world. Unconsolidated

£ million

		United Kingdom S.1		Public corporations S.11001		Private non-financial corporations S.11002 + S.11003	
		Assets	Liabilities	Assets	Liabilities	Assets	Liabilities
Financial account							
Net acquisition of financial assets/liabilities	**F.A/L**						
Monetary gold	F.11	–					
Special drawing rights	F.12	–1 397	–				
Monetary gold and special drawing rights	F.1	–1 397	–				
Currency	F.21	7 508	7 503	79		840	
Transferable deposits	F.22						
Deposits with UK MFIs[1]	F.22N1	265 463	285 587	239		27 151	
Deposits with rest of the world MFIs	F.22N9	111 903		–		11 026	
Other deposits	F.29	20 320	21 044	–446	–	88	
Currency and deposits	F.2	405 194	314 134	–128	–	39 105	
Short-term debt securities issued	F.31						
By UK central government	F.31N1	7 554	12 524	–		–315	
By UK local government	F.31N2	–	–				
By UK MFIs	F.31N5	13 768	20 237	–		1 360	
MMIs[2] by other UK residents	F.31N6	430	2 942	–		–2 580	1 953
MMIs by rest of the world	F.31N9	–19 494		–		1 425	
Long-term debt securities issued	F.32						
By UK central government	F.32N1	13 235	56 083	–		–23	
By UK local government	F.32N2	362	362	–			
By UK MFIs and other UK residents	F.32N5-6	–6 597	26 704	–	1 107	3 770	24 772
By rest of the world	F.32N9	–92 162		–		–608	
Debt securities	F.3	–82 904	118 852	–	1 107	3 029	26 725
Short-term loans	F.41						
By UK MFIs	F.41N1	73 021	35 915		299		15 192
By rest of the world MFIs	F.41N9		–44 463				3 002
Long-term loans	F.42						
Direct investment loans	F.421	31 727	25 002	–	–	28 336	16 970
Secured on dwellings	F.422	38 368	38 368	–			–231
Finance leasing	F.423	1 014	1 014		–59	546	324
Other long-term loans by UK residents	F.424N1	37 012	30 887.00	–174	1 907	–8 451	26 394
Other long-term loans by rest of the world	F.424N9		561		–		–
Loans	F.4	181 142	87 284.00	–174	2 258	20 431	61 651
Shares and other equity, excluding mutual funds' shares	F.51						
Listed UK shares	F.511N1	–17 805	–94 844	–		16 492	–97 353
Unlisted UK shares	F.512N1	–795.0	139 757	–	–	17 390.0	123 919
Other UK equity (including direct investment in property)	F.519N6	–1 691	–968		–1 691		723
UK shares and bonds issued by other UK residents	F.519N7	–	–	–	–	–	
Shares and other equity issued by rest of the world	F.519N9	–60 226		64		922	
Investment fund shares/units	F.52						
UK mutual funds' shares	F.52N1	1 972	2 031			20	
Rest of the world mutual funds' shares	F.52N9	2 910					
Equity and investment fund shares/units	F.5	–75 635.0	45 976	64	–1 691	34 824.0	27 289
Non-life insurance technical reserves	F.61	757	936	–		63	
Life insurance and annuity entitlements	F.62	19 617	20 437				
Pension schemes[3]	F.6M	63 360	63 360				9 862
Provisions for calls under standardised guarantees	F.66	–	–				
Insurance, pension and standardised guarantee schemes	F.6	83 734	84 733	–		63	9 862
Financial derivatives	F.71	21 616	–	–		–533	
Financial derivatives and employee stock options	F.7	23 495	1 880	–		–533	1 714
Other accounts payable/receivable	F.8	29 419	29 751	103	393	6 736	7 969
Total net acquisition of financial assets	**F.A**	563 048.0		–135		103 655.0	
Total net acquisition of financial liabilities	**F.L**		682 610.00		2 067		135 210
Net lending(+)/borrowing(-)							
Net lending(+)/borrowing(-) from the financial account	B.9f		–119 562.00		–2 202		–31 555.0
Statistical discrepancy between the financial and capital account	dB.9		2 763		–310		12 269
Net from the capital account	**B.9n**		–116 799		–2 512		–19 286

Source: Office for National Statistics; Bank of England

13.1 Flow of funds
2016

continued

Total economy: all sectors and the rest of the world. Unconsolidated

£ million

		Monetary financial institutions S.121+S.122+S.123		Other financial intermediaries and financial auxiliaries S.124 to S.127		Insurance corporations and pension funds S.128+S.129	
		Assets	Liabilities	Assets	Liabilities	Assets	Liabilities
Financial account							
Net acquisition of financial assets/liabilities	F.A/L						
Monetary gold	F.11						
Special drawing rights	F.12						
Monetary gold and special drawing rights	F.1						
Currency	F.21	663	7 363	–			
Transferable deposits	F.22						
Deposits with UK MFIs[1]	F.22N1	111 218	285 587	61 152		−1 154	
Deposits with rest of the world MFIs	F.22N9	99 983		2 408		−4 480	
Other deposits	F.29	–		8 251	3 188	–	
Currency and deposits	F.2	211 864	292 950	71 811	3 188	−5 634	
Short-term debt securities issued	F.31						
By UK central government	F.31N1	−1 553		9 523		1 625	
By UK local government	F.31N2	–		–			
By UK MFIs	F.31N5	−167	20 237	13 792		−3 124	
MMIs[2] by other UK residents	F.31N6	32		2 267	978	−186	
MMIs by rest of the world	F.31N9	−17 353		−7 645		1 770	
Long-term debt securities issued	F.32						
By UK central government	F.32N1	51 581		−52 774		14 177	
By UK local government	F.32N2	–		7		121	
By UK MFIs and other UK residents	F.32N5-6	−17 757	−1 472	11 142	5 742	−4 069	3 168
By rest of the world	F.32N9	−84 817		1 422		−12 488	
Debt securities	F.3	−70 034	18 765	−22 266	6 720	−2 174	3 168
Short-term loans	F.41						
By UK MFIs	F.41N1	73 021			6 849		4 378
By rest of the world MFIs	F.41N9				−52 836		3 809
Long-term loans	F.42						
Direct investment loans	F.421	–		1 672	6 384	1 719	1 648
Secured on dwellings	F.422	40 694		1 217		990	
Finance leasing	F.423	−24	84	492	60		
Other long-term loans by UK residents	F.424N1	724		30 983	−17 183	−624	−2 095
Other long-term loans by rest of the world	F.424N9		–		312		
Loans	F.4	114 415	84	34 364	−56 414	2 085	7 740
Shares and other equity, excluding mutual funds' shares	F.51						
Listed UK shares	F.511N1	−263	76	−5 805	2 330	−15 744	103
Unlisted UK shares	F.512N1	−4 220	−167	−344	9 199	−2 842	6 806
Other UK equity (including direct investment in property)	F.519N6		–				
UK shares and bonds issued by other UK residents	F.519N7	–	–	–		–	
Shares and other equity issued by rest of the world	F.519N9	−45		−29 457		−26 718	
Investment fund shares/units	F.52						
UK mutual funds' shares	F.52N1	59		166	2 031	20 580	
Rest of the world mutual funds' shares	F.52N9			2 603		307	
Equity and investment fund shares/units	F.5	−4 469	−91	−32 837	13 560	−24 417	6 909
Non-life insurance technical reserves	F.61	2		2		4	936
Life insurance and annuity entitlements	F.62	–					20 437
Pension schemes[3]	F.6M	–	528		410	13 686	49 792
Provisions for calls under standardised guarantees	F.66	–					
Insurance, pension and standardised guarantee schemes	F.6	2	528	2	410	13 690	71 165
Financial derivatives	F.71	19 474		152	–	1 061	
Financial derivatives and employee stock options	F.7	19 474	84	152	61	1 061	21
Other accounts payable/receivable	F.8	45	95	483	−1 858	8 694	7 825
Total net acquisition of financial assets	F.A	271 297		51 709		−6 695	
Total financial liabilities	F.L		312 415		−34 333		96 828
Net lending(+)/borrowing(-)							
Net lending(+)/borrowing(-) from the financial account	B.9f		−41 118		86 042		−103 523
Statistical discrepancy between the financial and capital accounts	dB.9		40 011		−108 827		84 175
Net from the capital account	B.9n		−1 107		−22 785		−19 348

Source: Office for National Statistics; Bank of England

13.1
continued

Flow of funds
2016

Total economy: all sectors and the rest of the world. Unconsolidated

£ million

		Central government S.1311		Local government S.1313		Households S.14	
		Assets	Liabilities	Assets	Liabilities	Assets	Liabilities
Financial account							
Net acquisition of financial assets/liabilities	F.A/L						
Monetary gold	F.11	–					
Special drawing rights	F.12	–1 397	–				
Monetary gold and special drawing rights	F.1	–1 397	–				
Currency	F.21		140			4 719	
Transferable deposits	F.22						
Deposits with UK MFIs[1]	F.22N1	–2 007		–2 582		70 401	
Deposits with rest of the world MFIs	F.22N9	2 958		101		–93	
Other deposits	F.29	1 251	17 856	1 493		9 663	
Currency and deposits	F.2	2 202	17 996	–988		84 690	
Short-term debt securities issued	F.31						
By UK central government	F.31N1		12 524	–1 726		–3	
By UK local government	F.31N2				–		
By UK MFIs	F.31N5	–		–657		1 678	
MMIs[2] by other UK residents	F.31N6	487		408		4	–
MMIs by rest of the world	F.31N9	2 309					
Long-term debt securities issued	F.32						
By UK central government	F.32N1		57 276	–114		93	
Other UK central government bonds/UK local government	F.32N2		–1 193		362	–572	
By UK MFIs and other UK residents	F.32N5-6	–	–6 613	–	–	530	–
By rest of the world	F.32N9	3 701				451	
Debt securities	F.3	6 497	61 994	–2 089	362	2 181	–
Short-term loans	F.41						
By UK MFIs	F.41N1		–81		127		9 336
By rest of the world MFIs	F.41N9		–2 398		–		2 950
Long-term loans	F.42						
Direct investment loans	F.421						
Secured on dwellings	F.422	–5 417		884			38 488
Finance leasing	F.423		632		–27		
Other long-term loans by UK residents	F.424N1	18 744	–8	3 725	2 182	–7 915	19 080
Other long-term loans by rest of the world	F.424N9	–	41		208		
Loans	F.4	13 327	–1 814	4 609	2 490	–7 915	69 854
Shares and other equity, excluding mutual funds' shares	F.51						
Listed UK shares	F.511N1	–2 485		–516		–8 844	
Unlisted UK shares	F.512N1	–3		–		–9 368	
Other UK equity (including direct investment in property)	F.519N6	–		–1 691		–	
UK shares and bonds issued by other UK residents	F.519N7	–		–		–	–
Shares and other equity issued by rest of the world	F.519N9	277				–3 629	
Investment fund shares/units	F.52						
UK mutual funds' shares	F.52N1					–20 807	
Rest of the world mutual funds' shares	F.52N9					–	
Equity and investment fund shares/units	F.5	–2 211		–2 207		–42 648	–
Non-life insurance technical reserves	F.61			11		666	
Life insurance and annuity entitlements	F.62					19 617	
Pension schemes[3]	F.6M				2 121	49 674	
Provisions for calls under standardised guarantees	F.66		–				
Insurance, pension and standardised guarantee schemes	F.6		–	11	2 121	69 957	
Financial derivatives	F.71	894				1 130	
Financial derivatives and employee stock options	F.7	894				3 009	
Other accounts payable/receivable	F.8	8 582	4 788	222	3 903	2 556	5 858
Total net acquisition of financial assets	F.A	27 894		–442		111 830	
Total financial liabilities	F.L		82 964		8 876		75 712
Net lending(+)/borrowing(-)							
Net lending(+)/borrowing(-) from the financial account	B.9f		–55 070		–9 318		36 118
Statistical discrepancy between the financial and capital accounts	dB.9		247		–152		–17 889
Net from the capital account	**B.9n**		–54 823		–9 470		18 229

Source: Office for National Statistics; Bank of England

Total economy: all sectors and the rest of the world. Unconsolidated

£ million

		Non-profit institutions serving households S.15		Rest of the world S.2	
		Assets	Liabilities	Assets	Liabilities
Financial account					
Net acquisition of financial assets/liabilities	F.A/L				
Monetary gold	F.11			–	–
Special drawing rights	F.12			–	–1 397
Monetary gold and special drawing rights	F.1			–	–1 397
Currency	F.21	1 207		286	291
Transferable deposits	F.22				
Deposits with UK MFIs[1]	F.22N1	1 045		20 124	
Deposits with rest of the world MFIs	F.22N9	–			111 903
Other deposits	F.29	20		724	
Currency and deposits	F.2	2 272		21 134	112 194
Short-term debt securities issued	F.31				
By UK central government	F.31N1	3		4 970	
By UK local government	F.31N2	–	–		
By UK MFIs	F.31N5	886		6 469	
MMIs[2] by other UK residents	F.31N6	–2	11	2 512	
MMIs by rest of the world	F.31N9	–			–19 494
Long-term debt securities issued	F.32				
By UK central government	F.32N1	295		42 848	
By UK local government	F.32N2	806		–	
By UK MFIs and other UK residents	F.32N5-6	1 506	–	33 301	
By rest of the world	F.32N9	177			–92 162
Debt securities	F.3	1 952	11	90 100	–111 656
Short-term loans	F.41			–44 463	37 106
By UK MFIs	F.41N1		–185		
By rest of the world MFIs	F.41N9		1 010		
Long-term loans	F.42			25 563	37 852
Direct investment loans	F.421			25 002	31 727
Secured on dwellings	F.422		–		
Finance leasing	F.423				–
Other long-term loans by UK residents	F.424N1	–	610		6 125
Other long-term loans by rest of the world	F.424N9			561	
Loans	F.4	–	1 435	–18 900	74 958
Shares and other equity, excluding mutual funds' shares	F.51				
Listed UK shares	F.511N1	–640		–77 039	
Unlisted UK shares	F.512N1	–1 408		140 552	
Other UK equity (including direct investment in property)	F.519N6	–		723	
UK shares and bonds issued by other UK residents	F.519N7	–	–	–	
Shares and other equity issued by rest of the world	F.519N9	–1 640			–60 226
Investment fund shares/units	F.52				
UK mutual funds' shares	F.52N1	1 954		59	
Rest of the world mutual funds' shares	F.52N9	–			2 910
Equity and investment fund shares/units	F.5	–1 734	–	64 295	–57 316
Non-life insurance technical reserves	F.61	9		179	
Life insurance and annuity entitlements	F.62			820	
Pension schemes[3]	F.6M		647	–	
Provisions for calls under standardised guarantees	F.66				
Insurance, pension and standardised guarantee schemes	F.6	9	647	999	–
Financial derivatives	F.71	–562	–	–	21 616
Financial derivatives and employee stock options	F.7	–562	–	4	21 619
Other accounts payable/receivable	F.8	1 998	778	–25	–357
Total net acquisition of financial assets	F.A	3 935		157 607	
Total financial liabilities	F.L		2 871		38 045
Net lending(+)/borrowing(-)					
Net lending(+)/borrowing(-) from the financial account	B.9f		1 064		119 562
Statistical discrepancy between the financial and capital accounts	dB.9		1 950		–2 763
Net from the capital account	B.9n		3 014		116 799

1 Monetary financial institutions
2 Money market instruments
3 F.63 Pension entitlements, F.64 Claims of pension funds on pension managers, F.65 Entitlements to non-pension benefits

Source: Office for National Statistics; Bank of England

13.2 Flow of Funds
2016
Total economy: all sectors and the rest of the world. Unconsolidated

£ billion

	AF.A/L	United Kingdom S.1 Assets	United Kingdom S.1 Liabilities	Public corporations S.11001 Assets	Public corporations S.11001 Liabilities	Private non-financial corporations S.11002 + S.11003 Assets	Private non-financial corporations S.11002 + S.11003 Liabilities
Financial balance sheet at end of period							
Total financial assets	**AF.A/L**						
Monetary gold	AF.11	9.4					
Special drawing rights	AF.12	8.9	11.1				
Monetary gold and special drawing rights	AF.1	18.3	11.1				
Currency	AF.21	87.8	89.1	0.9		6.8	
Transferable deposits	AF.22						
Deposits with UK MFIs[1]	AF.22N1	4 103.7	7 018.9	9.0		427.1	
Deposits with rest of the world MFIs	AF.22N9	2 614.3		–		200.3	
Other deposits	AF.29	200.4	202.8	3.5	–	3.4	
Currency and deposits	AF.2	7 006.2	7 310.8	13.4	–	637.7	
Short-term debt securities issued	AF.31						
By UK central government	AF.31N1	50.3	94.9	0.3		0.7	
By UK local government	AF.31N2	–					
By UK MFIs	AF.31N5	87.3	236.2	0.4		13.7	
MMIs[2] by other UK residents	AF.31N6	14.0	53.4	0.1		4.8	36.6
MMIs by rest of the world	AF.31N9	95.2				8.7	
Long-term debt securities issued	AF.32						
By UK central government	AF.32N1	1 391.8	1 934.6	0.5		2.4	
By UK local government	AF.32N2	4.4	4.4	–		–	
By UK MFIs and other UK residents	AF.32N5-6	981.2	2 083.4	–	24.0	45.2	331.0
By rest of the world	AF.32N9	1 008.4		0.1		13.0	
Debt securities	AF.3	3 632.7	4 406.9	1.4	24.0	88.5	367.6
Short-term loans	AF.41						
By UK MFIs	AF.41N1	2 331.8	1 234.7		2.0		353.7
By rest of the world MFIs	AF.41N9		756.4		–		126.1
Long-term loans	AF.42						
Direct investment loans	AF.421	253.4	409.3	–	0.7	230.2	375.6
Secured on dwellings	AF.422	1 366.4	1 366.4	–			4.1
Finance leasing	AF.423	39.2	39.2		0.6	7.3	26.8
Other long-term loans by UK residents	AF.424N1	1 090.1	633.1	1.1	16.6	38.7	272.1
Other long-term loans by rest of the world	AF.424N9		38.9		0.4		0.5
Loans	AF.4	5 080.9	4 478.0	1.1	57.5	276.1	1 159.0
Shares and other equity, excluding mutual funds' shares	AF.51						
Listed UK shares	AF.511N1	761.7	1 960.9	–	–	31.5	1 506.7
Unlisted UK shares	AF.512N1	695.0	1 797.2	0.3	1.5	77.4	1 025.5
Other UK equity (including direct investment in property)	AF.519N6	129.9	144.3		128.5		15.8
UK shares and bonds issued by other UK residents	AF.519N7	–	–	–		–	
Shares and other equity issued by rest of the world	AF.519N9	2 444.3		1.5		885.1	
Investment fund shares/units	AF.52						
UK mutual funds' shares	AF.52N1	1 086.0	1 088.5			0.8	
Rest of the world mutual funds' shares	AF.52N9	287.0					
Equity and investment fund shares/units	AF.5	5 403.9	4 990.9	1.8	130.1	994.8	2 547.9
Non-life insurance technical reserves	AF.61	46.6	57.6	–		3.9	
Life insurance and annuity entitlements	AF.62	633.9	641.0				
Pension schemes[3]	AF.6M	3 812.8	3 812.8				676.3
Provisions for calls under standardised guarantees	AF.66	–	–				
Insurance, pension and standardised guarantee schemes	AF.6	4 493.2	4 511.4	–		3.9	676.3
Financial derivatives	AF.71	5 399.3	5 356.7			37.0	57.3
Financial derivates and employee stock options	AF.7	5 404.7	5 362.2			37.0	62.3
Other accounts payable/receivable	AF.8	495.4	485.5	15.6	24.6	114.2	168.0
Total financial assets	AF.A	31 535.3		33.5		2 152.3	
Total financial liabilities	AF.L		31 556.6		236.2		4 981.0
Net financial assets/liabilities							
Financial net worth	**BF.90**		**−21.3**		**−202.8**		**−2 828.8**

Source: Office for National Statistics; Bank of England

13.2
continued

Flow of Funds
2016
Total economy: all sectors and the rest of the world. Unconsolidated

£ billion

		Monetary financial institutions S.121+S.122+S.123		Other financial intermediaries and financial auxiliaries S.124 to S.127		Insurance corporations and pension funds S.128+S.129	
		Assets	Liabilities	Assets	Liabilities	Assets	Liabilities
Financial balance sheet at end of period							
Total financial assets	AF.A/L						
Monetary gold	AF.11						
Special drawing rights	AF.12						
Monetary gold and special drawing rights	AF.1						
Currency	AF.21	12.0	84.3	0.1			
Transferable deposits	AF.22						
Deposits with UK MFIs[1]	AF.22N1	1 498.0	7 018.9	742.8		104.6	
Deposits with rest of the world MFIs	AF.22N9	1 923.1		371.9		40.7	
Other deposits	AF.29	–		16.4	34.3	–	
Currency and deposits	AF.2	3 433.2	7 103.2	1 131.2	34.3	145.2	
Short-term debt securities issued	AF.31						
By UK central government	AF.31N1	7.6		36.2		4.6	
By UK local government	AF.31N2	–		–			
By UK MFIs	AF.31N5	5.3	236.2	51.2		6.3	
MMIs[2] by other UK residents	AF.31N6	0.2		5.1	15.0	1.0	
MMIs by rest of the world	AF.31N9	41.2		31.9		6.7	
Long-term debt securities issued	AF.32						
By UK central government	AF.32N1	636.0		182.0		564.3	
By UK local government	AF.32N2	–		–		2.6	
By UK MFIs and other UK residents	AF.32N5-6	330.9	742.8	308.0	953.7	288.9	30.1
By rest of the world	AF.32N9	375.1		170.6		369.7	
Debt securities	AF.3	1 396.3	979.0	785.0	968.7	1 244.1	30.1
Short-term loans	AF.41						
By UK MFIs	AF.41N1	2 331.8	–		683.7		21.9
By rest of the world MFIs	AF.41N9				552.8		34.4
Long-term loans	AF.42						
Direct investment loans	AF.421	–	–	11.7	17.6	11.5	15.4
Secured on dwellings	AF.422	1 197.1		114.0		12.5	
Finance leasing	AF.423	2.4	2.8	29.5	2.4		
Other long-term loans by UK residents	AF.424N1	10.7	–	678.7	105.0	160.3	0.5
Other long-term loans by rest of the world	AF.424N9		–		31.0		
Loans	AF.4	3 542.0	2.8	833.9	1 392.6	184.3	72.2
Shares and other equity, excluding mutual funds' shares	AF.51						
Listed UK shares	AF.511N1	23.2	1.1	276.3	353.5	148.9	99.7
Unlisted UK shares	AF.512N1	85.7	255.5	233.9	489.3	6.1	25.3
Other UK equity (including direct investment in property)	AF.519N6						
UK shares and bonds issued by other UK residents	AF.519N7	–		–	–	–	–
Shares and other equity issued by rest of the world	AF.519N9	174.8		633.9		554.7	
Investment fund shares/units	AF.52						
UK mutual funds' shares	AF.52N1	2.5		102.7	1 088.5	683.5	
Rest of the world mutual funds' shares	AF.52N9			47.1		239.9	
Equity and investment fund shares/units	AF.5	286.2	256.5	1 294.0	1 931.3	1 633.0	125.0
Non-life insurance technical reserves	AF.61	0.1		0.1		0.2	57.6
Life insurance and annuity entitlements	AF.62	–					641.0
Pension schemes[3]	AF.6M	–	36.5		28.3	862.5	2 958.7
Provisions for calls under standardised guarantees	AF.66	–					
Insurance, pension and standardised guarantee schemes	AF.6	0.2	36.5	0.1	28.3	862.8	3 657.2
Financial derivatives	AF.71	3 339.4	3 286.6	1 893.0	1 876.2	135.9	133.9
Financial derivatives and employee stock options	AF.7	3 339.4	3 286.8	1 893.0	1 876.4	135.9	133.9
Other accounts payable/receivable	AF.8	0.1	6.1	32.6	1.7	40.7	87.7
Total financial assets	AF.A	11 997.2		5 969.8		4 246.0	
Total financial liabilities	AF.L		11 671.0		6 233.3		4 106.2
Net financial assets/liabilities							
Financial net worth	**BF.90**		**326.2**		**−263.5**		**139.8**

Source: *Office for National Statistics; Bank of England*

13.2

Flow of Funds
2016

continued

Total economy: all sectors and the rest of the world. Unconsolidated

£ billion

		Central government S.1311		Local government S.1313		Households S.14	
		Assets	Liabilities	Assets	Liabilities	Assets	Liabilities
Financial balance sheet at end of period							
Total financial assets	AF.A/L						
Monetary gold	AF.11	9.4					
Special drawing rights	AF.12	8.9	11.1				
Monetary gold and special drawing rights	AF.1	18.3	11.1				
Currency	AF.21		4.8			56.4	
Transferable deposits	AF.22						
Deposits with UK MFIs[1]	AF.22N1	12.8		25.4		1 258.2	
Deposits with rest of the world MFIs	AF.22N9	13.7		1.5		63.1	
Other deposits	AF.29	25.3	168.6	8.5		143.0	
Currency and deposits	AF.2	51.8	173.4	35.4		1 520.7	
Short-term debt securities issued	AF.31						
By UK central government	AF.31N1		94.9	0.9		–	
By UK local government	AF.31N2				–	–	
By UK MFIs	AF.31N5	–		0.7		6.3	
MMIs[2] by other UK residents	AF.31N6	0.7		1.9		0.2	–
MMIs by rest of the world	AF.31N9	6.8				–	
Long-term debt securities issued	AF.32						
By UK central government	AF.32N1		1 934.6	0.4		2.6	
By other UK central government bonds/UK local government	AF.32N2	–			4.4	1.4	
By UK MFIs and other UK residents	AF.32N5-6	0.8	0.2	0.2		7.2	1.5
By rest of the world	AF.32N9	77.3				1.6	
Debt securities	AF.3	85.6	2 029.7	4.1	4.4	16.6	–
Short-term loans	AF.41						
By UK MFIs	AF.41N1		3.5		10.3		150.7
By rest of the world MFIs	AF.41N9		5.2		–		29.5
Long-term loans	AF.42						
Direct investment loans	AF.421						
Secured on dwellings	AF.422	32.0		10.9			1 325.1
Finance leasing	AF.423		6.2		0.5		
Other long-term loans by UK residents	AF.424N1	175.4	0.4	6.4	74.3	18.7	156.0
Other long-term loans by rest of the world	AF.424N9		0.5		6.5		
Loans	AF.4	207.5	15.9	17.3	91.5	18.7	1 661.3
Shares and other equity, excluding mutual funds' shares	AF.51						
Listed UK shares	AF.511N1	24.6		3.6		219.1	
Unlisted UK shares	AF.512N1	18.2		0.7		235.7	
Other UK equity (including direct investment in property)	AF.519N6	2.6		125.9		1.4	
UK shares and bonds issued by other UK residents	AF.519N7	–				–	–
Shares and other equity issued by rest of the world	AF.519N9	6.1				133.8	
Investment fund shares/units	AF.52						
UK mutual funds' shares	AF.52N1					272.1	
Rest of the world mutual funds' shares	AF.52N9					–	
Equity and investment fund shares/units	AF.5	51.5		130.3		862.1	–
Non-life insurance technical reserves	AF.61			0.6		41.0	
Life insurance and annuity entitlements	AF.62					633.9	
Pension schemes[3]	AF.6M				68.7	2 950.2	
Provisions for calls under standardised guarantees	AF.66		–				
Insurance, pension and standardised guarantee schemes	AF.6		–	0.6	68.7	3 625.1	
Financial derivatives	AF.71	−6.5	1.7			0.2	0.7
Financial derivatives and employee stock options	AF.7	−6.5	1.7			5.7	0.7
Other accounts payable/receivable	AF.8	88.0	52.6	2.7	47.1	187.2	84.6
Total financial assets	AF.A	496.2		190.4		6 236.0	
Total financial liabilities	AF.L		2 284.2		211.7		1 746.6
Net financial assets/liabilities							
Financial net worth	**BF.90**		**−1 788.1**		**−21.3**		**4 489.4**

Source: Office for National Statistics; Bank of England

13.2
continued

Flow of Funds
2016

Total economy: all sectors and the rest of the world. Unconsolidated

£ billion

		Non-profit institutions serving households S.15		Rest of the world S.2	
		Assets	Liabilities	Assets	Liabilities
Financial balance sheet at end of period					
Total financial assets	AF.A/L				
Monetary gold	AF.11				–
Special drawing rights	AF.12			11.1	8.9
Monetary gold and special drawing rights	AF.1			11.1	8.9
Currency	AF.21	11.6		2.2	0.9
Transferable deposits	AF.22				
Deposits with UK MFIs[1]	AF.22N1	25.7		2 915.2	
Deposits with rest of the world MFIs	AF.22N9	–			2 614.3
Other deposits	AF.29	0.2		2.5	
Currency and deposits	AF.2	37.5		2 919.8	2 615.3
Short-term debt securities issued	AF.31				
By UK central government	AF.31N1	–		44.5	
By UK local government	AF.31N2	–	–		
By UK MFIs	AF.31N5	3.5		148.9	
MMIs[2] by other UK residents	AF.31N6	0.1	1.8	39.4	
MMIs by rest of the world	AF.31N9	–			95.2
Long-term debt securities issued	AF.32				
By UK central government	AF.32N1	3.5		542.8	
By UK local government	AF.32N2	0.3		–	
By UK MFIs and other UK residents	AF.32N5-6	2.7	1.5	1 102.3	
By rest of the world	AF.32N9	1.0			1 008.4
Debt securities	AF.3	11.2	3.3	1 877.8	1 103.6
Short-term loans	AF.41			756.4	1 097.1
By UK MFIs	AF.41N1		8.7		
By rest of the world MFIs	AF.41N9		8.2		
Long-term loans	AF.42			448.2	710.4
Direct investment loans	AF.421				
Secured on dwellings	AF.422		–		
Finance leasing	AF.423				
Other long-term loans by UK residents	AF.424N1	–	8.2		
Other long-term loans by rest of the world	AF.424N9				
Loans	AF.4	–	25.1	1 204.6	1 807.5
Shares and other equity, excluding mutual funds' shares	AF.51				
Listed UK shares	AF.511N1	34.4		1 199.2	
Unlisted UK shares	AF.512N1	37.0		1 102.1	
Other UK equity (including direct investment in property)	AF.519N6	–		14.4	
UK shares and bonds issued by other UK residents	AF.519N7	–	–	–	
Shares and other equity issued by rest of the world	AF.519N9	54.5			2 444.3
Investment fund shares/units	AF.52				
UK mutual funds' shares	AF.52N1	24.3		2.5	
Rest of the world mutual funds' shares	AF.52N9	–			287.0
Equity and investment fund shares/units	AF.5	150.2	–	2 318.2	2 731.3
Non-life insurance technical reserves	AF.61	0.6		11.0	
Life insurance and annuity entitlements	AF.62			7.1	
Pension schemes[3]	AF.6M		44.4	–	
Provisions for calls under standardised guarantees	AF.66				
Insurance, pension and standardised guarantee schemes	AF.6	0.6	44.4	18.1	–
Financial derivatives	AF.71	0.2	0.4	2 607.4	2 649.9
Financial derivatives and employee stock options	AF.7	0.2	0.4	2 607.4	2 649.9
Other accounts payable/receivable	AF.8	14.2	13.1	8.9	18.9
Total financial assets	AF.A	214.0		10 966.0	
Total financial liabilities	AF.L		86.3		10 935.4
Net financial assets/liabilities					
Financial net worth	**BF.90**		**127.7**		**30.6**

1 Monetary financial institutions
2 Money market instruments
3 AF.63 Pension entitlements, AF.64 Claims of pension funds on pension
   managers, AF.65 Entitlements to non-pension benefits

Source: Office for National Statistics; Bank of England

13.3.1 Flow of Funds - F.1 Monetary gold and special drawing rights

£ billion

		2010	2011	2012	2013	2014	2015	2016
Balance sheet assets								
Central government	NIFC	18.2	19.2	19.3	16.3	16.7	16.2	18.3
UK total	NYVN	18.2	19.2	19.3	16.3	16.7	16.2	18.3
Rest of the world	M98E	10.1	10.1	9.6	9.4	9.4	9.5	11.1
Balance sheet liabilities								
Central government	M98F	10.1	10.1	9.6	9.4	9.4	9.5	11.1
UK total	NYVS	10.1	10.1	9.6	9.4	9.4	9.5	11.1
Rest of the world	M9ML	9.1	9.4	9.1	9.0	9.0	9.1	8.9
Net acquisition of financial assets								
Central government	NWXM	–	0.3	0.1	–	–	0.1	−1.4
UK total	NQAD	–	0.3	0.1	–	–	0.1	−1.4
Rest of the world	NEWJ	–	–	–	–	–	–	–
Net acquisition of financial liabilities								
Central government	M9MK	–	–	–	–	–	–	–
UK total	NYPT	–	–	–	–	–	–	–
Rest of the world	M9MJ	–	0.3	0.1	–	–	0.1	−1.4

Source: Office for National Statistics; Bank of England

13.3.2 Flow of Funds - F.2 Currency and deposits

£ billion

		2010	2011	2012	2013	2014	2015	2016
Balance sheet assets								
Public corporations	NKDR	9.9	11.8	11.6	12.7	12.5	13.5	13.4
Private non-financial corporations	NKJZ	434.8	426.7	459.7	485.9	524.5	565.6	637.7
Monetary financial institutions	NNSX	3 072.5	3 463.9	3 483.4	3 252.6	2 987.0	2 925.1	3 433.2
Other financial intermediaries and financial auxiliaries	NLPL	1 363.7	1 336.1	1 252.0	1 218.4	1 085.7	951.2	1 131.2
Insurance corporations and pension funds	NIYD	120.1	130.7	130.7	146.1	146.5	137.0	145.2
Central government	NIFF	38.2	49.7	51.9	56.4	55.8	46.4	51.8
Local government	NJEL	27.0	28.1	34.1	31.0	32.1	36.1	35.4
Households	NIRV	1 180.1	1 218.1	1 273.7	1 321.9	1 375.3	1 430.3	1 520.7
NPISH[1]	NJKT	26.6	26.3	27.8	30.6	32.8	34.6	37.5
UK total	NYVT	6 272.9	6 691.3	6 724.8	6 555.6	6 252.1	6 139.7	7 006.2
Rest of the world	NLCV	3 021.4	3 227.9	2 979.9	2 690.2	2 681.2	2 546.0	2 919.8
Balance sheet liabilities								
Public corporations	NKGV	–	–	–	–	–	–	–
Monetary financial institutions	NNWB	6 670.8	7 017.5	7 047.9	6 823.4	6 473.3	6 352.2	7 103.2
Other financial intermediaries and financial auxiliaries	NJUF	11.1	21.0	20.9	30.4	35.8	31.2	34.3
Central government	NIIJ	127.8	136.6	134.5	126.5	144.4	155.3	173.4
UK total	NYVU	6 809.7	7 175.1	7 203.3	6 980.4	6 653.5	6 538.6	7 310.8
Rest of the world	NLFZ	2 484.6	2 744.1	2 501.3	2 265.3	2 279.8	2 147.1	2 615.3
Net acquisition of financial assets								
Public corporations	NCXU	–	2.1	-0.2	1.0	-0.2	0.9	-0.1
Private non-financial corporations	NEQE	16.1	-7.3	14.4	23.5	51.6	46.4	39.1
Monetary financial institutions	NGCA	134.1	174.5	128.5	-220.7	-38.9	-70.4	211.9
Other financial intermediaries and financial auxiliaries	NFJC	-7.5	-50.9	-102.9	-38.7	-127.3	-118.7	71.8
Insurance corporations and pension funds	NBSG	-3.3	13.2	-3.1	-4.0	4.7	-15.6	-5.6
Central government	NARQ	-14.6	12.5	5.3	6.8	5.6	-8.3	2.2
Local government	NBYO	-0.3	0.8	4.3	-2.2	0.5	3.8	-1.0
Households	NBLY	32.3	40.0	42.7	52.1	60.0	59.5	84.7
NPISH[1]	NCEW	-0.9	–	2.2	0.6	1.0	1.4	2.3
UK total	NQAK	155.7	184.9	91.2	-181.5	-43.0	-100.9	405.2
Rest of the world	NEWM	62.5	75.3	-119.4	-278.1	-7.9	-121.4	21.1
Net acquisition of financial liabilities								
Public corporations	A4FK	–	–	–	–	–	–	–
Monetary financial institutions	NGFE	39.7	143.8	164.6	-234.8	-127.1	-108.1	293.0
Other financial intermediaries and financial auxiliaries	NFMG	-9.2	9.9	-0.2	9.6	5.2	-4.7	3.2
Central government	NAUU	-8.0	9.2	-2.1	-7.9	18.0	10.9	18.0
UK total	NQCK	22.5	162.9	162.4	-233.1	-103.8	-102.0	314.1
Rest of the world	NEZQ	195.7	97.3	-190.6	-226.6	52.9	-120.3	112.2

1 Non-profit institutions serving households

Source: Office for National Statistics; Bank of England

13.3.3 Flow of Funds - F.3 Debt securities

£ billion

		2010	2011	2012	2013	2014	2015	2016
Balance sheet assets								
Public corporations	NKEA	2.3	2.3	1.5	1.4	1.4	1.4	1.4
Private non-financial corporations	NKKI	56.6	63.3	58.2	59.9	63.7	76.9	88.5
Monetary financial institutions	NNTG	1 256.1	1 295.2	1 348.9	1 305.7	1 346.5	1 295.2	1 396.3
Other financial intermediaries and financial auxiliaries	NLPU	524.1	518.0	518.7	507.7	731.6	710.1	785.0
Insurance corporations and pension funds	NIYM	853.6	946.5	1 002.1	1 002.5	1 096.5	1 098.3	1 244.1
Central government	NIFO	45.1	52.3	52.7	47.4	51.9	67.8	85.6
Local government	NJEU	2.9	2.5	3.1	4.6	6.2	6.3	4.1
Households	NISE	10.0	10.4	15.3	12.4	14.1	16.1	16.6
NPISH[1]	NJLC	9.2	7.1	7.0	8.0	9.5	9.5	11.2
UK total	NYWL	2 760.0	2 897.5	3 007.4	2 949.7	3 321.5	3 281.6	3 632.7
Rest of the world	NLDE	1 670.1	1 748.3	1 733.4	1 581.2	1 687.3	1 734.6	1 877.8
Balance sheet liabilities								
Public corporations	NKHE	18.9	15.1	14.0	18.6	21.4	22.8	24.0
Private non-financial corporations	NKZA	285.9	328.0	345.6	352.4	337.0	324.6	367.6
Monetary financial institutions	NNWK	1 110.9	1 024.2	966.7	842.2	885.3	875.5	979.0
Other financial intermediaries and financial auxiliaries	NLSY	836.9	862.3	867.5	836.0	954.0	955.8	968.7
Insurance corporations and pension funds	NJBQ	24.1	24.1	26.2	23.9	28.7	24.7	30.1
Central government	NIIS	1 129.5	1 391.3	1 478.5	1 485.3	1 747.4	1 766.8	2 029.7
Local government	NJHY	1.0	1.6	2.3	3.0	3.5	4.1	4.4
Households	NIVI	–	–	–	–	–	–	–
NPISH[1]	NJOG	1.3	1.4	1.4	1.7	2.5	3.0	3.3
UK total	NYWM	3 408.6	3 648.0	3 702.1	3 563.1	3 979.7	3 977.4	4 406.9
Rest of the world	NLGI	1 021.6	997.8	1 038.7	967.9	1 029.1	1 038.7	1 103.6
Net acquisition of financial assets								
Public corporations	NCYD	–	–	–0.8	–	–	–	–
Private non-financial corporations	NEQN	8.2	0.6	–3.3	4.0	15.4	12.5	3.0
Monetary financial institutions	NGCJ	–26.9	–30.1	45.5	–47.8	1.8	–48.5	–70.0
Other financial intermediaries and financial auxiliaries	NFJL	45.0	12.3	20.7	34.6	121.0	2.1	–22.3
Insurance corporations and pension funds	NBSP	24.8	10.3	8.0	16.9	–11.7	–3.9	–2.2
Central government	NARZ	6.9	7.8	2.0	–4.0	4.8	16.1	6.5
Local government	NBYX	0.7	–0.4	0.5	2.0	1.7	–0.1	–2.1
Households	NBMH	–3.1	–0.9	3.5	–2.4	1.2	0.2	2.2
NPISH[1]	NCFF	0.6	–	–2.3	1.9	1.5	–2.4	2.0
UK total	NQAL	56.1	–0.5	73.8	5.2	135.7	–24.0	–82.9
Rest of the world	NEWV	131.6	50.2	–79.6	76.1	48.0	56.7	90.1
Net acquisition of financial liabilities								
Public corporations	NENJ	0.4	0.4	3.2	3.4	3.7	2.2	1.1
Private non-financial corporations	NETR	12.4	27.5	2.8	22.5	8.6	20.7	26.7
Monetary financial institutions	NGFN	–38.4	–130.1	–95.8	–65.0	9.9	–15.0	18.8
Other financial intermediaries and financial auxiliaries	NFMP	57.0	68.8	–69.1	86.5	10.6	–50.8	6.7
Insurance corporations and pension funds	NBVT	0.3	1.2	0.2	1.5	2.4	3.1	3.2
Central government	NAVD	164.4	128.3	109.9	80.1	86.7	58.3	62.0
Local government	NCCB	–	0.6	0.7	0.7	0.5	0.6	0.4
Households	NBPL	–	–	–	–	–	–	–
NPISH[1]	NCIJ	0.2	0.5	–	0.4	0.8	0.4	0.011
UK total	NQCM	196.2	97.3	–48.1	130.2	123.2	19.5	118.9
Rest of the world	NEZZ	–8.5	–47.6	42.4	–48.9	60.5	13.3	–111.7

1 Non-profit institutions serving households

Source: Office for National Statistics; Bank of England

13.3.4 Flow of Funds - F.4 Loans

£ billion

		2010	2011	2012	2013	2014	2015	2016
Balance sheet assets								
Public corporations	NKFC	1.6	1.5	1.5	1.4	1.4	1.2	1.1
Private non-financial corporations	NKWY	288.5	264.5	286.3	300.8	316.1	267.3	276.1
Monetary financial institutions	NNUI	3 527.0	3 444.5	3 376.5	3 282.4	3 207.9	3 227.7	3 542.0
Other financial intermediaries and financial auxiliaries	NLQW	763.6	744.2	760.4	763.2	729.2	748.4	833.9
Insurance corporations and pension funds	NIZO	128.1	144.8	176.5	205.9	167.9	173.8	184.3
Central government	NIGQ	186.3	183.0	193.8	193.4	197.0	193.7	207.5
Local government	NJFW	7.5	8.8	11.4	12.3	13.8	15.8	17.3
Households	NITG	18.4	18.4	18.5	18.7	18.7	18.8	18.7
NPISH[1]	NJME	–	–	–	–	–	–	–
UK total	NYYP	4 921.0	4 809.7	4 824.9	4 778.1	4 652.0	4 646.7	5 080.9
Rest of the world	NLEG	1 219.0	1 180.6	1 344.3	1 307.7	1 329.0	1 136.9	1 204.6
Balance sheet liabilities								
Public corporations	NKIG	53.3	56.2	55.7	53.5	54.7	55.4	57.5
Private non-financial corporations	NLBC	1 162.7	1 116.4	1 175.6	1 141.1	1 093.5	1 093.8	1 159.0
Monetary financial institutions	NNXM	3.3	3.3	3.5	3.5	2.7	2.8	2.8
Other financial intermediaries and financial auxiliaries	NLUA	1 668.0	1 547.1	1 635.3	1 575.3	1 481.6	1 283.9	1 392.6
Insurance corporations and pension funds	NJCS	33.4	40.4	62.1	68.3	53.3	60.9	72.2
Central government	NIJU	10.1	10.7	9.7	10.1	10.7	15.8	15.9
Local government	NJJA	70.5	71.7	81.3	83.6	86.5	88.2	91.5
Households	NIWK	1 459.8	1 464.2	1 485.1	1 502.2	1 541.6	1 590.1	1 661.3
NPISH[1]	NJPI	18.8	21.1	22.7	21.6	22.0	22.6	25.1
UK total	NYYQ	4 479.9	4 331.3	4 531.1	4 459.4	4 346.8	4 213.5	4 478.0
Rest of the world	NLHK	1 660.2	1 659.0	1 638.1	1 626.4	1 634.2	1 570.1	1 807.5
Net acquisition of financial assets								
Public corporations	NCZF	–	–0.2	–0.1	–0.2	–0.1	–0.2	–0.2
Private non-financial corporations	NERP	–6.8	–1.7	–12.2	6.5	45.4	–2.4	20.4
Monetary financial institutions	NGDL	–1.7	–36.9	–17.7	–39.3	–79.1	50.6	114.4
Other financial intermediaries and financial auxiliaries	NFKN	50.1	–4.9	–19.0	45.5	5.8	13.4	34.4
Insurance corporations and pension funds	NBTR	0.4	12.7	5.2	3.1	–6.6	9.2	2.1
Central government	NATB	2.1	–3.6	10.2	–0.4	3.4	–3.9	13.3
Local government	NBZZ	1.3	1.4	2.6	2.1	3.2	3.6	4.6
Households	NBNJ	2.1	–2.1	0.3	–1.5	–9.0	–3.4	–7.9
NPISH[1]	NCGH	–	–	–	–	–	–	–
UK total	NQAN	47.5	–35.3	–30.7	15.9	–37.1	66.8	181.1
Rest of the world	NEXX	91.6	–39.5	20.3	–31.9	128.0	–169.0	–18.9
Net acquisition of financial liabilities								
Public corporations	NEOL	2.2	3.3	–0.4	–2.1	0.4	0.8	2.3
Private non-financial corporations	NEUT	–31.5	–27.3	4.8	29.2	37.3	1.7	61.7
Monetary financial institutions	NGGP	0.2	0.1	0.1	0.1	0.1	0.1	0.1
Other financial intermediaries and financial auxiliaries	NFNR	112.4	–78.2	46.6	–62.6	–30.7	–179.3	–56.4
Insurance corporations and pension funds	NBWV	–4.8	5.0	2.7	4.1	0.1	20.8	7.7
Central government	NAWF	–2.3	–2.0	0.2	0.5	0.6	9.3	–1.8
Local government	NCDD	2.9	1.9	10.4	0.9	1.7	1.1	2.5
Households	NBQN	9.5	19.1	16.5	26.6	42.3	53.4	69.9
NPISH[1]	NCJL	0.3	1.9	–1.0	–0.8	0.7	–0.4	1.4
UK total	NQCN	88.8	–76.2	79.9	–4.2	52.4	–92.7	87.3
Rest of the world	NFBB	50.3	1.4	–90.3	–11.8	38.5	–9.5	75.0

1 Non-profit institutions serving households

Source: Office for National Statistics; Bank of England

13.3.5 Flow of Funds - F.5 Equity and investment fund shares/units

£ billion

		2010	2011	2012	2013	2014	2015	2016
Balance sheet assets								
Public corporations	NKFU	0.9	0.9	1.5	2.2	1.7	1.7	1.8
Private non-financial corporations	NKXQ	861.9	890.3	878.1	903.1	873.3	913.3	994.8
Monetary financial institutions	NNVA	289.7	292.5	334.4	344.3	296.2	268.2	286.2
Other financial intermediaries and financial auxiliaries	NLRO	1 057.8	912.9	958.5	1 101.3	1 152.0	1 178.4	1 294.0
Insurance corporations and pension funds	NJAG	1 281.3	1 178.9	1 312.5	1 409.6	1 481.8	1 496.5	1 633.0
Central government	NIHI	80.0	60.0	91.7	71.2	73.0	57.3	51.5
Local government	NJGO	117.7	119.6	121.7	124.2	127.5	129.6	130.3
Households	NITY	717.7	671.7	652.5	718.9	792.6	801.6	862.1
NPISH[1]	NJMW	73.9	80.0	70.7	76.8	96.7	125.7	150.2
UK total	NYZZ	4 480.9	4 206.8	4 421.6	4 751.4	4 894.8	4 972.5	5 403.9
Rest of the world	NLEY	1 483.6	1 511.4	1 806.1	1 972.8	2 085.0	2 086.6	2 318.2
Balance sheet liabilities								
Public corporations	NKIY	120.5	121.8	123.7	125.2	127.2	128.9	130.1
Private non-financial corporations	NLBU	2 079.9	1 987.9	2 134.6	2 336.2	2 371.5	2 358.1	2 547.9
Monetary financial institutions	NNYE	174.4	210.7	229.0	224.0	236.5	245.6	256.5
Other financial intermediaries and financial auxiliaries	NLUS	1 490.0	1 355.9	1 533.3	1 681.6	1 793.0	1 811.6	1 931.3
Insurance corporations and pension funds	NJDK	64.6	55.5	74.3	95.9	114.4	124.2	125.0
UK total	NZAA	3 929.4	3 731.8	4 094.9	4 462.9	4 642.6	4 668.5	4 990.9
Rest of the world	NLIC	2 035.1	1 986.4	2 132.8	2 261.3	2 337.2	2 390.6	2 731.3
Net acquisition of financial assets								
Public corporations	NCZX	0.1	0.1	0.1	0.1	−0.4	0.1	0.1
Private non-financial corporations	NESH	36.3	63.7	31.1	24.5	−85.8	−3.3	34.8
Monetary financial institutions	NGED	6.0	−18.5	−17.7	−27.0	4.2	−34.8	−4.5
Other financial intermediaries and financial auxiliaries	NFLF	32.3	22.6	57.0	40.5	38.5	1.4	−32.8
Insurance corporations and pension funds	NBUJ	32.0	−29.4	4.2	−42.5	−9.3	19.8	−24.4
Central government	NATT	−0.3	−0.9	2.0	−29.7	−7.7	−13.4	−2.2
Local government	NCAR	−0.4	−0.2	−0.8	0.2	−0.5	−0.7	−2.2
Households	NBOB	−8.9	−15.9	−17.9	−0.2	−14.8	−45.5	−42.6
NPISH[1]	NCGZ	2.1	12.4	−3.3	−7.8	2.9	13.0	−1.7
UK total	NQAP	99.3	33.8	54.6	−41.9	−73.0	−63.5	−75.6
Rest of the world	NEYP	35.3	12.1	37.8	72.8	36.0	84.6	64.3
Net acquisition of financial liabilities								
Public corporations	NEPD	−0.6	−0.7	−0.9	−1.1	−1.9	−1.3	−1.7
Private non-financial corporations	NEVL	25.3	2.5	16.9	18.3	−19.5	26.9	27.3
Monetary financial institutions	NGHH	4.0	5.7	11.7	−7.9	1.8	9.2	−0.1
Other financial intermediaries and financial auxiliaries	NFOJ	53.1	26.6	−20.9	17.1	34.4	21.4	13.6
Insurance corporations and pension funds	NBXN	0.2	0.6	1.4	3.2	3.2	1.8	6.9
UK total	NQCS	82.0	34.7	8.2	29.6	18.0	58.0	46.0
Rest of the world	NFBT	52.6	11.3	84.2	1.3	−55.0	−36.9	−57.3

1 Non-profit institutions serving households

Source: Office for National Statistics; Bank of England

13.3.6 Flow of Funds - F.6 Insurance, pension & standardised guarantee schemes

£ billion

		2010	2011	2012	2013	2014	2015	2016
Balance sheet assets								
Public corporations	NPYB	–	–	–	–	–	–	–
Private non-financial corporations	NPYD	7.2	4.7	4.2	4.0	4.0	3.8	3.9
Monetary financial institutions	NPYR	0.2	0.1	0.1	0.1	0.1	0.2	0.2
Other financial intermediaries and financial auxiliaries	NPYP	0.2	0.1	0.1	0.1	0.1	0.1	0.1
Insurance corporations and pension funds	NPXR	494.9	777.3	658.1	504.3	853.4	792.3	862.8
Local government	NPXT	0.7	0.7	0.7	0.7	0.7	0.6	0.6
Households	NPXP	2 487.6	2 859.7	2 898.7	2 846.9	3 267.8	3 277.2	3 625.1
NPISH[1]	NPXV	0.6	0.6	0.6	0.6	0.6	0.6	0.6
UK total	NZBF	2 991.4	3 643.3	3 562.5	3 356.8	4 126.8	4 074.8	4 493.2
Rest of the world	NPYF	12.9	12.3	19.8	20.0	20.8	21.6	18.1
Balance sheet liabilities								
Private non-financial corporations	M9RJ	348.0	579.7	499.2	372.7	675.5	617.6	676.3
Monetary financial institutions	NPYS	24.7	37.7	29.7	20.5	36.4	33.8	36.5
Other financial intermediaries and financial auxiliaries	NPYQ	14.0	21.0	16.0	14.2	26.0	24.0	28.3
Insurance corporations and pension funds	NPXS	2 515.5	2 886.8	2 931.1	2 877.4	3 303.2	3 312.0	3 657.2
Central government	DM55	–	–	–	–	–	–	0.041
Local government	M9RL	74.2	85.0	73.4	67.7	62.2	68.5	68.7
NPISH[1]	NPXW	28.0	45.5	32.8	24.2	44.3	40.5	44.4
UK total	NZBG	3 004.4	3 655.5	3 582.2	3 376.8	4 147.6	4 096.4	4 511.4
Rest of the world	M9RN	–	–	–	–	–	–	–
Net acquisition of financial assets								
Public corporations	NPWL	–	–	–	–	–	–	–
Private non-financial corporations	NPWN	–4.0	–2.4	–0.6	–0.1	–	–0.2	0.1
Monetary financial institutions	NPWZ	–0.1	–0.1	–	–	–	–	0.002
Other financial intermediaries and financial auxiliaries	NPWT	–0.1	–0.1	–	–	–	–	0.002
Insurance corporations and pension funds	NPWB	11.4	11.7	12.3	13.5	13.0	12.7	13.7
Local government	NPWD	–0.1	–	–	–	–	–	0.011
Households	NPVZ	73.8	75.9	56.3	44.2	53.2	100.9	70.0
NPISH[1]	NPWF	–0.1	–	–	–	–	–	0.009
UK total	NQAW	80.8	85.1	68.1	57.5	66.2	113.4	83.7
Rest of the world	NPWP	–3.9	–0.3	3.1	–0.5	–0.2	0.4	1.0
Net acquisition of financial liabilities								
Private non-financial corporations	M9VY	8.3	8.4	8.8	9.7	9.4	9.2	9.9
Monetary financial institutions	NPXA	0.5	0.5	0.5	0.5	0.5	0.5	0.5
Other financial intermediaries and financial auxiliaries	NPWU	0.4	0.3	0.3	0.4	0.4	0.4	0.4
Insurance corporations and pension funds	NPWC	65.4	73.1	59.0	43.7	53.0	101.2	71.2
Central government	DM53	–	–	–	–	–	–	–
Local government	M9W2	1.8	1.8	1.9	2.1	2.0	2.0	2.1
NPISH[1]	NPWG	0.5	0.6	0.6	0.6	0.6	0.6	0.6
UK total	NQCV	77.0	84.8	71.1	57.0	66.0	113.8	84.7
Rest of the world	M9W4	–	–	–	–	–	–	–

1 Non-profit institutions serving households

Source: Office for National Statistics; Bank of England

13.3.7 Flow of Funds - F.7 Financial derivatives and employee stock options

£ billion

		2010	2011	2012	2013	2014	2015	2016
Balance sheet assets								
Private non-financial corporations	MMU8	25.3	29.7	28.6	25.6	30.0	31.0	37.0
Monetary financial institutions	MMV2	4 242.0	5 412.7	4 650.6	3 406.2	3 778.5	2 911.4	3 339.4
Other financial intermediaries and financial auxiliaries	MMV5	2 049.9	2 570.4	2 144.9	2 030.5	2 282.6	1 523.2	1 893.0
Insurance corporations and pension funds	MMV8	95.1	141.1	126.3	126.1	151.1	104.1	135.9
Central government	MMW3	2.0	2.7	3.3	2.9	2.1	2.1	−6.5
Households	MMW6	7.5	9.1	5.2	8.2	6.4	5.6	5.7
NPISH[1]	MMW7	–	–	0.1	0.4	0.5	0.2	0.2
UK total	MMU5	6 421.8	8 165.8	6 958.9	5 600.1	6 251.1	4 577.5	5 404.7
Rest of the world	MMW8	2 895.0	3 554.9	3 032.2	2 376.7	2 806.4	2 391.4	2 607.4
Balance sheet liabilities								
Private non-financial corporations	MMX4	39.9	52.0	46.8	40.6	51.5	55.4	62.3
Monetary financial institutions	MMX6	4 204.4	5 387.8	4 641.6	3 379.5	3 774.2	2 899.1	3 286.8
Other financial intermediaries and financial auxiliaries	MMX9	2 011.6	2 498.0	2 079.6	1 940.5	2 167.6	1 497.5	1 876.4
Insurance corporations and pension funds	MMY4	92.1	135.9	125.2	125.4	149.3	102.7	133.9
Central government	MMY7	2.7	3.3	2.4	1.3	1.1	2.2	1.7
Households	MMZ2	3.1	5.4	1.6	4.0	2.7	1.5	0.7
NPISH[1]	MMZ3	–	–	0.2	0.3	0.1	0.3	0.4
UK total	MMW9	6 353.9	8 082.5	6 897.5	5 491.5	6 146.5	4 558.7	5 362.2
Rest of the world	MMZ4	2 963.0	3 638.2	3 093.7	2 485.3	2 911.0	2 410.1	2 649.9
Net acquisition of financial assets								
Public corporations	MN5H	–	–	–	–	–	–	–
Private non-financial corporations	MN5I	−1.0	−8.1	4.4	3.4	−6.8	−3.1	−0.5
Monetary financial institutions	MN5K	−27.5	−14.6	−6.8	12.0	2.4	11.0	19.5
Other financial intermediaries and financial auxiliaries	MN5N	−18.3	25.6	−34.8	25.3	25.2	−89.9	0.2
Insurance corporations and pension funds	MN5Q	1.6	2.3	−5.0	−0.7	−0.3	−0.8	1.1
Central government	MN5T	−0.3	−0.1	0.6	–	−0.9	−1.2	0.9
Households	MN5W	1.6	1.3	1.9	2.1	1.4	2.3	3.0
NPISH[1]	MN5X	0.5	−0.3	−0.3	0.4	−0.1	−0.6	−0.6
UK total	MN5F	−43.3	6.1	−40.0	42.4	20.9	−82.4	23.5
Rest of the world	MN5Y	–	–	–	–	–	–	0.004
Net acquisition of financial liabilities								
Private non-financial corporations	MN64	1.4	1.5	1.5	1.5	1.6	1.7	1.7
Monetary financial institutions	MN66	0.1	0.1	0.1	0.1	0.1	0.1	0.1
Other financial intermediaries and financial auxiliaries	MN69	0.1	0.1	0.1	0.1	0.1	0.1	0.1
Insurance corporations and pension funds	MN6C	–	–	–	–	–	–	0.021
UK total	MN5Z	1.6	1.6	1.7	1.7	1.8	1.8	1.9
Rest of the world	MN6K	−44.9	4.5	−41.6	40.7	19.1	−84.2	21.6

1 Non-profit institutions serving households

Source: Office for National Statistics; Bank of England

13.3.8 Flow of Funds - F.8 Other accounts payable/receivable

£ billion

		2010	2011	2012	2013	2014	2015	2016
Balance sheet assets								
Public corporations	NKGO	13.0	13.9	13.4	14.6	15.3	15.5	15.6
Private non-financial corporations	NKYK	116.8	116.9	118.8	118.6	115.9	116.0	114.2
Monetary financial institutions	NNVU	0.2	0.1	0.1	0.1	0.1	0.1	0.1
Other financial intermediaries and financial auxiliaries	NLSI	19.1	22.1	27.2	27.6	21.1	27.9	32.6
Insurance corporations and pension funds	NJBA	37.0	31.0	31.3	34.3	34.4	31.1	40.7
Central government	NIIC	60.0	60.4	61.7	66.3	70.4	79.0	88.0
Local government	NJHI	1.4	0.9	0.9	0.9	1.7	2.4	2.7
Households	NIUS	132.3	136.3	180.9	179.2	189.5	184.1	187.2
NPISH[1]	NJNQ	7.2	7.1	8.6	9.4	10.6	12.3	14.2
UK total	NZBP	386.9	388.8	443.0	451.0	459.1	468.4	495.4
Rest of the world	NLFS	3.5	3.8	4.1	5.9	7.6	8.7	8.9
Balance sheet liabilities								
Public corporations	NKJS	18.2	19.0	19.0	19.9	23.3	24.3	24.6
Private non-financial corporations	NLCO	141.7	147.5	149.5	152.8	153.3	159.6	168.0
Monetary financial institutions	NNYY	12.4	7.5	6.6	5.7	5.1	5.5	6.1
Other financial intermediaries and financial auxiliaries	NLVM	0.2	0.1	-0.2	1.8	4.6	0.3	1.7
Insurance corporations and pension funds	NJEE	69.6	72.9	80.2	83.1	98.5	82.3	87.7
Central government	NILG	21.6	20.0	55.9	56.5	55.5	55.1	52.6
Local government	NJKM	26.7	28.5	31.1	33.2	35.2	43.3	47.1
Households	NIXW	81.2	73.8	76.3	75.6	70.2	79.6	84.6
NPISH[1]	NJQU	10.0	10.1	11.1	11.0	11.3	12.1	13.1
UK total	NZBQ	381.6	379.4	429.5	439.5	457.0	462.1	485.5
Rest of the world	NLIW	8.8	13.2	17.5	17.4	9.7	15.0	18.9
Net acquisition of financial assets								
Public corporations	NEBR	-3.4	0.6	2.6	1.0	0.7	0.8	0.1
Private non-financial corporations	NETB	-9.7	-0.1	10.4	-4.1	1.8	-2.1	6.7
Monetary financial institutions	NGEX	–	–	–	–	0.1	–	0.045
Other financial intermediaries and financial auxiliaries	NFLZ	-0.7	7.0	0.6	0.8	0.6	0.4	0.5
Insurance corporations and pension funds	NBVD	-9.1	-0.9	7.9	2.1	-0.7	-2.2	8.7
Central government	NAUN	3.2	0.7	2.1	4.9	4.5	9.4	8.6
Local government	NCBL	–	-0.4	–	–	0.9	0.7	0.2
Households	NBOV	-16.2	-6.3	10.8	-7.1	-1.6	-8.0	2.6
NPISH[1]	NCHT	-1.0	–	1.5	0.8	1.2	1.7	2.0
UK total	NQBK	-36.9	0.7	35.9	-1.6	7.4	0.7	29.4
Rest of the world	NEZJ	0.8	0.3	0.4	1.2	1.6	1.1	-0.025
Net acquisition of financial liabilities								
Public corporations	NEPX	-1.5	0.8	0.1	0.9	0.7	1.0	0.4
Private non-financial corporations	NEWF	2.8	6.0	4.7	0.4	2.3	5.9	8.0
Monetary financial institutions	NGIB	0.2	0.7	–	-0.4	-0.1	1.1	0.1
Other financial intermediaries and financial auxiliaries	NFPD	-17.0	-10.9	-37.6	-4.9	-7.5	-1.5	-1.9
Insurance corporations and pension funds	NBYH	-4.8	4.3	13.7	1.4	7.4	-17.5	7.8
Central government	NAXR	-10.9	0.1	44.4	-0.9	6.9	-2.0	4.8
Local government	NCEP	0.3	1.8	2.6	2.2	2.0	8.0	3.9
Households	NBRZ	-5.2	-2.7	7.8	0.8	-2.5	7.0	5.9
NPISH[1]	NCKX	-0.1	0.1	0.8	-0.1	0.2	0.7	0.8
UK total	NQDG	-36.1	0.2	36.5	-0.6	9.4	2.6	29.8
Rest of the world	NFCN	–	0.8	-0.2	0.1	-0.4	-0.9	-0.4

1 Non-profit institutions serving households

Source: Office for National Statistics; Bank of England

338

Glossary

A to B

Above the line

Transactions in the production, current and capital accounts, which are above the net lending (positive) or net borrowing (negative) (financial surplus or deficit) line in the presentation used in the economic accounts. The financial transactions account is below the line in this presentation.

Accruals basis

A method of recording transactions to relate them to the period when the exchange of ownership of the goods, services or financial asset applies (see also cash basis). For example, Value Added Tax accrues when the expenditure to which it relates takes place, but HM Revenue and Customs receives the cash some time later. The difference between accruals and cash results in the creation of an asset and liability in the financial accounts, shown as amounts receivable or payable (F.7).

Actual final consumption

The value of goods consumed by a sector but not necessarily purchased by that sector (see also final consumption expenditure, intermediate consumption).

Advance and progress payments

Payments made for goods in advance of completion and delivery of the goods and services. Also referred to as staged payments.

Asset boundary

Boundary separating assets included in creating core economic accounts (such as plant and factories, also including non-produced assets such as land and water resources) and those excluded (such as natural assets not managed for an economic purpose).

Assets

Entities over which ownership rights are enforced by institutional units, individually or collectively; and from which economic benefits may be derived by their owners by holding them over a period of time.

Balancing item

A balancing item is an accounting construct obtained by subtracting the total value of the entries on one side of an account from the total value for the other side.

Balance of payments

A summary of the transactions between residents of a country and residents abroad in a given time period.

Balance of trade

The balance of trade in goods and services. The balance of trade is a summary of the imports and exports of goods and services across an economic boundary in a given period.

Balance sheet

A statement, drawn up at a particular point in time, of the value of assets owned and of the financial claims (liabilities) against the owner of these assets.

Bank of England

This comprises S.121, the central bank sub-sector of the financial corporations' sector.

Bank of England – Issue Department

This part of the Bank of England deals with the issue of bank notes on behalf of central government. It was formerly classified to central government though it is now part of the central bank and monetary authorities sector. Its activities include, among other things, market purchases of commercial bills from UK banks.

Basic prices

These prices are the preferred method of valuing gross value added and output. They reflect the amount received by the producer for a unit of goods or services, minus any taxes payable, plus any subsidy receivable on that unit as a consequence of production or sale (that is, the cost of production including subsidies). As a result the only taxes included in the basic price are taxes on the production process – such as business rates and any Vehicle Excise Duty paid by businesses – that are not specifically levied on the production of a unit of output. Basic prices exclude any transport charges invoiced separately by the producer.

Below the line

The financial transactions account that shows the financing of net lending (positive) or net borrowing (negative) (formerly financial surplus or deficit).

Bond

A financial instrument that usually pays interest to the holder. Bonds are issued by governments as well as by companies and other institutions, for example, local authorities. Most bonds have a fixed date on which the borrower will repay the holder. Bonds are attractive to investors since they can be bought and sold easily in a secondary market. Special forms of bonds include deep discount bonds, equity warrant bonds, Eurobonds and zero coupon bonds.

British government securities

Securities issued or guaranteed by the UK government; also known as gilts.

C to D

Capital

Capital assets are those that contribute to the productive process so as to produce an economic return. In other contexts the word can be taken to include tangible assets (for example, buildings, plant and machinery), intangible assets and financial capital (see also fixed assets, inventories).

Capital formation

Acquisitions less disposals of fixed assets, improvement of land, change in inventories and acquisitions less disposals of valuables.

Capital stock

A measure of the cost of replacing the capital assets of a country held at a particular point in time.

Capital transfers

Transfers that are related to the acquisition or disposal of assets by the recipient or payer. They may be in cash or kind and may be imputed to reflect the assumption or forgiveness of debt.

Cash basis

The recording of transactions when cash or other assets are actually transferred, rather than on an accruals basis.

Certificate of deposit

A short-term interest-paying instrument issued by deposit-taking institutions in return for money deposited for a fixed period. Interest is earned at a given rate. The instrument can be used as security for a loan if the depositor requires money before the repayment date.

Chained volume measures

Chained volume measures are time series that measure gross domestic product (GDP) in real terms (that is, excluding price effects). Series are calculated in the prices of the previous year and in current price and all of these two-year series are then "chain-linked" together. The advantage of the chain-linking method is that the previous period's price structure is more relevant than the price structure of a fixed period from further in the past.

Cost, insurance and freight (CIF)

The basis of valuation of imports for customs purposes, it includes the cost of insurance premiums and freight services. These need to be deducted to obtain the free-on-board (FOB) valuation consistent with the valuation of exports that is used in the economic accounts.

An international classification that groups consumption according to its function or purpose. Thus the heading clothing, for example, includes expenditure on garments, clothing materials, laundry and repairs. Used to classify the expenditure of households.

Combined use table

Table of the demand for products by each industry group or sector, whether from domestic production or imports, estimated at purchasers' prices. It displays the inputs used by each industry to produce their total output and separates out intermediate purchases of goods and services. The table shows which industries use which products. Columns represent the purchasing industries; rows represent the products purchased.

Commercial paper

This is an unsecured promissory note for a specific amount, maturing on a specific date. The commercial paper market allows companies to issue short-term debt directly to financial institutions, who then market this paper to investors or use it for their own investment purposes.

Compensation of employees

Total remuneration payable to employees in cash or in kind. Includes the value of social contributions payable by the employer.

Consolidated accounts

Those accounts that are drawn up to reflect the affairs of a group of entities. For example, a ministry or holding company with many different operating agencies or subsidiary companies may prepare consolidated accounts reflecting the affairs of the organisation as a whole, as well as accounts for each operating agency or subsidiary.

Consolidated fund

An account of central government into which most government revenue (excluding borrowing and certain payments to government departments) is paid and from which most government expenditure (excluding loans and National Insurance benefits) is paid.

Consumption

See final consumption, intermediate consumption.

Consumption of fixed capital

The amount of capital resources used up in the process of production in any period. It is not an identifiable set of transactions but an imputed transaction, which can only be measured by a system of conventions.

All bodies recognised as independent legal entities that are producers of market output and whose principal activity is the production of goods and services.

Counterpart

In a double-entry system of accounting, each transaction gives rise to two corresponding entries. These entries are the counterparts to each other. Thus the counterpart of a payment by one sector is the receipt by another.

Debenture

A long-term bond issued by a UK or foreign company and secured on fixed assets. A debenture entitles the holder to a fixed interest payment or a series of such payments.

Depreciation

See consumption of fixed capital.

Derivatives (F.71)

Financial instruments whose value is linked to changes in the value of another financial instrument, an indicator or a commodity. In contrast to the holder of a primary financial instrument (for example, a government bond or a bank deposit), who has an unqualified right to receive cash (or some other economic benefit) in the future, the holder of a derivative has only a qualified right to receive such a benefit. Examples of derivatives are options and swaps.

Dividend and Interest Matrix (DIM)

The Dividend and Interest Matrix represents property income flows related to holdings of financial transactions. The gross flows are shown in D.4 property income.

Direct investment

Net investment by UK or foreign companies in their foreign or UK branches, subsidiaries or associated companies. A direct investment in a company means that the investor has a significant influence on the operations of the company, defined as having an equity interest in an enterprise resident in another country of 10% or more of the ordinary shares or voting stock. Investment includes not only acquisition of fixed assets, stock building and stock appreciation, but also all other financial transactions such as: additions to, or payments of working capital; other loans and trade credit; and acquisitions of securities. Estimates of investment flows allow for depreciation in any undistributed profits. Funds raised by the subsidiary or associate company in the economy in which it operates are excluded as they are locally raised and not sourced from the parent company.

That part of the market dealing with short-term borrowing. It is called the discount market because the interest on loans is expressed as a percentage reduction (discount) on the amount paid to the borrower. For example, for a loan of £100 face value when the discount rate is 5%, the borrower will receive £95, but will repay £100 at the end of the term.

Double deflation

Method for calculating value added by industry chained volume measures, which takes separate account of the differing price and volume movements of input and outputs in an industry's production process.

Dividend

A payment made to company shareholders from current or previously retained profits. Dividends are recorded when they become payable. See Dividend and Interest Matrix (DIM).

E to F

ECGD

See Export Credit Guarantee Department.

Economically significant prices

These are prices whose level significantly affects the supply of the good or service concerned. Market output consists mainly of goods and services sold at "economically significant" prices, while non-market output comprises those provided free or at prices that are not economically significant.

Employee stock options

An employee stock option is an agreement made on a given date (the "grant" date) under which an employee may purchase a given number of shares of the employer's stock at a stated price (the "strike" price), either at a stated time (the "vesting" date) or within a period of time (the "exercise" period) immediately following the vesting date.

Enterprise

An institutional unit producing market output. Enterprises are found mainly in the non-financial and financial corporations sectors but exist in all sectors. Each enterprise consists of one or more kind-of-activity units.

Environmental accounts

Satellite accounts describing the relationship between the environment and the economy.

Equity is ownership of a residual claim on the assets of the institutional unit that issued the instrument. Equities differ from other financial instruments in that they confer ownership of something more than a financial claim. Shareholders are owners of the company whereas bondholders are merely outside creditors.

European System of National and Regional Accounts (ESA)

An integrated system of economic accounts, which is the European version of the System of National Accounts (SNA).

European Investment Bank

This was set up to assist economic development within the European Union. Its members are the member states of the EU.

Exchange Cover Scheme (ECS)

A scheme first introduced in 1969 whereby UK public bodies raise foreign currency from overseas residents, either directly or through UK banks, and surrender it to the Exchange Equalisation Account in exchange for sterling for use to finance expenditure in the UK. HM Treasury sells the borrower foreign currency to service and repay the loan at the exchange rate that applied when the loan was taken out.

Exchange Equalisation Account (EEA)

The government account with the Bank of England in which transactions in reserve assets are recorded. These transactions are classified to the central government sector. It is the means by which the government, through the Bank of England, influences exchange rates.

Export credit

Credit extended abroad by UK institutions, primarily in connection with UK exports but also including some credit in respect of third country trade.

Export Credit Guarantee Department (ECGD)

A non-ministerial government department, classified to the public corporations sector, the main function of which is to provide insurance cover for export credit transactions.

Factor cost

In the System of National Accounts 1968 this was the basis of valuation that excluded the effects of taxes on expenditure and subsidies.

The expenditure on those goods and services used for the direct satisfaction of individual needs or the collective needs of members of the community, as distinct from their purchase for use in the productive process. It may be contrasted with actual final consumption, which is the value of goods consumed but not necessarily purchased by that sector (see also intermediate consumption).

Financial auxiliaries (S.126)

Auxiliary financial activities are ones closely related to financial intermediation but which are not financial intermediation themselves, such as the repackaging of funds, insurance broking and fund management. Financial auxiliaries therefore include insurance brokers and fund managers.

Financial corporations (S.12)

All bodies recognised as independent legal entities whose principal activity is financial intermediation and/or the production of auxiliary financial services.

Financial intermediation

Financial intermediation is the activity by which an institutional unit acquires financial assets and incurs liabilities on its own account by engaging in financial transactions on the market. The assets and liabilities of financial intermediaries have different characteristics so that the funds are transformed or repackaged with respect to maturity, scale, risk and so on, in the financial intermediation process.

Financial leasing

A form of leasing in which the lessee (the leaseholder) contracts to assume the rights and responsibilities of ownership of leased goods from the lessor (the legal owner) for the whole (or virtually the whole) of the economic life of the asset. In the economic accounts this is recorded as the sale of the asset to the lessee, financed by an imputed loan (F.42). The leasing payments are split into interest payments and repayments of principal.

Financial intermediation services indirectly measured (FISIM)

FISIM represents the implicit charge for the service provided by monetary financial institutions paid for by the interest differential between borrowing and lending rather than through fees and commissions.

Fixed assets

Produced assets that are themselves used repeatedly or continuously in the production process for more than one year. They comprise buildings and other structures, vehicles and other plant and machinery, and also plants and livestock that are used repeatedly or continuously in production, for example, fruit trees or dairy cattle. They also include intangible assets such as computer software, research and development, and artistic originals.

Economic flows reflect the creation, transformation, exchange, transfer, or extinction of economic value. They involve changes in the volume, composition, or value of an institutional unit's assets and liabilities. They are recorded in the production, distribution and use of income and accumulation accounts.

FOB (free on board)

A FOB price excludes the cost of insurance and freight from the country of consignment but includes all charges up to the point of the exporting country's customs frontier.

Futures

Forward contracts traded on organised exchanges. They give the holder the right to purchase a commodity or a financial asset at a future date.

G to H

Gilts

Bonds issued or guaranteed by the UK government. Also known as gilt-edged securities or British government securities.

Gold

The System of National Accounts (SNA) and the International Monetary Fund (IMF) (in the sixth edition of its Balance of Payments Manual) recognise three types of gold:

- monetary gold, treated as a financial asset

- gold held as a store of value, to be included in valuables

- gold as an industrial material, to be included in intermediate consumption or inventories

The present treatment is as follows.

In the accounts a distinction is drawn between gold held as a financial asset (financial gold) and gold held like any other commodity (commodity gold). Commodity gold in the form of finished manufactures together with net domestic and overseas transactions in gold moving into or out of finished manufactured form (as in, for example, jewellery, dentistry, electronic goods, medals and proof – but not bullion – coins) is recorded in exports and imports of goods.

All other transactions in gold (that is, those involving semi-manufactures, for example, rods and wire; or bullion, bullion coins or banking-type assets and liabilities denominated in gold, including official reserve assets) are treated as financial gold transactions and included in the financial account of the balance of payments.

The UK has adopted different treatment to avoid distortion of its trade in goods account by the substantial transactions of the London bullion market.

Grants

Voluntary transfer payments. They may be current or capital in nature. Grants from government or the European Union to producers are subsidies.

Gross

Main economic series can be shown as gross (as in, before deduction of the consumption of fixed capital) or net (as in, after deduction). Gross has this meaning throughout this publication unless otherwise stated.

Gross domestic product (GDP)

The total value of output in the economic territory. It is the balancing item on the production account for the whole economy. Domestic product can be measured gross or net. It is presented in the accounts at market (or purchasers') prices.

Gross fixed capital formation (GFCF)

Acquisitions less disposals of fixed assets and the improvement of land.

Gross national disposable income

The income available to the residents arising from gross domestic product and receipts from, less payments to, the rest of the world of employment income, property income and current transfers.

Gross national income (GNI)

GNI is gross domestic product less net taxes on production and imports, less compensation of employees and property income payable to the rest of the world, plus the corresponding items receivable from the rest of the world.

Gross value added (GVA) (B.1g)

The value generated by any unit engaged in production and the contributions of individual sectors or industries to gross domestic product. It is measured at basic prices, excluding taxes less subsidies on products.

Holding companies

A holding company is a purely financial concern, which uses its capital solely to acquire interests (normally controlling interests) in a number of operating companies.

Although the purpose of a holding company is mainly to gain control and not to operate, it will typically have representation on the boards of directors of the operating firms.

Holding companies provide a means by which corporate control can become highly concentrated through pyramiding. A holding company may gain control over an operating company, which itself has several subsidiaries.

Holding gains or losses

Profit or loss obtained by virtue of the changing price of assets being held. Holding gains or losses may arise from either physical or financial assets.

Households (S.14)

Individuals or small groups of individuals as consumers and in some cases as entrepreneurs producing goods and market services (where such activities cannot be hived off and treated as those of a quasi-corporation).

I to J

Imputation

The process of inventing a transaction where, although no money has changed hands, there has been a flow of goods or services. It is confined to a very small number of cases where a reasonably satisfactory basis for the assumed valuation is available.

Index-linked gilts

Gilts whose coupon and redemption value are linked to movements in the Retail Prices Index.

Institutional unit

Institutional units are the individual bodies whose data is amalgamated to form the sectors of the economy. A body is regarded as an institutional unit if it has decision-making autonomy in respect of its principal function and either keeps a complete set of accounts or is in a position to compile, if required, a complete set of accounts that would be meaningful from both an economic and a legal viewpoint.

Input-output

A detailed analytical framework based on supply and use tables. These are matrices showing the composition of output of individual industries by types of product and how the domestic and imported supply of goods and services is allocated between various intermediate and final uses, including exports.

Institutional sector

In the economic accounts the economy is split into different institutional sectors, that is, units grouped according broadly to their role in the economy. The main sectors are non-financial corporations, financial corporations, general government, and households and non-profit institutions serving households (NPISH). The rest of the world is also treated as a sector for many purposes within the accounts.

Intellectual property products include mineral exploration, computer software, research and development, and entertainment, literary or artistic originals. Expenditure on them is part of gross fixed capital formation. They exclude non-produced non-financial assets such as leases, transferable contracts and purchased goodwill, expenditure on which would be intermediate consumption.

Intermediate consumption

The consumption of goods and services in the production process. It may be contrasted with final consumption and capital formation.

International Monetary Fund (IMF)

A fund set up as a result of the Bretton Woods Conference in 1944, which began operations in 1947. It currently has 188 member countries (as of October 2014) including most of the major countries of the world. The fund was . set up to supervise the fixed exchange rate system agreed at Bretton Woods and to make available to its members a pool of foreign exchange resources to assist them when they have balance of payments difficulties. It is funded by member countries' subscriptions according to agreed quotas.

Inventories

Inventories consist of finished goods (held by the producer prior to sale, further processing, or other use) and products (materials and fuel) acquired from other producers to be used for intermediate consumption, or resold without further processing, as well as military inventories.

K to L

Kind-of-activity unit (KAU)

An enterprise, or part of an enterprise, that engages in only one kind of non-ancillary productive activity, or in which the principal productive activity accounts for most of the value added. Each enterprise consists of one or more kind-of-activity units.

Liability

A claim on an institutional unit by another body that gives rise to a payment or other transaction transferring assets to the other body. Conditional liabilities, where the transfer of assets only takes place under certain defined circumstances, are known as contingent liabilities.

Life assurance

An insurance policy that, in return for the payment of regular premiums, pays a lump sum on the death of the insured. In the case of policies limited to investments that have a cash value, in addition to life cover, a savings element provides benefits that are payable before death. In the UK, endowment assurance provides life cover or a maturity value after a specified term, whichever is sooner.

The ease with which a financial instrument can be exchanged for goods and services. Cash is very liquid whereas a life assurance policy is less so.

Lloyd's of London

The international insurance and reinsurance market in London.

M to N

Marketable securities

Securities that can be sold on the open market.

Market output

Output of goods and services sold at economically significant prices.

Merchant banks

Monetary financial institutions whose main business is primarily concerned with corporate finance and acquisitions.

Mixed income

The balancing item on the generation of income account for unincorporated businesses owned by households. The owner or members of the same household often provide unpaid labour inputs to the business. The surplus is therefore a mixture of remuneration for such labour and return to the owner as entrepreneur.

Monetary financial institutions (MFIs) (S.121 to S.123)

MFIs, as defined by the European Central Bank, consist of all institutional units included in the central bank (S. 121), deposit-taking corporations except the central bank (S1.22) and money market funds (S.123) sub-sectors.

Money market

The market in which short-term loans are made and short-term securities traded. "Short-term" usually applies to periods of under one year but can be longer in some instances.

The industrial classification used in the European Union. Revision 2 is the "Statistical classification of economic activities in the European Community in accordance with Commission Regulation (EC) No. 1893/2006 of 20th December 2006".

National income

See gross national disposable income and real national disposable income.

Net

After deduction of the consumption of fixed capital. Also used in the context of financial accounts and balance sheets to denote, for example, assets less liabilities.

Non-market output

Output of own account production of goods and services provided free or at prices that are not economically significant. Non-market output is produced mainly by the general government and non-profit institutions serving households (NPISH) sectors.

Non-observed economy

Certain activities may be productive and also legal but are concealed from the authorities for various reasons – for example, to evade taxes or regulation. In principle these, as well as economic production that is illegal, are to be included in the accounts but they are by their nature difficult to measure.

Non-profit institutions serving households (NPISH) (S.15)

These include bodies such as charities, universities, churches, trade unions and members' clubs.

O to P

Operating leasing

The conventional form of leasing, in which the lessee makes use of the leased asset for a period in return for a rental, while the asset remains on the balance sheet of the lessor. The leasing payments are part of the output of the lessor and the intermediate consumption of the lessee (see also financial leasing).

Operating surplus

The balance on the generation of income account. Households also have a mixed income balance. It may be seen as the surplus arising from the production of goods and services before taking into account flows of property income.

The most common type of share in the ownership of a corporation. Holders of ordinary shares receive dividends (see also equity).

Output for own final use (P.12)

Production of output for final consumption or gross fixed capital formation by the producer. Also known as own-account production.

Own-account production

Production of output for final consumption or gross fixed capital formation by the producer. Also known as output for own final use.

Par value

A security's face or nominal value. Securities can be issued at a premium or discount to par.

Pension funds (S.129)

The institutions that administer pension schemes. Pension schemes are significant investors in securities. Self-administered funds are classified in the financial accounts as pension funds. Those managed by insurance companies are treated as long-term business of insurance companies.

Perpetual inventory model (or method) (PIM)

A method for estimating the level of assets held at a particular point in time by accumulating the acquisitions of such assets over a period and subtracting the disposals of assets over that period. Adjustments are made for price changes over the period. The PIM is used in the UK accounts to estimate the stock of fixed capital and hence the value of the consumption of fixed capital.

Portfolio

A list of the securities owned by a single investor. In the balance of payments statistics, portfolio investment is investment in securities that does not qualify as direct investment.

Preference share

This type of share guarantees its holder a prior claim on dividends. The dividend paid to preference share holders is normally more than that paid to holders of ordinary shares. Preference shares may give the holder a right to a share in the ownership of the company (participating preference shares). However, in the UK they usually do not and are therefore classified as bonds (F.3).

See economically significant prices, basic prices, purchasers' prices.

Principal

The lump sum that is lent under a loan or a bond.

Production boundary

Boundary between production included in creating core economic accounts (such as all economic activity by industry and commerce) and production that is excluded (such as production by households that is consumed within the household).

Promissory note

A security that entitles the bearer to receive cash. These may be issued by companies or other institutions (see commercial paper).

Property income

Incomes that accrue from lending or renting financial or tangible non-produced assets, including land, to other units. See also tangible assets.

Public corporations (S.11001 and S.12001)

These are public trading bodies that have a substantial degree of financial independence from the public authority that created them. A body is normally treated as a trading body when more than half of its income is financed by fees. A public corporation is publicly controlled to the extent that the public authorities appoint a majority of the board of management, or when public authorities can exert significant control over general corporate policy through other means. Since the 1980s, many public corporations, such as British Telecom, have been privatised and reclassified within the accounts as private non-financial corporations. Public corporations can also exist in the financial sector.

Public sector

Central government, local authorities and general government.

Purchasers' prices

These are the prices paid by purchasers. They include transport costs, trade margins and taxes (unless the taxes are deductible by the purchaser from their own tax liabilities).

Q to R

Unincorporated enterprises that function as if they were corporations. For the purposes of allocation to sectors and sub-sectors they are treated as if they were corporations, that is, separate units from those to which they legally belong.

Three main types of quasi-corporation are recognised in the accounts:

- unincorporated enterprises owned by government that are engaged in market production

- unincorporated enterprises (including partnerships) owned by households

- unincorporated enterprises owned by foreign residents

The last group consists of permanent branches or offices of foreign enterprises and production units of foreign enterprises that engage in significant amounts of production in the territory over long or indefinite periods of time.

Real national disposable income (RNDI)

Gross national disposable income adjusted for changes in prices and in the terms of trade.

Related companies

Branches, subsidiaries, associates or parents.

Related import or export credit

Trade credit between related companies, included in direct investment.

Rental

The amount payable by the user of a fixed asset to its owner for the right to use that asset in production for a specified period of time. It is included in the output of the owner and the intermediate consumption of the user.

Rents (D.45)

The property income derived from land and sub-soil assets. It should be distinguished in the current system from rental income derived from buildings and other fixed assets, which is included in output (P.1).

Repurchase agreement (repo)/reverse repo

This is short for "sale and repurchase agreement". One party agrees to sell bonds or other financial instruments to other parties under a formal legal agreement to repurchase them at some point in the future – usually up to six months – at a fixed price. Reverse repos are the counterpart asset to any repo liability.

Repo or reverse repo transactions are generally treated as borrowing or lending within other investment, rather than as transactions in the underlying securities. The exception is for banks, where repos are recorded as deposit liabilities. Banks' reverse repos are recorded as loans, the same as for all other sectors. Legal ownership does not change under a "repo" agreement. It was previously treated as a change of ownership in the UK financial account but under the System of National Accounts is treated as a collateralised deposit (F.22).

Reserve assets

Short-term assets that can be very quickly converted into cash. They comprise the UK's official holdings of gold, convertible currencies, special drawing rights and changes in the UK reserve position in the International Monetary Fund (IMF). Also included between July 1979 and December 1998 are European Currency Units acquired from swaps with the European Co-operation Fund, European Monetary Institute (EMI) and the European Central Bank (ECB).

Residents

These comprise general government, individuals, private non-profit-making bodies serving households, and enterprises within the territory of a given economy.

Residual error

The term used in the former accounts for the difference between the measures of gross domestic product from the expenditure and income approaches.

Resources and uses

The term resources refers to the side of the current accounts where transactions that add to the amount of economic value of a unit or sector appear. For example, wages and salaries are a resource for the unit or sector receiving them. Resources are by convention put on the right side, or at the top of tables arranged vertically. The left side (or bottom section) of the accounts, which relates to transactions that reduce the amount of economic value of a unit or sector, is termed uses. To continue the example, wages and salaries are a use for the unit or sector that must pay them.

Rest of the world

This sector records the counterpart of transactions of the whole economy with non-residents.

S to T

Satellite accounts

Satellite accounts describe areas or activities not dealt with by core economic accounts. These areas or activities are considered to require too much detail for inclusion in the core accounts or they operate with a different conceptual framework. Internal satellite accounts re-present information within the production boundary. External satellite accounts present new information not covered by the core accounts.

Saving (B.8g)

The balance on the use of income account. It is that part of disposable income that is not spent on final consumption and may be positive or negative.

Secondary market

A market in which holders of financial instruments can re-sell all or part of their holding. The larger and more effective the secondary market for any particular financial instrument the more liquid that instrument is to the holder.

Sector

See institutional sector.

Securities

Tradable or potentially tradable financial instruments.

Standard Industrial Classification (SIC)

The industrial classification applied to the collection and publication of a wide range of economic statistics. The current version, SIC 2007, is consistent with NACE, revision 2. See the NACE section of the glossary for further details.

System of National Accounts (SNA)

The internationally agreed standard system for macroeconomic accounts. The latest version is described in System of National Accounts 2008.

Special drawing rights (SDRs) (F.12)

These are reserve assets created and distributed by decision of the members of the International Monetary Fund (IMF). Participants accept an obligation to provide convertible currency to another participant, when designated by the IMF to do so, in exchange for SDRs equivalent to three times their own allocation. Only countries with a sufficiently strong balance of payments are so designated by the IMF. SDRs may also be used in certain direct payments between participants in the scheme and for payments of various kinds to the IMF.

Special purpose entities (SPEs)

SPEs are generally organised or established in economies other than those in which the parent companies are resident; and engaged primarily in international transactions but in few or no local operations.

SPEs are defined either by their structure (for example, financing subsidiary, holding company, base company, regional headquarters), or their purpose (for example, sale and regional administration, management of foreign exchange risk, facilitation of financing of investment).

SPEs should be treated as direct investment enterprises if they meet the 10% criterion. SPEs are an integral part of direct investment networks as are, for the most part, SPE transactions with other members of the group.

Staged payments

See advance and progress payments.

Standardised guarantees

Standardised guarantees are normally issued in large numbers, usually for fairly small amounts, along identical lines. There are three parties involved in these arrangements; the debtor, the creditor and the guarantor. Either the debtor or creditor may contract with the guarantor to repay the creditor if the debtor defaults. The classic examples are export credit guarantees and student loan guarantees.

Subsidiaries

Companies owned or controlled by another company. Under Section 1159 of the Companies Act (2006) this means, broadly speaking, that another company either holds a majority of the voting rights in it, is a member of it and has the right to appoint or remove a majority of its board of directors, or is a member of it and controls alone (pursuant to an agreement with other members) a majority of the voting rights in it. The category also includes subsidiaries of subsidiaries.

Subsidies (D.3)

Current unrequited payments made by general government or the European Union to enterprises. Those made on the basis of a quantity or value of goods or services are classified as "subsidies on products" (D.31). Other subsidies based on levels of productive activity (for example, numbers employed) are designated "other subsidies on production" (D.39).

Suppliers' credit

Export credit extended overseas directly by UK firms other than to related concerns.

Supply table

Table of estimates of domestic industries' output by type of product. Compiled at basic prices and includes columns for imports of goods and services, for distributors' trading margins and for taxes less subsidies on products. The final column shows the value of the supply of goods and services at purchasers' prices. This table shows which industries make which products; columns represent the supplying industries, rows represent the products supplied.

Taxes

Compulsory unrequited transfers to central or local government or the European Union. Taxation is classified in the following main groups:

- taxes on production and imports (D.2)

- current taxes on income wealth and so on (D.5)

- capital taxes (D.91)

Technical reserves (of insurance companies) (F.61)

These reserves consist of pre-paid premiums, reserves against outstanding claims, actuarial reserves for life insurance and reserves for with-profit insurance. They are treated in the economic accounts as the property of policy-holders.

Terms of trade

Ratio of the change in export prices to the change in import prices. An increase in the terms of trade implies that the receipts from the same quantity of exports will finance an increased volume of imports, so measurement of real national disposable income needs to take account of this factor.

Transfers

Unrequited payments made by one unit to another. They may be current transfers (D.5 to 7) or capital transfers (D.9). The most important types of transfers are taxes, social contributions and benefits.

Treasury bills

Short-term securities or promissory notes that are issued by government in return for funding from the money market. Each week in the UK, the Bank of England invites tenders for sterling Treasury bills from the financial institutions operating in the market. European currency unit (ECU) or euro-denominated bills were issued by tender each month but this programme has now wound down; the last bill was redeemed in September 1999. Treasury bills are an important form of short-term borrowing for the government, generally being issued for periods of three or six months.

U to Z

Unit trusts

Institutions within sub-sector S.123 through which investors pool their funds to invest in a diversified portfolio of securities.

Individual investors purchase units in the fund representing an ownership interest in the large pool of underlying assets, giving them an equity stake. The selection of assets is made by professional fund managers. Unit trusts therefore give individual investors the opportunity to invest in a diversified and professionally managed portfolio of securities, without the need for detailed knowledge of the individual companies issuing the stocks and bonds.

They differ from investment trusts in that the latter are companies in which investors trade shares on the Stock Exchange, whereas unit trust units are issued and bought back on demand by the managers of the trust. The prices of unit trust units therefore reflect the value of the underlying pool of securities, whereas the price of shares in investment trusts are affected by the usual market forces.

Uses

See resources and uses.

Use table

See combined use table.

United Kingdom (UK)

Broadly, in the accounts, the UK comprises Great Britain plus Northern Ireland and that part of the continental shelf deemed by international convention to belong to the UK. It excludes the Channel Islands and the Isle of Man.

Valuables

Goods of considerable value that are not used primarily for production or consumption but are held as stores of value over time, for example, precious metals, precious stones, jewellery and works of art.

Valuation

See basic prices, purchasers' prices, factor cost.

Value added

The balance on the production account: output less intermediate consumption. Value added may be measured net or gross.

Value Added Tax (VAT) (D.211)

A tax paid by enterprises. In broad terms an enterprise is liable for VAT on the total of its taxable sales but may deduct tax already paid by suppliers on its inputs (intermediate consumption). Therefore, the tax is effectively on the value added by the enterprise. Where the enterprise cannot deduct tax on its inputs the tax is referred to as non-deductible. VAT is the main UK tax on products (D.21).

Background notes
What do you think?

We welcome your feedback on this publication. If you would like to get in touch, please contact us via email: blue.book.coordination@ons.gsi.gov.uk.

Release policy

This release includes data up to 2016. Data are consistent with Index of Production, published on 10 October 2017, the current price trade in goods data within UK trade, published on 10 October 2017 and Balance of Payments, Quarterly National Accounts and United Kingdom Economic Accounts, published on 29 September 2017.

National Accounts Work Plan

The Economic Statistics and Analysis Strategy (ESAS) is reviewed and updated annually in the light of changing needs and priorities, and availability of resources. Making explicit ONS's perceived priorities will allow greater scrutiny and assurance that these are the right ones. In addition, this ESAS will allow research and development priorities to be laid out, making it easier for external experts to see the areas where ONS would be particularly keen to collaborate.

Continuous improvement of sources, methods and communication

Prior to publication, we published a series of articles detailing the changes and the impact they would have within Blue Book 2017; these can be found on the National Accounts articles page on our website. This includes supplementary analyses of data to help with the interpretation of statistics and guidance on the methodology used to produce the national accounts.

National accounts classification decisions

The UK national accounts are produced under internationally agreed guidance and rules set out principally in the European System of Accounts (ESA 2010) and the accompanying Manual on Government Deficit and Debt-Implementation of ESA 2010 – 2016 edition (MGDD).

In the UK, we are responsible for the application and interpretation of these rules. Therefore we make classification decisions based upon the agreed guidance and rules.

Economic context

We publish the monthly Economic Commentary, giving economic commentary on the latest GDP estimate and our other economic releases. The next article will be published on 23 November 2017.

Important quality issues

Common pitfalls in interpreting series:

- expectations of accuracy and reliability in early estimates are often too high

- revisions are an inevitable consequence of the trade-off between timeliness and accuracy

- early estimates are based on incomplete data

Very few statistical revisions arise as a result of "errors" in the popular sense of the word. All estimates, by definition, are subject to statistical "error". In this context the word refers to the uncertainty inherent in any process or calculation that uses sampling, estimation or modelling. Most revisions reflect either the adoption of new statistical techniques or the incorporation of new information which allows the statistical error of previous estimates to be reduced. Only rarely are there avoidable "errors", such as human or system failures, and such mistakes are made quite clear when they do occur.

The quality of Blue Book estimates

Unlike many of the short-term indicators we publish, there is no simple way of measuring the accuracy of the Blue Book dataset. All estimates, by definition, are subject to statistical uncertainty and for many well-established statistics we measure and publish the sampling error and non-sampling error associated with the estimate, using this as an indicator of accuracy. Since sampling is typically done to determine the characteristics of a whole population, the difference between the sample and population values is considered a sampling error. Non-sampling errors are a result of deviations from the true value that are not a function of the sample chosen, including various systematic errors and any other errors that are not due to sampling.

The Blue Book dataset, however, is currently constructed from various data sources, some of which are not based on random samples or do not have published sampling and non-sampling errors available, making it very difficult to measure both error aspects and their impact on GDP. While development work continues in this area, like all other G7 national statistical institutes, we don't publish a measure of the sampling error or non-sampling error associated with this dataset.

Reliability

Estimates for the most recent quarters are provisional and are subject to revision in the light of updated source information. We currently provide an analysis of past revisions in the GDP and other statistical bulletins that present time series.

Our revisions to economic statistics page brings together our work on revisions analysis, linking to articles and revisions policies. Revisions to data provide one indication of the reliability of main indicators.

Further information

You can get the latest copies of this and all our other releases through the release calendar on our website.

Details of the policy governing the release of new data are available from the media relations office.

We are committed to ensuring that all information provided is kept strictly confidential and will only be used for statistical purposes. Further details regarding confidentiality can be found on our website in the respondent charters for businesses and households.

Code of practice

National Statistics are produced to high professional standards set out in the UK Statistics Authority's Code of Practice for Official Statistics. They undergo regular quality assurance reviews to ensure that they meet customer needs. They are produced free from any political interference.